lonely planet

San Francisco

"All you've got to do is decide to go
and the hardest part is over.

So go!"

TONY WHEELER, COFOUNDER – LONELY PLANET

THIS EDITION WRITTEN AND RESEARCHED BY
Alison Bing, John A Vlahides

Contents

Plan Your Trip 4

Explore San Francisco 48

Understand San Francisco 251

Survival Guide 287

San Francisco Maps 313

Left: Pacific Heights
p126

Above: MH de Young
Museum p193

Right: Ferry Plaza
Farmers Market p76

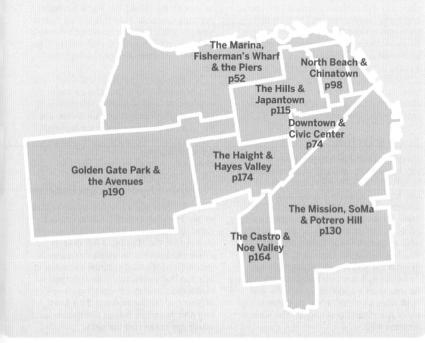

The Marina,
Fisherman's Wharf
& the Piers
p52

North Beach &
Chinatown
p98

The Hills &
Japantown
p115

Downtown &
Civic Center
p74

Golden Gate Park &
the Avenues
p190

The Haight &
Hayes Valley
p174

The Mission, SoMa
& Potrero Hill
p130

The Castro &
Noe Valley
p164

Welcome to San Francisco

Grab your coat and a handful of glitter, and enter the land of fog and fabulousness. So long, inhibitions; hello, San Francisco.

Outlandish Notions

Consider permission permanently granted to step up, strip down and go too far: other towns may surprise you, but in San Francisco you will surprise yourself. Good times and social revolutions tend to start here, from manic Gold Rushes to blissful hippie Be-Ins. If there's a skateboard move yet to be busted, a technology still unimagined, a poem left unspoken or a green scheme untested, chances are it's about to happen here. Yes, right now: this town has lost almost everything in earthquakes and dotcom gambles, but never its nerve.

Food & Drink

Every available Bay Area–invented technology is needed to make dinner decisions in this city, with the most restaurants and farmers markets per capita in North America, supplied by pioneering local organic farms. Following dinner, there's the pressing matter of a drink. A brief flirtation with respectability in 1906 convinced City Hall to ban women from bars, effectively driving the action underground through Prohibition. Today San Francisco celebrates its speakeasies and vintage saloons, and with Wine Country providing a steady supply of America's finest hooch – the West remains wild.

Natural Highs

California is one grand, sweeping gesture, a long arm cradling the Pacific. But then there's San Francisco, that seven-by-seven-mile peninsula that looks like a forefinger pointing upwards. Take this as your hint to look up: you'll find San Francisco's crooked Victorian rooflines, wind-sculpted treetops and fog tumbling over the Golden Gate Bridge.

Heads are perpetually in the clouds atop San Francisco's 43 hills. Cable cars provide easy access to Russian and Nob Hills, and splendid panoramas atop Coit Tower. But the most exhilarating highs are reached via Telegraph Hill's garden-lined stairway walks, windswept hikes around Land's End and climbs up rocky Corona Heights.

Neighborhood Microclimates

Microclimates add a touch of magic realism to San Francisco: when it's drizzling in the outer reaches of Golden Gate Park, it may be sunny in the Mission. A few degrees' difference between neighborhoods grants permission for salted caramel ice cream in Mission Dolores Park or a hasty retreat to the tropical heat at the California Academy of Sciences' rainforest dome. This town will give you goose bumps one minute, and warm you to the core the next.

Why I Love San Francisco

By Alison Bing, Author

On my way from Hong Kong to New York, I stopped in San Francisco for a day. I walked from the Geary St art galleries up Grant Ave to Waverly Place, just as temple services were starting. The breeze smelled like incense and roast duck. In the basement of City Lights bookstore, near the Muckraking section, I noticed a sign painted by a 1920s cult: 'I am the door.' It's true. San Francisco is the threshold between East and West, body and soul, fact and fiction. That was 18 years ago. I'm still here. You have been warned.

For more about our authors, see p344.

California St cable car, Financial District

San Francisco's
Top 10

Golden Gate Park (p192)

1 You may have heard that San Francisco has a wild streak a mile wide, but it also happens to be 4.5 miles long. Golden Gate Park lets San Franciscans do what comes naturally: roller-discoing, drum-circling, petting starfish, sniffing orchids and racing bison toward the Pacific. It's hard to believe these 1017 acres of lush terrain were once just scrubby sand dunes, and that San Franciscans have successfully preserved this stretch of green since 1866, ousting casinos and a theme-park igloo village. (CONSERVATORY OF FLOWERS, GOLDEN GATE PARK)

◉ *Golden Gate Park & the Avenues*

SFMOMA & SoMa Art Scene (p132 & p139)

2 New media art has been collected at San Francisco Museum of Modern Art (SFMOMA) since before anyone knew what to call it. Now the museum is undergoing a $480 million expansion – and if that sounds audacious, wait until you see the rest of the neighborhood. The Cartoon Art Museum showcases political cartoons too hot to print, the Contemporary Jewish Museum allows 600 artists to take liberties with *Mein Kampf,* and Electric Works shows North Korean propaganda posters. (SFMOMA)

◉ *The Misson, SoMa & Potrero Hill*

JOHN ELK III / LONELY PLANET IMAGES ©

Alcatraz (p54)

3 From its 19th century founding to hold Civil War deserters and Native American dissidents to its closure by Bobby Kennedy in 1963, Alcatraz was America's most notorious prison. No prisoner is known to have escaped alive – but after spending even a minute in D-Block solitary, listening to the sounds of city life across the bay, the 1.25-mile swim through riptides may seem worth a shot. For maximum chill factor, book the popular night tour to check out the gloomy jailhouse. On the return ferry to San Francisco, freedom never felt so good.

◉ *The Marina, Fisherman's Wharf & the Piers*

Golden Gate Bridge (p59)

4 Other suspension bridges impress with engineering, but none can touch the Golden Gate Bridge for showmanship. On sunny days it transfixes crowds with a radiant glow – a feat pulled off by 25 daredevil painters who maintain the bridge's luminous complexion by applying 1000 gallons of International Orange paint every week. When afternoon fog rolls in, the bridge puts on a magic show that's positively riveting: now you see it, now you don't and, abracadabra, it's sawn in half. Tune in tomorrow for its dramatic unveiling, just in time for the morning commute.

◉ *The Marina, Fisherman's Wharf & the Piers*

Ferry Building (p76)

5 San Francisco's monument to food stands tall and proud on Saturdays, when star chefs troll farmers market stalls for rare heirloom varietals and foodie babies blissfully teethe on organic peaches. Local farmers and food trucks have dedicated followings any rock star would envy, so anticipate waits for organic Dirty Girl tomatoes and Namu's sustainable Korean steak tacos. Bide your time exchanging recipe tips, then haul your picnic to Pier 2. With feet dangling over the sparkling bay and culinary bounty in hand, lunch and life exceed expectations. (FERRY PLAZA FARMERS MARKET, FERRY BUILDING)

◉ *Downtown & Civic Center*

Hilltop Vistas

6 Gravity seems unkind as you scale SF's steepest hills, with calf muscles and cable car wheels groaning – but all grumbling ends once you hit the summit. With wind-bent trees, Victorian turrets and the world at your feet atop Corona Heights Park (p166), Buena Vista Park (p177) or 41 of the city's other peaks, one word comes to mind: wheeeeee! Hilltop parks like Sterling Park (p119) and Ina Coolbrith Park (p119) are San Francisco's crowning glories. Wild parrots may mock your progress up Telegraph Hill to Coit Tower (p101) but, really, they can't expect to keep scenery like this to themselves.

(LAFAYETTE PARK)

Cable Cars *(p45)*

7 White-knuckle grips that cling to worn wooden benches give away San Francisco novices. Lurching uphill, you may exhale when the bell finally signals the summit. But don't look now: what goes up all 338ft of San Francisco's Nob Hill must come down. Maybe now is not the best time to mention that the brakes are still hand-operated, or that this Victorian steampunk invention has hardly changed since 1873. Once you reach the terminus, you're ready to take the next giddy ride standing, with nothing between you and eternity but a creaky hand strap.

◉ *Cable Cars*

North Beach Bars

(p110)

8 Friendly bartenders were once highly suspect in San Francisco. Circa 1849, a night that began with smiles and a 10¢ whiskey could end two days later, waking from a drugged sleep on a vessel bound for Patagonia. Now that Shanghai Kelly is no longer a danger to drinkers, San Franciscans can relax over historically correct cocktails at North Beach's re-vived Barbary Coast saloons. Today's scene would look familiar to long-gone sailors, with well-scuffed wooden floors, absinthe spoons and lighting dim enough to put a bordello madam at ease – plus reassuring barkeep backsass.

◉ *North Beach & Chinatown*

Marine Life at Fisherman's Wharf (p56)

9 Sea lions, sharks and jellyfish lurk along Fisherman's Wharf. Sea lions have lived the Californian dream since 1989, when they brought harems to Pier 39 yacht docks for sunning and canoodling. After disappearing in 2009, their return in 2010 was greeted with cheers and a brass band. Sharks circle nearby at Aquarium of the Bay, where the only barrier between visitors and bay waters is a glass tube. A less ominous underwater world can be glimpsed at the newly restored Aquatic Park Bathhouse, where jellyfish flutter across 1930s mosaics.

◉ *The Marina, Fisherman's Wharf & the Piers*

Neighborhood Boutiques (p39)

10 Terrariums, desert-island message bottles, necklaces made of shattered wind-shields: shopping looks strangely like installation art in San Francisco's indie boutiques. Although SF has spawned mega-retailers – Levi Strauss, Pottery Barn and the Gap are all headquartered downtown – zoning restrictions limit chain retailers in the city's neighborhoods. Where other cities might plunk another Walmart, here you'll find Victorian storefronts selling Icelandic gamelan music and organic-cotton Mayan minidresses. Local designers win pride of place on shelves, and killer sale racks put mall mark-ups to shame. (LOYAL ARMY CLOTHING, P186, THE HAIGHT)

🔒 *Shopping*

What's New

Urban Farming

Recent reports rank San Francisco the greenest city in North America – but you could probably guess that with a glance at SF's Green Festival urban farming programs or the beehive-covered freeway on-ramp at Hayes Valley Farm (p177). For tips on growing your own organic food, farming for kids and urban composting (now mandated by law in SF), check out workshops at SF's nonprofit sustainable gardening program, Garden for the Environment (www.gardenfortheenvironment.org).

Old-timey Saloons

The Barbary Coast is roaring back to life with historically researched whiskey cocktails and staggering absinthe concoctions in San Francisco's great Western saloon revival (p110).

SFMOMA Expansion

SF is more artistically gifted than ever, thanks to a donation of 1100 modern masterworks and a half-billion-dollar expansion in the works at San Francisco Museum of Modern Art (SFMOMA; p132).

Aquatic Park Bathhouse Restoration

Maintenance of this 1930s landmark uncovered long-lost deco woodcarvings and WPA murals – and with its Sargent Johnson mosaics gleaming and ocean liner structure finally shipshape, this maritime monument is a must-see (p58).

Outer Sunset Cool

The Ocean Beach chill factor brings pro surfers and hipsters alike to the Sunset, for artist-designed hoodies at Mollusk, soul-warming organic food at Outerlands and beachcomber-architect decor at General Store (p198).

Valencia Gallery Scene

Downtown is where the money is, but the Mission is where street artists and MFA students live – so arts nonprofits and upstart galleries around Valencia St spot emerging talent first (p138).

Foraged Fine Dining

No local chef's tasting menu is complete without wild chanterelles found beneath California oaks, miner's lettuce from Berkeley hillsides or SF-backyard nasturtium flowers. Daniel Patterson sets the standard at Coi (p108).

Permanent Pop-up Restaurants

When pop-up restaurants settle down, they establish regular hours at local bars, cafes and the Corner, a venue that hosts different pop-ups most nights (p144).

Acoustic Twang

Gunshots begin races, but most SF events begin with guitar chords. Lyrics including 'lonesome' and 'cowboy' recall SF's Western longitude, though there's latitude for authenticity at Hardly Strictly Bluegrass (p24).

Dandies

Dapper gents in are setting trends and throwing off SF's gaydar. Straight and gay men alike spiff up at Sui Generis and Revolver, and step out at Churchill (p171).

For more recommendations and reviews, see **lonelyplanet.com/san-francisco.**

Need to Know

Currency
US dollar ($)

Language
English

Visas
The US Visa Waiver program allows nationals of 27 countries to enter the US without a visa; see p299.

Money
ATMs widely available; credit cards accepted at most hotels, stores and restaurants. Farmers markets, food trucks and some bars are cash-only.

Cell Phones
Most US cell phones, apart from the iPhone, operate on CDMA, not the European standard GSM; check compatibility with your phone service provider.

Time
Pacific Standard Time (GMT/UTC minus eight hours)

Tourist Information
SF's Visitor Information Center (415-391-2000; www.onlyin sanfrancisco.com; Lower Level, Hallidie Plaza; 9am-5pm Mon-Fri, 9am-3pm Sat & Sun) Muni Passports, last-minute vacancy listings and accommodations deals.

Your Daily Budget

Budget less than $100
- Dorm bed $25–$30
- Burrito $6–$8
- Food-truck dishes $5–$10
- Mission galleries & murals free
- Live music at Hotel Utah/ Bottom of the Hill $5–$12
- Castro Theatre show $10

Midrange $100–$250
- Motel/downtown hotel $80–$180
- Ferry Building meal $15–$35
- Bar/pop-up restaurant meal $20–$45
- SFMOMA $18/$9 after 6pm Thursdays
- Symphony rush tickets $20–$25
- Muni Passport $14

Top end $250 plus
- Boutique hotel $150–$380
- Chef's tasting menu $65–$140
- City Pass (Muni plus five attractions) $69
- Alcatraz night tour $33
- Opera orchestra seats $30–$90

Advance Planning

Two months before Book your reservations at Chez Panisse or French Laundry; start walking to build stamina for Mission gallery or bar crawls.

Three weeks before Book Alcatraz tour, Chinatown Alleyway Tour or Precita Eyes Mission Mural Tour.

One week before Search for tickets to American Conservatory Theater, SF Symphony or SF Opera, and find out what else is on next weekend.

Useful Websites

- **SF Bay Guardian** (www. sfbg.com) Hot tips on local entertainment, arts, politics.
- **SFGate** (www.sfgate.com) *San Francisco Chronicle* news and event listings.
- **7x7** (www.7x7.com) Trend-spotting SF restaurants, bars and style.
- **Craigslist** (http://sfbay. craigslist.org) SF-based source for jobs, dates, free junk.
- **Lonely Planet** (www. lonelyplanet.com/san -francisco) Destination information, hotel bookings, traveler forum and more.

WHEN TO GO

Summer brings fog and chilly 55°F weather to SF; early fall is best for warm weather, street fairs and harvest cuisine.

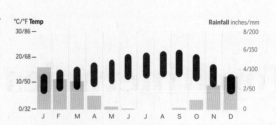

°C/°F **Temp**

Rainfall inches/mm

Arriving in San Francisco

San Francisco Airport (SFO)
Fast rides to downtown SF on BART cost $8.10; door-to-door shuttle vans cost $17; express bus fare to Temporary Transbay Terminal is $5; taxis cost $35 to $50.

Oakland International Airport (OAK) Take the AirBART shuttle ($3) to Coliseum station to catch BART to downtown SF ($3.80); take a shared van to downtown SF for $35 to $30; or pay $50 to $60 for a taxi to SF destinations.

Temporary Transbay Terminal (Map p330; Howard & Main Sts) Greyhound buses arrive/depart downtown SF's temporary depot (until 2017) at Howard & Main Sts.

Emeryville Amtrak station (EMY) Located outside Oakland, this depot serves LA–Seattle *Coast Starlight*, Chicago–Emeryville *California Zephyr* and other trains; Amtrak runs free shuttles to/from San Francisco's Ferry Building and Caltrain.

For much more on **arrival**, see p288.

Getting Around

For Bay Area transit options, departures and arrivals, call 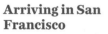511 or check www.511.org. A detailed Muni Street & Transit Map is available free online and at the Powell Muni kiosk ($3).

➡ **Cable cars** Frequent, slow and scenic, from 6am to 1am daily. Single rides cost $6; for frequent use, get a Muni Passport.

➡ **Muni streetcar & bus** Reasonably fast but schedules vary wildly by line; infrequent after 9pm. Fares cost $2.

➡ **BART** High-speed transit to East Bay, Mission St, SFO and Millbrae, where it connects with Caltrain.

➡ **Taxi** Fares cost about $2.25 per mile; meters start at $3.50.

For much more on **getting around**, see p288.

Sleeping

San Francisco is the birthplace of the boutique hotel, offering stylish rooms at a price: $100 to $200 midrange, plus 15.5% hotel tax (hostels exempt) and $35 to $50 for overnight parking. Some downtown hotels cost less, but proceed with caution: west of Mason is the sketchy, depressing Tenderloin. Motels are better options for parking and hostels offer value for solo travelers, but no privacy.

Useful Websites

➡ **B&B San Francisco** (www.bbsf.com) Personable, privately owned B&Bs and neighborhood inns.

➡ **SF Visitor Information Center Reservations** (www.onlyinsanfrancisco. com) Vacancies and deals; indispensible in high season and during major conventions.

➡ **Lonely Planet** (http://hotels.lonelyplanet.com) Expert author reviews, user feedback, booking engine.

For much more on **sleeping**, see p238.

Top Itineraries

Day One

North Beach (p98)

 Parrots squawk encouragement as you climb **Greenwich Street stairs** to **Coit Tower** for WPA murals and 360-degree panoramas. Amble downhill through **Washington Square** and down Columbus past **Columbus Tower**, and take a breather in the redwood grove beneath the **Transamerica Pyramid**.

> **Lunch** Hail dim sum carts for dumplings at City View (p109).

Chinatown (p98)

Compare traditional and contemporary, Chinese and Chinese American artists at **Chinese Culture Center**, and cross the pedestrian bridge to watch fierce chess matches in progress at **Portsmouth Square**. Wander through temple-lined **Waverly Place** and notorious **Ross Alley** to find your fortune at **Golden Gate Fortune Cookie Company**. Past the pagoda-topped tea and trinket shops of Grant Ave and down poetry-paved **Jack Kerouac Alley** is **City Lights bookstore**, the home of Beat poetry. Celebrate free spirits and free speech here and at the **Beat Museum** across the street.

> **Dinner** Reserve ahead for North Beach's best pasta at Cotogna (p84).

North Beach (p98)

 Prepare yourself for insane hats and razor-sharp wit at **Beach Blanket Babylon**, SF's most over-the-top drag satire (and that's saying something). Recap over nightcaps fit for Victorian swells and madams at **Comstock Saloon**.

Day Two

Golden Gate Park (p190)

Hop the Judah to Stanyan, then walk into the park to see carnivorous plants enjoying their insect breakfasts at **Conservatory of Flowers** and dahlias wet with dew in the **Dahlia Garden**. Follow Andy Goldworthy's artful sidewalk fault lines to find faultless Oceanic masks and tower-top views at the **MH de Young Museum**, then take a walk on the wild side in the rainforest dome of the **California Academy of Sciences**. Enjoy a moment of Zen with green tea at the **Japanese Tea Garden**, and bliss out in the secret redwood grove at the **San Francisco Botanical Garden**.

> **Lunch** Surfers hit Outerlands (p201) for grilled cheese and organic soup.

The Sunset (p190)

Find driftwood jewelry and DIY architecture books at **General Store**, and artist-designed hoodies and custom surfboards at **Mollusk**. Beachcomb **Ocean Beach** up to the **Beach Chalet** to glimpse 1930s WPA murals celebrating Golden Gate Park, and amber sunsets glimpsed through a pint of the house-brewed ale.

> **Dinner** Inspired organic Cal-Moroccan feasts satisfy cravings at Aziza (p198).

Japantown (p115)

Psychedelic posters and top acts make for rock-legendary nights at the **Fillmore**, or you could get in the swing with the jazz greats performing nightly at **Yoshi's**.

Day Three

SoMa (p130)

☼ Fuel up with an artful latte at the cafe at the rooftop sculpture garden of **SFMOMA**, then plot your descent through three floors of boundary-pushing, horizon-expanding art. Explore SF's multiculti roots at the **Museum of the African Diaspora** and **Contemporary Jewish Museum**, then find crafty new ideas at the **Museum of Craft & Folk Art**.

 Lunch La Taqueria makes the definitive Mission burrito (p142).

The Mission (p130)

☼ Walk 24th St past mural-covered bodegas to **Balmy Alley**, where the Mission muralist movement began in the 1970s. Stop for a 'secret breakfast' (bourbon and cornflake) ice cream sundae at **Humphry Slocombe**, then head up Valencia to another foodie favorite, **Ritual Coffee Roasters**. Pause for pirate supplies and Fish Theater at **826 Valencia**, and duck into **Clarion Alley** to see the Mission's ongoing outdoor art show. See San Francisco's first building, Spanish adobe **Mission Dolores**, and visit the memorial to native Ohlone who built it.

 Dinner Early walk-ins may score sensational small plates at Frances (p166).

The Castro (p164)

☾ Sing along to show tunes pounded out on the Mighty Wurlitzer organ before shows at deco-fabulous **Castro Theatre**. Party boys cruise over to **440 Castro** afterwards, while mixed straight/gay/male/female crowds clink glasses at **Blackbird**.

Day Four

Russian Hill (p115)

☼ Grab a leather strap on the **Powell-Hyde cable car** and hold on: you're in for hills and thrills. Hop off at Vallejo to follow stairway walks and side streets to four literary locations: hilltop **Ina Coolbrith Park**, named after San Francisco's over-the-top romantic poet; shady **Macondray Lane**, the backdrop for Armistead Maupin's *Tales of the City;* **Russell St**, where Jack Kerouac wrote *On the Road* in an attic; and **Sterling Park**, where sweeping bay views inspired SF's original 'King of Bohemia.'

 Lunch Za (p124) features cornmeal-crusted pizza and Anchor Steam beer.

The Piers (p52)

☼ Cover the waterfront, beginning with newly restored underwater murals and mosaics at **Aquatic Park Bathhouse**. You can save the world from Space Invaders at **Musée Mécanique**, or enter underwater stealth mode inside a real WWII submarine: **USS Pampanito**. Watch sea lions cavort at **Pier 39**, then follow your rumbling stomach to the **Ferry Building**.

 Dinner Try the local oysters and Dungeness crab at the Ferry Building (p86).

Alcatraz (p52)

☾ To end the evening with shivers, don't miss the boat for the night tour of **Alcatraz**. Once you return to freedom, hop on the vintage **F-Market line streetcar** to celebrate your great San Francisco escape with bubbly at **Waterbar**.

If You Like...

Museums

San Francisco Museum of Modern Art (SFMOMA) Big, bold exhibitions push artistic boundaries through the roof and into an entirely new wing. (p132)

MH de Young Museum Global art and craft masterworks with provocative ideas and enviable hand–eye coordination. (p193)

Asian Art Museum Sightsee halfway across the globe in an hour, from romantic Persian miniatures to daring contemporary Chinese installation art. (p77)

Legion of Honor Iconic impressionists, a sensational modern collection of 90,000 graphic artworks and weekend organ recitals amid Rodin sculptures. (p195)

Cartoon Art Museum Original drawings by comics legends, from R Crumb and Edward Gorey to Spiderman. (p139)

Free Shows

Stern Grove Festival Free concerts at Golden Gate Park's natural amphitheater, from Afrobeat jazz to SF Opera. (p23)

Hardly Strictly Bluegrass Festival Elvis Costello, Gillian Welch, banjo legend Earl Scruggs and other headliners play for free on three stages at Golden Gate Park. (p24)

Shakespeare in the Park Romeo, Juliet and company take over a former military base to provide

SABRINA DALBESIO / LONELY PLANET IMAGES ©

Contemporary Jewish Museum (p140)

free outdoor performances. (p23)

Amoeba Music concerts Rockers, DJs and hip-hop heroes give free shows in-store. (p186)

Giants Baseball Catch a glimpse of the action and join the party at the Embarcadero waterfront promenade behind left field. (p161)

Saloons

Comstock Saloon Vintage Victorian watering hole with lantern lighting, strong drink and dainty bar bites. (p110)

Elixir Serving spur-shaking cocktails since the Gold Rush – only now they're organic. (p148)

Homestead Front-parlor dive bar complete with stamped-tin ceiling, Boddington's on tap and peanuts in the shell. (p148)

Bloodhound Antler chandeliers, cocktails in Mason jars and a murder of crows on the ceiling. (p150)

Rickhouse Bartenders in newsboy caps pour vicious punch bowls and whiskey straight from the barrel. (p89)

Madrone Victorian art bar with an absinthe fountain and the ultimate saloon showdown: Michael Jackson versus Prince. (p184)

Vista Points

Coit Tower Up Greenwich St stairs, atop Telegraph Hill, inside the 1930s tower, and atop the viewing platform: 360-degree panoramas. (p101)

Land's End Shipwrecks, Golden Gate Bridge views and wind-blown Monterey pines line the scenic hike from Sutro Baths to Legion of Honor. (p195)

Sterling Park Poetic views of the Golden Gate Bridge from atop Russian Hill are worth jumping off the Powell-Hyde cable car to find. (p119)

Corona Heights Park Rocky outcropping with views over the Haight, Castro and Mission to the great bay beyond. (p166)

Local Hangouts

Trouble Coffee Soggy wet-suited surfers sit outside, but everyone else keeps warm inside at the scavenged-wood coffee bar. (p201)

Cole Valley Cafe Warm up when the fog rolls into Golden Gate Park at this upbeat, laid-back Haight coffeehouse. (p181)

Cafe Flore Glassed-in Castro corner venue that serves coffee with a side of local eye candy. (p170)

Mission Dolores Park Athletes, radical politicos, quasi-professional tanners, performance artists and toddlers: on sunny days, they all converge on this grassy hillside. (p134)

Japantown The unofficial living room of film festival freaks, Lolita Goths, anime aficionados and grandmas who fought for civil rights. (p118)

Avant-Garde Architecture

California Academy of Sciences Renzo Piano's LEED–certified green landmark, capped with a 'living roof' of California wildflowers. (p193)

MH de Young Museum Pritzker Prize–winning Swiss architects Herzog & de Meuron clad the museum in copper, slowly oxidizing green to match park scenery. (p193)

For more top San Francisco spots, see
⇒ Eating (p27)
⇒ Drinking & Nightlife (p31)
⇒ Entertainment (p34)
⇒ GLBT (p37)
⇒ Shopping (p39)
⇒ Sports & Activities (p41)
⇒ Cable Cars (p45)

Contemporary Jewish Museum Daniel Liebskind's creatively repurposed SF power station makes a powerful statement with a blue steel addition to form the Hebrew letter for life. (p140)

Federal Building Natural lighting and air circulation lightens the mood inside this government building, and saves taxpayer dollars. (p142)

Offbeat Shopping

826 Valencia Tri-corner hats, oyster-openers, lard recipes, tall tales and other essential pirate supplies. (p135)

Electric Works Balls of fluff, Chinese Cultural Revolution–era toys, David Byrne's diagrams explaining pop culture and fine-art prints of psychedelic cupcakes. (p140)

Loved to Death Morbid glamour, from genuine Victorian hair lockets to the taxidermy art wall. (p187)

Hollow Shelves laden with galvanized tin pails, driftwood candleholders, birdcages, Guinness cupcakes and tea: it's Alice in Wonderland retail. (p202)

Park Life Coolhunting made simple: skateboard decks sporting SF Victorian row houses, Russian prison tattoo books

PLAN YOUR TRIP IF YOU LIKE...

and backroom collage art installations. (p203)

Animals in Urban Habitats

Bison in Golden Gate Park Great shaggy beasts safely stampeding toward the Pacific in their park paddock. (p192)

Sea lions at Pier 39 These beach bums have been sticking it to the man since 1989, claiming squatters' rights to millionaires' yacht slips. (p56)

Wild parrots at Telegraph Hill By city decree, SF's official birds are the renegade parrots that turn Telegraph treetops red, yellow, green and blue. (p101)

Knock-kneed shorebirds at Crissy Field Once this airstrip was home to WWII warbirds, but it's been converted back into a coastal marshland sanctuary for shorebirds. (p60)

Mission bookstore cats Great vacation reads await discovery on Adobe Books' piled tables, but you'll have to convince the cats to move. (p158)

Hidden Alleyways

Balmy Alley Hot topics and artistic talents have surfaced since the 1970s in this alley covered in art by SF muralistas. (p134)

Spofford Alley Revolutions were plotted and bootlegger gun battles waged here – but peace has brought Chinese orchestras and mah-jong games here. (p100)

Jack Kerouac Alley This byway named after the Beat author is inscribed with his poetry, right on the road. (p102)

Bob Kaufman Alley A quiet alley, named for the spoken-word

artist who kept an anti-war vow of silence for 12 years. (p106)

Ross Alley Ladies who entered this notorious alley once risked their reputations, but now the most colorful characters are on the alleyway murals. (p100)

Macondray Lane A shady, cottage-lined lane was the perfect setting for a mysterious landlady in Armistead Maupin's *Tales of the City*. (p122)

Getting Naked

Baker Beach When the fog rolls into the clothing-optional north end of the beach, you'll get goose bumps in the most unusual places. (p61)

Pride Parade A handful of rainbow glitter is all you need to get out there and show some pride. (p23)

Bay to Breakers Racers streak across town wearing nothing but shoes and fanny packs to stash sunscreen. (p22)

Folsom Street Fair As you'll notice, it's possible to get tattooed and pierced absolutely everywhere – but don't stare unless you're prepared to compare. (p23)

Jane Warner Plaza You've arrived in the Castro when you spot nudists casually chatting at bistro tables at the F-line streetcar turnaround. (p166)

Historic Sites

Mission Dolores The first building in San Francisco was this Spanish adobe mission, built by conscripted Ohlone and Miwok labor. (p134)

Alcatraz 'The Rock' was a Civil War jail, an A-list gangster penitentiary, and contested territory

between Native Americans and the FBI. (p54)

City Lights Publishing poetry got City Lights founder Lawrence Ferlinghetti arrested – and won a landmark case for free speech. (p112)

Chinese Historical Society of America Julia Morgan built the elegant, tile-roofed brick Chinese YWCA, which now hosts shows chronicling turning points in Asian-American history. (p106)

City Hall History keeps getting made under this rotunda – the first 1960s sit-in, the first publicly gay elected official, the first citywide composting law. (p82)

Portsmouth Square The Gold Rush, dirty politics, kangaroo trials and burlesque shows all kicked off around Portsmouth Square. (p107)

Beaches

Baker Beach This cove was once an army base, but now it's packed with families, fishers and, at the north end, nudists. (p61)

Ocean Beach Beachcombing and bonfires are the preferred activities at SF's blustery 4-mile beach, where riptides limit swimming. (p198)

Santa Cruz This is the bay fictional character Gidget surfed, and made surfing a '60s pop-culture sensation; Santa Cruz remains California's classic surf destination.

Half Moon Bay When winter surf swells hit nosebleed heights, join the crowds on the dunes to watch Mavericks, California's death-defying surf contest. (p207)

Stinson Beach Marin's glorious stretch of sand is idyllic for sunset walks, but not swimming – too many sharks.

LEE FOSTER / LONELY PLANET IMAGES ©

(Above) Baker Beach (p61)
(Below) Vesuvio, Jack Kerouac Alley (p102)

SABRINA DALBESIO / LONELY PLANET IMAGES ©

Movie Locations

Nob Hill What a ride: Steve McQueen's muscle car goes flying over the summit in *Bullit* and somehow it lands in SoMa.

Sutro Baths San Francisco's splendid, dandified ruin made a suitable setting for the May–December romance in *Harold and Maude*. (p195)

Human Rights Campaign Action Center & Store Harvey Milk's camera shop in the movie *Milk* was the actual Castro location, now home to the GLBT civil rights organization (p172).

Bay Bridge Oops: when Dustin Hoffman sets out for Berkeley in *The Graduate,* he is heading the wrong way across the bridge.

Alcatraz Even America's highest security prison can't contain Clint Eastwood, who plots to escape with a spoon and razor-sharp wits in *Escape from Alcatraz*. (p54)

Fort Point Hitchcock was right: swirling noir-movie fog and giddy Golden Gate views make for a thrilling case of *Vertigo*. (p61)

PLAN YOUR TRIP IF YOU LIKE...

Month by Month

February

Lion dancing, warm days and alt-rock shows provide sudden relief from February drizzle.

☆ Noise Pop

Winter blues, be gone: discover your new favorite indie band and catch rockumentary premieres and rockin' gallery openings at get-to-know-you venues, all part of the Noise Pop Festival (www.noisepop.com); last week of February.

✨ Lunar New Year Parade

Chase the 200ft dragon, lion dancers, toddler kung fu classes and frozen-smile runners-up for the Miss Chinatown title through town, as lucky red envelopes and fireworks fall from the sky during Chinese New Year celebrations (www.chineseparade.com).

April

Reasonable room rates and weekends crammed with cultural events make for an excellent start to San Francisco spring, with only sporadic showers.

☆ Perpetual Indulgence in Dolores Park

Easter Sunday is an indulgent all-day event (p134; www.thesisters.org) at Mission Dolores Park: there's a morning Easter egg hunt for the kids, followed by the Bonnet Contest and the Hunky Jesus Contest, for those who prefer their messiahs muscle-bound.

✨ Cherry Blossom Festival

Japantown blooms and booms in April when the Cherry Blossom Festival (www.nccbf.org) turns out *taiko* drums, homegrown hip-hop and street shrines – plus food-stall yakitori and tempura galore.

☆ San Francisco International Film Festival

The nation's oldest film festival (www.sffs.org) is still looking stellar after more than 50 years, with 325 films, 200 directors and star-studded premieres; held end of April to early May at Sundance Kabuki Cinema (p126).

May

As inland California warms up to summer, fog settles over the Bay Area – but goose bumps haven't stopped San Francisco's naked joggers and conga lines yet.

🏃 Bay to Breakers

Run costumed or naked from Embarcadero to Ocean Beach for Bay to Breakers (www.baytobreakers.com), while joggers dressed as salmon run upstream. Race registration costs $44 to $48; held third Sunday in May.

✨ Carnaval

Brazilian or just faking it with a wax and a tan? Get head-dressed to impress, shake your tail feathers in the Mission and conga through the inevitable fog during Carnaval (www.carnavalsf.com); last weekend of May.

June

Since 1971, Pride has grown into a month-long extravaganza, with movie premieres and street parties culminating in the million-strong Pride Parade. In sun or fog, the Summer of Love returns to the Haight.

⭐ Haight Ashbury St Fair

Free music on two stages, plus macramé, tie-dye and herbal brownies surreptitiously for sale: all that's missing is the free love. Held every mid-June since 1978, when Harvey Milk helped make the first Haight fair (www.haightashburystreetfair.org) happen.

☆ San Francisco International Lesbian & Gay Film Festival

Here, queer and ready for a premiere for three decades, the oldest, biggest gay/lesbian/bisexual/transgender (GLBT) film fest (www.frameline.org) anywhere screens 250 films from 25 countries over two weeks in the second half of June.

⭐ Pride Parade

Come out wherever you are: SF goes wild for GLBT pride on the last Sunday of June, with 1.2 million people, seven stages, tons of glitter and ounces of thongs at the Pride Parade (www.sfpride.org). Crowds cheer same-sex newlyweds, gays in uniform and inspired drag.

July

Wintry summer days make bundling up advisable, but don't miss July barbecues and outdoor events, including charity hikes, free concerts and fireworks.

⭐ Independence Day

July 4 explodes with Fisherman's Wharf fireworks even in summer fog, celebrating San Francisco's dedication to life, liberty and the pursuit of happiness no matter the climate – economic, political or meteorological.

🏃 AIDS Walk

Until AIDS takes a hike, you can: this 10km fundraiser hike (www.aidswalk.net/sanfran) benefits 47 AIDS organizations. In nearly three decades, $74 million has been raised to fight the pandemic and support those living with HIV. Held the third Sunday in July.

☆ Stern Grove Festival

Music for free among the redwood and eucalyptus trees every summer since 1938. Stern Grove concerts (www.sterngrove.org) include world music and jazz, but the biggest events are July performances by the SF Ballet and SF Symphony and August arias from SF Opera.

September

Summer weather arrives at last and SF celebrates with more outrageous antics than usual: public spankings, free Shakespeare and combinations of the two at the Fringe Festival.

☆ Fringe Festival

More outrageous theatrical antics in SF than usual hit the stage at the Fringe Festival (www.sffringe.org) in late September, at discount prices. Book ahead, or chance it at the Exit Theater (p95) box office.

⭐ Folsom St Fair

Bondage enthusiasts emerge from dungeons worldwide for San Francisco's wild street party (www.folsomstreetfair.com), with public spankings for charity, leather, nudity and beer; held last Sunday of September, at Folsom St between 7th and 11th Sts.

☆ SF Shakespeare Festival

The play's the thing in the Presidio, outdoors and free of charge on sunny September weekends during the Shakespeare Festival (www.sfshakes.org). Kids' summer workshops are also held for budding Bards, culminating in performances throughout the Bay Area.

October

Expect golden sunshine and events for all kinds of aficionados: roots music, literary pub crawls, jazz greats and comics conventions.

⭐ Litquake

Stranger-than-fiction literary events take place the second week of October during SF's literary festival (www.litquake.org), with authors leading lunchtime story sessions and spilling trade secrets over drinks at the legendary Lit Crawl.

☆ **Hardly Strictly Bluegrass Festival**

The west goes wild for free bluegrass and rock with a twang at Golden Gate Park (www.strictlybluegrass. com), with three days of concerts and three stages of headliners, from Elvis Costello to Gillian Welch; held early October.

☆ **SF Jazz Festival**

Minds are blown by jazz greats and upstarts during the SF Jazz Festival (www. sfjazz.org), from Grammy-winning singing bassist Esperanza Spalding and saxophonist Joshua Redman to danceable acts like Goran Bregovic and his Wedding and Funeral Orchestra, and the bluesy pop-star India Arie; held late September through November.

November

Party to wake the dead and save the planet as San Francisco celebrates its Mexican history and green future.

✿ **Día de los Muertos**

Zombie brides and Aztec dancers in feather regalia party like there's no tomorrow on Día de los Muertos (Day of the Dead; www.dayofthedeadsf.org), paying respects to the dead along the way; held down 24th St on November 2.

✿ **Green Festival**

Energy-saving spotlights are turned on green cuisine, technology, fashion and booze during the three-day, mid-November Green Festival (www. greenfestivals.org).

(Top) Street performers on a float, Lunar New Year Parade (p22)

(Bottom) Competitor in costume, Bay to Breakers (p22)

With Kids

San Francisco has the fewest kids per capita of any US city and, according to SF SPCA data, about 19,000 more dogs than kids live here. Yet many locals make a living entertaining kids – from Pixar animators to video game designers – and this town is packed with attractions for kids.

Rainforest dome, California Academy of Sciences (p193)

SABRINA DALBESIO / LONELY PLANET IMAGES ©

Techies

Silicon Valley engineers encourage their kids' scientific curiosity at SF's hands-on discovery museums. San Francisco Children's Creativity Museum (p141) allows future tech to moguls design their own video games and animations, while the Exploratorium's MacArthur Genius Grant–winning interactive displays (p63) help kids figure out the physics of skateboarding for themselves, and kiddie gearheads are riveted by vintage steamships at the Hyde St Pier Historic Ships Collection (p57).

Nature Lovers

Kids fascinated by the underwater world shouldn't miss the Aquarium of the Bay (p58) or the Eel Forest and starfish petting zoo at the California Academy of Sciences (p193) – plus the added perks of penguins and a butterfly-filled rainforest dome.

Budding Artistes & Authors

Painting prodigies find new inspiration on Precita Eyes Mission Mural Tours – though parents may fear for their garage doors – and crafty kids can make their own SF souvenirs through hands-on programs at the Asian Art Museum (p77) and the Museum of Craft & Folk Art (p140).

A rest in the Poet's Chair at City Lights (p112) may inspire a haiku, but arts workshops are also available at the Cartoon Art Museum (p139) and 826 Valencia (p135).

Teen Hangouts

Haight St

Ogle boards and decks at SFO Snowboarding & FTC Skateboarding (p187), watch free shows at Amoeba Music (p186) and max out on cute at Loyal Army Clothing (p186).

Valencia St

Art-school-bound high schoolers dressed in hand-patched hoodies pore over hand-drawn zines at Needles & Pens (p158), Adobe Books (p158) and 826 Valencia, and

NEED TO KNOW

➡ **Change facilities** Best public facilities are at Westfield San Francisco Centre (p96) and San Francisco Main Library (p83).

➡ **Emergency care** San Francisco General Hospital (p295).

➡ **Babysitting** Available at high-end hotels or American Child Care (www.american childcare.com/san_francisco.html).

➡ **Strollers & car seats** Bring your own.

➡ **Diapers & formula** Available citywide at Walgreens (p296).

➡ **Kiddie menus** Mostly in cafes and downtown diners; call ahead about dietary restrictions.

mingle shyly over lattes and minicupcakes at Ritual Coffee Roasters (p149).

Junior Foodies

When spirits and feet begin to drag, there's plenty of ice cream and kid-friendly meals to pick them back up – look for the 🖽 symbol throughout this book. But discerning young diners may prefer finger sandwiches and tea cakes at Crown & Crumpet (p66) or the food-truck gourmet dining at Off the Grid (p69). For more of a culinary challenge, 18 Reasons (p161) offers classes on pickles and stinky cheeses, Humphry Slocombe (p144) has freaky ice cream flavors, and the Ferry Building (p86) lets kids graze gourmet goods from farmers and top chefs.

Active Kids

Golden Gate Park is a dream come true for kids with energy to burn. Hop on paddle-boats or tandem bikes at Stow Lake or strap on some rentals at Golden Gate Bike & Skate (p204) and head into the park on Sundays, when it's closed to traffic. After a Chinatown Alleyway Tour led by a local teen, head up to Chinatown Kite Shop (p114) for a long-tailed dragon model, and let it rip at Crissy Field. For action without all the walking, take a cable car joyride from downtown to Musée Mécanique (p57).

Weird & Creepy

Carnivorous flowers have insect breath at Conservatory of Flowers (p194), and kids will be holding their breath as they slip below decks on the submarine USS *Pampanito* (p57). Prison tours of Alcatraz fascinate kids, and keeps them on their best behavior for hours. For pirate supplies, don't miss 826 Valencia, and for assorted hummingbird bones, organic play-dough and a mounted teddy-bear head, hit the Paxton Gate children's store (p160).

Little Ones

Museums free to kids under 12

Kids are highly encouraged to explore art in San Francisco, with free admission to kids aged 12 and under at San Francisco Museum of Modern Art (SFMOMA; p132), Asian Art Museum (p77), Legion of Honor (p195), MH de Young Museum (p193) Museum of the African Diaspora (p140) and Contemporary Jewish Museum (p140).

Conveniently Located Playgrounds

Combine sightseeing with playtime at playgrounds located in Chinatown's historic Portsmouth Square and Old St Mary's Park, or head to the best-equipped playground in town at Golden Gate Park, where there are swings, monkey bars, play castles with slides and steep hillside slides for daredevil older siblings.

JUDY BELLAH / LONELY PLANET IMAGES ©

Prepared food at Boulette's Larder (p86)

 Eating

Other US cities boast bigger monuments, but San Francisco packs more flavor. Chef Alice Waters set the Bay Area standard for organic, sustainable, seasonal food back in 1971 at Chez Panisse, and today you'll find California's pasture-raised meats and organic produce proudly featured on Korean, Mexican, Chinese, Moroccan, Japanese, Ethiopian, Indian and Vietnamese menus. Congratulations — you couldn't have chosen a better time or place for dinner.

Fine Dining

SF restaurants take a flexible, California-casual approach to dining: jeans are acceptable, dietary limitations are cheerfully accommodated and well-informed servers will help you discover your new favorite dish. But SF's top chefs are very serious about sustainability – to taste the difference that local, organic, sustainably sourced ingredients make, try restaurants with the 🗷 icon.

Reserve ahead or take your chances in a restaurant-dense area like the Mission,

Japantown, the Avenues or North Beach. If you don't have a reservation, call to ask if there's room at the bar, seats for walk-ins or any last-minute cancellations. Most SF restaurants have online reservations through their websites or **OpenTable** (www.opentable.com), but if the system shows no availability, call the restaurant directly as some seats may be held for phone reservations and walk-ins. Places like French Laundry (p218), Chez Panisse (p209) and small, celebrated SF bistros like Frances (p166) offer limited seating, so call a month ahead and take what's available.

NEED TO KNOW

Price Ranges

In this book, the following price symbols apply, exclusive of drink, tax and tip:

→ $$$ over $30 a meal
→ $$ $15–$30 a meal
→ $ under$15 a meal

Tipping

Together, tax and tip add 25% to 30% to the bill. SF follows the US tipping standard: 20% to 25% is generous, 15% is the minimum, unless something went horribly wrong with service. Many restaurants add an automatic 18% service charge for parties of six or more.

Surcharges

Some restaurants tack on a 4% surcharge (or $1 to $2 per guest) to cover the cost of providing healthcare to restaurant employees as required by SF law. This surcharge is not something your server can deduct, but if you don't appreciate it, say so in a restaurant review online.

Opening Hours

Many restaurants are open seven days a week, though some close Sunday and/or Monday night. Lunch is usually noon to 3pm; dinner starts around 5:30pm with last service 9pm to 9:30pm weekdays or 10pm on weekends. Exceptions are noted in this book.

Feedback

Get local opinions and share your own experience at **Chowhound** (www.chow hound.chow.com/boards/1) and SF-based **Yelp** (www.yelp.com).

Bargain Gourmet

Even when you eat cheaply in San Francisco, you're spoiled for choice: $5 scores shrimp dumplings, gourmet tacos or a tasty roast beef *banh mi* (Vietnamese sandwich). The best selections of cheap eats can be found at farmers markets, food trucks and mom-and-pop eateries at the Avenues, the Mission and the gritty, gourmet Tenderloin. The US recession has brought prices at upscale SF restaurants down to earth, with affordable bar menus and midweek deals. Restaurants without liquor licenses typically offer free corkage, but otherwise it's usually $15 to $20. Look out for deals at top SF restaurants at **Blackboard Eats** (www. blackboardeats.com/san-francisco) and during **Dine About Town** (www.dineabouttown. com) in June and January.

Nontraditional Dining

BAR FOOD

Most upscale restaurants in SF offer an abbreviated, affordable menu at the bar– no reservations necessary. At bars that aren't attached to restaurants, food is often provided by caterers and food trucks. Try the following:

Kitchenette (www.kitchenettesf.com) Serves inspired, seasonal small plates under $10 at Heart (p148).

Tamale Lady The Tamale Lady guest-stars at Zeitgeist (p148) Wednesday through Friday.

Spencer on the Go (www.spenceronthego. com) Dishes French takeaway in front of Terroir Natural Wine Merchant (p151) Wednesday through Saturday nights.

Hapa SF (www.hapasf.com) Serves coconut free-range chicken skewers and other pan-Pacific dishes weekly at Vinyl Wine Bar (p184).

POP-UP RESTAURANTS

By night, pop-up restaurants take over SF galleries, storefronts and cafes. Visiting chefs prepare creative meals around a theme, eg foraged foods, hurricane fundraisers, winemaker dinners. Pop-ups often charge restaurant prices, but without advance menus, quality control, health-inspected facilities or professional service. Bring cash and arrive early: most pop-ups don't accept credit cards, and popular dishes run out fast.

Chef Eskender Aseged's **Radio Africa Kitchen** (www.radioafricakitchen.com) serves creative, organic Mediterranean-African fusion, **Ken-Ken Ramen** (www.twitter.com/ kenkenramen) makes slow-cooked, sustainable Japanese noodles, and **ForageSF** (www.foragesf.com) makes dinner with foraged ingredients. Look for announcements on **EaterSF** (http://sf.eater.com), **Grub Street San Francisco** (http://san francisco.grubstreet.com) and **Inside Scoop** (http://insidescoopsf.sfgate.com) for upcoming pop-ups.

SF's largest gathering of gourmet trucks is Off the Grid (p69), where 30 food trucks circle their wagons. Trucks and carts are cash-only businesses, and lines for popular trucks can take 10 to 20 minutes. Look for prominently displayed permits as your guarantee of proper food preparation, refrigeration and regulated working conditions.

For the best gourmet to go, try clamshell buns stuffed with duck and mango from **Chairman Bao** (www.facebook.com/chair manbao), free-range herbed roast chicken from **Roli Roti** (www.roliroti.com), organic Korean tacos from Namu (p199) and dessert from Kara's Cupcakes (p69) and the **Créme Brúleé Cart** (www.twitter.com/creme bruleecart).

You can track food trucks at **Roaming Hunger** (www.roaminghunger.com/sf/vendors) or on **Twitter** (@MobileCravings/sf-food-trucks, @streetfoodsf). Plan ahead for the annual **Street Food Festival** (www.sfstreetfoodfest.com).

Hands-on Cooking Events

Gourmet dinners taste better when you have a hand in making them with the Bay Area's passionate foodie community. Spots fill up quickly – sometimes within the hour of an even notification email – so subscribe to the organization's email list and act fast.

18 Reasons (www.18reasons.org) This not-for-profit is affiliated with Bi-Rite and hosts small educational dinners with local winemakers ($25 to $50), knife-skills and artisan food classes ($50 to $75) and occasional potlucks ($5).

Cook Here & Now (www.cookhereandnow.com) Hosts free, multi-culti community cooking events celebrating local, seasonal ingredients at San Francisco Parks & Recreation's Mission Arts Center. Sign-up is on a first-come, first-served basis.

La Cocina (www.lacocinasf.org) This non-profit offers cooking workshops ($65 to $95) and classes on starting a food business ($25), with proceeds providing training and professional kitchens for low-income culinary entrepreneurs.

Farmers Markets

NorCal idealists who headed back to the land in the 1970s started the nation's organic farming movement. Today the local bounty can be sampled in the US city with the most farmers markets per capita.

Ferry Building (www.cuesa.org; ☉Tues, Thu, Sat) The Ferry Building showcases California-grown, organic produce, artisan meats and gourmet prepared foods at moderate-to-premium prices at markets held in the morning year-round.

Alemany (www.sfgov.org/site/alemany) City-run Alemany has offered bargain prices for local and organic produce every Saturday year-round since 1945, plus stalls with ready-to-eat foods.

Heart of the City (www.hocfarmersmarket. org; UN Plaza; ☉7am-5pm Sun & Wed) Local produce (some organics) at good prices and prepared-food stalls for downtown lunches.

Inner Sunset (parking lot btwn 8th & 9th Aves, off Irving St; ☉9am-1pm) Local and some organic produce as well as artisan foods at moderate prices, plus kids programs on Sundays April through September.

Castro Farmers Market (Market St at Noe St; ☉4-8pm) Local and organic produce and artisan foods at moderate prices, cooking demos and live folk music March through December.

Eating by Neighborhood

➡ **The Marina, Fisherman's Wharf & the Piers** (p66) Seafood, fusion, food trucks at the Embarcadero.

➡ **Downtown & Civic Center** (p84) Vietnamese and brunch at Civic Center and the Tenderloin.

➡ **North Beach & Chinatown** (p108) Pizza, pasta, experimental Californian at North Beach.

➡ **The Mission, SoMa & Potrero Hill** (p142) Tacos, Italian-Californian fusion, vegetarian, pop-up restaurants at the Mission; bar bites, tasting menus, soup, sandwiches at SoMa.

➡ **The Castro & Noe Valley** (p166) Bistros and burgers at the Castro.

➡ **The Haight & Hayes Valley** (p180) Market menus, Japanese izakaya, dessert at Hayes Valley.

➡ **Golden Gate Park & the Avenues** (p198) Dim sum, Dungeness crab, Korean, modern Moroccan at the Avenues.

Lonely Planet's Top Choices

Coi (p108) Wild tasting menus featuring foraged morels, wildflowers and Pacific seafood are like licking the California coastline.

Benu (p146) Fine dining meets DJ styling in ingenious remixes of Eastern classics and the best ingredients in the West.

La Taqueria (p142) Some of SF's most memorable meals, wrapped in foil and under $8.

Frances (p166) Creative California farm-to-table fare, with French fine-dining finesse.

Aziza (p198) Sunshiny flavors evaporate Pacific fog in the Avenues, where California mysteriously bumps up against Morocco.

Best for NorCal Cuisine

Chez Panisse (p109)

French Laundry (p218)

Commonwealth (p143)

Jardinière (p183)

Delfina (p143)

Boulevard (p146)

Best al Fresco Frisco

Boulette's Larder (p86)

Café Claude (p87)

Starbelly (p167)

Il Cane Rosso (p86)

Cafe Flore (p170)

Belden Place (p84)

Best Meals under $10

Off the Grid (p69)

Rosamunde Sausage Grill (p180)

Blue Barn Gourmet (p69)

Saigon Sandwich Shop (p88)

Udupi Palace (p144)

Best Local Organic Fusion

Namu (p199)

Slanted Door (p86)

Acquerello (p123)

Juhu Beach Club (p146)

Mission Chinese (p145)

Best for Foodie Gifts

Bi-Rite (p145)

Loyal Army Clothing (p186)

Rainbow (p145)

Ferry Building (p86)

City Discount (p128)

Le Sanctuaire (p96)

Best for Dessert

Humphry Slocombe (p144)

Chantal Guillon Macarons (p183)

Three Twins Ice Cream (p180)

Kara's Cupcakes (p69)

Miette (p189)

Best for Brunch

Out the Door (p122)

Brenda's French Soul Food (p88)

Suppenküche (p183)

Butler & the Chef (p146)

Mission Beach Cafe (p145)

Best for Lunch

Barbacco (p85)

Bocadillos (p84)

Sentinel (p147)

Boxed Foods (p87)

Split Pea Seduction (p147)

Best Taquerias & SF-Mex

Chilango (p167)

Little Chihuahua (p181)

Mijita (p86)

Pancho Villa (p145)

Best Reinvented American Classics

Burgers: Zuni Cafe (p183)

Fries: Spruce (p199)

Pizza: Zero Zero (p146)

Chili: Greens (p68)

Hot dogs: Warming Hut (p69)

PB&J: Michael Mina (p84)

Drinking & Nightlife

No matter what you're having, SF bars, cafes and clubs are here to oblige. But why stick to your usual, when there are microbrews, California wines and local roasts to try? Adventurous drinking is abetted by local bartenders, who've been poring over Gold Rush saloon history and Prohibition-era cocktail recipes. SF baristas take their cappuccino-foam-drawing competition seriously, and they're gratified with any order that's fern-worthy.

Cocktails

Tonight you're gonna party like it's 1899. Before picking up their shakers at night, local bartenders spend days dusting off historic SF recipes. Gone are the mad-scientist's mixology beakers of two years ago: today SF's drink historians are judged by their absinthe fountains and displays of swizzle sticks from defunct ocean liners. Just don't be surprised if your anachronistic cocktail comes served in a cordial glass, punch bowl or Mason jar, instead of a tumbler, highball or martini glass. All that authenticity-tripping over cocktails may sound self-conscious, but after enjoying strong pours at SF's vintage saloons and speakeasies, consciousness is hardly an issue.

Happy hour specials or well drinks run $6 to $7, and gourmet choices with premium hooch run $8 to $14. Top-shelf SF Bay hooch includes No. 209 Gin, Hangar vodka and Old Potrero whiskey. If you tip $1 to $2 per drink, bartenders return the favor with heavy pours next round – that's why it's called getting tip-sy.

Wine

To get a glass of the good stuff, you don't need to commit to a bottle or escape to Wine Country. San Francisco restaurants and wine bars are increasingly offering topnotch, small-production California wines *alla spina* (on tap). *Alla spina* by the ounce or carafe is ecofriendlier than bottles and better value than flights, which usually include a clunker or two. Organically grown and biodynamic wines feature on most SF lists, along with solar-powered wineries and 'natural process' wines experimenting with wild-yeast fermentation.

Wine Country deals Plan your trip for late fall, when you can taste new releases and score harvest specials.

Food-truck pairings Consult the bar's Twitter feed or Facebook page – or see what trucks are in the area at www.roaminghunger.com/sf/vendors or @MobileCravings/sf-food-trucks on Twitter.

Cult wine retailers Bi-Rite (p145), PlumpJack Wines (p72) and California Wine Merchant (p70) sell hard-to-find wines at reasonable prices.

Beer

SF's first brewery was built before the city was in 1849, and it's been the default beverage ever since. You won't get attitude for ordering beer with fancy food here – in fact, you can get a pairing consult from the resident beer sommelier at Bar Crudo (p180), and City Beer Store & Tasting Room (p152) designs tasting plates to accompany beer. When in doubt, go local and seasonal: 21st Amendment's Hell or High Watermelon wheat beer is perfect in summer, and Anchor Steam's Christmas Ale keeps spirits bright.

Cost $4 to $7 a pint for draft microbrews, $2 PBRs.

Beer gardens Drink in the great outdoors at Zeitgeist, Beach Chalet (p201) and Wild Side West (p149).

House brews Doesn't get more local than beer brewed onsite at Magnolia Brewpub (p180) and Social (p202).

NEED TO KNOW

Smoking

Not legal indoors. Some bars have smoking patios, including Rye (p91), Rosewood (p111) and Irish Bank (p90), or backyards, such as El Rio (p148) and Zeitgeist (p148) – otherwise, you'll be puffing on the sidewalk.

Opening Hours

Downtown and SoMa bars draw happy hour crowds 4pm to 7pm; otherwise, bars are hopping by 9pm, with last call 10:30pm weekdays and 1:30am weekends. Clubs kick in around 10pm and many close at 2am, with a few exceptions like the Endup (p151).

Websites

To find out what's up where this weekend, check free weeklies *SF Weekly* (www.sfweekly.com) and *San Francisco Bay Guardian* (www.sfbg.com), and troll upcoming events on SFStation (www.sfstation.com), Squid List (www.squidlist.com/events), UrbanDaddy (www.urbandaddy.com/home/sfo) and Thrillist (www.thrillist.com/SF/new).

Meet brewers SF Brewers' Guild hosts meet-ups with local brewers: check the calendar at www.sfbrewersguild.org.

Cafe Scene

When San Francisco couples break up, the thorniest issue is: who gets the café? San Franciscans are fiercely loyal to specific roasts and baristas – especially in the Mission, Haight and North Beach – and most first Internet dates meet on neutral coffee grounds.

At some wifi-enabled cafes that serve as workplaces for telecommuting SF, you may actually get a look for laughing too loud. But there's a backlash afoot, and cafes are limiting wifi-usage, eliminating outlets and hosting events to revive SF's coffeehouse culture. When using free cafe wi-fi, remember: order something every hour, deal with interruptions graciously, don't leave laptops unattended, and know that watching porn in public is creepy, even in anything-goes SF.

Cost $2 for American coffee and $3 to $4 for espresso drinks.

Tipping Leave a buck in the tip jar for espresso drinks, especially when staying awhile.

Cell phones Texting is fine, but you'll see signs everywhere requesting 'No phone calls' – an SF barista's pet peeve.

Clubbing

DJs set the tone at clubs in SF, where the right groove gets everyone on the dance floor – gay, straight and a glorious swath of whatever. SF is relaxed about dress codes, though club bouncers do turn away people wearing flip-flops, shorts or T-shirts (unless they're fancy), especially at swing and salsa clubs. Otherwise, you'll usually only wait 10 minutes to get in anywhere, unless stumbling drunk. At fancy clubs, cocktail tables with cushy seating are usually reserved for groups who buy overpriced bottles of champagne or vodka ($150 to $300), and you might be reminded of this if you so much as lean on the armrest.

Most clubs charge $10 to $20 at the door. For discounted admission, show up before 10pm or sign up on the club's online guest list, usually indicated by a VIP or RSVP link.

Drinking by Neighborhood

➡ **The Marina, Fisherman's Wharf & the Piers** (p70) Straight bars in the Marina.

➡ **Downtown & Civic Center** (p89) Dives, chichi lounges, old-school gay bars in Civic Center & the Tenderloin.

➡ **North Beach & Chinatown** (p110) Barbary Coast saloons, eccentric bars, retro lounges in North Beach.

➡ **The Mission, SoMa & Potrero Hill** (p148) Hipster saloons, salsa clubs, women's and trans bars in the Mission; art lounges, wine bars, men's cruising bars, clubs in SoMa.

➡ **The Castro & Noe Valley** (p170) Gay bars in the Castro.

➡ **The Haight & Hayes Valley** (p183) Mean whiskey, serious beer, boho lounges in the Haight.

➡ **Golden Gate Park & the Avenues** (p201) Irish and tiki bars in the Richmond.

Lonely Planet's Top Choices

Smuggler's Cove (p184) Roll with the rum punches at this Barbary Coast shipwreck bar.

Zeitgeist (p148) Surly lady bartenders tap 40 microbrews, and the Tamale Lady cures late-night munchies in the beer garden.

Elixir (p148) Talk about pouring it on thick: bartenders mix seasonal, organic cocktails with house-infused liquor for charity.

Wine Country (p214) Drink in the scenery – literally – in America's most celebrated growing region.

Bar Agricole (p150) Drink your way to a history degree with well-researched cocktails – anything with hellfire bitters earns honors.

Best Researched Cocktails

Rye (p91)

Bourbon & Branch (p90)

Cantina (p89)

Alembic (p184)

Rickhouse (p89)

Best Wine Selections

RN74 (p150)

Hôtel Biron (p185)

Barrique (p91)

Terroir Natural Wine Merchant (p151)

California Wine Merchant (p70)

Best for Beer

Toronado (p183)

City Beer Store & Tasting Room (p152)

Church Key (p111)

Irish Bank (p90)

Best Bar Bites

Heart (p148)

Hog Island Oyster Company (p86)

Vinyl Wine Bar (p184)

Clock Bar (p90)

Comstock Saloon (p110)

Best Cafes

Caffe Trieste (p110)

Sightglass Coffee (p153)

Ritual Coffee Roasters (p149)

SFMOMA rooftop cafe (p132)

Borderlands (p149)

Trouble Coffee (p201)

Best Dance Clubs

Endup (p151)

DNA Lounge (p152)

El Rio (p148)

Ruby Skye (p90)

Rickshaw Stop (p91)

Temple (p152)

Best Happy Hours

Bar Crudo (p180)

Nojo (p183)

15 Romolo (p111)

Taverna Aventine (p91)

California Academy of Sciences Night Life (p193)

Exploratorium at night (p63)

Best for Date Nights

Top of the Mark (p125)

Burritt Room (p89)

Lush Lounge (p91)

Butterfly Bar (p124)

Dosa (p124)

Best Theme Bars

Specs' (p110)

Edinburgh Castle (p91)

Trad'R Sam's (p202)

Bigfoot Lodge (p125)

Tonga Room (p125)

Martuni's (p185)

⭐ Entertainment

SF is one of the top five US cities for the number of creative types per square mile – and when all those characters take the stage, look out. Though the city has a world-famous orchestra, opera, film festival, theater and ballet, the SF scene isn't all about marquee names: you can see cutting-edge dance, comedy and music for the price of an IMAX movie.

Comedy & Spoken Word

SF is always good for a laugh, so comics often try out new material here – recent headliners include Zach Galfianakis, Dave Chapelle and Tracy Morgan. The best guaranteed laughs are at Beach Blanket Babylon (p112) and monologues at the Marsh (p155). Historic clubs are in North Beach, with additional clubs Downtown. BATS Improv (p71) teaches improvisational comedy workshops.

Shy types hardly get a word in edgewise between the annual Litquake (p23), near-daily readings at San Francisco Main Library (p83), and such literary throw-downs as **Literary Death Match** (www.literarydeathmatch.com) and the monthly **Porchlight** (www.porchlightsf.com) storytelling series. Hemlock Tavern (p94) and Edinburgh Castle (p91) are legendary, but most Mission bars host events where you can take the stage.

Dance

Isadora Duncan once performed at the Palace of the Legion of Honor, but today you couldn't cram all of SF's soloists under one roof. SF supports the country's longest-running ballet company, the San Francisco Ballet (p93) and multiple independent local troupes at Yerba Buena Center for the Arts (p156). Calendar highlights include June's **San Francisco Ethnic Dance Festival** (www.worldartswest.org), events at cutting-edge **Counterpulse** (www.counterpulse.org) and sporadic performances by whip-smart **Chris Black/Potrzebie Dance Project** (www.potrzebie.com).

The Bay Area goes out on a limb with 'extreme dance,' experimental forms combining aerial performance, site-specific work, circus arts and modern movement. Experimental styles are championed at **Kunst Stoff** (www.kunst-stoff.org), **Zaccho Dance Theater** (www.zaccho.org) and Root Division (p138). **Dancers' Group** (www.dancersgroup.org) keeps a comprehensive calendar.

Film

Discerning SF film buffs support several historic movie palaces and world-class film festivals. Most independent theaters spare you the usual 20 minutes of commercials before features, and shows limited to over-21 audiences at Sundance Kabuki Cinema (p126) allow audiences to enjoy less noise and more beer with movies. On the second Thursday of each month, April through October, bring your blanket to free outdoor screenings at **Dolores Park Movie Night** (www.doloresparkmovie.org).

Festivals Beyond the San Francisco International Film Festival, SF hosts Lesbian & Gay, Jewish and Arab Film Festivals.

Tickets Most tickets run $10 to $13, with weekday matinees around $8. Buy tickets ahead online for premieres, festivals and limited engagements.

IMAX & 3D features Check upcoming schedules at AMC Loews Metreon 16 (p157) and Sundance Kabuki Cinema (p126).

Live Music

Anything goes on SF's music scene. A single club may host funk, reggae, bluegrass and hardcore punk all in the same week; check online calendars.

Bluegrass California's roots music has gone wild since its Gold Rush origins, and so can you at Hardly

Strictly Bluegrass Festival (p24). For toe-tapping bluegrass, don't miss SF public radio station **Bluegrass Signal** (www.kalw.org).

Funk & hip-hop Oakland has tougher rap and faster hyphy beats, but SF plays it loose and funky at Mezzanine (p156) and Independent (p185).

Jazz From Dave Brubeck's catchy time-outs to Broun Fellinis' progressive music, SF Jazz Festival (p24) covers the waterfront. Major jazz talents perform year-round at Yoshi's (p125), the centerpiece of SF's historic Fillmore Jazz District.

Punk Punk's not dead, with Jello Biafra appearances, Green Day musicals and smoking ska-core surfacing from underground SUB-Mission (p155) and Slim's (p156).

Rock Psychedelic rock made SF's '60s reputation at the Fillmore (p125), but alt-rock has helped keep the scene unpredictable and songs under 20 minutes.

Opera & Classical Music

Opera brought devastated San Francisco back to its feet after the 1906 earthquake (see p259), and it's been earning standing ovations since at San Francisco Opera. When opera season ends, enjoy vocal calisthenics from Grammy-winning **Chanticleer** (www.chanticleer.org), a 12-man chorus who perform around the Bay Area. San Francisco's **Pocket Opera Company** (www.pocketopera.org) performs opera librettos translated into English around the bay February through June.

You gotta love a city whose symphony conductor has rock-star status: the air is electric whenever Michael Tilson Thomas raises the baton with nine-time Grammy winning San Francisco Symphony. For world-class performances from vocalists, solo classical pianists and jazz ensembles at Herbst Theater, check **San Francisco Performances** (www.performances.org). Free classical concerts are held at 12:30pm Tuesdays at Old St Mary's Cathedral (p107).

Symphony & opera season Typically runs September through June; check **SF Classical Voice** (www.sfcv.org) for upcoming dates.

Music at Golden Gate Park SF Opera and SF Symphony perform gratis at Stern Grove Festival (p23).

Bargain tickets SF Opera offers the USA's least expensive basic opera tickets at $10 to $50; SF Symphony offers rush tickets on performance nights and open rehearsal tickets for $20 to $25.

NEED TO KNOW

Arts Calendar

Check the KQED Community (http://events.kqed.org) website, which includes listings for free and family events.

Discounts

Sign up for free at Gold Star Events (www.goldstarevents.com) to receive emails offering discounts on comedy, theater, concerts, opera and spas.

Half-price Tickets

Visit the TIX Bay Area (www.tixbayarea.org) website, or its ticket booth at Union Square, for cheap tickets to day-of or next-day shows.

Theater

Experimental theater sets SF apart from other US cities – Pulitzer Prize–winning *Angels in America* got its wings at American Conservatory Theater (ACT; p93) before winning Tonys on Broadway. In summer, **San Francisco Mime Troupe** (www.sfmt.org) performs free political-comedy satire in Mission Dolores Park and SF Shakespeare Festival (p23) performs gratis in the Presidio.

Theatre Bay Area (www.theatrebayarea.org) A comprehensive calendar of what's playing at 100 Bay Area companies.

Broadway shows Touring shows regularly stop in SF; see listings from production company **SHN** (www.shnsf.com).

Tickets Marquee shows run $35 to $150, but same-day, half-price tickets are often available and indie theater runs $10 to $30.

Entertainment by Neighborhood

➡ **Downtown & Civic Center** (p92) Symphony, opera, theater, live music, spoken word and comedy are in Downtown.

➡ **North Beach & Chinatown** (p112) Comedy, live music and spoken word in North Beach.

➡ **The Mission, SoMa & Potrero Hill** (p154) Dance, live music, experimental theater and spoken word are in the Mission and SoMa.

➡ **Golden Gate Park & the Avenues** (p202) Free opera, theater and concerts in Golden Gate Park.

Lonely Planet's Top Choices

San Francisco Symphony (p92) Sets the tempo for modern classical, with guests like Jessye Norman, Metallica and Rufus Wainwright.

Castro Theatre (p172) Organ overtures and revivals with enthusiastic audience participation raise this deco cinema's roof.

American Conservatory Theater (p93) Daring theater, from operas by Tom Waits and William S Burroughs to controversial David Mamet plays.

San Francisco Opera (p92) Divas like Renée Fleming bring down the house with classics and contemporary works including *Nixon in China*.

Oberlin Dance Collective (p154) Style and substance in balance, with muscular, meaningful original choreography.

Best Free Entertainment

Hardly Strictly Bluegrass Festival (p24)

Stern Grove Festival (p23)

San Francisco Mime Troupe (p34)

San Francisco Shakespeare Festival (p23)

Mission Dolores Park Movie Night (p34)

Best for Laughs

Cobb's Comedy Club (p112)

Punch Line (p94)

Purple Onion (p112)

Marsh (p155)

Beach Blanket Babylon (p112)

Best for Spoken Word

Litquake (p23)

City Lights (p112)

San Francisco Main Library (p83)

Hemlock Tavern (p94)

Make-out Room (p155)

Amnesia (p156)

Best for Dance

Yerba Buena Center for the Arts (p156)

San Francisco Ballet (p93)

San Francisco Ethnic Dance Festival (p157)

Carnaval (p22)

Best for Movies

San Francisco International Film Festival (p22)

Sundance Kabuki Cinema (p126)

Roxie Cinema (p154)

Bridge Theater (p202)

Balboa Theater (p202)

Best for Theater

Berkeley Repertory Theatre (p209)

Zellerbach Hall (p209)

Intersection for the Arts (p154)

Marsh (p155)

Exit Theater (p95)

Best Live Music Venues

Fillmore Auditorium (p125)

Great American Music Hall (p94)

Bimbo's 365 Club (p112)

Yoshi's (p213)

Bottom of the Hill (p156)

Mezzanine (p156)

⭐ GLBT

Doesn't matter where you're from, who you love or who's your daddy: if you're here, and queer, welcome home. San Francisco is America's pinkest city, and though New York Marys may call it the retirement home of the young – the sidewalks roll up early here –there's nowhere better to be out and proud.

Gay/Lesbian/Bi/Trans Scene

In San Francisco, you don't need to trawl the urban underworld for a gay scene. Here 'mos are mainstream, and hetero norms need not apply. Remember, this is where gay marriage first became legal in the US. If you're giving aggressive gaydar, the scene will find you: expect direct come-ons at stores, activist cafes and neighborhood bar patios. Drag shows are popular with San Franciscans of all persuasions, though you'll never need a professional reason to cross-dress – next to baseball, gender-bending is SF's favorite sport.

The intersection of 18th and Castro Sts is the heart of the gay men's casual cruising scene, but dancing queens head to South of Market (SoMa), the location of most thump-thump clubs and sex venues. Back in the 1950s, Sundays were gay old times in SF bars at events euphemistically called 'tea dances' – and Sundays remain the most happening nights in town. Weeknights, most guys stay home, and those looking for dates commandeer keyboards.

So where are all the ladies? They're busy scamming on their exes' exes at the Lexington Club (p148), screening documentaries at **Artists' Television Access** (www.atasite. org) or raising kids in Noe Valley and Bernal Heights. For dates, hit up the Mission, the preferred 'hood of alt-chicks, dykes, trans FTMs (female-to-males) and flirty femmes.

Party Planning

Find out where the party's happening on the weekend through these SF resources:

Betty's List (www.bettyslist.com) Parties, fund-raisers, power lesbian mixers.

Juanita More (www.juanitamore.com) The drag superstar throws fierce parties attended by hot boys, especially for Pride.

Honey Soundsystem (www.honeysoundsystem. com) Roving queer DJ collective stirs the pot with insane dance parties.

Cockblock (www.cockblocksf.com) Draws a happening les/gay crowd the second Saturday of the month at Rickshaw Stop (p91).

Fresh (www.freshsf.com) Sunday-night circuit party at Ruby Skye (p90).

Fem Bar Women's theme party and lounge scene first Sundays at Harlot.

Delicious Women hit the floor third Saturday afternoons at the Cafe (p171).

Craigslist (www.craigslist.org) Click on women-seeking-women or men-seeking-men to search for roving parties or post a query.

GLBT by Neighborhood

➡ **Downtown & Civic Center** (p89) Dive bars, trans venues and queer theater, especially in the Tenderloin.

➡ **The Mission, SoMa & Potrero Hill** (p148) Women's and trans bars, arts venues and community spaces in the Mission; raging dance clubs, leather bars, drag shows and men's sex clubs are in SoMa.

➡ **The Castro & Noe Valley** (p170) Gay history, men's cruising bars and testosterone-fuelled shopping in the Castro; GLBT family scene in Noe Valley.

NEED TO KNOW

News & Events

San Francisco Bay Times (www.sfbaytimes.com) has good resources for transsexuals; *Bay Area Reporter* (BAR; www.ebar.com) for news and listings; free nightlife advertorial mag *Gloss Magazine* (www.glossmagazine.net).

Women's Community Venues

Women's Building (p135) for organizations; Lyon-Martin Women's Health Services (p296) for health and support; Brava Theater (p155) and Femina Potens (www.feminapotens.org) for arts.

Support & Activism

LYRIC (www.lyric.org) for queer youth; Human Rights Campaign Action Center & Store (p172) for political organizing; GLBT History Museum (p166) for context; Under One Roof (p173) to support local AIDS organizations with souvenir purchases.

Lonely Planet's Top Choices

Pride (p23) The most extravagant celebration on the planet culminates in Pink Saturday parties and an exhilarating 1.2 million-strong Pride Parade.

Human Rights Campaign Action Center & Store (p172) Been there, signed the petition, bought the T-shirt supporting civil rights at Harvey Milk's camera storefront.

Castro Theatre (p166) San Francisco International Lesbian & Gay Film Festival premieres here as well as audience-participatory cult classics.

GLBT History Museum (p166) Proud moments and historic challenges, captured for posterity.

Aunt Charlie's (p92) Knock-down, drag-out winner for gender-bending shows and dance-floor freakiness.

Best Queer Dance Floors

Stud (p150)

Rebel Bar (p185)

Rickshaw Stop (p91)

Endup (p151)

440 Castro (p170)

Best for Women

Lexington Club (p148)

Wild Side West (p149)

El Rio (p148)

Harlot (p152)

Women's Building (p135)

Brava Theater (p155)

Best Daytime Scene

Mission Dolores Park (p134)

Baker Beach (p61)

Cafe Flore (p170)

Harvey Milk & Jane Warner Plazas (p166)

Samovar Tea Lounge (p171)

Hunky Jesus Contest (p22)

Best for Weeknights

Cat Club (p150)

Mix (p171)

New Conservatory Theater (p95)

Truck (p148)

Qbar (p171)

Best for Dinner Dates

Zuni Cafe (p183)

Delfina (p143)

L'Ardoise (p167)

Tataki (p167)

Jardinière (p183)

Commonwealth (p143)

Best Places to Stay

Parker Guest House (p249)

Inn on Castro (p249)

Willows (p249)

24 Henry (p249)

Best for Gay Old Times with Straight Friends

Mint (p186)

SF International Lesbian & Gay Film Festival (p23)

AsiaSF (p156)

Under One Roof (p173)

Blackbird (p170)

Shopping

All those rustic dens, well-stocked spice racks and fabulous outfits don't just pull themselves together – San Franciscans scour their city for it. Eclectic originality is San Francisco's style signature, and that's not one-stop shopping. But consider the thrill of the hunt: while shopping in SF, you can watch fish theater, make necklaces from zippers and trade fashion tips with drag queens.

Style Secrets

There's no shame in admitting you picked up staples at SoMa designer outlets or Union Square post-holiday sales – everyone loves a sweet deal – but locals are otherwise loath to patronize chain stores. Most will claim political reasons (supporting local designers, the economy, fellow workers of the world etc, etc) but the real reason is individualist vanity. Many San Franciscans would rather stay home Friday night than show up at a party in the same Gap sweater as three other people. Indie designers and vintage shops supply original SF style, and savvy shoppers trawl discount racks on SF's most boutique-studded streets: Haight, Valencia, Hayes, upper Grant, Fillmore, Union and Polk.

Adventures in Retail

To boost the shopping drama, San Francisco stores often pull double duty as nonprofits, event spaces and art galleries, and look more like natural history museums or pioneer farm sheds. For further adventures in retail, don't miss these shopping events:

Monster Drawing Rally (www.soex.org) Artists scribble furiously, and audience members snap up their work while still wet; February.

Noise Pop (www.noisepop.com) Concerts and rock-star pop-up shops; February.

Litquake (www.litquake.com) Score signed books and grab drinks with authors afterwards; September.

Alternative Press Expo (www.comic-con.org/ape) Comics, drawings, zines and crafts, plus workshops with comics artists; October.

Artpad (www.artpadsf.com) Independent art fair with live bands, rooftop video screenings and artistic mayhem.

KPFA Craft Fair (www.kpfa.org/craftsfair) The original hippie holiday crafts fair to support Berkeley's public radio station; December.

Celebration of Craftswomen (www.womensbuilding.org) Local craftswomen show off their skills and support the Women's Building; held at Fort Mason in December.

Shopping by Neighborhood

➡ **The Marina, Fisherman's Wharf & the Piers** (p71) Date outfits, girly accessories, wine, design in the Marina.

➡ **Downtown & Civic Center** (p95) Department stores, global megabrands, discount retail, Apple store.

➡ **The Hills & Japantown** (p126) Date outfits, girly accessories, wine and design in Pacific Heights.

➡ **The Mission, SoMa & Potrero Hill** (p158) Bookstores, local design collectives, artisan foods, art galleries, vintage whatever.

➡ **The Haight & Hayes Valley** (p186) Local and independent designers, home design, sweets and shoes in Hayes Valley; head shops, music stores, vintage, eccentric accessories, and skate, snow and surf gear in the Haight.

NEED TO KNOW

Business Hours

Most stores are open daily from 10am to 6–7pm, though hours often run 11am to 8pm Saturdays and 11am to 6pm Sundays. Stores in the Mission and the Haight tend to open later and keep erratic hours; many Downtown stores open until 8pm or 9pm.

Sales Tax

Factor SF city and CA state sales taxes into your shopping budget – combined, they tack 9.5% onto the price of your purchase. This tax is not refundable.

Returns

Try before you buy, and for gifts, ask about return policies. Many stores offer returns for store credit only, so when in doubt, consider a gift certificate – in California, they never expire and you can often use them for online.

Websites

Check Urban Daddy (www.urbandaddy.com) for store openings and events; Thrillist (www. thrillist.com) for guy gifts and gadgets; Refinery 29 (www.refinery29.com) for sales and trends; and Daily Candy (www.daily candy.com) for SF finds and deals.

Lonely Planet's Top Choices

City Lights (p112) If you can't find nirvana in the Poetry Chair

upstairs, try Lost Continents in the Basement.

826 Valencia (p135) Your friendly neighborhood pirate supply store and publishing house; proceeds support an on-site youth literacy program.

Under One Roof (p173) Volunteers ring up goods donated by local designers with sincere thanks – all proceeds support local AIDS organizations.

Park Life (p203) Making museum stores jealous with rising-star artists out back, limited-edition art books and design oddities in front.

Revolver (p187) Effortlessly clever indie-movie-star style and retro boho-chic; no clove cigarettes required.

Best SF Fashion Designers

Goorin Brothers Hats (p186)

Mission Statement (p159)

Nooworks (p158)

Dema (p159)

Al's Attire (p113)

Sunhee Moon (p160)

Best for Women

Velvet da Vinci (p128)

Eco Citizen (p128)

Gimme Shoes (p188)

Jeremy's (p160)

Candystore Collective (p159)

Ambiance (p173)

Best for Men

MAC (p188)

Sui Generis (p172)

Upper Playground (p187)

Room 4 (p160)

Nancy Boy (p188)

Best for the Person Who Has Everything

Electric Works (p140)

Good Vibrations (p159)

General Store (p203)

SCRAP (p158)

Madame S & Mr S Leather (p160)

Loved to Death (p187)

Best for Foodies

Ferry Building (p76)

Bi-Rite (p145)

Omnivore (p173)

PlumpJack Wines (p72)

Loyal Army Clothing (p186)

City Discount (p128)

Best for Eclectic Decor

Gravel & Gold (p158)

Accident & Artifact (p159)

ATYS (p72)

Branch (p160)

Prairie Collective (p186)

Peace Industry (p188)

Best for Reading Material

Adobe Books (p158)

Booksmith (p185)

Green Apple Books (p203)

Isotope (p189)

Books Inc (p172)

Kayo Books (p97)

Sports & Activities

San Franciscans love the outdoors, and their historic conservation efforts have protected acres of parks, beaches and woodlands to enjoy. This city lives for sunny days spent biking, skating, surfing and facing fierce competition, from disc golf to lawn bowling. Foggy days are spent at arts workshops and on trapezes, but evenings are for dancing and Giants games.

Spectator Sports

You can catch 49ers football and Giants baseball on cable anytime, anywhere – but SF is the place to see them on their home turf. The 49ers play at Candlestick Park (p162) south of the city, and the Giants play at AT&T Park (p161). You might be able catch some Giants action for free at the Embarcadero waterfront boardwalk – just look for the cluster of folding chairs with coolers.

Tickets Book through team websites, or try Ticketmaster (www.ticketmaster.com). If games are sold out, search the 'Tickets' category on www.craigslist.org.

Sports coverage *San Francisco Chronicle* (www.sfgate.com) is best for complete coverage, but *The Examiner* online (www.examiner.com/san_francisco) also has the latest sports stats and predictions.

Outdoor Activities

On sunny weekends, SF is out kite-flying, surfing or biking. Fog keeps temperatures perfect for exercising, but don't neglect sunscreen: UV rays penetrate SF's thin cloud cover.

BICYCLING

Every weekend thousands of cyclists cross the Golden Gate to explore the Marin Headlands and Mt Tamalpais. The first off-road races in the '70s kicked up dirt on Mt Tam, which remains the Bay Area's supreme mountain-biking challenge. Check out our biking tour (p67), which takes you from the waterfront over Golden Gate Bridge.

Many SF streets have bicycle lanes, and major parks have bike paths. The best and safest places to cycle in SF are Golden Gate Park, the Embarcadero and the wooded Presidio. The classic Sunday ride runs through Golden Gate Park, along John F Kennedy Dr (car-free on Sundays) to Ocean Beach (best when it's not too windy).

City biking maps San Francisco Bicycle Coalition (www.sfbike.org) produces *San Francisco Biking/Walking Guide,* which shows how to avoid traffic and hills – find it at local bike shops, Rainbow Grocery (p145) or at the Bicycle Coalition's website as a PDF.

Route planning Put your smart phone to work finding the perfect route using the San Francisco Bike Route Planner. (Google it on the fly, or pre-program your phone with the following address: www.amarpai.com/bikemap/bikemap.html.) You enter your starting address and destination, tick a box stating whether you want the most direct route or the most bike-friendly route and – ta-da! – a map appears showing you the optimal route, along with each street's grade.

Cycling guides Good books for Bay Area cyclists include *Bay Area Bike Rides,* by Ray Hosler, and *Cycling the San Francisco Bay Area: 30 Rides to Historic Sites and Scenic Places,* by Carol O'Hare. For tips, check the resources page of the Bicycle Coalition's website.

Critical Mass To prove your right of way in this bicycling city, pedal with the renegade mob Critical Mass (www.critical-mass.info) on the last Friday of the month. Bicyclists are legally allowed to 'take the lane,' as in ride down the center of the street, if hazards make riding on the shoulder unsafe. Some motorists get angry about this, so use caution and stand down if someone flips you off from a passing car.

NEED TO KNOW

Free Outdoor Activities

Lawn bowling, baseball, archery, disc golf: try something new gratis at Golden Gate Park.

Gear

From mountaineering to diving, they've got you covered at Sports Basement (p72).

Group Activities

Join groups kayaking, surfing and camping through the University of California San Francisco's Outdoors Programs (☑415-476-2078; www.outdoors.ucsf. edu); open to the public and a great way to meet people.

Rainy Day Adventures

Head to the Marina to Planet Granite (p73) rock-climbing gym and House of Air (p72) trampoline park, take a trapeze workshop at Circus Center Trapeze (p204), or hit Yerba Buena Center Ice Skating & Bowling (p162).

Riding naked Yes, it's legal in SF. World Naked Bike Ride (www.sfbikeride.org) takes place in early June to protest US dependence on fossil fuel. A clever compromise for shy types: body paint.

GOLF

Tee up and enjoy mild weather, clipped greens and gorgeous views. The top courses are public (see p204) and most offer deals on their websites, including Presidio Golf Course (p73).

RUNNING

Marina Green has a 2.5-mile jogging track and fitness course, and trails abound in Golden Gate Park, including a 400m synthetic track in Kezar Stadium at the park's southeast corner. Trails cover about 3 miles from the Panhandle to the ocean, and on Sundays cars are banned from John F Kennedy Dr, east of Crossover Dr. With its eucalyptus forests and ocean air, the Presidio is another runners' paradise. Lake Merced Park is a 368-acre island of country trails at the southwest end of the city that's ideal for long runs. Some of SF's major races, like Bay to Breakers (p22), are more festive than serious.

SKATING & SKATEBOARDING

In skate circles, SF is best known as the home of roller disco and the skateboard magazine **Thrasher** (www.thrashermagazine. com). Inline skaters make commando raids every Friday night along the waterfront, and disco-skate in Golden Gate Park on Sundays. Potrero del Sol/La Raza Skatepark (p161) is the city's newest skatepark, with bowls and ramps – though you'll want to clear out of the area by sunset, when the neighborhood scene can get sketchy. Haight St is urban skating at its obstacle-course best, especially the downhill slide from Baker to Pierce.

For signature SF skateboards and skate gear, hit Mission Skateboards (p158) and SFO Snowboarding & FTC Skateboarding (p187); for decks and trucks, Upper Playground (p187). If you'd rather rent your wheels, Golden Gate Park Bike & Skate (p204) rents inline and four-wheeled roller skates in good weather.

TENNIS

There are free public tennis courts all over San Francisco, including popular courts at Mission Dolores Park and Sterling Park. For other free public courts, contact **San Francisco Recreation & Park Department** (☑415-831-2700; www.parks.sfgov.org; ☉9am-4pm). Call ahead to reserve one of 21 Golden Gate Park **courts** (☑415-753-7131; fees adult $4-6, kids free; ☉4-6pm Wed, 9am-5pm Thu & Fri).

Water Sports & Activities

SAILING

Sailing the bay is work: currents are strong, winds erratic and cold, and tidal currents ferocious. Know what you're doing, or else hit the water aboard a skippered sailboat cruise, cocktail in hand. Sailing is best April through August, when the westerlies are most reliable, but diehards sail year-round. Classes and rentals are available in SF from Spinnaker Sailing (p162) or City Kayak (p162). Sail the bay on a catamaran with Adventure Cat (p72) or take a booze cruise with Red & White Fleet (p72).

Whale-watching season peaks mid-October through December, when gray whales migrate from the Bering Sea to Baja California – the longest annual mammal migration in the world. Whales cruise the coastline and are easy to spot from land, especially from Point Reyes. Book whale-watching tours through Oceanic Society Expeditions (p72).

SURFING & WINDSURFING

Surfing is best in winter, when storms churn up swells 12ft or higher. Santa Cruz is the top destination, followed by the challenging (and shark-prone) Stinson Beach in Marin County. SF's Ocean Beach is surfed by locals at daybreak in winter, but these Pacific swells are not for beginners. Check the surf report before you suit up (☑415-273-1618). A safer bet is bay windsurfing and bodysurfing off the beach at Crissy Field.

Hit up Aqua Surf Shop (p189) for board rentals, and Mollusk (p203) for specialty boards and gear. San Francisco Surf Company (p72) offers classes for beginners.

SWIMMING

To picture the Northern California beach scene, think Hitchcock. Wind and fog are the dominant summer weather patterns, and the waters around SF are frigid. Four-mile-long Ocean Beach (p198) is best for romantic walks: its currents are dangerous for swimming. Try Santa Cruz instead for calmer waters and warmer beaches. Hardy swimmers determined to brave SF's chilly waters head to Aquatic Park. Baker Beach (p61) is popular with sunbathers, walkers, surf fishers and nudists (at the northern end); swimming is feasible close to shore when the tide is coming in.

Local pools Koret Pool (p189) and Embarcadero YMCA have well-kept pools; city pool schedules are listed at www.parks.sfgov.org.

TI2Y Swim Swim 1.5 miles from Treasure Island (TI) to Embarcadero YWCA.

Alcatraz Sharkfest Swim Swimmers ferry to Alcatraz, then swim 1.5 miles back to Aquatic Park. Entry costs $175; reservations and information available through **Envirosports** (www.envirosports.com).

Indoor Activities

ART WORKSHOPS

When (not if) San Francisco leaves you with excess artistic inspiration, pursue your vision with hands-on classes. Transform industrial scraps into mosaics at SCRAP (p158), silkscreen protest posters at Mission Cultural Center for Latino Arts (p161), bind your own coffee-table art book at San Francisco Center for the Book (p162) and join craft sessions already in progress at Museum of Craft & Folk Art (p140).

DANCE

Here in the home of Isadora Duncan and the standard-setting San Francisco Ballet (p93), dance festivals are held year-round and international dance companies are hosted at Yerba Buena Center for the Arts (p156).

You don't need years of training to take the floor: a brief lesson will get you lindy-hopping at Golden Gate Park, tango-ing at Mission Cultural Center and creating an interpretive-dance ode to SF at Oberlin Dance Collective (p154). Live music venues across town offer dance classes before kicking off the evening's entertainment, from Bimbo's 356 Club (p112) in North Beach to Mission clubs.

YOGA

With hundreds of studios in town, if you're a serious devotee of a particular tradition, you'll find it in SF with a quick internet search; otherwise, try Yoga Tree (p163).

Sports & Activities by Neighborhood

➡ **The Marina, Fisherman's Wharf & the Piers** (p72) Running, biking, windsurfing, kayaking, skating, yoga in the Marina.

➡ **The Mission, SoMa & Potrero Hill** (p161) Arts, dance, skateboarding, street biking, yoga at the Mission; swimming, kayaking, sailing, yoga in SoMa.

➡ **Golden Gate Park & the Avenues** (p204) Surfing, biking, swimming, golf, archery in and around the Avenues.

Lonely Planet's Top Choices

Golden Gate Park (p192) The ultimate urban sports field: fly-casting, running, roller disco, croquet, biking and more.

San Francisco Giants (p161) Go Giants to watch and learn how the World Series is won – bushy beards, women's underwear and all.

Potrero del Sol/La Raza Skatepark (p161) Skate the bowl or watch in awe as pro street skaters hit air and padded kindergartners scoot along.

Oceanic Society Expeditions (p72) Watch whales breach, blow and splash on their annual Pacific migration.

Mission Cultural Center for Latino Arts (p161) Pick up Afro-Peruvian dance moves, printmaking skills and inspiration at this community center.

Best Urban Outdoor Sports Venues

Crissy Field (p60)

Mission Dolores Park (p134)

Sterling Park (p119)

Fort Funston (p198)

Marina Green (p42)

Best for Water Sports

Santa Cruz (p235)

City Kayak (p162)

San Francisco Surf Company (p72)

Aquatic Park (p58)

Baker Beach (p61)

Best on Wheels

Golden Gate Park Bike & Skate (p204)

Wheel Fun Rentals (p205)

Mission Skateboards (p158)

SFO Snowboarding & FTC Skateboarding (p187)

Mt Tamalpais (p227)

Golden Gate Bridge (p59)

Best Outdoor Escapes

Muir Woods (p227)

Point Reyes (p232)

Napa Valley & Sonoma Valley Wine Country (p214)

Stinson Beach (p228)

San Francisco Botanical Garden (p194)

Coastal Trail (p195)

Best for DIY Art Inspiration

Needles & Pens (p158)

Museum of Craft & Folk Art (p140)

Goodwill As-Is Store (p161)

Flax (p188)

Mission Murals (p133)

Southern Exposure (p139)

Best Indoor Activities

Circus Center Trapeze (p204)

House of Air (p72)

Planet Granite (p73)

Yerba Buena Center Ice Skating & Bowling (p162)

Best Low-impact Challenges

Lawn Bowling Club (p204)

San Francisco Croquet Club (p205)

San Francisco Disc Golf (p205)

Golden Gate Municipal Golf Course (p204)

AIDS Walk (p23)

Cable Cars

A creaking hand brake seems to be the only thing between you and a cruel fate as your 15,000-pound cable car picks up speed downhill, careening toward oncoming traffic. But Andrew Hallidie's 1873 contraptions have held up miraculously well on San Francisco's breakneck slopes, and groaning brakes and clanging brass bells only add to the carnival-ride thrills.

History

Legend has it that the idea of cable cars occurred to Hallidie in 1869, as he watched a horse carriage struggle up Jackson St – until one horse slipped on wet cobblestones and the carriage went crashing downhill. Such accidents were considered inevitable on steep San Francisco hills, but Hallidie knew better. His father was the Scottish inventor of wire cable, which Hallidie had put to work hauling ore out of mines during the Gold Rush. If hemp-and-metal cable could haul rocks through High Sierras snowstorms, surely it could transport San Franciscans through fog.

The 'Wire rope railway' wasn't a name that inspired confidence, and skeptical city planners granted the inventor just three months to make his contraption operational by August 1, 1873. Hallidie had missed his city deadline by four hours when his cable car was poised on Jones St ready for the descent. The cable car operator was terrified, and Hallidie himself is said to have grabbed the brake and steered the car downhill.

By the 1890s, 53 miles of track crisscrossed the city. Hallidie became a rich man, and even ran for mayor; defamed as an opportunistic Englishman despite his civic contributions and US citizenship, he lost. He remained a lifelong inventor, earning 300 patents and becoming a prominent member of California Academy of Sciences.

TRIALS BY FIRE

Before Hallidie came along, hermits had the run of Nob Hill. No sane person wanted to climb this windswept 338ft crag after a long

day's work downtown – until Hallidie's cable cars provided easy access to breathtaking views on the summit. But without a windbreak between them, Nob Hill mansions went up in flames in the 1906 earthquake and fire. Luckily, a fleet of cable cars stored outside the fire zone was saved, and grand buildings such as Grace Cathedral soon sprouted up around revived lines.

THE CABLE CAR LADY TO THE RESCUE

The Powell-Hyde turnaround at Fisherman's Wharf is named for Friedel Klussmann, a genteel botany enthusiast. She became better known as 'The Cable Car Lady' in 1947, when she began rallying her local ladies' gardening club against the mayor's plans to replace the city's two Powell St cable car lines with buses. Her campaign was derided by the mayor, who scoffed at his opponent as a dotty, sentimental Luddite.

Klussmann and her fellow gardeners responded to harsh words with hard numbers: cable cars brought in more tourism dollars than the city spent on upkeep, and buses were less effective and more costly. The dispute was brought to a public vote: the mayor lost to the ladies by a landslide. When the insolvent California St line was imperiled in 1952, the Cable Car Lady rallied to rescue it. Upon Klussmann's death at age 90 in 1986, cable cars citywide were draped in black.

Technology & Operation

Today the cable car seems more like a steampunk carnival ride than modern transport, but it remains the killer app to conquer San Francisco's highest hills. Cable cars still can't move in reverse, and require burly

NEED TO KNOW

Operating Hours

Cable car lines operate from about 6am to 1am daily, with scheduled departures every three to 12 minutes; for detailed schedules, see http://transit.511.org.

Cost

If you're planning to stop en route, get a Muni Passport (p290); one-way tickets cost $6, with no on-and-off privileges.

Boarding

The Powell St and California St cable car turnarounds usually have queues, but they move fast. To skip the queue, head further up the line and jump on when the cable car stops. Cable cars may make rolling stops, especially on downhill runs. To board on hills, act fast: leap onto the baseboard and grab the closest leather hand strap.

Stops

Cable cars stop at almost every block on the California St and Powell-Mason lines, and every block on the north–south stretches of the Powell-Hyde line; detailed transit maps are available free online at www.sfmuni.com or at the Powell St turnaround kiosk for $3.

Child Safety

This Victorian transport is certainly not childproof. You won't find car seats or seat belts on these wooden benches; kids love the open-air seating in front, but holding small children securely inside the car is safer.

Accessibility

Cable cars are not accessible for people with disabilities.

Signage

To help distinguish the two Powell lines, Powell-Mason is signed in yellow and Powell-Hyde has red signage.

gripmen and one buff gripwoman to lean hard on hand-operated brakes to keep them from careening downhill. The city receives many applicants for this job, but 80% fail the strenuous tests of upper-body strength and hand-eye coordination, and rarely reapply.

Although cables groan piteously with uphill effort, they seldom fray and have rarely broken in more than a century of near-continuous operation. The key to the cable car's amazing safety record is the cable grip wheel: clips click into place and gradually release to prevent cables from slipping. To watch this clever Victorian technology in action, visit the Cable Car Museum.

Powell-Hyde Cable Car

The ascent up Nob Hill feels like the world's longest roller-coaster climb – but on the Powell-Hyde car, the biggest thrills are still ahead. This cable car bobs up and down hills, with the Golden Gate Bridge popping in and out of view on Russian Hill. This isn't a million-dollar view, it's a $40 million view. That's how much Oracle CEO and America's Cup enthusiast Larry Ellison paid in 2011 to buy his neighbor's house atop Russian Hill, since his own bay view was partially obstructed by trees.

Hop off the cable car at Lombard St to walk the zig-zagging route to North Beach. But Russian Hill's best scenery is hidden nearby. Duck into Russell St to spot Jack Kerouac's Love Shack where he wrote *On the Road,* or follow stairway walks to shady Macondray Lane and blooming Ina Coolbrith Park. Russian Hill's priceless panorama belongs not to a billionaire, but penniless poet George Sterling: Sterling Park, where views of sailboats bobbing on the bay are framed by wind-sculpted pines. Top that with a root-beer float at Swensen's or a sundae downhill at Ghirardelli Ice Cream.

Powell-Mason Cable Car

The Powell-Hyde line may have multi-million-dollar vistas, but the Powell-Mason line has more culture. Detour atop Nob Hill for San Francisco–invented martinis with 360-degree panoramas at Top of the Mark, then resume the ride to Chinatown, the Chinese Historical Society of America and temple-lined Waverly Pl. The route cuts through North Beach at Washington Sq, where you're surrounded by pizza possibilities and Diego Rivera murals at the nearby San Francisco Art Institute. The terminus at Bay and Taylor Sts is handy

San Francisco's Cable Cars

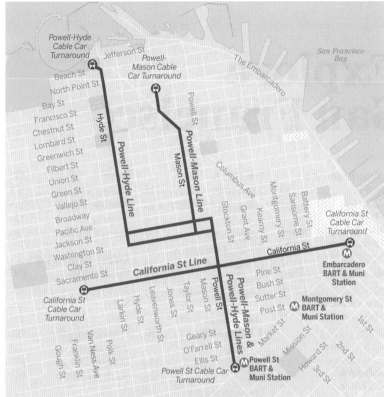

to visit two truly riveting attractions: USS *Pampanito* and Musée Mécanique.

California St Cable Car

History buffs and crowd-shy visitors prefer San Francisco's oldest cable car line: the California St cable car, which has been in operation since 1878. This divine ride west heads through Chinatown past Old St Mary's Cathedral and climbs Nob Hill to Grace Cathedral. Hop off at Polk St for Swan Oyster Depot, tempting boutiques and cocktails with Sasquatch at Bigfoot Lodge. The Van Ness Ave terminus is a few blocks west of Alta Plaza Park and Lafayette Parks, which are both ringed by stately Victorians. From here, brave the gauntlet of Fillmore St boutiques to Japantown.

Explore
San Francisco

SAN FRANCISCO'S
TOP SIGHTS

Neighborhoods at a Glance

❶ The Marina, Fisherman's Wharf & the Piers (p52)

Since the Gold Rush, the waterfront here has been the point of entry for new arrivals. It remains a major attraction for sea lion antics and old-school video games, it's and the getaway to and from Alcatraz. To the west, the Marina has chic boutiques in a former cow pasture and organic dining along the water-front. At the adjoining Presidio, you'll encounter Shakespeare on the loose, a mildly amused Yoda and public nudity at a former army base.

❷ Downtown & Civic Center (p74)

Downtown has all the urban amenities: art galleries, swanky hotels, first-run theaters, a mall full of brand names and XXX cinemas. Civic Center is a zoning conundrum, with

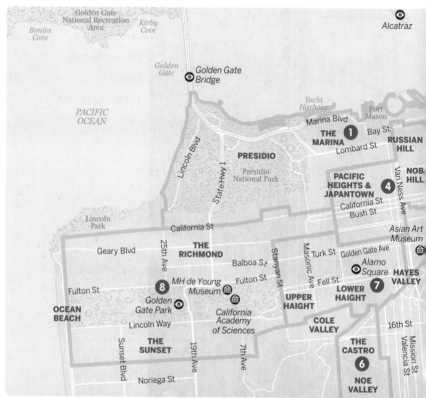

great performances and Asian art treasures on one side of City Hall, and dive bars and soup kitchens on the other.

❸ North Beach & Chinatown (p98)

In North Beach wild parrots circle overhead, while the idle chatter in Italian cafes and bohemian bars below runs from soccer to filmmaking over the sound of opera on the jukebox. On the main streets of Chinatown, dumplings and rare teas are served under pagoda roofs, but in its historic back alleys you'll find temple incense, mah jong tile clatter and distant echoes of revolution.

❹ The Hills & Japantown (p115)

Russian and Nob Hills are the stomping grounds of eccentric millionaires and hardcore urban hikers, with cable cars delivering customers to hilltop bars and high-fashion boutiques. When you see sushi picnics in the fountains, cutting-edge fashion in starchy Victorian storefronts and rock at the legendary Fillmore, you'll know you've arrived in Japantown.

❺ The Mission, SoMa & Potrero Hill (p130)

The best way to enjoy the Mission is with a book in one hand and a burrito in the other, amid murals, sunshine and the usual crowd of documentary filmmakers and novelists. The Mission is difficult to define and never entirely exclusive: largely Latin American 24th St also attracts Southeast Asians, lesbians and dandies. Silicon Valley refugees take to Potrero Hill, while barflies and artists lurk in the valley below. Some are drawn to South of Market (SoMa) for high technology, others for high art, but everyone gets down and dirty on the dance floor.

❻ The Castro & Noe Valley (p164)

Rainbow flags wave their welcome to party boys, career activists and leather daddies in the Castro, while over the hill in Noe Valley, megastrollers brake for bakeries and boutiques, as moms load up on sleek shoes and strong coffee.

❼ The Haight & Hayes Valley (p174)

Hippies reminisce and punks lose their sneers in the Haight, land of flower-power souvenirs, anarchist comic books, free concerts and skateboards. Fashionistas raid boutiques for local designs, while Zen monks drift past on the sidewalks of Hayes Valley.

❽ Golden Gate Park & the Avenues (p190)

Around Golden Gate Park, hardcore surfers and gourmet adventurers find a home where the buffalo roam and the MH de Young's tower rises above it all. The foggy Avenues are a grey area of unexpected overlap, with authentic Irish bars, organic Cali-Moroccan cuisine and Japanese convenience stores.

NEIGHBORHOODS AT A GLANCE

The Marina, Fisherman's Wharf & the Piers

THE PRESIDIO | FORT MASON | COW HOLLOW

Neighborhood Top Five

❶ Strolling across the **Golden Gate Bridge** (p59) just as the fog clears, revealing magnificent views of downtown San Francisco and sailboats plying the waves below.

❷ Feeling cold winds blow through **Alcatraz** (p54) and imagining the misery of prison life.

❸ Giggling at the shenanigans of braying and barking sea lions at **Pier 39** (p56).

❹ Poking into hidden courtyards and finding indie boutiques along **Union St** (p71).

❺ Marveling at 19th-century arcade games at the **Musée Mécanique** (p57).

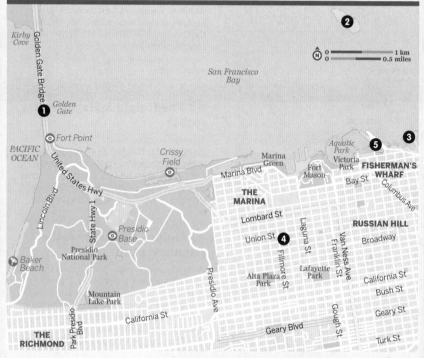

For more detail of this area, see Map p315, p317 and p318 ➡

Explore the Marina, Fisherman's Wharf & the Piers

Fisherman's Wharf is the epicenter of tourism in San Francisco; the few remaining fishermen moor their boats around Pier 45. Locals don't usually visit the Wharf. The area gets packed by early afternoon: the earlier you come, the better – unless you don't mind strolling through crowds, in which case afternoon is better. Summertime fog usually clears by midday (if it clears at all), so save the Golden Gate Bridge for the early afternoon – but be forewarned that afternoon fog blows in around 4pm. Carry a jacket and don't wear shorts, unless you're here during the rare heat wave (locals spot the tourists by their short pants). Most people walk far more than they expect to when exploring the waterfront, so wear comfortable shoes and sunscreen. Cow Hollow and the Marina have good shopping, bars and restaurants. Explore these areas later in the day, after working hours but while shops are still open, when the busy sidewalks provide a glimpse of how San Franciscans entertain themselves near the waterfront.

Local Life

➜ **Nature walks** San Franciscans love the outdoors – joggers and dog walkers flock to the waterfront trails at Crissy Field (p60) and the wooded hills of the Presidio for ocean breezes and knockout views.

➜ **Barhopping** The Marina District bars on Fillmore St, from Union St to Chestnut St, are ground zero for party-girl sorority sisters and the jocks who love them. Not all locals approve.

➜ **City views** For dramatic views of Fisherman's Wharf and the San Francisco skyline – and a break from the crowds – hop on a ferry at Pier 39.

Getting There & Away

➜ **Streetcar** Historic F Market streetcars run along Market St, then up the Embarcadero waterfront to Fisherman's Wharf.

➜ **Cable car** The Powell-Hyde and Powell-Mason lines run up Powell St to the Wharf; the Mason line is quicker, but the hills are better on the Hyde line.

➜ **Bus** Major routes to the Wharf and/or the Marina from downtown include the 19, 30, 47 and 49.

➜ **Parking** At the Wharf, there are garages at Pier 39 and Ghiradelli Square (enter on Beach St, between Larkin and Polk Sts). At the Marina, there's parking at Crissy Field and Fort Mason. The Presidio is the only place it's easy to park – and free.

Lonely Planet's Top Tip

To gain breathing room from the tourist crowds, head west of Ghiradelli Square. Make your way to the northernmost end of Van Ness Ave, then cut west along the waterfront pedestrian–bicyclist path, through Fort Mason to the Marina Green. Aim for the bobbing masts of the yacht club, along Marina Blvd, stopping to explore piers jutting into the bay, but keeping your eye on the prize: the Golden Gate Bridge.

✖ Best Places to Eat

➜ Gary Danko (p66)
➜ Greens (p68)
➜ A16 (p68)
➜ Betelnut (p68)
➜ Friday night food trucks (p69)

For reviews, see p66 ➜

🍸 Best Places to Drink

➜ Buena Vista Cafe (p70)
➜ Pier 23 (p70)
➜ Betelnut (p68)
➜ Lou's Pier 47 (p70)
➜ California Wine Merchant (p70)

For reviews, see p70 ➜

☉ Best for Waterfront Vistas

➜ Golden Gate Bridge (p59)
➜ Warming Hut (p69)
➜ Crissy Field (p60)
➜ San Francisco Municipal pier at Aquatic Park (p58)
➜ Sea lions at Pier 39 (p56)

TOP SIGHTS
ALCATRAZ

Alcatraz: for almost 150 years, the name has given the innocent chills and the guilty cold sweats. Over the years it's been the nation's first military prison, a forbidding maximum-security penitentiary and disputed territory between Native American activists and the FBI. So it's no surprise that the first step you take off the ferry and onto 'the Rock' seems to cue ominous music: dunh-dunh-dunnnnh!

Early History

It all started innocently enough back in 1775, when Spanish lieutenant Juan Manuel de Ayala sailed the *San Carlos* past the 12-acre island that he called Isla de Alcatraces (Isle of the Pelicans). In 1859 a new post on Alcatraz became the first US West Coast fort, and it soon proved handy as a holding pen for Civil War deserters, insubordinates and those who had been court-martialed. Among the prisoners were Native American scouts and 'unfriendlies,' including 19 Hopis who refused to send their children to government boarding schools where speaking Hopi and practicing their religion were punishable by beatings. By 1902 the four cell blocks of wooden cages were rotting, unsanitary and ill-equipped for the influx of US soldiers convicted of war crimes in the Philippines. The army began building a new concrete military prison in 1909, but upkeep was expensive and the US soon had other things to worry about: WWI, financial ruin and flappers.

DON'T MISS...

- ➡ Self-guided audio tour
- ➡ Solitary-confinement cells on D block
- ➡ Waterfront vistas along the Agave Trail

PRACTICALITIES

- ➡ Alcatraz Cruises
- ☑ 415-981-7625
- ➡ www.nps.gov/alca traz for park info, www. alcatrazcruises.com, for ferry reservations
- ➡ ferry departs Pier 33
- ➡ admission daytime adult/child/family $26/16/79; night tours adult/child $33/19.50
- ➡ ferry departs every half hour btwn 9am-3:55pm, night tours 6:10pm & 6:45pm

Prison Life

In 1922, when the 18th Amendment to the Constitution declared selling liquor a crime, rebellious Jazz Agers weren't prepared to give up their tipple – and gangsters kept the booze coming. Authorities were determined to make a public example of criminal ringleaders, and in 1934 the Federal Bureau of Prisons took over Alcatraz as a prominent showcase for its crime-fighting efforts. The Rock averaged only 264 inmates, but its roster read like an America's Most Wanted list. A-list criminals doing time on Alcatraz included Chicago crime boss Al 'Scarface' Capone, dapper kidnapper George 'Machine Gun' Kelly, hot-headed Harlem mafioso and sometime poet 'Bumpy' Johnson, and Morton Sobell, the military contractor found guilty of Soviet espionage along with Julius and Ethel Rosenberg. Today, first-person accounts of daily life in the Alcatraz lockup are included on the excellent self-guided audio tour.

But take your headphones off for just a moment, and you'll notice the sound of carefree city life traveling from across the water: this is the torment that made perilous escapes into riptides worth the risk. Although Alcatraz was considered escape-proof, in 1962 the Anglin brothers and Frank Morris floated away on a makeshift raft and were never seen again. Security and upkeep proved prohibitively expensive, and finally the island prison was abandoned to the birds in 1963.

Indian Occupation

Native Americans claimed sovereignty over the island in the '60s, noting that Alcatraz had long been used by the Ohlone people as a spiritual retreat. But federal authorities refused their proposal to turn Alcatraz into a Native American study center. Then on the eve of Thanksgiving, 1969, 79 Native American activists broke a Coast Guard blockade to enforce their claim. Over the next 19 months, some 5600 Native Americans would visit the occupied island. Public support eventually pressured President Richard Nixon to restore Native territory and strengthen self-rule for Native nations in 1970. Each Thanksgiving Day since 1975, an 'Un-Thanksgiving' ceremony has been held at dawn on Alcatraz, with Native leaders and supporters showing their determination to reverse the course of colonial history. After the government regained control of the island, it became a national park, and by 1973 it had already become a major tourist draw. Today the cell blocks, 'This is Indian land' water-tower graffiti and rare wildlife are all part of the attraction.

NEED TO KNOW

Book Alcatraz tours well ahead, at least two weeks for self-guided daytime visits, longer for ranger-led night tours. When visiting by day, we like booking the first or last boat of the day because there are fewer people. Visiting Alcatraz means walking – a lot. The ferry drops you off at the bottom of a big hill, which you'll have to ascend to reach the cell block. The path is paved, but if you're out of shape you'll be panting by the top. Wear sturdy shoes, as you may want to explore some of the unpaved bird-watching trails at the top of the hill. Most people spend two to three hours on the island, but if you bring lunch you can linger longer. You only need to reserve the outbound boat, not the return, so take your time. Weather changes fast and it's often windy on Alcatraz – wear layers and long pants. There is no food available on the island, only bottled water; carry snacks.

TOP SIGHTS
ALCATRAZ

TOP SIGHTS
FISHERMAN'S WHARF

Where fisherman once snared sea life, San Francisco now traps tourists. Clam chowder in a sourdough bowl? Check. 'I escaped Alcatraz' T-shirts? Check. The Wharf may not be the 'real San Francisco,' but it's always lively and still retains some authenticity and even a few surprises. Stick near the waterfront, where sea lions bray, street performers scare unsuspecting passersby, and an aquarium and carousel entice wide-eyed kids. Once you've explored the tall ships at Pier 45, consult mechanical fortune tellers at Musée Mécanique, then high-tail it away to discover the real SF.

Pier 39

The focal point of Fisherman's Wharf isn't the waning fishing fleet, but the carousel, carnival-like attractions, shops and restaurants of **Pier 39** (Map p315; www.pier39.com; Beach St & the Embarcadero; 🚋; Ⓜ Embarcadero & Stockton St, 🚋 Powell-Mason). Developed in the 1970s to revitalize tourism, the pier draws thousands of tourists daily, but it's really just a big outdoor shopping mall.

By far the best reason to walk the pier is to spot the famous sea lions, who took over this coveted waterfront real estate in 1989. They've been making a public display ever since – canoodling, belching, scratching their backsides and gleefully shoving one another off the docks. These unkempt squatters became San Francisco's favorite mascots. However, because California law requires boats to make way for marine mammals, yacht owners have had to relinquish valuable slips to accommodate as many as 1300 sea lions who 'haul out' onto the docks between January and July. They gather on the west side of the pier; follow the signs.

DON'T MISS...

→ Sea lions at Pier 39
→ Musée Mécanique
→ San Francisco Maritime National Historic Park
→ Aquatic Park

PRACTICALITIES

→ Map p315
→ www.fishermans wharf.org
→ Embarcadero and Jefferson St waterfront, from Pier 39 to Van Ness Ave
→ admission free
→ 🚋 Powell-Mason, Powell-Hyde

Musée Mécanique

A flashback to penny arcades, the **Musée Mécanique** (Map p315; www.museemechanique.org; Shed A, Pier 45; ☉10am-7pm; ⊞; ⓜJefferson & Taylor Sts, ⬚Powell-Mason, Powell-Hyde) houses a mind-blowing collection of vintage mechanical amusements. Sinister, freckle-faced Laughing Sal has creeped out kids for over a century, but don't let this manic mannequin deter you from the best arcade west of Coney Island. Prices have spiked in the last century: a quarter, not a penny, lets you start brawls in Wild West saloons, peep at belly dancers through a vintage Mutoscope and even learn a cautionary tale about smoking opium.

San Francisco Maritime National Historical Park

Four Bay Area ships are currently open as museums at the **Maritime National Historical Park** (Map p315; www.nps.gov/safr; Hyde St Pier, 499 Jefferson St; adult/child $5/free; ☉9:30am-5pm Oct-May, to 7pm Jun-Sep; ⬚Powell-Hyde). Moored along the Hyde St Pier, standouts include the elegant 1891 schooner *Alma* and the steamboat *Eureka,* the world's largest ferry c 1890. For more mariner action, check out the steam-powered paddle-wheel tugboat *Eppleton Hall* and the magnificent triple-masted, iron-hulled *Balclutha,* an 1886 British vessel, which brought coal to San Francisco and took grain back to Europe via the dreaded Cape Horn.

USS Pampanito

The **USS Pampanito** (Map p315; www.maritime.org/pamphome.htm; Pier 45; adult/child/family $9/5/20; ☉9am-8pm Thu-Tue, to 6pm Wed; ⬚Powell-Hyde), a WWII-era US navy submarine, completed six wartime patrols, sunk six Japanese ships, battled three others and lived to tell the tale. Submariners' stories of tense moments in underwater stealth mode will have you holding your breath – beware, claustrophobics – and all those cool brass knobs and mysterious hydraulic valves make 21st-century technology seem overrated.

SS Jeremiah O'Brien

It's hard to believe the historic 10,000-ton **SS Jeremiah O'Brien** (Map p315; www.ssjeremiahobrien.org; Pier 45; adult/child $10/5; ☉9am-4pm; ⓜJefferson & Taylor Sts, ⬚Powell-Hyde) was turned out by San Francisco's ship builders in under eight weeks. It's harder still to imagine how she dodged U-boats on a mission delivering supplies to allied forces on D-Day. Of the 2710 Liberty ships launched during WWII, this is the only one still fully operational. Visit on

WHAT THE...?

Keep your eyes peeled for the notorious 'Bushman' of Pier 39, who lurks behind branches of eucalyptus trees, then leaps out and shouts 'Ugga bugga!' to scare the bejeezus out of unsuspecting tourists, then (even more shocking) hits them up for change. If you spot him first, stick around and watch how others react. Things don't always go as planned.

About two-thirds of all the waterways in California drain into San Francisco Bay, which is why there was once such a thriving community of fishermen along the waterfront. Dams and diversions, built in the mid-20th century, redirected nearly every river in the state, decimating local fish populations.

FISHERMEN AT PIER 47

A few third- and fourth-generation fishermen remain in the bay, but to survive the drop in salmon and other local stocks some captains now use their boats for whale-watching and bay tours, making a living off the city's new lifeblood: tourism. Find the remaining fleet around Pier 47.

'steaming weekends' (usually the third weekend of each month), or check the website for upcoming four-hour cruises.

Aquarium of the Bay

Sharks circle overhead, manta rays sweep shyly by and seaweed sways all around at **Aquarium of the Bay** (Map p315; www.aquariumofthebay.com; Pier 39; adult/child $17/8; ⊙9am-8pm summer, 10am-6pm winter; M49, F; ⍾), where a series of conveyer belts guide you through glass tubes surrounded by sea life from San Francisco Bay. Not for the claustrophobic, perhaps, but the thrilling fish-eye view leaves kids and parents wide-eyed and humming *Little Mermaid* tunes.

San Francisco Carousel

A chariot awaits to whisk you and the kids past the Golden Gate Bridge, Alcatraz and other SF landmarks hand-painted onto this Italian **carousel** (Map p315; www.pier39.com; Pier 39; admission $3; ⊙11am-7pm; ⍾; MEmbarcadero & Stockton St), twinkling with 1800 lights at the bayside end of Pier 39. The carnival music is loud enough to drown out the screams of a tiny tot clinging for dear life to a high-stepping horse.

Aquatic Park Bathhouse (Maritime Museum)

The quirky **Maritime Museum** (Map p318; www.maritime.org; 900 Beach St; admission free; ⍾; MBeach & Polk Sts, ⍰Powell-Hyde) was a casino and public bathhouse when built in 1939 by the Depression-era Work Projects Administration (WPA). Beautifully restored murals depict the mythical lands of Atlantis and Mu, and the handful of exhibits include maritime ephemera and cool dioramas. Notice the entryway slate carvings by celebrated African American artist Sargent Johnson, and the back veranda's toad and seal sculptures by SF's own Beniamino Bufano.

Ghirardelli Square

Willy Wonka would tip his hat to Domingo Ghirardelli (gear-ar-*del*-ee), whose business became the West's largest chocolate factory in 1893. After the company moved to the East Bay, developers reinvented the factory as a mall and landmark ice-cream parlor in 1964. Today, **Ghirardelli Square** (www.ghirardellisq.com; 900 North Point St; ⊙10am-9pm; MBeach & Polk Sts, ⍰Powell-Hyde) has entered its third incarnation as a boutique luxury timeshare/spa complex with wine-tasting rooms – care for a massage and a merlot with your Ghirardelli chocolate sundae? The square looks quite spiffy, with local boutiques, along with the charming tearoom Crown & Crumpet and a branch of the ever-tempting Kara's Cupcakes. And, of course, there's still **Ghirardelli Ice Cream** for chocolate souvenirs.

Aquatic Park

Eccentricity along Fisherman's Wharf is mostly staged, but at **Aquatic Park** (Map p315; northern end of Van Ness Ave; admission free; ⍾; ⍰Powell-Hyde), it's the real deal: extreme swimmers dive into the bone-chillingly cold waters of the bay in winter, eccentrics mumble conspiracy theories at panoramic Victoria Park, and wistful tycoons contemplate sailing far away from their Blackberries. To get perspective on the Wharf, wander out the municipal pier, at the foot of Van Ness Ave.

Beniamino Bufano's St Francis Statue

A winsome **statue** (Map p315; cnr Taylor & Beach Sts; admission free; MPowell & Beach Sts; ⍰Powell-Mason) of SF's favorite saint by its favorite sculptor – so what's it doing in a parking lot? Technically this was only a model for Bufano's massive black granite St Francis in Grace Cathedral, but there's something so San Francisco about this version, with exposed toes hanging ten like a surfer.

TOP SIGHTS
GOLDEN GATE BRIDGE & THE MARINA

The city's most spectacular icon towers 80 stories above the roiling waters of the Golden Gate, the narrow entrance to San Francisco Bay. Hard to believe SF's northern gateway lands not into a tangle of city streets, but into the Presidio, an army base turned national park, where forested paths and grassy promenades look largely as they have since the 19th century.

Golden Gate Bridge

San Francisco's famous suspension bridge, painted a signature shade called International Orange, was almost nixed by the navy in favor of concrete pylons and yellow stripes. Joseph B Strauss rightly receives a lot of praise as the engineering mastermind behind this iconic marvel, but without the aesthetic intervention of architects Gertrude and Irving Murrow and the incredibly quick work of daredevil workers, this 1937 landmark might have been just another traffic bottleneck.

How It Came to Be

Nobody thought it could happen, and it wasn't until the early 1920s that the City of San Francisco began to seriously investigate the possibility of building a bridge over the treacherous, windblown strait. The War Department owned the land on both sides, and it didn't want to take chances with ships, so safety and solidity were its primary goals. But the green light was given to the counterproposal by Strauss and the Murrows for a subtler suspension span, economic in form, that harmonized with the natural

DON'T MISS...

➡ Fort Point

➡ The cross-section of suspension cable near the toll plaza

➡ Midday summer fog clearing, when bridge towers emerge from clouds

➡ The municipal pier behind the Warming Hut

PRACTICALITIES

➡ Map p317

➡ www.goldengate bridge.org/visitors

➡ off Lincoln Blvd

➡ Southbound toll $6, northbound free; carpools (three or more) free 5am-9am & 4pm-6pm

➡ Ⓜ Golden Gate Bridge Parking Lot, all Golden Gate Transit buses

BEST PLACES TO SEE IT

Cinema buffs believe Hitchcock had it right: seen from below at Fort Point, the bridge induces a thrilling case of *Vertigo*. Fog aficionados prefer the lookout at Vista Point in Marin, on the sunnier north side of the bridge, to watch gusts of clouds rush through the bridge cables. Crissy Field is a key spot to appreciate the span in its entirety, with windsurfers and kite-fliers adding action to your snapshots. Unlike the Bay Bridge, the Golden Gate Bridge provides access to cyclists and pedestrians (see the bicycling tour, p67).

On the foggiest days, up to one million gallons of water, in the form of fog, blow through the Golden Gate each hour.

THE OTHER SIDE

The picture-perfect Golden Gate has a surprisingly dark side: it's the world's number-one suicide site. A suicide-prevention net is being installed to curb numbers. For more on this, *The Bridge* (2006) is an excellent documentary.

environment. Before the War Department could insist on an eyesore, laborers dove into the treacherous riptides of the bay and got the bridge underway in 1933. Just four years later workers balanced atop swaying cables to complete what was then the world's longest suspension bridge – nearly 2 miles long, with 746ft suspension towers, higher than any construction west of New York.

Crossing the Bridge

Pedestrians take the eastern sidewalk. Dress warmly. From the parking area and bus stop (off Lincoln Blvd), a pathway leads past the toll plaza, then it's 1.7 miles across. If walking the 3.4 miles round-trip seems too much, bus to the north side via Golden Gate Transit, then walk back (for instructions, see www.goldengatebridge.org/visitors). Note: pedestrian access is open in summer from 5am to 9pm, and in winter from 5am to 6pm.

By bicycle, follow the 49-mile Dr signs along Lincoln Blvd, through the Presidio, to the parking lot right before the toll plaza. Facing the snack bar, go right, toward the flower beds, then follow the bicycle path that crosses under the roadway to the western sidewalk, reserved for bikes only. Bicycles cross 24 hours, but travel the eastern sidewalk certain hours; for details, see www.goldengatebridge.org.

The 28 Muni bus runs from Fort Mason (Laguna & Bay Sts) to the toll plaza, which is on the SF side, then continues down 19th Ave. Marin County-bound Golden Gate Transit buses (routes 70 and 80 run frequently; $3.65 one-way) are the fastest, most comfortable way from downtown; get off at the toll plaza. To cross by bus without then penetrating deep into Marin (as Golden Gate Transit buses do), take the 76 Muni (Sundays only) to the Marin Headlands.

Crissy Field

War is for the birds in this military airstrip turned waterfront nature preserve called **Crissy Field** (Map p317; www.crissyfield.org; btwn Mason St & Golden Gate Promenade; MBroderick & Jefferson Sts), with knockout views of the Golden Gate. Where military aircraft once zoomed in for a landing, bird-watchers now huddle in the silent rushes of a reclaimed tidal marsh. Joggers pound beachside trails, and the only security alerts are raised by puppies suspiciously sniffing surfers. On foggy days, stop by the certified-green Warming Hut (p69) or **Crissy Field Center** (603 Mason St; 9am-5pm) to browse regional nature books and thaw out over fair-trade coffee.

Baker Beach

Picnic amid wind-sculpted pines, fish from craggy rocks or frolic nude at the mile-long sandy **Baker Beach** (Map p317; ☺sunrise-sunset; ⓜBaker Beach), with spectacular views of the Golden Gate Bridge. Crowds come on weekends, especially on fog-free days; get here early. For nude sunbathing (mostly straight girls and gay boys), head to the north end. Families in clothing stick to the south end, nearer to the parking lot. Mind the currents and the c-c-cold water.

Presidio Base

Explore that splotch of green on the map between Baker Beach and Crissy Field, and you'll find a parade grounds, Yoda and Mickey Mouse, a centuries-old adobe wall and a pet cemetery. What started out as a Spanish fort built by conscripted Ohlone people in 1776 is now a treasure hunt of oddities, set in an urban **Presidio National Park** (Map p317; ☑415-561-4323; www.nps.gov/prsf; ☺dawn-dusk; ⓜPresidio Blvd & Simonds Loop).

Begin your adventures by heading to the parade grounds to get a trail map and shuttle bus schedule at the **visitors center** (Bldg 105, Montgomery St & Lincoln Blvd; ☺ 9am-5pm) (verify location before heading here; it's slated to move), then take advantage of rock-star photo ops among the decrepit barracks. This is where Jerry Garcia began and ended his ignominious military career by going AWOL nine times in eight months before twice being court-martialed and co-founding the Grateful Dead. Mickey Mouse fans head to the Walt Disney Family Museum (p63), while fans of the macabre hike to the **Pet Cemetery**, off Crissy Field Ave, where handmade tombstones mark the final resting places of hamsters and kittens. East of the parade grounds, towards the Palace of Fine Arts, lies the **Letterman Campus**, home to nonprofits and *Star Wars* filmmaker George Lucas, whose offices require a special pass – but you can pay your respects to the Yoda statue out front.

To find site-specific temporary art, such as environmental artist Andy Goldsworthy's *Wood Line,* giant S-curves of fallen eucalyptus trunks on the forest floor (between Lovers Lane and Presidio Blvd), consult the **Presidio Trust** (www.presidio.gov/experiences), which also publishes good hiking maps to scenic overlooks.

PresidioGo (☑415-561-5300; www.presidio.gov/directions/presidiogoshuttle; fare free) buses loop around the park from the **Presidio Transit Center** (215 Lincoln Blvd). Weekday service runs every 30 minutes, 6:30am to 7:30pm; weekends, it's every 60 minutes, 11am to 6pm, and includes weekend-only stops at Fort Point and Warming Hut. Download the bus map and schedule from the PresidioGo website before coming.

Fort Point

Fort Point (Map p317; ☑415-556-1693; www.nps.gov/fopo; Marine Dr; admission free; ☺10am-5pm Fri-Sun; ⓜGolden Gate Bridge Parking Lot) came about after an eight-year makeover from a small Spanish fort to a triple-decker, brick-walled US military fortress. Completed in 1861 with 126 cannons, just in time to protect the bay against certain invasion by Confederate soldiers during the Civil War...or not, as it turned out. Without firing a single shot, Fort Point was abandoned in 1900 and became neglected once the Golden Gate Bridge was built over it – engineers even added an extra span to preserve it.

Alfred Hitchcock saw deadly potential in Fort Point, and shot the trademark scene from *Vertigo* here of Kim Novak leaping from the lookout to certain death into the bay...or not, as it turned out. Fort Point has since given up all pretense of being deadly, and now has a gift shop, Civil War displays and panoramic viewing decks.

On Saturday mornings, March through October, staff demonstrate how to catch crabs from the pier; reservations required.

SIGHTS

⊙ The Marina & Cow Hollow

The Marina generally refers to everything north of busy Lombard St, west of Van Ness Ave; Cow Hollow refers to the area around Union St, just south of Lombard St, on the slope below Pacific Heights.

`FREE` WAVE ORGAN   MONUMENT
Map p318 (www.exploratorium.edu; Marina Small Craft Harbor jetty; ⊙daylight hours; 🚌) An Exploratorium project worth investigating, the Wave Organ is a sound system of PVC tubes and concrete pipes capped with found marble from San Francisco's old cemetery, built right into the tip of the yacht harbor jetty. Depending on the waves, winds and tide, the tones emitted by the organ can sound like nervous humming from a dinnertime line chef or spooky heavy breathing over the phone in a slasher film. Access to the organ is free, but a bit of a hike from the Exploratorium.

CHURCH OF ST MARY THE VIRGIN   CHURCH
Map p318 (☑415-921-3665; www.smvsf.org; 2325 Union St; ⊙9am-5pm Sun-Fri; 🚇Union & Steiner Sts) You might expect to see this rustic arts and crafts building on the slopes of Tahoe instead of Pacific Heights, but this episcopal church is full of surprises. The structure dates from 1891, but the church has kept pace with its progressive-minded parish, with homeless community outreach and 'Unplugged' all-acoustic Sunday services led by hip young reverend Jennifer Hornbeck.

`FREE` VEDANTA SOCIETY   TEMPLE
Map p317 (☑415-922-2323; www.sfvedanta. org; 2963 Webster St; 🚇Fillmore & Union Sts) Meandering through the Marina, you'll pass Mexican-inspired art deco, Victorian mansions, generic bay window boxes – and, hello, what's this? A riotous 1905 mishmash of architectural styles, with red turrets representing major world religions and the Hindu-inspired Vedanta Society's organizing principle: 'the oneness of existence.' The society founded a new temple in 1959, but its architectural conundrum remains. The only thing missing is a finger pointing at the moon, with a caption reading 'Thou art that.' The temple is not open to the public.

OCTAGON HOUSE   HISTORICAL BUILDING
Map p318 (☑415-441-7512; 2645 Gough St; admission donation $3; ⊙noon-3pm 2nd & 4th Thu & 2nd Sun of month, closed Jan; 🚇Union & Gough Sts) Crafty architects are always trying to cut corners on their clients, and here architect William C McElroy succeeded. This is one of the last examples of a brief San Franciscan vogue for octagonal houses in the 1860s, when it was believed that houses catching direct sunlight from eight angles was good for your health. Three afternoons a month you can peruse the collection of colonial antiques and peek inside a time capsule that McElroy hid under the stairs.

⊙ Fisherman's Wharf & Fort Mason

FISHERMAN'S WHARF   LANDMARK
Fisherman's Wharf includes the following sights: Pier 39 (p56), Musée Mécanique (p57), San Francisco Maritime National Historical Park (p57), USS *Pampanito* (p57), SS *Jeremiah O'Brien* (p57), Aquarium of the Bay (p58), San Francisco Carousel (p58) and Beniamino Bufano's St Francis Statue (p58).

HOW TO KNOW IF IT'S FOGGY AT THE COAST

San Francisco is famous for its summertime microclimates (p251). Downtown may be sunny and hot, while the Golden Gate is fogged-in and 20°F (10°C) colder. Thanks to satellite imagery, you can get a view of the fog line over the California coast (during daylight hours only) and immediately know if clouds are hugging the shoreline and – most importantly – how many layers to pack before trekking to the Golden Gate Bridge. Go to the National Oceanic & Atmospheric Administration (NOAA; www. wrh.noaa.gov/mtr) website for San Francisco, navigate to the 'Satellite imagery' page, and click on the '1km visible satellite' for Monterey, California. SF is the thumb-shaped peninsula, surrounded by bays to its right. Voilà!

ⓘ FINDING WATERFRONT ADDRESSES

When searching for addresses on the waterfront, remember that even-numbered piers lie *south* of the Ferry Building and odd-numbered piers *north* of the Ferry Building. All even-numbered piers are south of Market St.

FORT MASON CENTER　　CULTURAL BUILDINGS

Map p318 (☏415-441-3400; www.fortmason.org; Marina Blvd & Laguna St; 🚌Marina Blvd & Laguna St) San Francisco takes subversive glee in turning military installations into venues for nature, fine dining and out-there experimental art. Evidence: Fort Mason, a former shipyard and the embarkation point for WWII troops shipping out for the Pacific. The military mess halls are gone, replaced by vegan-friendly Greens, a restaurant run by a Zen community. Warehouses now host cutting-edge theater at Magic Theater, the home base of Pulitzer Prize–winning playwright Sam Shepard, and improvised comedy workshops at BATS Improv. The dockside Herbst Pavilion counts major arts events and fashion shows among its arsenal – see the website for upcoming performances and events.

⊙ The Presidio

MARINA　　LANDMARK

The Marina includes the following sights: Baker Beach (p61), Crissy Field (p60), Presidio Base (p61) and Fort Point (p61).

GOLDEN GATE BRIDGE　　LANDMARK

See p59.

EXPLORATORIUM　　MUSEUM

Map p317 (☏415-561-0360; www.exploratorium. edu; 3601 Lyon St; adult/child $15/10, 1st Wed of month free; ⊙10am-5pm Tue-Sun; ♿; 🚌28, 30, 43) Is there a science to skateboarding? Do robots have feelings? Do toilets really flush counterclockwise in Australia? Head to the Exploratorium to get fascinating scientific answers to all the questions you always wanted to ask in science class. Try out a punk hairdo courtesy of the static-electricity station, and feel your way – in darkness – through the maze of the highly recommended **Tactile Dome** (☏415-561-0362); admission to the Tactile Dome is extra on top

of general admission, patrons must be over seven years old, and advance reservations are required. Note, in 2013, the Exploratorium is slated to move to Pier 13.

FREE **PALACE OF FINE ARTS**　　MONUMENT

Map p317 (www.lovethepalace.org; Palace Dr; 🚌28, 30, 43) Like a fossilized party favor, this romantic, ersatz Greco-Roman ruin is the memento San Francisco decided to keep from the 1915 Panama–Pacific International Exposition. The original was built in wood, burlap and plaster as a picturesque backdrop by celebrated Berkeley architect Bernard Maybeck, but by the 1960s it was beginning to crumble. The structure was recast in concrete, so that future generations could gaze up at the rotunda relief to glimpse 'Art under attack by materialists, with idealists leaping to her rescue.' Further renovations in 2010 restored the palace to its former glory. Plan to pose for pictures by the swan lagoon.

SWEDENBORGIAN CHURCH　　CHURCH

Map p317 (☏415-346-6466; www.sfswedenbor gian.org; 2107 Lyon St; ⊙hours vary; 🚌Jackson & Presidio Sts) Radical ideals in the form of distinctive buildings make beloved SF landmarks; this standout 1894 example is the collaborative effort of 19th-century Bay Area progressive thinkers, such as naturalist John Muir, California Arts & Crafts leader Bernard Maybeck and architect Arthur Page Brown. Church founder Emanuel Swedenborg was an 18th-century Swedish theologian, a scientist and an occasional conversationalist with angels, who believed that humans are spirits in a material world unified by nature, love and luminous intelligence – a lovely concept, embodied in an equally lovely building. Enter the church through a modest brick archway, and pass into a garden, sheltered by trees from around the world. Inside, nature is everywhere – in the hewn-maple chairs, mighty madrone trees supporting the roof, and in scenes of Northern California that took muralist William Keith 40 years to complete.

WALT DISNEY FAMILY MUSEUM　　MUSEUM

Map p317 (☏415-345-6800; www.disney.go.com/ disneyatoz/familymuseum; 104 Montgomery St; adult/child $20/12; ⊙Wed-Mon 10am-6pm; 🚌Presidio Blvd & Simonds Loop) An 1890s military barracks houses 10 galleries that tell the exhaustively long story of Walt Disney. Opened in 2009, the museum gets high marks for design, integrating 20,000 sq ft

SILICONVALLEYSTOCK / ALAMY ©

RICHARD CUMMINS / LONELY PLANET IMAGES ©

RICHARD CUMMINS / LONELY PLANET IMAGES ©

STEPHEN SAKS / LONELY PLANET IMAGES ©

3

1. Exploratorium (p63)
San Francisco's hands-on museum of weird science.

2. Palace of Fine Arts (p63)
Bernard Maybeck's 1915 Palace of Fine Arts was intended as a temporary structure, but the beloved fake ruin was recast in concrete in the 1960s.

3. Forbes Island (p66)
This houseboat turned island is now a restaurant strong on grilled meats and atmosphere.

4. Cow Hollow
Cow Hollow has good shops, bars and restaurants along Union St.

of contemporary glass-and-steel exhibition space with the original 19th-century brick building, but it's definitely geared toward grown-ups and will bore kids after an hour (too much reading). In typical Disney style, the exhibits are impeccably presented, with lavish detail in a variety of media, including a jaw-dropping scale model of Disneyland that will delight die-hard Mouseketeers, but budgeteers may prefer to save their $20 toward a trip to Anaheim.

✗ EATING

Fisherman's Wharf is where the fishing fleet unloads its morning catch. From mid-November to June, the local specialty is fresh caught Dungeness crab. Look for roiling cauldrons in front of restaurants near the docks at the foot of Taylor St. Though Wharf restaurants are fine for a quick bowl of chowder or a crab Louis, most are overpriced and there's nothing groundbreaking about the cooking. If you're seriously into food, wander the Wharf from west to east before lunch (if you're coming by cable car, take the Powell-Hyde line), then head to the Ferry Building (p76), either on foot or the F-Market line streetcar, which goes right there.

Major Marina dining destinations are on Chestnut St from Fillmore to Divisadero Sts, and Union St between Fillmore St and Van Ness Ave, but there's fun, funky fare on Lombard St. Greens gives reason to trek to Fort Mason.

✗ Fisherman's Wharf

GARY DANKO CALIFORNIAN $$$
Map p315 (☑415-749-2060; www.garydanko.com; 800 North Point St; 3-/5-course menus $68/102; ⊘dinner; MNorth Point & Hyde St, ☐Powell-Hyde) Smoked-glass windows prevent passersby from tripping over their tongues at the sight of exquisite roasted lobster with trumpet mushrooms, blushing duck breast with rhubarb compote, trios of crème brûlée and the lavish cheese cart. Take your server's seasonal recommendations of three to five courses and prepare to be impressed. Gary Danko has won multiple James Beard Awards for providing impeccable dining experiences, from inventive salad courses like oysters with caviar and lettuce cream

to the casually charming server who hands you tiny chocolate cakes as a parting gift. Reservations essential.

FORBES ISLAND GRILL $$$
Map p315 (☑415-951-4900; www.forbesisland. com; Pier 41; mains $28-40; ⊘5-10pm Wed-Sun; ☑; MJefferson & Powell St) No man is an island, except for an eccentric millionaire named Forbes Thor Kiddoo. A miniature lighthouse, thatched hut, waterfall, sandy beach and swaying palms transformed his moored houseboat into the Hearst Castle of the bay. Today this bizarre domicile is a restaurant strong on grilled meats and atmosphere. Reserve in advance and catch boat shuttles from Pier 39; landlubbers dining below deck should bring their motion-sickness meds.

EAGLE CAFÉ AMERICAN $$
Map p315 (☑415-433-3689; www.eaglecafe. com; Pier 39, 2nd fl, Ste 103; mains $10-20; ⊘7:30am-9pm; ☑; MEmbarcadero & Stockton St, ☐Powell-Mason) The best breakfast and lunch spot on Pier 39 is here. The Eagle's food is simple and straightforward – pancakes and omelets, crab-salad sandwiches and juicy burgers. The views are good, the prices right, and they even accept reservations, which you should definitely make on weekends to save yourself a long wait.

CROWN & CRUMPET CAFE $$
(☑415-771-4252; www.crownandcrumpet.com; 207 Ghirardelli Sq, North Point & Larkin St; dishes $8-12; ⊘10am-9pm Mon-Fri, 9am-9pm Sat, 9am-6pm Sun; ☑; MNorth Point & Larkin St, ☐Powell-Hyde) Designer style and rosy cheer usher tea time into the 21st century: girlfriends rehash hot dates over scones with strawberries and champagne, and dads and daughters clink porcelain cups after choosing from 38 kinds of tea. Weekend reservations recommended.

GRANDEHO'S KAMEKYO II JAPANESE $$
Map p315 (☑415-673-6828; 2721 Hyde St; mains $10-20; ⊘lunch & dinner Mon-Fri, dinner Sat & Sun; MNorth Point & Hyde St, ☐Powell-Mason) A reliable spot to slurp udon and nosh sushi while touring the Wharf. This storefront Japanese satisfies for friendly service and reasonable lunchtime prices (considering the neighborhood), and makes a good pit stop before hopping the Powell-Hyde cable car out front.

BOUDIN BAKERY BAKERY $
Map p315 (www.boudinbakery.com; Jefferson St at Mason St; dishes $7-15; ⊘11am-9:30pm) Dating

START **MARITIME MUSEUM**
FINISH **PIER 41**
DISTANCE **EIGHT MILES**
DURATION **TWO TO FOUR HOURS**

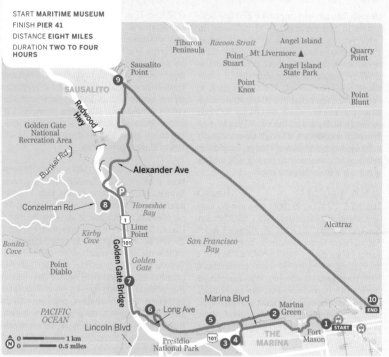

Neigborhood Bicycle Ride
Freewheeling Over The Bridge

The deco design of the ❶ **Maritime Museum** (p58), a 1939 creation of the Work Projects Administartion (WPA), is crawling with public art.

Joggers, Frisbee-throwers and kite-fliers congregate at ❷ **Marina Green** on weekends. A right turn bisects the two boat marinas, and at the end is the curious Wave Organ (p62).

Dig how your voice echoes inside this flashback to the 1915 Panama–Pacific International Expo at the ❸ **Palace of Fine Arts** (p63). Pose for photos under the Greco-Roman arches reflected in the pond.

Ditch the bike and exercise your senses in the wacky, one-of-a-kind ❹ **Exploratorium** (p59) – especially if you have kids in tow.

Head to ❺ **Crissy Field** (p60) to watch windsurfers and kiteboarders attempt one of the windiest beaches in SF. Take the Golden Gate Promenade, a foot-and-bike path skirting the field toward Fort Point and Warming Hut.

Fuel up on organic sandwiches and coffee at ❻ **Warming Hut** (p69). Afterwards, backtrack to Long Ave and hang a sharp right up super-steep Lincoln Blvd to the bridge.

With everyone craning their necks, it's no surprise that bicycles sometimes collide on the ❼ **Golden Gate Bridge** (p59). Keep your eyes peeled. Seriously. You'll be grateful you brought a windbreaker if the fog blows in when you're halfway across.

Lock your bike at the ❽ **Marin Headlands** and hike into the tempting rolling hills – the steep, winding Coastal Trail leads to Rodeo Beach (5 miles). Turn left after the bridge onto Conzelman Rd. Or just enjoy the views and pedal past.

Swanky ❾ **Sausalito** (p228) and its bayside setting are worth strolling to when your legs need stretching. Get drinks on the deck at **Paradise Bay** (1200 Bridgeway).

Take the ferry from Sausalito back to ❿ **Pier 41** at Fisherman's Wharf.

to 1849, Boudin was one of the first five businesses in San Francisco, and still uses the same yeast starter in its sourdough bread. Though you can find better bread elsewhere these days, Boudin's food court remains a Wharf staple for clam chowder in a hollowed-out bread bowl. The best reason to come is the remarkably well-curated bread-baking museum, which chronicles SF's role in the Gold Rush and the city's long love affair with sourdough. Though there's usually a $3 museum admission charge, employees tell us you're welcome to peek inside for free if nobody's manning the door.

IN-N-OUT BURGER
BURGERS $

Map p315 (☑800-786-1000; www.in-n-out.com; 333 Jefferson St; meals under $10; ☺10:30am-1am Sun-Thu, to 1:30am Fri & Sat; 🖢; ⓜJones & Beach Sts, 🚋Powell-Hyde) Gourmet burgers have taken SF by storm, but In-N-Out has had a good thing going for 60 years: prime chuck beef, processed on-site, plus fries and shakes made with ingredients you can pronounce, all served by employees paid a living wage. Ask for yours off the menu 'wild style,' cooked in mustard with grilled onions.

GHIRARDELLI ICE CREAM
ICE CREAM $

Map p315 (☑415-771-4903; www.ghirardellisq. com; 900 North Point St, West Plaza; dishes $4-8; ☺10am-11pm; 🖢; ⓜNorth Point & Larkin St, 🚋Powell-Hyde) Mr Ghirardelli sure makes a swell sundae. The legendary Cable Car comes with Rocky Road ice cream, marshmallow topping and enough hot fudge to satisfy a jonesing chocoholic.

✖ The Marina

A16
ITALIAN $$

Map p318 (☑415-771-2216; www.a16sf.com; 2355 Chestnut St; pizza $12-18, mains $18-26; ☺lunch Wed-Fri, dinner daily; ⓜDivisadero & Chestnut Sts) Like a high-maintenance date, this Neapolitan pizzeria demands reservations and then haughtily makes you wait in the foyer. The housemade mozzarella *burrata* and chewy-but-not-too-thick-crust pizza makes it worth your while. Skip the spotty desserts and concentrate on adventurous appetizers, including house-cured *salumi* platters and delectable marinated tuna.

BETELNUT
ASIAN $$

Map p318 (☑415-929-8855; www.betelnut restaurant.com; 2030 Union St; dishes $10-20; ☺11:30am-11pm Sun-Thu, 11:30am-midnight Fri & Sat; ⓜUnion & Laguna Sts) Palm-frond ceiling fans whirl overhead at high-energy Betelnut, a Marina District spin on the Chinese beer house. It serves fiery pan-Asian street foods designed to pair with house-label brews and fresh-fruit cocktails. Best dishes: Szechuan string beans, Celia's lettuce cups and succulent glazed pork ribs. Plan to share. Up-tempo lounge beats set a party mood, making this a great spot to start a night on the town. Make reservations.

GREENS
VEGETARIAN, CALIFORNIA $$

Map p318 (☑415-771-6222; www.greensres taurant.com; Fort Mason Center, Bldg A; mains lunch $15-17, dinner $17-24; ☺lunch Tue-Sat, dinner Mon-Sat, brunch Sun; 🖢🖘; ⓜMarina Blvd & Laguna St) Career carnivores won't realize there's no meat in the hearty black-bean chili with crème fraîche and pickled jalapeños, or that roasted eggplant *panino* (sandwich), packed with hearty flavor from ingredients mostly grown on a Zen farm in Marin. On sunny days, get yours to go so you can enjoy it on a wharfside bench, but if you're planning a sit-down weekend dinner or Sunday brunch you'll need reservations.

MAMACITA
MEXICAN $$

Map p318 (☑415-346-8494; www.mamacitasf. com; 2317 Chestnut St; dishes $10-18; ☺dinner; ⓜDivisadero & Chestnut Sts) One of the city's best for sit-down Mexican makes everything from scratch – tortillas, tamales and two dozen fresh-daily sauces for wide-ranging dishes, from spit-roasted goat to duck *carnitas*. The knock-out cocktail menu lists 60 tequilas, which explains the room's deafening roar. Make reservations.

ROSE'S CAFÉ
CALIFORNIAN $$

Map p318 (☑415-775-2200; www.rosescafesf. com; 2298 Union St; mains lunch $10-17, dinner $17-28; ☺8am-10pm; 🖢🖘; ⓜUnion & Fillmore Sts) Follow your salads and housemade soups with rich organic polenta with gorgonzola and thyme, or a simple grass-fed beef burger, then linger over espresso or tea. Shop if you must, but return to this sunny corner cafe from 4pm to 6pm for half-price wine by the glass. Great breakfasts, too.

JUDY'S CAFE
BREAKFAST $

Map p318 (☑415-922-4588; www.judyscafesf. com; 2268 Chestnut St; mains $9-13; ☺7am-4pm;

FOOD TRUCK FRIDAYS

The most happening Friday-night food scene occurs at **Off the Grid** (www.offthegridsf. com), in the parking lot of Fort Mason Center (Map p318). Scores of Bay Area food trucks gather here for an appreciative crowd of local eaters, who graze from truck to tent, sampling everything from coconut curry to crème brûlée. The hours are from 5pm to 10pm, but we recommend arriving before 6:30pm to avoid long waits. Cash only. After dinner, stroll the waterfront and watch the sun slip behind the Golden Gate.

⊕; Ⓜ Chestnut & Scott Sts) Locals queue up for giant breakfasts at Judy's, a storefront diner with standouts like sourdough French toast, enormous omelets and great pumpkin bread. Expect to wait. Cash only.

BARNEY'S BURGERS
BURGERS **$**

Map p318 (☎ 415-563-0307; www.barneysham burgers.com; 3344 Steiner St; dishes $8-12; ⊙11am-10pm Mon-Sat, 11am-9:30pm Sun; ⊅⊕; Ⓜ Chestnut & Fillmore Sts) Don't let the name fool you. Yes, its many varieties of all-natural beef and turkey burgers are great, but Barney's also makes big, healthy salads and even serves organic tofu for vegetarians. And, yum, those milkshakes.

BLUE BARN GOURMET
SANDWICHES, SALADS **$**

Map p318 (☎ 415-441-3232; www.bluebarngour met.com; 2105 Chestnut St; $9-12; ⊙11am-8:30pm Sun-Thu, to 7pm Fri & Sat; Ⓜ Chestnut & Fillmore Sts) Toss aside thoughts of ordinary salads. For $8.75, build a mighty mound of organic produce, topped with six fixings: artisan cheeses, caramelized onions, heirloom tomatoes, candied pecans, pomegranate seeds, even Meyer grilled sirloin. For something hot, try the toasted panini oozing with Manchego cheese, fig jam and salami.

LA BOULANGE
SANDWICHES, BAKERY **$**

Map p318 (☎ 415-440-4450; www.laboulange bakery.com; 1909 Union St; dishes $7-11; ⊙7am-6pm; ⊅⊕; Ⓜ Union & Laguna Sts) Even the most die-hard boutique trawler needs to refuel sometime, and La Boulange offers caffeine and house-baked carbo-loading in the middle of the Union St strip. La Combo is a $7.25 lunchtime deal to justify your next Union St boutique purchase: half a *tartine* (open-faced sandwich) with soup or salad, plus all the Nutella and pickled *cornichons* (gherkins) you desire from the condiments bar.

REAL FOOD
GROCERIES **$**

Map p318 (☎ 415-567-6900; www.realfoodco. com; 3060 Fillmore St; ⊙8am-9pm; Ⓜ Union & Lyon Sts) The deli cases at this organic grocery are packed with housemade prepared foods, including respectable sushi, roasted eggplant-and-tomato salad, free-range herb-turkey sandwiches and organic gingerbread. On sunny days, grab a seat on the patio. If you like what you taste, sign up for a cooking class (see the website).

KARA'S CUPCAKES
BAKERY, DESSERT **$**

Map p318 (☎ 415-563-2253; www.karascup cakes.com; 3249 Scott St; cupcakes $3; ⊙10am-8pm Mon-Sat, to 6pm Sun; Ⓜ Chestnut & Scott Sts) Proustian nostalgia washes over fully grown adults as they bite into cupcakes that recall childhood magician-led birthday parties. Varieties range from yummy chocolate marshmallow to classic carrot cake with cream-cheese frosting, all meticulously calculated for maximum glee.

✗ The Presidio

WARMING HUT
CAFE, SANDWICHES **$**

Map p317 (☎ 415-561-3040; 983 Marine Dr, The Presidio; dishes $4-6; ⊙9am-5pm; Ⓜ Richardson Blvd & Francisco St) Wetsuited windsurfers and Crissy Field kite-fliers thaw out with fair-trade coffee, organic pastries and organic hot dogs at Warming Hut, while browsing an excellent selection of field guides and sampling honey made by the Presidio honeybees. This ecoshack below the Golden Gate Bridge has walls ingeniously insulated with recycled denim and a heartwarming concept: all purchases fund Crissy Field's ongoing conversion from US army airstrip to wildlife preserve.

PRESIDIO SOCIAL CLUB
AMERICAN **$$**

Map p317 (☎ 415-885-1888; www.presidioso cialclub.com; 563 Ruger St, The Presidio; mains $12-24; ⊙11:30am-10pm Mon-Fri, 10am-10pm Sat & Sun; Ⓜ Lombard & Lyon Sts) Inside an atmospheric converted army building within the Presidio, this is a good spot for weekend brunch before hiking, or a lingering afternoon meal with classic cocktails. The comfort-food menu includes dishes like crab sandwiches, mac-n-cheese, and flat-iron steak with French fries.

🍷 DRINKING & 🍸 NIGHTLIFE

Marina District watering holes – which author Armistead Maupin called 'breeder bars' – cater to frat boys and bottle blonds. Many San Franciscans categorically refuse to set foot in them. The epicenter of the scene is at Fillmore and Greenwich Sts.

TOP CHOICE BUENA VISTA CAFE   BAR

Map p315 (☎415-474-5044; www.thebuenavista. com; 2765 Hyde St; ☺9am-2am Mon-Fri, 8am-2am Sat & Sun; 🚋Powell-Hyde) Warm your cockles with a prim little goblet of bitter-creamy Irish coffee, introduced to the US at this destination bar that once served sailors and cannery workers. The creaky Victorian floor manages to hold up carousers and families alike, served community-style at round tables overlooking the Wharf.

CALIFORNIA WINE MERCHANT   BAR

Map p318 (www.californiawinemerchant.com; 2113 Chestnut St; ☺10am-midnight Mon-Wed, 10am-1:30am Thu-Sat, 11am-11pm Sun; 🚋Chestnut & Fillmore Sts) Part wine store, part wine bar, this little shop on busy Chestnut St caters to grey-at-the-temples professionals and neighborhood wine aficionados, and serves half-glasses. Arrive early to score a table, or stand and gab with the locals.

BRAZEN HEAD   PUB

Map p318 (☎415-921-7600; www.brazenheadsf. com; 3166 Buchanan St; ☺4pm-1am; 🚋Laguna & Chestnut Sts) You have to know where you're going to find the Brazen Head, a tiny atmospheric pub with low lighting and cozy nooks, where hand-holding couples dine on good onion soup and pepper steak, a world away from the guffawing frat kids on Chestnut St.

MATRIXFILLMORE   LOUNGE

Map p318 (www.matrixfillmore.com; 3138 Fillmore St; ☺8pm-2am Mon-Sun; 🚋Fillmore & Union Sts) The neighborhood's most notorious up-market pick-up joint provides a fascinating glimpse into the lives of single, Marina swankers. Treat it as a comic sociological

study, while digging the stellar cocktails, blazing fireplace and sexy lounge beats. Bring your credit card.

BUS STOP   BAR

Map p318 (☎415-567-6905; 1901 Union St; ☺10am-2am; 🚋Union & Laguna Sts) Bus Stop has 18 flickering TV screens and a manly crowd that roars when their team scores. If your girlfriend wants to shop, but you must watch the game, wait here as she trawls through surrounding Union St boutiques.

☆ ENTERTAINMENT

TEATRO ZINZANNI   THEATER

(☎415-438-2668; www.zinzanni.org; Pier 29, Embarcadero; admission $117-145; ☺Wed-Sun dinner, Sun lunch; 🚋Embarcadero & Sansome St) Inside a 19th-century *Spiegeltent* (an opulent Belgian traveling-circus tent) top circus talent flies overhead, a celeb-diva croons and clowns pull wacky stunts as you dig into a surprisingly good five-course dinner or Sunday lunch. This ain't no B-grade dinner theater: a 'clown-wrangler' seeks out world-class talent in Europe and Asia, and the acts, menu and performers are refreshed quarterly. Former stars have included Joan Baez and Broadway's Liliane Montevecchi. Dress for dinner, and arrive early to see the over-the-top harmonium and boutique selling tiaras and ostrich-feather opera gloves (ideal if you're underdressed). Expect audience participation – especially if you're a looker. Reservations essential.

PIER 23   LIVE MUSIC

(☎415-362-5125; www.pier23cafe.com; Pier 23; admission $10; ☺shows 5-7pm Tue, 6-8pm Wed, 7-10pm Thu, 10pm-midnight Fri & Sat, 4-8pm Sun; 🚋Embarcadero & Greenwich St) It looks like a surf shack, but this old waterfront restaurant on Pier 23 regularly features R&B, reggae, Latin bands, mellow rock and the occasional jazz pianist. Wander out to the bayside patio to soak in views. The dinner menu features pier-worthy options like batter-fried oysters and whole roasted crab.

LOU'S PIER 47   LIVE MUSIC

Map p315 (☎415-771-5687; www.louspier47.com; 300 Jefferson St; admission $3-10; ☺shows 4pm-midnight Sun-Thu, 4pm-1am Fri, noon-1am Sat; 🚋Jones & Beach Sts) The Wharf has little nightlife, which is why we're glad for stalwart Lou's, which presents live blues seven nights a week and Saturday afternoon (when there's no cover). Good backup if you're staying nearby and don't want to travel.

MAGIC THEATER
THEATER

Map p318 (☎415-441-8822; www.magictheatre.org; 3rd fl, Bldg D, Fort Mason Center; tickets $25-55; ⓜMarina Blvd & Laguna St) The Magic is known for taking risks and staging provocative plays by playwrights such as Bill Pullman, Terrence McNally, Edna O'Brien, David Mamet and longtime playwright-in-residence Sam Shepard. Watch the next generation break through in professionally staged works written by teenagers as part of the Young California Writers Project.

BATS IMPROV
THEATER

Map p318 (☎415-474-8935; www.improv.org; 3rd fl, Bldg B, Fort Mason Center; admission $15; ⓥweekend shows 8pm; ⓜMarina Blvd & Laguna St) Bay Area Theater Sports explores all things improv, from audience-inspired themes to wacked-out musicals at completely improvised weekend shows. Or take center stage yourself at an improv-comedy workshop (held on weekday nights and weekend afternoons). Think fast: classes fill quickly. Admission prices vary depending on the show/workshop.

🛍 SHOPPING

ELIZABETHW
BEAUTY PRODUCTS

Map p315 (www.elizabethw.com; 900 North Point St; ⓥ10am-9pm Mon-Sat, 10am-7pm Sun; ⓜNorth Point & Larkin St, ☖Powell-Hyde) Local scent-maker elizabethW supplies the tantalizing aromas of changing seasons without the sweaty brows or frozen toes. 'Sweet Tea' smells like a Georgia porch in summertime; 'Vetiver' like autumn in Maine. For a true SF fragrance, 'Leaves' is as audaciously green as Golden Gate Park in January.

MINGLE
CLOTHING, ACCESSORIES

Map p318 (www.mingleshop.com; 1815 Union St; ⓥ11am-7pm; ⓜUnion & Laguna Sts) To break up the khaki monotony of the Gap and wrest free of H&M trends, get out there and mingle with SF designers. Local designers keep this boutique stocked with hot Cleopatra-collar dresses, mod ring-buckled bags and plaid necklaces, all for less than you'd pay for Marc Jacobs on mega-sale. Men emerge from Mingle date-ready in dark tailored denim and black Western shirts with white piping – the SF version of a tux.

MY ROOMMATE'S CLOSET
CLOTHING, ACCESSORIES

Map p318 (www.myroommatescloset.com; 3044 Fillmore St; ⓥ11am-6pm, noon-5pm Sun; ⓜUnion & Fillmore Sts) All the half-off bargains and none of the clawing dangers of a sample sale. You'll find cloud-like Catherine Malandrino chiffon party dresses, executive Diane Von Furstenburg wrap dresses and designer denim at prices approaching reality.

PAST PERFECT
ANTIQUES, HOUSEWARES

Map p318 (☎415-929-7651; 2224 Union St; ⓥ11am-7pm; ⓜUnion & Fillmore Sts) So this is how Pacific Heights eccentrics fill up those mansions: Fornasetti face plates, Danish teak credenzas and Lucite champagne buckets. The store is a collective, so prices are all over the place – some sellers apparently believe their belongings owe them back rent, while others are happy just to unload their ex's mother's prized spoon collection.

UKO
CLOTHING, ACCESSORIES

Map p318 (☎415-563-0330; 2070 Union St; ⓥ11am-6:30pm Mon-Sat, noon-5:30pm Sun; ⓜUnion & Buchanan Sts) Laser-cut, draped and micro-pleated are the fashion-forward signatures of Uko's inventive garments for men and women. Get bonus fashion IQ points for clever jackets with hidden pockets-within-pockets, Cop-Copine wrap skirts with oddly flattering flaps, and silver drop earrings that add an exclamation point to your look.

CHLOE ROSE
CLOTHING, ACCESSORIES

Map p318 (www.chloeroseboutique.com; 1824 Union St; ⓜUnion & Laguna Sts) If your airline lost your luggage and you're pouting about not having that perfect party dress to wear to dinner, take heart: Chloe Rose will restore your sexy silhouette and doll you up with such pretty jewelry that you can tell the airline just to write you a check instead.

MARMALADE SF
CLOTHING

Map p318 (www.marmaladesf.com; 2059 Union St; ⓜUnion & Buchanan Sts) With such a sexy collection of girly-girl clothes, all by local and indie designers, and personalized service hell-bent on helping you find your own personal style, it's hard to believe nothing at Marmalade costs over $100.

SAN FRANCISCO SURF COMPANY
OUTDOOR GEAR

Map p318 (www.sfsurfcompany.com; 2181 Union St; ⊙Wed-Mon; MFillmore & Union Sts) If you've come to Cali to surf, the dudes at this chill boutique will trick you out with the latest gear and clothing, and tell you where to find the best breaks. Also teaches beginners; by reservation.

PLUMPJACK WINES
WINE

Map p318 (www.plumpjack.com; 3201 Fillmore St; ⊙11am-8pm Mon-Sat, to 6pm Sun; MFillmore & Lombard Sts) Discover a new favorite California vintage under $30 at the distinctive wine boutique that won partial-owner and former-mayor Gavin Newsom respect from even Green Party gourmets. A more knowledgeable staff is hard to find anywhere in SF, and they'll set you up with the right bottles to cross party lines. PlumpJack Wines also has a store in Noe Valley (Map p337; 4011 24th St, Noe Valley).

ATYS
HOUSEWARES

Map p318 (www.atysdesign.com; 2149b Union St; ⊙11am-6:30pm Mon-Sat, noon-6pm Sun; MUnion & Fillmore Sts) Tucked away in a courtyard, this design showcase offers version 2.0 of essential household items: a mirrored coat rack, a rechargeable flashlight that turns a wineglass into a lamp, and a zero-emissions, solar-powered toy airplane.

SPORTS BASEMENT
OUTDOOR GEAR

Map p317 (www.sportsbasement.com; 610 Old Mason St; ⊙9am-9pm Mon-Fri, 8am-8pm Sat & Sun; MBroderick & Jefferson Sts) All you triathletes who desperately need your gait analyzed or your kids outfitted with rental snowboards, you've come to the right place. This 80,000 sq ft sports-and-camping equipment emporium was once a US army PX, which is why you'll find hiking boots near the Fresh Produce sign. Dig those closeout prices. Check the website for weekly speakers and classes.

🏃 SPORTS & ACTIVITIES

BLAZING SADDLES
BICYCLING

Map p315 (☑415-202-8888; www.blazingsaddles. com; 2715 Hyde St; bike hire per hour $8-15, per day $32-88; ⊙8am-7:30pm, weather permitting; ⊕; ⊡Powell-Hyde) Blazing Saddles is tailored to visitors, with a main shop on Hyde St and five rental stands around Fisherman's Wharf, convenient for biking the Embarcadero or to the Golden Gate Bridge. Reserve online for a 10% discount; rentals includes all extras (bungee cords, packs etc).

OCEANIC SOCIETY EXPEDITIONS
WHALE-WATCHING

Map p318 (☑415-474-3385; www.oceanic-society. org; trips per person $100-120; ⊙office 8:30am-5pm Mon-Fri, trips Sat & Sun; MBroderick & Jefferson Sts) The Oceanic Society runs top-notch, naturalist-led, ocean-going weekend boat trips – sometimes to the Farallon Islands – during both whale-migration seasons. Cruises depart from the yacht harbor (Scott St & Marina Blvd) and last all day. Kids must be 10 years or older. Reservations required.

ADVENTURE CAT
SAILING

Map p315 (☑415-777-1630; www.adventurecat. com; Pier 39; adult/child $35/15, sunset cruise $50; ⊕; MEmbarcadero & Stockton St) There's no better view of San Francisco than from the water, especially at twilight on a fogless evening aboard a sunset cruise. Adventure Cat uses catamarans, with a windless indoor cabin for grandmums and a trampoline between hulls for bouncy kids. Three daily cruises depart March through October; weekends-only November through February.

RED & WHITE FLEET
BAY CRUISE

Map p315 (☑415-673-2900; www.redandwhite. com; Pier 43-1/2; adult/child $24/16; ⊕; MJefferson & Powell Sts) A one-hour bay cruise gives you perspective on San Francisco's geography and the chance to see the Golden Gate Bridge from water level. Brave the wind and sit on the outdoor upper deck. Audio tours in multiple languages provide narrative. On-board alcohol subdues naysayers.

HOUSE OF AIR
TRAMPOLINE PARK

Map p317 (☑415-345-9675; www.houseofairsf. com; 926 Old Mason St, Crissy Field; adult/child $14/10; ⊙10am-10pm Mon-Thu, 10am-11pm Fri, 9am-9pm Sun; ⊕; MBroderick & Jefferson Sts) If you ever resented your gym teacher for not letting you jump as high as you wanted on the trampoline, you can finally get your way at this incredible trampoline park, with multiple areas to jump, including the Matrix, where you can literally bounce off the walls on 42 attached trampolines the size of a basketball court. Little kids have dedicated play areas. Reservations strongly recommended, especially weekends.

PLANET GRANITE   ROCK CLIMBING
Map p317 (☏415-692-3434; www.planetgranite.com; 924 Old Mason St, Crissy Field; day use adult $13-18, child $10; ⏲6am-11pm Mon-Fri, 8am-8pm Sat, 8am-6pm Sun; Ⓜ Broderick & Jefferson Sts) Take in spectacular bay views through a wall of glass as you ascend false-rock structures in this kick-ass 25,000-sq-ft climbing center – the ideal place to train for an expedition to Yosemite. Master top ropes as high as 45ft or test your strength ascending giant boulders and vertical-crack climbing walls, then finish your workout in the full gym or stretch in a yoga session. Check the website for class schedules.

PRESIDIO GOLF COURSE   GOLF
Map p317 (☏415-561-4661; www.presidiogolf.com; Arguello Blvd & Finley Rd; 18 holes SF resident $65-85, non-resident $125-145; ⏲sunrise-sunset; Ⓜ Sacramento & Cherry Sts) Whack balls with military-style precision on the course once reserved exclusively for US forces. The Presidio course, now operated by the Arnold Palmer company, overlooks the bay and is considered one of the country's best. Book up to 30 days in advance on the website, which sometimes lists specials, too. Rates include cart.

Downtown & Civic Center

UNION SQUARE | THE TENDERLOIN | FINANCIAL DISTRICT | JACKSON SQUARE

Neighborhood Top Five

1 Ooh-ing and ahh-ing as you travel 6000 years back in time at the **Asian Art Museum** (p77), marveling at the largest viewable collection of Eastern art outside Asia.

2 Drinking in spectacular bay views while eating your way through the **Ferry Building** (p86).

3 Hearing impresario Michael Tilson Thomas conduct Mahler or Beethoven at the **San Francisco Symphony** (p92).

4 Lying on the marble stairs at **City Hall** (p82) and gazing up at the world's fifth-largest dome.

5 Congratulating yourself for not wearing shorts and freezing your butt off aboard the **cable cars** (p79).

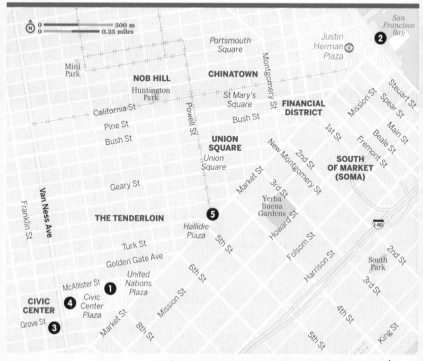

For more detail of this area, see Map p316, p320 and p322 →

Explore Downtown

Start your day assembling a picnic at the Ferry Building, then ride the California St cable car to the top of Nob Hill. From here, you can decide to walk east into Chinatown and North Beach, north to Russian Hill and Fisherman's Wharf, west toward Polk St and Pacific Heights and Japantown, or south to Civic Center and the Asian Art Museum.

Montgomery St is the main street in the buttoned-up Financial District, which extends to the Embarcadero waterfront. Downtown's main epicurean destination, the waterfront Ferry Building, marks the foot of Market St. Two miles up Market St, Civic Center refers to the governmental buildings behind City Hall, which abut the less-than-savory Tenderloin and lower Polk St. The Polk St north of Geary St has happening bars and indie boutiques, but they mostly lie beyond Civic Center around Russian and Nob Hills. Shoppers and gallery-hoppers will love Union Square.

A word of warning: most first-time visitors are thrown by the grittiness of some downtown areas, including lower Powell St, the Downtown destination of two cable car routes. Downtown is generally safe, but the streets west of Powell St and south of Geary St are rife with panhandlers and junkies.

Local Life

➡ **Markets** The farmers markets at the Ferry Building (p76) draw food-savvy locals.

➡ **Waterfront walks** Locals walk south toward the Bay Bridge for expansive vistas and stellar public art.

➡ **Cheap eats** The Tenderloin is full of cheap ethnic restaurants, but walking here is not for the faint of heart: when in doubt, take a taxi.

Getting There & Away

➡ **Streetcar** Historic F-Market line streetcars run above Market St, then along the Embarcadero to Fisherman's Wharf.

➡ **Cable car** The Powell-Hyde and Powell-Mason lines link Downtown with the Wharf (the Mason line is shorter, the Hyde line more scenic); the California St line runs west up Nob Hill.

➡ **Bus** Market St–bound Muni lines serve downtown: 2, 5, 6, 14, 21, 30, 31, 38, 41, 45 and 71.

➡ **Metro** The J, K, L, M and N metro lines run under Market St.

➡ **BART** Downtown stations are Embarcadero, Montgomery and Powell.

Lonely Planet's Top Tip

Most tourists begin their trips at Powell St as it's near many hotels and it's the route of Wharf-bound cable cars. However, they often get stuck waiting in the long lines at the Powell St cable car turnaround at Market St, held hostage by panhandlers and bad street performers. Either queue up for the Powell St cable car well before noon or get your fix on the lesser-traveled California St line.

✗ Best Places to Eat

➡ Ferry Building (p86)
➡ Gitane (p85)
➡ Slanted Door (p86)
➡ Cotogna (p84)
➡ Wayfare Tavern (p84)

For reviews, see p84 ➡

☕ Best Places to Drink

➡ Rickhouse (p89)
➡ Barrique (p91)
➡ Edinburgh Castle (p91)
➡ Cantina (p89)
➡ Bix (p91)

For reviews, see p89 ➡

☆ Best Places for Live Performances

➡ San Francisco Symphony (p92)
➡ San Francisco Opera (p92)
➡ Rrazz Room (p93)
➡ Café Royale (p93)
➡ Biscuits & Blues (p93)

For reviews, see p92 ➡

Other towns have gourmet ghettos, but San Francisco puts its love of food front and center at the Ferry Building. The once-grand port was overshadowed by a 1950s elevated freeway until 1989, when the freeway turned out to be less than earthquake-proof. The freeway above the waterfront was demolished and the Ferry Building again emerged as the symbol of San Francisco. Only now, it's become its own destination, marking your arrival onto America's most-happening food scene.

DON'T MISS...

➡ The grand arrivals hall

➡ The Embarcadero waterfront promenades

➡ Wild parrots at Justin Herman Plaza

➡ Views of SF from a departing ferry

➡ Vaillancourt Fountain

PRACTICALITIES

➡ Map p316

➡ www.ferrybuilding marketplace.com

➡ Market St & the Embarcadero

➡ ⏱10am-6pm Mon-Fri, 9am-6pm Sat, 11am-5pm Sun

➡ Ⓜ&ⓇEmbarcadero

Ferry Building

Like a grand salute, the Ferry Building's trademark 240ft tower greeted dozens of ferries daily after its 1898 inauguration. But with the opening of the Bay Bridge and Golden Gate, ferry traffic subsided in the 1930s. Then the new overhead freeway obscured the building's stately facade and car fumes turned it black. Only after the 1989 earthquake did city planners snap to and realize what they'd been missing: with its grand halls and bay views, this was the perfect place to develop a new public commons.

Even before building renovations were completed in 2003, the Ferry Plaza Farmers Market began operating out front on the sidewalk. While some complained the prices were higher than at other markets, there was no denying this one offered seasonal, gourmet treats and local specialty foods not found elsewhere. Artisanal goat cheese, fresh-pressed California olive oil, wild boar and organic vegetables soon captured the imagination of SF's professional chefs and semiprofessional eaters.

Today the organic gourmet action also continues indoors, where select local shops sell wild-harvested mushrooms, gold-leaved chocolates, sustainably farmed oysters and caviar, as well as myriad other temptations. Standout shops and restaurants provide further reasons to miss your ferry. For restaurants, see p86.

You can still catch ferries here (p292), and on a sunny day, it may become the highlight of your trip. Otherwise, simply walk along the waterfront promenades flanking the Ferry Building north and south, and get a taste of life by the water in the new San Francisco.

Justin Herman Plaza

The plaza at the foot of Market St, across the Embarcadero from the Ferry Building, may lack visual aesthetics – the Vaillancourt Fountain was intentionally designed to be ugly, mirroring the freeway that once roared above – but Justin Herman Plaza draws big crowds. Lunchtime concert-goers, Critical Mass protesters, lawn bowlers, wintertime ice-skaters, Friday-night roller skaters, and internet daters screening potential mates from behind the fountain's wall of water all flock here. But the most thrilling sight is the wild parrots of Telegraph Hill. Follow the poplar trees leading north to lush **Sue Bierman Park** (Map p316; Clay & Drumm Sts), a patch of green where you can picnic and watch squawking green birds zip through the branches.

TOP SIGHTS
ASIAN ART MUSEUM

The largest viewable collection of Asian art outside Asia covers 6000 years and thousands of miles of terrain. A trip through the galleries is a treasure-hunting expedition, from racy Rajasthan palace miniatures to the largest collection of Japanese sculptural baskets outside Japan to the jewel-box gallery of lustrous Chinese jade – just don't bump into those priceless Ming vases.

To give some idea of Asia's virtuosity, the Asian Art Museum has amassed 17,000 prime examples of the region's ingenuity and artistry. Consider the diplomatic backbends curators had to do to put such a diverse collection into proper perspective. Where the UN falters, this museum succeeds in bringing Taiwan, China and Tibet together, uniting Pakistan and India, and striking a harmonious balance between Japan, Korea and China.i Granted, the Chinese collection takes up two wings and South Asia only one, but that healthy cultural competition has served to encourage donations of South Asian artifacts. Given the city's 150-year history as North America's gateway to Asia, the collection is also quintessentially San Franciscan, drawing on longstanding local ties and distinguished local collections.

The building itself is another feat of diplomacy. Italian architect Gae Aulenti's clever repurposing of the old San Francisco Main Library building left intact the much-beloved granite bas-relief on the building's face, the entryway's travertine arches and the polished stone staircase inside. Two new indoor plazas for oversize installations were also added.

Begin your tour of the collection by taking a single-file escalator up to the top floor. The curatorial concept is to follow the geographical path of Buddhism through Asia from the top floor down, beginning on the 3rd floor with India, and then – wait, isn't that Iran, followed by the Sikh kingdoms, then Indonesia? By the time you've cruised past 3000-plus Zoroastrian artifacts and splendid Balinese shadow puppets, all theological quibbles will yield to astonishment – and possibly exhaustion. If museums wear you out fast – or you're short on time – either find art from your favorite Asian country or head directly for the Chinese collections.

The Asian also emphasizes educational programs, which keep pan-generational crowds thronging the place. Hands-on workshops for kids and evening lectures with noted art historians are boons for parents and couples on date night.

Make a day of it with lunch at **Café Asia** (200 Larkin St; ⊙10am-4:30pm Tues, Wed, Fri-Sun, 10am-8:30pm Thu; dishes $5-14), where sunny days mean *bento* boxes on the balcony terrace. On Thursdays every other month, from 5pm to 9pm, hipsters are in charge with **Matcha**, an urban-contemporary event series with a changing lineup, but always music and cocktails. Think DJs spinning Japanese hip-hop, tattoo artists giving live demos, sake-makers pouring tastings, and crafty types making Chinese paper lanterns to ward off hungry ghosts.

DON'T MISS...

➡ 3000-year-old Chinese ritual bronzes

➡ Rare Japanese scrolls and screens

➡ Gilt-bronze Buddha from the year 338

➡ Architectural detail on the building's facade

➡ Café Asia

PRACTICALITIES

➡ Map p322

➡ ☎415-581-3500

➡ www.asianart.org

➡ 200 Larkin St

➡ adult/child $12/ free, 1st Sun of month free

➡ ⊙10am-5pm Tue-Sun, to 9pm Thu Feb-Sep

➡ Ⓜ&ⓇCivic Center

SIGHTS

⊙ Financial District & Jackson Square

FERRY BUILDING   LANDMARK
See p76.

JUSTIN HERMAN PLAZA   SQUARE
See p76.

TRANSAMERICA PYRAMID & REDWOOD PARK   NOTABLE BUILDING
Map p316 (www.thepyramidcenter.com; 600 Montgomery St; ⊙9am-6pm Mon-Fri; ⓜ&ⓡEmbarcadero) The defining feature of San Francisco's skyline was built during the Jet Age, atop the wreck of a whaling ship abandoned in the 1849 Gold Rush, at the site of a saloon frequented by Mark Twain and the newspaper office where Sun Yat-sen drafted his Proclamation of the Republic of China.

Architect William Pereira maximized light in the narrow streets below with his pyramid design, but even before its 1972 inauguration his pointy office tower was derided as Pereira's Prick. Critics claimed Pereira's Hollywood special-effects background was too apparent in the 853ft streamlined tower, which looked ready for blastoff. But others found the quirky landmark perfectly suited to SF. Even those who still love to hate it adore Redwood Park, the half-acre stand of redwoods at its base.

Another redeeming feature was the view – note the past tense. Since September 11, the viewing platform at the tip of the pyramid has been closed to visitors for 'security reasons.' If you're determined to get virtually queasy witnessing the slight half-foot sway at the top of the Pyramid in a strong wind, you can do so by visiting the virtual observation deck.

JACKSON SQUARE   NEIGHBORHOOD
Map p316 (www.jacksonsquaresf.com; around Jackson & Montgomery Sts; ⓜ&ⓡEmbarcadero) Local ad agencies and antiques dealers are more subtle about wheedling money from unsuspecting consumers than were the previous occupants of this former dock area. Notorious saloon owner Shanghai Kelly and madam Miss Piggot once conked new arrivals on the head and delivered them to ships in need of crew. (Despite their efforts, many ships were abandoned as sailors left to seek their fortune in San Francisco.)

Along the former waterfront bounded by Washington St, Columbus Ave, Pacific Ave and Sansome St, Italianate buildings with tall windows and cast-iron shutters were erected to house whiskey dealers, lawyers, loan offices and other necessary Barbary Coast evils. Architects and gallery owners liked the high ceilings and low rents, and they successfully lobbied for historic status for the Jackson Square area in 1971. Since then, many of the elegant storefronts have been taken over by upscale interior-design showrooms.

AP HOTALING WAREHOUSE   HISTORICAL BUILDING
Map p316 (451-55 Jackson St) 'If, as they say, God spanked the town/For being over-frisky/Why did He burn His churches down/And spare Hotaling's whiskey?' The snappiest comeback in SF history was this saloon-goers' retort after Hotaling's 1866 whiskey warehouse survived the 1906 earthquake and fire. Many considered this divine retribution for Barbary Coast debauchery. A bronze plaque with this ditty still graces the resilient Italianate building.

EMBARCADERO CENTER   NOTABLE BUILDING
Map p316 (www.embarcaderocenter.com; Sacramento St; ⊙10am-5pm; ⓜ&ⓡEmbarcadero; ⓡCalifornia St) The skyscrapers of the Embarcadero Center, joined by overhead walkways, form an urban-sprawl mall and have little to recommend them beyond some good public art and the crowd-pleasing Embarcadero Center Cinema (p94). They connect to the north with Golden Gateway Center – a 1950s-designed modernist housing development on the site of the city's former wholesale vegetable market – anchored by One Maritime Plaza (née the Alcoa Building, 300 Clay St), the city's first skyscraper to use crisscrossing-steel seismic reinforcements.

⊙ Union Square

FREE **49 GEARY**   ART GALLERY
Map p320 (☏415-788-9818; www.sfada.com; 49 Geary St; ⊙10:30am-5:30pm Tue-Fri, 11am-5pm Sat; ⓜ&ⓡPowell St) Pity the collectors silently nibbling endive in austere Chelsea galleries – at 49 Geary, openings mean unexpected art, goldfish-shaped crackers and outspoken crowds. Four floors of gal-

leries feature standout international and local works including eclectic, eye-popping photography ranging from the 19th to 21st centuries at Fraenkel Gallery to sculptor Seth Koen's minimalist pieces at Gregory Lind. Beat the crowds by coming on weekdays for quieter contemplation.

FREE **77 GEARY** ART GALLERY

Map p320 (77 Geary St; ⊙10:30am-5:30pm Tue-Fri, 11am-5pm Sat; MⓈ&ⓇPowell St) The most intriguing art usually appears in what looks like the wrong place, and 77 Geary's unmarked entryway is no exception. Get seduced on the mezzanine by the minimalism of **Patricia Sweetow Gallery** (www.patriciasweetowgallery.com) and shaken up on the 2nd floor by the political art of **Togonon Gallery** (www.togonongallery.com). For beauty with brains, see **Marx & Zavattero** (www.marxzav.com) next door for David Hevel's neo-baroque, middle-America-meets-Hollywood taxidermy sculptures and Paul Mullins' tragic-comic exploration of rural contentment. Sensitive meets sensational at **Rena Bransten Gallery** (www.renabranstengallery.com), featuring shows such as Hung Liu's mirage-like portraits of found ancestors and collaged stills from 'unwatchable' movies by a man who should know: *Polyester* cult-sensation John Waters.

UNION SQUARE SQUARE

Map p320 (intersection of Geary, Powell, Post & Stockton Sts; MⓈ&ⓇPowell St; ⓇPowell-Mason, Powell-Hyde) Louis Vuitton is more top-of-mind than the Emancipation Proclamation, but Union Square – bordered by department stores and mall chains – was named after pro–Union Civil War rallies held here 150 years ago. A misguided renovation paved the place and installed benches narrow enough to keep junkies from nodding off, turning this once-lovely park into a fancy prison exercise yard. Redeeming features include Emporio Rulli (p85), the half-price theater-ticket booth (p35) and the stellar people-watching.

**POWELL ST CABLE CAR
TURNAROUND** LANDMARK

Map p320 (cnr Powell & Market Sts; MⓈ&ⓇPowell St) Stand awhile at Powell and Market Sts and you'll spot arriving cable car operators leaping out, gripping trolleys and slooowly turning them around by hand on a revolving wooden platform. Cable cars can't go in reverse and this terminus is where the Powell-Mason and Powell-Hyde lines end

and begin. Riders line up late morning to early evening for the city's famous moving historic landmarks – so do panhandlers, street performers and preachers on megaphones. Some find the scene colorful, others find it unnerving. If you're worried about time, count heads and do the math: cable cars hold 60 people maximum (29 seated, 31 standing), but leave the terminus with fewer as to leave room for passengers to board along the route. They depart the turnaround every five to ten minutes at peak times. Powell-Mason cars are quickest to the Wharf; Powell-Hyde cars are more scenic and traverse more hills. For more on choosing the right cable car line, see p45).

PALACE HOTEL HISTORICAL BUILDING

Map p320 (☎415-512-1111; www.sfpalace.com; 2 New Montgomery St; MⓈ&ⓇMontgomery St) The city's most storied hotel opened in 1875, and was gutted during the 1906 earthquake and fire. Opera-star Enrico Caruso was staying here that day, and he reportedly ran into the street, swearing he'd never return to San Francisco. The current building opened in 1909. Ten years later, Woodrow Wilson gave his League of Nations speech here, and in 1923 US President Warren G Harding died upstairs. Visit by day to see the opulent Garden Court and its luminous stained-glass domed ceiling, then pop into the **Pied Piper Bar** to see Maxfield Parrish's mural of the Pied Piper. Afterwards have drinks across the street at House of Shields (p152) and see the gorgeous mahogany back bar, which was originally intended to frame the Parrish mural, but proved too small.

BOHEMIAN CLUB HISTORICAL BUILDING

Map p320 (624 Taylor St; MⓈSutter & Taylor Sts; ⓇPowell-Mason, Powell-Hyde) The most infamous, secretive club in all San Francisco was founded in the 19th century by bona fide bohemians, but they couldn't afford the upkeep so allowed the ultra-rich to join. Now the roster lists an odd mix of power elite and famous artists: apparently both George W Bush and Bob Weir are current members. On the Post St side of the club's ivy-covered brick wall, look for the plaque honoring Gold Rush–era author Bret Harte, which depicts characters from his works. On the extreme right is 'The Heathen Chinee.' It's not a racist attack – quite the opposite – but a reference to the eponymous 1870 satirical poem Harte wrote mocking anti-Chinese sentiment in Northern

1. Union Square (p79)
This square was named after pro–Union Civil War rallies held here 150 years ago.

2. Ferry Plaza Farmers Market, Ferry Building (p76)
The farmers market sells seasonal, gourmet treats and local specialty foods.

3. War Memorial Opera House (p92)
Opera divas bring down the house with classic and contemporary works performed in this lavish building.

DOWNTOWN ROOFTOP GARDENS

Above the busy sidewalks, there's a serene world of public rooftop gardens that provide perspective on Downtown's skyscraper-canyons. Here's a short list of favorites.

One Montgomery Terrace (Map p322; 50 Post St/1 Montgomery St; ⊙10am-6pm Mon-Sat) Great Market St views of old and new SF. Enter through Crocker Galleria, take the elevator to the top, then ascend stairs or enter Wells Fargo at One Montgomery and take the elevator to 'R.'

Sun Terrace (Map p316; 343 Sansome St; ⊙10am-6pm Mon-Fri) Knockout vistas of the Financial District and Transamerica Pyramid from atop a slender art-deco skyscraper. Take the elevator to level 15.

Orchard Garden Hotel (Map p320; 466 Bush St; ⊙7am-9pm) Green space above the Chinatown Gate, with south-facing, big-sky Downtown views.

Fairmont Hotel (950 Mason St; ⊙24hr) Traverse the lobby toward the Pavilion Room, then out glass doors to a deliciously kitsch rooftop courtyard – our favorite.

California. Ironically, upon publication the poem had the opposite effect and became a rallying cry against Chinese immigration. Things are seldom what they seem at the Bohemian Club.

**XANADU GALLERY: FOLK ART
INTERNATIONAL** NOTABLE BUILDING
Map p320 (☑415-392-9999; www.folkartintl.com; 140 Maiden Lane; ⊙10am-6pm Tue-Sat; Ⓜ&ⓇPowell St) Shrink the Guggenheim and plop it inside a brick box with a sunken Romanesque archway, and there you have Frank Lloyd Wright's 1949 Circle Gallery Building, which since 1979 has been the home of Xanadu Gallery. The nautilus shell ramp in the atrium leads you on a world tour of high-end folk art, from Fijian war clubs to mounted nose ornaments from the Andes.

JAMES FLOOD BUILDING HISTORICAL BUILDING
Map p320 (cnr Market & Powell Sts; Ⓜ&ⓇPowell St) This 1904 stone building survived the 1906 earthquake and retains much of its original character, notwithstanding the ground-level Gap flagship. Upstairs there are long, labyrinthine halls lined with frosted-glass doors, just like in a noir movie – and that's no coincidence. Back in 1921 the San Francisco office of the infamous Pinkerton National Detective Agency hired a young private investigator named Dashiell Hammett, now better known as the author of the 1930 noir classic *The Maltese Falcon*.

LOTTA'S FOUNTAIN MONUMENT
Map p320 (Market St at Kearny St; Ⓜ&Ⓡ Montgomery St) Lotta Crabtree made a kill-ing as San Francisco's diminutive opera diva, and she never forgot the city that paid for her trademark cigars. At the age of 28, the already-wealthy performer commissioned this cast-metal pillar thrice her size with a spigot fountain as a present to the people of San Francisco. It was a useful gift indeed during the 1906 fire, when it became the sole source of water downtown.

◉ Civic Center &
the Tenderloin

ASIAN ART MUSEUM MUSEUM
See p77.

FREE **CITY HALL** HISTORICAL BUILDING
Map p322 (☑tour info 415-554-6023, art exhibit line 415-554-6080; www.ci.sf.ca.us/cityhall; 400 Van Ness Ave; ⊙8am-8pm Mon-Fri, tours 10am, noon & 2pm; 🚹; Ⓜ&ⓇCivic Center) That mighty beaux arts dome pretty much covers San Francisco's grandest ambitions and fundamental flaws. It was designed by John Bakewell and Arthur Brown Jr in 1915 to outdo Paris for flair and outsize the capitol building dome in Washington, DC. The dome was a little unsteady until its retrofit after the 1989 earthquake, when ingenious technology enabled the dome to swing on its base without raising alarm.

The gold leafing on the dome's exterior is a reminder of dot-com–era excess. But from the inside, the splendid rotunda has ringing acoustics, and if that dome could talk, it would tell of triumph and tragedy. Anti-McCarthy sit-in protesters were hosed off the grand staircase in 1960, but finally ran

McCarthy out of town. Harvey Milk was assassinated here in 1978. And in 2004, the cheers heard around the world were from families and friends of the 4037 same-sex couples who celebrated their marriages here, thanks to Mayor Newsom's short-lived challenge to California state marriage law. Take the elevator one flight down to discover intriguing public art exhibits, which range from photographs of senior subcultures to work by blind artists.

Free docent tours of City Hall meet at the tour kiosk near the Van Ness Ave entrance, but City Hall is best seen in action. If you want insight into how San Francisco government works – or doesn't, as the case may be – the Board of Supervisors meets Tuesdays at 2pm in City Hall; check the agenda and minutes online. Theoretically, visitors may be removed for 'boisterous' behavior, but this being San Francisco, democracy in action can get pretty rowdy without fazing seen-it-all security guards.

GLIDE MEMORIAL UNITED METHODIST CHURCH
CHURCH

Map p322 (☑415-674-6090; www.glide.org; 330 Ellis St; ☺celebrations 9am & 11am Sun; ⓂⓇPowell St) The 100-member Glide gospel choir kicks off Sunday celebrations, and the welcome is warm for whoever comes through the door – the diverse, 1500-plus congregation includes many who'd once lost all faith in faith. After the celebration ends, the congregation keeps the inspiration coming, providing a million free meals a year and housing for formerly homeless families – now that's hitting a high note.

SAN FRANCISCO MAIN LIBRARY
NOTABLE BUILDING

Map p322 (☑415-557-4400; www.sfpl.org; 100 Larkin St; ☺10am-6pm Mon & Sat, 9am-8pm Tue-Thu, noon-5pm Fri & Sun; ☏♿; ⓂⓇCivic Center) The vast skylight dome sheds plenty of light through San Francisco's Main Library. And this being San Francisco, the library actively appeals to broad audiences – to wit the African American Center, Chinese Center, the James C Hormel Gay & Lesbian Center, and the Center for San Francisco History. Besides its eclectic collection of San Franciscans and (some of) their favorite books, the library quietly boasts an excellent high-profile author-reading and lecture series, plus intriguing ephemera exhibits in the 6th-floor Skylight Gallery.

Artistic touches include Alice Aycock's spiral staircase between the 5th and 6th floors, and artist Ann Chamberlain's 2nd-floor wallpaper made of cards from the old card catalog, with running commentary provided by 200 San Franciscans. Just don't go looking for all the books listed on the cards.

LUGGAGE STORE GALLERY
ART GALLERY

Map p322 (☑415-255-5971; www.luggagestore gallery.org; 1007 Market St; ☺noon-5pm Wed-Sat; ⓂⓇCivic Center) A dandelion pushing through the cracks in the sidewalk, this plucky nonprofit gallery has for two decades brought signs of life to one of the toughest blocks in the Tenderloin. The art sprawls across the spacious 2nd-floor gallery, rising above the street without losing sight of it: this space was the launching pad for renowned graffiti satirists.

Two Luggage Store regulars you might recognize around town are Rigo and Brazilian duo Ogemeos. Rigo did the 'One Tree' mural that looks like a one-way sign by the 101 Fwy on-ramp in SoMa. And the Ogemeos did the mural of a defiant kid holding a lit firecracker atop the gallery building. With such oddly touching works, poetry nights and monthly performing-arts events, this place puts the tender in the Tenderloin.

◢ ARTS COMMISSION GALLERY
ART GALLERY

Map p322 (☑415-554-6080; www.sfacgallery. org; 401 Van Ness Ave; ☺noon-5pm Wed-Sat; ⓂVan Ness Ave) Get in on the next art movement at this lobby-level public gallery featuring international perspectives and local talents. You never know what you might find. As well as hanging shows and hosting receptions in its gallery, the commission also sponsors wide-ranging works in the rotunda of City Hall.

UNITED NATIONS PLAZA
SQUARE

Map p322 (Market St btwn Hyde & Leavenworth Sts; ☺6am-midnight; ⓂⓇCivic Center) This vast brick-paved triangle commemorates the signing of the UN charter in San Francisco. It offers a clear view of City Hall, sundry Scientologists drumming up converts and the odd drug deal in progress. Thankfully, the wonderful **Heart of the City Farmers Market** (Map p322; www.hocfarmersmarket.org; 7am-5pm Wed & Sun) provides a fresher perspective on the Tenderloin.

✖ EATING

The sustainable-food temple known as the Ferry Building (see p76) houses several foodie shrines under one roof. It features chef-operated lunch counters, high-end take-out and a farmers market on Tuesday and Thursday from 10am to 2pm, and Saturdays from 8am to 2pm. At dinnertime, Downtown is best known for its high-end houses, like Fleur de Lys and Michael Mina, but at lunchtime most eateries cater to office workers, with meals around $10. The Financial District is quiet at night, when only midrange and top-end restaurants stay open. The Tenderloin – west of Powell St, south of Geary St, north of Market St – feels sketchy and sometimes rough, but as always in San Francisco, superior dining rewards the adventurous. Note that some cheap eats in the 'Loin close earlier than their posted hours.

✖ Financial District & Jackson Square

MICHAEL MINA CALIFORNIAN $$$
Map p316 (☑415-397-9222; www.michaelmina. net; 252 California St; lunch $49-59, dinner $35-42; ☉lunch Mon-Fri, dinner daily; Ⓜ&ⓇMontgomery St, ⓖCalifornia St) San Francisco's favorite culinary son and winner of the James Beard Award has reinvented his posh namesake restaurant, which spawned an empire of 16 others around the country. Gone is the multicourse, silver-service European luxe, in favor of more lighthearted, á la carte French-Japanese cooking that blurs the lines between formal and casual. There's still caviar, but also a foie gras PB&J. Signature mains still include lobster pot pie, but now it's served deconstructed. The cavernous dining room, with its massive mirrors

angled just-right for people-watching, feels austerely elegant, and the bar is a happening spot for cocktails and small bites. Reservations essential.

COTOGNA ITALIAN $$
Map p316 (☑415-775-8508; www.cotognasf.com; 470 Pacific Ave; mains $14-24; ☉lunch & dinner Mon-Sat; ✍; ⓂPacific Ave & Montgomery St) Chef-owner Michael Tusk won the 2011 James Beard Award for best chef. Ever since, it's been hard to book a table at Cotogna (and its fancier big sister Quince, next door), but it's worth planning ahead to be rewarded with his authentic rustica Italian cooking that magically balances a few pristine flavors. Pastas are outstanding, and pizzas have tender-to-the-tooth crusts. The $24 prix-fixe menu is a steal.

WAYFARE TAVERN AMERICAN $$$
Map p316 (☑415-772-9060; www.wayfare tavern.com; 558 Sacramento St; mains $19-29; ☉11am-11pm Mon-Sat, 5pm-11pm Sun; Ⓜ&ⓇMontgomery Sts; ⓖCalifornia St) The decor nods to Colonial Americana and old San Francisco, with exposed brick and polished wood, barkeeps in white jackets, trophy heads on the wall, and enough decorative bric-a-brac to cause frissons over potential earthquakes. The cooking – deviled eggs, buttermilk fried chicken, steak tartare, pot roast – gives excellent insight into the traditional-American culinary repertoire, but the backslapping-businessman clientele can get loud; sit upstairs. Book two to three weeks ahead, one month for weekends.

BOCADILLOS BASQUE $$
Map p316 (☑415-982-2622; www.bocasf.com; 710 Montgomery St; dishes $9-15; ☉7am-10pm Mon-Fri, 5-10:30pm Sat; ⓂClay & Montgomery Sts) Forget multipage menus and giant portions, and have your choice of two small sandwiches on toasted rolls, with a green

---

ALFRESCO DINING ON WARM NIGHTS

During the odd heat wave in SF, when it's too hot to stay indoors without air-con (which nobody in SF has) and warm enough to eat outside, two downtown streets become the go-to destinations for dining alfresco: Belden Place (www.belden-place. com) and Claude Lane. Both are pedestrian alleyways lined with restaurants, which set up side-by-side tables in the street, creating scenes remarkably like Paris in summertime. The food is better on Claude Lane, notably at sexy Gitane and Cafe Claude. But the scene on Belden is more colorful, especially at restaurants Plouf, Tiramisu and Café Bastille – which are otherwise not outstanding, but so much fun.

QUICK BITES WHILE SHOPPING

A few of our favorite places to recharge between boutiques:

Emporio Rulli (Map p320; ☎415-433-1122; www.rulli.com; Union Square; ◐7:30am-7:30pm; Ⓜ&ⓇPowell St) Artisinal Italian pastries, powerful espresso and prosciutto sandwiches at outdoor tables in Union Square.

Mocca on Maiden Lane (Map p320; ☎415-956-1188; 175 Maiden Lane; ◐8am-6pm Mon-Fri, 8:30am-4pm Sat; Ⓜ&ⓇPowell St) Order steak sandwiches, seafood salads and cheesecake inside, then carry outside to umbrella tables in a chic pedestrian alley; cash only.

Rotunda (Map p320; ☎415-362-4777; www.neimanmarcus.com; 150 Stockton St; ◐11am-5pm Mon-Sat; Ⓜ&ⓇPowell St) Favored by ladies in Chanel suits, who come for lobster club sandwiches and proper afternoon tea beneath the gorgeous stained-glass dome at Neiman Marcus.

Bio (Map p320; ☎415-362-0255; 75 O'Farrell St; ◐8am-6pm; Ⓜ&ⓇPowell St) Healthful sandwiches, vegan salads, gluten-free quiches and multiple varieties of kombucha, but no seating (picnic at Union Square).

Cafe Claude (p87) The ideal spot to collapse with your shopping bags when you realize it's 4pm and you've forgotten to eat lunch – and, oh, wouldn't a glass of wine be nice, too?

---

salad, for just $10 at this downtown favorite for tapas and small plates. The juicy lamb burgers, snapper ceviche with Asian pears, and Catalan sausages are just-right Basque bites, made better with wine by the glass.

KOKKARI   GREEK $$$

Map p316 (☎415-981-0983; www.kokkari.com; 200 Jackson St; mains $21-35; ◐lunch Mon-Fri, dinner daily; ☝) This one Greek restaurant where you'll want to lick your plate instead of break it, with starters like grilled octopus with a zing of lemon and oregano, and a signature lamb, eggplant and yogurt moussaka as rich as the Pacific Stock Exchange. Reserve ahead to avoid waits, or make a meal of hearty Mediterranean apps at the happening bar.

BARBACCO   ITALIAN $$

Map p316 (☎415-955-1919; www.barbaccosf. com; 220 California St; mains lunch $10-13, dinner $11-17; ◐11:30am-10pm Mon-Fri, 5:30-10pm Sat; Ⓜ&ⓇEmbarcadero; ⓒCalifornia St) A lunch counter for the new millennium, Barbacco's best seats are stools along the open kitchen, unless you want to meet downtown bankers at the communal tables lining the exposed-brick wall. Plan to share earthy-delicious small plates – fried brussels sprouts, bruschetta of house-cured sardines and lemon-aioli egg salad, and chicken thighs braised with olives, escarole and almonds. The iPad wine list is annoying (don't downtowners go out

to lunch to get *away* from their screens?), but includes 3oz pours at fair prices, allowing you to taste multiple varietals without going broke.

🌿 MIXT GREENS   SALADS $

Map p316 (www.mixtgreens.com; 120 Sansome St; salads $8-11; ◐10:30am-3pm Mon-Fri; ☝; Ⓜ&ⓇMontgomery St) Stockbrokers line up out the door for generous organic salads, like humanely raised, herb-marinated chicken with chipotle dressing or mango, jicama and roasted peanuts with tangy Thai vinaigrette. Grab a stool or get yours to go in a compostable corn container to enjoy bayside near the Ferry Building.

✖ Union Square

GITANE   BASQUE, MEDITERRANEAN $$

Map p320 (☎415-788-6686; www.gitanerest aurant.com; 6 Claude Lane; mains $15-25; ◐5:30pm-midnight Tue-Sat, bar to 1am; ☝; Ⓜ&ⓇMontgomery St) Slip out of the Financial District and into something more comfortable at this sexy jewel-box bistro – a dimly lit mash-up of French boudoir and '70s chic, with lipstick-red lacquered ceilings reflecting tasseled silks, tufted leather and velvet snugs. The menu draws inspiration from Basque, Spanish and Moroccan traditions, with standout stuffed squash blossoms, lamb tartare, semolina-crusted sardines,

EATING AT THE FERRY BUILDING

Slanted Door (Map p316; ☎415-861-8032; www.slanteddoor.com; 1 Ferry Bldg; lunch $13-24, dinner $18-36; ⊙lunch & dinner; Ⓜ&Ⓡ Embarcadero) San Francisco's most effortlessly elegant restaurant harmonizes California ingredients, continental influences and Vietnamese flair. Owner-chef Charles Phan enhances top-notch ingredients with bright flavors, heaping local Dungeness crab atop cellophane noodles and garlicky Meyer Ranch 'shaking beef' on watercress. The wildly successful venture is still a family establishment, with Phan family members serving multistar meals for here and to go at Out the Door (p122). Book two weeks ahead for lunch, one month for dinner – or call at 5:30pm for last-minute cancelations.

La Mar Cebicheria (Map p316; ☎415-397-8880; www.lamarcebicheria.com; Pier 1½, The Embarcadero; lunch $13-20, dinner $20-30; ⊙lunch & dinner; Ⓜ&Ⓡ Embarcadero) Big and bustling, La Mar has spectacular bay views and a snappy electric-blue and polished-wood decor. The key ingredient in its collaged plates of Peruvian *cebiche* is *leche de tigre*, the 'milk of the tiger,' a marinade of lime, chili and brine that 'cooks' the fish without a fire, and is said to have aphrodisiac properties. Sunny days are prime for flirting outside by the bay over a plate of pristine, spicy *cebiche classico* of sustainably caught California halibut, habanero, Peruvian corn and yam, with a side order of crispy-delicious housemade empanadas.

Hog Island Oyster Company (Map p316; ☎415-391-7117; www.hogislandoysters.com; 1 Ferry Bldg; 6 oysters $15-17; ⊙11:30am-8pm Mon-Fri, 11am-6pm Sat & Sun Ⓜ&Ⓡ Embarcadero) Slurp the bounty of the North Bay, with a view of the East Bay, at this Ferry Building favorite for sustainably farmed oysters. Take yours au naturel, with caper *beurre blanc,* spiked with bacon and paprika or perhaps classic-style, with lemon and shallots. Mondays and Thursdays between 5pm and 7pm are happy hours indeed for shellfish fans, with half-price oysters and $4 pints.

Boulette's Larder (Map p316; ☎415-399-1155; www.bouletteslarder.com; 1 Ferry Bldg; mains $18-23; ⊙9am-3pm Mon-Fri, noon-3pm Sat, 11am-3pm Sun; Ⓜ&Ⓡ Embarcadero) Dinner theater doesn't get more literal than brunch at Boulette's communal table, strategically placed inside a working kitchen, amid a swirl of chefs preparing fancy French take-out dinners for commuter gourmands. Inspired by their truffled eggs or beignets? Get spices and mixes to go at the pantry counter.

Plant Cafe Organic (Map p316; ☎415-984-1973; www.theplantcafe.com; Pier 3; mains lunch $11-15, dinner $14-22; ⊙lunch & dinner; ☝; Ⓜ&Ⓡ Embarcadero) Solar panels provide the power and most ingredients come from within a 30 minutes radius of SF at this locavore favorite, just north of the Ferry Building. The high-ceilinged, post-industrial space, with exposed ductwork and hanging glass-tungsten bulbs, has knockout bay views and a gastro-pub vibe. Red meat is notably absent on the veg-heavy menu, but there's fish, chicken and duck. Book ahead for weekend dinner or Sunday brunch, or get to-go salads and sandwiches from the adjoining cafe.

Il Cane Rosso (Map p316; ☎415-391-7599; www.canerossosf.com; 1 Ferry Bldg; mains $13; ⊙breakfast, lunch & dinner; Ⓜ&Ⓡ Embarcadero) Il Cane Rosso serves seasonal-regional, earthy-delicious breakfasts and lunches, and soul-satisfying three-course dinners for $25 (5pm to 9pm), in a tiny space that seats you in the kitchen. If it's warm enough, snag an outdoor table overlooking the bay. The menu changes daily and you can't book, but this is great food for not a lot of money.

Mijita (Map p316; ☎415-399-0814; www.mijitasf.com; 1 Ferry Bldg; dishes $4-5; ⊙10am-7pm Mon-Wed, to 8pm Thu-Sat, to 4pm Sun; ☝☝; Ⓜ&Ⓡ Embarcadero) At this order-at-the-counter taco shop, owner-chef Traci Des Jardins puts her signature stamp on her Mexican grandmother's standbys. Expect fresh local produce for tangy-savory jicama and grapefruit salad with pumpkin seeds, and sustainably harvested fish cooked with the minimum of oil in seriously addictive Baja fish tacos. Wash it all down with melon *agua frescas* (fruit-flavored drinks) bayside, with envious seagulls circling overhead.

sautéed radishes, silky pan-seared scallops and *tagines* (Moroccan stews). Make reservations and dress sharp. Or drop by for craft cocktails at the swank little bar.

FLEUR DE LYS   FRENCH $$$

Map p320 (☑415-673-7779; www.fleurdelyssf.com; 777 Sutter St; menus $72-95; ☺dinner Mon-Sat; ✎; Ⓜ&Ⓡ Powell St) Long before celebrity chef Hubert Keller took his show on the road to Vegas and *Top Chef Masters,* this was the ultimate over-the-top SF destination. There's nothing subtle about the swanky sultan's tent interior. It's perfectly suited for princely repasts, involving gnocchi graced with chanterelles, hazelnut-encrusted scallops, halibut crowned with rhubarb coulis and truffle, and a king's ransom of foie gras on every other dish. Vegetarians are entitled to five-course feasts for a surprisingly reasonable $72.

SONS & DAUGHTERS   CALIFORNIAN $$$

Map p320 (☑415-391-8311; www.sonsanddaughterssf.com; 708 Bush St; 4-course menu $58; ☺dinner; Ⓡ Powell-Hyde, Powell-Mason) Sons & Daughters is a breath of culinary fresh air in a city that can get haughty about food. The young chefs here incorporate unusual elements in their white-tablecloth, farm-to-table cooking, but manage to keep the food accessible, with dishes like potato-skin consommé and black-truffle ice cream. The happening little storefront bistro has no ridiculous month-ahead reservations policy (though you should definitely book), making it ideal for an impromptu night out.

CAFE CLAUDE   FRENCH $$

Map p320 (☑415-392-3505; www.cafeclaude.com; 7 Claude Lane; mains $10-20; ☺11:30am-10:30pm Mon-Sat, 5:30pm-10:30pm Sun; Ⓜ&Ⓡ Montgomery St) Hidden on a little alleyway, Cafe Claude is the perfect French cafe, with zinc bar, umbrella tables outside and staff chattering *en français.* Lunch is served till a civilized 5pm, and a jazz combo plays during dinner Thursday to Saturday, when regulars dine on classics like *coq au vin* and steak tartare. The food is solidly good, but it's the romance of the scene that's so special.

HECHO   JAPANESE, LATIN $$$

Map p320 (☑415-835-6400; www.hechosf.com; 185 Sutter St; dishes $7-19; ☺lunch & dinner; Ⓜ&Ⓡ Montgomery St) Hecho's formula is simple: top-grade, thick-cut sushi and succulent meats grilled over Japanese charcoal,

served with seasonal sakes and tequila – 80 different kinds. In a break with downtown chic, mirroring the menu's rustic frankness, Hecho's decor has a dressed-down, varnished-wood look, but chairs aren't comfy enough to linger long. Thursday to Sunday, it's open until 1am – one of few downtowners to serve so late.

FARMERBROWN   NEW AMERICAN $$

(☑415-409-3276; www.farmerbrownsf.com; 25 Mason St; mains $12-23; ☺dinner Tue-Sun, weekend brunch bar 10am-2pm; Ⓜ&Ⓡ Powell St) This rebel from the wrong side of the block dishes up mean seasonal watermelon margaritas with a cayenne salt rim (genius), ribs that stick to yours, and coleslaw with a kick that'll leave your lips buzzing. Chef-owner Jay Foster works with local organic and African-American farmers to provide food with actual soul, in a setting that's rusted and cleverly repurposed as a shotgun shack. Harried service – it's always busy – and afro-funk beats match the uptempo crowd.

KATANA-YA   JAPANESE $

Map p320 (☑415-771-1280; 430 Geary St; dishes $7-12; ☺11:30am-2am Mon-Fri, noon-2am Sat & Sun; Ⓜ&Ⓡ Powell St) A glorified closet of a restaurant, Katana-Ya is the place for a late-night bite after the theater, or anytime you're willing to brave a couple of sketchy Tenderloin blocks for steaming bowls of udon and ramen, with broth so savory it's almost dense. Avoid the bland sushi. After a night's drinking, the curries seem to have curative properties. Expect waits at peak times.

BOXED FOODS   SANDWICHES, SALADS $

Map p320 (www.boxedfoodscompany.com; 245 Kearny St; dishes $8-10; ☺8am-3pm Mon-Fri; ✎; Ⓜ&Ⓡ Montgomery St) Organic, local, seasonal ingredients make outrageously flavorful lunches, whether you choose the zesty strawberry salad with mixed greens, walnuts and tart goat cheese or the Boxed BLT, with crunchy applewood smoked bacon. Get yours to go to the Transamerica Pyramid and Redwood Park, or grab one of the tables out back.

MURACCI'S CURRY   JAPANESE $

Map p320 (www.muraccis.com; 307 Kearny St; dishes $8-10; ☺11am-6pm Mon-Thu, to 5pm Fri; ✎; Ⓜ&Ⓡ Montgomery St) On foggy days, warm up from the inside out with a steaming curry-topped *katsu* (pork cutlet), grilled chicken rice-plate or classic Japanese comfort-food curry – neither spicy nor sharp, but gently tingling, faintly sweet and powerfully savory. Chipper counter staff take your order, then call your name when your food is ready.

📷 BREAD & COCOA   CAFE, SANDWICHES $

Map p320 (www.breadandcocoa.com; 199 Sutter St; dishes $6-9; ⊙7am-6pm Mon-Fri, 8:30am-5pm Sat & Sun; 📷; Ⓜ&ⓇMontgomery St) Local, artisanal ingredients add a fresh zing to sandwiches, such as roast-chicken panini with pesto, and tangy Humboldt Fog cheese with prosciutto, organic tomato and arugula. These sandwiches may not be huge for $8 to $10, but their flavor sure is.

✖ Civic Center & the Tenderloin

📷 MILLENNIUM   VEGETARIAN $$$

Map p322 (☎415-345-3900; www.millennium restaurant.com; 580 Geary St; set menu $39-72; ⊙dinner; 📷; Ⓜ&ⓇPowell St) If all vegetarian food could be this satisfying and opulent, there could be cattle roaming the streets of SF and no one would give them a second glance. Seasonal first courses include grilled semolina flatbread topped with caramelized onions, wilted spinach and a flourish of almond romesco. This is followed by a peppery pastry roulade that opens with a fork's touch to reveal a creamy center of golden potatoes and smoky *achiote* (chili) chard. And it's topped off with a saffron-scented rice pudding with mango sorbet. Book ahead for aphrodisiac dinners and vegetarian Thanksgiving.

BRENDA'S FRENCH SOUL FOOD   CREOLE, SOUTHERN $

Map p322 (☎415-345-8100; www.frenchsoul food.com; 652 Polk St; mains $8-12; ⊙8am-3pm Sun-Tue, 8am-10pm Wed-Sat; ⓂVan Ness Ave) Chef-owner Brenda Buenviaje blends New Orleans–style Creole cooking with French technique to create 'French soul food.' Expect updated classics like red beans and rice, serious biscuits and grits, amazing Hangtown fry (eggs scrambled with salt pork and fried oysters), good shrimp-stuffed po' boys, and fried chicken served with collard greens and hot-pepper jelly. Take the fire off the spicy cooking with sweet-watermelon tea.

📷 FARM:TABLE   AMERICAN $

Map p322 (☎415-292-7089; www.farmtablesf. com; 754 Post St; dishes $6-9; ⊙7:30am-6pm Mon-Fri, 8am-6pm Sat, 9am-3pm Sun; ⓂPost & Jones Sts) A tiny storefront with one wooden communal table inside, two tables and a stand-up counter outside, farm:table uses seasonal, regional organics in its foodie-smart breakfasts and lunches, posting the daily-changing menu on Twitter (@farm table). Good place to chill with locals. Great coffee. Cash only.

PAGOLAC   VIETNAMESE $

Map p322 (☎415-776-3234; 655 Larkin St; mains $6-12; ⊙5-9:30pm Tue-Sun; 📷; ⓂLarkin & O'Farrell Sts) Right in the hard heart of the Tenderloin is this inviting nook that's warm with low light and friendly faces. The special tasting menu of seven courses of beef may be overkill for anyone who's not a famished gaucho, but sugarcane shrimp and barbecued chicken are tasty alternatives. Pagolac also does good *pho* (Vietnamese soup) with meatballs and *bo tai chanh* (lemon-marinated rare steak slices).

SAI JAI THAI   THAI $

Map p322 (☎415-673-5774; 771 O'Farrell St; ⊙11am-10:45pm; ⓂLarkin & O'Farrell Sts) Mom and the cooks shout at each other in Thai, hardly anyone speaks English and the room is grungy, but the cooking's spot on. Just make sure when they ask how hot, you reply, 'Spicy like for Thai people!' Alas, no beer.

SHALIMAR   INDIAN $

Map p322 (☎415-928-0333; www.shalimarsf. com; 532 Jones St; dishes $5-10; ⊙noon-midnight; ⓂGeary & Jones Sts) Follow your nose to tandoori chicken straight off the skewer and naan bread still bubbling from the oven at this fluorescent-lit, linoleum-floored downtown Indian dive. Watch and learn as foodies, who demand five-star service elsewhere, meekly fetch their own water pitchers and tamarind sauce from the fridge.

SAIGON SANDWICH SHOP   VIETNAMESE $

Map p322 (☎415-474-5698; 560 Larkin St; sandwich $3.50; ⊙6:30am-5:30pm; ⓂLarkin & Eddy Sts) Order your $3.50 *banh mi* (Vietnamese sandwich) when the ladies of the Saigon call you, or you'll get skipped. Act fast and be rewarded with a baguette piled high with your choice of roast pork, chicken, pâté, meatballs and/or tofu, plus pickled carrots, cilantro, jalapeño and thinly sliced onion.

🍷 DRINKING & NIGHTLIFE
⚑

The only downside to Downtown drinking is the downtown crowd: too-loud deal-making by dudes in suits, with after-hours office flirting between co-workers. It's fun when it's going well, but it gets sloppy on Friday nights. For more texture and grit, head to the Tenderloin to drink with 20-something hipsters. Drinks are cheapest in the 'Loin and get increasingly pricey as you move towards the Financial District. Most Downtown bars have good happy-hour specials; otherwise drinks cost upwards of $10 (or more) east of Powell St, but drop in price in the Tenderloin.

🍷 Union Square

RICKHOUSE   BAR

Map p320 (www.rickhousebar.com; 246 Kearny St; ⊙Mon-Sat; Ⓜ&ⓇMontgomery St) Like an old shotgun shack plunked downtown, Rickhouse is lined floor to ceiling with repurposed whisky casks imported from Kentucky and backbar shelving from an Ozark Mountains nunnery that once secretly brewed hooch. The emphasis is (naturally) on whiskey, including some killer hard-to-find bourbons. But we most like coming with a posse and ordering the citrusy Pisco Punch, served vintage-style in a garage-sale punch bowl, complete with cups dangling off the side.

CANTINA   BAR

Map p320 (www.cantinasf.com; 580 Sutter St; ⊙Mon-Sat; ⓂSutter & Mason Sts) All the Latin-inspired cocktails (think tequila, cachaça and pisco) are made with fresh juice – there's not even a soda gun behind the bar – at this mixologist's dream bar that's mellow enough on weeknights for quiet conversation. The all-local crowd includes many off-duty bartenders – always a good sign. DJs spin on weekends.

BURRITT ROOM   LOUNGE

Map p320 (www.crescentsf.com; 417 Stockton St; Ⓜ&ⓇMontgomery St) Upstairs at the Crescent Hotel, Burritt works shabby-chic, with distressed-wood paneling and century-old tile floors, red-velvet sofas, brick walls and gaudy chandeliers that create the effect of an abandoned building co-opted by swank squatters, who prefer champagne cocktails over swill, and punchbowls over pints.

TUNNEL TOP   BAR

Map p320 (www.tunneltop.com; 601 Bush St; ⊙Mon-Sat; ⓂSutter & Stockton Sts) You can't tell who's local and who's not in this happening, chilled two-story bar, with exposed beams, beer-bottle chandelier and little mezzanine where you can spy on the crowd below. The owners are French, and their Gallic friends throng the place, tapping their toes to conscious hip-hop (think Common, not Little Wayne) and boom-boom house music, the SF soundtrack. Cash only.

DOWNTOWN & CIVIC CENTER DRINKING & NIGHTLIFE

OLD-SCHOOL TOURIST FAVORITES

Downtown is chockablock with tourist joints that fit the bill under certain circumstances – like, when you're traveling with screaming hungry kids and you just want to have a couple of cocktails and be left alone, but realize you're on vacation and should go somewhere atmospheric. Fear not: we've got you covered.

Tommy's Joynt (Map p322; ☑415-775-4216; www.tommysjoynt.com; 1101 Geary St; mains $4-9; ⊙11am-2am; 🚻; ⓂGeary St & Van Ness Ave) Open and unchanged since 1947 – with enough ephemera and animal heads on the walls to prove it – Tommy's is the classic for *hof brau* (cafeteria-style) meals of turkey, corned beef and buffalo stew.

Johnny Foley's (Map p320; ☑415-954-0777; www.johnnyfoleys.com; 243 O'Farrell St; mains $14-24; ⊙11:30am-1:30am; 🚻; Ⓜ&ⓇPowell St) Great-looking vintage bar and grill, with tile floors and gorgeous woodwork, live music nightly and passable Irish-pub grub.

Lefty O'Douls (Map p320; ☑415-982-8900; www.leftyodouls.biz; 333 Geary St; mains $7-11; ⊙7am-2am; 🚻; Ⓜ&ⓇPowell St) Floor-to-ceiling kitsch, baseball memorabilia, sports on TV, live music and *hof brau* – Lefty's is tourist central and reliably fun on game nights.

LOCAL KNOWLEDGE

HUSH-HUSH HOOCH

Psst – keep a secret? Speakeasies, those Prohibition-era underground gin joints, still exist in SF. We're not telling how, but once you've found the phone number or website for **Bourbon & Branch**, you can make a reservation to get the location (an unmarked door in the Tenderloin) and password for entry. Inside, studded leather banquettes, mirrored oak tables and red velvet walls evoke the roaring 1920s. The original speakeasy basement – complete with bullet holes and secret escape routes – and the room hidden behind the fake bookcase are perfect for super-private parties. Keep it under your hat.

CLOCK BAR
LOUNGE

Map p320 (☎415-397-7000; www.michaelmina.net; Westin St Francis Hotel, 335 Powell St; Ⓜ&ⓇPowell St; ⓇPowell-Mason, Powell-Hyde) If it's in season, it goes into the glass at this top-end mixology bar, the brainchild of celeb-chef Michael Mina. Ooh and aah over truffled popcorn while sampling knockout cocktails in cozy leather-and-wood snugs. Arrive early or reserve ahead, or expect to stand. Dress sharp.

GOLD DUST LOUNGE
BAR

Map p320 (247 Powell St; ⓒ7am-2am; Ⓜ&ⓇPowell St) Precarious Victorian brass chandeliers hover over a bar full of visitors and a twangy rockabilly band at this Union Square anachronism, where the gold paint has lost its glitter and pints are no longer cheap. But there's something of a time-machine effect in the swinging doors, coat stands and nude paintings – you almost expect someone to beckon you to a brothel upstairs.

IRISH BANK
PUB

Map p320 (www.theirishbank.com; 10 Mark Lane; ⓒ11:30am-2am; ⓇCalifornia St) Perfectly pulled pints and thick-cut fries with malt vinegar, plus juicy burgers, brats and anything else you could possibly want with lashings of mustard are staples at this cozy Irish pub. There are tables beneath a big awning in the alley out front, ideal for smokers – even on a rainy night.

LE COLONIAL
NIGHTCLUB

Map p320 (www.lecolonialsf.com; 20 Cosmo Pl; ⓂMontgomery St; ⓇPowell-Mason, Powell-Hyde) Time-travel to colonial French-Vietnam at this sexy downtowner with attentive service and tasty, if overpriced, Southeast Asian cooking. The draw is the scene: after 10pm Friday and Saturday, the 2nd-floor lounge becomes a nightclub and everyone dances. Make a night of it with dinner, or head directly upstairs to the pink-lit bar, with its rattan decor and low-slung stools, and order a Singapore sling. The sometimes-touristy, dressed-up crowd varies, but after 10pm skews toward 20- and 30-somethings.

RUBY SKYE
NIGHTCLUB

Map p320 (www.rubyskye.com; 420 Mason St; admission $10-25; ⓒ9pm-late Fri & Sat, sometimes Thu & Sun; Ⓜ&ⓇPowell St) The city's premiername nightclub occupies a vintage theater reminiscent of classic NY clubs, with reserveable balcony boxes. The who's-who of the world's DJs play here – think Danny Tenaglia, Dimitri from Paris, Christopher Lawrence and Paul Van Dyk. The very mainstream crowd sometimes gets messy (hence gruff security), but when your fave DJ's playing, who cares? The Funktion-One sound system is state of the art.

VESSEL
NIGHTCLUB

Map p320 (www.vesselsf.com; 85 Campton Pl; admission varies; ⓒ10pm-2am Wed-Sat; Ⓜ&ⓇPowell St) The crowd dresses sharp at Vessel, a midsized subterranean clublounge with kick-ass sound and mesmerizing lighting, which sometimes books bigname DJs (think Louie Vega). We prefer the more-local Wednesday to Thursday scene over the sometimes-suburban weekend crowd, which takes longer to get its drink on and dance. Get on the list.

CELLAR
NIGHTCLUB

Map p320 (www.cellarsf.com; 685 Sutter St; cover varies; ⓂSutter & Taylor Sts) The slightly grungy, subterranean Cellar has two dance floors with dueling sound systems. It's best weeknights when you want to party, but don't want to fuss with fancier clubs. Recommended when there's no cover (check the website); otherwise, it's not worth $10.

JOHN'S GRILL BAR

Map p320 (www.johnsgrill.com; 63 Ellis St; ⊙11am-10pm; M&R Powell St; R Powell-Mason, Powell-Hyde) It could be the martinis, the low lighting or the *Maltese Falcon* statuette upstairs, but something about Dashiell Hammett's favorite bar lends itself to hardboiled tales of lost love and true crimes, confessed while chewing toothpicks. That is, until the tourists filling the joint snap you back into the present.

Financial District & Jackson Square

BARRIQUE BAR

Map p316 (☎415-421-9200; www.barriquesf.com; 461 Pacific Ave; ⊙3pm-10pm Tue-Sat; M Pacific Av & Montgomery St) Farm-to-table is to restaurants what Barrique is to wine bars. Here your glass of high-end, small-batch vino comes straight from the cask, directly from the vineyard, sans label. Though there's a bottle list, stick to barrel tastings for the full experience. Sitting up front in the brick-walled space provides better people-watching, but we prefer the white-leather sofas out back, near the casks, to watch blending in action. Cheese and charcuterie plates – artisinal and organic, natch – keep your buzz in check.

TAVERNA AVENTINE BAR

Map p316 (☎415-981-1500; www.aventinesf.com; 582 Washington St; ⊙11:30am-midnight Mon-Fri, 8:30pm-2am Sat; M Clay & Montgomery Sts) In the days of the Barbary Coast, the 150-year-old building that houses the Aventine fronted on the bay, and you can still see salt-water marks on the brick walls in the parlor downstairs. But the main action happens upstairs, where the high ceilings, brick-walled space and creative reuse of wood lends a vintage vibe and bartenders whip up bourbon and Scotch cocktails in the old-new fashion. The place packs for happy hour, from 3pm to 7pm Monday to Friday.

BIX BAR

Map p316 (☎415-433-6300; www.bixrestaurant. com; 56 Gold St; M Pacific Av & Montgomery St) Down a little alleyway at Jackson Square, Bix evokes 1930s supper clubs, with mahogany paneling and white-jacketed barmen shaking cocktails. This was one of the bars that jump-started the martini craze of the 1990s, and it's as swank as ever. The restaurant is solid, but the bar is great, with nightly live piano and sometimes a jazz trio. Look sharp and swagger.

Civic Center & the Tenderloin

EDINBURGH CASTLE BAR

Map p322 (☎415-885-4074; www.castlenews.com; 950 Geary St; M Geary & Polk Sts) SF's finest old-school monument to drink comes complete with dart boards, pool tables, rock bands, occasional literary readings and locals acting out (as is our habit). Photos of bagpipers, the *Trainspotting* soundtrack on the jukebox and a service delivering vinegary fish and chips in newspaper are all the Scottish authenticity you could ask for, short of haggis.

LUSH LOUNGE BAR

Map p322 (☎415-771-2022; www.thelushlounge sf.com; 1221 Polk St; M Polk & Post Sts) Snag a wooden table by the steel-front fireplace and order anything in stemware – martinis are the specialty (15 different varieties) at this industrial-cool bar, but we also recommend the lemon drops and cosmos. Lush Lounge marks the line on Polk St where grit ends and hip begins. Ideal for couples and small groups of all sexual persuasions.

RYE BAR

Map p322 (☎415-474-4448; www.ryesf.com; 688 Geary St; M Geary & Leavenworth Sts) Rye's stark-style design mixes concrete, steel and polished wood, and its leather sofas are a sexy spot for a basil gimlet or anything else made with herb-infused spirits or fresh-squeezed juice. The smokers patio is actually a cage overlooking the sidewalk, and it offers a glimpse of who's inside. It packs after 10pm; arrive early.

RICKSHAW STOP NIGHTCLUB

Map p322 (☎415-861-2011; www.rickshawstop. com; 155 Fell St; admission $5-35; ⊙6pm-2am Wed-Sat) Finally a club where 18 to 21-year-olds can (sometimes) get in for the high-school prom they wish they'd attended. DIY-looking, red-velvet curtains line the black-box walls of this former TV studio, which hosts a changing lineup that appeals to alterna-20-somethings who style life on a shoestring. Thursday's Popscene (18 plus) is always happening. Other nights range from

Bollywood to lesbian. Check the calendar online.

WHISKEY THIEVES BAR
Map p322 (☎415-409-2063; 839 Geary St) It's worth braving junkies on the sidewalk to discover the incredible selection of unusual whiskeys at this Tenderloin dive, where the backbar is subdivided by category – Irish, Scotch, Bourbon and Rye. Seven dollars gets you a shot and a PBR. Party-kid hipsters get their drink on fast, feeding the juke box between rounds of pool.

222 HYDE NIGHTCLUB
Map p322 (☎415-345-8222; www.222hyde.com; 222 Hyde St; ⊙Tue-Sun; Ⓜ&ⓇCivic Center) Various DJs spin at this tiny shotgun club with kick-ass sound system and big booming bass. It's good for a no-fuss night with local 20-somethings. The bar even serves pizza. The dance floor is down a flight of stairs out back – watch your step! – you wouldn't be the first to fall on your ass.

HA-RA BAR
Map p322 (☎415-673-3148; 875 Geary St; ⊙3:30pm-2am Mon & Tue, 9:30am-2am Wed-Sun) If you're alone with your journal, or need a place for a tête-à-tête that may end in tears, bring a fiver for the jukebox, select Miles Davis and cozy up in this often-empty vintage-1947 classic dive. Take note of the flashback-to-the-1950s, black-and-white photo of the couple dancing, then look at the wall sconces and you'll realize you're standing in the exact same spot – only now it's filled with ghosts, not bee-boppers.

DECO LOUNGE GAY BAR
Map p322 (☎415-346-2025; www.decosf.com; 510 Larkin St; ⊙10am-2am Sun-Thu, to 4am Fri & Sat; ⓂLarkin & Eddy Sts) There's usually a party at this indecorous dive club, where the all-male clientele rocks into the wee hours. Theme nights range from disco-queen to shirtless-bear extravaganzas, and drink specials embolden patrons to enter occasional wet-jockstrap contests. Sports queens watch Giants games off hours.

AUNT CHARLIE'S GAY BAR
Map p322 (☎415-441-2922; www.auntcharlies lounge.com; 133 Turk St; admission $5; Ⓜ&ⓇPowell St) On one of Downtown's worst blocks, divey-chic Aunt Charlie's brings vintage pulp-fiction covers to life with the Hot Boxxx Girls, the city's best classic drag show,

Friday and Saturday nights at 10pm (call for reservations). Thursday is Tubesteak Connection ($5), when bathhouse anthems, vintage porn and early '80s disco draw throngs of art-school gay boys. Other nights, it's the classic old-school dump.

☆ ENTERTAINMENT

SAN FRANCISCO SYMPHONY LIVE MUSIC
Map p322 (☎415-864-6000; www.sfsymphony. org; tickets $30-125; Davies Symphony Hall, 201 Van Ness Ave; ⓂVan Ness Ave) The SF Symphony often wins Grammys, thanks to celebrity-conductor and musical-director Michael Tilson Thomas, the world's foremost Mahler impresario. When he's not on the podium, other famous conductors take the baton. The orchestra is joined by the Grammy-winning Symphony Chorus for serious choral works, such as Beethoven's *Missa solemnis*. During festivals over summer and at Christmas, look for stars like Bernadette Peters, Pink Martini and Peabo Bryson.

The best sound is in the cheap seats in the center terrace, but the loge is most comfy and glam and has the best sight lines. If you're on a budget, sit in the front section of AA, BB, HH or JJ; or sit behind the stage in the center terrace – the sound doesn't blend evenly, but you get the musicians' perspective and look into the conductor's eyes (likewise in pricier side terrace seats). Call the **rush-ticket hotline** (☎415-503-5577) after 6:30pm to find out whether the box office has released $20 next-day tickets, which you must pick up in person on the day of performance: choose the side terrace over the front orchestra – unless you want to be 10ft from the strings, but the sound is uneven so close to the stage. During intermission, head all the way upstairs and stand on the flying-saucer-like balconies for bird's-eye views of City Hall.

SAN FRANCISCO OPERA LIVE MUSIC
Map p322 (☎415-864-3330; www.sfopera.com; War Memorial Opera House, 301 Van Ness Ave; tickets $10-350; ⓂVan Ness Ave) SF has been obsessed with opera since the Gold Rush, and it remains a staple on the social calendar. Blue bloods like Ann Getty *always* book the Tuesday A-series – the best nights to spot fabulous gowns and tuxedos. The gorgeous 1932 hall is cavernous and echoey, but there's no more glamorous seat in SF than the velvet-curtained boxes, complete

LOCAL KNOWLEDGE

FRIDAY NIGHT SKATES

On Friday nights at 8:30pm, a renegade crowd of thrill-seeking skaters gathers at Justin Herman Plaza, at the foot of Market St in front of the Ferry Building. They bust out boom boxes and show off moves, before setting out at 9pm toward Pier 39 and the Marina, then back Downtown via Chinatown and Union Square. Typically you'll spot a couple dozen skaters rolling in an amorphous mob, but on a warm Friday night, over 150 may show up. If you want to join, check the **California Outdoor Rollersports Association** (CORA; www.cora.org/friday.phtml) website for details. The closest place to rent skates is at **Bike & Roll** (☑415-771-8038; www.bikeandroll.com; 353 Jefferson St; skates per hour/day $7/25) at Fisherman's Wharf; reserve skates several days ahead.

with champagne service. The best mid-range seats for sight lines and sound are in the front section of the dress circle. The balcony has the best sound but you'll need binoculars to see the stage, unless you come on 'Opera Vision' nights, when a huge screen shows the action on stage. (Don't sit directly beneath the flickering high-def monitors; if you come to the opera to get away from TV, you'll hate the balcony during these performances.)

Hang in the back of the hall with die-hard opera buffs with standing-room-only tickets: starting at 10am, the box office sells 150 standing-room spots ($10, cash only); two hours before curtain, they release 50 more. Snag an empty seat after intermission, when somnambulant seniors go home. Pre-order intermission cocktails at reserved tables in the lower-lobby cafe. Smokers and thrill-seekers: head to the Grand Tier outdoor terrace to overlook City Hall and Downtown's twinkling lights – one of SF's best nighttime views. If you're walking by during a performance, wander into the box-office lobby and watch the stage monitors for a teaser.

SAN FRANCISCO BALLET   DANCE
Map p322 (☑415-861-5600, tickets 415-865-2000; www.sfballet.org; War Memorial Opera House, 301 Van Ness Ave; tickets $10-120; MVan Ness Ave) The San Francisco Ballet is America's oldest ballet company, and the first to premier the *Nutcracker*, which it performs annually. In San Francisco, its home is the War Memorial Opera House, but it also appears at other venues now and then; check the website. For more on seat selection, see the San Francisco Opera listing.

CAFÉ ROYALE   LOUNGE
Map p322 (☑415-441-4099; www.caferoyale-sf.com; 800 Post St; admission free; ☺3pm-midnight Sun-Thu, to 2am Fri & Sat; MPost & Leavenworth

Sts) A Parisian tiled floor and semicircular fainting couches lend atmosphere and acoustics to this artsy-cool lounge, which hosts live jazz, film screenings, theatrical presentations, readings by local writers and sometimes even belly dancing. Otherwise it's a charming cafe and wine bar with good drink prices, a pool table and an entirely local crowd. Serves food till 7pm.

RRAZZ ROOM   LIVE MUSIC
Map p320 (☑415-394-1189; www.therrazzroom.com; 222 Mason St; tickets from $30; M&RPowell St, RPowell-Mason, Powell-Hyde) The city's premier cabaret theater hosts a variety of jazz, pop and comedy acts, ranging from Broadway divas like Betty Buckley and Pia Zadora to local celebs like Connie Champagne and Wesla Whitfield. Great for a night on the town.

AMERICAN CONSERVATORY THEATER   THEATER
Map p320 (ACT; ☑415-749-2228; www.act-sf.org; 415 Geary St; MGeary & Mason Sts; RPowell-Mason, Powell-Hyde) Breakthrough shows destined for the big time in London or New York sometimes pass muster at the turn-of-the-century Geary Theater, which has hosted ACT's landmark productions of Tony Kushner's *Angels in America* and Robert Wilson's *Black Rider,* with a libretto by William S Burroughs and music by the Bay Area's own Tom Waits.

BISCUITS & BLUES   LIVE MUSIC
Map p320 (☑415-292-2583; www.biscuitsand blues.com; 401 Mason St; admission $5-20; ☺music 8-11:30pm Wed-Sat; M&RPowell St) With a steady lineup of top-notch blues and jazz talent, Biscuits & Blues has rightly earned a reputation as one of America's best blues clubs. And the name isn't a gimmick – the joint serves hot biscuits, catfish and chicken for the full Southern experience

(make reservations). Acts sometimes perform Tuesdays; big names fetch up to $35.

STARLIGHT ROOM — LIVE MUSIC

Map p320 (☎415-395-8595; www.harrydenton. com; 21st fl, 450 Powell St; cover varies, often free; ⊗8:30pm-2am Tue-Sat; Ⓜ&ⓇPowell St; ⓟPowell-Mason, Powell-Hyde) Views are mesmerizing from the 21st floor of the Sir Francis Drake Hotel, where khaki-clad tourists let down their hair and dance to live bands on weekends and DJs on weekdays. On Sundays, there's a kooky drag-show brunch (make reservations).

HEMLOCK TAVERN — LIVE MUSIC

Map p322 (☎415-923-0923; www.hemlock tavern.com; cover free-$10; 1131 Polk St; Ⓜ Sutter & Polk Sts) When you wake up tomorrow with peanut shells in your hair (weren't they all over the floor?) and a stiff neck from rocking entirely too hard to the Family Curse (weren't they great?), you'll know it was another successful night at the Hemlock. Weekday nights, stand-up comedy and literary readings are anything but staid among this motley crowd of raucous, party-hardy San Franciscans.

GREAT AMERICAN MUSIC HALL — LIVE MUSIC

Map p322 (☎415-885-0750; www.musichallsf.com; 859 O'Farrell St; admission $12-35; ⊗box office 10:30am-6pm Mon-Fri & on show nights; Ⓜ O'Farrell & Polk Sts) Once a bordello, the rococo Great American Music Hall is one of SF's coolest places for shows. A balcony with table seating rims the main standing-room floor area, the sound system is top-notch, and there are food and drinks. Music ranges from rock, alt-rock and country to jazz and blues.

FREE JAZZ — LIVE MUSIC

Map p316 (☎866-920-5299; www.sfjazz.org; 3 Embarcadero Center; ⊗box office 11am-5:30pm Mon-Fri; Ⓜ&ⓇEmbarcadero Center) Presents jazz – from post-bebop to blues – during festivals and summer-concert series at various venues, often at symphony hall with major luminaries such as Wynton Marsalis. Also hosts free outdoor concerts around town, including Union Square on Thursday evenings in August. A new SF Jazz Center theater opens autumn 2012.

PUNCH LINE — COMEDY

Map p316 (☎415-397-4337; www.punchlinecom edyclub.com; 444 Battery St; admission $12-23 plus 2-drink minimum; ⊗shows 8pm Tue-Thu, Sun, 8pm & 10pm Fri & Sat; Ⓜ&ⓇEmbarcadero) Known for launching promising talent (think Robin Williams, Chris Rock, Ellen DeGeneres and David Cross), this historic standup venue is small enough for you to see into performers' eyes. Strong drinks keep you laughing, even when jokes sometimes bomb.

EMBARCADERO CENTER CINEMA — CINEMA

Map p316 (☎415-267-4893; www.landmark theatres.com; top fl, 1 Embarcadero Center; adult/child $10.50/8; Ⓜ&ⓇEmbarcadero) Forget blockbusters – here locals queue up for the latest Almodóvar film and whatever won best foreign film at the Oscars. The snack bar caters to discerning tastes with good local coffee, fair-trade chocolate and popcorn with real butter.

COMMONWEALTH CLUB — LECTURES

Map p320 (☎415-597-6700; www.common wealthclub.org; 595 Market St; Ⓜ&ⓇMontgomery St) You know you've arrived when the Commonwealth Club asks you to speak. Every US president since Teddy Roosevelt has spoken at the club, the longest-running, most influential public-affairs forum in the US. Intellectual luminaries and other important figures speak at over 400 annual events. Topics range from politics and economics to culture and society. Many programs are broadcast on public radio stations nationwide, including local affiliate KQED-FM (88.5).

CITY ARTS & LECTURES — LECTURES

Map p322 (☎box office 415-392-4400; www.city arts.net; Herbst Theater, 401 Van Ness Ave; tickets from $17; Ⓜ&ⓇCivic Center) The city's foremost lecture series hosts an all-star lineup of today's most celebrated artists, writers and intellectuals, from Joan Didion to David Sedaris and Madeline Albright to Tina Fey. Most take place at the Herbst Theater, and are broadcast on local public-radio station KQED-FM (88.5); check the website for schedules.

WARFIELD — LIVE MUSIC

Map p320 (☎800-745-3000; www.thewarfield theatre.com; 982 Market St; admission varies; ⊗box office 10am-4pm Sun & 90min before curtain on show nights; Ⓜ&ⓇPowell St) Famous names play this former vaudeville theater, including the Beastie Boys and PJ Harvey; when Furthur (formerly the Grateful Dead) play, the balcony fills with pot smoke.

EXIT THEATER
THEATER

Map p320 (☎415-673-3847; www.theexit.org; 156 Eddy St; admission $15-20; Ⓜ&ⓇPowell St) Experimental theater in this tiny venue provides an escape from the musical-and-melodrama treadmill. It's also home to the annual San Francisco Fringe Festival, a mass exodus from the norm.

NEW CONSERVATORY THEATRE
THEATER

Map p322 (☎415-861-8972; www.nctcsf.org; 25 Van Ness Ave; tickets $10-30; ⓂVan Ness Ave) This respected gay company draws playwrights like Terrance McNally and continually shows new works. There's usually a boy partially naked on stage, earning it the nickname 'Nude Conservatory Theatre,' but it's never a strip show. Shows range from camp to dead serious.

MITCHELL BROTHERS O'FARRELL THEATER
LOUNGE

Map p322 (☎415-776-6686; www.ofarrell.com; 895 O'Farrell St; admission $20-40; ⊙11:30am-1:30am Mon-Sat, 5:30pm-1:30am Sun; ⓂGeary & Polk Sts) This infamous strip joint remains open, long after one of the founding brothers murdered the other. Jim and Artie Mitchell opened the theater in 1969 and began making porn, including the legendary *Deep Throat,* starring Marilyn Chambers. At its prime, the Mitchells' multimillion-dollar empire included a production company and 11 California theaters. But the Mitchell brothers went the way of Cain and Abel, when Jim shot and killed Artie in 1991. He was convicted of voluntary manslaughter and served six years; a heart attack killed him in 2007. Despite its tawdry background, the O'Farrell Theater is generally regarded as a classy place (with a capital k). Even if you don't go inside, ask to see the little porn museum just inside the door.

SHOPPING

Union Square

H&M
CLOTHING, ACCESSORIES

Map p320 (www.hm.com; 150 Powell St; Ⓜ&ⓇPowell St, ⓇPowell-Mason; Powell-Hyde) What IKEA is to home furnishing, H&M is to fashion: suspiciously affordable, perpetually crowded, not really made for the long haul and perfect for parties. With limited-edition runs and special collections by designers like splashy British colorist Matthew Williamson (and lesser ones like, oof, Madonna) you won't have to worry that your closet looks exactly like everyone else's – unless you bought it at IKEA. There are several outlets in town, but the one on Powell St is the biggest, with a vast men's section.

LOEHMANN'S
CLOTHING, ACCESSORIES

Map p320 (www.loehmanns.com; 222 Sutter St; ⓂMontgomery St) The most revealing Downtown fashion choice isn't what shoes you wear, but which floor you choose in this discount designer superstore. North Beach artists drift to the middle floor for almost-free Free People smocks; Pacific Heights charity fundraisers hit the top floor for discounted Prada shirtdresses; and gift shoppers converge around 40%-off red-tagged Kate Spade clutches in main-floor accessories. Pace yourself: women's shoes and an impressive men's section are across the street.

GUMP'S
JEWELRY, HOUSEWARES

Map p320 (www.gumps.com; 135 Post St; Ⓜ&ⓇMontgomery St) San Francisco's original department store opened in 1861, importing luxury items from the Far East. Today it's famous for its jade, silk, rugs, porcelain and housewares – if you're a guest in someone's home and want to express your gratitude with the perfect high-end hostess gift, this is the place.

MARGARET O'LEARY
CLOTHING, ACCESSORIES

Map p320 (www.margaretoleary.com; 1 Claude Lane; ⊙Tue-Sat; Ⓜ&ⓇMontgomery St) Ignorance of the fog is no excuse in San Francisco, but should you confuse SF for LA (the horror!) and neglect to pack the obligatory sweater, Margaret O'Leary will sheathe you in knitwear, no questions asked. The San Francisco designer's specialties are warm, whisper-light cardigans in cashmere, organic cotton or ecominded bamboo yarn.

ORIGINAL LEVI'S STORE
CLOTHING, ACCESSORIES

Map p320 (☎415-501-0100; www.us.levi.com; 300 Post St; Ⓜ&ⓇPowell St; ⓇPowell-Mason, Powell-Hyde) The flagship store in Levi Strauss' hometown sells classic jeans that fit without fail, plus limited-edition pairs made of tough Japanese selvage and eco-organic cotton denim. Start with the impressive discount racks (30% to 60% off), but don't hold out for sales – denim fanatics Tweet their finds here, so rare lines like 1950s prison-model denim sell out fast. They'll hem your jeans for $10.

BARNEYS
DEPARTMENT STORE

Map p320 (www.barneys.com; 77 O'Farrell St; Ⓜ&ⓇPowell St; ⓇPowell-Mason, Powell-Hyde) The high-end New York fashion staple known for its inspired window displays and up-to-70%-off sales has hit the West Coast. Barneys showcases emerging designers; well-priced, well-fitted sportswear on its co-op label; and exclusive ecoconscious lines by Philip Lim, Theory, and its own affordable Green Label, focusing on clean lines with a clean conscience.

MACY'S
DEPARTMENT STORE

Map p320 (www.macys.com; 170 O'Farrell St; ◷10am-9pm Mon-Thu, 10am-11pm Fri, 9am-11pm Sat, 11am-7pm Sun; Ⓜ&ⓇPowell St; ⓇPowell-Mason, Powell-Hyde) Five floors of name brands, plus a basement food court. The men's department is across the street so they won't have to worry their pretty little heads about where to find boxer briefs and Kenneth Cole shirts, while women have to brave the perfume police and fend off slightly insulting free makeover offers just to check out the shoe sale (totally worth it).

BRITEX FABRICS
FABRICS

Map p320 (www.britexfabrics.com; 146 Geary St; ◷Mon-Sat; Ⓜ&ⓇPowell St; ⓇPowell-Mason, Powell-Hyde) No reality design show can compare with the four floors of nonstop fashion drama at Britex. First floor: designers bicker over who gets first dibs on caution-orange chiffon. Second floor: glam rockers dig through a velvet goldmine. Third floor: Hollywood stylists squeal 'To die for!' over '60s Lucite buttons. Top floor: fake fur flies and remnants roll as costumers prepare for Burning Man, Halloween and your average SF weekend.

LE SANCTUAIRE
FOOD, DRINK

Map p320 (www.le-sanctuaire.com; 5th fl, 315 Sutter St; ◷10:30am-4:30pm Mon-Fri, by appointment; ⓂSutter & Stockton Sts; ⓇPowell-Mason & Powell-Hyde) Mad scientists, thrill seekers and professional chefs get buzzed, speakeasy-style (read: appointment only), at this culinary curiosity shop. Here you'll find anchovy juice, spherifiers to turn fruit into caviar, salt for curing meats and, of course, that hallmark of molecular gastronomy: foaming agents. Check the website for classes on making smoked watermelon with

vacuum sealers and using liquid nitrogen to make powdered lard – alas, suspending disbelief with gellants isn't on the schedule.

DSW
SHOES

Map p320 (www.dswshoe.com; 111 Powell St; Ⓜ&ⓇPowell St; ⓇPowell-Mason, Powell-Hyde) The basement clearance section is where recovering shoe hounds come after they've sworn that they've bought their last pair for the season. Diligent research has uncovered 40% to 60% off Marc Jacobs flats, Betsy Johnson wedges and an inexplicable bonanza of limited-edition Pumas.

WESTFIELD SAN FRANCISCO CENTRE
DEPARTMENT STORE

Map p320 (www.westfield.com/sanfrancisco; 865 Market St; ◷most shops 10am-8:30pm Mon-Sat, 11am-7pm Sun; Ⓙ; Ⓜ&ⓇPowell St; ⓇPowell-Mason, Powell-Hyde) Wait, is this suburbia? Sure looks like it inside this nine-level chain-store city, with Bloomingdale's and Nordstrom, plus 400 other retailers and a movie theater. Supposedly there's a 'distinctive boutique' concept to this mall, which translates to the same amount of stuff crammed into smaller stores. Best/only reasons to brave this behemoth: post-holiday sales, H&M's Spanish cousin Mango, bathrooms (including lounges with baby-changing tables) and a respectable basement food court.

🏛 Financial District

FERRY PLAZA WINE MERCHANT
FOOD, DRINK

Map p316 (www.fpwm.com; 1 Ferry Plaza; Ⓜ&ⓇEmbarcadero) Stock up on California wines after you've sipped a few – start with viogniers, work your way to cabs, swishing and spitting to maintain your capacity to taste. Savvy staff describe wines in a fun, informative way, ensuring a good time. The bar is jammed on Saturdays, but otherwise staff will take the time to suggest pairings and exciting new releases.

RECCHIUTI CHOCOLATES
FOOD, DRINK

Map p316 (www.recchiuticonfections.com; 1 Ferry Bldg; Ⓜ&ⓇEmbarcadero) No San Franciscan can resist Recchiuti: Pacific Heights parts with old money for its *fleur de sel* caramels; Noe Valley's child foodie prodigies prefer S'more Bites to the campground variety; and the Mission splurges on chocolates designed by developmentally disabled artists from Creativity Explored (p134) – part of the proceeds benefit the nonprofit gallery.

SUR LA TABLE   HOUSEWARES

Map p316 (www.surlatable.com; 1 Ferry Bldg; Ⓜ&ⓇEmbarcadero) Can't fathom life without an espresso maker and citrus reamer? You'll never need to, thanks to these understanding salespeople. For the hippie gourmet, there's a windowsill grow-light for sprouting, ahem, herbs, and for the young aspiring chef, a cupcake-frosting set. Look for free demos that show how to master technique with your new gear.

JAPONESQUE   HOUSEWARES

Map p316 (www.japonesquegallery.com; 824 Montgomery St; ⊙Tue-Sat; ⓂPacific Av & Montgomery St) Wabi-sabi is not something you smear on sushi, but the fine appreciation for organic forms and materials you can experience first-hand at Japonesque. Owner Koichi Hara stocks antique Japanese bamboo baskets and contemporary ceramics, alongside Ruth Rhoten's molten silver vases and Hiromichi Iwashita's graphite-coated, chiseled-wood panels that look like bonfire embers.

🏛 Civic Center & the Tenderloin

KAYO BOOKS   BOOKSTORE

Map p322 (www.kayobooks.com; 814 Post St; ⊙Thu-Sat; ⓂPost & Leavenworth Sts) Juvenile delinquents will find an entire section

EDEN & EDEN

Detour from reality at **Eden & Eden** (Map p316; www.edenandeden.com; 560 Jackson St; ⓂKearny St), a Dadaist design boutique, where anchors float on silk dresses, clouds rain on pillows, architectural blueprints serve as placemats and Ozzy Osbourne has been transformed into a stuffed mouse wearing batwings. Prices are surprisingly down to earth for far-out, limited-edition finds from local and international designers.

dedicated to their life stories here, where vintage pulp fiction, true crime and erotica titles ending in exclamation points (including the succinct *Wench!*) induced John Waters to endorse this place on NPR. You might find a first edition Dashiell Hammet gumshoe caper, a wayward nun's tale filed under Catholic Guilt or *Women's Medical Problems* in the Bizarre Nonfiction section.

MAGAZINE   MAGAZINES

Map p322 (www.themagazinesf.com; 920 Larkin St; ⊙Mon-Sat; ⓂGeary & Larkin Sts) No place carries a better selection of vintage magazines. The Magazine's old wooden shelves contain everything from 1940s pinup mags, 1970s *Vanity Fair* and decades-old issues of *Playboy,* to the *Saturday Evening Post, Tiger Beat* and pulp novels with titles like *Aliens Ate My Baby*. Most cost a mere 35¢.

North Beach & Chinatown

Neighborhood Top Five

1 Wandering **Chinatown alleyways** (p100) to hear mah jong tiles, temple gongs and Chinese orchestras – the sounds of a community that's survived fire, earthquakes and even politicians.

2 Climbing Filbert St Steps past heckling parrots and fragrant gardens to panoramic **Coit Tower** (p101).

3 Reflecting in the Poet's Chair and celebrating free speech at **City Lights** (p112).

4 Time-traveling through the old Chinatown at the **Chinese Historical Society of America** (p106), then returning to the present at the **Chinese Culture Center** (p106).

5 Bar-crawling like Jack Kerouac to historic North Beach hotspots: **Specs'**, **Tosca Cafe** and **Vesuvio** (p110).

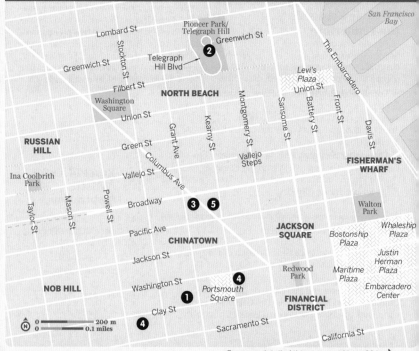

For more detail of this area, see Map p324 ➡

Explore North Beach & Chinatown

From downtown, enter Dragon Gate onto Chinatown's main tourist drag, Grant Ave. The street is lined with pagoda-topped Chinatown deco buildings purpose-built in the 1920s by Look Tin Eli and other Chinatown merchants to attract curiosity seekers and souvenir shoppers – clearly their plan worked like a charm. It's hard to believe this cheerfully inauthentic, vintage-neon-signed attraction was once notorious, brothel-lined Dupont St – at least until you see the fascinating displays on 19th-century Chinatown at the Chinese American Historical Society. Duck into Chinatown's historic alleyways to glimpse a neighborhood that's survived against daunting odds, and detour for dim sum at City View.

Cross over into North Beach via Jack Kerouac Alley and City Lights bookstore, San Francisco's literary landmark and spiritual home to the Beat movement. Espresso at Caffe Trieste is all the additional inspiration necessary to free your inner 'beatnik' on the North Beach walking tour, or hike up garden-lined Filbert St steps to giddy panoramas and daring murals at Coit Tower. Descend in time for a happy hour bar crawl or dinner reservations at Coi, and you might be taken for a local.

Local Life

→ **Hangouts** Join regular crowds of writers at Caffe Trieste (p110), martial arts masters at Washington Square and skaters at Old St Mary's Park.

→ **Foodie discoveries** Even been-there, eaten-that San Franciscans find new taste sensations at Jai Yun (p110), Red Blossom Tea Company (p113) and the herbal apothecaries lining Stockton St.

→ **Local celebrity sightings** Keep an eye out for Robin Williams at Cobb's Comedy Club (p112), Sean Penn at Tosca Cafe (p111), Francis Ford Coppola at Columbus Tower (p102), and Tom Waits and Carlos Santana at 101 Music (p113).

→ **Five-dollar bargains** Fly a butterfly kite from Chinatown Kite Shop (p114), rummage sale toy bins at Double Punch (p113) and carbo-load at Tony's Coal-fired Pizza & Slice House (p109).

Getting There & Away

→ **Bus** The key routes passing through downtown, Chinatown and North Beach are 1, 30, 41 and 45.

→ **Cable car** From Downtown or the Wharf, take the Powell-Mason and Powell-Hyde lines through Chinatown and North Beach. The California St cable car passes through the southern end of Chinatown.

Lonely Planet's Top Tip

Wild hawks and parrots circle above North Beach as though looking for a parking spot. The weekend parking situation is so dire that locals tend to avoid North Beach and Chinatown – forgetting there's public parking underneath Portsmouth Square. You may also luck into a spot at Good Luck Parking Garage, where spots are stenciled with fortune-cookie wisdom: 'You are not a has-been.'

Best Places to Eat

→ Coi (p108)
→ Jai Yun (p110)
→ City View (p109)
→ Ristorante Ideale (p108)
→ Molinari (p109)

For reviews, see p108 →

Best Places to Drink

→ Specs' (p110)
→ Caffe Trieste (p110)
→ Comstock Saloon (p110)
→ Tosca Cafe (p111)
→ 15 Romolo (p111)

For reviews, see p110 →

Best Places for Artistic Inspiration

→ City Lights (p112)
→ Chinese Culture Center (p106)
→ Coit Tower (p101)
→ Bob Kaufman Alley (p106)
→ Li Po (p111)
→ Jack Kerouac Alley (p102)

For reviews, see p102 →

 TOP SIGHTS
CHINATOWN ALLEYWAYS

Forty-one historic alleyways packed into Chinatown's 22 blocks have seen it all since 1849: gold rushes and revolution, incense and opium, fire and icy receptions. These narrow backstreets are lined with towering buildings because there was nowhere to go but up in Chinatown after 1870, when laws limited Chinese immigration, employment and housing.

Waverly Place

Off Sacramento St are the flag-festooned balconies of Chinatown's historic temples, where services have been held since 1852 – even in 1906 while the altar was still smoldering at **Tien Hou Temple** (125 Waverly Place; ⊙hours vary).

Ross Alley

Ross Alley (Map p324) was known as Mexico, Spanish and Manila St after the women who staffed its notorious back-parlor brothels. Colorful characters now fill alleyway murals, and anyone can make a fortune the easy way at Golden Gate Fortune Cookie Company.

Spofford Alley

As sunset falls on sociable **Spofford Alley** (Map324), you'll hear clicking mah jong tiles and a Chinese orchestra warming up. But generations ago, you might have overheard Sun Yat-sen and his conspirators at number 36 plotting the 1911 overthrow of China's last dynasty.

Commercial St

Across Portsmouth Square from San Francisco's City Hall, this euphemistically named hot spot caught fire in 1906. The city banned Commercial St's 25¢ Chinese brothels in favor of 'parlor houses,' where basic services were raised to $3 and watching cost $10.

DON'T MISS...

➡ Waverly Place
➡ Golden Gate Fortune Cookie Company
➡ Spofford Alley

PRACTICALITIES

➡ Map p324
➡ btwn Grant Ave & Stockton St, California St & Broadway
➡ Ⓜ Stockton St; 🚋 Powell St, California St

TOP SIGHTS
COIT TOWER

The exclamation point on San Francisco's skyline is Coit Tower, the stark white deco tower that eccentric heiress Lillie Hancock Coit left a fortune to build as a monument to San Francisco firefighters. The tower has been a lightning rod for controversy for its colorful, provocative 1930s Works Project Administration (WPA) murals – but there's no debating the 360-degree panoramas from Coit Tower's viewing platform.

DON'T MISS...

➡ WPA murals
➡ The 360-degree viewing platform panorama
➡ Filbert St Steps

PRACTICALITIES

➡ Map p324
➡ Telegraph Hill Blvd
➡ adult/child $4.50/2
➡ ⊘10am-6pm
➡ Ⓜ39

WPA Murals & Viewing Platform

Coit Tower's lobby murals are positioned high above the city, but they're grounded in the realities of California's Great Depression. The murals show San Franciscans at work and play, lining up at soup kitchens and organizing dock-workers' unions, partying despite Prohibition and reading library books in Chinese, Italian and English – including *The Communist Manifesto*.

For a federally funded project, these murals were highly controversial. But the red-baiting backfired: San Franciscans embraced the tower and its murals as beloved city landmarks. To see murals hidden inside Coit Tower's stairwell, take the free tours at 11am Saturdays. Take the elevator up to the tower's panoramic open-air platform 210ft above San Francisco to spot two bridges, cable cars and the bay.

Telegraph Hill

In the 19th century, a ruthless entrepreneur began quarrying Telegraph Hill and blasting away roads, and this garden-lined cliffside boardwalk became the main uphill route. City Hall eventually stopped the quarrying of Telegraph Hill, but the view of the bay from **Filbert St Steps** (Map p324) is still (wait for it) dynamite. The climb is steep, but it leads past sculpture gardens, hidden cottages along a wooden boardwalk called **Napier Lane**, sweeping vistas of the Bay Bridge, and colorful wild parrot flocks that have claimed the trees of Telegraph Hill.

◉ SIGHTS

Standing atop the Filbert St Steps, you can understand what Italian fishermen, Beat poets and wild parrots saw in North Beach: tough climbs and giddy vistas, a place with more sky than ground, an area that was civilized but never entirely tamed. Coit Tower adds a monumental exclamation point to the scenery, lifting North Beach out of the fog of everyday life.

Across Columbus Ave is Chinatown, survivor of gold booms and busts, anti-Chinese riots and bootlegging wars, trials by fire and earthquake. Yet Chinatown repeatedly made history, providing labor for America's first cross-country railroad, creating original Chinatown deco architecture, and leading the charge for China's revolution and US civil rights.

◉ North Beach

COIT TOWER LANDMARK
See p101.

TELEGRAPH HILL LANDMARK
See p101.

JACK KEROUAC ALLEY STREET
Map p324 (btwn Grant & Columbus Aves; Ⓜ Columbus Ave) Fans of *On the Road* and *Dharma Bums* will appreciate how fitting it is that Kerouac's namesake alleyway offers a poetic and slightly seedy shortcut between Chinatown and North Beach via favorite Kerouac haunts, City Lights bookstore (p112) and Vesuvio (p111) – Kerouac took his books, Buddhism and drink to heart.

BEAT MUSEUM MUSEUM
Map p324 (☏ 1-800-537-6822; www.thebeatmuseum.org; 540 Broadway; admission $5; ⊙ 10am-7pm Tue-Sun; Ⓜ Columbus Ave) The Beat goes on and on – OK, so it rambles a little – at this truly obsessive collection of SF literary-scene ephemera c 1950–69. The banned edition of Allen Ginsberg's *Howl* is the ultimate free-speech trophy, and the 1961 check for $10.08 that Jack Kerouac wrote to a liquor store has a certain dark humor, but those Kerouac bobble-head dolls are the real head-shakers.

Enter the museum through a turnstile at the back of the museum store, grab a ramshackle reclaimed theater seat, redolent with the accumulated odors of poets, pot and pets, and watch fascinating films about the Beat era's leading musicians, artists, writers, politicos and undefinable characters. Upstairs there are shrines to individual Beats with first-hand remembrances and artifacts, including first editions of books that expanded the American outlook to include the margins. Downstairs in the store, you can buy poetry chapbooks and obscure Beat titles you won't find elsewhere; entry to this part is free, and so are readings held here (check website).

COLUMBUS TOWER HISTORICAL BUILDING
Map p324 (916 Kearny St; Ⓜ Kearny St) Like most SF landmarks worthy of the title, this one has a seriously checkered career. Built by shady political boss Abe Ruef in 1905, the building was finished just in time to be reduced to its steel skeleton in the 1906 earthquake and fire. The new copper cladding was still shiny in 1907 when not-so-honest Abe was convicted of bribing city supervisors. By the time he emerged bankrupt from San Quentin State Prison, the cupola was oxidizing green.

Towering artistic aspirations found a home here, too. Grammy-winning folk group The Kingston Trio bought the tower in the 1960s, and the Grateful Dead recorded in the basement. Since the 1970s, Columbus Tower has been owned by Francis Ford Coppola, and film history has been made here by Coppola's American Zoetrope filmmaking studio, *The Joy Luck Club* director Wayne Wang and Academy Award–winning actor/director Sean Penn.

WASHINGTON SQUARE PARK
Map p324 (Columbus Ave & Union St; Ⓜ Columbus Ave) Wild parrots, tai chi masters, nonagenarian churchgoing *nonnas* (grandmothers) and Ben Franklin are the company you'll keep on this lively patch of lawn. The parrots keep their distance in the treetops, but like anyone else in North Beach, they can probably be bribed into friendship with a focaccia from Liguria Bakery (p108) on the square's northeast corner.

The 1897 statue of Ben Franklin is a nonsequitur, and the taps below his feet falsely advertise mineral water from Vichy, France. This is yet another example of a puzzling public artwork courtesy of a certifiable SF eccentric, Henry D Cogswell, who made his fortune fitting miners with gold fillings.

START **CITY LIGHTS BOOKSTORE**
END **LI PO**
DISTANCE **1.5 MILES**
DURATION **TWO HOURS**

Neigborhood Walk
North Beach Beat

At ❶ **City Lights bookstore** (p112), the home of Beat poetry and free speech, pick up some poetry to inspire your journey into the heart of literary North Beach – Lawrence Ferlinghetti's *San Francisco Poems* is a good choice.

Head to ❷ **Caffe Trieste** (p110) for potent espresso and opera on the jukebox in the back booth, where Francis Ford Coppola allegedly drafted *The Godfather*.

At ❸ **Washington Square**, you'll spot parrots in the treetops and octogenarians making smooth tai chi moves: pure poetry in motion. On the corner, focaccia hot from a 100-year-old oven makes ❹ **Liguria Bakery** (p108) a worthy pit stop for hungry historical novelists.

Quiet ❺ **Bob Kaufman Alley** (p106) was named for the legendary street-corner poet, who broke a 12-year vow of silence when he walked into a North Beach cafe and recited his poem *All Those Ships That Never Sailed*: 'Today I bring them back/Huge and transitory/And let them sail/Forever.'

At the ❻ **Beat Museum** don't be surprised to hear a Dylan jam session by the front door or see Allen Ginsberg naked in documentary footage screened inside the museum: the Beat goes on here in rare form.

Begin your literary bar crawl at ❼ **Specs'** (p110) amid merchant-marine memorabilia, tall tales and regulars blowing off steam over pints of Anchor Steam.

Jack Kerouac once blew off Henry Miller to go on a bender at ❽ **Vesuvio** (p111), where raucous evenings often ended with the *On the Road* author getting booted onto the street now named for him: ❾ **Jack Kerouac Alley**. Kerouac's words embedded in the alley sum up North Beach nights: 'The air was soft, the stars so fine, and the promise of every cobbled alley so great...'

Follow the literary lead of Kerouac and Ginsberg and end your night in a vinyl booth at ❿ **Li Po** (p111), with another beer beneath the gold Buddha's forgiving gaze.

NORTH BEACH & CHINATOWN SIGHTS

1. Caffe Trieste (p110)

Linger over a legendary espresso at Caffe Trieste, where Francis Ford Coppola drafted *The Godfather*.

2. Chinatown (p100)

Chinatown's historic Tien Hou Temple has held services since 1852.

3. City Lights (p112)

City Lights bookstore is San Francisco's literary landmark and spiritual home to the Beat movement.

SAINTS PETER & PAUL CHURCH CHURCH

Map p324 (☑415-421-0809; www.stspeterpaul.
san-francisco.ca.us; 666 Filbert St; ⊙7:30am-
4pm; Ⓜ Columbus Ave) Wedding cake was the
apparent inspiration for this 1924 triple-
decker cathedral with its lacy white towers, and in its downtime between Catholic
masses in Italian, Chinese and Spanish,
the church pulls a triple wedding shift
on Saturdays. Joe DiMaggio and Marilyn
Monroe had their wedding photos taken
here, though they weren't permitted to
marry in the church because both had
been divorced (they got hitched at City
Hall instead).

True to North Beach literary form,
there's poetry by Dante in a glittering mosaic inscription over the grand triple entryway that brings to mind Beat poets and
Beatles alike: 'The glory of Him who moves
all things/Penetrates and glows throughout
the universe.'

⊙ Chinatown

CHINATOWN ALLEYWAYS ALLEYWAYS

See p100.

CHINESE CULTURE CENTER ART GALLERY

Map p324 (☑415-986-1822; www.c-c-c.org; 3rd
fl, Hilton Hotel, 750 Kearny St; gallery admission
free, donation requested, tours adult/child $25/20;
⊙10am-4pm Tue-Sat; Ⓜ Kearny St) You can see
all the way to China on the 3rd floor of the
Hilton inside this cultural center, which
hosts exhibits of traditional Chinese arts, including China's leading brush-painters; Xian
Rui (Fresh & Sharp) cutting-edge art installations, recently featuring Stella Zhang's
ethereal indoor sails and discomfiting tooth-
pick-studded pillows; and a new 'Art at Night'
series showcasing Chinese-inspired art, jazz
and food. In odd-numbered years, don't miss
the Present Tense Biennial, where 30-plus
Bay Area artists are invited to give their personal takes on Chinese culture.

For more first-hand experiences of Chinese culture, check the center's schedule for
upcoming concerts, hands-on arts workshops for adults and children, Mandarin
classes, genealogy services, arts festivals in
Chinatown's historic alleyways and Chinatown Heritage Walking Tours.

CHINESE HISTORICAL SOCIETY OF AMERICA MUSEUM

Map p324 (CHSA; ☑415-391-1188; www.chsa.
org; 965 Clay St; adult/child $5/2, 1st Thu of
month free; ⊙noon-5pm Tue-Fri, 11am-4pm Sat;
Ⓜ Stockton St; 🚃 California St) Picture what it
was like to be Chinese in America during
the Gold Rush, the transcontinental railroad construction or the Beat heyday at
the nation's largest Chinese American historical institute. Intimate vintage photos,
an 1880 temple altar and Francis Wong's
mesmerizing miniatures of Chinatown
landmarks are seen alongside the Daniel
KE Ching collection of thousands of vintage advertisements, toys and postcards
conveying Chinese stereotypes. Sleuthing
by CHSA historians continue to uncover
lost and neglected artifacts, including Jake
Lee's fascinating watercolors of Chinese
American history, painted in the 1960s for
a Chinatown restaurant.

WORTH A DETOUR

BOB KAUFMAN ALLEY

What, you mean your hometown doesn't have a street named after an African American Catholic-Jewish-voodoo anarchist Beat poet who refused to speak for 12 years?
The man revered in France as the 'American Rimbaud' was a major poet who helped
found the legendary *Beatitudes* magazine in 1959 and a spoken-word bebop jazz artist who was never at a loss for words, yet he felt compelled to take a Buddhist vow of
silence after John F Kennedy's assassination, which he kept until the end of the Vietnam War.

Kaufman's life was hardly pure poetry: he was a teenage runaway, periodically
found himself homeless, was occasionally jailed for picking fights in rhyme with police,
battled methamphetamine addiction with varying success and once claimed his goal
was to be forgotten. Yet like the man himself, the hidden **Bob Kaufman Alley** (Map
p324; off Grant Ave near Filbert St; Ⓜ Columbus Ave) named in his honor is offbeat, streetwise and often profoundly silent.

CHINATOWN HERITAGE WALKING TOURS

Local-led, kid-friendly **Chinatown Heritage Walking Tours** (☏415-986-1822; www.c-c-c.org; adult/child $30/25; ⊙tours 10am, noon & 2pm Tue-Sat) guide visitors through the living history and mythology of Chinatown in two hours, winding through backstreets to key historic sights: Golden Gate Fortune Cookie Factory, Tien How Temple and Portsmouth Square. All proceeds support Chinatown community programming at the Chinese Culture Center; bookings can be made online or by phone. Groups of four or more should book two days in advance.

Rotating art and history exhibits are across the courtyard in CHSA's graceful red-brick, green-tile-roofed landmark building, built as Chinatown's YWCA in 1932 by Julia Morgan, one of California's first women architects and the chief architect of Hearst Castle. Check CHSA's website for openings and events, including ever-popular **Chinatown Food Walking Tours**.

PORTSMOUTH SQUARE   PARK

Map p324 (733 Kearny St; Ⓜ Kearny St; 🚊 California St) Since apartments in Chinatown's narrow brick buildings are small, Portsmouth Square is the neighborhood's living room. The square is named after John B Montgomery's sloop, which pulled up near here in 1846 to stake the US claim on San Francisco. Bronze plaques and monuments dot the perimeter of the historic square and a monument bearing a ship with golden sails is dedicated to adventure author Robert Louis Stevenson, who found inspiration here c 1879. But the presiding deity at this park is the Goddess of Democracy, a bronze replica of the statue made by Tiananmen Square protesters in 1989.

First light is met with outstretched arms by tai chi practitioners. By afternoon toddlers rush the playground slides, and tea crowds collect at the kiosk under the pedestrian bridge to joke and dissect the day's news. The checkers and chess played on concrete tables in gazebos late into the evening aren't mere games, but 365-day obsessions, come rain or shine. Chinese New Year brings a night market to the square, featuring Chinese opera, calligraphy demonstrations and cell-phone charms of the goddess Guan Yin for better reception.

OLD ST MARY'S CATHEDRAL   CHURCH

Map p324 (☏415-288-3800; www.oldsaintmarys.org; 660 California St; ⊙11am-6pm Mon-Tue, to 7pm Wed-Fri, 9am-6:30pm Sat, 9am-4:30pm Sun; Ⓜ Stockton St; 🚊 California St) Many thought it a lost cause, but California's first cathedral, inaugurated in 1854, tried for decades to give San Francisco some religion – despite its location in brothel central. Hence the stern admonition on the church's clock tower: 'Son, observe the time and fly from evil.'

Eventually the archdiocese abandoned attempts to convert Dupont St whoremongers and handed the church over to America's first Chinese community mission, run by the activism-oriented Paulists. During WWII, the church served 450,000 members of the US armed services as a recreation center and cafeteria. The walls of the church miraculously withstood the 1906 earthquake and fire, which destroyed one of the district's biggest bordellos directly across the street, making room for **St Mary's Square**. Today, skateboarders do tricks of a different sort in the park, under the watchful eye of Beniamino Bufano's 1929 pink granite and steel statue of Chinese revolutionary Sun Yat-sen.

CHINESE TELEPHONE EXCHANGE   HISTORICAL BUILDING

Map p325 (743 Washington St; Ⓜ Stockton St; 🚊 California St) California's earliest adopters of advanced technology weren't in Silicon Valley, but right here in Chinatown. This triple-decker tiled pagoda caused a sensation in 1894 not for its looks, but its smarts. To connect callers to the right person, switchboard operators had to speak fluent English and five Chinese dialects as well as memorize at least 1500 Chinatown residents by name, residence and occupation. The switchboard was open 365 days a year, and the manager and assistant managers lived on-site.

Since anyone born in China was prohibited by law from visiting San Francisco throughout the 1882–1943 Chinese Exclusion era, this switchboard was the main means of contact with family and business partners in China for 60 years. The exchange operated until 1949, and the landmark was bought and restored by Bank of Canton in 1960.

DRAGON'S GATE · MONUMENT

Map p324 (intersection of Grant Ave & Bush St; Ⓜ Stockton St; 🚋 California St) Enter the Dragon archway and you'll find yourself on the once-notorious street known as Dupont in its red-light heyday. Sixty years before the family-friendly overhaul of the Las Vegas Strip, Look Tin Eli and a group of forward-thinking Chinatown businessmen pioneered the approach here in Chinatown, replacing seedy attractions with more tourist-friendly ones.

After consultation with architects and community groups, Dupont St was transformed into Grant Ave, with deco-chinoiserie dragon lamps and tiled pagoda rooftops, and police were reluctantly persuaded to enforce the 1914 Red Light Abatement Act in Chinatown. By the time this gate was donated by Taiwan in 1970 grandly proclaiming that 'everything in the world is in just proportions,' Chinatown finally had a main street that did the community greater justice.

GOOD LUCK PARKING GARAGE · LANDMARK

Map p324 (735 Vallejo St; Ⓜ Stockton St; 🚋 Mason St) Each parking spot at this garage comes with fortune-cookie wisdom stenciled onto the asphalt: 'The time is right to make new friends' or 'Stop searching forever – happiness is right next to you.' These omens are brought to you by artist Harrell Fletcher and co-conspirator Jon Rubin, who also gathered the vintage photographs of the Chinese and Italian ancestors of local residents that grace the entry tiles like heraldic emblems.

🍴 EATING

When choosing an Italian restaurant in North Beach, use this rule of thumb: if a host has to lure you inside with, 'Ciao, bella!', keep walking. Try smaller neighborhood restaurants on side streets off Grant Ave and Washington St, where staff gossip in Italian.

Ignore menus in Chinatown, where the best dishes are loaded onto dim sum carts or listed in Chinese. Try dim sum places along Stockton St, and wander off Grant Ave to find basement eateries long beloved by starving artists, including Jack Kerouac, Allen Ginsberg and the Beats.

🍴 North Beach

🏆 TOP CHOICE COI · CALIFORNIAN $$$

Map p324 (📞 415-393-9000; www.coirestaurant. com; 373 Broadway; set menu $145; ⏱ 5:30-10pm Wed-Sat; Ⓜ Columbus Ave) Chef Daniel Patterson's wildly inventive, 11-course menu ($145 per person) is a Hwy 1 road trip, all unexpected curves and giddy heights. With skillful handling, California's specialty produce wows at every turn – especially black-and-green noodles made from Manilla clams and seaweed. Wild foods top it all: purple ice-plant petals are strewn atop warm duck's tongue, and wild-caught abalone makes a positively salacious salad course. With a wink at the Broadway strip joint next door, Coi's interior seems borrowed from a '70s Big Sur nudist colony, with shaggy cushions, grass-cloth walls, terrariums and framed moss – but the seasonal flavors and intriguing wine pairings ($95; generous enough for two to share) will have you living for the moment.

RISTORANTE IDEALE · ITALIAN $$

Map p324 (📞 415-391-4129; 1315 Grant Ave; pasta $11-18; ⏱ 5:30-10:30pm Mon-Sat, 5-10pm Sun; Ⓜ Columbus Ave) Italian regulars are stunned that a restaurant this authentic borders the Pacific, with Roman chef Maurizio Bruschi's *bucatini ammatriciana* (Roman tube pasta with savory tomato-pancetta-pecorino sauce) served properly al dente. There's also ravioli and ricotta gnocchi made by hand in-house, and a well-priced selection of robust Italian wines served by wisecracking Tuscan waitstaff. Portions are lavishly American, but seafood and meat preparations remain strictly Italian to highlight freshness and flavors released in cooking – unlike North Beach's many sundried-tomato-pesto-on-everything imposters.

LIGURIA BAKERY · BAKERY $

Map p324 (📞 415-421-3786; 1700 Stockton St; focaccia $2-4; ⏱ 8am-1pm Mon-Fri, from 7am Sat & Sun; Ⓜ Columbus Ave; 🚋 Mason St) Bleary-eyed art students and Italian grandmothers are in line by 8am for the cinnamon-raisin focaccia hot out of the 100-year-old oven, leaving 9am dawdlers a choice of tomato or classic rosemary and 11am stragglers out of luck. Take what you can get, and don't kid yourself that you're going to save it for lunch.

CAFÉ JACQUELINE
FRENCH $$$

Map p324 (☑415-981-5565; 1454 Grant Ave; soufflés $16-25; ☺5:30-11pm Wed-Sun; ⒨Columbus Ave) The secret terror of top chefs is the classic French soufflé: only when the ingredients are in golden-mean proportions, whipped into perfect peaks, baked at the right temperature and removed from the oven not a second too early or late will a soufflé rise to the occasion. Chef Jacqueline's soufflés float across the tongue like fog over the Golden Gate Bridge, and with the right person across the tiny wooden table to share that seafood soufflé, dinner could hardly get more romantic – until you order the chocolate for dessert.

CINECITTÁ
PIZZA $

Map p324 (☑415-291-8830; 663 Union St; pizzas $9-15; ☺noon-10pm Sun-Thu, to 11pm Fri & Sat; ⚲⚄; ⒨Columbus Ave; ⒢Mason St) That tantalizing aroma you followed into this 22-seat eatery is thin-crust Roman pizza, probably the ever-popular Travestere (fresh mozzarella, arugula and prosciutto), served with sass by Roman owner Romina. Vegetarians prefer the Funghi Selvatici, with wild mushrooms, zucchini and sundried tomato, but that saliva-prompting aroma that elicits exclamations from Italian regulars is the O Sole Mio, with capers, olives, mozzarella and anchovies. Go local with drinks – Anchor Steam is on tap or Claudia Springs Zin (bottles are half-off Mondays and Tuesdays) – and save room for housemade tiramisu.

BRIOCHE BAKERY
BAKERY, SANDWICHES $

Map p324 (☑415-765-0412; www.briochecafe.com; 210 Columbus Ave; pastries $2-6; ☺7am-8pm; ☎⚄⚲; ⒨Columbus Ave) When Gold Rush miners first found gold here they treated themselves to 'Frenchy food,' on what was once San Francisco's Barbary Coast. Now you too can start your day striking it rich with flaky cinnamon twists and not-too-sweet *pain au chocolat* (chocolate croissants). You'll be back later for the decadent North Beach–inspired tartine with *prosciutto di Parma,* pear, and herbed ricotta, drizzled with honey.

MOLINARI
DELI $

Map p324 (☑415-421-2337; 373 Columbus Ave; sandwiches $5-8; ☺9am-5:30pm Mon-Fri, 7:30am-5:30pm Sat; ⒨Columbus Ave) Grab a number and a crusty roll, and when your number rolls around, the guys behind the counter will stuff it with translucent sheets of *prosciutto di Parma,* milky buffalo mozzarella, tender marinated artichokes or slabs of the legendary house-cured salami (the city's best). While you wait, load up on essential Italian groceries for later, like truffle-filled gnocchi, seasoned *pecorino* (sheep's cheese) and aged balsamic vinegar.

TONY'S COAL-FIRED PIZZA & SLICE HOUSE
PIZZA $

Map p324 (☑415-835-9888; www.tonyspizza napoletana.com; 1556 Stockton St; slices $4-5; ☺noon-11pm Wed-Sun; ⒨Columbus Ave; ⒢Powell St) Fuggedaboudit: this may be San Francisco, but you can still grab a cheesy, thin-crust slice to go in a New York minute from nine-times world champion pizza-slinger Tony Gemignani. What? You were expecting meatball subs and Kosher salt shakers? Done. Difference here is you can take that slice to sunny Washington Square and watch tai chi practice and wild parrots in the trees year-round. Sorry, Manhattan – whaddayagonnado?

NAKED LUNCH
SANDWICHES $

Map p324 (☑415-577-4951; www.nakedlunch sf.com; 504 Broadway; sandwiches $8-12; ☺11:30am-2pm Tue-Sat; ⒨Columbus Ave; ⒢Powell St) Unpredictable, utterly decadent cravings worthy of a William S Burroughs novel are satisfied by the ever-changing menu at this lunch stall tucked between XXX entertainment venues. Foie gras, duck prosciutto and black truffle salt are liable to sprawl across a sandwich, keeping company with naughty salty-sweet, artisan-made *chicharrones* (fried pork rinds) and sweet-talking Southern cinnamon iced tea.

✖ Chinatown

CITY VIEW
DIM SUM $

Map p324 (☑415-398-2838; 662 Commercial St; dishes $3-5; ☺11am-2:30pm Mon-Fri, 10am-2:30pm Sat & Sun; ⒨Kearny St; ⒢California St) Dim sum aficionados used to cramped quarters and surly service are wowed by impeccable shrimp and leek dumplings, tender asparagus, crisp Peking duck, and coconut-dusted custard tarts, all dished up from carts with a flourish in a spacious, sunny room. Try to arrive on the early or late side of lunch, when your server has the time to explain what exactly it is that smells so good in those bamboo steamers.

YUET LEE CHINESE, SEAFOOD **$$**

Map p324 (☎415-982-6020; 1300 Stockton St; mains $11-18; ⊙11am-3am Wed-Mon; 🍴; MStockton St; 🚃Powell St) With a radioactive green paint job and merciless fluorescent lighting, this Chinese seafood diner isn't for first dates, rather for drinking buddies and committed couples who have nothing to hide and are willing to share outstanding batter-dipped, salt-and-pepper calamari and tender roast duck.

HOUSE OF NANKING CHINESE **$$**

Map p324 (☎415-421-1429; 919 Kearny St; mains $9-15; ⊙11am-10pm Mon-Fri, noon-10pm Sat, noon-9pm Sun; MKearny St) Meekly suggest an interest in seafood, nothing deep-fried, perhaps some greens, and your brusque server nods, snatches the menu and, within minutes, returns with Shanghai specialties: meltaway scallops, fragrant sautéed pea shoots, garlicky noodles and a tea ball that blossoms in hot water. Expect bossy service, a wait for a shared table and a strict cash-only policy – but also bright, fresh flavors at reasonable prices.

GOLDEN STAR VIETNAMESE **$**

Map p324 (☎415-398-1215; 11 Walter Lum Pl; noodles $5-8; ⊙10am-9pm; MKearny St) Elementary school cafeterias could outclass the Golden Star for atmosphere – but if you know *pho* (Vietnamese noodle soup), this is the place to go. Five-spice chicken *pho* is the house specialty that warms the bones on a foggy day, but on a hot day, branch out and get the *bun* (rice vermicelli) topped with thinly sliced grilled beef, imperial rolls, mint and ground peanuts. Except in understandable cases of extreme noodle gluttony, your bill will be under $8 (cash only).

🍷 DRINKING & NIGHTLIFE

🍷 North Beach

TOP CHOICE SPECS' BAR

Map p324 (12 William Saroyan Pl; ⊙5pm-2am) If you've ever wondered what you do with a drunken sailor, here's your answer: march that sailor down this hidden pedestrian alley and stow him away in the back of the bar, where he can wax nostalgic over Seven Seas mementos. With all the Merchant Marine memorabilia on the walls, your order is obvious: one pint of Anchor Steam, coming right up.

TOP CHOICE CAFFE TRIESTE CAFE

Map p324 (601 Vallejo St; ⊙6:30am-11pm Sun-Thu, to midnight Fri & Sat; 🛜; MColumbus Ave) Poetry on bathroom walls, opera on the jukebox, live Italian and gypsy folk music weekly, and regular sightings of Beat poet laureate Lawrence Ferlinghetti: this is North Beach at its best, as it's been since the 1950s. Linger over a legendary espresso, join aging anarchists debating how best to bring down the government, or scribble your screenplay under the Sicilian mural just as young Francis Ford Coppola did. Perhaps you've heard of the movie: it was called *The Godfather*.

COMSTOCK SALOON BAR

Map p324 (155 Columbus Ave; ⊙11:30am-2am Mon-Fri, 2pm-2am Sat; MColumbus Ave) Welcome to the Barbary Coast, where fortunes were made and squandered, burlesque dancers had hearts or at least teeth of gold,

---

WORTH A DETOUR

JAI YUN

There's no need to worry about what to order at **Jai Yun** (Map p324; ☎415-981-7438; www.menuscan.com/jaiyun; 680 Clay St; ⊙by reservation only 11am-2pm Mon-Wed & Fri, 6:30-9:30pm Fri-Wed; MKearny St, 🚃California St): there's no menu, since chef Ji Nei creates the market-inspired, Shanghai style bill of fare based on what's fresh that day (mention any food allergies or aversions when you book). Fingers crossed, the day's specialties will include tender abalone, translucent housemade rice noodles with cured pancetta, and addictive, paper-thin marinated lotus root. Lunches are a better deal for 6 to 10 small plates ($18 to $35 per person prix-fixe), while dinners are proper feasts of 20 plus tiny, sensational dishes ($55 to $70 per person). Never mind that servers often rely on hand-gestures with non–Mandarin-speakers – the sophisticated, fascinating flavors will leave you assured in your impeccable taste. Cash only, and the wine selection is limited – bring your own reisling for $20 corkage.

and well-researched cocktails at Victorian Comstock Saloon remain period-perfect: the Pisco Punch is made with real pineapple gum, and the Hop Toad with Jamaican rum, bitters and apricot brandy would make sea captains abandon ship. The adjacent restaurant is the kind of place where you might take a madam gone respectable for a 'pig in a blanket' (sausage in a fluffy biscuit), beef shank and bone marrow pot pie or decadent maple bourbon cake.

TOSCA CAFE   BAR
Map p324 (www.toscacafesf.com; 242 Columbus Ave; ☺5pm-2am Tue-Sun; Ⓜ Columbus Ave) Sean Penn, Bobby DeNiro and Sofia Coppola might lurk in the VIP room, but they'll probably be basing their next character study on regulars sipping *caffe corretto* (espresso 'corrected' with liquor) in the retro red-vinyl booth next to yours. Opera on Tosca's jukebox (with genuine 45rpm platters) sometimes has to compete with the thump-thump of Larry Flynt's Hustler Club next door, but Tosca wins for classic movie-star sex appeal.

15 ROMOLO
Map p324 (☏415-398-1359; www.15romolo.com; 15 Romolo Pl; ☺5pm-2am; Ⓜ Columbus Ave) Strap on your spurs and prepare for an adventure: finding this Western saloon tucked inside an alleyway wedged between North Beach burlesque joints calls for a stiff drink. Arrivals are swiftly rewarded at the dark-wood bar with Victorian-inspired cocktails that stay on the manly side of dainty – the Pimm's Cup strikes a rigorous gin/cucumber/bitters ratio, and the honey vodka and basil-spiked Track 42 has just a dab of egg white. Happy hour runs from 5:00pm to 7:30pm daily, and if the mood and menu strikes you, stick around for spiffed-up pub grub like smoked pulled-pork sliders and fries with Madras curry ketchup – but bear in mind bathrooms are limited.

CHURCH KEY   BAR
Map p324 (1402 Grant Ave; ☺5pm-midnight; Ⓜ Columbus Ave) Foggy North Beach nights call for a beer, but warm ones deserve two – ideally from the selection of 55 international craft brews at Church Key. Whether your favorite beer is Brazilian or Kiwi, bacon-flavored or pomegranate-scented, look for the discreet white key sign over the door and head on back to the copper-topped bar for a consultation with well-versed bartenders. There are only a couple of wines on the menu and no cocktails – but with potent 10% to 12% beer, you won't miss them. Cash only.

VESUVIO   BAR
Map p324 (www.vesuvio.com; 255 Columbus Ave; ☺6am-2am; Ⓜ Columbus Ave) Guy walks into a bar, roars and leaves. Without missing a beat, the bartender says to the next customer, 'Welcome to Vesuvio, honey – what can I get you?' It takes a lot more than a barbaric yawp to get Vesuvio's regulars to glance up from their microbrewed beer and anesthetizing absinthe. Kerouac blew off Henry Miller to go on a bender here, and after knocking back his namesake drink (a small bucket of rum, tequila and OJ) with neighborhood characters, you'll get why.

🍷 Chinatown

LI PO   BAR
Map p324 (☏415-982-0072; 916 Grant Ave; ☺2pm-2am; Ⓜ Stockton St) Beat a hasty retreat from Grant Ave souvenir shops to the retro red booths where Allen Ginsberg and Jack Kerouac debated the meaning of life and literature under the patient gaze of the golden Buddha by the bar. Enter the faux-grotto doorway and try not to bump your head on the red lanterns as you place your order: beer or Chinese mai tai, made with *baiju* (rice liquor), better known as white lightning.

ROSEWOOD   BAR
Map p324 (☏415-951-4886; 732 Broadway; ☺5:30pm-2am Wed-Fri, 7pm-2am Sat; Ⓜ Stockton St) This unmarked bar delivers on its name with sleek floor-to-ceiling, rosewood-paneled walls, dim lighting and low-slung tufted black-leather sofas. Basil gimlets and crafty DJs drum up dance-floor action and intrigue on the bamboo-enclosed smokers' patio – arrive before 10pm if you're here for casual conversation.

EZ5   BAR
Map p324 (☏415-362-9321; www.ez5bar.com; 684 Commercial St; cover free; ☺4pm-2am Mon-Fri, 8pm-2am Sat; Ⓜ Kearny St) Need a day off? EZ5 obliges happy hour from 4pm to 8pm weekdays, offering sweet deals on Day Off sweet-sour lemon vodka cocktails. The '80s are in the house, with cherry-red

vinyl seating and classic video games like Ms Pac Man – which comes in handy on a slow night. Karaoke and Jell-o shots take the edge off Monday nights, and Fi-Di ties loosen once DJs start spinning house and hip-hop around 9pm to 10pm.

⭐ ENTERTAINMENT

BEACH BLANKET BABYLON   LIVE MUSIC

Map p324 (BBB; ☑415-421-4222; www.beach blanketbabylon.com; 678 Green St; admission $25-100; ⊙shows 8pm Wed, Thu & Fri, 6:30pm & 9:30pm Sat, 2pm & 5pm Sun; MStockton St; ⊠Mason St) Since 1974, San Francisco's longest-running musical-cabaret Beach Blanket Babylon has spoofed current events with topical comedy that changes so often that stagehands giggle along with the audience. Heads of state and pop-culture figureheads alike are played by actors in campy giant wigs and hats, and no subject is above mockery: Queen Elizabeth, Prince Charles and Duchess Camilla saw the show, but that didn't stop one of BBB's resident drag queens from satirizing the royal wedding. Spectators must be over 21 to handle the racy humor, except at cleverly sanitized Sunday matinees. Reservations essential; arrive one hour early for best seats.

COBB'S COMEDY CLUB   COMEDY

Map p324 (☑415-928-4320; www.cobbscomedy club.com; 915 Columbus Ave; admission $18-33, plus 2-drink minimum; ⊙shows 8pm & 10:15pm; MColumbus Ave) There's no room to be shy at Cobb's, where bumper-to-bumper shared tables make for an intimate (and vulnerable) audience. The venue is known for launching local talent and giving big-name acts from HBO's Dave Chapelle to NBC's Tracy Morgan a place to try risky new material. Check the website for shows.

PURPLE ONION   COMEDY

Map p324 (☑415-956-1653; www.caffemac aroni.com; 140 Columbus Ave; admission $10-15; ⊙check website; MColumbus Ave) Legendary comics including Woody Allen, Robin Williams and Phyllis Diller clawed their way up from underground at this grotto nightclub. Recently, comics have been taking back the stage from lackluster lounge acts, and the club's enjoying a renaissance – Zach Galifianakis shot an excruciatingly funny comedy special here. Bookings are sporadic; see online event calendar.

BIMBO'S 365 CLUB   LIVE MUSIC

Map p324 (☑415-474-0365; www.bimbos365 club.com; 1025 Columbus Ave; tickets from $20; ⊙check website; ⊠Powell-Mason) This vintage-1931 speakeasy still plays it fast and loose with strong drink, a polished parquet dance floor where Rita Hayworth once kicked up her heels in the chorus line, and live shows by the likes of Cibo Matto, Ben Harper and Coldplay. Cash only, and bring something extra to tip the ladies' powder room attendant – this is a classy joint.

🛍 SHOPPING

🛍 North Beach

TOP CHOICE CITY LIGHTS   BOOKSTORE

Map p324 (☑415-362-8193; www.citylights.com; 261 Columbus Ave; ⊙10am-midnight; MColumbus Ave) 'Abandon all despair, all ye who enter,' orders the sign by the door to City Lights bookstore, written by founder and San Francisco poet laureate Lawrence Ferlinghetti. This commandment is easy to follow upstairs in the sunny **Poetry Room**, with its piles of freshly published verse, a designated **Poet's Chair** and literary views of laundry strung across Jack Kerouac Alley. Poetic justice has been served here since 1957, when City Lights won a landmark free speech ruling over Allen Ginsberg's incendiary epic poem *Howl,* and went on to publish Lenny Bruce, William S Burroughs, Angela Davis and Zapatista Subcomandante Marcos, among others. When you abandon despair, you make more room for books.

ARIA   ANTIQUES, COLLECTIBLES

Map p324 (☑415-433-0219; 1522 Grant Ave; ⊙11am-6pm Mon-Sat, noon-5pm Sun; MColumbus Ave) Find inspiration for your own North Beach epic poem under Nelson lamps on Aria's battered shelves, piled with anatomical drawings of starfish, love-potion bottles, castle keys lost in gutters a century ago, and even a bucket of paint-spattered brushes (not for sale). Hours are erratic whenever owner-chief scavenger Bill Haskell is out treasure-hunting.

101 MUSIC
MUSIC

Map p324 (☑415-392-6369; 1414 Grant Ave; ⊘10am-8pm Tue-Sat, noon-8pm Sun; Ⓜ Columbus Ave) You'll have to bend over those bins to let DJs and hardcore collectors pass (and, hey, wasn't that Tom Waits?!), but among the $3 to $10 discs are obscure releases *(Songs for Greek Lovers)* and original recordings by Nina Simone, Janis Joplin, and San Francisco's own anthem-rockers, Journey. At the sister shop at 513 Green St, don't bonk your head on the vintage Les Pauls, and check out the sweet turntables that must've cost some kid a year's worth of burger-flipping c 1978.

AL'S ATTIRE
CLOTHING, ACCESSORIES

Map p324 (www.alsattire.com; 1314 Grant Ave; ⊘11am-7pm Mon-Sat, noon-5pm Sun; Ⓜ Columbus Ave) Hepcats and slick chicks get their duds at Al's, where vintage styles are reinvented in noir-novel twill, dandy high-sheen cotton and midcentury flecked tweeds. Prices aren't exactly bohemian, but turquoise wing-tips are custom-made to fit your feet, and svelte hand-stitched jackets have silver-screen star quality. Ask about custom orders for weddings and other shindigs.

ROCK POSTERS & COLLECTIBLES
ANTIQUES

Map p324 (www.rockposters.com; 1851 Powell St; ⊘10am-6pm Tue-Sat; Ⓜ Columbus Ave, ⓠMason St) Anyone who hazily remembers the '60s may recall long-lost bands (and brain cells) in this trippy temple to the rock gods. Nostalgia isn't cheap, so expect to pay hundreds for first-run psychedelic Fillmore concert posters featuring Jimi Hendrix or the Grateful Dead. But you can still find deals on handbills for 1970s local acts like Santana, Dead Kennedys, and Sly and the Family Stone.

DOUBLE PUNCH
TOYS, ART

Map p324 (www.doublepunch.com; 1821 Powell St; ⊘11am-7pm Mon-Sat, to 6pm Sun; Ⓜ Columbus Ave; ⓠMason St) Art and collectible toys line these walls, making Double Punch doubly dangerous for collectors with kids. Artworks in the upstairs gallery are originals by emerging local artists (the San Francisco Art Institute is right up the block), and toys are limited edition – though since LucasFilm is based in San Francisco, *Star Wars* action figures are usually in stock. Prices run high for graffiti artist Brian Donnelly's rare KAWS figurines, but check the $5 bargain bin for kid-friendly finds.

LOLA OF NORTH BEACH
GIFTS, STATIONERY

Map p324 (www.lolaofnorthbeach.com; 1415 Grant Ave; ⊘11am-6:30pm Mon-Sat, to 5:30pm Sun; Ⓜ Columbus Ave; ⓠMason St) Answers to all your SF gifting quandaries, from artsy souvenirs (ticket stub album for all those cleverly designed SF museum tickets) to Beatnik baby showers (onesies with a typewriter tapping out 'So my story begins...'), plus California-made soy travel candles that smell like sunshine.

🏛 Chinatown

GOLDEN GATE FORTUNE COOKIE COMPANY
FOOD, DRINK

Map p324 (☑415-781-3956; 56 Ross Alley; ⊘8am-7pm; Ⓜ Stockton St; ⓠPowell St) You too can say you made a fortune in San Francisco after visiting this bakery, where cookies are stamped out on old-fashioned presses and folded while hot – just as they were back in 1909, when they were invented in San Francisco for the **Japanese Tea Garden** (p194). You can make your own customized cookies (50¢ each) or pick up a bag of the risqué adult fortune cookies – no need to add 'in bed' at the end to make these interesting. Cash only; 50¢ tip for photo requested.

CLARION MUSIC CENTER
MUSIC

Map p324 (www.clarionmusic.com; 816 Sacramento St; ⊘11am-6pm Mon-Fri, 9am-5pm Sat; Ⓜ&ⓠCalifornia St) The minor chords of the *erhu* (Chinese string instrument) will pluck at your heartstrings as you walk through Chinatown's alleyways, and here you can try your hand at the bow yourself with a superior or student model. With the impressive range of congas, gongs and hand-carved tongue drums, you could become your own multiculti, one-man band. Check the website for concerts, workshops and demonstrations by masters.

RED BLOSSOM TEA COMPANY
FOOD, DRINK

Map p324 (www.redblossomtea.com; 831 Grant Ave; ⊘10am-6:30pm Mon-Sat, 10am-6pm Sun; Ⓜ Stockton St; ⓠPowell St) Crook your pinky: it's always teatime at Red Blossom, featuring 100 specialty teas imported by brother-sister team Alice and Peter Luong. Make your selection from shiny canisters lining wooden shelves, or go with namesake blossoms – tightly wound balls of tea that unfurl into flowers in hot water – and score a free sample with purchase.

CHINATOWN KITE SHOP   GIFTS
Map p324 (www.chinatownkite.com; 717 Grant Ave; ⊙10am-8.30pm; Ⓜ Kearny St; 🚋 Powell St)
Be the star of Crissy Field and wow any kids in your life with a fierce 6ft-long flying shark, a surreal set of flying legs or a flying panda bear that looks understandably stunned. Pick up a two-person, papier-mâché lion dance costume and invite a date to bust ferocious moves with you next lunar new year.

FAR EAST FLEA MARKET   GIFTS
Map p324 (📞 415-989-8588; 729 Grant Ave; ⊙10am-10pm; Ⓜ Stockton St- 🚋 Powell St) The shopping equivalent of crack, this bottomless store is dangerously cheap and certain to make you giddy and delusional. Of course you can get that $8.99 samurai

TEA TASTING

Several Grant Ave tea importers have tasting bars where you can sample their teas. Places that offer free tastings usually expect you to make a purchase, and the hard sell may begin before you finish sipping. For a more relaxed, enlightening teatime experience, Red Blossom Tea Company (p113) offers half-hour tea classes with freshly brewed tastings from a daily tasting menu – plus a brief immersion course on preparing tea for maximum flavor ($30 for up to four participants). Drop in weekdays or call ahead on weekends; seating is limited.

sword through airport security! There's no such thing as too many bath toys, bobbleheads and Chia Pets! Step away from the dollar Golden Gate snow globes while there's still time…

The Hills & Japantown

PACIFIC HEIGHTS | RUSSIAN HILL | NOB HILL

Neighborhood Top Five

1 Stepping off the Powell-Hyde cable car atop twisty **Lombard St** (p117) and taking in the spectacular hilltop vistas.

2 Marveling at afternoon fog blowing through the Golden Gate, from atop **Sterling Park** (p119).

3 Soaking naked in silence in the communal Japanese baths at **Kabuki Springs & Spa** (p129).

4 Eating sushi and catching a live band at **Yoshi's** (p125).

5 Shopping for Japanimé and quirky ephemera at the vintage-'60s **Japan Center** (p118)

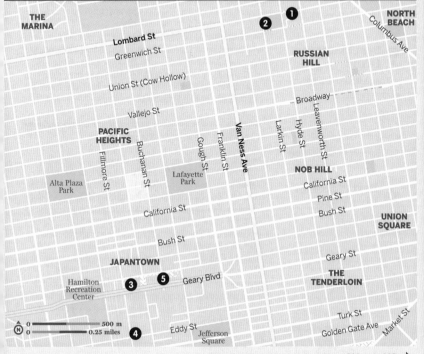

For more detail of this area, see Map p326 and p328 ➡

Lonely Planet's Top Tip

Cable cars serve Russian and Nob Hills, but the Powell St lines have notoriously long waits at their terminuses. Alternatively take the California St line, which rarely has queues. Ride west from the foot of Market St to Van Ness Ave, then walk to Pacific Heights and Japantown; but instead of taking California St west of Van Ness, walk along Sacramento St (one block north of California) – it passes Lafayette Park.

✗ Best Places to Eat

➡ Acquerello (p123)
➡ Swan Oyster Depot (p123)
➡ Tataki (p122)
➡ Out the Door (p122)
➡ Pizzeria Delfina (p123)

For reviews, see p122 ➡

☕ Best Places to Drink

➡ Tonga Room (p125)
➡ Amélie (p125)
➡ Butterfly Bar (p124)
➡ 1300 on Fillmore (p124)
➡ Bigfoot Lodge (p125)

For reviews, see p124 ➡

☆ Best Places for Live Music

➡ Yoshi's (p125)
➡ Boom Boom Room (p126)
➡ Fillmore Auditorium (p125)
➡ Rasella's (p126)
➡ Sheba Piano Lounge (p125)

For reviews, see p125 ➡

Explore the Hills & Japantown

Tackle Japantown and Pacific Heights at the same time. The neighborhoods are immediately adjacent to each other and connect via Fillmore St. Start at the intersection of Geary Blvd and Fillmore St, work your way through Japantown, then head north on Fillmore St to window-shop boutiques. Continue uphill until the street becomes residential, around Jackson St, then head west a block to Alta Plaza Park for spectacular hilltop city views – there's a fantastic playground here, too.

Russian and Nob Hills are likewise adjacent to each other, but because of their ultra-steep gradients, they're not as easy to explore on foot. Fortunately they're both accessible via cable car. Nob Hill stands between downtown and Chinatown; Russian Hill abuts Fisherman's Wharf and North Beach. Consider combining the hills with one of these other neighborhoods. Polk St is the main shopping and nightlife strip near Russian Hill; Fillmore St in Pacific Heights is swankier.

Local Life

➡ **Jazz** The city's top jazz clubs (p125) lie south of Geary St, along Fillmore St; wander between piano bars and jazz clubs before deciding which you like best.

➡ **Cinema** Locals come to Japantown for dinner and a movie at Sundance Kabuki Cinema (p126), which serves food and wine in its main theater.

➡ **Shopping** Most visitors only see the inside of the mall at Japan Center (p118), but there's also shopping *outside* the mall, along Post St, from Webster St to Laguna St.

➡ **Canines** Dog lovers flock to Alta Plaza Park for a pug parade on the first Sunday of the month, from 1pm to 4pm – only in San Francisco.

Getting There & Away

➡ **Bus** The 1, 2, 3 and 38 buses connect downtown with Japantown and Pacific Heights; the 22 connects Japantown and Pacific Heights with the Marina and the Mission. Bus 10 links Russian and Nob Hills with Pacific Heights. Bus 27 runs from downtown to Nob Hill. Buses 41 and 45 run from downtown to Russian Hill.

➡ **Cable car** The Powell-Hyde cable car serves Russian and Nob Hills; the Powell-Mason line serves Nob Hill; and the California St line runs between downtown, Nob Hill and the easternmost edge of Pacific Heights.

➡ **Parking** Street parking is hard to find, but possible. Find garages at Japan Center on Fillmore St (between Geary and Post Sts) and Post St (between Webster and Buchanan Sts).

OREN HARVEY / LONELY PLANET IMAGES ©

TOP SIGHTS
LOMBARD ST

You've seen its eight switchbacks in a 1000 photographs and maybe in a few movies and TV shows, too. Hitchcock used it in *Vertigo*, MTV shot episodes of *The Real World* here, and Barbra Streisand and Ryan O'Neal came flying down the twisty street in the classic-cinema car chase in *What's Up, Doc?* Everyone knows Lombard St as the 'world's crookedest street,' but is it really true?

Russian Hill, as it descends Lombard St, has a natural 27% grade – far too steep for automobiles in the 1920s. Lombard St property owners came up with the idea to install a series of curves. The result is what you see today: a red-brick street with eight sweeping turns, divided by lovingly tended flower beds and 250 steps rising on either side.

Once the street started appearing on postcards in the 1950s, the tourist board dubbed it the 'world's crookedest street,' which is factually incorrect. Vermont St, on Potrero Hill, between 20th and 22nd Sts, deserves this cred, but don't bother trekking across town: Lombard St is (way) prettier. To avoid throngs of tourists, come early morning, but chances are it'll be foggy; for sun-lit pictures, try timing your visit for midafternoon.

Don't try anything funny. The recent clampdown on renegade skaters means that the Lombard St thrills featured in the *Tony Hawk's Pro Skater* video game will remain strictly virtual, at least until the cops get slack. Until 2008, every Easter Sunday for seven years adults had arrived at the crest of Lombard St toting plastic toy tricycles for the annual Bring Your Own Big Wheel Race. But after vehement complaints from kill-joy residents, the art-prankster organizers moved their toy-joyride to – where else? – Vermont St. Check www.jonbrumit.com/byobw.html for the latest.

DON'T MISS...

➡ Snapping pictures from the bottom of the hill, looking up

➡ Arriving via the Powell-Hyde cable car

➡ Seeing Lombard St from Coit Tower, the next hill over

PRACTICALITIES

➡ Map p326

➡ 900 block of Lombard St

➡ 🚋Powell-Hyde

SIGHTS

⊙ Japantown & Pacific Heights

JAPAN CENTER
NOTABLE BUILDING

Map p328 (www.sfjapantown.org; 1625 Post St; ☺10am-midnight; Ⓜ Post & Webster Sts) Entering this oddly charming mall is like walking onto a 1960s Japanese movie set – the fake-rock waterfall, indoor wooden pedestrian bridges, rock gardens and curtained wooden restaurant entryways have hardly aged since the mall's grand opening in 1968. If not for the anachronistic Tare Panda cell-phone charms and Harajuku fashion mags displayed at Kinokuniya Books & Stationery (p127), Japan Center would be a total time warp.

PEACE PAGODA
MONUMENT

Map p328 (Peace Plaza, Japan Center; Ⓜ Post & Webster Sts) When San Francisco's sister city of Osaka, Japan, made a gift of Yoshiro Taniguchi's five-tiered concrete stupa to the people of San Francisco in 1968, the city seemed stupefied about what to do with the minimalist monument, and kept clustering boxed shrubs around its stark nakedness. But with some well-placed cherry trees and low, hewn-rock benches in the plaza, the pagoda is finally in its element, au naturel.

RUTH ASAWA FOUNTAINS
MONUMENT

Map p328 (Buchanan St pedestrian mall, at Post St; Ⓜ Sutter & Buchanan Sts) Sit inside the fountain, splash around and stay awhile: celebrated sculptor and former WWII internee Ruth Asawa designed these fountains to be lived in, not observed from a polite distance. Bronze origami dandelions sprout from polished-pebble pools, with benches built right in for bento-box picnics. On rare warm days along this wind-tunnel pedestrian block, kids frolic and weary shoppers enjoy footbaths under the dandelions.

IKENOBO IKEBANA SOCIETY
GALLERY

Map p328 (☎415-567-1011; Japan Center, 1737 Post St, Suite 385 Kineketsu Bldg; Ⓜ Geary Blvd & Webster St) The oldest and largest society outside Japan for *ikebana* (the Japanese art of flower-arranging) has the displays to prove it: a curly willow branch tickling a narcissus in an abstract *jiyubana* (freestyle) arrangement, or a traditional seven-part *rikka* landscape featuring pine and iris.

Even shoppers hell-bent on iron teapots and *maneki neko* (waving kitty) figurines can't resist stopping to stare at the arrangements.

COTTAGE ROW
STREET

Map p328 (off Bush St btwn Webster & Fillmore Sts; Ⓜ Fillmore & Sutter Sts) Take a detour to days of yore, when San Francisco was a sleepy seaside fishing village and before houses got all uptight, upright and Victorian. Easygoing 19th-century California clapboard cottages hang back along a brick-paved pedestrian promenade and let plum trees and bonsai take center stage. The homes are private, but the minipark is public, ideal for a sushi picnic.

KONKO TEMPLE
TEMPLE

Map p328 (☎415-931-0453; www.konkofaith. org; 1909 Bush St; ☺8am-6pm Mon-Sat, to 3pm Sun; Ⓜ Sutter & Laguna Sts) Inside the low-roofed, high-modernist temple, you'll find a handsome blond-wood sanctuary with a lofty beamed ceiling, vintage photographs of Konko events dating back 70 years, and friendly Reverend Joanne Tolosa, who'll answer questions about the temple or its Shinto-based beliefs, then leave you to contemplation. On New Year's Day, the temple invites visitors to jot down a remembrance, regret and wish on a slip of paper to affix to a tree and to receive a blessing with sacred rice wine.

HAAS-LILIENTHAL HOUSE
HISTORIC BUILDING

(☎415-441-3004; www.sfheritage.org/haas-lilien thal-house; 2007 Franklin St; adult/child $8/5; ☺noon-3pm Wed & Sat, 11am-4pm Sun; Ⓜ Van Ness Ave & Jackson St) A grand Queen Anne–style Victorian with its original period splendor c 1882, this family mansion looks like a Cluedo game come to life – Colonel Mustard could definitely have committed murder with a rope in the dark-wood ballroom, or Miss Scarlet with a candlestick in the red-velvet parlor. One-hour tours are led by volunteer docents devoted to Victoriana.

AUDIUM
SOUND SCULPTURE

Map p328 (☎415-771-1616; www.audium.org; 1616 Bush St; admission $20; ☺performances 8:30pm Fri & Sat, arrive by 8:15pm; Ⓜ Van Ness Av & California St, Ⓐ California St) Sit in total darkness as Stan Shaff plays his hour-plus compositions of sounds emitted by his sound chamber, which sometimes degenerate into 1970s sci-fi sound effects before resolving into oddly endearing Moog synthesizer wheezes. The

Audium was specifically sculpted in 1962 to produce bizarre acoustic effects and eerie soundscapes that only a true stoner could enjoy for two solid hours.

⊙ Russian & Nob Hills

LOMBARD ST   STREET
See p117.

STERLING PARK   PARK
Map p326 (www.rhn.org/pointofinterestparks.html; Greenwich & Hyde Sts; 🚲; 🚋Powell-Hyde) 'Homeward into the sunset/Still unwearied we go/Till the northern hills are misty/With the amber of afterglow.' Poet George Sterling's *City by the Sea* is almost maudlin – that is, until you watch the sunset over the Golden Gate Bridge from the hilltop park named in his honor.

Sterling was a great romancer of all that San Francisco offered – nature, idealism, free love and opium – and was frequently broke. But as the toast of the secretive, elite Bohemian Club (p79), San Francisco's high society indulged the poet in his eccentricities, including carrying a lethal dose of cyanide as a reminder of life's transience. Broken by his ex-wife's suicide and loss of his best friend, novelist Jack London, the 'King of Bohemia' apparently took this bitter dose in 1926 inside his apartment at the club. Within two years, his influential friends had this park – with zigzagging paths and stirring, Sterling views – named after him.

If you're not left breathless by these hilltop views, play tennis on the adjacent public court named after San Francisco's Alice Marble, the 1930s tennis champ who recovered from tuberculosis to win Wimbledon and to serve as a US secret agent among the Nazis during WWII. Sure puts a little posttennis panting into perspective, doesn't it?

FREE DIEGO RIVERA GALLERY   GALLERY
Map p326 (📞415-771-7020; www.sfai.edu; 800 Chestnut St; ⏰9am-5pm; 🚇Stockton St & Columbus Ave, 🚋Powell-Hyde) Diego Rivera's 1931 *The Making of a Fresco Showing a Building of a City* is a *trompe l'oeil* fresco within a fresco, showing the artist himself as he pauses to admire his work, as well as the work in progress that is San Francisco. The fresco covers an entire wall in the Diego Rivera Gallery at the San Francisco Art Institute, on your left through the entryway courtyard. For a memorable San Francisco

vista, head to the terrace cafe for espresso and panoramic bay views.

INA COOLBRITH PARK   PARK
Map p326 (Vallejo St; 🚋Powell-Mason) On the San Francisco literary scene, all roads eventually lead to Ina Coolbrith, California's first poet laureate; colleague of Mark Twain and Ansel Adams; mentor of Jack London, Isadora Duncan, George Sterling and Charlotte Perkins Gilman; and lapsed Mormon (she kept secret from her bohemian posse that her uncle was Mormon prophet Joseph Smith). The tiny park is a fitting honor, long on romance and exclamation-inspiring vistas. Climb past gardens, decks and flower-framed apartment buildings and, as the fog blows in, listen to the whooshing wind in the treetops.

JACK KEROUAC'S LOVE SHACK   HISTORIC SITE
Map p326 (29 Russell St; 🚇Union & Hyde Sts, 🚋Powell-Hyde) This modest house on a quiet alley was the source of major literature and major drama from 1951 to 1952, when Jack Kerouac shacked up with Neal and Carolyn Cassady and their baby daughter to pound out his 120ft-long scroll draft of *On the Road*. Jack and Carolyn became lovers at her husband Neal's suggestion, but Carolyn frequently kicked them both out – though Neal was allowed to move back for the birth of their son John Allen Cassady (named for Jack, and Allen Ginsberg).

GRACE CATHEDRAL   CHURCH
Map p326 (📞415-749-6300; www.gracecathedral.org; 1100 California St; except for services, suggested donation adult/child $3/2; ⏰8am-6pm, services 8:30am & 11am (with choir) Sun; 🚋California St) This Episcopal church has been rebuilt three times since the Gold Rush, and the current French-inspired, reinforced concrete cathedral took 40 years to complete. But Grace keeps pace with the times. Its commitment to pressing social issues is embodied in its AIDS Memorial Chapel, which has a bronze altarpiece by artist-activist Keith Haring. Here his signature figures are angels taking flight – especially powerful imagery as this was his last work before he died of AIDS in 1990. Grace's spectacular stained-glass windows include a series dedicated to human endeavor, including one of Albert Einstein uplifted in a swirl of nuclear particles. Day and night you'll notice people absorbed in thought while walking the outdoor, inlaid stone labyrinth, meant to guide

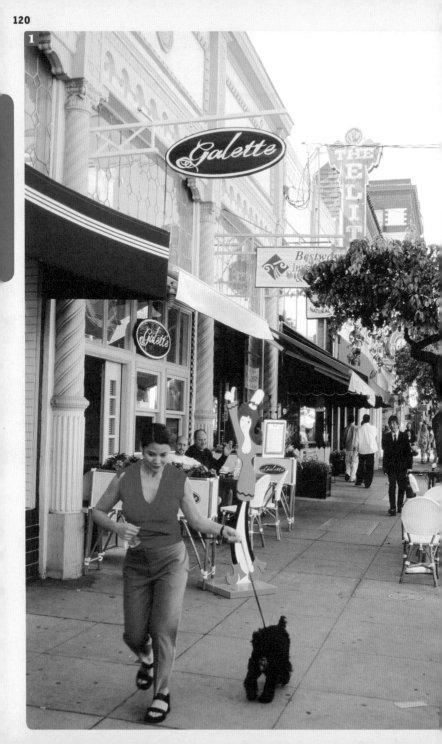

2

3

Pacific Heights (p126)
ndow-shop boutiques along
more St.

2. Fillmore Auditorium (p125)
Jimi Hendrix, Janis Joplin and the
Doors have all played at the historic
Fillmore.

3. Peace Pagoda (p118)
The Peace Pagoda was a gift from
San Francisco's sister city of Osaka,
Japan.

restless souls through three spiritual stages: releasing, receiving and returning. Check the website for events at the indoor labyrinth, which include meditation services and yoga.

MACONDRAY LANE   STREET

Map p326 (btwn Jones & Leavenworth Sts; MUnion & Jones Sts, RPowell-Mason) This scenic route down from Ina Coolbrith Park, via a steep stairway and past gravity-defying wooden cottages, is so charming that it looks like something out of a novel. And so it is: Armistead Maupin used this as the model for Barbary Lane in his *Tales of the City* series.

MASONIC AUDITORIUM   CULTURAL BUILDING

Map p326 (☑415-776-7457; www.masonicauditorium.com; 1111 California St; ☺10am-3pm Mon-Fri; RCalifornia St) Conspiracy theorists, jazz aficionados and anyone exploring immigrant roots should know about Masonic Auditorium. Built as a temple to freemasonry in 1958, the building regularly hosts headline acts. And every other Tuesday morning it hosts mass US-citizenship swearing-in ceremonies. If you're looking for confirmation that California is run by a secret club, here you have it: many of the nation's founding fathers were Freemasons, including George Washington, and the same can be said about California's. It's all captured in the modernist stained-glass windows, which depict founders of Freemasonry in California and their accomplishments – if you can decipher the enigmatic symbols and snippets of fabric embedded in the glass. The frieze below the windows has soil and gravel samples from all 58 California counties, plus Hawaii for some reason known only to those in on the secret handshake. Downstairs a visitors center reveals some of the society's intriguing secrets.

FREE CABLE CAR MUSEUM   HISTORIC SITE

Map p326 (☑415-474-1887; www.cablecarmuseum.org; 1201 Mason St; ☺10am-6pm Apr-Sep, to 5pm Oct-Mar; ☑; RPowell-Mason, Powell-Hyde) Grips, engines, braking mechanisms... if terms like these warm your gearhead heart, you will be completely besotted with the Cable Car Museum, housed in the city's still-functioning cable car barn. See three original 1870s cable cars and watch as cables glide over huge bull wheels – as awesome a feat of physics now as when the mechanism was invented by Andrew Hallidie in 1873.

PACIFIC-UNION CLUB   HISTORIC BUILDING

Map p326 (1000 California St; RCalifornia St) The only Nob Hill mansion to survive the 1906 earthquake and fire is a squat neoclassical brownstone, which despite its grandeur lacks architectural imagination. Today it's a private men's club. The exclusive membership roster lists newspaper magnates, both Hewlett and Packard of Hewlett-Packard, several US secretaries of defense and government contractors (insert conspiracy theory here). Democrats, people of color and anyone under 45 are scarce on the published list, but little else is known about the 800-odd, all-male membership: members can be expelled for leaking information. Cheeky cross-dressing protesters have pointed out that there's no specific ban on transgender or transvestite visitors supping in its main dining room or walking through the front door – privileges denied women.

✗ EATING

Japan Center is packed with restaurants, but some more intriguing Japanese restaurants lie along Post St and in the Buchanan Mall, across Post St. Upper Fillmore St is lined with restaurants, but many emphasize style over flavor. Along Hyde St on Russian Hill, you'll be glad you climbed to prime picnic spots and neighborhood bistros, but if the walk afterwards seems anticlimactic, hop a cable car.

✗ Japantown & Pacific Heights

TATAKI   JAPANESE, SUSHI $$

Map p328 (☑415-931-1182; www.tatakisushibar.com; 2815 California St; dishes $12-20; ☺lunch Mon-Fri, dinner daily; MDivisadero & California Sts) Pioneering sushi chefs Kin Lui and Raymond Ho rescue dinner and the oceans with sustainable delicacies: silky Arctic char drizzled with yuzu-citrus and capers happily replaces at-risk wild salmon; and the Golden State Roll is a local hero, featuring spicy, line-caught scallop, Pacific tuna, organic-apple slivers and edible 24-karat gold leaf.

OUT THE DOOR   VIETNAMESE $$$

Map p328 (☑415-923 9575; www.outthedoors.com; 2232 Bush St; mains lunch $12-18, dinner

$18-28; ☺8am-4:30pm & 5:30pm-10pm Mon-Fri, 8am-3pm & 5:30pm-10pm Sat & Sun; ⓂFillmore & Pine Sts) Offshoot of the famous Slanted Door (p86). Jumpstart early shopping with stellar French beignets and Vietnamese coffee, or salty-sweet Dungeness crab frittatas. Lunchtime's rice plates and noodles are replaced at dinner with savory clay-pot meats and fish. Make reservations.

PIZZERIA DELFINA   PIZZA $$

Map p328 (☑415-440-1189; www.pizzeriadelfina. com; 2406 California St; pizzas $11-17; ☺5-10pm Mon, 11am-10pm Tue-Thu, 11:30am-11pm Fri, noon-11pm Sat, noon-10pm Sun; ⓂFillmore & Sacramento Sts) Pizzeria Delfina derives success from simplicity: fresh-from-the-farm ingredients in copious salads, and house-cured meats on tender-to-the-tooth, thin-crusted pizzas – this is one place you actually *want* anchovies on your pizza. Inside gets loud; sit on the sidewalk. Expect a wait at peak meal times; come early or late.

NIJIYA SUPERMARKET   JAPANESE, SUSHI $

Map p328 (☑415-563-1901; www.nijiya.com; 1737 Post St; ⓂGeary Blvd & Webster St) Picnic under the Peace Pagoda with sushi or teriyaki bento boxes fresh from the deli counter and a swig of Berkeley-brewed Takara Sierra Cold sake from the drinks aisle, and you'll have change from a $20 for mango-ice-cream-filled *mochi* (chewy Japanese cakes with savory or sweet fillings).

BENKYODO   JAPANESE $

Map p328 (☑415-922-1244; www.benkyodocom pany.com; 1747 Buchanan St; ☺8am-5pm Mon-Sat; ⓂSutter & Buchanan Sts) The perfect retro lunch counter cheerfully serves an old-school egg-salad sandwich or pastrami for $4. Across the aisle, glass cases display teriyaki-flavored pretzels and $1 *mochi* made in-house daily – come early for popular varieties of green tea and chocolate-filled strawberry, but don't be deterred by savory, nutty lima-bean paste.

SAPORRO-YA   JAPANESE $$

Map p328 (☑415-563-7400; 1581 Webster St, Suite 202; noodles $8-11; ☺11am-11pm Mon-Sat, 11am-10pm Sun; ⓂGeary Blvd & Webster St) Locals favor this 2nd-floor noodle house for no-fuss meals of homemade ramen, served in big earthenware bowls on Formica tables in a room that's barely changed since the 1970s. Giant-sized combination dinners complete the menu, but noodles are the thing here.

BUN MEE   VIETNAMESE, SANDWICHES $

Map p328 (☑415-800-7698; www.bunmee.co; 2015 Fillmore St; dishes $6-12; ☺11am-10pm; ⓂFillmore & Pine Sts) The lines out the door are evidence of Bun Mee's perfect Vietnamese sandwiches; five-spice chicken is the classic, but the pork belly is sublime. Rice bowls and salads present alternatives to non-sandwich lovers. The tiny storefront packs; consider picnicking at nearby Alta Plaza Park.

GROVE   AMERICAN $

Map p328 (☑415-474-1419; 2016 Fillmore St; dishes $8-12; ☺7am-11pm; 📶🔥; ⓂFillmore & Pine Sts) Rough-hewn recycled wood, bric-a-brac in the rafters, and a stone fireplace lend a ski-lodge aesthetic to this Fillmore St cafe, where Pacific Heights locals recover from hangovers with made-to-order breakfasts, hunch over laptops with salads and sandwiches, and gab fireside with warm-from-the-oven cookies and hot cocoa.

SOPHIE'S CREPES   DESSERT $

Map p328 (1581 Webster, suite 275, Japan Center; dishes $4-8; ☺11am-9pm Sun-Thu, 11am-10pm Fri & Sat; ⓂGeary Blvd & Webster St) Crowds line up for Sophie's made-to-order crepes and sundaes. As interesting as the ice-cream selection (try the red bean) are the posses of Lolita Goth girls eating here, who take their fashion cues from filmmaker Tim Burton.

✖ Russian & Nob Hills

ACQUERELLO   CALIFORNIAN, ITALIAN $$$

Map p326 (☑415-567-5432; www.acquerello. com; 1722 Sacramento St; 3-/5-course menu $64/90; ☺5:30-9:30pm Tue-Sat; ⓂPolk & Sacramento Sts, 🚋California St) A converted chapel is a fitting location for a meal that'll turn Italian culinary purists into true believers in Cal-Italian cuisine. Chef Suzette Gresham's generous pastas and ingenious seasonal meat dishes include heavenly quail salad, devilish lobster *panzerotti* (stuffed dough pockets in a spicy seafood broth), and venison loin chops. An anteroom where brides once steadied their nerves is now lined with limited-production Italian vintages, which the sommelier will pair by the glass.

SWAN OYSTER DEPOT   SEAFOOD $$

Map p326 (☑415-673-1101; 1517 Polk St; dishes $10-20; ☺8am-5:30pm Mon-Sat; ⓂPolk & Sacramento Sts, 🚋California St) Superior flavor without the superior attitude of most seafood restaurants. The downside is an inevitable wait for the few counter seats, but the upside of the high turnover is unbelievably fresh seafood. On sunny days, place an order to go, browse Polk St boutiques, then breeze past the line to pick up your crab salad with Louie dressing and the obligatory top-grade oysters with mignonette sauce. Hike or take a bus up to Sterling Park for superlative seafood with ocean views.

FRASCATI CALIFORNIAN, ITALIAN $$$
Map p326 (☑415-928-1406; www.frascatisf.com; 1901 Hyde St; mains $20-30; ☺5:30pm-9:45pm Mon-Sat, 5:30-9pm Sun; ⊞Powell-Hyde) 'Clang clang clang went the trolley, zing zing zing went my heartstrings.' That classic Judy Garland tune makes sense after a romantic evening at this hilltop neighborhood charmer, with storefront windows looking out to passing cable cars. The Mediterranean menu skews Italian and French, with flavor-rich dishes like duck confit, pork chops with ratatouille, and a simple roast chicken with lemon-oregano jus. Make reservations.

ZA PIZZA $
Map p326 (☑415-771-3100; www.zapizzasf.com; 1919 Hyde St; ☺noon-10pm Sun-Wed, to 11pm Thu-Sat; ⓜUnion & Hyde Sts, ⊞Powell-Hyde) You don't get a gourmet, cornmeal-dusted, thin-crust slice like this every day. Pizza lovers brave the uphill climb for pizza slices piled with fresh ingredients, a pint of Anchor Steam and a cozy bar setting – all for under $10.

CHEESE PLUS DELI $
Map p326 (www.cheeseplus.com; 2001 Polk St; ☺10am-7pm; ⓜPolk St & Pacific Ave) Foodies, rejoice: here's one deli where they won't blink an eye if you say you'd rather have the aged, drunken goat cheese than provolone on your sandwich. For $8, you get a salad loaded with oven-roasted turkey and sustainable Niman Ranch bacon, but the specialty is the classic $7 grilled cheese, made with the artisan cheese du jour.

SWENSEN'S ICE CREAM $
Map p326 (www.swensensicecream.com; 1999 Hyde St; ☺noon-10pm Tue-Thu, to 11pm Fri-Sun; ⓜHyde & Union Sts, ⊞Powell-Hyde) Bite into your ice-cream cone, and get an instant brain-freeze and a hit of nostalgia besides. Oooh-ouch, that peppermint stick really takes you back, doesn't it? The 16-ounce

root beer floats are the 1950s version of Prozac, but the classic hot fudge sundae is pure serotonin with sprinkles on top.

🍷 DRINKING & NIGHTLIFE

🍶 Japantown & Pacific Heights

BUTTERFLY BAR LOUNGE
Map p328 (www.thehotelmajestic.com; 1500 Sutter St; ☺5-11pm Tue-Sat; ⓜSutter & Gough Sts) The Hotel Majestic's intimate 20-seat lounge resembles an elegant library bar in an English manor house, with a gorgeous collection of rare butterflies adorning the walls. Great martinis. Bring a date.

1300 ON FILLMORE LOUNGE
Map p328 (www.1300fillmore.com; 1300 Fillmore St; ☺4:30pm-10pm Sun-Thu, 4:30pm-midnight Fri & Sat; ⓜFillmore & Eddy Sts) Reviving swank south of Geary, 1300 on Fillmore's enormous heavy doors open into a double-high living-room space, with Oriental rugs, tufted-leather sofas, and floor-to-ceiling, black-and-white portraits of jazz luminaries. There's good Southern-inspired food, and on Sundays gospel brunch (reservations required) – big with the after-church crowd.

DOSA BAR
Map p328 (☑415-441-3672; www.dosasf.com; 1700 Fillmore St; ⓜFillmore St & Geary Blvd) Baubled glittering chandeliers hang from high ceilings at Dosa, an otherwise expensive (and good) Indian restaurant with a happening bar scene of sexy, non-snooty locals. It's good for snazzy cocktails, but if you're wearing dumpy clothes, you'll feel out of place.

HARRY'S BAR BAR
Map p328 (www.harrysbarsf.com; 2020 Fillmore St; ☺4pm-2am Mon-Thu, 11:30am-2am Fri-Sun; ⓜFillmore & Pine Sts) Cap off a shopping trip at Harry's mahogany bar with Bloody Marys made properly with horseradish or freshly muddled *mojitos*. A Pacific Heights mainstay, Harry's appeals to aging debutantes who love getting politely hammered.

FILLMORE ST JAZZ BAR CRAWL

The Fillmore St Jazz District was once the 'Harlem of the West,' back in the '40s and '50s, when Ella Fitzgerald and Duke Ellington played clubs near Fillmore and Geary. The 'hood fell victim to urban blight in the '70s and '80s, but lately has bounced back, particularly since the opening of Yoshi's and the **Jazz Heritage Center** (www.jazzheritagecenter.org; 1320 Fillmore St).

Start the evening at Geary and Fillmore and head south, listening at doors of clubs to find what turns you on. John Lee Hooker's Boom Boom Room (p126) marks the gateway to the neighborhood. You can see right onto the stage at Rassella's (p126), but if you don't like the sound, cross the street to the more intimate **Sheba Piano Lounge** (www.shebapianolounge.com; 1419 Fillmore St; ☉5pm-midnight, later on weekends) for piano jazz and a fireplace. Even if you don't catch an act at Yoshi's, pop into the lobby-level Lush Life Gallery to see ephemera of jazz greats. End with drinks on tufted-leather sofas at 1300 on Fillmore, where photos of jazz luminaries line the walls.

🍸 Russian & Nob Hills

TONGA ROOM
LOUNGE

Map p326 (www.fairmont.com; 950 Mason St, lower lvl, Fairmont Hotel; ☉5-11:30pm Sun, Wed & Thu, 5:30pm-12:30am Fri & Sat; cover $5-8; 🚇California St) Tonight's San Francisco weather: 100% chance of tropical rainstorms every 20 minutes, but only around the top-40 band playing on the island in the middle of the indoor pool – you're safe in your grass hut. For a more powerful hurricane, order one in a plastic coconut. Come before 8pm to beat the cover charge.

AMÉLIE
BAR

Map p326 (www.ameliesf.com; 1754 Polk St; 🚇Polk & Washington Sts, 🚋Powell-Hyde) This *très* cool neighborhood wine bar, painted to look like red wine splashing, serves well-priced vintages – happy-hour flights of three cost just $10 – with delish cheese and charcuterie plates. Weekends get too crowded, but on weekdays it's an ideal spot to cozy up with your sweetheart.

BIGFOOT LODGE
BAR

Map p326 (www.bigfootlodge.com; 1750 Polk St; 🚇Polk & Washington Sts, 🚋California St) Log-cabin walls, antler chandeliers, taxidermy animals everywhere you look – you'd swear you were at a state park visitors center, but for all the giggly-drunk 20-somethings. If you're looking for your gay boyfriend, he's wandered across the street to the Cinch.

TOP OF THE MARK
BAR

Map p326 (www.topofthemark.com; 999 California St; cover $5-15; ☉5pm-midnight Sun-Thu, 4pm-1am Fri & Sat; 🚋California St) So what if it's touristy?

Nothing beats twirling in the clouds in your best cocktail dress to a full jazz orchestra on the city's highest dance floor. Check the online calendar to ensure a band is playing the night you're coming. Expect $15 drinks.

CINCH
GAY BAR

Map p326 (www.thecinch.com; 1723 Polk St; ☉9am-2am Mon-Fri, 6am-2am Sat & Sun; 🚇Polk & Washington Sts) The last of the old-guard Polk St gay bars still has an old-timey saloon vibe, with pool, pinball, free popcorn and a big smokers patio where you get yelled at if you spark a joint (but people do it anyway).

☆ ENTERTAINMENT

YOSHI'S
LIVE MUSIC

Map p328 (☏415-655-5600; www.yoshis.com; 1300 Fillmore St; ☉shows 8pm & sometimes 10pm; 🚇Fillmore & Eddy Sts) San Francisco's definitive jazz club draws the world's top talent and hosts appearances by the likes of Leon Redbone and Nancy Wilson, along with occasional classical and gospel acts. We suggest buying tickets in advance – if you're with a group, we like the round, high-back booths (table numbers 30 to 40), but there's not a bad seat. Make a night of it with great sushi in the swingin' restaurant up front.

FILLMORE AUDITORIUM
LIVE MUSIC

Map p328 (☏415-346-6000; www.thefillmore.com; 1805 Geary Blvd; admission $20-40; ☉box office 10am-4pm Sun, 7:30-10pm show nights; 🚇Fillmore St & Geary Blvd) Jimi Hendrix, Janis Joplin, the Doors – they all played the Fillmore. Now you might catch the Indigo Girls,

Duran Duran or Tracy Chapman in the historic 1250-capacity standing-room theater (if you're polite and lead with the hip, you might squeeze up to the stage). Don't miss the priceless collection of psychedelic posters in the upstairs gallery.

BOOM BOOM ROOM — LIVE MUSIC

Map p328 (☎415-673-8000; www.boomboom blues.com; 1601 Fillmore St; admission $5-15; ☺4pm-2am Tue-Sun; Ⓜ Fillmore St & Geary Blvd) Cooking continuously since the '30s, this place is an authentic relic from the jumping post–WWII years of Fillmore St. Blues, soul and New Orleans funk, by top touring talent, play six nights a week. A large dance floor, killer cocktails and cool photos lining the walls may have you lingering till 2am. Shows start around 9pm.

RASSELAS — LIVE MUSIC

Map p328 (☎415-346-8696; www.rasselasjazz club.com; 1534 Fillmore St; 2-drink minimum; ☺8pm-midnight Sun-Thu, to 1am Fri & Sat; Ⓜ Fillmore St & Geary Blvd) Doubling as a good Ethiopian restaurant, Rasselas big windows let you look inside to see (and hear) who's playing before you commit. Live jazz every night (and occasionally salsa on Fridays) make this our favorite Upper Fillmore backup when we're wishy-washy about where to go.

RED DEVIL LOUNGE — LIVE MUSIC

Map p326 (☎415-921-1695; www.reddevillounge. com; 1695 Polk St; cover varies; ☺nights vary; Ⓜ Polk & Washington Sts) The up-and-coming and formerly famous (think Vanilla Ice and Sugar Hill Gang) play this narrow, intimate club. Your once-fave stars may have lost their luster, but the strong drinks haven't. Mondays are movie nights, Tuesdays open mic.

ENCORE KARAOKE LOUNGE — LOUNGE

Map p326 (☎415-775-0442; www.encorekaraoke sf.com; 2nd fl, 1550 California St; ☺3pm-2am; Ⓜ Polk & California Sts, Ⓒ California St) Our favorite karaoke bar, Encore is a throwback to 1970s rumpus rooms, with low-slung swiveling chairs of stitched Naugahyde, a pool table to keep you busy and a friendly crowd of raucous regulars who cheer when you nail a number.

SUNDANCE KABUKI CINEMA — CINEMA

Map p328 (☎415-929-4650; www.sundance cinemas.com/kabuki.html; 1881 Post St; adult/ child $11/8; Ⓜ Geary Blvd & Fillmore St) Cinema-going at its best. Reserve a stadium seat, belly up to the bar and order from the bistro, which serves everything from rib-eye steak to mac-n-cheese. A multiplex initiative by Robert Redford's Sundance Institute, Kabuki features big-name flicks and festivals – and it's green, with recycled-fiber seating, reclaimed-wood decor and local chocolates and booze. Note: expect a $1 to $3 surcharge to see a movie not preceded by commercials. Validated parking available.

CLAY THEATER — CINEMA

Map p328 (☎415-267-4893; www.landmark theatres.com; 2261 Fillmore St; adult/child & matinee $10.50/8; Ⓜ Fillmore & Sacramento Sts) In business since 1913, the single-screen Clay regularly screens a mix of both independent and foreign films. On Saturdays (and occasionally Fridays) at midnight, look for classics like *The Rocky Horror Picture Show*.

LUMIERE THEATER — CINEMA

Map p326 (☎415-267-4893; www.landmark theatres.com; 1572 California St; adult/child & matinee $10.50/8; Ⓜ Polk & California Sts, Ⓒ California St) Right off Polk St, the rough-at-the-edges Lumiere has one large screening room and two smaller rooms, all with seats that need replacing. But we love the programming – a mix of first-run art-house, foreign and documentary films.

VIZ CINEMA — CINEMA

Map p328 (☎415-525-8600; www.vizcinema. com; 1746 Post St, inside New People; tickets $12; Ⓜ Geary Blvd & Webster St) Catch up on current-release Japanese films, animé and documentaries at this underground 143-seat theater with HD projection and kick-ass sound. Also hosts the Asian-American Film Festival.

🛍 SHOPPING

🛍 Japantown & Pacific Heights

NEST — HOUSEWARES, GIFTS

Map p328 (www.nestsf.com; 2300 Fillmore St; Ⓜ Fillmore & Sacramento Sts) Make your nest cozier with the one-of-a-kind accessories from this well-curated collection, including Provençal quilts, beaded jewelry, craft kits and papier-mâché trophy heads for the kids' room, and mesmerizing century-old bric-a-brac and toys.

BENEFIT
BEAUTY PRODUCTS

Map p328 (www.benefitcosmetics.com; 2117 Fillmore St; M Fillmore & Sacramento Sts) Get cheeky with BeneTint, the dab-on liquid blush made from roses, or raise some eyebrows with Brow Zings tinted brow wax – they're two of Benefit's signature products invented in San Francisco by the twin-sister team. Surgery is so LA: in SF, overnight Angelinas swear by LipPlump and Lindsay Lohan dark-eye-circles are cured with Ooh La Lift.

CLARY SAGE ORGANICS
BEAUTY PRODUCTS

Map p328 (www.clarysageorganics.com; 2241 Fillmore St; M Fillmore & Sacramento Sts) To top off your spa day at Kabuki Springs & Spa (p129), Clary Sage designs its own line of yoga-wear and will outfit you with effortlessly flattering tunics made from organic California cotton, organic plant-based cleansers and lotions with light, delectable scents, and homeopathic flower-essence stress remedies.

KINOKUNIYA BOOKS & STATIONERY
BOOKSTORE

Map p328 (☑415-567-7625; 1581 Webster St; M Geary Blvd & Webster St) Like warriors in a showdown, the bookstore, stationery and manga divisions of Kinokuniya compete for your attention. Only you can decide where your loyalties lie: with stunning photography books and Harajuku fashion mags upstairs, vampire comics downstairs, or the stationery department's *washi* paper, super-smooth Sakura gel pens and pig notebooks with the motto 'what lovely friends, they will bring happy.'

HER
CLOTHING, ACCESSORIES

Map p328 (www.her-sf.com; 2053 Fillmore St; ☺Tue-Sun; M Fillmore & Pine Sts) Count on Her for universally flattering Ella Moss dresses and pencil skirts that slim your curves. You could get the star treatment with a personal shopper from Her dispatched to your hotel, but then you'd miss the smoking-hot sales rack for deals of up to 70% off.

MARC BY MARC JACOBS
CLOTHING, ACCESSORIES

Map p328 (www.marcjacobs.com; 2142 Fillmore St; M Fillmore & Sacramento Sts) The USA's hippest designer usually charges prices to match, but here alongside the $800 jackets and $300 sandals are bins of accessories under $25 – chunky resin bangles, snappy belts and limited-edition clutches.

NEW PEOPLE
CLOTHING, GIFTS

Map p328 (www.newpeopleworld.com; 1746 Post St) An eye-popping three-story emporium devoted to Japanese art and pop culture, New People is reason alone to visit Japantown. Get inspired by contemporary artists at **Superfrog Gallery**, then try on Lolita fashions (imagine *Alice in Wonderland*) at 2nd-floor **Baby the Stars Shine Bright**, and traditional Japanese clothing emblazoned with contemporary graphics at **Sou-Sou**. At **New People Shop**, find funky *kawaii* (Japanese for all things cute), like origami kits and cute-as-Pikachu Japanimation cards and t-shirts.

SOKO HARDWARE
HOUSEWARES

Map p328 (☑415-931-5510; 1698 Post St; ☺9am-5:30pm Mon-Sat; M Sutter & Buchanan Sts) *Ikebana,* bonsai, tea ceremony and Zen rock-garden supplies are all here at fair prices.

KATSURA GARDEN
GARDENS

Map p328 (☑415-931-6209; 1581 Webster St; M Geary Blvd & Webster St) For a little something special, consider a bonsai. Katsura Garden can set you up with a miniature juniper that looks like it grew on a windswept molehill, or a stunted maple that will shed five tiny, perfect red leaves next autumn.

ICHIBAN KAN
GIFTS

Map p328 (☑415-409-0472; 22 Peace Plaza, Suite 540; M Sutter & Buchanan Sts) It's a wonder you got this far in life without penguin soy-sauce dispensers, 'Men's Pocky' chocolate-covered pretzels, extra-spiky Japanese hair wax, soap dishes with feet, and the ultimate in gay gag gifts, the handy 'Closet Case' – all for under $5.

KOHSHI
GIFTS

Map p328 (www.kohshisf.com; 1737 Post St, Suite 335; ☺Mon closed; M Geary Blvd & Webster St) Fragrant Japanese incense for every purpose, from long-burning sandalwood for meditation to cinnamon-tinged Gentle Smile to atone for laundry left too long, plus lovely gift ideas: gentle charcoal soap, cups that look like crumpled paper, and purple Daruma figurines for making wishes.

JONATHAN ADLER
HOUSEWARES

Map p328 (www.jonathanadler.com; 2133 Fillmore St; M Fillmore & Sacramento Sts) Vases

THE HILLS & JAPANTOWN SHOPPING

with handlebar mustaches and cookie jars labeled 'Quaaludes' may seem like hold-overs from a Big Sur bachelor pad c 1974, but they're snappy interior inspirations from California pop potter (and *Top Design* judge) Jonathan Adler. Don't worry whether that leather pig foot-stool matches your mid-century couch – as Adler says, 'Mini-malism is a bummer.'

ZINC DETAILS   HOUSEWARES

Map p328 (www.zincdetails.com; 1905 Fillmore St) Pacific Heights chic meets Japantown mod at Zinc Details, with items like orange lacquerware salad-tossers, a sake dispenser that looks like a Zen garden boulder, and bird-shaped soy dispensers. If you can't find what you need here, try up the street at Zinc's 2410 California St location.

CROSSROADS   CLOTHING, ACCESSORIES

Map p328 (www.crossroadstrading.com; 1901 Fill-more St; MFillmore & Pine Sts) Pssst, fashionis-tas: you know those designers you see lining Fillmore St? Many of their creations wind up at Crossroads for a fraction of retail, thanks to Pacific Heights clotheshorses who tire of clothes fast and can't be bothered to hang onto receipts. That's why this Cross-roads store is better than the other ones in the city (including Market and Haight Sts). For even better deals, trade in your own old stuff and browse the half-price rack.

🏠 Russian & Nob Hills

🌿 ECO CITIZEN   CLOTHING, ACCESSORIES

Map p326 (www.ecocitizenonline.com; 2255 Polk St; MPolk & Green Sts) Idealism meets street chic in this boutique of ecofriendly, fair-traded fabulousness, from artisinal-made Afghani gold charm message necklaces, to Vivienne Westwood T-strap heels made of nontoxic PVC (recyclable on-site). Prices are reasonable and sales a steal – $50 could get you a fair-trade cashmere dress or SF-made Turk+Taylor recycled hot-air-balloon windbreaker.

STUDIO   GIFTS

Map p326 (www.studiogallerysf.com; 1815 Polk St; ⊙11am-8pm Wed-Fri, to 6pm Sat & Sun, by ap-pointment Mon & Tue; MPolk & Washington Sts, 🚡California St) Spiff up your pad with locally made arts and crafts at bargain prices, such as Chiami Sekine's collages of boxing bears and Monique Tse's fat-free cupcakes

made of blown glass. For a visual remem-brance of your visit to SF, Studio is the place, with small prints of local haunts by Elizabeth Ashcroft and architectural etch-ings by Alice Gibbons.

CITY DISCOUNT   HOUSEWARES

Map p326 (🗗415-771-4649; 1542 Polk St; MPolk & Sacramento Sts, 🚡California St) Bargains never tasted so sweet: heart-shaped Le Creuset cas-seroles, frighteningly effective Microplane graters, Brika espresso makers and other specialty gourmet gear, all at 30% to 50% off the prices you'd pay downtown. Hard-to-find appliance replacement parts, parchment pa-per and cooking tips are all readily available from dedicated foodie counter staff.

VELVET DA VINCI   JEWELRY

Map p326 (www.velvetdavinci.com; 2015 Polk St; ⊙11am-6pm Tue-Sat, to 4pm Sun; MPolk St & Pa-cific Ave, 🚡Powell-Hyde) You can actually see the ideas behind these handcrafted gems: Lynn Christiansen puts her food obses-sions into a purse that looks like whipped cream, and Enric Majoral's Mediterranean meditations yield rings that appear to be made of sand. Shows here reveal brilliance behind the baubles; during the Ethical Metalsmiths' 'Radical Jewelry Makeover,' the public was invited to bring broken trin-kets to be recycled into new jewelry, with sales supporting a campaign for respon-sible sourcing practices.

CRIS   CLOTHES, ACCESSORIES

Map p326 (🗗415-474-1191; 2056 Polk St; MPolk St & Broadway, 🚡Powell-Hyde) The best-looking windows on Polk St are consistently at Cris, a consignment shop specializing in con-temporary high-end fashion by big-name designers like Ballenciaga, Lanvin, Marni, Alexander Wang and Chloé, all in beauti-ful condition, at amazing prices, carefully curated by an elegant Frenchwoman with an eagle's eye and duchess's taste. Also great for handbags by Prada, Dolce-Gabana, ya-da-yada-yada…

PICNIC   CLOTHING, HOMEWARES

Map p326 (www.picnicsf.com; 1806-8 Polk St; MPolk & Washington Sts, 🚡Powell-Hyde) The kind of boutique gals hope to find when they're out for a girly-girl afternoon, look-ing to fall in love with a new indie designer, Picnic caters to women of childbearing age, who say c-u-u-u-t-e! to the pretty tops, smart skirts, hand-crafted jewelry and cozy home decor.

HYDE & SEEK ANTIQUES   ANTIQUES

Map p326 (☑415-776-8865; 1913 Hyde St; ☻noon-6pm Wed-Sat; ⓜUnion & Hyde Sts, ⓖPowell-Hyde) Like the home of a long-lost eccentric aunt, this tiny storefront is full of surprises: a briefcase that opens to reveal a full tartan bar, a Danish-design silver calla lily, a Native basket more tightly wound than your boss – all at reasonable prices.

SPORTS & ACTIVITIES

KABUKI SPRINGS & SPA   SPA

Map p328 (☑415-922-6000; 1750 Geary Blvd; admission $22-25; ☻10am-9:45pm, co-ed Tue, women only Wed, Fri & Sun, men only Mon, Thu & Sat; ⓜGeary Blvd & Fillmore Sts) Our favorite urban retreat is a spin on communal, clothing-optional, Japanese baths. Scrub yourself down with salt in the steam room, soak in the hot pool, then the cold plunge, and reheat in the sauna. Rinse and repeat. The look befits the location – slightly dated Japanese modern, with vaulted lacquered-wood ceilings, tile mosaics and low lighting. Men and women alternate days, except on Tuesdays, when bathing suits are required (arrive before 5pm to beat the line). Plan two hours' minimum, plus a 30-to-60-minute wait at peak times (add your name to the waitlist, then go next door to slurp noodles or catch a movie; when you return, breeze right in). Communal bathing gets discounted with massage appointments; book ahead and come on the gender-appropriate day.

The Mission, SoMa & Potrero Hill

Neighborhood Top Five

1 Looking into the future at **SFMOMA** (p132), which has showcased cutting-edge photography and new media works since before they were even considered art. Groundbreaking stuff, literally: a half-billion-dollar expansion is under way to house world-class collections that have doubled in size since 1995.

2 Seeing garage doors, billboards and storefronts transformed into canvases with over 400 **Mission murals** (p133).

3 Watching puffer fish completely immersed in their roles inside the Fish Theater at **826 Valencia** (p135).

4 Drinking up, getting down and acting out in hot and heavy **SoMa clubs** (p150).

5 Tasting the nation's next culinary sensation at the wildly inventive, fanatically fresh **Mission restaurants** (p142).

For more detail of this area, see Map p330 and p334 ➡

Explore the Mission, SoMa & Potrero Hill

Get to know San Francisco from the inside out, from SFMOMA and SoMa galleries to mural-covered Mission alleys. Score a whole new look at Mission boutiques and count on Mission and Potrero Hill nonprofits for the ultimate SF souvenir: a new creative talent, discovered at a hands-on arts workshop or dance class. Book ahead for fusion fare at Benu or extravagant vegetables at Commonwealth, or trawl the Mission by day and SoMa by night for gourmet street food. Become the toast of SoMa clubs with moves that would cause scandals back home – ever since its bathhouse heyday in the 1970s, SoMa has highly encouraged outrageous behavior on the dance floor. Once you've watched the sun rise over SoMa freeway on-ramps outside EndUp, you're practically a local.

Local Life

➡ **DIY** Make a children's pop-up book at SF Center for the Book (p162), skate the bowl at Potrero del Sol/ La Raza Skatepark (p161), upcycle office supplies into art at SCRAP (p158) and concoct edible perfumes at 18 Reasons (p161) and stories at 826 Valencia (p135).

➡ **Late-night munchies** Savor four-star bar fare at Bar Agricole (p150), graze gourmet food trucks outside Bloodhound (p150) or score tamales in the beer garden at Zeitgeist (p148).

➡ **Look the part** Define your own Mission hipster style with local designers at Mission Statement (p159), Nooworks (p158) and Dema (p159).

Getting There & Away

➡ **Bus** In SoMa, the 30 and 45 lines run down 4th St from Union Square and the 14 runs through SoMa to the Mission District along Mission St. The 27 runs from Mission to Nob Hill via SoMa, the 47 runs along Harrison through SoMa and up Van Ness to Fisherman's Wharf, while the 19 runs up 8th and Polk Sts to the wharf. In the Mission, bus 49 follows Mission St and Van Ness Ave to the wharf, while the 33 links Potrero and the Mission to the Castro, the Haight and Golden Gate Park.

➡ **Streetcar** All of the Market St streetcars serve the upper part of SoMa. The N line heads south along the Embarcadero and connects SoMa to the Haight and Golden Gate Park. The T Muni line from Downtown via SoMa stops along 3rd St between 16th and 22nd, in Potrero's Dogpatch district. The J streetcar heads from Downtown through the Mission.

➡ **BART** Stations at 16th and 24th Sts serve the Mission.

Lonely Planet's Top Tip

This is where almost all of SF's best nightlife is, and although you should be fine in the daytime, it's not always the safest area to walk alone at night. Recruit a friend and be alert in the Mission east of Valencia, in Potrero Hill below 18th St and in SoMa west of 5th St, especially around 6th St (aka Skid Row). Don't bring the bling – this isn't LA – and don't leave belongings unattended.

Best Places to Eat

➡ Benu (p146)
➡ La Taqueria (p142)
➡ Commonwealth (p143)
➡ Delfina (p143)
➡ Humphry Slocombe (p144)

For reviews, see p142 ➡

Best Places to Drink

➡ Bar Agricole (p150)
➡ Zeitgeist (p148)
➡ Elixir (p148)
➡ Bloodhound (p150)
➡ Heart (p148)

For reviews, see p148 ➡

Best Reasons to Stay Up Late

➡ Pogoing at Bottom of the Hill (p156)
➡ Ghettodisco at EndUp (p151)
➡ Throwback Thursdays at Cat Club (p150)
➡ Dancing with drag queens at AsiaSF (p156)

For reviews, see p154 ➡

THE MISSION, SOMA & POTRERO HILL

From its start in 1935, San Francisco Museum of Modern Art (SFMOMA) dared to be different to other museums. Instead of ignoring the elephant in the room – the Great Depression – SFMOMA made a point of addressing the issues of the day through its contemporary art collection, featuring Diego Rivera's poignant paintings of laborers and Dorothea Lange's haunting Works Project Administration (WPA) photographs of Dust Bowl families. Since photography had flourished in Northern California since early the Gold Rush days, SFMOMA got a head start on other museum collections with groundbreaking photography by local pioneers Eadweard Muybridge, Ansel Adams, Pirkle Jones, Imogen Cunningham and Edward Weston, among others.

But when SFMOMA outgrew its Civic Center home and moved to architect Mario Botta's light-filled brick box in 1995, it became clear just how far this museum was prepared to push the art world. The new museum showed its backside to New York and leaned full tilt towards the western horizon, taking risks on then-unknown SF artist Matthew Barney and his poetic videos involving industrial quantities of Vaseline, and Larry Sultan's revealing photographs of bored porn stars between takes in suburban California homes.

DON'T MISS...

➡ Photography collection
➡ Rooftop sculpture garden and cafe
➡ New media art shows
➡ Atrium installation
➡ Fisher Collection

PRACTICALITIES

➡ Map p330
➡ ☎415-357-4000
➡ www.sfmoma.org
➡ 151 3rd St
➡ adult/child $18/ free, half-price Thu after 6pm, first Tue of month free
➡ ⏲11am-6pm Fri-Tue, to 9pm Thu
➡ Ⓜ&Ⓡ Montgomery St

New Media, New Directions

Finally SFMOMA had room to launch international traveling shows, ranging from Olafur Eliasson's reality-distorting room installations to retrospectives of great postwar Japanese photographers Shomei Tomatsu and Daido Moriyama. The 1995 reopening coincided with the tech boom, and new media art took off in the SFMOMA galleries at roughly the same time as new technologies in the San Francisco Bay Area.

Ongoing Expansion

Collectors took notice of SFMOMA's bold direction, and donations doubled SFMOMA's holdings since 1995 – including the recent gift of over 1100 major modern works by the Fisher family (founders of SF-based clothiers the Gap, Old Navy and Banana Republic). A $480 million expansion is currently under way with Norway-based Snøhetta architects to accommodate the museum's expanded collection of paintings and photography, alongside emerging niches: video art, conceptual architecture, wall-drawing installations and relational art.

Museum Itinerary

There are regular, free gallery tours, but exploring on your own gives you the thrill of discovery, which is what SFMOMA is all about. Begin with the 3rd-floor photography galleries, then head up through the 4th- and 5th-floor rotating contemporary exhibits. The rooftop sculpture garden offers extraordinary views of the city, plus there's reviving Blue Bottle cappuccino and color-blocked Mondrian Cake at the rooftop cafe.

From here, work your way down through the galleries via the dramatic stairwell for vertiginous perspectives over the rotating atrium installation. Tack on additional time to browse art books, cleverly designed housewares and statement jewelry in SFMOMA's shop.

TOP SIGHTS
MISSION MURALS

Diego Rivera has no idea what he started. Inspired by works by the Mexican maestro's Depression-era works in San Francisco, generations of Mission muralists have covered neighborhood alleys and community institutions with some 400 murals to show political dissent, community pride and graffiti-art bravado. Barflys can be merciless in these streets, relieving themselves on notable works by muralists who've gone on to become art stars – but when historic Balmy Alley works are tagged, muralists carefully restore them.

24th St & Around

When 1970s Mission *muralistas* disagreed with US foreign policy in Latin America, they took to the streets with paintbrushes in hand – beginning with Balmy Alley (p134). Bodegas, taquerias and community centers lining 24th St are now covered with murals of mighty Mayan goddesses and Aztec warriors, honoring the Mission District's combined native and Mexican origins. At the corner of 24th and Bryant, the Galería de la Raza (p135) has reserved billboard space for its Digital Mural Project, broadcasting messages such as 'Trust your struggle.'

Valencia St & Around

Before Barry McGee and Chris Johansen sold out shows at international art fairs, they could be found at Clarion Alley (p135), gripping spray-paint cans. In 1993–94 an all-star team of seven muralists and local volunteers covered the Women's Building (p135) with *Maestrapeace,* featuring icons of female strength. Atop literary nonprofit 826 Valencia (p135) is a gold-leafed mural celebrating human attempts to communicate by Chris Ware, known for his acclaimed graphic novel *Jimmy Corrigan, Smartest Kid on Earth.*

DON'T MISS...

➡ Balmy Alley
➡ Clarion Alley
➡ *Maestrapeace*
➡ Chris Ware's mural at 826 Valencia
➡ Digital Mural Project at Galería de la Raza

PRACTICALITIES

➡ Map p334
➡ 24th St btwn Mission & Potrero; Valencia St btwn 17th & 20th Sts
➡ admission free
➡ ⓡ24th St Mission or 16th St Mission

◉ SIGHTS

The Mission is a crossroads of contradictions, and at its heart is Mission St, San Francisco's faded 'miracle mile' of deco cinemas now occupied by 99¢ stores and shady characters, surrounded by colorful murals and trend-setting restaurants. Further east, Potrero Hill has become a bedroom community for Silicon Valley tech execs, with art and culinary schools springing up in warehouses downhill. Wander South of Market St (SoMa), and discover corporate HQs from Embarcadero to 3rd St, museums and galleries from 2nd to 4th, Skid Row between 6th and 8th, and nightclubs from 9th to Van Ness.

◉ The Mission

MISSION DOLORES   CHURCH

Map p334 (☑415-621-8203; www.mission dolores.org; 3321 16th St; adult/child $5/3; ☺9am-4pm Nov-Apr, to 4:30pm May-Oct; ⓜ&ⓡ16th St Mission) The city's oldest building and its namesake, the whitewashed adobe Misión San Francisco de Asis was founded in 1776 and rebuilt in 1782 with conscripted Ohlone and Miwok labor in exchange for a meal a day – note the ceiling patterned after native baskets. Recent restorations in the old mission revealed a hidden mural behind the altar, which had been painted by Ohlone artisans: a sacred heart, pierced by a sword and dripping with blood.

The building's nickname, Mission Dolores (Mission of the Sorrows), was taken from a nearby lake, but it turned out to be tragically apt. With harsh living conditions and little resistance to introduced diseases, some 5000 Ohlone and Miwok died in mission measles epidemics in 1814 and 1826. In the cemetery beside the adobe mission, a replica Ohlone hut commemorates their mass burial in the graveyard, among early Mexican and European settlers.

Along with the Ohlone memorial, the cemetery is packed with graves dating from the Gold Rush. Alongside mission founders are Don Luis Antonio Arguello, the first governor of Alta California under Mexican rule, and Don Francisco de Haro, the first mayor of San Francisco. Hitchcock fans looking for the grave of Carlotta Valdes will be disappointed: the tomb was only a prop for the film *Vertigo*.

Today the modest adobe mission is overshadowed by the adjoining ornate Churriguera-esque basilica, built in 1913 after an 1876 brick Gothic cathedral collapsed in the 1906 earthquake. The front doors are usually only open during services, so you'll need to pass through the original mission structure and cross a courtyard to enter a side door.

Your eyes may take a moment to adjust once you're inside, because most of the light is filtered through the basilica's splendid stained-glass windows. The choir windows show St Francis beaming beatifically against an orange background, and lower windows along the nave feature the 21 California missions from Santa Cruz to San Diego and mission builders Father Junípero Serra and Father Francisco Palou. True to Mission Dolores' name, seven panels depict the *Seven Sorrows of Mary:* one above the main door, and three on each of the side balconies.

MISSION DOLORES PARK   PARK

Map p334 (Dolores St, btwn 18th & 20th Sts; ⓜ18th St, ⓡ16th St Mission) The site of quasi-professional Castro tanning contests, a small kids' playground (currently under reconstruction), free movies on summer nights and a Hunky Jesus Contest (p22) every Easter, this sloping park is also beloved for its year-round political protests and other favorite local sports. Flat patches are generally reserved for soccer games, candlelight vigils and ultimate Frisbee, and the tennis and basketball courts are open to anyone who's got game.

CREATIVITY EXPLORED   ART GALLERY

Map p334 (☑415-863-2108; www.creativity explored.org; 3245 16th St; donations welcome; ☺10am-3pm Mon-Fri, to 7pm Thu, 1-6pm Sat; ⓜ&ⓡ16th St Mission) Brave new worlds are captured in celebrated artworks that have appeared in museum retrospectives, in major collections from New York to New Zealand and even on Marc Jacobs handbags – all by the local developmentally disabled artists who create at this nonprofit center. Intriguing themes range from superheroes to architecture, and openings are joyous celebrations with the artists, their families and rock-star fan base.

BALMY ALLEY   STREET

Map p334 (btwn 24th & 25th Sts; ⓜ&ⓡ24th St Mission) Inspired by 1930s WPA and Diego Rivera murals in San Francisco, and outraged by US foreign policy in Central America, Mission activist artists set out in the 1970s to transform the political landscape, one mural-covered garage door at a time.

Balmy Alley showed personal perspectives on international events, with early works by muralist groups such as the Mujeres Muralistas (Women Muralists) and Placa (meaning 'mark-making') transforming fences and garages into artistic statements.

Today, a one-block walk down Balmy Alley leads past three decades of murals, from an early memorial for El Salvador activist Archbishop Óscar Romero to an homage to the golden age of Mexican cinema. Precita Eyes (p297) restores these murals, commissions new ones by San Francisco artists and leads muralist-led tours that cover 50 to 70 Mission murals within an eight-block radius of Balmy Alley. On November 1, the annual Mission parade Día de los Muertos (Day of the Dead; p24) begins here.

826 VALENCIA
CULTURAL SITE

Map p334 (☎415-642-5905; www.826valencia. com; 826 Valencia St; ☺noon-6pm; ⋈18th St) 'No buccaneers! No geriatrics!' warns the sign above the vat of sand where kids rummage for buried pirates' booty. The treasures are theirs for the taking, if they offer barter for it at the front counter – a song, perhaps, or a knock-knock joke.

This eccentric nonprofit Pirate Supply Store selling eye patches, message bottles, scoops from an actual tub o' lard and Mc-Sweeney's literary magazines is the front for a nonprofit offering free writing workshops and tutoring for youth, plus the occasional adult program on starting a magazine or scripting video games (check the website for listings). Step behind the velvet curtain into the Fish Theater, where a bug-eyed puffer fish is immersed in Method acting. The ichthyoid antics may not be quite up to Sean Penn standards, but as the sign says, 'Please don't judge the fish.'

CLARION ALLEY
STREET

Map p334 (btwn 17th & 18th Sts, off Valencia St; ⋈&⋒16th St Mission) Trial by fire is nothing compared to Clarion Alley's street-art test: unless a piece is truly inspired, it's going to get peed on or painted over. Very few pieces survive for years, such as Andrew Schoultz's mural of gentrifying elephants displacing scraggly birds, or the silhouette of kung-fu-fighting feminists that make Charlie's Angels look like chumps. Incontinent art critics seem to have taken over the east end of the alley – pee-eew! – so topical murals like the new one honoring the Arab Spring usually go up on the west end.

GALERÍA DE LA RAZA
ART GALLERY

Map p334 (☎415-826-8009; www.galeriadelaraza. org; 2857 24th St; donations welcome; ☺noon-6pm Wed-Sat, to 7pm Tue; ⋈&⋒24th St Mission) Art never forgets its roots at this nonprofit showcase for Latino art since 1970. Recent standouts include Sayuri Guzman's group portrait of Latinas connected by their long, braided hair, a group show exploring SF's Latin gay culture, and Enrique Chagoya's post–September 11 dinosaurs escaping the TV and rampaging through suburban living rooms. On the gallery wall outside is the Digital Mural Project, a billboard featuring slogans like '*Venceremos*/We shall overcome' instead of the usual cigarette advertisements.

WOMEN'S BUILDING
NOTABLE BUILDING

Map p334 (☎415-431-1180; www.womensbuilding. org; 3543 18th St; ⋈18th St; ⋒16th St Mission) The nation's first female-owned-and-operated community center has been quietly doing good work with 170 women's organizations since 1979, but the 1994 addition of the *Maestrapeace* mural showed this building for the landmark that it truly is. An all-star team of *muralistas* covered the building with women trailblazers, including activist Rigoberta Menchu, poet Audre Lorde and former US Surgeon-General Dr Jocelyn Elders.

FREE CALIFORNIA COLLEGE OF THE ARTS
ART GALLERY

Map p334 (☎1-800-447-1278; www.cca.edu; 1111 8th St at 16th St; ☺11am-7pm Tue & Thu, to 6pm Wed, Fri & Sat; ⋈16th St) A generous endowment and big-name curators allow the Wattis Institute to take on ambitious, sweeping shows like 'Americana: 50 States, 50 Months, 50 Exhibitions,' which runs through 2012 in a high-concept road trip from Alabama to Wyoming. See also **PLAySPACE** (☺3-7pm Tue-Thu, noon-2pm Sat Sep-May), an experimental exhibition space curated by MFA candidates in the college's curatorial studies program. Recent PLAySPACE projects resituated domestic objects in the wild, and remixed the Smithsonian's American Folk Music Anthology.

FREE ELEANOR HARWOOD GALLERY
ART GALLERY

Map p334 (☎415-867-7770; www.eleanorharwood. com; 1295 Alabama St; ☺11am-6pm Wed-Sat; ⋈&⋒24th St Mission) Hidden on a residential Mission side street is this treasure-box showcase for Bay Area talents, including Francesca Pastine, who creates haunting drawings

THOMAS WINZ / LONELY PLANET IMAGES ©

1. Mission Dolores Park (p134)

This sloping park is beloved for its sports, year-round political protests and the Hunky Jesus Contest at Easter.

2. San Francisco Museum of Modern Art (p132)

SFMOMA houses three floors of boundary-pushing, horizon-expanding art.

3. Mexican food (p142)

The city's best burritos can be found in the Mission.

LEE FOSTER / LONELY PLANET IMAGES ©

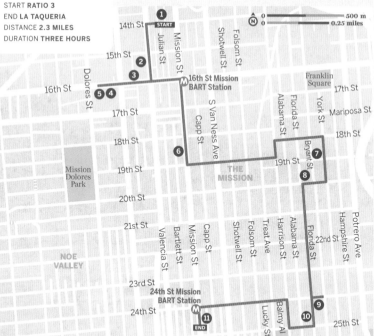

START **RATIO 3**
END **LA TAQUERIA**
DISTANCE **2.3 MILES**
DURATION **THREE HOURS**

Neigborhood Walk
Mission Gallery Hop

➤ The underground art scene surfaces in Mission galleries and art nonprofits, where you'll find artworks more affordable than in Downtown galleries and more portable than Mission murals. Here museum-worthy art isn't hung in pristine white boxes but in unfinished back-alley lofts like **1 Ratio 3**, where gallerist and former Whitney curator Chris Perez highlights SF talent before it hits the selling floor at Miami Basel. Jazz musicians jam downstairs at **2 Intersection for the Arts**, but the think pieces in the upstairs gallery raise an even bigger ruckus – one provocative recent show compared Latino and Asian American versions of California. Around the corner and past the sleeping cats at **3 Adobe Books**, a back gallery addresses bookish topics, inviting artists to alter and create altars for their favorite books. **4 Creativity Explored** showcases works by developmentally disabled artists, including John McKenzie's carefully inked word poems: 'war is weird/war is pushy/war is old-fashioned.'

Next door at **5 Needles & Pens** are shelves of artist's zines and a corner gallery crammed with art – recently, Nigel Peake's collapsing landscapes. You can see the stars rising among the next generation of streetwise Mission School artists here and at **6 Incline Gallery**, a gallery along the rear entry ramp of a Valencia St warehouse. Read between carefully drawn lines at **7 Guerrero Gallery**, and you'll find wry, spot-on social critiques. But before you get too comfortable observing from the sidelines, **8 Southern Exposure** pulls you into the action with community art pieces that invite your participation. Works by Latino artists at **9 Galería de la Raza** show that it's possible to envision a different world without forgetting your roots, while **10 Eleanor Hardwood Gallery** is an escape hatch from reality into meticulous imaginary worlds. But if you can't live on art alone, head to nearby **11 La Taqueria** for a burrito that counts as two gourmet meals.

by blacking out newspaper column inches like a censor, leaving only the margins. The gallery's breakthrough stars include US Venice Biennale artist Emily Prince, whose daily drawings form poignantly personal catalogs: all the hats in her house, say, or all the US soldiers killed in Iraq.

SOUTHERN EXPOSURE   ART GALLERY
Map p334 (☎415-863-2141; www.soex.org; 3030 20th St; donations welcome; ◷noon-6pm Thu-Sat; ⓜBryant St, ⓡ24th St Mission) Art really ties the room together at nonprofit Southern Exposure, where works are carefully crafted not just with paint and canvas but a sense of community. Recent projects have included collaborative drawings made by local youth in juvenile detention and an installation transforming the gallery into a public art market hall modeled after a farmers market, where artists hawk their wares with distinctive cries. Don't miss So-Ex's annual Monster Drawing Rally, where major Bay Area artists draw live and the audience snaps up works for $60 while the ink's still wet.

FREE GUERRERO GALLERY   ART GALLERY
Map p334 (☎415-400-5168; www.guerrerogallery.com; 2700 19th St; ◷11am-7pm Tue-Sat; ⓜBryant St, ⓡ16th St Mission) Social critiques can come across heavy-handed in words, but the artists featured at Guerrero Gallery have a way of slyly slipping them into captivating art. Witness Hilary Pecis' creepy, Disney-fied collaged version of heaven with castles, doves and white kittens, and New Bohemia's old-fashioned signs with hand-painted slogans that deadpan 'Monetize Your Ignorance.'

RATIO 3   ART GALLERY
Map p334 (☎415-821-3371; www.ratio3.org; 1447 Stevenson St; ◷11am-6pm Wed-Sat; ⓜ16 St, ⓡ16th St Mission) Art-fair buzz begins in San Francisco exactly where it should: down a back alley between a porn studio and a Greek Orthodox church, in an unfinished loft space with pristine white walls. While some gallery artists are recognizable from frequent *Artforum* and Miami Basel appearances, gallerist Chris Perez also showcases artworks that remain inexplicably unknown – including Ruth Laskey's sublime geometric weavings, or meticulous paintings by pioneering SF street artist Margaret Kilgallen.

FREE AMPERSAND
INTERNATIONAL ARTS   ART GALLERY
Map p334 (☎415-285-0170; www.ampersandintlarts.com; 1001 Tennessee St; ◷noon-5pm Thu, Fri & by appointment; ⓜ3rd St) Curator Bruno Mauro really takes his work home with him: since 1999 his live/work Dogpatch loft studio has doubled as an installation space for Bay Area and international artists (there's a sister space in Paris). Recent shows have featured Tara Foley's Jungian cityscapes, and Lori Gordon's installation of snippets of overheard conversations turned into newspaper headlines and placard slogans.

FREE ROOT DIVISION   ART GALLERY
Map p334 (☎415-863-7668; www.rootdivision.org; 3175 17th St; donations welcome; ◷2-6pm Wed-Sat; ⓜ&ⓡ16th St Mission) Everyone's a winner at this arts nonprofit, which offers artists subsidized studio space in exchange for providing low-cost community art classes, from painting to electronics for artists. Guest curators keep the gallery program lively, and private classes with resident artists are also available ($100 for three hours).

FREE INCLINE GALLERY   ART GALLERY
Map p334 (www.inclinegallerysf.com; 766 Valencia St; ◷5-8pm Thu & Fri, 11am-4pm Sat & Sun; ⓜ&ⓡ16th St Mission) Ramp up your art collection at Incline, where SF's emerging talents begin upward career trajectories with shows hung along a warehouse's sloping, skylit stairwell. Wall art installations add discoveries around every corner, while prices remain surprisingly down to earth – many well-crafted original works are in the double or low triple digits.

◉ SoMa

SAN FRANCISCO MUSEUM OF MODERN
ART (SFMOMA)   ART GALLERY
See p132.

CARTOON ART MUSEUM   MUSEUM
Map p330 (☎415-227-8666; www.cartoonart.org; 655 Mission St; adult/student $7/$5, 1st Tue of month is 'pay what you wish' day; ◷11am-5pm Tue-Sun; ⓜ&ⓡMontgomery St) Introducing this place to comics fans would be an insult: of course you recognize John Romita's amazing *Spiderman* cover drawings, and you were probably raised on the alphabet

from Edward Gorey's *Gashlycrumb Tinies*, starting with 'A is for Amy who fell down the stairs/B is for Basil assaulted by bears...' But even fanboys will learn something from lectures about 1930s efforts to unionize overworked women animators, and shows on underground comics legends like Spain Rodriguez and Trina Robbins.

Founded on a grant from Bay Area cartoon legend Charles M Schultz of *Peanuts* fame, this bold museum isn't afraid of the dark, racy or political, including R Crumb drawings from the '70s and a retrospective of political cartoons from the *Economist* by Kevin 'Kal' Kallaugher. Lectures and openings are rare opportunities to mingle with comic legends, Pixar studio heads and obsessively knowledgeable collectors.

CONTEMPORARY JEWISH MUSEUM   MUSEUM
Map p330 (☏415-344-8800; www.thecjm. org; 736 Mission St; adult/child $10/free, after 5pm Thu $5; ⊙11am-5pm Fri-Tue, 1-8pm Thu; Ⓜ&ⓇMontgomery St) That upended brushed-steel box balancing improbably on one corner isn't a sculpture but a gallery for the Contemporary Jewish Museum, a major new San Francisco landmark that opened in 2008 but had been around since 1984. Before Daniel Libeskind signed on to design New York's much-debated September 11 memorial, his design for this museum was already causing a stir in SF, with its blue-steel cladding and shape drawn from the Hebrew word *l'chaim*, 'to life' – a fine idea in theory, but one best appreciated from a helicopter. The steel structure is merged with the 1881 brick facade of the Jesse St Power substation, an early industrial structure charmingly decorated with cherubs and garlands.

The exhibits inside are thoughtfully curated, compelling and heavy-hitting. Standout recent shows have included *Warhol's Jews: Ten Portraits Reconsidered;* Linda Ellia's *Our Struggle: Artists Respond to Mein Kampf,* for which 600 artists from 17 countries were each invited to alter one page of Hitler's book; and a retrospective of the life and work of audacious author and modern art instigator Gertrude Stein, raised across the bay in Oakland.

MUSEUM OF THE AFRICAN DIASPORA   MUSEUM
Map p330 (☏415-358-7200; www.moadsf.org; 685 Mission St; adult/student $10/5; ⊙11am-6pm Wed-Sat, noon-5pm Sun; Ⓜ&ⓇMontgomery St) A three-faced divinity by Ethiopian icon painter Qes Adamu Tesfaw, a stereotype in silhouette by American Kara Walker, a regal couple by British sensation Chris Ofili: this museum has assembled a standout international cast of characters to tell the epic story of diaspora. Memorable recent shows range from Romare Bearden's graphic riffs on trains, jazz and family to quilts by India's Siddi community, descended from 16th-century African slaves. Themed interactive displays vary in interest and depth, but don't miss the moving video of slave narratives narrated by Maya Angelou.

MUSEUM OF CRAFT & FOLK ART   ART GALLERY
Map p330 (☏415-227-4888; www.mocfa.org; 51 Yerba Buena Lane; adult/child $5/free; ⊙11am-6pm Wed-Sat; Ⓜ&ⓇMontgomery St) Vicarious hand cramps are to be expected from a trip to this small but utterly absorbing museum, where remarkable handiwork comes with equally fascinating back stories. Recent shows showcased Korean *bojagi* (hand-pieced textiles), playful modern takes on iconic Mexican handicrafts, and internationally acclaimed SF artist Clare Rojas' urban folklore mural installations. DIY crafts workshops are held on first Thursdays from 6pm to 8pm, and second Saturdays from 2pm to 4pm; see the website for lectures and special kids' events.

FREE CATHARINE CLARK GALLERY   ART GALLERY
Map p330 (☏415-399-1439; www.cclark gallery.com; 150 Minna St; ⊙11am-6pm Tue-Sat; Ⓜ&ⓇMontgomery St) Art revolutions are instigated at Catharine Clark, a showcase for such gorgeous provocations as Al Farrow's miniature religious monuments made from ammunition, and Masami Teraoka's paintings of geishas and goddesses banding together like superheroines to fend off wayward priests. Don't miss the video/new media room, featuring works such as Anthony Discenza's mesmerizing digital remix of suburban dream homes.

FREE ELECTRIC WORKS   ART GALLERY
Map p330 (☏415-626-5496; www.sfelectricworks. com; 130 8th St; ⊙11am-6pm Tue-Fri, to 5pm Sat; Ⓜ&ⓇCivic Center) In the gallery/printmaking studio that calls itself 'The Land of Yes,' anything is possible – including David Byrne's diagrams revealing the overlap between hairstyles and long division, Talia Greene's portraits of Victorians with beards of swarming bees and Sandow Birk's mod-

WPA MURALS AT RINCON ANNEX POST OFFICE

Russian-born painter Anton Refregier won the Works Project Administration's (WPA) largest commission to depict the history of Northern California in 1941, but WWII intervened. When Refregier began again in 1945, he was lobbied by interest groups to present their version of history, and it took three years and 92 changes to make everyone happy. The murals were deemed 'communist' by McCarthyists in 1953, but they're now protected as a National Landmark.

The colorful chronology begins over the old **US Post Office** (Map p330; 101 Spear St; admission free; M&REmbarcadero) window with **Preaching & Farming at Mission Dolores**, where emaciated native workers do the heavy lifting while a friar expounds. A few scenes later, **Finding Gold at Sutter's Mill** shows the diversity of early Gold Rush arrivals: Latino, Asian and African American '49ers are depicted, plus sundry pirates. The version of history Refregier presents is not all rosy: **Vigilante Days** shows a man pulling a gun while another hangs from a noose, and **Beating the Chinese** shows red-faced attackers perpetrating 1870s anti-Chinese riots, alongside newspaper denunciations. **San Francisco as a Cultural Center** is a cultural collage with a wink: opera flyers, men of letters and burlesque dancers all gather under a glowing moon. The **Waterfront/1934 Strike** shows the history-changing dock-workers' strike organized just outside Rincon Center, and **War and Peace** concludes the cycle with very pointed (and given the artist's experience, quite personal) anticensorship imagery, moving from Nazi book burning to postwar promises for 'Freedom from fear/want/of worship/speech.'

ern take on Dante's *Inferno,* starring traffic-jammed LA as hell and San Francisco as a foggy purgatory. The small but select gallery store is what museum stores ought to be, with arty must-haves like beeswax crayons, Klein bottles, vintage Chinese toys dating from the Cultural Revolution and sculpted marble soda cans; the sale of some artist books and print editions benefit nonprofits.

CALIFORNIA HISTORICAL SOCIETY MUSEUM
MUSEUM

Map p330 (415-357-1848; www.california historicalsociety.org; 678 Mission St; adult/child $3/1; noon-4:30pm Wed-Sat; M&RMontgomery St) Get the lowdown on California history at this exhibition space devoted entirely to the state's history. Galleries show themed highlights from the museum's vast collection of more than half a million photographs, paintings and ephemera. Recent exhibits have shown how the Golden State built its reputation for movies, fresh food and the good life through silent-movie posters, vintage fruit labels and tourism brochures – and how that mythology washes with historical realities.

History buffs will want to make a date at the fascinating **research library** (noon-5pm Wed-Fri by reservation) for access to rare books, photos and manuscripts. The library has the definitive collection on the American Civil Liberties Union and the People's

Temple, among other California-centric subjects. Call ahead if you want to research a specific topic so staff can pull the appropriate materials from the vault.

CHILDREN'S CREATIVITY MUSEUM
MUSEUM

Map p330 (415-820-3320; www.zeum.org; 221 4th St; admission $10; 11am-5pm Tue-Sun; M&RPowell St) No velvet ropes or hands off here: kids have the run of the place, with high-tech displays that double dare them to make their own music videos, claymation movies and soundtracks. Jump right into a live-action video game, and sign up for workshops with the Bay Area's superstar animators, techno-whizzes, robot-builders and belly dancers. The vintage 1906 **Loof Carousel** out front operates until 6pm daily, and one $3 ticket covers two rides.

YERBA BUENA GARDENS
PARK

Map p330 (415-541-0312, 415-820-3550; www.yerbabuenagardens.com; 3rd & Mission Sts; sunrise-10pm; M&RMontgomery St) A spot of green in the swath of concrete South of Market. With Yerba Buena Center for the Arts and SFMOMA on one side and the Metreon cinema on the other, this is a prime spot for sun and downtime in between art and a movie. Free noontime concerts in the summer feature world music, hip-hop and jazz. The show-stopping centerpiece is Houston Cornwell and Joseph De Pace's

SOUTH PARK OR BUST

'Dot-com' was the magic word in San Francisco in the mid-'90s, when venture capitalists and 20-something techies plotted website launches in cafes ringing **South Park** (Map p330; 2nd, 3rd, Bryant & Brannan Sts; Ⓜ4th St). But when online pet food and ice cream delivery services failed to deliver profits, South Park became a dot-com ghost town, adding yet another bust to its checkered history.

Speculation is nothing new to South Park, which was planned by a real-estate developer in the 1850s as a bucolic gated community. A party to honor Crimean War victory was thrown here in 1855, in the hopes of attracting some of San Francisco's Gold Rush millionaires – but it degenerated into a cake-throwing food fight, and the development never took off. But this turf proved fertile ground for wild ideas: as a plaque around the corner indicates, 601 3rd St was the **birthplace of Jack London**, best-selling author of *The Call of the Wild, White Fang* and other Wild West adventure stories.

After WWII, Filipino American war veterans formed a quiet community here – at least until dot-com HQs suddenly moved in and out of the neighborhood. South Park offices weren't vacant for long before Web 2.0 moved in, including a scrappy start-up with an outlandish notion that soon everyone would be communicating in online haiku. Twitter has since moved its operations and 200 million users Downtown.

sleek Martin Luther King Jr Memorial Fountain, a wall of water that runs over the Reverend's immortal words: '...until justice rolls down like waters and righteousness like a mighty stream.'

A pedestrian bridge over Howard St links the popular esplanade to an often overlooked playground and family entertainment complex. Kids with energy and creativity to spare won't want to miss this complex, which includes the hands-on Children's Creativity Museum and carousel, a small bowling alley and an ice rink.

FREE BAER RIDGWAY   ART GALLERY

Map p330 (☎415-777-1366; www.baerridgway.com; 172 Minna St; ☉11am-6pm Tue-Sat; Ⓜ&ⓇMontgomery St) Awkwardness strikes a perfect balance in the uncanny, mad-in-San Francisco works highlighted at Baer Ridgway, from Castenada Reiman's architectural landscapes made of piled landscape paintings to Travis Collinson's fish-eyed Flemish portraits of modern loners.

FREE CROWN POINT PRESS   ART GALLERY

Map p330 (☎415-974-6273; www.crownpoint.com; 20 Hawthorne St; ☉10am-6pm Mon-Sat; ⓂMission St, ⓇMontgomery) Bet you didn't think anyone could capture Chuck Close's giant portraits, Wayne Thiebaud's Pop Art pastries or Australian Aboriginal artist Dorothy Napangardi's dreamings on paper. Yet here they are: color, woodcut portraits produced by carving and printing 51 separate blocks of wood; color gravures within glass pastry cases; and salt tracings of Mina Mina in mesmerizing sugar-lift etchings. Such are the mysterious powers of Crown Point Press printmakers, who work with artists to turn singular visions into large-scale paper multiples. When master printmakers are at work, you're often invited to watch – and if you want to make your own, you can pick up some how-to books and tools.

FEDERAL BUILDING   NOTABLE BUILDING

Map p330 (Mission & 7th Sts; Ⓜ&ⓇCivic Center) The revolutionary green design of this government office building by 2005 Pritzker Architecture Prize–winner Thomas Mayne means huge savings in energy consumption, not to mention taxpayer dollars. The ingenious layout eliminates internal political battles over corner offices, providing direct sunlight, natural ventilation and views for 90% of work stations. Detractors claim it looks like a fortress, but it adds a green mark of distinction to the otherwise low, blandly industrial SoMa warehouse skyline.

✕ EATING

✕ The Mission

TOP CHOICE LA TAQUERIA   MEXICAN $

Map p334 (☎415-285-7117; 2889 Mission St; burritos $6-8; ☉11am-9pm Mon-Sat, to 8pm Sun; ☑; Ⓜ&Ⓡ24th St Mission) Rabble-rouser, are you?

Ask a group of San Franciscans where to get the best burrito in town, then as voices rise, quietly slip off to La Taqueria. There's no debatable saffron rice, spinach tortilla or mango salsa here – just perfectly grilled meats, flavorful beans and classic tomatillo or mesquite salsa wrapped in a flour tortilla. They're purists at La Taqueria – if you don't want beans, you'll pay extra because they pack in more meat – but add-ons of spicy pickled vegetables and *crema* (Mexican sour cream) are true burrito bliss.

TOP CHOICE COMMONWEALTH   CALIFORNIAN $$

Map p334 (415-355-1500; www.common wealthsf.com; 2224 Mission St; small plates $5-16; 5:30-10pm Tue-Thu & Sun, to 11pm Fri & Sat; ; & 16th St Mission) California's most imaginative farm-to-table dining isn't in some quaint barn, but the converted cinderblock Mission dive where chef Jason Fox serves crispy hen with toybox carrots cooked in hay (yes, hay), and sea urchin floating on a bed of farm egg and organic asparagus that looks like a tide pool and tastes like a dream. Savor the $65 prix-fixe knowing $10 is donated to charity.

DELFINA   CALIFORNIAN, ITALIAN $$$

Map p334 (415-552-4055; www.delfinasf.com; 3621 18th St; mains $18-27; 5:30-10pm Sun-Thu, to 11pm Fri & Sat; ; 18th St, 16th St Mission) Simple yet sensational seasonal California cuisine with a slight Italian accent: Sonoma duck with Barolo-roasted cherries, housemade pasta with local wild boar ragu, profiteroles with coffee gelato and candied almonds. Since this is the one California-cuisine restaurant all of SF's picky eaters agree on, make reservations now, arrive early and prepare for a wait with a glass of wine – though when you get a whiff of the sensational wild mushroom pizza at Delfina Pizza next door, you might want to sign up there instead.

LOCANDA   ITALIAN $$

Map p334 (415-863-6800; www.locandasf.com; 557 Valencia St; share plates $10-24; 5:30pm-midnight; & 16th St Mission) The vintage Duran Duran Rome concert poster in the bathroom is your first clue that Locanda is all about cheekily authentic Roman fare. Truly scrumptious tripe melting into rich tomato-mint sauce is a must, piazza bianco with figs and prosciutto quickly becomes an obsession, and you'll want the large plate of Roman fried artichokes and sweetbreads –

possibly all to yourself. Pasta dishes are small and not as inspiring as dishes chef Anthony Strong invents from market-fresh organic ingredients and gives a faux-Roman name, like 'tartuco cream' corn soup.

ICHI SUSHI   SUSHI $$

Map p334 (415-525-4750; 3369 Mission St; www.ichisushi.com; 11:30am-10pm Tue-Thu, to 11pm Fri, 5:30-11pm Sun, 5:30-10pm Mon; Mission St, 24th St Mission) Alluring on the plate and positively obscene on the tongue, Ichi Sushi is a sharp cut above other fish thanks to clever culinary engineering. Silky, sustainably sourced fish is sliced with a jeweler's precision, balanced atop well-packed rice, and topped with tiny but powerfully tangy dabs of gelled yuzu and a microscopic brunoise of spring onion and chili daikon that make soy sauce unthinkable.

MAVERICK   CALIFORNIAN $$

Map p334 (415-695-1223; www.sfmaverick. com; 3316 17th St; share plates $12-25; 5:30-10pm Mon-Thu, to 11pm Fri & Sat, 5-9pm Sun, brunch 10:30am-2:30pm Sat & Sun; & 16th St Mission) Cowboys start California dreaming at this tiny Mission bistro, where pasture-raised meats are spruced up with sensational California-grown sides – think Southern fried chicken with pan-seared broccoli rabe and whiskey gravy, or sweetbreads with pickled cherries and edible nasturtium flowers.

MR POLLO   ECUADORIAN $$

Map p334 (415-374-5546; 2823 Mission St; 4-dish tasting menu $15; breakfast, lunch & dinner; ; & 24th St Mission) Mission-Mex devotees are in for a culinary awakening at this outpost of South American cuisine, with organic, market-fresh ingredients. Meals here are cooked to order and can't be rushed, so settle in for a two-hour parade of salt-pork *arepas* (flash-fried meat), empanadas (meat pies) and housemade lychee ice cream. Currently this bolt-hole hidden among Mission St dollar stores seats about 15, and there's at least a 20-minute wait – but since the Food Network talent-scouted chef/owner Manny Torres Gimenez, it's expanding.

RANGE   CALIFORNIAN $$$

Map p334 (415-282-8283; www.rangesf.com; 842 Valencia St; mains $20-28; 5:30-10pm Sun-Thu, to 11pm Fri & Sat; ; 18th St, 16th St Mission) Inspired American dining is alive

SF À LA MODE: TOP 5 LOCAL ICE CREAMS

Humphry Slocombe (Map p334; ☎415-550-6971; www.humphryslocombe.com; 2790 Harrison St; ice cream $2.75-5; ⏱noon-9pm Mon-Thu, to 10pm Fri-Sun; Ⓜ24th St Mission) Indie-rock organic ice cream may permanently spoil you for Top 40 flavors: once Thai curry peanut butter and strawberry goat cheese have rocked your taste buds, cookie dough seems so obvious, and ordinary sundaes can't compare to Sonoma olive oil ice cream drizzled with 20-year aged balsamic.

Mitchell's Ice Cream (Map p334; ☎415-648-2300; www.mitchellsicecream.com; 688 San Jose Ave; ice cream $3-6; ⏱11am-11pm; ⓂMission St) An otherwise nondescript Mission block is thronged with grinning grown-ups and kids doing happy dances as they make their Mitchell's selections: will it be a classic like Kahlua mocha cream or a tropical flavor like *macapuno* (young coconut)? The avocado and *ube* (purple yam) are acquired tastes, but they've been local favorites for generations – Mitchells has kept San Francisco coming back for seconds since 1953.

Bi-Rite Creamery (Map p334; ☎415-626-5600; www.biritecreamery.com; 3692 18th St; ice cream $3-7; ⏱11am-10pm Sun-Thu, to 11pm Fri & Sat; Ⓜ18th St) Velvet ropes at clubs seem pretentious in laid-back San Francisco, but at organic Bi-Rite Creamery they make perfect sense: as soon as SF temperatures nudge past 70 degrees, the line wraps around the corner for legendary salted caramel ice cream with housemade hot fudge. Also worth the wait is the Sonoma honey-lavender ice cream packed into an organic waffle cone – but for a quicker fix, try the balsamic strawberry soft serve at the soft-serve window (open 1pm to 9pm daily).

Mr & Mrs Miscellaneous (Map p334; ☎415-970-0750; 699 22nd St; ice cream $3-5; ⏱11:30am-6pm Tue-Sat, to 5pm Sun; Ⓜ22nd St) Black and Tan beer, toasted-sesame halva, cinnamon-y *horchata* and browned butter are among the many savory Miscellaneous flavors that make this ice creamery worth the climb up Potrero Hill.

and well at Range. Lowly pork shoulder becomes an eye-opener rubbed with coffee and served with bafflingly smooth grits, and wild nettle pasta stuffed with local goat cheese is a study in decadence. Celebrated pastry chef Michele Polzine's impeccable dessert soufflés will leave you weak in the knees, but although the beer fridge is a repurposed medical cabinet ominously emblazoned with the words 'Blood Bank,' Range won't actually cost you an arm or a leg.

UDUPI PALACE
INDIAN $

Map p334 (☎415-970-8000; www.udupipalaceca.com; 1007 Valencia St; mains $8-10; ⏱11am-10pm Mon-Thu, to 10:30pm Fri-Sun; ⓂValencia St, Ⓡ24th St Mission) Tandoori in the Tenderloin is for novices – SF foodies swoon over the bright, clean flavors of South Indian *dosa* (a light, crispy pancake made with lentil flour) dipped in mildly spicy vegetable *sambar* (soup) and coconut chutney. Don't miss the *medhu vada* (savory lentil donuts with *sambar* and chutney) or *bagala bhath* (yogurt rice with cucumber and nutty toasted mustard seeds).

TARTINE
BAKERY $

Map p334 (☎415-487-2600; www.tartinebakery.com; 600 Guerrero St; pastries $3-6, sandwiches $10-13; ⏱8am-7pm Mon, 7:30-7pm Tue & Wed, 7:30-8pm Thu & Fri, 9am-8pm Sat & Sun; ☎; Ⓜ18th St, Ⓡ16th St Mission) Riches beyond your wildest dreams: butter-intensive *pain au chocolat,* cappuccino with ferns drawn in dense foam and *croque monsieurs* turbo-loaded with ham, two kinds of cheese and béchamel. Don't be dismayed by the inevitable line out the door – it moves fast – but be aware that lolling in Dolores Park is the only possible post-Tartine activity.

CORNER
POP-UP $

Map p334 (☎415-875-9278; 2199 Mission St St; dishes $8; ⏱hours vary; Ⓜ18th St, Ⓡ16th St Mission) Forget *Top Chef,* the ultimate culinary trial for SF chefs is a night at the Corner. Successful chefs are invited back for command performances and may generate enough buzz to open permanent restaurants – but this is a tough crowd to impress. Recent encores have been granted to Ken Ken Ramen's housemade Japanese noodles with slow-cooked pork and Cat's Head Barbecue's sweet-tea marinated chicken.

OLD JERUSALEM
MIDDLE EASTERN $

Map p334 (☑415-642-5958; www.oldjerusalemsf.com; 2976 Mission St; mains $7-11; ☉11am-10pm Sun-Thu, to 11pm Fri & Sat; Ⓜ&🚇24th St Mission) Foodies scouring the Mission for the ultimate taco shouldn't overlook this outpost of Middle Eastern authenticity, complete with Dome of the Rock poster and pristine hummus – it doesn't overdo the tahini or garlic, or put roasted red peppers where they don't belong. Get the classic felafel, *shwarma* (marinated, roasted lamb) or *shish taouk* (marinated grilled chicken) with all the fixings: hummus, onion, eggplant, potato and tangy purple sumac, with optional hot-pepper paste.

MISSION BEACH CAFE
CALIFORNIAN $$

Map p334 (☑415-861-0198; www.missionbeachcafesf.com; 198 Guerrero St; brunch mains $8-13; ☉9am-2:30pm & 5:30-10pm Mon-Sat, to 11pm Fri & Sat, 9am-3:30pm Sun; Ⓜmarket St) Brunch gets an upgrade to first class with farm-fresh organic ingredients: pancakes come with strawberries and bourbon syrup, while *huevos rancheros* (ranch-style eggs) are served with heritage beans and sustainably raised pulled pork. The crowning glory is the veggie eggs Benedict with wild mushrooms, caramelized onions and truffle sauce, loaded onto an English muffin made by the in-house pastry chef.

MISSION CHINESE
CALIFORNIAN, CHINESE $$

Map p334 (Lung Shan; ☑415-863-2800; www.missionchinesefood.com; 2234 Mission St; dishes $9-16; ☉11:30am-10:30pm Mon & Tue, Thu-Sun; Ⓜ&🚇16th St Mission) Lovers of spicy food, Chinese takeout and sustainable meat converge on this gourmet dive. Creative, meaty mains like tingly lamb noodles are big enough for two – if not for vegetarians or the salt-shy – and satisfy your conscience, too: 75¢ from each main course is donated to San Francisco Food Bank. Look/live for the appearance of pork dumplings on the menu. Corkage is $10 for wine and $1 to $2 for beer; cash only, parties of eight or less only.

PANCHO VILLA
MEXICAN $

Map p334 (☑415-864-8840; www.sfpanchovilla.com; 3071 16th St; burritos $7-8.50; ☉10am-noon; Ⓜ&🚇16th St Mission) The hero of the downtrodden and burrito-deprived, delivering a fresh, heaping condiments bar and tinfoil-wrapped meals the girth of your forearm. The line moves fast going in, and as you leave, the door is held open for you and your newly acquired Pancho's paunch.

FOREIGN CINEMA
CALIFORNIAN $$$

Map p334 (☑415-648-7600; www.foreigncinema.com; 2534 Mission St; ☉6-10pm Mon-Thu, 5:30-11pm Fri & Sat, 5:30-10pm Sun, brunch 11am-3pm Sat & Sun; ☑; Ⓜ&🚇24th St Mission) Reliably tasty dishes like cocoa-rubbed bavette steak and five-spice quail are the main attractions, but Luis Buñuel and François Truffaut provide an entertaining backdrop

SF'S TOP 3 GOURMET GROCERIES

Bi-Rite (Map p334; ☑415-241-9760; www.biritemarket.com; 3639 18th St; ☉9am-9pm; 🚇16th St Mission) Nemesis of grocery budgets and ally of gourmands whose cooking repertoire is limited to reheating, Bi-Rite is a San Francisco foodie's version of breakfast at Tiffany's. Local artisan chocolates, sustainable cured meats and organic fruit are displayed like jewels, and the selection of Californian wines and cheeses is downright dazzling. Across the street is organic Bi-Rite Creamery (p144).

Duc Loi (Map p334; 2200 Mission St; ☉8am-8pm; Ⓜ18th St, 🚇16th St Mission) Stretch your culinary imagination with a browse through the refrigerated grocery case of organic lettuces and pan-Asian herbs fresh from the Central Valley, the wall of Mayan spices and tropical tree barks, and an entire aisle of international cookies and Japanese condiments.

Rainbow Grocery (Map p330; ☑415-863-0620; www.rainbowgrocery.org; 1745 Folsom St; ☉9am-9pm) The legendary cooperative attracts masses to buy eco/organic/fair-trade products in bulk, drool over the bounty of local cheeses and flirt in the all-natural skincare aisle. To answer your questions about where to find what in the Byzantine bulk section, ask a fellow shopper – staff can be elusive. Small though well-priced wine and craft beer selections; no meat products.

with movies screened in the courtyard, and subtitles you can follow when the conversation lags. For the red-carpet treatment, there's valet parking ($12) and a well-stocked oyster bar.

🍴 MISSION PIE   AMERICAN, BAKERY $

Map p334 (📞415-282-1500; www.missionpie. com; 2901 Mission St; ⊘7am-9pm Mon-Thu, 7am-10pm Fri, 8am-10pm Sat, 9am-9pm Sun; 🅁24th St Mission) Like mom used to make, only better: from savory chicken pot pies ($7) to all-American apple ($5 per slice with free organic whipped cream), made with organic, seasonal ingredients.

✖ SoMa

🏆 BENU   CALIFORNIAN FUSION $$$

Map p330 📞415-685-4860; www.benusf.com; 22 Hawthorne St; mains $25-40; ⊘5:30-10pm Tue-Sat; Ⓜ&🅁Montgomery) SF has refined fusion cuisine over 150 years, but no one rocks it quite like chef/owner Corey Lee (formerly of Napa's French Laundry), who remixes local, sustainable fine-dining staples and Pacific Rim flavors with a SoMa DJ's finesse. Velvety Sonoma foie gras with tangy, woodsy yuzu-sake glaze makes taste buds bust wild moves, while Dungeness crab and black truffle custard bring such outsize flavor to faux-shark's fin soup, you'll swear there's Jaws in there. The tasting menu is steep ($160) and beverage pairings add $110, but you won't want to miss star sommelier Yoon Ha's flights of fancy – including a rare 1968 Madeira with your soup.

ZERO ZERO   PIZZA $$

Map p330 (📞415-348-8800; www.zerozerosf. com; 826 Folsom St; ⊘noon-2:30pm & 5:30-10pm Sun-Thu, to 11pm Fri & Sat; Ⓜ&🅁Powell St) The name is a throw-down of Neapolitan pizza credentials – '00' flour is used exclusively for Naples' famous puffy-edged crust – and these pies deliver on that promise, with inspired SF-themes toppings. The Geary is an exciting offering involving Manila clams, bacon and chilies, but the real crowd-pleaser is the Castro, which, as you might guess, is turbo-loaded with house-made sausage.

BOULEVARD   CALIFORNIAN $$$

Map p330 (📞415-543-6084; www.boulevard restaurant.com; 1 Mission St; mains $28-39; ⊘11:30am-2pm & 5:30-10pm Mon-Thu, to 10:30 Fri & Sat; Ⓜ&🅁Embarcadero) The quake-surviving, 1889 belle epoque Audiffred Building is a fitting locale for Boulevard, which remains one of San Francisco's most solidly reliable and effortlessly graceful restaurants. Chef Nancy Oakes has a light, easy touch with classics like juicy pork chops, finesses Dungeness crab salad with fresh basil, watermelon and yogurt, and ends East–West coastal rivalries with Maine lobster stuffed inside California squid.

JUHU BEACH CLUB   INDIAN $

Map p330 (📞415-298-0471; www.facebook. com/juhubeachclub; 320 11th St; dishes $4-8; ⊘11:30am-2:30pm Mon-Fri; Ⓜolsom St) SoMa's gritty streets are looking positively upbeat ever since reinvented *chaat* (Indian street snacks) popped up inside Garage Café, serving lunchtime pork vindaloo buns, aromatic grilled Nahu chicken salad and the aptly named, slow-cooked shredded-steak 'holy cow' sandwich.

🍴 CITIZEN'S BAND   CALIFORNIAN $

Map p330 (📞415-556-4901; www.citizensbandsf. com; 1198 Folsom St; ⊘11:30am-2pm & 5:30-11pm Tue-Fri, 10am-2pm & 5:30-11pm Sat, 10am-2pm & 5:30-9:30pm Sun; Ⓜolsom St, 🅁Civic Center) The name refers to CB radio, and the menu here is retro American diner with a California difference: mac-n-cheese with Sonoma jack cheese and optional truffle, wedge-lettuce salads with local Point Reyes blue cheese, and local Snake River kobe beef burgers (the best in town). Don't miss small-production local wines and after-lunch treats from the pop-up cupcake shop on the premises.

BUTLER & THE CHEF   FRENCH $

Map p330 (📞415-896-2075; www.thebutler andthechefbistro.com; 155a South Park St; brunch mains $9-12; ⊘8am-3pm Tue-Sat, 10am-3pm Sun; ⓂTownsend St) All the French classics you'd never expect to find among SoMa warehouses are here, from the *croque monsieur* (pressed ham and cheese) with Niman Ranch ham, Emmenthal cheese and béchamel on organic bread, to light, flaky-crusted quiche Lorraine studded with Niman Ranch bacon. The cafe tables are tiny: mind your elbows or they'll wind up in your French onion soup, made with rich beef stock and a proper *crouton* topped with melting Gruyère.

YOON HA, HEAD SOMMELIER, BENU

Drinking in the Bay Area Scenery
Even though I worked in Napa, I still find the tasting rooms along Silverado Trail full of surprises, including some exceptional white wines. Everyone knows about the well-researched wine list at RN74 (p150), but have you had its cocktails? Rye (p91) is also on top of its mixology, and Bar Agricole (p150) doesn't serve beginner cocktails – they're strong enough that you have to respect them with little sips, and know they're going to take three times as long to finish.

Pop-up Pairings
All the food trucks and pop-up restaurants in San Francisco let you play around with the pairing possibilities, without a big investment. Look for Sonoma's versatile coastal pinot noirs and cool-climate chardonnays that aren't over-oaked, so they're better at the table. Mr Pollo (p143) doesn't have a license yet, and complex flavors like [chef] Manny's empanadas present a great creative corkage challenge.

How Wine Pairing is Like Air Traffic Control
Finding room on the palate for wine is like landing a plane: it works better if you have a wide airstrip. [Benu] chef Corey Lee has me taste menu items early on, and asks what four flavors come to the forefront. Once all those flavors are perfectly aligned, that creates a solid platform for wine – it just takes aim.

Becoming a Wine Aficionado
Look, I was raised in a nonwine culture, in Seoul, Korea. Growing up, we never had wine at the table. I had to learn everything, but I worked hard and enjoyed it. Nothing is innate. Just keep drinking.

HEAVEN'S DOG
CHINESE $$
Map p330 (☑415-863-6008; www.heavensdog.com; 545 Mission St; small plates $6-22; ☺5pm-1am Mon-Sat, 4:30-9pm Sun; Ⓜ&ⓇCivic Center) California Chinese fare from Chinatown-raised, James Beard Award–winning chef Charles Phan meets its match with cruise-liner cocktail pairings. Time your arrival for one of SF's best happy hours (5pm to 6:30pm), when pre-Prohibition cocktails gleaned from vintage resort recipes are $6 to $9 and accompanied by $6 orders of pork belly buns and shiitake *shu mai* (open-topped dumplings). Stick around for dinners of salt-and-pepper squid with a refreshing Biarritz Monk Buck, with Armagnac, Chartreuse, organic ginger, lemon and soda.

SENTINEL
SANDWICHES $
Map p330 (☑415-284-9960; www.thesentinelsf.com; 37 New Montgomery St; sandwiches $9; ☺7:30am-2:30pm Mon-Fri; Ⓜ&ⓇMontgomery St) Rebel SF chef Dennis Leary is out to revolutionize lunchtime take-out, taking on the classics with top-notch seasonal ingredients. Tuna salad gets radical with chipotle mayo and the snap of crisp summer vegetables, and corned beef crosses borders with Swiss cheese and housemade Rus-sian dressing. Menus change daily; come prepared for about a 10-minute wait, since every sandwich is made to order.

TROPISUEÑO
MEXICAN $
Map p330 (☑415-243-0299; www.tropisueno.com; 75 Yerba Buena Lane; ☺11am-10:30pm; Ⓜ&ⓇPowell St) Last time you enjoyed casual Mexican dining this much, there were probably balmy ocean breezes and hammocks involved. Instead, you're steps away from SFMOMA, savoring an *al pastor* (marinated pork) burrito with mesquite salsa and grilled pineapple and sipping a margarita with a chili-salted rim. The organic rustic decor and the location are upscale, but the prices are about what you'd pay in the Mission, give or take a buck and a BART ride.

SPLIT PEA SEDUCTION
SOUPS, SANDWICHES $
Map p330 (☑415-551-2223; www.splitpeaseduction.com; 138 6th St; lunches $6-10; ☺8am-5pm Mon-Fri; Ⓜ&ⓇCivic Center) Right off Skid Row are unexpectedly healthy, homey gourmet soup-and-sandwich combinations, including seasonal soups like potato and housemade pesto with a signature *crostata* (open-faced sandwich), such as blue

cheese with persimmon jam and toasted hazelnuts.

TU LAN
VIETNAMESE $

Map p330 (☎415-626-0927; 8 6th St; ⊙11am-9:30pm Mon-Sat; Ⓜ&Ⓡ Civic Center) Sidewalks don't get skankier than the one you'll be waiting on, but try complaining after your heap of velvety Vietnamese chicken curry or tangy tomato-onion prawns. One dish under $10 easily fills two starving artists.

🍷 DRINKING & NIGHTLIFE

🍸 The Mission & Potrero

 TOP CHOICE ZEITGEIST
BAR

Map p330 (www.zeitgeistsf.com; 199 Valencia St; ⊙9am-2am; Ⓡ16th St Mission) You've got two seconds flat to order from tough-gal barkeeps who are used to putting macho bikers in their place – but with 40 beers on draft available by the pint or pitcher, beer lovers are at a loss for words. When it's warm, regulars head straight to the bar's huge graveled beer garden to sit at long picnic tables and smoke out. Bring cash for the bar and SF's beloved Tamale Lady, who makes regular late-night appearances to serve homemade tamales steaming from a crock pot with sides of hot sauce and wisdom: 'Be nice to your mother, and your date too.'

⌀ ELIXIR
BAR

Map p334 (www.elixirsf.com; 3200 16th St; ⊙3pm-2am Mon-Fri, noon-2am Sat & Sun; Ⓡ16th St Mission) Do the planet a favor and have another drink at SF's first certified-green bar in an actual 1858 Wild West saloon, serving knockout cocktails made with seasonal organic fruit juices and local, organic, even biodynamic spirits. Invent your own or consult the resident mixologist – *ayiyi*, those peach margaritas with ancho-chili-infused tequila – and mingle over darts and a killer jukebox. Drink-for-a-cause Wednesdays encourage imbibing, with proceeds supporting local charities.

EL RIO
NIGHTCLUB

Map p334 (☎415-282-3325; www.elriosf. com; 3158 Mission St; admission $3-8; ⊙5pm-

2am Mon-Thu, 4pm-2am Fri, noon-2am Sun; Ⓜ&Ⓡ24th St Mission) The DJ mix at El Rio takes its cue from the patrons: eclectic, funky and sexy, no matter your orientation. The club rightly boasts about the back garden, its 'Totally Fabulous Happy Hour' from 5pm to 9pm Tuesday to Friday, and free oysters on the half shell on Fridays at 5:30pm. Sunday afternoons are the busiest, especially when salsa bands rock (lessons at 3pm); check the calendar for Saturday night events. Drawback: the distance from other bars on slow nights.

HEART
BAR

Map p334 (www.heartsf.com; 1270 Valencia St; ⊙5pm-11pm Sun, Mon & Wed, to midnight Thu-Sat; Ⓜ&Ⓡ24th St Mission) Friendly, arty, gourmet: this wine bar is all Heart. Check the website to arrive when Kitchenette pop-up is serving five-star organic, seasonal meals (share plates $4 to $12) – that masala cauliflower panna cotta will have you licking the jam jar it came in (ahem). The pinot noir is entirely too good for dribbly Mason jars, but there's no resisting the wine menu descriptions: one malbec is 'for kids who ate dirt' and a French white shows 'more soul than Marvin Gaye.'

HOMESTEAD
BAR

Map p334 (2301 Folsom St; ⊙5pm-1am; Ⓜ18th St, Ⓡ16th St Mission) Your friendly Victorian corner dive c 1893, complete with carved-wood bar, roast peanuts in the shell, cheap draft beer and Victorian tin-stamped ceiling. On any given night, SF's creative contingent pack the place to celebrate an art opening, dance show or fashion launch – and when Iggy Pop or David Bowie hits the jukebox, watch out.

LEXINGTON CLUB
LESBIAN BAR

Map p334 (3464 19th St; ⊙3pm-2am; ⓂMission St) SF's all-grrrrl bar can be cliquish at first, so be strategic: compliment someone on her skirt (she made it herself) or tattoo (she designed it herself) and casually mention you're undefeated at pinball, pool or thumb-wrestling. When she wins (because she's no stranger to the Lex), pout just a little and maybe she'll buy you a $4 beer.

TRUCK
GAY BAR

Map p334 (www.trucksf.com; 1900 Folsom St; ⊙11am-2am Mon-Fri, 4pm-2am Sat, 2pm-2am Sun; ⓂMission St) Truck is relentlessly clique-ish, with local artists, out-of-face drag queens, off-duty DJs and underground celebs, but draws a happy crowd and serves burgers and fries. The scene is gay neighborhood bar most nights, but Wednesday is drag night, and Friday Truck Wash lines 'em up and hoses 'em down. Dirty boys: get the password for Tuesday's speakeasy for $1 bourbon shots all night.

RITUAL COFFEE ROASTERS   CAFE
Map p334 (www.ritualroasters.com; 1026 Valencia St; ⊙6am-10pm Mon-Fri, 7am-10pm Sat, 7am-9pm Sun; ⓐ; Ⓜ&Ⓡ24th St Mission) Cults wish they inspired the same devotion as Ritual, where lines head out the door for house-roasted cappuccino with ferns in the foam and specialty drip coffees with some genuinely bizarre flavor profiles – believe the whiteboard descriptions claiming certain coffee beans taste like grapefruit or hazelnut. Electrical outlets are limited to encourage conversation instead of IMing, so you can eavesdrop on people plotting their next dates, art projects and political protests.

MEDJOOL SKY TERRACE   BAR
Map p334 (www.medjoolsf.com; 2522 Mission St; ⊙5-11pm Sun-Thu, to 2am Fri & Sat; Ⓜ&Ⓡ24th St Mission) SF's best open-air rooftop bar has knockout views of vintage Mission street marquees, Mediterranean small plates and basic but tasty cocktails (cash-only). Go early for sunsets and prime spots by heat lamps; instead of heading into the downstairs restaurant, take the hotel elevator to the top floor.

WILD SIDE WEST   LESBIAN BAR
(☑415-647-3099; 424 Cortland Ave; ⊙2pm-2am Mon-Sat, to midnight Sun; Ⓜ Mission St) The wildest thing about this historic neighborhood women's saloon is the overgrown beer garden, with frog lawn statues, water features, porch swings and year-round Christmas lights. On chilly nights, shoot pool at a table where (local legend has it) Janis Joplin once got lucky, then flirt with the crafty gals at the sewing-machine table by the fireplace. Best on weekends; straight girls welcome, but boys are out of place here.

LATIN AMERICAN CLUB   BAR
Map p334 (3286 22nd St; ⊙6pm-2am Mon-Fri, 2pm-2am Sat-Sun; Ⓜ Mission St) Margaritas go the distance here – just don't stand up too fast. *Ninja pinatas* and *papel picado* (cut-paper banners) add a festive atmosphere, and rosy lighting, and generous pours enable shameless flirting outside your age range.

PHONE BOOTH   BAR
Map p334 (1398 S Van Ness Ave; ⊙2pm-2am; Ⓡ24th St Mission) Twenty-something sexually ambiguous art-school students squeeze around tiny cocktail tables to get wasted on cheap drinks, shoot pool, munch free popcorn, feed a killer jukebox, smoke cigs indoors (shh!) and – on a good night – make out in the dim red light.

THEE PARKSIDE   BAR
Map p334 (www.theeparkside.com; 1600 17th St; ⊙2pm-2am; Ⓜ16th St) A motley Potrero Hill crowd of art-school profs, Google VPs, chefs-in-training and Zynga gaming engineers converge for live twangy and hardcore bands on weekends ($5 to $15 cover); other events range from cutthroat ping-pong tournaments to local design showcase Indie Mart. The sunny back patio is dog-friendly and smoker-happy, and dishes are good and the BBQ is cheap.

DOC'S CLOCK   BAR
Map p334 (www.docsclock.com; 2575 Mission St; ⊙6pm-2am Mon-Thu, 4pm-2am Fri & Sat, 8pm-midnight Sun; Ⓜ Mission St) Follow the siren call of the dazzling neon sign into this mellow, green-certified dive for your choice of 14 local craft brews, free shuffleboard, Pac-Man, tricky old pinball games and easy conversation. Happy hours run 6pm to 9pm daily and all day Sundays, and the first Saturday of the month is 4pm to 8pm Doggie Happy Hour, with proceeds to support city dog rescues.

BORDERLANDS   CAFE
Map p334 (☑415-970-6998; www.borderlands-cafe.com; 870 Valencia St; ⊙8am-9pm; Ⓜ Mission St) A delicious outlier in high-tech SF, Borderlands has deliberately unplugged their wi-fi and provided lo-fi reading material: racks of paperback mysteries available for thumbing or purchase, starting at a 1950s purchase price of 50¢. West Coast coffeehouse culture is staging a comeback here, complete with creaky wood floors, top-notch hot chocolate and sociable sofas for actual offline conversation.

ATLAS CAFE   CAFE
Map p334 (www.atlascafe.net; 3049 20th St; ⊙6:30am-10pm Mon-Fri, 8am-10pm Sat, 8am-8pm Sun; ⓐ; Ⓜ Mission St) A bohemian magnet, with serious coffee, art by regulars hanging

on the walls and discussions of novels in progress on the sunny back patio. Brunch becomes lunch with creative, vegetarian-friendly sandwiches (get the beetloaf, or yam and feta), soups and organic salads. Packed weekends, especially during occasional weekend bluegrass jams.

SAVANNA JAZZ — LIVE MUSIC

Map p334 (📞415-285-3369; www.savanna jazz.com; 2937 Mission St; live music cover $5-10; ☉shows 7:30pm Wed-Sun; 🚇24th St Mission) The carpets are sticky, the lights dim, the drinks strong and the music hot at this midsized black-box showroom and bar. It's mostly swing and bebop, and the place jumps Wednesday evenings for ever-popular Lindy-hop parties (lesson kicks off at 6:30pm).

BERETTA — BAR

Map p334 (📞415-695-1199; www.berettasf.com; 1199 Valencia St; ☉5:30pm-1am Mon-Fri, 11am-1am Sat & Sun; Ⓜ&🚇24th St Mission) After shopping locally and seasonally on Valencia St, nothing hits the spot like Beretta's lip-smacking local, seasonal cocktails, made with fresh everything. Drink before and after peak dinner hours, when the small storefront restaurant-and-bar gets packed and deafeningly loud. You might be inclined to come back for cocktail classes.

🍸 SoMa

[TOP CHOICE] BAR AGRICOLE — BAR

Map p330 (📞415-355-9400; www.baragricole. com; 355 11th St; 6-10pm Sun-Wed, 6pm-late Thu-Sat; Ⓜ10th St) Drink your way to a history degree with well-researched cocktails: Bellamy Scotch Sour with egg whites passes the test, but Tequila Fix with lime, pineapple gum and hellfire bitters earns honors. And talk about an overachiever – for its modern wabi-sabi design with natural materials and sleek deck, Agricole won a James Beard Award for restaurant design. Bar bites here are a proper pig-out, including pork pâté with aspic fried farm egg with crispy pork belly.

[TOP CHOICE] BLOODHOUND — BAR

Map p330 (www.bloodhoundsf.com; 1145 Folsom St; ☉4pm-2am; Ⓜ Mission St) The murder of crows painted on the ceiling is definitely an omen: nights at Bloodhound often assume mythic proportions. Vikings would feel at home amid these white walls and antler chandeliers, while bootleggers would ap-

preciate the reclaimed barnwood walls and top-shelf booze served in Mason jars. Shoot pool or chill on leather couches until your jam comes on the jukebox – it won't be long. SF's best food trucks often park out front, and you can bring your eats inside and ask the barkeep to suggest a pairing.

CAT CLUB — CLUB

Map p330 (www.catclubsf.com; 1190 Folsom St; admission $5 after 10pm; ☉9pm-3am Tue-Sun; Ⓜ&🚇Civic Center) You'll never really know your friends until you've seen them belt out A-ha's 'Take on Me' at 1984, Cat Club's Thursday-night retro dance party, where the euphoric bi/straight/gay/undefinable scene is like some surreal John Hughes movie. Come back to belt at karaoke Tuesdays, jump to '90s power pop at Saturday's Club Vogue, and shuffle winsomely at Friday and Sunday goth/new wave nights. The two small rooms get sweaty fast at special theme nights like Bondage-a-Go-Go and queer-stripcore Blowpony; check the online calendar.

STUD — GAY CLUB

(📞415-252-7883; www.studsf.com; 399 9th St; admission $5-8; ☉5pm-3am; 🚇10th St) The Stud has rocked the gay scene since 1966, but has branched out beyond the obvious leather daddies and preppy twinks into whole new categories of gay good times. Check the schedule for rocker-grrrl Monday nights, anything-goes Meow Mix Tuesday drag variety shows, raunchy comedy and karaoke Wednesdays, art/drag dance parties on Fridays and drag-disco-performance-art cabaret whenever hostess DJ MC MF Anna Conda gets the notion. Dress up and talk dirty, and you may never have to buy your own drink.

RN74 — BAR

Map p330 (www.michaelmina.net; 301 Mission St; ☉11:30am-1am Mon-Fri, 5pm-1am Sat, 5-11pm Sun; Ⓜ Mission St, 🚇Embarcadero) Wine collectors and encyclopedia authors must envy the Rajat Parr–designed wine menu at RN74, a succinct yet sweeping volume that somehow manages to include obscure Italian and Austrian entries, long-lost French vintages and California's most definitive account of cult wines. Settle into a couch for the duration of your self-guided wine adventure, and don't skip bar menu food pairings created by star chef Michael Mina.

TOP 5 DANCE VENUES

Couples-dancing has never gone out of style here. SF was at the forefront of the swing revival, and salsa and tango are perennial favorites. The following host dance nights in most genres, from cha-cha and swing to tango and waltz. Admission ranges between $5 and $10; when bands perform, the price rises to about $25. Swing events tend to move venues; check www.oldtimey.net and www.lindylist.com for the latest.

Cafe Cocomo (Map p334; ☑415-410-4012; www.cafecocomo.com; 650 Indiana St; admission $10-15; ☺7pm-midnight Mon, 6pm-midnight Thu, 6pm-2am Sat; Ⓜ16th St) *Muy caliente* (very hot) Cocomo is one of the top salsa clubs nationwide, with big bands keeping the dance floor kicking on Thursday and Saturday nights. To cool down, there's a mezzanine overlooking the dance-floor action and a big patio garden outside. Lessons precede parties; dress suave to pass the doormen (they've got a thing against baseball caps).

Metronome Dance Collective (Map p334; ☑415-871-2462; www.metronomedance collective.com; 1830 17th St; Ⓜ16th St) Always wished you could tango, swing or ballroom dance? This dancing school has one of the largest floors in the city, and top-ranked dance pros teach classes for beginners, advanced dancers and kids plus wedding workshops; see the website for details.

Verdi Club (Map p334; ☑415-861-9199; www.verdiclub.net; 2424 Mariposa St; Ⓜ Bryant St) Thursday-night tango at the Verdi is an eye-popper, with *bandoneón* (free-reed instrument) players and sharply dressed dancers circling the floor. Wear silk or a pencil-thin moustache, and blend right in. Lindy-hoppers take over Tuesday nights. Other nights vary; check the website.

Dance Mission (Map p334; www.dancemission.com; 3316 24th St; Ⓡ24th St Mission) Step out and find your niche at this Mission institution, featuring contact improv, dance jams and classes. The 140-seat theater showcases women performers, dance troupes and choreographers.

Roccapulco Supper Club (Map p334; www.roccapulco.com; 3140 Mission St; admission $10-15; ☺8pm-2am; Ⓡ24th St Mission) Get your salsa, rumba and *bachata* (Dominican dance) on at this high-ceilinged, stadium-sized Latin venue that books sensational touring acts like El Grupo Niche. This is a straight bar, ripe with cologne and hormones; single women new to the scene may feel more comfortable in a group.

ENDUP　　　　　　　　　　GAY CLUB

Map p330 (www.theendup.com; 401 6th St; admission $5-20; ☺10pm-4am Mon-Thu, 11pm-11am Fri, 10pm Sat-4am Mon; Ⓜ Bryant St) Anyone left on the streets of San Francisco after 2am on weekends is subject to the magnetic force of the EndUp's marathon dance sessions. It's the only club with a 24-hour license and though straight people do come here, it remains best known for its gay Sunday tea dances, in full force since 1973. Regulars arrive in time for popular reggae and 'Ghettodisco' sets on Saturdays (check the web) and bring a change of clothes for work Monday. Forget the Golden Gate Bridge: once you EndUp watching the sunrise over the freeway ramp here, you've officially arrived in SF.

🖋 **TERROIR NATURAL WINE MERCHANT**　　　　　　　BAR

Map p330 (www.terroirsf.com; 1116 Folsom St; ☺10pm-2am Tue-Sat; Ⓜ&Ⓡ Civic Center) Whether you're drinking red or white, your wine is green here – Terroir specializes in natural-process and biodynamic wines made from organic grapes, with impressive lists from key producers in France and Italy. Quality doesn't come cheap – expect to pay $10 to $16 a glass – but you can get bargain French takeaway from the **Spencer on the Go** food truck often parked out front and enjoy it with your wine.

SHINE　　　　　　　　　BAR, CLUB

Map p330 (www.shinesf.com; 1337 Mission St; admission free-$10; ☺9pm-2am Wed-Sat; Ⓜ Van Ness) Underground house parties erupt at tiny, offbeat Shine, decorated with disco balls and gold fabric wall panels that look like someone's Burning Man craft project. The DJs are hype for such a small bar, and when the beats heat up, barstools get shoved aside and the whole place becomes a dance floor; check the online calendar. Dig the photo booth, and the tricky bathroom mirror – people primping in the mirror have no idea anyone using the facilities can watch them rub lipstick off their teeth with a finger.

111 MINNA
BAR, CLUB

Map p330 (www.111minnagallery.com; 111 Minna St; admission free-$15; M&RMontgomery St) A superhero here to rescue the staid Downtown scene, 111 Minna is a street-wise art gallery by day (open from noon to 5pm Wednesday to Saturday) that transforms into a happening lounge space and club by night (evening hours vary). After-work events are networky but usually interesting – one recent week featured green professional happy hours, Japanime fan clubs and a gay teen support group fundraiser – until 9pm, when '90s and '80s dance parties take the back room by storm. Don't miss monthly free Sketch Tuesdays, when artists make work for sale to the audience.

HARLOT
CLUB

Map p330 (www.harlotsf.com; 46 Minna St; admission free-$20; 5pm-2am Wed-Fri, 9pm-2am Sat; M&RMontgomery St) Back when SoMa was the stomping ground of sailors, alleys were named for working girls, and Harlot pays them homage. Vampire bordello is the vibe here, with intense red lighting, velvet curtains revealing exposed-brick walls and table-sized photos of pinups wearing nothing but boa constrictors (watch where you put down that cocktail). Before 9pm it's a lounge, but after that the killer sound system pumps – especially with house on Thursdays, indie-rock on Wednesdays and monthly women-only Fem Bar parties. Weekends get suburban, but everyone cuts loose, so who cares? Dress funky to get past the doormen.

HOUSE OF SHIELDS
BAR

Map p330 (39 New Montgomery St; 2pm-2am Mon-Fri, 7pm-2am Sat; M&RMontgomery St) Flash back 100 years at this recently restored mahogany bar, with original c 1908 chandeliers hanging from high ceilings and old-fashioned cocktails without the frippery. This is the one bar in SF that slumming Nob Hill socialites and Downtown

bike messengers can agree on – especially after a few $5 cocktails in dimly lit corners.

DNA LOUNGE
NIGHTCLUB

Map p330 (www.dnalounge.com; 375 11th St; admission $3-25; 9:30pm-3am Fri & Sat, other nights vary; MMarket St) One of SF's last mega clubs hosts live bands and big-name DJs, with two floors of late-night dance action just seedy enough to be interesting (the cops keep trying and failing to shut this rowdy joint down). Second-and-fourth Saturdays are Bootie, the kick-ass original mash-up party (now franchised worldwide); Monday's 18-and-over night is the goth dance party called (of course) Death Guild with free tea service. Choose your night from the website – events ranging from seriously silly PopRocks to major drag king competitions – and dress the part. Early arrivals may hear crickets.

CITY BEER STORE & TASTING ROOM
BAR

Map p330 (www.citybeerstore.com; 1168 Folsom St; noon-10pm Tue-Sat, to 6pm Sun; MCivic Center) Sample exceptional local and Belgian microbrewed beer from the 300-brew menu (6oz to 22oz, depending how thirsty you are) at SF's top beer store. Create your own tastings of stouts or red ales, or pick a point on the globe at random and drink your way home via unknown artisan brews. Line your stomach with cheese and salami plates, and assemble your own six-pack to go. Check the website for bottle release parties and tapping events.

TEMPLE
NIGHTCLUB

Map p330 (www.templesf.com; 540 Howard St; admission $20; 10pm-4am Thu-Sun; M&RMontgomery St) The city's greenest club is an *izakaya* (bar snack) and sustainably sourced sushi bar before 10pm, when it turns into a glowing LED-lit nightclub serving drinks in biodegradable cups. Buddha presides over the sleek, all-white upstairs room with slick stone floors; downstairs are two smaller rooms with midsized dance floors that harness the energy of stomping feet to generate electricity. DJs spin the gamut from dub to hip-hop to techno; Fridays are consistently good for house, and it's usually $5 before 11pm if you're on the guest list. Dress like you mean it.

BUTTER
BAR

Map p330 (www.smoothasbutter.com; 354 11th St; 6pm-2am Thu-Sat, 8pm-2am Sun; M11th St) Lowbrow and loving it: everyone's chasing Tang cocktails with PBR and wailing to rock anthems here, while across the street at VIP clubs they're still politely waiting for the good times to start. You'll never pay $10 for a drink at this tiny, happening bar, leaving plenty of cash for Tater Tots, mini corn dogs and deep-fried Twinkies...dude, if you want nutrition, what're you doing in a bar called Butter? Check the website for events with even cheaper drinks, including infamous Trailer Trash Thursdays and genuinely sloppy Sunday karaoke.

WATERBAR
BAR

Map p330 (www.waterbarsf.com; 399 The Embarcadero; ⊘11:30am-9:30pm Sun-Mon, to 10pm Tue-Sat; MℝEmbarcadero) The giant glass column aquariums and picture-window vistas of the Bay Bridge at Waterbar are SF's surest way to impress a date over drinks. Leave the dining room to Silicon Valley strivers trying hard to impress investors, and make a beeline for the oval bar, where seating is closer, plates and prices are smaller, and oysters are piled temptingly around ice sculptures. There's a chorus of crack, pop and fizz as orders arrive: raw local Tomales Bay mollusks with shallot/wine mignonette and Napa bubbly by the glass.

CLUB SIX
CLUB

Map p330 (☏415-863-1221, 415-531-6593; www.clubsix1.com; 60 6th St; admission $5-15; ⊘7pm-midnight Mon, 9pm-2am Tue-Thu, to 4am Fri & Sat; MMarket St, ℝPowell St) Smack on Skid Row, but don't be daunted: inside Club Six defines casual cool, with lumpy sofas, worn hardwood floors and easy beats. Weekly parties cover hip-hop, house, world and dancehall reggae, drawing a mixed crowd with an up-for-anything attitude. Visit the street-level lounge when there's live music or dive into the thick of it on the basement dance floor.

1015 FOLSOM
NIGHTCLUB

Map p330 (www.1015.com; 1015 Folsom St; admission $10-20; ⊘10pm-2am Thu-Sat; MMission St) One of the city's biggest clubs, 'Ten-Fifteen' has been eclipsed by Temple and Ruby Skye but still draws huge postcollegiate crowds for Friday house DJ headliners and some serious dancers for Saturday Pura Latin nights. The main hall is enormous, and four other dance floors mean you could lose your posse if you're momentarily entranced by videos projected onto the 400ft water wall. If you're a sound purist, 1015's basement has one of the best systems in the city.

Be prepared for a pat-down before you enter; there's a serious no-drugs (or weapons) policy. Usually free before 10:15pm, though drinks run $10 to $15; see the calendar for events in the main hall and adjacent room at 103 Harriet. Public transit is hard to come by, and this is a sketchy area, so plan to drive or take taxis.

83 PROOF
BAR

Map p330 (www.83proof.com; 83 1st St; ⊘2pm-midnight Mon & Tue, 2pm-2am Wed-Fri, 8pm-2am Sat; MℝMontgomery St) On average weeknights when the rest of Downtown is dead, the piano player here has to bang on the keys to be heard over the buzzing crowd and flirting over basil gimlets on the mezzanine. High ceilings make room for five shelves of top-shelf spirits behind the bar, so trust your bartender to make a mean cucumber martini that won't hurt at work tomorrow.

MIGHTY
CLUB

Map p334 (www.mighty119.com; 119 Utah St; admission $10-20; ⊘10pm-4am Thu-Sat; M16th St) In a former warehouse sequestered in a no-man's land between SoMa, the Mission and Potrero Hill, Mighty packs a wallop with its awesome sound system, underground dance music, urban vibe, graffiti-esque art and cool local crowd who don't fuss about dress codes. Weekend DJs (occasionally big names) veer towards electronic, dance-house and hip-hop; on other nights, events vary wildly from geek-out SF Next Tech meet-ups and nonprofit benefit literary readings to gay Mustache Parties (check website).

SIGHTGLASS COFFEE
CAFE

Map p330 (www.sightglasscoffee.com; 270 7th St St; ⊘7am-6pm Mon-Sat, 8am-6pm Sun; ℝCivic Center) San Francisco's newest cult coffee is roasted in a SoMa warehouse – and if you're in the neighborhood, you won't need to be told where to find it. Follow the wafting aromas of the signature Owl's Howl Espresso to a cappuccino, and sample the family-grown, high-end 100% bourbon-shrub coffee.

DADA
BAR

Map p330 (www.dadasf.com; 86 2nd St; ⊘4pm-2am Mon-Wed, 3pm-2am Thu & Fri, 8pm-2am Sat; MℝMontgomery) Happy hour flavored martinis for $5 to $7 until 9pm and rotating local art shows take the commercial edge off Downtown, and restore the art-freak factor to SoMa. The high ceilings can make the scene loud when the DJ gets going, but that doesn't stop impassioned debates about the future of photography.

LONE STAR SALOON
GAY BAR

Map p330 (☑415-863-9999; www.lonestarsaloon.com; 1354 Harrison St; ☺noon-2am; Ⓜ Harrison St) Like bears to a honeycomb, big guys with fur are drawn to Lone Star. There's a huge back patio with a friendly bar, a highly competitive pool table, and so you don't have to wait, a trough urinal – plus a lone outhouse stall for shy cubs. There's no women's bathroom, because this is a guys' scene, with the rare exception of Buffy the Vampire Slayer fanboy nights. Busiest Thursday through Sunday.

☆ ENTERTAINMENT

☆ The Mission

TOP CHOICE ROXIE CINEMA
CINEMA

Map p334 (☑415-863-1087; www.roxie.com; 3117 16th St; admission $6-10; Ⓜ&Ⓡ16th St Mission) A little neighborhood nonprofit cinema with major international clout for helping distrib-

ute and launch indie films Stateside, and for showing controversial films and documentaries banned elsewhere. Film buffs should monitor this calendar, because tickets to film festival premieres, rare revivals and the raucous annual Oscars telecast sell out fast – but if the main show is sold out, check out documentaries in the teensy Little Roxy next door instead. No ads and personal introductions to every film.

TOP CHOICE OBERLIN DANCE COLLECTIVE
DANCE

Map p334 (ODC; ☑415-863-9834; www.odctheater.org; 3153 17th St; Ⓡ16th St Mission) For nearly 40 years, ODC has been redefining dance with risky, raw performances and the sheer joy of movement. ODC's season runs from September to December, and its stage presents year-round shows featuring local and international artists. Its Dance Commons is a hub and hangout for the dance community and offers 200 classes a week; all ages and all levels are welcome.

TOP CHOICE INTERSECTION FOR THE ARTS
THEATER

Map p334 (☑415-626-2787; www.theintersection.org; 446 Valencia St; admission $5-20; Ⓜ&Ⓡ16th St Mission) Watch this nonprofit

---

GAY & READY TO PLAY: SOMA SEX CLUBS

Powerhouse (Map p330; www.powerhouse-sf.com; 1347 Folsom St; ☺4pm-2am; Ⓜ10th St) Thursdays through Sundays are best at Powerhouse, an almost-rough-trade SoMa bar for leathermen, shirtless gym queens and the occasional porn star. Draft beer is cheap, and specials keep the crowd loose. Smokers grope on the (too-smoky) back patio, while oddballs lurk in the corners. Don't bring girls.

Blow Buddies (Map p330; ☑415-777-4323; www.blowbuddies.com; 933 Harrison St; admission $12, plus $8 membership fee; ☺Thu-Sun; Ⓜ5th St) The original owner was a Disney fetishist and set out to recreate, with exacting detail, Disneyland-like attractions, with mazes and specialty-fetish rooms spread over 6000 sq ft of indoor-outdoor warehouse space. It's still the best sex club in town, and hot water, soap and mouthwash are supplied. Sundays around 8pm are best, but other nights can be positively dreary: count coats in the coat-check through the barred window by the entrance to make sure there are at least 30 (call about the Wednesday night fetish parties). Note: no cologne, or they won't let you in.

Kok Bar (Map p330; www.kokbarsf.com; 1225 Folsom St; ☺6pm-2am Mon-Thu, 4pm-2am Fri & Sat; Ⓜ10th St) Formerly known as Chaps, this bar still delivers on its 1970s reputation for leather, kink and cruising, plus pool tables and pinball for slow nights and jock straps for sale for the overdressed. Best between 9pm (look for happy hour specials) and midnight, Thursday to Saturday, after which everyone goes to Powerhouse.

Hole in the Wall (Map p330; www.holeinthewallsaloon.com; 1369 Folsom St; ☺noon-2am; Ⓜ10th St) When the Hole moved here, it lost its legendary filthiness because it would otherwise have lost its license. It still has the best erotic posters in SF – not to mention a stained-glass window – and remains ground zero for sexy weirdos swinging from chains dangling over the bar.

MISSION THEATERS ON A MISSION

Marsh (Map p334; ☑415-826-5750; www.themarsh.org; 1062 Valencia St; tickets $15-35; Ⓜ&Ⓡ24th St Mission) Choose your seat wisely: you may spend the evening on the edge of it. With one-acts and one-off stagings of works-in-progress that involve the audience in the creative process, this is San Francisco experimental theater at its most exciting. A sliding-scale pricing structure allows everyone to participate, and a few reserved seats are sometimes available ($50 per ticket). Check the website for show schedules, workshops and work-in-progress readings.

Jewish Theater (Map p334; ☑415-522-0786; www.tjt-sf.org; 470 Florida St; tickets free-$35; Ⓜ16th St) Since 1978 this theater has presented original works focusing on Jewish and American cultural issues, from comedies capturing vaudeville's influence on hip-hop to a gutsy one-man show performing a dozen different voices from the Israeli–Palestinian conflict. Borscht Belt comedy, music, storytelling, and serious and comic drama all share the company's main stage in the Mission.

Brava Theater (Map p334; ☑415-641-7657; www.brava.org; 2781 24th St; Ⓜ24th St) Brava's been producing women-run theater for more than 20 years, hosting acts from comedian Sandra Bernhardt to V-day monologist Eve Ensler, and it's the nation's only company with a mission to produce original works by women of color and lesbians. Nodding to the neighborhood's Mexican heritage, Brava posts hand-painted billboards like the kind you'd see in old Mexico – check out the lobby displays.

arts space – since its founding in 1965, riveting and entirely unforeseen events have unfolded at Intersection. The tiny downstairs theater sizzles with hot jazz drawn from Latin, Asian and African American traditions, in between acclaimed theater premieres of adapted works by Pulitzer Prize–winner Junot Diaz, National Book Award–winner Denis Johnson and American Book Award–winning poet Jessica Hagedorn. Meanwhile in the upstairs gallery, tears are shed, arguments raised and careers launched by provocative art installations that seek to transform the space and the community along with it. If you arrive between shows, check out the literary series, workshops and open rehearsals; check the website for details.

ELBO ROOM
LIVE MUSIC

Map p334 (☑415-552-7788; www.elbo.com; 647 Valencia St; admission $5-15; ☺5pm-2am; Ⓜ&Ⓡ16th St Mission) Funny name, because there isn't much to speak of upstairs on show nights with crowd-favorite funk, dancehall dub DJs and offbeat indie bands like Uni and Her Ukelele. Come any night for $2 pints from 5pm to 9pm at the chilled downstairs bar (admission free).

RED POPPY ART HOUSE
THEATER

Map p334 (☑415-826-2402; www.redpoppyart house.org; 2698 Folsom St; Ⓡ24th St Mission) Like walking into an underground house

party where the guests have wildly varied skill sets: Ethiopian jazz vocals, performance poetry set to digital photographs, South Indian classical saxophone, wall-drawing with a conductor's baton. Check the event and workshop lineup on the website; admission is usually by sliding scale donation (typically $5 to $15). Otherwise, this corner storefront is open to passersby on Saturday afternoons and whenever someone's working on a project.

SUB-MISSION
LIVE MUSIC

Map p334 (☑415-255-7227; www.sf-submission. com; 2183 Mission St; shows $5-13; ☺7pm-late Fri & Sat; Ⓡ24th St Mission) Punk comes roaring out from the underground at SUB-Mission, with local Latin ska punk inflaming weeknights and visiting bands from LA to Canada on weekends leaving anyone within earshot with a nasty itch for more. Everything you'd expect from an underground Mission punk club is here: anarchic sets, unlockable bathrooms, surly bartenders and cheap, tasty tacos to cure whatever's wrong with your punk-ass.

MAKE-OUT ROOM
LIVE MUSIC

Map p334 (☑415-647-2888; www.makeoutroom. com; 3225 22nd St; cover free-$10; ☺6pm-2am; Ⓜ&Ⓡ24th St Mission) Velvet curtains and round booths help you settle in for the evening's entertainment, which ranges from punk-rock fiddle to '80s one-hit-wonder DJ

THE MISSION, SOMA & POTRERO HILL ENTERTAINMENT

WORTH A DETOUR

BOTTOM OF THE HILL

Quite literally at the bottom of Potrero Hill, **Bottom of the Hill** (Map p334; ☎415-621-4455; www.bottomofthehill.com; 1233 17th St; admission $5-12; ☺shows begin 9-10pm Tue-Sat; Ⓜ16th St) is definitely out of the way but always top of the list for seeing fun local bands, from notable alt-rockers like Deerhoof to newcomers worth checking out by name alone (Yesway, Stripmall Architecture, Excuses for Skipping). The big smokers patio is ruled by a cat that enjoys music more than people – totally punk rock. Anchor Steam on tap, but it's cash-only bar; check the website for lineups.

mash-ups and the painfully funny Mortified readings, when the power of margaritas convinces grown men to read aloud from their own teenage journals. Booze is a bargain, but the bar is cash-only.

AMNESIA
LIVE MUSIC

Map p334 (☎415-970-0012; www.amnesiathebar.com; 853 Valencia St; admission free-$10; ☺5:30pm-2am; Ⓜ Valencia St, Ⓡ16th St Mission) A closet-sized Boho dive with outsized swagger, serving cold Belgian beer and red-hot jazz to ragtag hipsters. Just to keep the crowds guessing, musical acts range from bluegrass to gypsy punk, plus Tuesday open mics, random readings and cinema shorts; check the calendar or just go with the flow.

LITTLE BAOBAB
LIVE MUSIC

Map p334 (☎415-643-3558; www.bissapbaobab.com; 3388 19th St; ☺6pm-2am Mon-Sat; Ⓜ18th St) A Senegalese restaurant early in the evening, Baobab brings on the DJ or live act around 9pm – and before you can say 'tamarind margarita,' tables are getting shoved out of the way to make more room on the dance floor. Reggae, salsa, Afrobeat and cameo appearances by Michael Franti get the Mission in a universal groove.

☆ SoMa

SLIM'S
LIVE MUSIC

Map p330 (☎415-255-0333; www.slims-sf.com; 333 11th St; tickets $11-28; ☺5pm-2am; Ⓜ Market St) Guaranteed good times by Gogol Bordello, Tenacious D, the Expendables and AC/DShe (a hard-rocking female tribute band) fit the bill at this midsized club owned by R&B star Boz Skaggs – but at any moment, legends like Prince and Elvis Costello might show up to play sets unannounced. Shows are all ages, though shorties may have a hard time seeing once the floor starts

bouncing. Come early to score burgers and fries with balcony seating; credit cards accepted, with $20 minimum.

MEZZANINE
LIVE MUSIC

Map p330 (☎415-625-8880; www.mezzaninesf.com; 444 Jessie St; admission $10-40; Ⓜ Market St, Ⓡ Powell St) Big nights come with bragging rights at the Mezzanine, with the best sound system in SF bouncing off the brick walls and crowds hyped for breakthrough hip-hop and R&B shows by Wyclef Jean, Quest Love, Method Man, Nas and Snoop Dogg. Mezzanine also hosts throwback new-wave nights and books classic alt bands like the Dandy Warhols and Psychedelic Furs; check the calendar.

YERBA BUENA CENTER FOR THE ARTS
LIVE MUSIC

Map p330 (YBCA; ☎415-978-2787; www.ybca.org; 700 Howard St; tickets free-$35; Ⓜ&Ⓡ Powell St) Rock stars would be jealous of art stars at YBCA openings, which draw overflow crowds of impeccably hip art groupies coat-checking their skateboards and shaggy faux furs to see live hip-hop by Mos Def, 1960s smut film festivals, spontaneous light shows set to the music of unrehearsed bands, and Vik Muniz' documentary on making art from trash. Most touring dance and jazz companies perform at YBCA's main theater (across the sidewalk from the gallery).

ASIASF
NIGHTCLUB

Map p330 (☎415-255-2742; www.asiasf.com; 201 9th St; per person from $35; ☺7-11pm Wed & Thu, 7pm-2am Fri, 5pm-2am Sat, 7-10pm Sun, reservation line 1-8pm; Ⓜ&Ⓡ Civic Center) First ladies of the world, look out: these dazzling Asian ladies can out-hostess you in half the time and less than half the clothes. Cocktails and Asian-inspired dishes are served with a tall order of sass and one little secret: your servers are drag stars. Every hour, the ladies get up on the red bar and work it like a runway on fire. The house choreographer has worked with Michael and Janet Jackson, so when the pop starts to pound, it's look out, Lady Gaga. Teasing is all in good fun, so don't take it seriously if (OK, when) your server flirts with your date or threatens to steal your shoes. Gaggles of girlfriends squeal and blushing straight businessmen play along, but once the inspiration and drinks kick in, everyone mixes it up on the downstairs dance floor. The three-course 'Menage à Trois Menu' runs $39, cocktails around $10 and, honey, those tips are well earned.

HOTEL UTAH SALOON   LIVE MUSIC
Map p330 (☑415-546-6300; www.hotelutah. com; 500 4th St; shows $5-10; ☺11:30am-2am Mon-Fri, 2pm-2am Sat & Sun; Ⓜ4th St) The ground-floor bar of this Victorian hotel became ground zero of the underground scene in the '70s, when upstarts Whoopi Goldberg and Robin Williams took the stage – now it's a sure bet for Monday Night Open Mics, indie-label debuts and local favorites like Riot Earp, Saucy Monkey and the Dazzling Strangers. Back in the '50s the bartender graciously served Beats, grifters and Marilyn Monroe, but snipped the ties of businessmen when they leaned across the bar; now you can wear whatever,

as long as you're buying, but there's a $20 credit card minimum.

BRAINWASH   LIVE MUSIC
Map p330 (☑415-861-3663; www.brainwash. com; 1122 Folsom St; ☺7am-10pm Mon-Thu, 7am-11pm Fri & Sat, 8am-10pm Sun; ☎; Ⓜ Civic Center) The barfly's eternal dilemma between going out and doing laundry is finally solved, right here in this bar-cafe with live music most nights and comedy on Thursdays. Last wash is at 8:30pm and the kitchen closes at 9pm, so plan your presoaking and order of Wash Load Nachos accordingly.

AMC LOEWS METREON 16   CINEMA
Map p330 (☑415-369-6201; www.amc theatres.com; 101 4th St; adult/child $11.50/8.50; Ⓜ&Ⓡ Powell St) Housed in a mega-entertainment complex, the 16-screen Metreon has comfortable reclining stadium seats with clear views of digital projection screens, plus 3D screenings ($3 extra per ticket) and an IMAX theater ($6 extra per ticket, or $7 for 3D screenings). The cinema occupies the top floor of a notoriously failed mall complex, but if a Target megastore moves in as planned, the food court options downstairs should expand.

DANCE AT YERBA BUENA CENTER FOR THE ARTS

Gallery shows with overflow opening crowds create scenes at Yerba Buena Center for the Arts, but the biggest, boldest moves in town are made right across the sidewalk. The theater main stage at Yerba Buena hosts the annual **Ethnic Dance Festival** (www.sfethnicdancefestival.org) and the regular season of **Liss Fain Dance** (www. lissfaindance.org), San Francisco's champions of muscular modern movement. Better yet, you never have to wait long for an encore, because three other major SF dance companies perform their home seasons on this stage.

Alonzo King's Lines Ballet (☑415-863-3040; www.linesballet.org) Long, lean dancers perform complicated, angular movements that showcase their impeccable technical skills. Recent shows have included a knockout kung-fu-meets-ballet joint work with Shaolin monks, which explored a synthesis of Eastern and Western forms, pairing dance with martial arts. King also offers classes and workshops.

Smuin Ballet (☑415-495-2234; www.smuinballet.org) Smuin riled the dance world in 2009 when it dubbed its work 'Ballet, but Entertaining' – as if the form wasn't – but the tag line captures the populist spirit of this long-running dance company. Though balletic in form, the works are by turns wacky and humorous, poignant and touching, and always have mass appeal – ideal for those who like dance performances but find the whole idea of interpretive dance a tad precious.

Joe Goode Performance Group (☑415-561-6565; www.joegoode.org) An early adaptor of narrative performance art into dance, maverick Joe Goode has an international reputation and a rigorous national touring schedule, yet regularly graces the Yerba Buena stage. His dancers are phenomenal exponents of their craft – and they're not kept silent: in Joe Goode works, the dancers use their voices as well as their bodies.

THE MISSION, SOMA & POTRERO HILL ENTERTAINMENT

🛍 SHOPPING

🛍 The Mission

TOP CHOICE ADOBE BOOKS & BACKROOM GALLERY
BOOKSTORE, ART

Map p334 (www.adobebooksbackroomgallery. blogspot.com; 3166 16th St; ⊙11am-midnight; Ⓜ&Ⓡ16th St Mission) Come here for every book you never knew you needed used and cheap, plus zine launch parties, poetry readings and art openings. To get to the Backroom gallery, first you have to navigate the obstacle course of sofas, cats, art books and German philosophy. But it's worth it: artists who debuted here have gone on to success at international art fairs and Whitney Biennials.

TOP CHOICE GRAVEL & GOLD
HOUSEWARES, GIFTS

Map p334 (www.gravelandgold.com; 3266 21st St; ⊙noon-7pm Tue-Sat, noon-5pm Sun; Ⓜ&Ⓡ24th St Mission) Get in touch with your roots and back to the land, without ever leaving sight of a Mission sidewalk. Gravel and Gold celebrates the 1960s to '70s hippie homesteader movement with every fiber of its being and its hand-dyed smocked dresses – which you can try on among psychedelic murals behind a patched curtain, of course. The proud purveyor of rare vintage artifacts like silkscreened Osborne Woods peace postcards and limited-edition books on DIY Mendocino shingle-shack architecture, Gravel and Gold also answers to a higher California calling: getting a whole new generation excited about the organic connections between art and nature.

NEEDLES & PENS
GIFTS, BOOKS

Map p334 (www.needles-pens.com; 3253 16th St; ⊙noon-7pm; Ⓜ&Ⓡ16th St Mission) Do it yourself or DIY trying: this scrappy zine/craft/how-to/art gallery delivers the inspiration to create your own magazines, rehabbed T-shirts or album covers. Nab Jay Howell's *Punks Git Cut* comic illustrating failed fighting words, Nigel Peake's pen-and-ink aerial views of patchworked farmland, and alphabet buttons to pin your own credo onto a handmade messenger bag.

SCRAP (SCROUNGERS' CENTER FOR RE-USABLE ART PARTS)
DIY

Map p334 (www.scrap-sf.org; 801 Toland St; ⊙9am-5pm Mon-Sat; Ⓜ Totland St) Renew, recycle and rediscover your creativity with postindustrial salvage arts and crafts from SCRAP – you'd be shocked what perfectly good raw materials San Francisco throws out. Take a workshop at SCRAP for inspiration, and make your very own recycled glass mosaic, necklace from zippers or Joseph Cornell–inspired diorama. Classes are held two Saturdays a month (see website for locations); the entrance to SCRAP is at the confluence of Hwy 101 and Hwy 280.

MISSION SKATEBOARDS
CLOTHING, ACCESSORIES

Map p334 (www.missionsk8boards.com; 3045 24th St; ⊙11am-7pm; Ⓜ&Ⓡ24th St Mission) Street creds come easy with locally designed Mission decks, custom tees to kickflip over and cult shoes at this shop owned by SF street-skate legend Scot Thompson. This shop is handy to Potrero del Sol/La Raza Skatepark (p161), and for newbies too cool for kneepads, SF General. Check the website for events, including street races and documentary premieres.

AQUARIUS RECORDS
MUSIC STORE

Map p334 (www.aquariusrecords.org; 1055 Valencia St; ⊙10am-9pm Mon-Wed, to 10pm Thu-Sun; ⓂValencia St, Ⓡ16th St Mission) When pop seems played out, this is the dawning of the age of Aquarius Records, featuring Armenian blues, Oakland warehouse-party bands and rare Japanese releases. Recent staff favorites include *Sounds of North American Frogs*, groovy '60 Brazilian tropicalia from Os Mutantes, woozy folk from New Zealand's Torlesse Super Group and SF's own Prizehog, enthusiastically described as 'dirgey doom pop slowcore!'

NOOWORKS
CLOTHING

Map p334 (www.nooworks.com; 395 Valencia St; ⊙11am-7pm Sat, to 5pm Sun & Mon; Ⓜ&Ⓡ16th St Mission) Artist-designed graphic prints make Nooworks the cream of the Mission's new crop of designers, with easy-going cotton minis getting a Mission edge with a 1930s Mayan print. Surreal men's tees featuring a bewigged Bach cat and buttery-soft teal leather hobo bags are good to go to any gallery.

COMMUNITY THRIFT
CLOTHING, ACCESSORIES

Map p334 (www.communitythriftsf.org; 623 Valencia St; ⊙10am-6:30pm; ⓂValencia St, Ⓡ16th St Mission) When local collectors and retailers have too much of a good thing, they donate it to Community Thrift, where proceeds go to community organizations –

all the more reason to gloat over your $5 totem-pole teacup, $12 vintage smock dress and that $35 art deco cigar humidor you found out back by the furniture. Donate your castoffs (until 5pm daily) and show some love to the Community.

BLACK & BLUE TATTOO BODY ART

Map p334 (www.blackandbluetattoo.com; 381 Guerrero St; ☺noon-7pm; M&R16th St Mission) This women-owned tattoo parlor gets it in ink with designs that range from graphic octopus-tentacle armbands to shoulder-to-shoulder spans of the Golden Gate Bridge. Check out the artists' work at the shop or online first for ideas, then book a consultation with the artist whose work interests you. Once you've talked over the design, you can book your tattoo – you'll need to show up sober, well-fed and clear-headed for your transformation.

VOYAGER GIFTS, ACCESSORIES

Map p334 (www.thevoyagershop.com; 365 Valencia St; ☺noon-7pm Sun-Fri, to 10pm Fri & Sat; M&R16th St Mission) Postapocalyptic art-school surf-shack is the general vibe at this art-installation storefront gallery. The communal love-child of Revolver (p187) and Mollusk (p203) plus sundry Mission bookstores and galleries, items for sale range from '70s-stye rough leather belts and cultish Dutch Scotch and Soda jeans to surfboards and some 5000 art books.

DEMA CLOTHING, ACCESSORIES

Map p334 (www.godemago.com; 1038 Valencia St; ☺11am-7pm Mon-Fri, noon-7pm Sat, noon-6pm Sun; M&R24th St Mission) BART from Downtown lunches to Mission art openings in vintage-inspired chic by San Francisco's own Dema Grimm. House specialties are flattering bias-cut dresses and floaty silk blouses in original prints, with buttons that look like gumdrops. Like any indie designer, Dema's not dirt cheap, but you get what you pay for here in squealed compliments; check bins and sales racks for deals up to 80% off.

MISSION STATEMENT CLOTHING, ACCESSORIES

Map p334 (www.missionstatementsf.com; 3458 18th St; ☺noon-7pm Wed-Mon; M18th St, R16th St Mission) Finally: locally designed, fashion-forward clothing and accessories that keep real bodies and real budgets in mind. Sofie Ølgaard's silk mini-dresses make anyone look leggy, Vanessa Gade's circle-chain necklaces bring a touch of infinity to low neck-

lines, and Estrella Tadao's reconstructed '70s men's suit jackets with zip-up lapels fend off SF fog. The counter staff are designers, so if that yellow wrap cardigan doesn't fit just so, they'll get one made to order for you.

GOOD VIBRATIONS CLOTHING, ACCESSORIES

Map p334 (☎415-522-5460; www.goodvibes.com; 603 Valencia St; ☺10am-9pm Sun-Thu, to 11pm Fri & Sat; M&R16th St Mission) 'Wait, I'm supposed to put that where?' The understanding salespeople in this worker-owned cooperative are used to giving rather, um, explicit instructions, so don't hesitate to ask. Margaret Cho is on the board, so you know they're not shy here. Check out the antique vibrators in the museum display by the door, and imagine getting up close and personal with the one that looks like a floor waxer – then thank your stars for modern technology.

ACCIDENT & ARTIFACT GIFTS, ACCESSORIES

Map p334 (www.accidentandartifact.com; 381 Valencia St; ☺noon-6pm Thu-Sun; M&R16th St Mission) A most curious curiosity shop, even by Mission standards. Decorative dried fungi and redwood burls make regular appearances on the scavenged wood displays alongside vintage Okinawan indigo textiles and artfully redrawn topographical maps. Better curation than most galleries, and priced accordingly.

CANDYSTORE COLLECTIVE CLOTHING, ACCESSORIES

Map p334 (www.candystorecollective.com; 3153 16th St; ☺noon-7pm Mon-Sat, to 6pm Sun; M&R16th St Mission) Jars of Pixie Stix and tasty little numbers for men and women by American indie designers are the pride of this greenery-sprouting storefront. Peppermint mini-dresses printed with rampaging zoo animals stand out in Mission bar crowds, while black organic-cotton duffle coats keep graffiti artists warm by night. Don't miss intoxicating Yosh perfumes, hippo-shaped lockets, trunk shows and 70%-off sales bins.

FABRIC8 CLOTHING, ACCESSORIES

Map p334 (www.fabric8.com; 3318 22nd St; ☺11am-7pm Sat-Mon, 1-7pm Tue-Thu, 11am-9pm Fri; M&R24th St Mission) Pull into this Astro-turfed-garage-turned-indie-design-boutique for a Mission-style overhaul. Rings sprout tiny volcanic geodes and Muni buses find their wings on T-shirts, while soft-sculpture mushrooms just want to make friends. Don't miss the bathtub fish tank, the backyard sculpture gallery or gallery openings with Mission food carts.

SUNHEE MOON
CLOTHING, ACCESSORIES

Map p334 (www.sunheemoon.com; 3167 16th St; ⊙noon-7pm Mon-Fri, to 6pm Sat & Sun; Ⓜ&Ⓡ16th St Mission) Minding your girlish figure so you don't have to, Sunhee Moon creates svelte shirtdresses and flattering fern-print tunics to make those curves work for you. You'll never need to wait for a sale, since there's always a rack with 20% to 50% off – yet another excuse to splurge on locally designed, free-form hoop earrings.

PAXTON GATE
GIFTS

Map p334 (www.paxton-gate.com; 824 Valencia St; ⊙11am-7pm; ⓂValencia St, Ⓡ16th St Mission) Salvador Dalí probably would've shopped here for all his taxidermy and gardening needs. What with puppets made with animal skulls, terrariums sprouting from lab specimen jars and teddy bear heads mounted like hunting trophies, this place is beyond surreal. The new kids' shop down the street (766 Valencia St) maximizes playtime with volcano-making kits, sea-monster mobiles and solar-powered dollhouses.

ROOM 4
CLOTHING, ACCESSORIES

Map p334 (☎415-647-2764; www.room4.com; 904 Valencia St; ⊙1-7pm Mon-Fri, noon-7pm Sat, noon-5pm Sun; ⓂMission St, Ⓡ16th St Mission) Spare yourself years of arduous thrifting, and head to this tiny treasure-box boutique for the good stuff: trippy green and orange swirled enamel dishes; free-form driftwood lamps; creepy portraits of big-eyed toddlers in the rain; and Pendleton plaid wool shirts and brass trucker belt buckles with unisex appeal.

🏠 SoMa

SFMOMA MUSEUM STORE
BOOKS, GIFTS

Map p330 (www.sfmoma.org/museumstore; 151 3rd St; ⊙10am-6:30pm Mon-Wed & Fri-Sun, to 9:30pm Thu; ⓂMarket St, Montgomery St, ⓡMontgomery St) Design fetishists may have to be pried away from the glass shelves and display cases, which brim with cereal bowls that look like spilt milk, Pantone color-swatch espresso cups and watches with a face to match Mario Botta's black-and-white SFMOMA facade. Contemporary art books will keep aspiring collectors absorbed for hours, and kids will be entranced

by William Wegman's video of dogs spelling out the alphabet.

JEREMY'S
CLOTHING, ACCESSORIES

Map p330 (www.jeremys.com; 2 South Park St; ⊙11am-6pm Mon-Wed & Fri, 11am-8:30pm Thu, noon-6pm Sun; ⓂTownsend St) No South Park excursion would be complete without swapping stories about your all-time-best bargains from Jeremy's. Runway modeling, window displays and high-end customer returns translate to jaw-dropping bargains on major designers for men and women. Men's stuff gets picked over faster, but you could score a skinny Prada suit at half off if you work fast. Brave the lines to try before you buy – returns are possible for store credit, but only within seven days.

🅿 BRANCH
HOUSEWARES

Map p330 (www.branchhome.com; 345 9th St; ⊙9:30am-5:30pm Mon-Fri; Ⓜ10th St) When you're looking for original home decor with a sustainable edge, it's time to Branch out. Whether you're in the market for a cork chaise lounge, beechwood-fiber bath towel or a tiny bonsai in a reclaimed breathmint tin, Branch has you covered – and yes, they ship.

MADAME S & MR S LEATHER
CLOTHING, ACCESSORIES

Map p330 (www.madame-s.com; 385 8th St; ⊙11am-7pm; Ⓜ&ⓇCivic Center) Only in San Francisco would an S&M superstore outsize Home Depot, with such musts as suspension stirrups, latex hoods and, for that special someone, a chrome-plated codpiece. If you've been a very bad puppy, there's an entire department catering to you here, and gluttons for punishment will find home decor inspiration in Dungeon Furniture.

GENERAL BEAD
JEWELRY, GIFTS

Map p330 (www.genbead.com; 637 Minna St; ⊙noon-6pm; Ⓜ&ⓇCivic Center) Blind beading ambition will seize you when you're upstairs among the racks of bagged bulk beads, where visions of holiday gifts for the entire family appear like mirages: multi-tiered necklaces, sequined seascapes, mosaic frames, even lampshades. To practice restraint, order smaller quantities downstairs from the bead-bedecked staff behind the counter, who will ring you up on bejeweled calculators.

GAMA-GO
CLOTHING, ACCESSORIES

Map p330 (www.gama-go.com; 335 8th St; ⊙noon-6pm Mon-Fri, to 5pm Sat & Sun; Ⓜ&ⓇCivic Center) Every one of SF-designer Gama-Go's products seems calibrated to hit the fascination nerve: a hand-shaped cleaver called the Karate Chopper, T-shirts with a roaring powder-blue yeti, and a tape measure disguised as a cassette tape. Gama-Go is distributed nationally, but here in the showroom you'll find 70% off last season's lines and score 15% off all purchases from noon to 2pm daily.

ISDA & CO OUTLET
CLOTHING, ACCESSORIES

Map p330 (www.isda-and-co.com; 21 South Park St; ⊙10am-6pm Mon-Sat; ⓂTownsend St) Sharp SF urban professionals aren't born into casual Friday elegance – they probably clawed their way up through racks of artfully draped shirts and sculpted cardigans at this local designer outlet. Colors are mostly variations on a graphite-gray theme, but the lean silhouette is shamelessly flattering.

SAN FRANCISCO FLOWER MART
FLOWERS

Map p330 (www.sfflmart.com; 640 Brannan St; ⊙10am-3pm Mon-Sat; Ⓜ4th St) When you're in San Francisco, in love and in the doghouse, do what the locals do: bring armloads of relentlessly cheerful sunflowers, bask in forgiveness and never let on that you got them cheap at the Flower Mart. Many of the 80 flower and plant vendors offer seasonal flowers grown locally, not flown in, so you can enjoy your greenery the green way.

GOODWILL 'AS IS' SHOP
CLOTHING, ACCESSORIES

Map p330 (www.sfgoodwill.org; 86 11th St; ⊙8am-3pm Mon-Sat; Ⓜ&ⓇCivic Center) 'Ooh, that wedding dress would look fierce with some blood on it!' Getting to the bottom of the bin before the regular crowds of emerging designers, vintage resellers, drag queens, serial costume-partiers and the rest of San Francisco's fashion rebels isn't always easy, but items cost $2.50 and the commentary is priceless.

🏃 SPORTS & ACTIVITIES

⬜CHOICE AT&T PARK
BASEBALL

Map p334 (☎415-972-2000; http://sanfrancisco.giants.mlb.com; AT&T Park; tickets $5-135; ⓂN) The San Francisco Giants, SF's 2010 World Series–winning National League baseball team, plays 81 home games from April to October in this ballpark, which changes its name with every telecom merger. The Giants pack huge crowds and often make the playoffs, with superstitious practices that might seem eccentric elsewhere but endear them to SF: the entire team has been known to sport bushy beards and the pitcher to wear women's underwear on winning streaks. Games are frequently sold out, but season-ticket holders often sell unwanted tickets through the team's Double Play Ticket Window on the website.

On nongame days a behind-the-scenes **tour** (☎415-972-2400; tickets $12.50; ⊙10:30am & 2:30pm) includes visits to the clubhouse, dugout and field. There's also a mini replica of the field, the world's largest baseball glove, and a kids' play structure in that hideous giant Coca-Cola bottle that pretends to be a sculpture. Bonus: on the east side of the park, you can stand at the archways along the waterfront promenade and watch a few innings for free.

18 REASONS
CLASSES

(☎415-252-9816; www.18reasons.org; 593 Guerrero St; ⊙6:30am-5pm Mon-Sat, 7am-4:30pm Sun; ⓂChurch St) Go gourmet at this local food community nonprofit affiliated with Bi-Rite (p145), offering artisan cheese and wine tastings, knife-skills and edible perfume workshops and more – check the website for upcoming classes and family-friendly events.

MISSION CULTURAL CENTER FOR LATINO ARTS
CLASSES

Map p334 (☎415-643-5001; www.missionculturalcenter.org; 2868 Mission St; ⊙5-10pm Mon, 10am-10pm Tue-Fri, 10am-5:30pm Sat; Ⓜ&Ⓡ24th St Mission) Join a class in tango, capoeira or Afro-Peruvian dance; make arts and crafts with the kids; or create a protest poster at the printmaking studio at this happening cultural center. Teachers are friendly, and participants range from *niños* (kids) to *abuelos* (grandparents). Check the online calendar for upcoming gallery openings; don't miss Day of the Dead altar displays in November.

POTRERO DEL SOL/LA RAZA SKATEPARK
SKATING

Map p334 (www.sfgov.org; 25th & Utah Sts; Ⓜ&Ⓡ24th St Mission) An isolated, scrubby park that had been abandoned to gangs became NorCal's hottest urban skatepark in 2008 with support from the city's Recreation

THE MISSION, SOMA & POTRERO HILL SPORTS & ACTIVITIES

WORTH A DETOUR

SAN FRANCISCO 49ERS

The **49ers** (☎415-656-4900; www.sf49ers.com; Monster Park; tickets $25-100; Ⓜ️T & shuttle buses) were the dream team of the National Football League (NFL) during the 1980s and early '90s, but the team has been in a sorry state of late, finishing at the very bottom of the heap in the 2004 season and not making the playoffs since. Clearly, these five-time Super Bowl champs will be rebuilding for some years to come, but fan loyalty has not flagged. Yet the team keeps threatening to leave San Francisco, perhaps as a ploy to get voters to approve a bond measure to build a new, updated stadium closer to the city instead of old Candlestick Park, rather unfortunately dubbed 'Monster Park' after its current corporate sponsor. Book tickets through www.ticketmaster.com, and factor in $20 to park in the stadium lot, due to recent car break-ins during games.

and Park department. Day and night under strategically placed lights, newbies and pros blast ollies off the hip of these concrete bowls. There are downsides: the bathroom is often off-limits due to misuse or stench, and graffiti on the concrete can make for a slippery ride. Wait for a clean area of the bowl to bust big moves, and leave room for little skaters. For gear, hit up Mission Skateboards (p158).

CITY KAYAK   KAYAKING
Map p330 (☎415-357-1010; www.citykayak.com; South Beach Harbor; kayak rentals per hr $35-65, 3hr lesson & rental package $59, tours $65-75; Ⓜ️Embarcadero) You haven't seen San Francisco until you've seen it from the water, and the next best thing to Sir Francis Drake's ship the *Golden Hind* is a kayak. Newbies can venture calm waters near the Bay Bridge, and experienced paddlers might hit the choppy waters beneath the Golden Gate Bridge or take a moonlight tour with all-inclusive rentals. First-timers can take lessons and head out alone or with an escorted tour; check the website for details.

SAN FRANCISCO CENTER FOR THE BOOK   CLASSES
Map p334 (☎415-565-0545; www.sfcb.org; 300 De Haro St; admission free; ☺10am-5pm Mon-Fri; Ⓜ️16th St) Anyone who can't get enough of the sight, sound and smell of a freshly cracked book will achieve a whole new level of obsession with the center's displays and classes on elaborate Coptic binding and wooden typesetting machines. Beyond traditional techniques, the center offers hands-on classes that show you how to make books that fit into matchboxes, pop up into cityscapes and unfold into prison guard towers.

SPINNAKER SAILING   BOATING
(Map p330; ☎415-543-7333; www.spinnaker-sailing.com; Pier 40; lessons $375; ☺10am-5pm;

Ⓜ️Embarcadero) Do 'luff,' 'cringle' and 'helms-a-lee' mean anything to you? If yes, captain a boat from Spinnaker and sail into the sunset. If not, charter a skippered vessel, or take classes and learn to talk like a sailor – in a good way.

BAKAR FITNESS & RECREATION CENTER   SWIMMING
Map p334 (☎415-514-4545; http://mbfitness.ucsf.edu; 1675 Owens & 16th Sts; day pass $15; ☺5:30am-10pm Mon-Fri, 7:30am-8pm Sat & Sun; Ⓜ️16th St) The view from the dizzyingly high, six-lane, 25yd rooftop pool is enough to make you forget you came here to swim. Located at the UCSF Mission Bay campus, this pool and patio overlook the ballpark to the Bay Bridge. Water-based exercise classes are offered in a second pool, one level below.

EMBARCADERO YMCA   SWIMMING
Map p330 (☎415-957-9622; www.ymcasf.org/embarcadero; 169 Steuart St; day pass $15; ☺5:30am-9:45pm Mon-Fri, 8am-7:45pm Sat, 9am-5:45pm Sun; Ⓜ️&Ⓡ️Embarcadero) Downtown professionals flock to this clean, modern YMCA, with extensive gym equipment, swimming pool, basketball court and massage services. Each locker room has a steam room. Bring a lock for your locker or else use the tiny penny lockers by the swimming pool.

YERBA BUENA CENTER ICE SKATING & BOWLING   ICE SKATING, BOWLING
Map p330 (☎415-820-3532; www.skatebowl.com; 750 Folsom St; skating adult/child $8/6 plus $3 skate rental, bowling per game $5.50-9 plus $3 shoe rental; ☺bowling 10am-10pm Sun-Thu, to midnight Fri & Sat; Ⓜ️&Ⓡ️Powell St) Built on the rooftop of the Moscone Convention Center, the ice and bowling centers are a huge draw for families. Unlike most rinks, this one is bright and nat-

urally lit with walls of windows; the bowling alley has just 12 lanes but serves beer. Check the website or call for skating times.

YOGA TREE YOGA
Map p334 (☎415-647-9707; www.yogatreesf.com; 1234 Valencia St; drop-in classes $18; ☺10am-10pm; ᵫ24th St Mission) Yoga-lovers will find instant community in this clean, warm, colorful studio, which has personable, high-quality instructors, great deals on introductory classes (three sessions for $20) and drop-in classes, primarily in Hatha yoga. Massage and private lessons are available too, and there are four other locations to choose from: the Castro, Hayes Valley, Haight and another Mission location on Shotwell.

The Castro & Noe Valley

Neighborhood Top Five

1 Catching a classic film at the **Castro Theatre** (p172) and hearing the Mighty Wurlitzer's pipes roar before showtime.

2 Climbing **Corona Heights** (p166) at sunset and watching Market St light up below.

3 Dodging baby strollers on **24th St** (p173) as you window-shop indie stores.

4 Watching sexy strangers in **Jane Warner Plaza** (p166), by the F-Market line terminus.

5 Not going over the handlebars while biking down SF's steepest road, **22nd St** (p166).

For more detail of this area, see Map p336 and p337 ➡

Explore the Castro & Noe Valley

The Castro's main crossroads is the intersection of Market and Castro Sts. Noe Valley is over the (big) hill at Castro and 24th Sts. You can explore both neighborhoods in a few hours.

Mornings are quiet in both neighborhoods. The Castro is busiest afternoons and evenings, especially on weekends, when crowds come to people-watch, shop and drink; at night expect to see 20-somethings stumbling down Castro. Noe Valley is best at midday and in the afternoon – there's not much open after 7pm, just a few bars and restaurants.

If the 21st St Hill atop Castro St proves too much, bus 24-Divasadero connects the two neighborhoods, but it's notorious for gaps in service: expect to wait or check www.nextmuni.com for real-time arrivals. In Noe Valley, shops on 24th St extend between Diamond and Sanchez Sts; and on Church St, the restaurants and shops continue until the last stop on the J-Church line, around 29th St. Castro-area shops line Market St, between Church and Castro Sts; and Castro St, from Market to 19th Sts, with a few scattered along 18th St. Both neighborhoods are surrounded by residential streets, good for strolling, with many pretty Victorians.

Local Life

➡ **Hangouts** The Wednesday afternoon Castro Farmers Market (March through November) provides the best glimpse of locals, especially from a sidewalk table at the Cafe Flore (p170).

➡ **Drinking** The Castro is packed with bars, but most don't get going till evening. Pick up a copy of *BarTab* magazine – supplement to the local, gay *Bay Area Reporter* newspaper – to find what's on.

➡ **What (not) to wear** You may be tempted to flaunt your gym-toned physique in the sexy Castro, but once the afternoon fog blows in, locals spot tourists by their shorts and tank tops. Carry a jacket – or shiver.

Getting There & Away

➡ **Metro** K, L and M trains run beneath Market St to Castro Station. J trains serve Noe Valley.

➡ **Streetcar** Vintage streetcars operate on the F-Market line, from Fisherman's Wharf to Castro St.

➡ **Bus** The 24 and 33 lines operate to the Castro, but may have long waits between buses. The 24 and 48 lines serve Noe Valley.

Lonely Planet's Top Tip

Historic streetcars run like toy trains along the waterfront and up Market St, from Fisherman's Wharf to the Castro, via Downtown. Trouble is, service can be sporadic. To save time, take a train or bus and check their arrival times at www.nextmuni.com, which uses GPS tracking. If the F-Market line is running slow, take the underground K, L or M lines, which move (much) faster up Market St.

✖ Best Places to Eat

➡ Frances (p166)
➡ Starbelly (p167)
➡ Anchor Oyster Bar (p167)
➡ Chow (p167)
➡ Chilango (p167)

For reviews, see p166 ➡

🍷 Best Places to Drink

➡ Cafe Flore (p170)
➡ Blackbird (p170)
➡ 440 Castro (p170)
➡ Moby Dick (p170)
➡ Twin Peaks Tavern (p170)

For reviews, see p170 ➡

🔒 Best Places to Shop

➡ Sui Generis (p172)
➡ Ambiance (p173)
➡ Omnivore (p173)
➡ Cliff's Variety (p172)
➡ Neon Monster (p173)

For reviews, see p165 ➡

⊙ SIGHTS

CASTRO THEATRE
THEATER

Map p336 (☑415-621-6120; www.thecastrotheatre.com; 429 Castro St; Ⓜ Castro St) The city's grandest cinema opened in 1922. The Spanish-Moorish exterior yields to mishmash styles inside, from Italianate to Oriental. Ask nicely and staff might let you peak without buying a ticket. For the best photos of the blue-and-pink lights, shoot from across the street.

GLBT HISTORY MUSEUM
MUSEUM

Map p336 (☑415-777-5455; www.glbthistory.org/museum; 4127 18th St; admission $5; Ⓜ Castro St) America's first gay-history museum cobbles ephemera from the community – Harvey Milk's campaign literature, matchbooks from long-gone bathhouses, the dress Laura Linney wore as Mary Anne Singleton in the TV remake of *Tales of the City* – together with harder-hitting installations, such as audiovisual interviews with Gore Vidal and pages of the 1950s penal code banning homosexuality. Though it's fascinating to see pieces of the gay collective past, the curatorial vision sometimes feels a bit timid. Still, it's well worth a look, and you can pick up great gay-SF souvenir T-shirts, including one of Milk, emblazoned with his famous inspirational quotation, 'You gotta give 'em hope.'

HARVEY MILK & JANE WARNER PLAZAS
SQUARE

Map p336 (Market & Castro Sts; Ⓜ Castro St) A huge, irrepressibly cheerful rainbow flag lords over Castro and Market Sts, officially dubbed Harvey Milk Plaza. Look closer and spot a plaque honoring the man whose lasting legacy to the Castro is civic pride and political clout; see text and images of his life, down the stairs beside the Muni station. Across Castro St, by the F-train terminus, at Jane Warner Plaza (named for a recently deceased, much-loved lesbian police officer), kids too young for the bars congregate at public tables and chairs. This a good place to take in local color – on warm days several oddball nudists congregate to shock tourists. Welcome to the Castro.

CORONA HEIGHTS PARK
PARK

Map p336 (bounded by 16th St & Roosevelt Way; Ⓜ Castro St) Urban hikers scramble up the rocky 520ft summit of Corona Heights (aka Museum Hill or Red Rocks) for jaw-dropping eastward 180-degree views. Come evening, the city unfurls below in a carpet of light. Take tiny Beaver St uphill to the steps through the bushes, then cut right of the tennis courts and up the trail. For an easier hike, enter via the Roosevelt Way side.

Near the summit is the family-ready **Randall Junior Museum** (☑415-554-9600; www.randallmuseum.org; admission free; ⊙10am-5pm Tue-Sat), with live-animal exhibits and hands-on workshops (check the website for details); downstairs is the **Golden Gate Model Railroad Club** (www.ggmrc.org; admission free; ⊙10am-4pm Sat), a jaw-dropping collection of working vintage Lionel trains.

NOBBY CLARKE MANSION
HISTORICAL BUILDING

Map p336 (250 Douglass St, at Caselli Ave; Ⓜ Castro St) Built in 1892 by a wealthy attorney who recognized that the weather was sunnier here than atop fashionable Nob Hill, this gorgeous turreted mansion went uninhabited after its construction: Snob Hill socialites dubbed the house 'Nobby Clarke's Folly' and his wife refused to move in. It served briefly as a hospital; now it's an apartment building. Spot the disco ball in the top turret window and you'll definitely know that you're not on Nob Hill.

22ND ST HILL
STREET

Map p337 (22nd St, btwn Church & Vicksburg Sts) The prize for steepest street is shared between two SF blocks: Filbert St (between Hyde and Leavenworth Sts) and this block of 22nd. Both streets have a 31.5% grade (17-degree slope), but there's less traffic here. Nothing quite beats the thrill of cycling down 22nd, grabbing two fistfuls of brakes and trying not to go over the bars – not for the faint of heart.

✖ EATING

Most Castro restaurants lie on Market St, from Church to Castro Sts, and around the intersection of Castro and 18th Sts. In Noe Valley, find quick lunch spots along 24th St, between Church and Diamond Sts.

TOP CHOICE FRANCES
CALIFORNIAN $$

(Map p336; ☑415-621-3870; www.frances-sf.com; 3870 17th St; mains $14-27; ⊙5-10.30pm Tue-Sun) Chef/owner Melissa Perello earned a Michelin star for fine dining, then ditched downtown to start this market-inspired neighborhood bistro. Daily menus showcase bright, seasonal flavors and luxurious textures: cloudlike sheep's milk ricotta gnocchi with crunchy breadcrumbs and broccolini, grilled calamari with preserved Meyer lemon, and artisan wine served by the ounce, directly from Wine Country.

STARBELLY   CALIFORNIAN, PIZZA **$$**

Map p336 (☑415-252-7500; www.starbellysf. com; 3583 16th St; dishes $6-19; ⊘11:30am-11pm, till midnight Fri & Sat; ⓂCastro St) The seasonal small plates at always-busy Starbelly include standout *salumi,* market-fresh salads, scrumptious pâté, roasted mussels with housemade sausage and thin-crusted pizzas. The barnlike rooms get loud with revelers; sit on the heated patio for quieter conversation. If you can't score a table, consider its neighboring burger joint, **Super Duper Burger** (www.superdupersf.com; 2304 Market St; ⊘11am-11pm) for all-natural burgers and milkshakes.

ANCHOR OYSTER BAR   SEAFOOD **$$**

Map p336 (www.anchoroysterbar.com; 579 Castro St; mains $15-25; ⊘11:30am-10pm Mon-Sat, 4-9:30pm Sun; ⓂCastro St) Since its founding in 1977, Anchor's formula has been simple: seafood classics, like local oysters, crab cakes, clam chowder and copious salads. The nautical-themed room seats just 24 at shiny stainless-steel tables; you can't make reservations, but you can sit at the marble-top bar to shorten the wait.

CHOW   AMERICAN **$$**

Map p336 (☑415-552-2469; www.chowfoodbar. com; 215 Church St; mains $9-14; ⊘11am-11pm; ☑; ⓂChurch St) Chow's diverse menu appeals to all tastes, with everything from pizza to pork chops and Thai-style noodles to spaghetti and meatballs. The wood-floored room is big, loud and always busy. Avoid tables alongside the bar (you'll get jostled); request a table on the back patio for quiet(er) conversations. Call ahead for the 'no-wait' list.

CHILANGO   MEXICAN **$$**

Map p336 (☑415-552-5700; www.chilango restaurantsf.com; 235 Church St; dishes $8-12; ⊘11am-10pm; ⓂChurch St) Upgrade from taqueria to sit-down restaurant at this casual Mexican spot that uses all-organic ingredients in its Mexico City–derived cooking. Meals are served at tile-top tables with Frida Kahlo images embedded within. Everything is made to order, including guacamole and tortillas. Favorite dishes: filet-mignon tacos, duck *flautas* (deep-fried

flour tortilla with filling) and succulent *carnitas* (roast pork).

L'ARDOISE   FRENCH **$$**

Map p336 (☑415-437-2600; 151 Noe St; mains $16-19; ⊘dinner Tue-Sat; ⓂNoe & Market Sts) For date night with an all-local crowd, this storefront neighborhood charmer on a leafy side street is perfectly placed for strolling hand-in-hand after dining on classic French-bistro fare. Dim lighting adds sex appeal, but the room gets noisy – especially on weekends – when the cheek-by-jowl tables fill. Make reservations.

LA MÉDITERRANÉE   MIDDLE EASTERN **$$**

Map p336 (☑415-431-7210; www.lamediterranee. net; 288 Noe St; mains $12-15; ⊘11am-10pm Sun-Thu, to 11pm Fri & Sat; ☑⊞; ⓂCastro St) Zesty, lemon-laced Lebanese fare at friendly prices makes La Méd the Castro's neighborhood meet-up spot. Chicken kebabs on rice pilaf are pleasingly plump; the *kibbe* is a harmonious blend of pine nuts, ground lamb and cracked wheat; and the smoky eggplant in the baba ghanoush was roasted for hours and isn't the least bit bitter about it.

SUSHI TIME   JAPANESE, SUSHI **$$**

Map p336 (☑415-552-2280; www.sushitime-sf. com; 2275 Market St; dishes $8-15; ⊘5-10:30pm Mon-Sat; ☑; ⓂCastro St) Barbie, GI Joe and Hello Kitty make cameos on the *maki* (sushi roll) menu at this surreal sushi spot downstairs from a bookstore and gym, Tokyo-style. Devour sashimi in the tiny glassed-in patio like a shark in an aquarium, and notice how your munching mysteriously synchronizes with the J-pop on the stereo. Happy hour specials before 6pm.

TATAKI   SUSHI **$$**

(☑415-282-1889; www.tatakisushibar.com; 1740 Church St; dishes $12-20; ⊘dinner; ⓂChurch & 29th Sts) Sister to the groundbreaking Pacific Heights sushi bar (p122), this second branch of Tataki has the same high standards for sustainably sourced fish, smartly paired with unusual ingredients. And it's right on the J-Church streetcar line.

LOVEJOY'S TEA ROOM   BAKERY **$$**

Map p337 (☑415-648-5895; www.lovejoystearoom. com; 1351 Church St; tea $10-15; ⊘11am-6pm Wed-Sun; ⓂChurch & Clipper Sts) All the chintz you'd expect from an English tearoom, but with a San Francisco crowd: curators talk video-installation art over Lapsang souchong, scones

1. Castro Theatre (p172)
The city's grandest cinema opened in 1922.

2. Revelers in costume, the Castro
Hit the Castro's legendary bars and clubs for a memorable night out.

3. Streetcars
Vintage streetcars operate along Market St in the Castro.

4. Noe Valley (p164)
Grab some lunch and stroll the pretty streets of Noe Valley, the Castro's more subdued neighbor.

CHEAP EATS: THE CASTRO & NOE VALLEY

Burgermeister (Map p336; www.burgermeistersf.com; 138 Church St; burgers $8-12; ⊘11am-11pm; ⛟; ⓜChurch St) All-natural burgers and fries.

Casa Mexicana (Map p336; ☑415-551-2272; 180 Church St; ⊘11am-10pm; ⛟; ⓜChurch St) Good burritos.

Mollie Stone's Markets (Map p336; www.molliestones.com; 4201 18th St; ⊘7am-11pm; ⓜCastro St) High-end grocery with prepared foods.

Taqueria Zapata (Map p336; 4150 18th St; dishes $5-9; ⊘11am-10pm; ⛟; ⓜCastro St) Good burritos.

Noe Valley Bakery (Map p337; www.noevalleybakery.com; 4073 24th St; dishes $4-8; ⊘7am-7pm Mon-Fri, to 6pm Sat & Sun; ⛟; ⓜCastro & 24th St) Sandwiches on house-baked bread, croissants and éclairs.

Barney's Burgers (Map p337; www.barneyshamburgers.com; 4138 24th St; burgers $8-12; ⊘11am-10pm; ☑⛟; ⓜCastro & 24th St) All-natural burgers and big salads.

and clotted cream, while dual dads take their daughters and dolls out for 'wee tea' of tiny sandwiches, petits fours and hot chocolate.

CATCH
SEAFOOD **$$**

Map p336 (☑415-431-5000; www.catchsf.com; 2362 Market St; $12-17; ⊘lunch Mon-Fri, dinner daily, brunch Sat & Sun; ⬚Castro St) 'Catch' as in 'of the day' – Dungeness crab, oysters, sole – not necessarily a reference to that silver fox by the fireplace. Try the vat-sized cioppino, and maneuver away from the piano to hear the hot dish being served by fellow diners.

🍷 DRINKING & NIGHTLIFE

Castro bars open earlier than in other neighborhoods; on weekends most open at noon.

TOP CHOICE CAFE FLORE
CAFE

Map p336 (☑415-621-8579; www.cafeflore.com; 2298 Market St; ⊘7am-midnight Sun-Thu, to 2am Fri & Sat; 🛜; ⓜCastro St) You haven't done the Castro till you've lollygagged on the sun-drenched patio at the Flore – everyone winds up here sooner or later. Weekdays present the best chance to meet neighborhood regulars, who colonize the tables outside. Weekends get packed. Great happy hour drink specials, like two-for-one margaritas. Pretty good food, too. Wi-fi weekdays only.

BLACKBIRD
GAY BAR

Map p336 (☑415-503-0630; www.blackbird bar.com; 2124 Market St; ⊘3pm-2am Mon-Fri, noon-2am Sat & Sun; ⓜChurch St) The Castro's

lounge-bar draws a mix of guys in tight T-shirts and their gal-pals. The look is sleek and clean, but not overstyled. We dig the macabre news clippings on the walls, the cocktails are strong, and there's a good selection of wines and craft beers by the glass. Bartenders provide eye candy. Ideal spot to begin a Castro pub crawl, but it gets packed weekends.

440 CASTRO
GAY BAR

Map p336 (☑415-621-8732; www.the440.com; 440 Castro St; ⊘noon-2am; ⓜCastro St) The most happening bar on the street, 440 Castro draws bearded, gym-fit 30-something dudes – especially for Thursday's 'CDXL', when go-go boys twirl – and an odd mix of Peter Pans for Monday's underwear night.

MOBY DICK
GAY BAR

Map p336 (☑415-861-1199; www.mobydicksf.com; 4049 18th St; ⊘2pm-2am Mon-Fri, noon-2am Sat & Sun; ⓜCastro St) The name overpromises, but not for the giant fish tank behind the bar, which provides a focal point for shy boys who would otherwise look at their shoes. Weekdays it's a mellow spot for pool, pinball and meeting neighborhood 20-to-40-somethings.

TWIN PEAKS TAVERN
GAY BAR

Map p336 (☑415-864-9470; www.twinpeakstav ern.com; 401 Castro St; ⊘noon-2am Mon-Fri, 8am-2am Sat & Sun; ⓜCastro St) Don't call it the glass coffin. Show some respect: Twin Peaks was the first gay bar in the world with windows opening to the street. The jovial crowd skews (way) over 40, but they're not chicken hawks (or they wouldn't hang here), and they love it when happy kids show up and join the party. Ideal for a tête-à-tête after a film at the Castro, or for cards, Yahtzee or backgammon (BYO).

MIX
GAY BAR

Map p336 (☎415-431-8616; www.sfmixbar.com; 4086 18th St; ☺6am-2am; Ⓜ Castro St) The last Castro bar to open at 6am, the Mix is a must on a pub crawl. We like the low-ceilinged pool and bar area, but prefer the open-air back smokers patio. Expect gal-next-door lesbians, 20-something gay boys, trannie pals and the odd stumbling drag queen. Great drink specials keep everyone wasted. Mondays there's free pool.

CHURCHILL
BAR

Map p336 (www.churchillsf.com; 198 Church St; Ⓜ Church St) Another gay bar bites the dust and goes straight(-ish), but you'd never know from the stylin' decor – a mash-up of recycled wood, nautical rope strung across the ceiling, vintage blown-glass lanterns and tufted sofas that evoke 1940s cool and dockworker hot, making this the best-looking bar in the 'hood. Welcoming bartenders craft stellar whiskey drinks.

SAMOVAR TEA LOUNGE
CAFE

Map p336 (☎415-626-4700; www.samovartea.com; 498 Sanchez St; ☺10am-10pm; Ⓜ Castro St) Styled in soothing Zen-chic, Samovar's sunny Castro location specializes in organic, fair-trade teas and provides a cozy alternative to the neighborhood's ubiquitous bars. Sandwiches and cheese plates, designed to pair with tea, provide reason to linger.

JUMPIN' JAVA
CAFE

Map p336 (☎415-431-5282; 139 Noe St; ☺7am-8pm; 🛜; Ⓜ Noe & Market Sts) Alterna-dorks hunch over MacBooks and trade passing glances at the Castro's quietest cafe, nicknamed 'Laptop Library.' Nobody talks. Bring a computer or be bored. Packed weekends. Fun fact: this chapter was penned here.

PILSNER INN
GAY BAR

Map p336 (☎415-621-7058; www.pilsnerinn.com; 225 Church St; ☺10am-2am; Ⓜ Church St) A fave of gay-softball leagues, the Pilsner is the classic neighborhood joint, with big smokers patio, pinball and pool. Good meeting point if your group is splitting in two directions, SoMa and the Castro.

LOOKOUT
GAY BAR

Map p336 (☎415-431-0306; www.lookoutsf.com; 3600 16th St; Ⓜ Castro St) To hook up with locals, swill margaritas at one of Lookout's drag or sports-team fundraisers. Hot rugby players come Sunday afternoons for Jock. Please, no catcalling from the balcony over the street.

CAFE
GAY NIGHTCLUB

Map p336 (www.cafesf.com; 2369 Market St; Ⓜ Castro St) The Cafe packs a just-over-21 crowd – especially Fridays for Boy Bar – into its upstairs dance floor with kick-ass sound and high-tech lighting. Parties range from Latino to lesbian; check the calendar. If you're not up for dancing, cruise the open-air smokers lounge, or shoot pool beneath trippy lights that make it hard to aim after your second cocktail.

QBAR
GAY BAR

Map p336 (☎415-864-2877; www.qbarsf.com; 456 Castro St; Ⓜ Castro St) Twenty-somethings pack shoulder-to-shoulder to shout over ear-splitting pop and dance on a tiny dance floor. Occasional go-go boys add spice; smokers pack the front room. Wednesday's Booty Call is a staple. 'Too many girls!' declare old-timers, who stay far away.

TOAD HALL
GAY BAR

Map p336 (☎415-621-2811; www.toadhallbar.com; 4146 18th St; Ⓜ Castro St) Posses of pals get their drink on at Toad Hall, which has killer drink specials, a chill smokers patio, tiny dance floor and friendly bartenders. Its name comes from the Castro's original gay bar, which had been forgotten until resurrected in the film *Milk*, but this place bears no resemblance.

MIDNIGHT SUN
GAY BAR

Map p336 (☎415-861-4186; 4067 18th St; Ⓜ Castro St) This video bar is a favorite of khaki-clad suburbanites who aren't entirely comfortable socializing unless there's something specific to divert their attention. The *Dynasty* era marked its heyday, but crowds still come for *American Idol,* and it remains a reliable place to...well, watch TV. Best time: early evening.

BADLANDS
GAY BAR

Map p336 (☎415-626-9320; www.badlands-sf.com; 4121 18th St; Ⓜ Castro St) The Castro's long-standing dance bar gets packed with gay college boys, their screaming straight girlfriends and chicken hawks. If you're over 30, you'll feel old. Weekends, expect a line.

TRIGGER — GAY NIGHTCLUB

Map p336 (www.clubtrigger.com; 2344 Market St; MCastro St) The crowd skews toward 20-something at Trigger, where music blares too loudly to talk, but the dance floor is usurped by stand-and-model boys who are too busy texting to dance. Better to watch go-go boys from the upstairs balcony – assuming it's not cordoned off for faux VIPs. We love the spontaneous, 10-minute drink specials.

☆ ENTERTAINMENT

CASTRO THEATRE — CINEMA

Map p336 (☎415-621-6120; www.thecastrotheatre. com; 429 Castro St; adult/child $10/7.50; MCastro St) The Mighty Wurlitzer organ rises from the orchestra pit before evening performances, and the audience cheers as the organist plays classics from the Great American Songbook, ending with (sing along, now): 'San Francisco open your Golden Gate/You let no stranger wait outside your door...' If there's a cult classic on the bill, such as *Whatever Happened to Baby Jane,* expect audience participation. Otherwise, the crowd is behaved and rapt. Note: sound echoes in the balcony.

CAFÉ DU NORD/SWEDISH AMERICAN HALL — LIVE MUSIC

Map p336 (☎415-861-5016; www.cafedunord.com; 2170 Market St; cover varies; MChurch St) You never know what's doing at Café du Nord, a former basement speakeasy, with bar and showroom. Rockers, chanteuses, comedians, raconteurs and burlesque acts perform nightly, and the joint still looks like it must've in the '30s. The hall upstairs, with balcony seating and Scandinavian woodwork, hosts miscellaneous events. Check the online calendar.

🛍 SHOPPING

🛍 The Castro

SUI GENERIS — CLOTHING, ACCESSORIES

Map p336 (www.suigenerisconsignment.com; men's shop 2231 Market St, women's shop 2265 Market St; MCastro St) Emerge with confi-

dence from his-and-her designer-consignment boutiques knowing you won't spot another person working your new look. The well-curated collection of contemporary and vintage clothing skews dressy. Best for those who fit runway-model sizes, but with relatively fat wallets.

CLIFF'S VARIETY — HOUSEWARES

Map p336 (www.cliffsvariety.com; 479 Castro St; MCastro St) None of the hardware maestros at Cliff's will raise an eyebrow if you express a dire need for a jar of rubber nuns, silver body paint and a case of cocktail toothpicks, though they might angle for an invitation. The window displays at Cliff's, a community institution since 1936, are a local landmark.

UNIONMADE — CLOTHING, SHOES

Map p336 (www.unionmadegoods.com; 493 Sanchez St; MCastro St) Upgrade your casual-Friday look with Unionmade's cool mix of classic labels – American-heritage brands like Pendleton and Levi's Vintage, plus European staples like Il Bisonte leather goods.

BOOKS INC — BOOKSTORE

Map p336 (www.booksinc.net; 2275 Market St; ⊙10am-10pm; MCastro St) The Castro's indie bookstore has new-release hardcovers, good fiction, extensive magazines and many travel books. Check the bulletin boards for schedules of readings and literary happenings.

DE LA SOLE — SHOES

Map p336 (www.delasole.com; 549 Castro St; MCastro St) SF gets its kicks at De La Sole, from mod Duckie Brown-Florsheim wingtips, to radiator-vented sandals by Montreal brand Industry. Says the sales rep to a customer squeezing into a 60% off Palladium boot: 'Don't worry, it won't always be so tight.' Chimes in a fellow customer, without missing a beat: 'That's what they all say.'

HUMAN RIGHTS CAMPAIGN ACTION CENTER & STORE — GIFTS, CLOTHING

Map p336 (www.hrc.org; 575 Castro St; MCastro St) If this storefront seems familiar, you're right: this was once Harvey Milk's camera shop and one of the locations used in the Academy Award–winning *Milk*. Now it's home to the HRC, the GLBT lobbying group and its affiliated shop. Make more than a fashion statement in signature HRC tees designed by Marc Jacobs, Kenneth Cole and other fashion-forward thinkers, with proceeds supporting civil-rights initiatives. Hopeful romantics head here to sign marriage-equality petitions and pop the question with rings inscribed on the inside with *aequalitas* (equality).

UNDER ONE ROOF
GIFTS, HOUSEWARES

Map p336 (www.underoneroof.org; 518a Castro St; MCastro St) All the fabulous gifts under this roof are donated by local designers and businesses, so AIDS service organizations get 100% of the proceeds from your etched San Francisco–skyline martini glasses and adorable Jonathan Adler vase. Those sweet sales clerks are volunteers, so show them love for raising $11 million to date.

KENNETH WINGARD
HOUSEWARES

Map p336 (www.kennethwingard.com; 2319 Market St; MCastro St) Upgrade from ho-hum IKEA to mod housewares that are positively scrumptious: glossy tangerine bud vases, vintage tiki-fabric cushions and mood-setting, ecofriendly, cork-shaded lamps, all priced for mass consumption.

WORN OUT WEST
ACCESSORIES

Map p336 (582 Castro St; MCastro St) Left your gear at home? Pick up leathers, original-cut Levi's 501s, cockrings and tank tops at this old-school-Castro used-clothing store, and dress like a local. Good fetish wear at great prices. Not much for gals, alas.

PHOTOWORKS
PHOTO PROCESSING

Map p336 (www.photoworkssf.com; 2077a Market St; MChurch St) Quick proquality photo processing and printing for film and digital shooters, plus bonus creative services: digital pics can be printed on classic Ilford black-and-white paper or even canvas.

🔒 Noe Valley

AMBIANCE
CLOTHING, ACCESSORIES

Map p337 (www.ambiancesf.com; 3985 & 3989 24th St; MChurch & 24th Sts) Expect to emerge clutching some little number requiring you to hit the town: swingy skirts for Lindy-hopping in Golden Gate Park, or DNA-pattern jackets for biotech lectures. The shoe-and-sale store next door encourages

you to keep the retail rush going, as do Ambiance's two sister stores. Visit 1458 Haight St for teen-appropriate prom dresses, and 1858 Union St in the Marina for cocktail attire.

OMNIVORE
BOOKSTORE

Map p337 (www.omnivorebooks.com; 3885a Cesar Chavez St; MChurch & 27th Sts) Salivate over signed cookbooks by chef-legend Alice Waters, A16's 'James Beard Rising Star Chef' Nate Appelbaum, and signed copies of *Omnivore's Dilemma* by Michael Pollan. Check the in-store events calendar for standing-room-only events with star chefs, and don't miss the collection of vintage cookbooks and rarities such as a Civil War–era recipe book, written longhand.

NEON MONSTER
BOOKSTORE, TOYS

Map p337 (www.neonmonster.com; 901 Castro St; ☺Tue-Sun; MCastro & 22nd Sts) A cuddly Cyclops is the mascot of this toy boutique, comic-book gallery and graphic-novel shop that also carries a collection of snappy silk-screen T-shirts and vinyl records that you can play in the shop to confirm their quality. Welcome back to the analogue world, with nary a screen in sight.

ISSO
CLOTHING, ACCESSORIES

Map p337 (www.issosf.com; 3789 24th St; MChurch & 24th Sts) 'Made, found or designed in the Bay Area' is the motto of this purveyor of women's apparel that also designs its own line – expect classic styles updated with little zings, such as angle-pocket pencil skirts made of vintage fabric. Local designers, such as SheBible and Nopal Apparel, round out the collection.

🏷 GLOBAL EXCHANGE FAIR TRADE CRAFT CENTER
GIFTS, HOUSEWARES

Map p337 (www.globalexchangestore.org; 4018 24th St; MCastro & 24th Sts) Consumerism with a heart of gold: wild splurges on splashy Rwandan laptop bags, fair-trade chocolate, sweatshop-free sneakers from Pakistan and crates of smiling, organic Egyptian-cotton carrots seem somehow noble, since the proceeds go right back to the community cooperatives that made them via nonprofit Global Exchange.

The Haight & Hayes Valley

Neighborhood Top Five

1 Bringing the Summer of Love back to **Haight St** (p176): wearing flowers, making a manifesto, singing freestyle folk songs on the corner of Haight and Ashbury Sts, or following in the footsteps of psychedelic-rock giants.

2 Planting pumpkins on a freeway ramp and harvesting gardening tips at non-profit **Hayes Valley Farm** (p177).

3 Taste-testing 400 brews at **Toronado** (p183), 250 spirits at **Alembic** (p184) and 200 rums at **Smuggler's Cove** (p184).

4 Escaping shopping-mall sameness and scoring **original SF style** in Hayes Valley and Haight boutiques (p186).

5 Dining at a top table: star-chef Traci Des Jardins' **Jardinière** (p183) or the hilltop picnic tables at **Alamo Square** (p181).

For more detail of this area, see Map p338 and p329 ➡

Explore Hayes Valley & the Haight

Stroll Hayes Valley trendy restaurants and glam boutiques, then discover its down-to-earth side: the Zen Center and Hayes Valley Farm. If the fog lifts by noon, detour for a picnic lunch atop Alamo Square Park. Otherwise, hop the bus straight to the Upper Haight for a walking tour through hippie history. Browse your way down Haight St for a moveable feast of Rosamunde sausages, Toronado beer and Three Twins ice cream that will prepare you to take on the world – possibly even karaoke at the Mint, the Scorpion Bowl at Smuggler's Cove or the poles on the Rebel Bar's dance floor.

Local Life

➡ **Cheap eats and fancy drinks** Locals economize – sort of – with Rosamunde sausages (p180) and Toronado Belgian ales (p183), oyster po'boy sliders and rare bourbon at Alembic (p184), and food truck BBQ ribs and California cult pinots at Vinyl Wine Bar (p184).

➡ **Musical stylings** Go acoustic on the corner of Haight and Ashbury Sts (p176), belt it out at the Mint (p186), sing along at Martuni's (p185) or rock out at free concerts at Amoeba Music (p186).

➡ **Hangouts** Aspiring flower children and original-issue hippies gather at Coffee to the People (p184), local designers work the counters at Hayes Valley boutiques (p187) and skaters hit Haight St's downhill slide into the Lower Haight (p176).

Getting There & Away

➡ **Bus** Number 21 heads from Downtown west through Hayes Valley along Hayes St, 49 runs up Van Ness Ave along the eastern edge of Hayes Valley, and 5 passes along the north side. Market St buses 6 and 71 run up Haight St to Golden Gate Park, passing the south end of Hayes Valley. The 22 links the Lower Haight to the Mission and Potrero Hill to the south, and Japantown, Pacific Heights and the Marina to the north. Number 24 connects the Haight to the Castro and Pacific Heights via Divisadero. Bus 43 connects the Upper Haight with the Presidio and the Marina, and 33 runs through the Upper Haight between the Richmond and the Mission.

➡ **Streetcar** The N line runs between Downtown and Ocean Beach through the Lower Haight, passing the Upper Haight to the north.

➡ **BART** Civic Center BART is four blocks east of Hayes Valley.

Lonely Planet's Top Tip

Ever since the '60s, America's youth have headed to the Haight as a place to fit in, no questions asked. But in 2010 San Francisco passed the controversial Sit/Lie Law, making daytime sidewalk loitering punishable by $50 to $100 fines. Critics claim the law targets vulnerable homeless teens in the Haight – with 1300 shelter beds to accommodate 6500 to 13,000 homeless, many youth have no place to go. Spare change is a short-term fix; consider donations to youth-service nonprofits.

THE HAIGHT & HAYES VALLEY

✗ Best Places to Eat

➡ Jardinière (p183)
➡ Bar Jules (p183)
➡ Rosamunde Sausage Grill (p180)
➡ Three Twins Ice Cream (p180)
➡ Zuni Cafe (p183)

For reviews, see p180 ➡

☙ Best Places to Drink

➡ Smuggler's Cove (p184)
➡ Toronado (p183)
➡ Alembic (p184)
➡ Aub Zam Zam (p184)
➡ Hôtel Biron (p185)

For reviews, see p183 ➡

☉ Best Places to Unleash Your Inner Freak

➡ Haight St (p176)
➡ Noc Noc (p184)
➡ Rebel Bar (p185)
➡ Loved to Death (p187)

 TOP SIGHTS
HAIGHT ST

SABRINA DALBESIO / LONELY PLANET IMAGES ©

Was it the fall of 1966 or the winter of '67? As the Haight saying goes, if you can remember the Summer of Love, man, you probably weren't there. The fog was laced with Nag Champa incense and burning draft cards, entire days were spent contemplating Day-Glo Grateful Dead posters, and the corner of Haight and Ashbury Sts became the turning point of a generation.

Unlikely Landmarks

Flashbacks are a given in the Haight, which still has its swinging '60s tendencies. Only a very mysterious, very local illness could explain the number of neighborhood medical marijuana clubs, and tie-dyes and ideals have never entirely gone out of fashion here – hence the highly prized vintage psychedelic rock tees on the wall at Wasteland (p186) and Bound Together Anarchist Book Collective (p186). Some '60s memories are better left behind: habits were kicked in the neighborhood's many rehabs, and many an intimate itch has been mercifully treated gratis at the Haight Ashbury Free Clinic (p296). To relive the highlights of the era, a short walking tour (p182) passes the former flophouses of the Haight's most famous and infamous residents.

Lower & Upper Haight

Since the '60s, Haight St has divided into two major splinter factions, divided by a **Divisadero St** strip of indie boutiques, trendy bars and restaurants. The **Upper Haight** specializes in potent coffee, radical literature and retail therapy for rebels, while the **Lower Haight** has better bars, more economic and ethnic diversity, and a pot-club mellow occasionally disrupted by gang activity northeast of Fillmore and Haight Sts. Haight St has its share of grit, but it remains a magnet.

DON'T MISS...
➡ Haight Flashback walking tour
➡ Mysterious 4:20 clock at Haight & Ashbury Sts
➡ *Anarchists of the Americas* mural at Bound Together Anarchist Book Collective
➡ Lower Haight bars

PRACTICALITIES
➡ Map p338
➡ Haight St btwn Fillmore & Stanyan Sts
➡ Ⓜ Haight St

◉ SIGHTS

Weekends are quite a scene in the Upper Haight, with hippies reliving their glory days trailed by teenage relatives pretending not to know them, suburban punks wearing too much aftershave and Harajuku hipsters dragging suitcases full of prime vintage attire for resale in Tokyo. But also in the mix are Green Party candidates for sheriff, cafe regulars who greet one another by name and street musicians who play a mean banjo.

Small yet high-maintenance Hayes Valley is securely tucked between the Lower Haight and Civic Center, and is best known for high-end boutiques and low-key landmarks: the Zen Center and Hayes Valley Farm.

◉ The Haight

HAIGHT ST   STREET
See p176.

BUENA VISTA PARK   PARK
Map p338 (Haight St btwn Central Ave & Baker St; MHaight St) True to its name, this park founded in 1867 offers sweeping views of the city beyond century-old cypresses to the Golden Gate Bridge as rewards for hiking up the steep hill. When SF went up in flames in 1906, this was where San Franciscans found refuge and watched the town smolder; on your way downhill, take Buena Vista Ave West to spot Victorian mansions that date from that era. Hanging around after the park closes at sunset for boozing or cruising is risky, given recent criminal activity at night.

GRATEFUL DEAD HOUSE   NOTABLE BUILDING
Map p338 (710 Ashbury St; MHaight St) Like most of the surviving members of the Grateful Dead, this Victorian sports more than just a touch of gray – but back in the 1960s this was the candy-colored flophouse where Jerry Garcia and bandmates blew minds, amps and brain cells. The mom-and-pop flower shop up the block has done brisk business selling bouquets that get left on the steps here ever since Jerry's membership in the Dead took a turn for the literal.

HUNTER S THOMPSON CRASH PAD   NOTABLE BUILDING
(318 Parnassus Ave; MStanyan St) How this building survived Hunter S Thompson's tenancy here during the mid-'60s is anyone's guess. On the otherwise unremarkable bay-windowed facade, you might notice patched bullet holes – mementos of parties that invariably degenerated into Hell's Angels orgies and shoot-outs. Gonzo journalism was born when Thompson narrowly survived to tell the tale in his book *Hell's Angels: The Strange and Terrible Saga of the Outlaw Motorcycle Gang,* and state his motto: 'When the going gets weird, the weird turn pro.'

THE HAIGHT & HAYES VALLEY SIGHTS

A WILD IDEA: HAYES VALLEY FARM

A freeway on-ramp is no place for a pumpkin...or is it? After the 1989 earthquake damaged the freeway on-ramp at Fell St, a 2-acre stretch of asphalt was left to crumble into urban blight – until a group of renegade community gardeners began the wildest urban permaculture experiment in the West. With labor donated by neighbors and support ranging from Project Homeless Connect to the mayor, asphalt has been pulled up, the soil certified lead-safe and organic compost laid down.

The nonprofit **Hayes Valley Farm** (☑415-863-3136; www.hayesvalleyfarm.com; entry 450 Laguna St at Fell St; ☺noon-5pm Sun, Wed & Thu; MHayes St) is subject to future city development plans, and there have been some setbacks, as when community beehives key for pollination were vandalized. But the crops have hit the highway, with orange California poppies and blue lupine taking over the sidewalk and a bumper crop of nitrogen-rich fava beans. According to garden organizers, there may be pumpkins for Halloween.

Visitors are welcome three days a week, and there's no need to call ahead to volunteer. Just show up Sundays, Wednesdays and Thursdays by 12:30pm, and after a brief orientation, community farmers will put you to work. Check the website for other community events in the garden, including free outdoor yoga, Monday kids' activities and sliding-scale workshops on sustainable urban garden design.

SABRINA DALBESIO / LONELY PLANET IMAGES ©

1. Amoeba Music (p186)
The West Coast's most eclectic collection of new and used music and video.

2. Bound Together Anarchist Book Collective (p186)
Free thinkers come here for organic farming manuals, prison literature and radical comics.

3. Alamo Square (p181)
Grand Victorian homes ring Alamo Square.

4. Zuni Cafe (p183)
Zuni Cafe has been turning basic menu items into gourmet staples since 1979.

◉ Hayes Valley

ZEN CENTER
HISTORIC BUILDING

Map p329 (☑415-863-3136; www.sfzc.org; 300 Page St; ◷9:30am-12:30pm & 1:30-5pm Mon-Fri, 8:30am-noon Sat; Ⓜ️Hayes St) No, this isn't a spa, but an active spiritual retreat since 1969 for the largest Buddhist community outside Asia. The graceful landmark building was designed by Julia Morgan, California's first licensed female architect, better known as chief architect of Hearst Castle and the Chinatown YWCA (see p106). Morgan built this Italianate brick structure in 1922 to house Emanu-el Sisterhood, a residence for low-income Jewish working women, and you can see ironwork stars of David on the first-floor loggia. With its large, open courtyard and casement windows, the building has inspired and illuminated people of all faiths.

The center is open to the public for visits, meditation (see the website for the meditation schedule) and Zen workshops, and also offers overnight stays by prior arrangement for intensive meditation retreats.

✖️ EATING

✖️ The Haight

TOP CHOICE ROSAMUNDE SAUSAGE GRILL
SAUSAGES $

Map p338 (☑415-437-6851; 545 Haight St; sausages $4-6; ◷11:30am-10pm; Ⓜ️Haight St) Impress a dinner date on the cheap: load up classic Brats or duck-fig links with complimentary roasted peppers, grilled onions, whole-grain mustard and mango chutney, and enjoy with your choice of 100 beers at Toronado (p183), next door.

THREE TWINS ICE CREAM
ICE CREAM $

Map p338 (☑415-487-8946; www.threetwins icecream.com; 254 Fillmore St; cone $2.25-3.25; ◷noon-10:30pm Mon-Thu, 11am-11pm Fri & Sat, 11am-10:30pm Sun; Ⓜ️Haight St) Lower Haight's kids, locavores and pot club regulars agree: Three Twins has the finest seasonal, certified organic ice creams in town. Fall means cardamom, winter is an excuse for Meyer lemon cookie, spring brings honey orange blossom and summer is all about Strawberry Je Ne Sais Quoi, with a dash

of balsamic vinegar. For a taste sensation, get bittersweet chocolate or vanilla almond drizzled with Sonoma olive oil and sea salt.

BAR CRUDO
SEAFOOD $$

Map p338 (☑415-409-0679; www.barcrudo. com; 655 Divisadero St; small plates $10-14; ◷5-11pm Mon-Sat, to 10pm Sun; Ⓜ️Divisidero St) An international idea that's pure California: choice morsels of fresh seafood served raw Italian-style, with pan-Asian condiments and East–West beers. Start with Japanese Hitachino white ale and raw fluke with coconut milk and grapefruit, and graduate to potent Belgian Tripel ales with wasabi-spiked Arctic char. Don't miss Tuesday to Sunday happy hour from 5pm to 6:30pm, when specials include $1 local oysters.

RAGAZZA
PIZZA $$

Map p338 (☑415-255-1133; www.ragazzasf.com; 311 Divisadero St; pizza $13-18; ◷5-10pm Mon-Thu, to 10:30 Fri & Sat; ✏️ 🚼; Ⓜ️Divisadero St) 'Girl' is what the name means, as in, 'Oooh, girl, did you try the nettle pizza?!' Since it comes with Boccalone pancetta, portobello mushrooms and nutty provolone, you definitely should. Locally cured, humanely raised pork is the breakout star of many Ragazza pies, from the Amatriciana with pecorino, bacon and egg to the Calabrian chili with cauliflower and pork belly. Squash blossom pizza with truffle cheese needs no such embellishment, though a glass of Greco di Tufo wine couldn't hurt.

MAGNOLIA BREWPUB
CALIFORNIAN, AMERICAN $$

Map p338 (☑415-864-7468; www.magnoliapub. com; 1398 Haight St; mains $11-20; ◷noon-midnight Mon-Thu, to 1am Fri, 10am-1am Sat, 10am-midnight Sun; Ⓜ️Haight St) Organic pub grub and samplers of homebrews keep the conversation flowing at communal tables, while grass-fed Prather Ranch burgers satisfy stoner appetites in the side booths – it's like the Summer of Love all over again, only with better food. Magnolia smells vaguely like a brewery because it is one, which can be a problem at brunch but is definitely an asset otherwise. Features seasonal microbrew ales and wheat beers you won't find elsewhere.

ZIRYAB
MIDDLE EASTERN $$

Map p338 (☑415-522-0800; www.ziryabgrill.com; 528 Divisadero St; mains $10-16; ◷4-11:30pm Mon-Thu, noon-12:30pm Fri & Sat, noon-11pm Sun; ✏️; Ⓜ️Divisadero St) Banish all traumatic memo-

TOP SIGHTS
ALAMO SQUARE

San Franciscans seldom miss an opportunity to show off, as you can see from the outrageous Victorian homes ringing Alamo Square Park. When San Franciscans struck it rich in the Gold Rush, they upgraded from Downtown tenements to grand houses embellished to the eaves with woodwork and gilding. These ornaments served a practical purpose: rows of houses were hastily constructed using a similar template, and citizens needed to know which stairs to stumble up after long Barbary Coast nights.

Since Alamo Square homes were built on bedrock away from Downtown, several were spared San Francisco's 1906 earthquake and fire. But modern real estate magnates consider Gold Rush tastes garish enough to bring down property values, so many of SF's 'Painted Ladies' have been painted marketably bland beige. The pastel, cookie-cutter Painted Ladies of famed **Postcard Row** on Alamo Square's east side literally pale in comparison with the colorful characters along the north side of the park, and along parallel McAllister and Golden Gate Sts. Here you'll spot true Barbary Coast baroque: facades bedecked with fish-scale shingles, swagged stucco garlands and gingerbread trim dripping from peaked roofs. On sunny days, claim a hilltop picnic table and see the city skyline framed by wind-sculpted pines.

DON'T MISS...

➡ Postcard Row
➡ Hilltop shoe planters
➡ Easterward views of Downtown skyline
➡ Hillside picnic tables

PRACTICALITIES

➡ Map p338
➡ Btwn Hayes & Scott Sts
➡ Admission free
➡ Ⓜ Hayes St

THE HAIGHT & HAYES VALLEY ALAMO SQUARE

---

ries of dry chicken *shwarmas* with this succulent, organic poultry rolled in flatbread and sealed by hummus with a tantalizing whiff of curry. The vegan lentil soup is so robust it'll make your voice drop an octave, and the hookahs on the front porch provide solace to smokers rendered furtive by SF's antismoking laws.

COLE VALLEY CAFE
CAFE $

Map p338 (✉415-668-5282; www.colevalleycafe.com; 701 Cole St; sandwiches $5-6; ☺6:30am-8:30pm Mon-Fri, to 8pm Sat & Sun; 🛜📷🚼; Ⓜ Haight St) Powerful coffee and chai, free wi-fi, chocolate-chip pumpkin cake and hot gourmet sandwiches – go for the lip-smacking thyme-marinated chicken with lemony avocado spread, or smoky roasted eggplant with peppers and pesto. Chef/owner Jawad knows the entire neighborhood by name and lunch order, and has a kind word for everyone.

🖼 LITTLE CHIHUAHUA
MEXICAN $

Map p338 (✉415-255-8225; www.thelittlechihuahua.com; 292 Divisadero St; tacos/burritos

$4/7; ☺11am-11pm Mon-Fri, 10am-11pm Sat & Sun; Ⓜ Haight St) Who says sustainable, organic food has to be expensive or French? Charbroiled tomatillos, sustainable fish, Niman Ranch meats and organic veggies add up to sensational tacos, washed down with $3 draft beer or housemade organic *agua fresca* (fruit drink).

AXUM CAFE
ETHIOPIAN $

Map p338 (✉415-252-7912; www.axumcafe.com; 698 Haight St; mains $7-14; ☺5:30-10pm Mon-Fri, 12:30-10pm Sat & Sun; 📷; Ⓜ Haight St) Whether you've got a hot date with a vegan, the hunger of an athlete or the salary of an activist, Axum's vegetarian platter for two with spongy *injera* bread is your saving grace. Dig in with your bare hands, and try not to hog lip-tingling red lentils and mellow yellow chickpeas.

ESCAPE FROM NEW YORK PIZZA
PIZZA $

Map p338 (✉415-668-5577; www.escapefromnewyorkpizza.com; 1737 Haight St; slices $3-4; ☺11:30am-midnight Sun-Thu, to 2am Fri & Sat; 📷🚼; Ⓜ Haight St) The Haight's obligatory

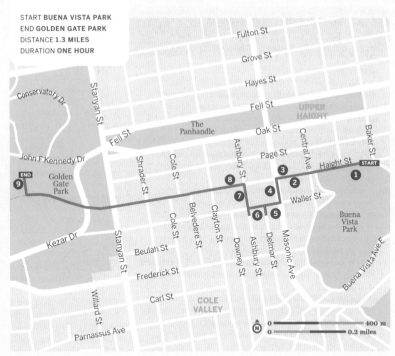

START **BUENA VISTA PARK**
END **GOLDEN GATE PARK**
DISTANCE **1.3 MILES**
DURATION **ONE HOUR**

Neighborhood Walk
Haight Flashback

➡ Start your trip back in time in ❶ **Buena Vista Park**, with panoramic city views that moved surviving San Franciscans to tears after the fire of 1906.

Heading west up Haight St, you may recognize Emma Goldman and Sacco and Vanzetti in the *Anarchists of the Americas* mural at ❷ **Bound Together Anarchist Book Collective** – if you don't, staff can provide you with some biographical comics by way of introduction. Continuing west, you can't miss ❸ **Magnolia Brewpub**, the corner microbrewery and organic eatery named after a Grateful Dead song.

At ❹ **1235 Masonic Ave**, you might once have glimpsed the Simbionese Liberation Army. This was once a safehouse where the SLA is believed to have held Patty Hearst, the kidnapped heiress turned revolutionary bank robber.

Turning right off Masonic Ave onto Waller St, you'll notice a narrow lane leading uphill. In 1978 ❺ **32 Delmar St** was the site of Sid Vicious' overdose that finally broke up the Sex Pistols.

Pay your respects to the former flophouse of Jerry Garcia, Bob Weir and Pigpen, plus sundry Deadheads, at the ❻ **Grateful Dead House** at 710 Ashbury St. In October 1967, antidrug cops raided the house and arrested everyone in it (Garcia wasn't home). Down the block, ❼ **635 Ashbury St** is one of many known San Francisco addresses for Janis Joplin, who had a hard time hanging onto leases in the 1960s – but, as she sang, 'Freedom's just another word for nothin' left to lose.'

At the corner of Haight and Ashbury, you'll notice that the ❽ **clock** overhead always reads 4:20, better known in 'Hashbury' as International Bong Hit Time. Follow the beat of your own drummer to the drum circle at ❾ **Hippie Hill in Golden Gate Park**, where free spirits have gathered since the '60s to tune in, turn on and attempt to hit a workable groove.

mid-bender stop for a hot slice. Pesto with roasted garlic and potato will send you blissfully off to carbo-loaded sleep, but the sundried tomato with goat cheese, artichoke hearts and spinach will recharge you to go another round.

✗ Hayes Valley

TOP CHOICE JARDINIÈRE   CALIFORNIAN $$$

(Map p329; ☑415-861-5555; www.jardiniere. com; 300 Grove St; mains $19-37; ☺5-10:30pm Tue-Sat, to 10pm Sun & Mon; Ⓜ Van Ness) Her formidable reputation as Iron Chef, Top Chef Master and James Beard Award winner precedes her, but star chef Traci Des Jardins is better known at her namesake restaurant Jardinière as a champion of sustainable, salacious California cuisine. She has a way with California's organic vegetables, free-range meats and sustainably caught seafood that's probably illegal in other states, lavishing braised oxtail ravioli with summer truffles and stuffing crispy pork belly with salami and fig. Go Mondays, when $45 scores three decadent courses with wine pairings.

🍴 BAR JULES   CALIFORNIAN $$

Map p329 (☑415-621-5482; www.barjules.com; 609 Hayes St; mains $10-26; ☺6-10pm Tue, 11:30am-3pm & 6-10pm Wed-Sat, 11am-3pm Sun; Ⓜ Hayes St) Small, local and succulent is the credo at this corridor of a neighborhood bistro. The short daily menu thinks big with flavor-rich, sustainably minded offerings like local duck breast with cherries, almonds and arugula, a local wine selection and the dark, sinister 'chocolate nemesis.' Even with reservations, waits are a given – but so is simple, tasty food.

ZUNI CAFE   CALIFORNIAN, AMERICAN $$$

Map p329 (☑415-552-2522; www.zunicafe.com; 1658 Market St; mains $14-29; ☺11:30am-11pm Tue-Thu, to midnight Fri & Sat, 11am-11pm Sun; Ⓜ Market St) Gimmickry is for amateurs – Zuni has been turning basic menu items into gourmet staples since 1979. Reservations and fat wallets are handy, but the see-and-be-seen seating is a kick and the food is beyond reproach: Caesar salad with house-cured anchovies, crispy wood-brick-oven-roasted free-range chicken with horseradish mashed potatoes, and mesquite-grilled organic-beef burgers on focaccia (pile of shoestring fries $6 extra, and recommended).

🍴 NOJO   JAPANESE $$

Map p329 (☑415-896-4587; www.nojosf.com; 231 Franklin St; small plates $4-12; ☺5-10pm Wed, Thu, Sun & Mon, to 11pm Fri & Sat; Ⓜ Hayes St) Everything you could possibly want skewered and roasted at happy hour, except maybe your boss. The house specialty is Japanese *izakaya* (bar snacks), especially grilled chicken yakitori (kebabs), panko-crusted anchovies and spicy beef heart slathered with earthy soy-based sauce. Plates are tasting-portion size, and you'll need that room for the house sundae: Humphry Slocombe black sesame and white miso ice creams with rice crackers. Top-notch produce, wine and beer selection, all locally sourced.

SUPPENKÜCHE   GERMAN $$

Map p329 (☑415-252-9289; www.suppenkuche. com; 525 Laguna St; mains $10.50-20; ☺dinner 5-10pm daily, brunch 10am-2:30pm Sun; Ⓜ Hayes St) Feast on housemade Bratwurst sausages and spaetzle oozing with cheese, and toast your new friends at the unvarnished communal table with a 2L glass boot of draft beer – then return to cure inevitable hangovers with Sunday brunches of inch-thick 'Emperor's Pancakes' studded with brandied raisins.

CHANTAL GUILLON MACARONS   DESSERT $

Map p329 (☑415-864-2400; www.chantalguillon. com; 437 Hayes St; macarons $1.60; ☺11am-7pm Tue-Sat, noon-6pm Sun & Mon; Ⓜ Hayes St) Sorry, Oreo: the competition for the ultimate sandwich cookie is down to Chantal Guillon's Sicilian pistachio and passion-fruit French macarons. Declare a winner from sunny sidewalk seats, or go for a second championship round: caramel *fleur-de-sel* salt and Early Grey.

🍷 DRINKING & NIGHTLIFE

🍸 The Haight

TOP CHOICE TORONADO   PUB

Map p338 (www.toronado.com; 547 Haight St; ☺11:30am-2am; Ⓜ Haight St) Glory hallelujah, beer lovers: your prayers have been heard. Be humbled before the chalkboard altar

LOCAL KNOWLEDGE

TRIPLE THREAT: VINYL WINE BAR

Combine three food trends – gourmet food trucks, wine on tap and pop-up restaurants – swirl vigorously, and voilá: **Vinyl Wine Bar** (Map p338; ☑415-621-4132; wwww.facebook.com/vinylwinebar; 359 Divisadero St; ⊗5:30-11pm Mon-Thu, to midnight Fri-Sun; MDivisadero St). It all started as a creative workaround: people drink more wine with food, but the former cafe venue didn't have a restaurant license. Trucked-in culinary options ranging from fresh pasta to soul food draw diverse foodie crowds, and tantalizing pairing possibilities. Care for an Austrian Grüner Veltliner with those grits, or maybe you'd prefer to blend your own wine to accompany that asparagus ravioli in sheep's milk sauce? Check Vinyl's Facebook page, and explore pairing options expanded to the power of three.

that lists 50-plus beers on tap and hundreds more bottled, including spectacular seasonal microbrews. Bring cash, come early and stay late, with a sausage from Rosamunde (p180) next door to accompany ale made by Trappist monks.

ALEMBIC BAR
Map p338 (www.alembicbar.com; 1725 Haight St; ⊗noon-2am; MHaight St) Haight St's spiffiest, tiniest bar has hammered tin ceilings, rough-hewn wood floors and 250 choices of specialty hooch – plus throngs of artisan bourbon drinkers and cocktail research historians proudly standing behind the 'No Red Bull/No Jägermeister' sign. Bar snacks here aren't elementary peanuts, but advanced-degree artisan cheeses, pickled quail eggs and iced duck hearts.

AUB ZAM ZAM BAR
Map p338 (1633 Haight St; ⊗3pm-2am; MHaight St) Arabesque arches, an *Arabian Nights*–style mural, 1930s jazz on the jukebox and top-shelf cocktails at low-shelf prices keep restless romantics happy for the night at this Haight St mainstay. Legendary founder Bruno was a character who'd throw you out for ordering a vodka martini, but he was a softie in the end, bequeathing his beloved bar to regulars who had become friends. Cash only.

COFFEE TO THE PEOPLE CAFE
Map p338 (1206 Masonic Ave; ⊗6am-8pm Mon-Fri, to 9pm Sat & Sun; 🛜📶🚻; MHaight St) Coffee breaks here may induce flashbacks, what with the radical bumper stickers on the tables, hippie macramé on the walls, shelves of consciousness-raising books and enough fair-trade espresso to revive the Sandinista movement. Five percent of your purchase goes to support community organizations, and baristas donate 3% of their tips to

send children in coffee-growing regions to school.

MADRONE BAR
Map p338 (☑415-241-0202; www.madronelounge.com; 500 Divisadero St; ⊗5pm-2am Tue-Sat, 6pm-2am Sun & Mon; MDivisadero St) A changing roster of DJs and giggling cuties come as a surprise in a Victorian bar decorated with rotating art installations and a tree-trunk bar, a bomb-shaped disco ball and an absinthe fountain – but nothing tops the jaw-dropping mash-ups at the Saturday-monthly Prince vs Michael Jackson party, when the place packs.

NOC NOC BAR
Map p338 (www.nocnocs.com; 557 Haight St; ⊗5pm-2am; MHaight St) Who's there? Near-sighted graffiti artists, anarchist hackers moonlighting as electronica DJs, and other characters straight out of an R Crumb comic, that's who. Happy hour is from 5pm to 7pm daily, but be warned: those sake cocktails will knock-knock you off your scavenged steampunk stool.

UVA ENOTECA BAR
Map p338 (www.uvaenoteca.com; 568 Haight St; ⊗5-11pm Mon-Thu, to 11:30pm Fri, 11am-2:30pm & 5-11:30pm Sat, 11am-2:30pm & 5-10pm Sun; MHaight St) Boys with shags and girls with bangs discover the joys of Bardolino and Barbera by the tasting glass, served with inventive small plates of local veggies, cheese and charcuterie boards by a staff of tattooed Lower Haight hotties.

Hayes Valley

TOP CHOICE SMUGGLER'S COVE BAR
(www.smugglerscovesf.com; 650 Gough St; ⊗5pm-2am; MVan Ness) Yo-ho-ho and a bottle of rum...or wait, make that a Dead

Reckoning tawny port cocktail with Angostura bitters, Nicaraguan rum and vanilla liqueur, unless someone wants to share the flaming Scorpion Bowl? Pirates are bedeviled by choice at this shambling Barbary Coast shipwreck of a tiki bar, hidden speakeasy-style behind a tinted door. With tasting flights from a selection of 200 specialty rums and 70 historic cocktail recipes gleaned from rum-running around the world, you won't be dry-docked for long.

HÔTEL BIRON BAR
Map p329 (www.hotelbiron.com; 45 Rose St; ☺5pm-2am; ⓂMarket St) An oenologist's dream walk-in closet that serves as a wine bar, with standout Californian, Provençal and Tuscan vintages, and a ceiling made of corks. The vibe is French underground, with exposed-brick walls, surreally romantic art, a leather couch and just a few tables for two. Barkeeps let you keep tasting until you find what you like; pair with decadent cheese plates.

MARTUNI'S GAY BAR
Map p329 (http://martunis.ypguides.net; 4 Valencia St; ☺2pm-2am; ⓂMarket St) Slip behind the velvet curtains to see who's tickling the ivories at the city's last piano bar, where gay and straight, salt-and-pepper regulars seem to have committed the Great American Songbook to memory. You'll be singing too, after a couple of top-notch watermelon, apricot or Godiva chocolate martinis under $10.

PISCO LATIN LOUNGE BAR
Map p329 (www.piscosf.com; 1817 Market St; ☺5pm-midnight Mon-Thu & Sun, to 1am Fri & Sat; ⓂMarket St) The pisco sour has been the toast of SF since the Peruvians arrived in the early days of the Gold Rush, before the word 'vegan' was coined. So although Pisco serves Nuevo Latino small bites like quinoa risotto balls and yucca fries at its walnut bar, the signature drink is strictly traditional: pisco sour made with lime, pisco liquor, and a swirl of bitters atop frothy egg whites.

MOMI TOBY'S REVOLUTION CAFÉ CAFE
Map p329 (528 Laguna St; ☺7:30am-10pm Mon-Thu, to 11pm Fri, 8am-10pm Sat & Sun; ⓂHayes St) For once, a cafe that's not an internet port. Dig the boho scene, with artists on both sides of the counter, swilling coffee and wine. Bask in the sun at outdoor tables, or snag a window seat inside and mingle with locals over leisurely happy hours (4pm to 7pm daily). There's another location in the Mission that hosts Classical Revolution concerts on Sundays.

☆ ENTERTAINMENT

INDEPENDENT LIVE MUSIC
Map p338 (☑415-771-1421; www.theindependentsf.com; 628 Divisadero St; tickets $13-20; ☺box office 11am-6pm Mon-Fri, to 9:30pm show nights, doors 7:30pm or 8:30pm; ⓂDivisadero St) One of the city's coolest live-music venues, the Independent showcases funky soul acts (Nikka Costa, Sergent Garcia), indie dreamers (Kimya Dawson, Blonde Redhead) and cult rock (Meat Puppets, Ted Nugent), plus such wacky events as the US Air Guitar Championships. Ventilation is poor, but drinks are cheap.

REBEL BAR GAY CLUB
Map p329 (☑415-431-4202; 1760 Market St; ☺5pm-3am Mon-Thu, to 4am Fri, 11am-4am Sat & Sun; ⓂMarket St) Funhouse southern biker bar disco, complete with antique mirrored walls, signature Hell's Angel cocktail (Bulleit bourbon, Chartreuse and OJ) and all those exposed pipes (ahem). Rebel looks badass, but it's SF all the way: bartenders are flirty, there's vinegary Carolina-style BBQ at the in-house pop-up restaurant, and the crowd is not above bouncing to Gaga. The crowd is mostly 30-something, gay and tribally tattooed, but you can bring anyone who's not easily scandalized. On a good night, all four poles get thoroughly worked.

BOOKSMITH BOOK READINGS
Map p338 (☑415-863-8688; www.booksmith.com; 1644 Haight St; ☺10am-10pm Mon-Sat, to 8pm Sun; ☝; ⓂHaight St) SF is one of America's top three book markets, and authors who swing through town on tours make Booksmith's Author Series a literary destination. Recent readings include *Sandman* and *Coraline* author Neil Gaiman, legendary rock critic Greil Marcus and controversial 'tiger mother' Amy Chua. Check online calendar for book swaps and Saturday morning kids' story hour.

SF LESBIAN GAY BISEXUAL TRANSGENDER COMMUNITY CENTER GAY CENTER
Map p329 (☑415-865-5555; www.sfcenter.org; 1800 Market St; ☺noon-6pm; ⓂMarket St) The glass-walled teal Victorian is a gorgeous place to see and be seen, but because of

poor endowment, too-high rental rates and weak programming, it hasn't panned out as a GLBT community hangout. Still, it's worth a look to see if something's on during Pride month (June).

SHOPPING

The Haight

AMOEBA MUSIC   MUSIC STORE
Map p338 (www.amoeba.com; 1855 Haight St; ⊙10:30am-10pm Mon-Sat, 11am-9pm Sun; MHaight St) Enticements are hardly necessary to lure the masses to the West Coast's most eclectic collection of new and used music and video, but Amoeba offers listening stations, a free music zine with uncannily accurate reviews, a free concert series that recently starred Elvis Costello and Shonen Knife, and a foundation that's saved more than 1000 acres of rainforest.

BOUND TOGETHER ANARCHIST BOOK COLLECTIVE   BOOKSTORE
Map p338 (www.boundtogetherbookstore.com; 1369 Haight St; ⊙11:30am-7:30pm; MHaight St) Given the state of the economy lately, an anarchist bookstore seems like the go-to place for answers. Since 1976 this volunteer-run, nonprofit bookstore has kept free thinkers supplied with organic farming manuals, prison literature and radical comics, while coordinating the Anarchist Book Fair and restoring its 'Anarchists of the Americas' storefront mural – makes us tools of the state look like slackers.

GOORIN BROTHERS HATS   ACCESSORIES
Map p338 (www.goorin.com; 1446 Haight St; ⊙11am-7pm Sun-Fri, to 8pm Sat; MHaight St) Peacock feathers, high crowns and local-artist-designed embellishments make it easy for SF hipsters to withstand the fog while standing out in a crowd. Straw fedoras with striped tie-silk bands bring the shade in style, as do flat-brim baseball caps with warrior embroidery by Hawaiian San Franciscan tattoo artist Orly Lacquiao.

PRAIRIE COLLECTIVE   GIFTS, ACCESSORIES
Map p338 (www.prairiecollective.com; 262 Divisadero St; ⊙11am-6pm Wed-Mon, noon-4pm Sun; MHaight St) Three local designers are head-

KARAOKE AT THE MINT

Die-hard singers pore over giant books of 30,000 tunes in every genre at mixed-straight-gay karaoke bar the **Mint** (☏415-626-4726; www.themint.net; 1942 Market St; ⊙noon-2am; MMarket St), where big voices rattle pennies in the basement of the US mint just uphill. Coinage won't get you far here, though: standard karaoke-jockey tip is $1 a song. Billy Idol is fair game for a goof, but only serious belters take on Barbra.

ing back to nature while putting down roots in a San Francisco storefront with mellow pups-in-residence Bernie and Lil' Boy. Studio Choo's wildflower arrangements burst from antique medicine bottles, Magpie & Rye's tree-trunk bowls and macramé-covered pebble paperweights usher the outdoors into offices, and vintage flour sacks find new purpose in life thanks to found-design specialists the Cloak and Cabinet Society. The boutique is a miniature Mendocino getaway, with its upscale beach-shed look and honeyed aromas of handmade beeswax candles.

PIEDMONT BOUTIQUE   CLOTHING, ACCESSORIES
Map p338 (www.piedmontsf.com; 1452 Haight St; ⊙11am-7pm; MHaight St) 'No food, no cell phones, no playing in the boas,' says the sign at the door, but inside, that last rule is gleefully ignored by cross-dressers, cabaret singers, strippers and people who take Halloween dead seriously. All the getups are custom-designed in-house and built to last – so, like certain escorts, honey, they're not as cheap as they look.

LOYAL ARMY CLOTHING   CLOTHING, ACCESSORIES
Map p338 (www.loyalarmy.com; 1728 Haight St; ⊙11am-7pm Mon-Sat, 11:30am-7pm Sun; 🖢; MHaight St) Food with high self-esteem is a recurring theme on this San Francisco designer's cartoon-cute tees, totes and baby clothes: a bag of chips says 'All that and me!', while California rolls brag to nigiri sushi 'That's how we roll!' and a butter pat on pancakes squeals 'I'm a hot mess!' But the most popular character is the San Francisco fogbank: most of the clouds are silver and smiling, but there's always one that has fangs.

WASTELAND
CLOTHING, ACCESSORIES

Map p338 (www.wastelandclothing.com; 1660 Haight St; ⊙11am-8pm Mon-Sat, noon-7pm Sun; Ⓜ Haight St) The catwalk of thrift, this vintage superstore adds instant style with barely worn Marc Jacobs smocks, '70s Pucci maxi-skirts and a steady supply of go-go boots. Hip occasionally verges on hideous with fringed sweaters and patchwork suede jackets, but at these prices you can afford to take fashion risks.

REVOLVER
CLOTHING, ACCESSORIES

Map p338 (www.revolversf.com; 136 Fillmore St; ⊙noon-8pm; Ⓜ Haight St) Entering this boutique is like wandering into the bedroom of some stoner-dandy Western novelist, with easy pieces in natural, nubby fabrics strewn across wooden crates and clocks made from linen-bound antique books ticking noisily on the walls. Don't miss the store-within-a-store in the rear gallery, which was recently wallpapered with maps, strung with feisty air plants in miniature glass terrariums, and stocked with American-made suede saddle shoes and Japanese linen sundresses.

UPPER PLAYGROUND
CLOTHING, ACCESSORIES

Map p338 (☑415-861-1960; www.upperplayground.com; 220 Fillmore St; ⊙noon-7pm; Ⓜ Haight St) Blend into the SF scenery with locally designed 'Left Coast' hoodies, geek-chic tees featuring the state of California stuffed into a tube sock, and collegiate pennants for city neighborhoods (the Tenderloin totally needs a cheering section). Men's gear dominates, but there are women's tees, kids' tees in the back room and slick graffiti art in Fifty24SF Gallery next door.

XAPNO
GIFTS, CLOTHING

Map p338 (☑415-863-8199; www.xapno.com; 678 Haight St; ⊙11am-7pm Tue-Thu & Sun, 10am-9pm Fri & Sat; Ⓜ Haight St) Antique typewriter ribbon tins, bracelets locally made from pocket-watch faces, succulents dripping from hanging nautilus shells: such unusual gifts lead grateful recipients to believe you've spent weeks and small fortunes in San Francisco curiosity shops. But Xapno regularly stocks rare finds at reasonable prices, and will wrap them for you, too. Hours are erratic.

LOVED TO DEATH
GIFTS, CLOTHING

Map p338 (☑415-551-1036; www.lovedtodeath.net; 1681 Haight St; ⊙11:30am-7pm Mon-Sat, noon-7pm Sun; Ⓜ Haight St) Herds of deer stare unblinking from the walls alongside devotional ex-voto miniatures, a beady-eyed hawk and a rusty saw. The signs here are definitely ominous, and for sale. Taxidermy is a recurring theme in San Francisco decor lately, but this ghoulish gallery goes beyond the pale with Victorian Lolita Goth bat-winged lockets and, for ruthless romantics, heart-shaped cast-iron locks. Not for the faint of heart, or vegans – though as store proprietors point out, no animal has been killed specifically for these designs.

SFO SNOWBOARDING & FTC SKATEBOARDING
OUTDOOR GEAR

Map p338 (☑415-626-1141; www.sfosnow.com; 1630-32 Haight St; ⊙11am-7pm; Ⓜ Haight St) Big air and big style are the tip at this local snowboard and skateboard outfitter. Show some local flair as you grab air on a Western Edition deck with drawings of ramshackle Victorian houses, or hit the slopes with Tahoe-tested gear (mostly for dudes, some unisex). Ask clued-in staff about upcoming SF street games and Tahoe snow conditions.

BRAINDROPS
BODY ART

Map p338 (☑415-621-4162; www.braindrops.net; 1324 Haight St; ⊙noon-7pm Sun-Thu, to 8pm Fri & Sat; Ⓜ Haight St) New Yorkers and Berliners fly in for original custom designs by top tattoo artists here – bring design ideas to your consultant, or trust them to make suggestions. Piercings are done here gently without a gun, with body jewelry ranging from pop-star opal belly-button studs to mondo jade ear spools.

Ⓗ Hayes Valley

TOP CHOICE RELIQUARY
CLOTHING, ACCESSORIES

Map p329 (☑415-431-4000; www.reliquarysf.com; 537 Octavia Blvd; ⊙11am-7pm Tue-Sat, noon-6pm Sun; Ⓜ Hayes St) Earthy and urbane is not an oxymoron, but a lifestyle choice achievable through years of meditation and/or a shopping spree at Reliquary. Owner Leah Bershad was once a designer for the Gap, but the folksy jet-set aesthetic here is the exact opposite of khaki-and-fleece global domination. Half the stock is well-traveled vintage – ikat silk kimonos, Santa Fe woolen blankets, silver jewelry banged together by Humboldt hippies – and the rest are cult American designs like Court

GANGS OF SAN FRANCISCO T-SHIRTS

Watch out, because **Laureano Faedi** (☑415-621-2431; www.gangsofsanfrancisco.com; 66 Gough St; ☉noon-6pm Tue-Sat, to 4pm Sun; Ⓜ Hayes St) is about to get all historical on your T-shirt – and if that sounds quaintly threatening, wait until you see his logos. The Brazil-born SF silk-screener has unearthed insignia for every thuggish clique to claim an SF street corner, from the San Francisco Vigilance Committee – known for conducting kangaroo trials and swift hangings during SF's Gold Rush era – to the Richmond Beer Town Brawlers, who malingered near Golden Gate Park c 1875–96.

denim, Majestic tissue-tees and Claire Vivier pebble-leather clutches.

FLIGHT 001   ACCESSORIES

Map p329 (☑415-487-1001; www.flight001.com; 525 Hayes St; ☉11am-7pm Mon-Sat, to 6pm Sun; Ⓜ Hayes St) Having a nice flight in the zero-legroom era is actually a possibility with the in-flight assistance of Flight 001. Clever carry-ons built to fit international size regulations come with just the right number of pockets for rubber alarm clocks, travel Scrabble sets and the first-class Jet Comfort Kit with earplugs, sleep mask, booties, neck rest, candy and cards.

POLANCO   ACCESSORIES, HOUSEWARES

Map p329 (☑415-252-5753; 393 Hayes St; ☉noon-6pm Mon, 11:30am-6:30pm Tue-Sat, 1-6pm Sun; Ⓜ Hayes St) Contemporary folk art by Mexican and Chicano artists mix traditional techniques and new ideas at Polanco, from Artemio Rodriguez's woodcuts of Day of the Dead skeletons sporting Mohawks to Gabriel Mendoza's surrealist *retratos* (portraits) of professionals literally consumed by their work. Don't miss the Oaxacan devil masks embedded with actual goat's horns, or the Frida Kahlo–esque earrings of silver hands cupping tiny hearts.

NANCY BOY   BEAUTY PRODUCTS

Map p329 (☑415-552-3636; www.nancyboy.com; 347 Hayes St; ☉11am-7pm Mon-Fri, to 6pm Sat & Sun; Ⓜ Hayes St) All you closet pomaders and after-sun balmers: wear those products with pride, without feeling like the dupe of some cosmetics conglomerate. Clever Nancy Boy knows you'd rather pay for the product than for advertising campaigns featuring the starlet du jour, and delivers locally made products with effective plant oils that are tested on boyfriends, never animals.

GIMME SHOES   SHOES

Map p329 (☑415-864-0691; www.gimmeshoes.com; 416 & 381 Hayes St; ☉11am-7pm Mon-Sat,

noon-6pm Sun; Ⓜ Hayes St) Don't let SF hills become your arch-rivals: head to Gimme Shoes and kick up those high-end heels. Bide your time and those Philip Lim wood platforms and Vivienne Westwood pirate boots at the spotlit 381 Hayes showcase might hit the 40%-to-60%-off racks across the street at 416 Hayes. Men have their pick of sleek pearl grey Costume National oxfords or soft-soled John Varvatos Fillmore ankle boots.

MAC   CLOTHING, ACCESSORIES

Map p329 (☑415-863-3011; www.modernappealingclothing.com; 387 Grove St; ☉11am-7pm Mon-Sat, noon-6pm Sun; Ⓜ Hayes St) 'Modern Appealing Clothing' is what it promises and what it delivers with structured looks from Belgian minimalist Dries Van Noten, New Wave revivals from Van Beirendonck and splashy limited-edition tees designed by developmentally disabled artisans at Oakland's Creative Growth. Staff are on your side, rooting for you to score something from the 40%-to-75%-off sales rack. Check out the second location showcasing California designers on Dogpatch's artisan shopping strip at 1003 Minnesota.

PEACE INDUSTRY   HOUSEWARES

Map p329 (☑415-255-9940; www.peaceindustry.com; 597 Hayes St; ☉10am-6pm Mon-Fri, 11am-6pm Sat, 11am-5pm Sun; Ⓜ Hayes St) Persian carpets usually take credit for grand entrances, but Peace Industry's cooperative-made Iranian felted wool rugs have graphic pop art appeal achieved with vegetable dyes and a spongy, ticklish texture underfoot. Get back to nature with a dewdrop pattern in off-white and brown wool or go arty with a Salvador Dalí curled mustache pattern.

FLAX   ART SUPPLIES

Map p329 (☑415-552-2355; www.flaxart.com; 1699 Market St; ☉9:30am-7pm Mon-Sat; ♿; Ⓜ Market St) People who swear they lack artistic flair suddenly find it at Flax, where an entire room of specialty papers, racks of plump paint tubes in luscious colors and a wonderland of hot-glue guns practically make the collage for you. Art projects for kids start here, and the vast selections of pens and notebooks are novels waiting to happen.

MIETTE   FOOD

Map p329 (☎415-626-6221; www.miettecakes. com; 449 Octavia Blvd; ☺noon-7pm Sun-Fri, 11am-7pm Sat; ⓂHayes St) Pure candy heaven: racks of licorice twists, a table of artisan chocolate bars and a fully stocked cup-cake counter. Tots load up on Pixie Stix and chocolate fire trucks, while adults ogle salty French caramels and dark chocolates spiked with chili. Ask for help first, so you don't get caught with your hand in the candy jar.

GREEN ARCADE   BOOKSTORE

Mapp329(☎415-431-6800;www.thegreenarcade. com; 1680 Market St; ☺noon-8pm Mon-Sat, to 7pm Sun; ⓜ; ⓂMarket St) Everything you al-ways wanted to know about mushroom foraging, worm composting and running for office on an environmental platform. This bookstore emphasizes helpful how-to books over eco-apocalypse treatises, so you'll leave with a rosier outlook on making the world a greener place.

ISOTOPE   BOOKSTORE

Map p329 (☎415-621-6543; www.isotopecomics. com; 326 Fell St; ☺11am-7pm Tue-Fri, to 6pm Sat & Sun; ⓜ; ⓂHayes St) The toilet seats signed by famous cartoonists over the front counter show just how seriously Isotope takes com-ics. Newbies tentatively flip through Daniel Clowes and Chris Ware in the graphic-novel section, while fanboys load up on Berke-ley's Adrian Tomine or the latest from SF's Last Gasp Publishing and head upstairs to lounge with local cartoonists.

LOTUS BLEU   HOUSEWARES

Mapp329(☎415-861-2700;www.lotusbleudesign. com; 325 Hayes St; ☺11am-6pm Tue-Fri, to 7pm Sat, noon-5pm Sun; ⓂHayes St) French whim-sy, Vietnamese design and San Franciscan psychedelic color keep eyes open wide in this compact design boutique packed from basement to rafters with fuchsia felt bull's-eye pillows, French laminated-canvas totes and lacquer breakfast trays.

RESIDENTS APPAREL
GALLERY   CLOTHING, ACCESSORIES

Map p329 (☎415-621-7718; www.ragsf.com; 541 Octavia Blvd; ☺noon-7pm; ⓜ; ⓂHayes St) Lo-cal designers make eclectic SF chic easy at this certified-green cooperative boutique. Take your pick of limited-edition screen-printed tees, locally made dark denim (no sweatshops here, thank you), reconstructed vintage dresses and one-of-a-kind jewelry in silver, gemstones and found feathers.

FIDDLESTICKS   GIFTS, CLOTHING

Map p329 (☎415-565-0508; www.shopfiddle sticks.com; 540 Hayes St; ☺11am-7pm Mon-Sat, to 6pm Sun; ⓜ; ⓂHayes St) Baby shower gifts are a done deal here with teensy superhero capes, eensy organic-cotton elephant one-sies and weensy moon boots. Gifts under $30 for big sisters and brothers include an igloo dollhouse and toy recycling trucks made from recycled green plastic.

🏃 SPORTS & ACTIVITIES

AQUA SURF SHOP   SURFING

Map p338 (☎415-876-2782; www.aquasurfshop. com; 1742 Haight St; ☺11am-7pm; rental per day board/wetsuit $25/15; ⓂHaight St) This laid-back, tiki-themed surf shop has wax for your board, reversible polka-dot biki-nis and signature hoodies to brave chilly Ocean Beach. Even kooks (newbies) be-come mavericks with Aqua's wetsuit rent-als, tide updates and lesson referrals.

AVENUE CYCLERY   CYCLING

Map p338 (☎415-387-3155; www.avenuecyclery. com; 756 Stanyan St; bikes per hr/day $8/30; ☺10am-6pm Mon-Sat, to 5pm Sun; ⓜ; ⓂHaight St) In one of the more bicycle-friendly parts of the city, Avenue Cyclery has an extensive selection of bicycles for rent (price includes helmet) and for sale.

KORET POOL   SWIMMING

Map p338 (☎415-422-6821; www.usfca.edu/koret; Parker Ave & Turk St; adult/child $15/10; ☺6am-9pm Mon-Fri, 8am-6pm Sat & Sun; ⓂStanyan St) For a serious lap swim, head to this Olympic-sized pool at the University of San Francisco, with 40ft ceilings and over-sized windows. Admission includes use of the full gym as well.

Golden Gate Park & the Avenues

Neighborhood Top Five

1 Doing what comes naturally in **Golden Gate Park** (p192): skipping, lolling or Lindy-hopping through America's most outlandish stretch of urban wilderness alongside strange flowers and stranger art, and racing the buffalo towards the Pacific Ocean.

2 Following Andy Goldsworthy's sidewalk fault lines to earth-shaking art inside the **MH de Young Museum** (p193).

3 Enjoying sunsets on the wildflower-topped roof and wild nights at **California Academy of Sciences** (p193).

4 Numbing toes in the Pacific and expanding horizons to Asia at **Ocean Beach** (p198).

5 Finding foodie nirvana in the foggy outer reaches of the **Richmond** and the **Sunset** (p198) districts.

For more detail of this area, see Map p342 ➡

Explore Golden Gate Park & the Avenues

Civilization is overrated, with its traffic jams and office blocks – but by the time you reach the Conservatory of Flowers in Golden Gate Park, that's all behind you. Hang out with blue butterflies in the rainforest dome at the California Academy of Sciences, or globe-trot from Egyptian goddesses to James Turrell light installations in MH de Young Museum's worldly arts exhibits. Enjoy a moment of Zen and green tea in the Japanese Tea Garden, then summit Strawberry Hill for views over Stow Lake to the Pacific as red-tailed hawks swoop past.

Wander to the Botanical Garden for respite in the redwood grove before hopping the N streetcar all the way to Ocean Beach. Stroll the four-mile stretch of sand to the Richmond for dinner at Aziza and drinks at Trad'r Sam's, or stay put in the Sunset for surf-shopping at Mollusk and dinner at Outerlands or Thanh Long. With food and fog like this, you must be in heaven.

Local Life

➡ **Sporting life** Take on new challenges in Golden Gate Park, including roller disco, fly-casting, disc golf and Lindy-hopping (p204).

➡ **Foggy days** Stay warm with Trouble Coffee (p201), hoodies from Mollusk (p203), matinees at the Balboa Theater (p202), and rainforest strolls inside the California Academy of Sciences (p193) and Conservatory of Flowers (p194).

➡ **Goose bumps, guaranteed** Get delicious chills with bare feet on Ocean Beach (p198), eerily lifelike ceremonial masks at MH de Young Museum (p193), cliff's-edge views along the Coastal Trail (p195) and ice-cream cocktails at Trad'r Sam's (p202).

➡ **Outposts of cool** Outlandishness isn't just an aesthetic, but a way of life at Park Life (p203) art openings, Hollow (p202) art-installation coffee breaks, and musical interludes in the garden at General Store (p203).

Getting There & Away

➡ **Bus** Numbers 1 and 38 run from Downtown to the Richmond. Buses 5 and 21 head from Downtown along the north edge of Golden Gate Park, while number 2 runs the length of Clement St past the Legion of Honor. Bus 71 hooks around Golden Gate Park on the Sunset side.

➡ **Streetcar** The N line runs from Downtown, through the Sunset to Ocean Beach.

Lonely Planet's Top Tip

Hear that echo across Golden Gate Park? It's probably a concert, and very likely free. Opera divas, indie acts, bluegrass greats and hip-hop heavies take turns rocking SF gratis, from the wintry days of June through golden October afternoons. Most concerts are held in Sharon Meadow or Polo Fields on weekends; for upcoming events, consult the calendar (p22).

✦ Best Places to Eat

➡ Aziza (p198)
➡ Namu (p199)
➡ Kabuto (p199)
➡ Outerlands (p201)
➡ Thanh Long (p200)

For reviews, see p198 ➡

⬤ Best Places to Drink

➡ Beach Chalet (p201)
➡ Trouble Coffee (p201)
➡ Social (p202)
➡ Hollow (p202)
➡ Plough & the Stars (p202)

For reviews, see p201 ➡

◉ Best Urban Wildlife Sightings

➡ Bison (p192)
➡ Bank swallows (p198)
➡ White alligator (p193)
➡ Sea lions (p198)
➡ Snowy plover (p198)

For reviews, see p195 ➡

TOP SIGHTS
GOLDEN GATE PARK

When San Franciscans refer to 'the park,' there's only one that gets the definite article: Golden Gate Park. Everything San Franciscans hold dear is here: free spirits, free music, redwoods, Frisbee, protests, fine art, bonsai and buffalo.

On the northeast end of the park, you'll find the **Dahlia Garden**, Conservatory of Flowers (p194) and the sheltered, contemplative valley of the **AIDS Memorial Grove**. On the southeast corner is a **children's playground**, while further west is a baseball diamond, pagan altars on the hill behind and the **Shakespeare Garden**, featuring 150 plants mentioned in Shakespeare's writings.

The scenery turns surreal at the California Academy of Sciences (p193), Renzo Piano's LEED–certified home for 38,000 weird and wonderful animals under a 'living roof' of California wildflowers. Across the Music Concourse, you can see from Oceania to California via ancient Egypt inside Herzog & de Meuron's sleek MH de Young Museum (p193), clad with copper that's oxidizing green to blend into the park.

This scenery seems far-fetched now, but Mayor Frank McCoppin's park project seemed impossible in 1866. Even Frederick Law Olmstead, architect of New York's Central Park, was daunted by the prospect of transforming 1017 acres of dunes into park. San Francisco's green scheme fell to young, tenacious civil engineer William Hammond Hall, who insisted that instead of casinos, hotels and an igloo village, primary park features should include botanical gardens (p194), the Japanese Tea Garden (p194) and boating on scenic Stow Lake (p194).

DON'T MISS...

➡ MH de Young Museum

➡ California Academy of Sciences

➡ San Francisco Botanical Garden

➡ Japanese Tea Garden

➡ Conservatory of Flowers

PRACTICALITIES

➡ Map p342

➡ ☎415-831-2700

➡ www.sfrecpark.org

➡ Btwn Stanyan St & Great Hwy, Fulton St & Lincoln Way

➡ Admission free

➡ ☉sunrise-sunset

➡ ⓂStanyan, Irving, Fulton Sts

To the west around Martin Luther King Jr Dr are the polo fields where the 1967 Human Be-In took place, and free concerts are still held. At the park's wild western edge, quixotic **bison** stampede in their paddock towards **windmills** and Ocean Beach sunsets.

MH de Young Museum

The oxidized copper building keeps a low profile, but there's no denying the park's star attraction: the **MH de Young Museum** (Map p342; ☑415-750-3600; www. famsf.org/deyoung; 50 Hagiwara Tea Garden Dr; adult/child $10/free, discount with Muni ticket $2, 1st Tue of month free; ⊗9:30am-5:15pm Tue-Sun, to 8:45pm Fri mid-Jan–Nov; ⋈9th Ave). The cross-cultural collection featuring African masks and Meso-American sculpture alongside California crafts and American painting has been broadening artistic horizons for a century, and its new home designed by Swiss architects Herzog & de Meuron (of Tate Modern fame) is equally daring. The seemingly abstract pattern on the facade is drawn from aerial photography of the park, and clever light-wells illuminate surprises around every corner.

The 144ft twisting sci-fi medieval armored tower is the one architectural feature that seems incongruous with the park setting, but it offers spectacular views on clear days to the Pacific and Golden Gate Bridge. Access to the tower viewing room is free, and worth the wait for the elevator by Ruth Asawa's mesmerizing filigreed pods.

Upstairs, don't miss 19th-century Oceanic ceremonial oars and stunning Afghani rugs from the 11,000-plus textile collection. Blockbuster basement shows range from Queen Nefertiti's treasures to Balenciaga's sculptural gowns, but even more riveting are main floor installations – look for SF artist Al Farrow's metal cathedrals made from reclaimed guns and environmental artist Andy Goldsworthy's artificial fault line running from the sidewalk right into the museum.

California Academy of Sciences

Leave it to San Francisco to dedicate a glorious four-story monument entirely to freaks of nature: **California Academy of Sciences** (Map p342; ☑415-379-8000; www.calacademy.org; 55 Music Concourse Dr; adult/child $29.95/24.95, discount with Muni ticket $3; ⊗9:30am-5pm Mon-Sat, 11am-5pm Sun; ⋈9th Ave). The Academy's tradition of weird science dates from 1853, with thousands of live animals and 46 scientists now under a 2½-acre wildflower-covered roof. Butterflies flutter through the glass rainforest dome, a rare **white alligator** stalks a swamp and Pierre the Penguin paddles his tank in the African Hall. In the

WILD NIGHTS AT THE ACADEMY

The penguins nod off to sleep, but night owls roam after-hours events at the California Academy of Sciences. Kids may not technically sleep during Academy Sleepovers, but they might kick off promising careers as research scientists. At over-21 NightLife Thursdays, rainforest-themed cocktails are served and strange mating rituals may be observed among shy internet daters. Book ahead online.

Though a local newspaper cautioned that Golden Gate Park's scenic benches led to 'excess hugging,' San Franciscans have flocked to the park since its inception. On a single sunny day in 1886, almost a fifth of the city's entire population made the trip to the park.

HUNGRY?

The Academy Café offers the most reliable food inside the park, but inexpensive, tasty alternatives line 9th Ave between Lincoln and Judah in the Sunset, and are just a couple of blocks away on Balboa between 5th and 8th in the Richmond.

GOLDEN GATE PARK & THE AVENUES GOLDEN GATE PARK

basement aquarium, kids duck inside a glass bubble to enter an eel forest, find Nemos in the tropical-fish tanks and befriend starfish in the aquatic petting zoo.

The views inside and outside Renzo Piano's acclaimed LEED–certified green building are sublime: you can glimpse into infinity in the Planetarium or ride the elevator to the blooming rooftop for park panoramas. Main floor displays explain conservation issues affecting California's ecosystem, and you can actually eat those words – the cafeteria sells treats made with local, organically grown ingredients.

San Francisco Botanical Garden

Sniff your way around the world inside the 70-acre **San Francisco Botanical Garden** (Map p342; ☑415-661-1316; www.strybing.org; 1199 9th Ave; admission $7; ☺9am-6pm Apr-Oct, 10am-5pm Nov-Mar; Ⓜ9th Ave). Almost anything grows in the peculiar microclimates of this corner of Golden Gate Park, from South African savannah grasses to Japanese magnolias, New Zealand cloud-forest mosses to Mexican cacti. The Mediterranean fragrance garden is designed to touch, smell and taste, and the California native-plant section explodes with color when wildflowers bloom in early spring. Don't miss the redwood grove, murky lily pond with giant koi or the lake where blue egrets gamely pose for photos. Free tours take place daily; for details, stop by the bookstore inside the entrance. Last entrance is one hour before closing.

Japanese Tea Garden

Inchworm-backed bridges, five-tiered pagodas and miniature waterfalls offer photo-ops galore in the **Japanese Tea Garden** (Map p342; www.japaneseteagardensf. com; Hagiwara Tea Garden Dr; adult/child $7/5, Mon, Wed & Fri before 10am free; ☺9am-6pm Mar-Oct, to 4:45pm Nov-Feb; Ⓜ9th Ave). Since 1894 this 5-acre garden has blushed with cherry blossoms in spring, turned flaming red with maple leaves in fall and lost all track of time in the meditative Zen Garden. Green tea and fortune cookies – legendarily invented for this garden's inauguration – are served in the open-air tea pavilion year-round.

But the signature attraction is the 100-year-old **bonsai grove** tended for decades by landscape designer Makoto Hagiwara, whose family returned from WWII Japanese American internment camps to discover their prized miniature evergreens had been sold. The Hagiwaras spent two decades tracking down the trees, and returned them to their rightful home. Free tours cover the garden's history Mondays and Saturdays at 9:30am.

Conservatory of Flowers

Flower power is alive and well at San Francisco's **Conservatory of Flowers** (Map p342; ☑415-666-7001; www.conservatoryofflowers.org; Conservatory Dr West; adult/child $5/3; ☺sunrise-sunset). Inside this recently restored 1878 Victorian greenhouse, orchids command center stage like opera divas, lilies float contemplatively in ponds and carnivorous plants give off odors that smell exactly like insect belches.

Stow Lake

A park within the park, **Stow Lake** (Map p342; www.sfrecpark.org/StowLake.aspx; ☺sunrise-sunset; Ⓜ9th Ave) offers steep hikes up a picturesque island called Strawberry Hill, with red-tailed hawks circling overhead. Huntington Falls tumble down the 400ft hill into the lake, near a romantic Chinese pavilion that fairly begs for soap-opera scenes. Pedal boats, row boats and bikes are available at the 1946 **boathouse** (☑415-752-0347; per hr paddleboats/canoes/rowboats $24/20/19, tandem bikes $15, bikes $8; ☺rentals 10am-4pm).

TOP SIGHTS
GOLDEN GATE PARK

◉ SIGHTS

Populist millionaire Adolph Sutro built a public railway in the 1890s to transport Downtown tenement-dwellers to breezy Ocean Beach. Modest tract homes sprang up along the line in the Richmond District, and transplanted immigrant communities thrived alongside the park's botanical transplants. South of Golden Gate Park are candy-colored Sunset District homes, with top-value ethnic eateries along Irving St and surf hangouts around Judah and 45th.

◉ The Richmond

GOLDEN GATE PARK   PARK
Golden Gate Park includes the following sights: MH de Young Museum (p193), California Academy of Sciences (p193), San Francisco Botanical Garden (p194), Japanese Tea Garden (p194), Conservatory of Flowers (p194) and Stow Lake (p194).

COASTAL TRAIL   LANDMARK
Map p342 (⊘sunrise-sunset; Ⓜ Judah St) Suit up and hit your stride on the 9-mile Coastal Trail, starting at Fort Funston, crossing 4 miles of sandy Ocean Beach, wrapping around the Presidio and then ending at Fort Mason. Casual strollers can pick up the trail near Sutro Baths, head around Land's End for a peek at Golden Gate Bridge, and then duck into the Legion of Honor at Lincoln Park.

LEGION OF HONOR   MUSEUM
Map p342 (☑415-750-3600; http://legionofhonor. famsf.org; 100 34th Ave; adult/child $10/6, discount with Muni ticket $2, 1st Tue of month free; ⊘9:30am-5:15pm Tue-Sun; Ⓜ Clement St) Never doubt the unwavering resolve of a nude model. This marble-clad replica of Paris' Legion d'Honneur was a gift to San Francisco from Alma de Bretteville Spreckels, a larger-than-life sculptor's model who married well and donated her fortune to create this monumental tribute to Californians killed in France in WWI. The Legion's world-class collection is wildly eclectic, from Monet water lilies to John Cage soundscapes, ancient Iraqi ivories to R Crumb comics. The centerpiece of 'Big Alma's' legacy is Rodin's *The Kiss* – but at 4pm on weekends, pipe organ recitals steal the show in the Rodin gallery. Don't miss rotating shows from the Legion's Achenbach

Foundation for Graphic Arts, a major modern collection of 90,000 works on paper.

LINCOLN PARK   PARK
Map p342 (Clement St; ⊘sunrise-sunset; Ⓜ Clement St) John McLaren took time out from his 56-year job as Golden Gate Park's superintendent to establish lovely Lincoln Park, the official western terminus of the cross-country Lincoln Hwy. A partially paved path with a couple of flights of stairs covers rugged coastline from the Legion of Honor to the Cliff House, part of the 9-mile Coastal Trail. Terrific views of the Golden Gate and low-tide sightings of coastal shipwrecks are highlights of the 45-minute hike around Land's End; pick up the trailhead north of the Legion of Honor.

SUTRO BATHS   PARK
Map p342 (www.nps.gov/prsf; ⊘sunrise-sunset; Ⓜ 48th Ave) Hard to imagine from these ruins, but Victorian dandies and working stiffs converged here for bracing baths and workouts in itchy wool rental swimsuits. Mining magnate Adolph Sutro built hot and cold indoor pools to accommodate 10,000 unwashed masses in 1896, but the masses apparently preferred dirt, and the place was finally closed in 1952. Head through the sea-cave archway at low tide for end-of-the-world views of Marin Headlands.

FREE CLIFF HOUSE   NOTABLE BUILDING
Map p342 (☑415-386-3330; www.cliffhouse. com; 1090 Point Lobos Ave) Populist millionaire Adolph Sutro imagined this place as a working-man's paradise, and in 1863 it was a much-needed escape from Downtown tenements. After an 1894 fire, Sutro rebuilt the Cliff House as a palatial eight-story Victorian resort with art galleries, dining rooms and an observation tower. It miraculously survived the 1906 earthquake, only to be destroyed by fire the following year. The 1909 stark neoclassical replacement built by Sutro's daughter Emma remained popular for its saloon and restaurant.

In 2004, a $19 million facelift turned the Cliff House into an upscale (read: overpriced) restaurant with all the charm of a fast-food outlet. But two popular attractions remain: sea lions barking on Seal Rock and the **Camera Obscura** (☑415-750-0415; www.giantcamera.com; 1096 Point Lobos Ave; adult/child $3/2; ⊘11am-sunset), a Victorian invention that projects the sea view outside onto a parabolic screen.

ROBERTO GEROMETTA / LONELY PLANET IMAGES ©

1. Ocean Beach (p198)
Beachcombing and bonfires are favored at SF's blustery 4-mile beach.

2. MH de Young Museum (p193)
Global art and craft masterworks are on display at the MH de Young Museum in Golden Gate Park.

3. California Academy of Sciences (p193)
The rainforest dome at the California Academy of Sciences is filled with butterflies.

4. Wing Lee (p200)
Line up for Chinese steamed buns at Wing Lee in the Richmond.

FORT FUNSTON'S PLUCKY LITTLE CLIFF-DWELLERS

Fort Funston is a refuge for the smallest birds in North America: **bank swallows**. They may be little, but they throw all 10g to 20g of themselves into their work, burrowing holes 4ft deep into Fort Funston's sandstone cliffs to provide safe havens for their tiny chicks. Heftier females are highly desirable mates, since they can handle their share of the heavy lifting of nest-building and hauling insects to feed chicks. These plucky little birds are endangered in California, but as many as a couple of hundred bank swallows have been spotted recently in Fort Funston's cliffs, alongside starlings that squat in old nests. Bring binoculars from April to June, and you may spot chicks finding their wings.

COLUMBARIUM   NOTABLE BUILDING

Map p342 (☑415-771-0717; www.neptune-soci ety.com; 1 Loraine Ct; ☉8:30am-5pm Mon-Fri, 10am-3pm Sat & Sun; ⓂGeary St) The ancient Roman innovation of memorial buildings came in handy in San Francisco in 1898, when real estate was already hitting a premium on the seven-by-seven peninsula. The neoclassical Columbarium was largely abandoned to raccoons and mushrooms from 1934 until 1979, when it was restored by the Neptune Society, a cremation advocacy group. After pioneering gay city Supervisor Harvey Milk was killed by a political opponent, his funerary niche was established here. Today the restored domed Columbarium is lined with art nouveau stained-glass windows and more than 5000 niches, honoring dearly beloved relations, dogs and rabbits. It's between Stanyan St and Arguello Blvd, off Anza St.

◉ The Sunset

OCEAN BEACH   BEACH

Map p342 (☑415-561-4323; www.parksconser vancy.org; ☉sunrise-sunset; Ⓜ48th Ave) Bikinis, Elvis sing-alongs and clambakes are not the scene here – think more along the lines of wetsuits, pagan rituals and toasted marshmallows. Bonfires are permitted in the artist-designed fire pits, but follow park rules about fire maintenance and alcohol (not allowed) or you could get fined. On rare sunny days the waters may beckon, but only hardcore surfers and sea lions should brave these riptides. At the south end of the beach, beachcombers may spot sand dollars and the remains of a 19th-century shipwreck. Stick to paths in the fragile dunes, where skittish, knock-kneed snowy plover shorebirds shelter in winter.

FORT FUNSTON   PARK

(☑415-561-4323; www.parksconservancy.org; Skyline Blvd; ⓂJudah St) Grassy dunes up to 200ft high at Fort Funston give you an idea of what the Sunset looked like before it was paved over in the 20th century. The fort is protected as part of the Golden Gate National Recreation Area, and it attracts butterflies and migrating birds. In this defunct military installation, you'll find 146-ton WWII guns pointing out to sea and abandoned Nike missile silos near the parking lot. Nuclear missiles were never launched from Ft Funston, but on any sunny, breezy day, flocks of hang gliders launch and land here.

The National Park Service is gradually replacing invasive ice plants with native California plants such as dune sagebrush, coastal buckwheat and sand verbena. Volunteers are welcome to join the effort at the Fort Funston Native Plant Nursery (see website for details). If you're driving, bicycling or walking here, follow the Great Hwy south and turn right on Skyline Blvd; the park entrance is past Lake Merced, on the right-hand side.

✖ EATING

✖ The Richmond

 AZIZA   MOROCCAN, CALIFORNIAN $$

Map p342 (☑415-752-2222; www.aziza-sf.com; 5800 Geary Blvd; mains $16-29; ☉5:30-10:30pm Wed-Mon; ☑; ⓂGeary Blvd) Mourad Lahlou's inspiration is Moroccan and his produce organic Californian, but his flavors are out of this world: Sonoma duck confit melts into caramelized onion between flaky layers of pastry *basteeya,* while sour cherries rouse slow-cooked local lamb shank from its barley bed. Chef Mourad has his own Food Network show and is opening a restaurant Downtown, but he continues to pioneer Moroccan–California crossroads cuisine at Geary and 22nd – and pastry chef Melissa Chou's Moroccan mint tea Bavarian deserves its own landmark.

TOP CHOICE **NAMU** KOREAN, CALIFORNIAN $$

Map p342 (☎415-386-8332; www.namusf.com; 439 Balboa St; small plates $8-16; ⊙6-10:30pm Sun-Tue, 6pm-midnight Wed-Sat, brunch 10am-3pm Sat & Sun; M Balboa St) SF's unfair culinary advantages – top-notch organic ingredients, Silicon Valley inventiveness and deep roots in Pacific Rim cuisine – are showcased in Namu's Korean-inspired soul food. Don't miss the complimentary housemade kimchi, ultra-savory shiitake mushroom dumplings and Namu's original take on *bibimbap:* organic vegetables and a Sonoma farm egg served sizzling on rice in a stone pot, with optional (and recommended) marinated Marin Sun Farms grass-fed steak. The drink menu stresses *soju* (grain liquor), but a more original option is Natural Process Alliance's organic Napa sauvignon blanc wine, dispensed from a reused metal canteen.

KABUTO CALIFORNIAN, SUSHI $$

Map p342 (☎415-752-5652; www.kabutosushi.com; 5121 Geary Blvd; sushi $6-10; ⊙11:30am-2:30pm & 5:30-10:30pm Tue-Sat, 5:30-10:30pm Sun; M Geary Blvd) Strict Tokyo traditionalists and seafood agnostics alike squeal over the innovative sushi served in this converted vintage hot-dog drive-in. Every night there's a line out the door to witness sushi chef Eric top nori-wrapped sushi rice with foie gras and olallieberry reduction, *hamachi* (yellowtail) with pear and wasabi mustard, and – eureka! – the '49er oyster with sea urchin, caviar, a quail's egg and gold leaf, chased with rare sake. Reserve ahead; seats groups up to four.

NAMU'S KOREAN TACOS

If Namu's earthy, pan-Pacific flavors leave you craving more, head to the Ferry Building farmers market on Thursdays or Saturdays to find its stall serving 'Korean tacos': Marin Sun beef short ribs, tomatoes, rice and a dollop of spicy mayo in a nori seaweed wrapper (two for $5).

TON KIANG RESTAURANT DIM SUM $$

Map p342 (☎415-387-8273; www.tonkiang.net; 5821 Geary Blvd; dim sum $3-7; ⊙10am-9pm Mon-Thu, to 9:30pm Fri, 9:30am-9:30pm Sat, 9am-9pm Sun; ⬤; M Geary Blvd) The reigning champion of dim sum runs laps around the competition, pushing trolleys laden with fragrant, steaming bamboo baskets. Choose some on aroma alone, or ask for the *gao choy gat* (shrimp and chive dumplings), *dao miu gao* (pea tendril and shrimp dumplings) and *jin doy* (sesame balls) by name. A running tally is kept at your table, so you could conceivably quit while you're ahead of the $20 mark – but wait, here comes another cart...

SPRUCE CALIFORNIAN $$$

(☎415-931-5100; www.sprucesf.com; 3640 Sacramento St; mains $14-30; ⊙11:30am-2:30pm Mon-Fri, 5-10pm Sun-Thu, 5-11pm Fri & Sat; M California St) VIP all the way, with Baccarat crystal chandeliers, tawny leather chairs and your choice of 1000 wines. Ladies who lunch dispense with polite conversation, tearing into grass-fed burgers on house-baked English muffins loaded with pickled onions, zucchini grown on the restaurant's own organic farm and an optional slab of foie gras. Want fries with that? Oh yes you do: Spruce's are cooked in duck fat.

SPICES CHINESE $

Map p342 (☎415-752-8884; www.spicesrestaurantonline.com; 294 8th Ave; mains $6.95-12.95; ⊙11am-11pm; M Geary Blvd) The menu reads like an oddly dubbed Hong Kong action flick, with dishes labeled 'fire-burst!!' and 'stinky!', but the chefs can call zesty pickled Napa cabbage with chili oil, silky ma-po tofu and brain-curdling spicy chicken whatever they want – it's definitely worthy of exclamation. When you head toward the kitchen for the bathroom, the chili aroma will make your eyes well up – or maybe that's just gratitude. Cash only.

PPQ DUNGENESS ISLAND SEAFOOD $$$

Map p342 (☎415-386-8266; 2332 Clement St; crab mains $20-30; ⊙11am-10pm Wed-Mon; ⬤; M Geary Blvd) Dungeness crab season lasts most of the year in San Francisco, which means now is a fine time to enjoy one whole atop garlic noodles or dredged in peppercorn-laced flour and lightly fried, for a market price of about $20 per person. Ignore everything else on the menu, and put that bib to work.

GENKI
DESSERT, GROCERIES **$**

Map p342 (☑415-379-6414; www.genkicrepes. com; 330 Clement St; crepes $5; ☺2-10:30pm Mon, 10:30am-10:30pm Tue-Thu & Sun, 10am-11:30pm Fri & Sat; ⓂGeary Blvd) Life is always sweet at Genki, with aisles of packaged Japanese gummy candies nonsensically boasting flavors 'shining in the cheeks of a snow-country child,' a dozen variations on tapioca bubble tea, and French crepes by way of Tokyo with green-tea ice cream and Nutella. Stock up in the beauty supply and Pocky aisle to satisfy sudden hair-dye or snack whims.

HOUSE OF BAGELS
BAKERY **$**

Map p342 (☑415-752-6000; www.houseofbagels. com; 5030 Geary Blvd; bagels $1-3; ☺6am-6pm; ⓂGeary Blvd) New Yorkers console themselves that SF has better weather and produce, but they have better bagels – at least until they try the poppy-seed bagel (boiled, not steamed, then baked) with lox schmear (cream cheese spread) at this mainstay of SF's Russian Jewish neighborhood. Since you're in San Francisco, no one will mock you for ordering the Italian asiago cheese bagel, and you'll be glad you did.

HALU
JAPANESE **$$**

Map p342 (☑415-221-9165; 312 8th Ave; yakitori $2.50-4, ramen $10-11; ☺5-10pm Tue-Sat; ⓂGeary Blvd) Between the rare Beatles memorabilia plastering the walls and adventurous foods drifting by on skewers, dinner at this snug five-table joint feels like stowing away on the Yellow Submarine. Ramen is respectably toothsome, but the house specialty is yakitori, small bites crammed onto sticks and barbecued. Get anything wrapped in bacon – scallops, quail eggs, mochi rice cake – and if you're up for offal, have a heart.

BURMA SUPERSTAR
BURMESE **$$**

Map p342 (☑415-387-2147; www.burmasuper star.com; 309 Clement St; mains $9-22; ☺11am-3:30pm & 5-10pm Mon-Thu, to 10:30pm Sat & Sun; ⓂGeary Blvd) Yes, there's a wait, but do you see anyone walking away? Blame it on creamy, fragrant catfish curries and *la pat*, a traditional Burmese green-tea salad tarted up with lime and dried shrimp. Reservations aren't accepted, so ask the host to call you at the cafe across the street, and enjoy a glass of wine – or if you can't wait for that tea salad, head down the street to its casual small-plates sister restaurant, **B Star Bar** (127 Clement St).

WING LEE
DIM SUM **$**

Map p342 (☑415-831-7883; 501 Clement St; dim sum $1.60-3.50; ☺10am-5pm; ⓂGeary St) How do you feed two famished surfers for $10? Just Wing Lee it. Line up with small bills and walk away loaded with shrimp and leek dumplings, BBQ pork buns (baked or steamed), chicken *shu mai* (open-topped dumplings), potstickers and crispy sesame balls with a chewy red bean center. Fluorescent-lit lunch tables aren't made for dates, but these dumplings won't last long, anyway.

FIRST KOREAN MARKET
KOREAN **$**

Map p342 (☑415-221-2565; 4625 Geary Blvd; dishes $3-6; ☺9am-8pm; ⓂGeary Blvd) Kimchi and *kimbap* cravings are well and truly satisfied at First Korean, where you'll find entire rows of the spicy fermented veggies (better than pickles) and sesame-oil-laced Korean seaweed, vegetable and rice rolls (not to be confused with sushi), plus Korean BBQ wings (a snack worthy not only of Super Bowls, but Olympics).

✖ The Sunset

THANH LONG
VIETNAMESE **$$**

Map p342 (☑415-665-1146; www.anfamily.com/ restaurants/thanhlong_restaurant; 4101 Judah St; mains $10-18; ☺5-9:30pm Tue-Thu & Sun, to 10pm Fri & Sat; ♿; ⓂJudah St) Since 1971 San Franciscans have lingered in the Sunset after sunset for two reasons, both at Thanh Long: roast pepper crab and garlic noodles. One crab serves two (market price runs $34 to $40) with noodles ($9), but shaking beef and mussels make a proper feast. The wine list offers good-value local pairings, especially Navarro's dry gewürztraminer.

SUNRISE DELI
MIDDLE EASTERN **$**

Map p342 (☑415-664-8210; 2115 Irving St; dishes $4-7; ☺9am-9pm Mon-Sat, 10am-8pm Sun; ♿; ⓂJudah St) A hidden gem in the fog belt, Sunrise dishes up what is arguably the city's best smoky baba ghanoush, *mujeddrah* (lentil-rice with crispy onions), garlicky *foul* (fava bean spread) and crispy falafel, either to go or to enjoy in the old-school cafe atmosphere. Local Arab American hipsters confess to passing off the Sunrise's specialties as their own home cooking to older relatives.

YUM YUM FISH
JAPANESE, SUSHI **$**

Map p342 (☑415-566-6433; www.yumyumfish sushi.com; 2181 Irving St; sushi $1-8; ☺10:30am-

OUTERLANDS

When windy Ocean Beach leaves you feeling shipwrecked, drift into this beach-shack bistro for organic California comfort food. Lunch at **Outerlands** (Map p342; ☑415-661-6140; www.outerlandssf.com; 4001 Judah St; sandwiches & small plates $8-9; ☉11am-3pm & 6-10pm Tue-Sat, 10am-2:30pm Sun; Ⓜ Judah St) means open-faced sandwiches on crusty house-baked bread – pastrami brisket with pickled slaw as a menu mainstay – or the $9 grilled artisan cheese combo with seasonal housemade soup, especially if it's pumpkin or leek. Dinners get fancy, with slow-cooked pork shoulder slouching into green-garlic risotto and almond financiers with cherry-tarragon coulis. Arrive early and sip wine outside until seats open up indoors.

7:30pm; ☑; Ⓜ Judah St) Watch and learn as Yum Yum's sushi chef lovingly slices generous hunks of fresh sashimi, preparing a platter to order with your special *maki* needs in mind. Rolls can be made specially for vegans for as little as a dollar per order, and if you want sustainable sushi, bring your Seafood Watch Card (see p269) and order accordingly.

NANKING ROAD BISTRO   CHINESE $
Map p342 (☑415-753-2900; 1360 9th Ave; mains $7-12; ☉11:30am-10pm Mon-Fri, noon-10pm Sat & Sun; ☑ⓖ; Ⓜ Irving St) Northern regional Chinese food is underrepresented in historically Cantonese SF, but the breakaway stars of Nanking Road's menu are clamshell *bao* (bun) folded over crispy Beijing duck and a definitive *kung pao* chicken lunch special ($7), with the right ratio of chili to roast peanuts. Chinese opera characters stare you down from massive paintings as though to ensure you finish your vegetables – with caramelized eggplant and smoky dry-braised string beans, that's not hard.

SAN TUNG   DIM SUM $
Map p342 (☑415-242-0828; www.santungrestaurant.com; 1031 Irving St; mains $8-13; ☉11am-9:30pm Thu-Tue; Ⓜ Irving St) When you arrive at 5:30pm on a Sunday and already the place is packed, you might think you've hit a family dinner rush – but no, it's this crowded *all* the time. Blame it on the dry braised chicken wings – tender, moist morsels that defy the very name – and housemade dumplings and noodles. You'll be smacking your lips with the memory when the bill comes: a three-course meal for two for $20.

UNDERDOG   SAUSAGES $
Map p342 (☑415-665-8881; www.underdogorganic.com; 1634 Irving St; hot dogs $4-5; ☉11:30am-9pm; ☑ⓖ; Ⓜ Irving St) For cheap, organic meals on the run in a bun, Underdog is the

clear winner. The roasted garlic and Italian pork sausages are USDA certified-organic, and the smoky veggie chipotle hot dog could make dedicated carnivores into fans of fake meat.

☕ DRINKING & NIGHTLIFE

BEACH CHALET   BREWERY, BAR
Map p342 (www.beachchalet.com; 1000 Great Hwy; ☉9am-10pm Sun-Thu, to 11pm Fri & Sat; Ⓜ 48th Ave) Pacific sunsets are even more impressive glimpsed through a pint glass of the Beach Chalet's microbrewed beer, with live music on Tuesdays and Fridays. If there's a wait, wander downstairs to see 1930s Works Project Administration (WPA) frescoes highlighting San Francisco history and the development of Golden Gate Park. On sunny weekends, hit the Chalet's Golden Gate Park backyard bar for cocktails and raucous Sunday brunch buffets with bottomless champagne.

TROUBLE COFFEE   CAFE $
Map p342 (www.troublecoffee.com; 4033 Judah St; ☉7am-8pm Mon-Fri, 8am-8pm Sat, 8am-5pm Sun; Ⓜ Judah St) Coconuts are unlikely near blustery Ocean Beach, but here comes trouble with the 'Build Your Own Damn House' $8 breakfast special: coffee, thick-cut cinnamon-laced toast and an entire young coconut. The hewn-wood bench out front is permanently damp from surfers' rears, but house-roasted 'The Hammer' espresso at the reclaimed wood counter indoors breaks through any morning fog.

540 CLUB   BAR
Map p342 (www.540-club.com; 540 Clement St; ☉11am-2am; Ⓜ Geary St) Unless you're a

master criminal, this is the most fun you'll ever have inside a bank. Look for the neon pink elephant over the archway, and enter the converted savings and loan office to find minor mayhem already in progress, thanks to absinthe, $2 PBR, Punk Rock BBQ and Catholic School Karaoke (see website for events). Under vaulted ceilings, bartenders pull a dozen brews on tap – including bitter Guinness, blond Leffe and wheat Hoegaarden – to loosen you up for friendly games of darts or pool.

SOCIAL
BREWERY

Map p342 (www.socialkitchenandbrewery.com; 1326 9th Ave; ⊙5pm-midnight Mon-Thu, to 2am Fri, 11:30am-2am Sat, to midnight Sun; MIrving St) In every Social situation, there are a couple troublemakers – specifically L'Enfant Terrible, a dark Belgian ale with an attitude, and bitter but golden Rapscallion. This snazzy, skylit modern building looks like an architect's office but tastes like a neighborhood brewpub, which just happens to serve addictive lime-laced brussels-sprout chips – but hey, hogging the bowl is anti-Social.

BITTER END
PUB

Map p342 (441 Clement St; ⊙4pm-2am Mon-Fri, 11am-2am Sat & Sun; MGeary Blvd) Don't be bitter if tricky Tuesday-night trivia games don't end with decisive wins – near-victories are fine excuses for another beer or alcoholic pear cider at this local haunt with proper creaky wood floors, Irish bartenders and passable pub grub. Sore losers can always challenge trivia champs to a friendly grudge match at the pool tables and dart board on the balcony.

TRAD'R SAM'S
BAR

Map p342 (6150 Geary Blvd; ⊙11am-2am; MGeary Blvd) Island getaways in rattan booths at this threadbare tiki lounge will cure that Ocean Beach chill. You won't find beer on tap, but you may discover an ice-cream island in your cocktail. Classic-kitsch lovers order the Hurricane, which comes with two straws to share for a reason: drink it by yourself and it'll blow you away.

☆ ENTERTAINMENT

BRIDGE THEATER
CINEMA

Map p342 (☑415-267-4893; www.landmarkthe atres.com; 3010 Geary Blvd; adult/child $10.50/8) One of SF's last single-screen theaters, the Bridge screens international independent films from yakuza gangster thrillers to film-festival sensations.

BALBOA THEATER
CINEMA

Map p342 (☑415-221-8184; www.balboamov ies.com; 3630 Balboa St; adult/child $10/7.50; MBalboa St) First stop, Cannes; next stop, Balboa and 37th, where Russian documentaries split the bill with art-house darlings like Woody Allen. Filmmakers vie for marquee spots at this 1926 neighborhood movie palace, which has just one screen and a director who also programs for Telluride Festival.

PLOUGH & THE STARS
BAR

Map p342 (☑415-751-1122; www.theploughand stars.com; 116 Clement St; ⊙3pm-2am Mon-Thu, 2pm-2am Fri-Sun, showtime 9pm; MGeary Blvd) Bands who sell out shows from Ireland to Appalachia and headline San Francisco's Hardly Strictly Bluegrass Festival (see p24) turn up to jam on weeknights, taking breaks to clink pint glasses at long union-hall-style tables. Mondays are compensated for no live music with an all-day happy hour, plus free pool and blarney from regulars; expect modest cover charges for Friday and Saturday shows.

WORTH A DETOUR

HOLLOW
Between simple explanations and Golden Gate Park, there's **Hollow** (Map p342; ☑415-242-4119; www.hollowsf.com; 1493 Irving St; ⊙8am-5pm Mon-Fri, 9am-5pm Sat & Sun; MIrving St): an enigma wrapped in a mystery inside an espresso bar. House coffee is made with SF's cultish Ritual roasts, and the secret ingredient in the cupcakes is Guinness – but that doesn't begin to explain those shelves. Magnifying glasses, galvanized tin pails, deer antlers and monster etchings are inexplicably for sale here, obsessive-compulsively organized into a kind of shelf haiku. There are only a couple of marble tables, so expect a wait among like-minded eccentrics.

SUMMER MOVIE MADNESS IN THE AVENUES

Weekends in summer, the **Bridge Theater** (Map p342; ☑415-267-4893; www.landmark theatres.com; 3010 Geary Blvd; ticket $13) hosts Midnight Mass, featuring camp, horror and B-grade movies such as *Showgirls* and *Mommie Dearest,* with each screening preceded by a drag show spoofing the film. Local celeb Peaches Christ wrangles the always-raucous crowd; reserve ahead.

At the **Balboa Theater** (Map p342; ☑415-221-8184; www.balboamovies.com; 3630 Balboa St; tickets $15-20; Ⓜ Balboa St), summertime brings the occasional superhero flick and lots of classic ballet, dance, opera, jazz and Shakespeare performances screened in their entirety.

BYO blanket to outdoor Friday movie nights in summer at the Beach Chalet (p201), where admission is free with your purchase of house-brewed beer.

🛍 SHOPPING

TOP CHOICE PARK LIFE
ART, BOOKS

Map p342 (☑415-386-7275; www.parklifestore. com; 220 Clement St; ☺11am-8pm; Ⓜ Geary Blvd) Is Park Life a design store, an art gallery or an indie publisher? All of the above, with limited-edition scores that include piggy-bank lamps with fluorescent-coil tails, artist-designed statement tees with drawn-on pockets or bold semicolons, and Park Life's own publications by graffiti artist Andrew Schoultz. The back gallery showcases think pieces with sneaky humor, such as Ian Johnson's portrait of Miles Davis radiating prismatic thought waves and Erik Scollon's fist pump cast in tarnished disco-ball porcelain.

GREEN APPLE BOOKS
BOOKSTORE

Map p342 (☑415-387-2272; 506 Clement St; ☺10am-10:30pm Sun-Thu, to 11:30pm Fri & Sat; Ⓜ Geary Blvd) Blissed-out booklovers emerge blinking into the sunset after an entire day browsing three floors of new releases, used titles and staff picks more reliable than *New York Times* reviews. Local favorites are easy to spot in the local interest section – look for the local author tag. You can sell your books here, but be prepared for rejection: they can afford to be picky. Don't miss the fiction and music annex two doors down.

MOLLUSK
OUTDOOR GEAR

Map p342 (☑415-564-6300; www.mollusk surfshop.com; 4500 Irving St; ☺10am-6:30pm; Ⓜ Judah St) The high-impact store sign painted by Tauba Auerbach before she hit the Whitney Biennial is the first hint that this is the source of West Coast surfer cool. Visits by celebrity shapers (surfboard mak-

ers) yield limited-edition boards you won't find elsewhere, and signature Mollusk T-shirts and hoodies by local artists buy you nods of recognition on Ocean Beach. Coffee-table books on early California surfing and collages by local surfer/international, art fair sensation Thomas Campbell give kooks (newbies) vicarious surf-subculture thrills.

GENERAL STORE
GIFTS, ACCESSORIES

Map p342 (☑415-682-0600; 4035 Judah St; ☺11am-7pm Mon-Fri, 10am-7pm Sat & Sun; Ⓜ Judah St) Anyone born in the wrong place or time to be a NorCal hippie architect can still look the part, thanks to A) beards and B) General Store. Pine-lined walls showcase handcrafted recycled-leather boots, antique turquoise necklaces, brass bicycle bells, egg-shaped terrariums and vintage how-to books. Don't miss local art openings here, when smokers flirt dangerously on the hay bales out front and folkies strum in the backyard garden.

WISHBONE
GIFTS

Map p342 (www.wishbonesf.com; 601 Irving St; ☺11:30am-7pm Mon, Tue & Thu-Sat, to 6pm Sun; Ⓜ Irving St) Certain gifts never fail to please: explode-in-your-mouth Pop Rocks candy, smiling toast coin purses, and blue ribbons that proclaim 'Computer Whiz!' Gifts here will gratify hip parents, from a bath towel that doubles as a pirate's cape to the onesie silkscreened to look like a BART card.

SEEDSTORE
CLOTHING

Map p342 (www.seedstoresf.com; 212 Clement St; ☺11am-7pm Mon-Fri, to 8pm Sat, to 6pm Sun; Ⓜ Geary St) Less like entering a store than raiding the wardrobe of a modern spaghetti Western star. The old-timey shingle hung over the door is misleading: no gardening supplies are sold here, but you will find Joe's Jeans, Superdry military-style jackets, BB Dakota riding pants, filmy Free People peasant blouses and vintage Navajo-pattern cardigans.

🏃 SPORTS & ACTIVITIES

GOLDEN GATE PARK BIKE & SKATE SPORTS
Map p342 (☎415-668-1117; www.goldengatepark bikeandskate.com; 3038 Fulton St; skates per hr $5-6, per day $20-24, bikes per hr $3-5, per day $15-25, tandem bikes per hr/day $15/75, discs $6/25; ☺10am-6pm; Ⓜ Fulton St) Besides bikes and skates (both quad-wheeled and inline), this little rental shop just outside the park rents disc putters and drivers for the nearby free Frisbee golf course. Call ahead to confirm it's open if the weather looks iffy.

CIRCUS CENTER TRAPEZE SPORTS
Map p342 (☎415-759-8123, ext 810 for trapeze enrolment; www.circuscenter.org; 755 Frederick St; 2hr workshop $45; 🚇; Ⓜ Irving St) If you've ever dreamed of running away and joining the circus, indulge your fantasy at this circus-arts school, where adults and kids learn everything from contortionist tricks to the flying trapeze. Serious pupils with red-rubber noses attend the school's Clown Conservatory, the only clown-training school in the US.

LAWN BOWLING CLUB SPORTS
Map p342 (☎415-487-8787; http://sflb.filesfor friends.com; Bowling Green Dr, Golden Gate Park; Ⓜ Stanyan St) Pins seem ungainly and bowling shirts unthinkable once you've joined the sweater-clad enthusiasts on America's first public bowling green. Free lessons are available from member volunteers at noon on Wednesdays and Saturdays; call to confirm volunteer availability. Flat-soled shoes are mandatory, but otherwise people dress for comfort and the weather – though all-white clothing has been customary at club social events since 1901.

FREE LINDY IN THE PARK DANCE
Map p342 (www.lindyinthepark.com; John F Kennedy Dr btwn 8th & 10th Ave; ☺11am-2pm Sun; 🚇; Ⓜ Fulton St) Sundays swing at the free Lindy-hopping dance party in Golden Gate Park, at the outdoor bandshell between the MH de Young Museum and the California Academy of Sciences (weather permitting). All are welcome; dancers range from first-timers to semiprofessionals, hipsters to grandparents. Free half-hour lessons begin at noon, but you can always just watch or wing it.

SF'S TOP 3 URBAN GOLF COURSES

Golden Gate Municipal Golf Course (Map p342; ☎415-751-8987; www.goldengate parkgolfcourse.com; 47th Ave & Fulton St, Golden Gate Park; adult/child Mon-Thu $15/5, Fri-Sun $19/7; ☺6am-8pm; 🚇; Ⓜ Fulton St) Golden Gate Park has a challenging nine-hole, par-27 course built on sand dunes, with some 100yd drop-offs, 180yd elevated greens and Pacific views. No reservations are taken, but it's busiest before 9am weekdays and after school. On weekend afternoons, bide your time waiting with excellent clubhouse wood-fired BBQ sandwiches (their secret: Anchor Steam beer in the sauce). Equipment rentals and practice range available; kids welcome.

Lincoln Park Golf Course (Map p342; ☎415-221-9911; www.lincolnparkgc.com; 34th Ave & Clement St, Lincoln Park; Mon-Thu $37, Fri-Sun $41, cart $26; ☺sunrise-sunset; Ⓜ Clement St) For game-sabotaging views, the hilly, 18-hole Lincoln Park course wraps around Land's End and the Legion of Honor to face Golden Gate Bridge. This course has the most iconic SF vistas, so watch out for daydreaming hikers and brides posing for wedding pictures – fore!

Harding Park Municipal Golf Course (☎415-664-4690; www.harding-park.com; 99 Harding Rd at Skyline Blvd; 9-hole course Mon-Thu $26, Fri-Sun $31, 18-hole course Mon-Thu $150, Fri-Sun $170; ☺6:30am-7pm; Ⓜ Skyline Blvd) San Francisco's bargain public course is a lush 18-hole landscape partially shaded by cypress trees beside the ocean, plus the Jack Fleming nine-hole course, where walk-ins are welcome. Cart is included with 18-hole greens fees, or costs $14 with nine holes; call to reserve tee times.

GREAT OUTDOORS ACTIVITIES

Whether you're looking for a game or are content to watch, you're in the right place: Golden Gate Park has baseball and softball diamonds, four soccer fields and 21 tennis courts. But atypical athletes also find their niches in the park's fly-casting pools, archery range, Lawn Bowling Club, horseshoe pitch, model-yacht marina, disc golf course, big-band shell for Lindy-hopping and blacktop reserved for weekend roller disco.

John F Kennedy Dr is closed to motor vehicles east of Crossover Dr (around 8th Ave) on Sundays year-round and Saturdays from June to October to accommodate runners, skateboarders, unicyclists and meandering dreamers. To plan a picnic, concert or protest in the park and get detailed park maps, check in at **McLaren Lodge** (Map p342; cnr Fell & Stanyan Sts; ☺8am-5pm Mon-Fri) at the eastern entrance of the park, under the splendid cypress that's the city's official tree. For information about free park walking tours, call **Friends of Recreation & Parks** (☏415-263-0991).

FREE **SAN FRANCISCO CROQUET CLUB** SPORTS
(☏415-928-5525; www.croquetworld.com/sfcc.html; Stern Grove, 19th Ave & Wawona St; ♿; M19th Ave) Croquet is not just for mad queens and chi-chi garden parties anymore. These folks are hardcore about their wickets, but nonmembers can join free sessions on the first three Saturdays of the month, and kids are always welcome.

FREE **SAN FRANCISCO DISC GOLF** SPORTS
Map p342 (www.sfdiscgolf.org; Marx Meadow Dr at Fulton St btwn 25th & 30th Ave; MFulton St) If you love to throw Frisbees, head to the tranquil woods of Golden Gate Park to find a permanent 18-hole disc-golf course, enjoyed by cultish veterans and reckless beginners. You can rent a bag of flying saucers at Golden Gate Park Bike & Skate, and limber up for tournaments, which kick off Sundays from 8:30am to 10am.

SAN FRANCISCO MODEL YACHT CLUB SPORTS
Map p342 (☏415-386-1037; www.sfmyc.org; Spreckels Lake, Golden Gate Park; ♿; MFulton St) Kids go nuts for the impeccable scale-model yachts that sail on an oversized fountain called Spreckels Lake. Collectors lovingly build and maintain these ship-shape crafts in the adjacent clubhouse, and occasionally throw miniature regattas (check the website). Turtles sunbathe on the shore – Spreckels Lake has become a refuge for wayward and abandoned turtles.

WHEEL FUN RENTALS SPORTS
Map p342 (☏415-668-6699; www.wheelfunrentals.com; 50 Stow Lake Dr, Golden Gate Park; skates per hr/day $6/20, bikes $8/25, tandems $12/40; ☺9am-7pm; MMusic Concourse Dr) Glide around Golden Gate and dip into the Sunset on a reasonable rental. To cruise the waterfront, head to its second location in the Marina at Fort Mason (call for directions; it's in a parking lot).

FLYCASTING CLUB SPORTS
Map p342 (www.ggacc.org; McLaren Anglers' Lodge & Casting Pools, John F Kennedy Dr, Golden Gate Park; MFulton St) Across from the buffalo paddock in Golden Gate Park are casting pools with targets open to the general public. Fly casters practice here in their waders, gracefully setting a fly from a thin line that looks about a mile long. Check the website for upcoming free casting lessons.

GOLDEN GATE PARK & THE AVENUES SPORTS & ACTIVITIES

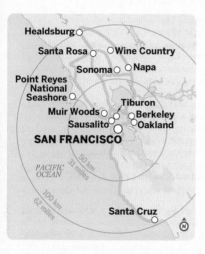

Day Trips from San Francisco

Berkeley (p207) & Oakland (p210)
The East Bay is home to a world-famous university, kick-ass music scene, fussy Gourmet Ghetto, gritty streets and summer weather 20° F warmer than in SF.

Napa Valley (p214) & Sonoma Valley (p219)
Fancy-pants Napa put America on the world's viticulture map, but historic Sonoma retains its folksy ways. Expect pastoral landscapes and great wine.

Muir Woods & Muir Beach (p227)
The world's tallest trees lord over the primordial forest and rugged seacoast, just across the Golden Gate.

Sausalito & Tiburon (p228)
Picturesque towns, perfect for strolling, are a ferry ride away in Marin County. Linger bayside, glass of wine in hand.

Point Reyes National Seashore (p232)
Wildlife hikes are incredible on windswept Point Reyes – spot sea lions, herds of elk, migratory birds and whales.

Hwy 1 to Santa Cruz (p235)
Pumpkin patches and hidden beaches line the coastal route to the classic NorCal surf town, complete with boardwalk and rickety wooden rollercoaster.

Berkeley

Explore

The main destinations of day-trippers are downtown Berkeley and the University of California (UC) campus. Just north of the campus, in North Berkeley on Shattuck Ave, lies the city's famous Gourmet Ghetto. Berkeley is also home to a large South Asian community, as evidenced by the abundance of sari shops on University Ave. The hills above Berkeley are crisscrossed by hiking trails through Tilden Regional Park, which has bird's-eye views over the Bay Area.

The Best...

➡ **Sight** University of California, Berkeley (p207)

➡ **Place to Eat** Chez Panisse (p209)

➡ **Place to Drink** Caffe Strada (p210)

Top Tip

If you're coming to explore the UC campus and downtown Berkeley during the day, avoid driving or taking the BART during rush hour (7am to 10am and 4pm to 7pm).

Getting There & Away

Car Bay Bridge to I-80 east; take University Ave exit.

BART Downtown Berkeley BART station is the most convenient.

Bus AC Transit (☑510-817-1717; www.actransit.org) operates buses from San Francisco's Temporary Transbay Terminal (Howard & Main Sts), with connecting service throughout Berkeley and Oakland.

Need to Know

➡ **Area Code** ☑510

➡ **Location** 14 miles northeast of San Francisco.

➡ **Berkeley Convention & Visitors Bureau** (☑510-549-7040, 800-847-4823; www.visitberkeley.com; 2030 Addison St #102; ⊙9am-1pm & 2-5pm Mon-Fri) Tourist office.

◉ SIGHTS

UNIVERSITY OF CALIFORNIA, BERKELEY
UNIVERSITY

The Berkeley campus of the University of California – aka 'Cal' – is California's oldest, founded in 1866. From Telegraph Ave, enter the campus via Sproul Plaza and Sather Gate, ground zero for people-watching, soapbox oration and pseudo-tribal drumming. Alternatively, enter from Center and Oxford Sts, near the Downtown Berkeley BART station. The **Campanile** (elevator rides $2; ⊙10am-4pm Mon-Fri, to 5pm Sat, to 1:30pm & 3-5pm Sun; ♿), officially Sather Tower, was modeled on St Mark's Basilica in Venice. The 328ft spire has knockout views. Look into the carillon of 61 bells, some as big as a Volkswagen; recitals take place daily at 7:50am, noon and 6pm, with a longer piece Sundays at 2pm. At the **UC Berkeley Art Museum** (☑510-642-0808; http://bampfa.berkeley.edu; 2626 Bancroft Way; adult/student $10/7, 1st Thu of month free; ⊙11am-5pm Wed-Sun), 11 galleries showcase works from ancient Chinese to cutting-edge contemporary. The complex also houses a bookstore, cafe, sculpture garden and the much-loved, avant-garde Pacific Film Archive (p210). In Kroeber Hall, the **Phoebe Hearst Museum of Anthropology** (☑510-643-7648; http://hearstmuseum.berkeley.edu; admission free; ⊙10am-4:30pm Wed-Sat, noon-4pm Sun) showcases the diversity of indigenous human cultures, with artifacts from ancient Peru, Egypt and Africa. There's also a large collection highlighting native California cultures.

TELEGRAPH AVE
STREET

Telegraph Ave is the heart of Berkeley's student village, with a constant flow of shoppers, vagrants and vendors. Expect an odd mix of greying hippies, too-cool hipsters and ponytailed panhandlers. It's not for everyone – some find it trashy and obnoxious – but when you're on the hunt for books, maps and CDs, this is the place. **Amoeba** and **Rasputin** carry some of the Bay Area's most diverse collections of music.

PEOPLE'S PARK
PARK

(btwn Haste St & Dwight Way; 🚌1 AC Transit) Just east of Telegraph Ave, People's Park rose to fame in the late '60s as the epicenter of political battles, but since then it has served as an unofficial dayroom for Berkeley's homeless. A restoration spruced it up, and occasional

East Bay

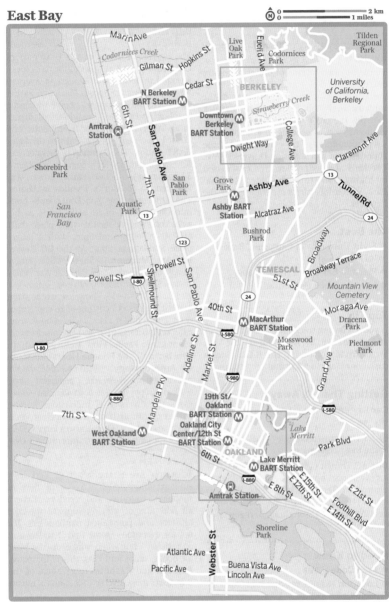

festivals still happen, but really it's a mangy patch of trampled grass.

TILDEN REGIONAL PARK PARK
(www.ebparks.org; [i]) For a better park, head to the Berkeley hills for hiking trails, picnic areas, swimming at Lake Anza and plenty of kids stuff, like pony rides and a steam train. There's a small fee for most activities. AC Transit bus 67 runs here weekends and holidays from Downtown Berkeley BART, but only stops at the entrances weekdays.

EATING & DRINKING

CHEZ PANISSE TOP CHOICE CALIFORNIAN $$$

(☎510-548-5525; www.chezpanisse.com; 1517 Shattuck Ave; cafe $18-29, restaurant set menu $65-95; ⊙cafe lunch & dinner Mon-Sat, restaurant dinner Mon-Sat; 🚍7, 9, 43 AC Transit) The temple of Alice Waters – doyenne of California cuisine – remains at the pinnacle of Bay Area dining. Book one month ahead for the legendary prix-fixe meals in the cozy Craftsman-style dining room. Note: there are no

Berkeley

variations to the daily restaurant menu. If you'd prefer to choose, book the less-expensive, but equally lovely, upstairs cafe.

CHEESE BOARD PIZZA COLLECTIVE
PIZZA $

(☎510-549-3055; www.cheeseboardcollective.coop; 1512 Shattuck Ave; pizza slice $2.50; ☺lunch & dinner Tue-Sat; ☐7, 9, 43 AC Transit) A Gourmet Ghetto mainstay, with a fantastic variety of artisanal cheeses and killer goat-cheese pizzas.

VIK'S CHAAT CORNER
INDIAN $

(2390 4th St; meals under $8; ☺11am-6pm Tue-Fri, to 8pm Sat & Sun; ☐9, 19, 51 AC Transit) Our favorite Berkeley cheap-eats serves freshly made, order-at-the-counter Indian classics – no tikka masala here. Daily specials include curries served with all the trimmings, for a mere $6 to $8.

LA NOTE
FRENCH, MEDITERRANEAN $

(☎510-843-1535; www.lanoterestaurant.com; 2377 Shattuck Ave; mains $10-13; ☺8am-2:30pm daily, 6-10pm Thu-Sat; ☐Downtown Berkeley) A good spot to fuel up before exploring, La Note serves a French-cafe menu of omelettes, *croques monsieurs,* niçoise salads and baguette sandwiches.

JUICE BAR COLLECTIVE
CAFE $

(www.thejuicebar.org; 2114 Vine St; dishes $3-6; ☺10am-4:30pm; ☐7, 9, 43 AC Transit) A tiny storefront cafe, Juice Bar makes tasty polenta pizzas, quiches, sandwiches and delish smoothies.

CAFFE STRADA
CAFE

(2300 College Ave; ☺7am-midnight; ☐7, 51 AC Transit) Students get wired on the giant patio and study, talk philosophy or make eyes. Good pastries.

JUPITER
BAR

(2181 Shattuck Ave; ☐Downtown Berkeley) For the best social introduction to Berkeley's bar scene, head to Jupiter's back patio. Live bands most nights.

⭐ **ENTERTAINMENT**

BERKELEY REPERTORY THEATRE
THEATER

(☎510-845-4700; www.berkeleyrep.org; 2025 Addison St; ☐Downtown Berkeley) Some San Franciscans cross the bay only for the top-notch pro theater at Berkeley Rep.

ZELLERBACH HALL
LIVE MUSIC

(☎510-642-9988; www.calperfs.berkeley.edu; UC Berkeley campus; ☐Downtown Berkeley) The concrete-box acoustics are terrible for non-amplified classical, but Zellerbach remains the premier East Bay stage, showcasing top-flight dance and music performances by international ensembles.

PACIFIC FILM ARCHIVE
CINEMA

(☎510-642-1124; http://bampfa.berkeley.edu; 2575 Bancroft Way; adult/child $9.50/6.50; ☐Downtown Berkeley) Internationally renowned for daily sc reenings that explore the art of film-making, including rare, new and historic prints from around the globe. Pick up tickets at the **box office** (2621 Durant Ave; ☺11am-5pm).

Oakland

Explore

Oakland is to San Francisco what Brooklyn is to Manhattan: a less-expensive address for bohemian refugees. Oakland is half the size of San Francisco, has a huge African American community and many architectural gems from the early 20th century. A little saltwater lake sits in the middle of downtown. It's a city of neighborhood joints, local grocers, and small nightclubs and restaurants. Oakland's downtown is best explored on a weekday; it's dead at night (except for the club scene; see boxed text p211). Wander past historic buildings and poke into colorful shops. With easy access from San Francisco via BART and ferry, you can comfortably spend a half day exploring downtown, Chinatown and Jack London Square on foot.

The Best...

➡ **Sight** Lake Merritt (p213)
➡ **Place to Eat** Wood Tavern (p213)
➡ **Place to Drink** Cafe Van Kleef (p211)

Top Tip

By far the most romantic way to reach Oakland is by ferry from Downtown San Francisco, but check the evening returns carefully: service ends early.

NIGHTLIFE ACROSS THE BAY

Oakland and Berkeley have a wealth of unpretentious, often-unadvertised talent with die-hard local followings. Everyone knows famous Yoshi's (p213), the Bay Area's leading jazz club, but there are many lesser-known, live-music hubs that put you smack in the middle of the East Bay's raw, soulful scene.

Cafe Van Kleef (☎510-763-7711; www.cafevankleef.com; 1621 Telegraph Ave, Oakland; ⊠19th St) Bebop, jazz, R&B, rock, funk – you name it, it plays in this narrow bar full of knickknacks and collectibles. Lip-smacking freshly squeezed Greyhounds (gin and grapefruit) and a party-down crowd.

Freight & Salvage (☎510-548-1761; www.freightandsalvage.org; 2020 Addison St, Berkeley; admission $5-22; ⊠51, 52, 72 AC Transit) An all-ages, alcohol-free coffeehouse and performance venue for traditional, regional and ethnic music – fiddle, folk, strings and soul.

Paramount Theatre (☎510-465-6400; www.paramounttheatre.com; 2025 Broadway, Oakland; ⊠19th St) A gorgeous art-deco theater featuring everything from the symphony to big-name comedy and rock acts such as Morrissey.

Stork Club (☎510-444-6174; www.storkcluboakland.com; 2330 Telegraph Ave, Oakland; admission $5; ⊗shows 9pm; ⊠59 AC Transit) Punk, funk, rockabilly and reggae are showcased here.

Uptown (☎510-451-8100; www.uptownnightclub.com; 1928 Telegraph Ave, Oakland; admission varies; ⊠19th St) Local rock bands and occasional celebs play this mammoth bar with a big outdoor smoking patio. You never know who might appear – Green Day came unannounced in 2009.

Getting There & Away

Travel time 20 minutes by car or BART.

Car Bay Bridge to I-880; take the Broadway exit to downtown.

BART The Richmond and Pittsburg/Bay Point lines run through downtown Oakland. Get off at the 12th St or 19th St exits. Pittsburg/Bay Point trains stop at Rockridge and at College Ave.

Ferry Oakland–Alameda Ferries (☎510-522-3300; www.eastbayferry.com) sails to Jack London Square from the Ferry Building and Pier 41 (30 minutes, $6.25).

Bus AC Transit (☎510-817-1717, 511; www.actransit.org) operates buses from San Francisco's Temporary Transbay Terminal (Howard & Main Sts), with connecting service throughout Berkeley and Oakland.

Need to Know

➡ **Area Code** ☎510
➡ **Location** 16 miles east of San Francisco
➡ **Oakland Convention & Visitors Bureau** (☎510-839-9000; www.oaklandcvb.com; 463 11th St, btwn Broadway & Clay St; ⊗9am-5pm Mon-Fri; ⊠Oakland City Center) Tourist office.

◉ SIGHTS

DOWNTOWN NEIGHBORHOOD

(Broadway & Clay St, 12th & 14th Sts; ⊠Oakland City Center) The pedestrian-friendly City Center forms downtown's heart. The twin towers of **Ronald Dellums Federal Building** are on 12th St. Highlighting the skyline on 13th and Franklin Sts is the **1923 Tribune Tower**, an Oakland icon with a red-neon clock, home to the *Oakland Tribune;* and on 14th and Clay Sts, the beautiful 1914 Beaux Arts **City Hall**.

Old Oakland (Washington St, btwn 8th & 10th Sts), just west of Broadway, is lined with restored historic buildings from the 1860s to 1880s, home to several upscale restaurants. There's a lively Chinese-influenced **farmers market** here Friday mornings.

East of Broadway, **Chinatown** centers on Franklin and Webster Sts, and dates back to the 1870s. It's much smaller than San Francisco's – and not touristy.

JACK LONDON SQUARE SQUARE

(www.jacklondonsquare.com; Broadway; ⊠51 AC Transit, ⊠Oakland) Jack London Square bears the name of the writer who raised hell on the waterfront. The sanitized marina strip feels like an outdoor mall, but it's a good jumping-off point: this is where

Oakland

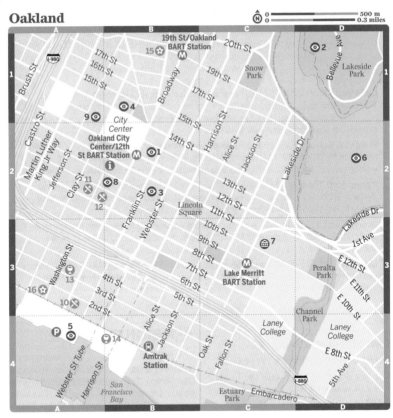

Oakland

ferries arrive from SF. Franklin Delano Roosevelt's official yacht, the **Potomac** (Floating White House; ☎510-627-1215; www. usspotomac.org), is usually moored beside the ferry landing and is definitely worth

a look. Sundays there's a **farmers market** (☉10am-2pm).

OAKLAND MUSEUM OF CALIFORNIA MUSEUM (☎510-238-2200; www.museumca.org; 1000 Oak St; adult/child $12/6, 1st Sun of month free;

⊙11am-5pm Wed-Sat, to 9pm Fri; ⓡLake Merritt) This museum has excellent permanent collections on California history, regional natural sciences and works by local artists, including fine prints by Californian photographers Ansel Adams and Dorothea Lange.

LAKE MERRITT
LAKE

(along Lakeside Dr; ⓡLake Merritt) Oakland's visual centerpiece, Lake Merritt is a gorgeous place to stroll, jog or lollygag on sunny days. Once a tidal marsh teeming with waterfowl, it became a lake in 1869 with the damming of an arm of the Oakland estuary. It still supports migratory birds and remains connected to the estuary, but its 155 acres are briny and unfit for swimming. You'll spot hundreds of Canada geese (and their droppings) along a 3.5-mile perimeter path.

CHILDREN'S FAIRYLAND
AMUSEMENT PARK

(☎510-452-2259; www.fairyland.org; Grand & Belle vue Aves; admission $8; ⊙10am-4pm daily summer, Wed-Sun spring & fall, Fri-Sun winter; ⓠ12 AC Transit, ⓡ19th St) On the northern side of Lake Merritt at Lakeside Park, Children's Fairyland was apparently Walt Disney's inspiration for Disneyland. It has a weirdly dilapidated charm; little kids love it. The adjacent **boating center** (☎510-238-2196; 568 Bellevue Ave; ⊙10:30am-4pm Mar-Oct, Sat & Sun Nov-Feb) rents canoes, rowboats, kayaks, pedal boats and sailboats for $10 to $18 per hour.

✖ EATING & DRINKING

WOOD TAVERN
AMERICAN $$$

(☎510-654-6607; www.woodtavern.net; 6317 College Ave; lunch $10-20, dinner $19-26; ⊙11:30am-10pm; ⓡRockridge) The daily-changing New American brasserie-style menu features what's in season, with earthy, soulful dishes like pan-roasted lemon-rosemary chicken, chopped salads, cheese boards, charcuterie plates and great burgers. Very local, happening crowd. Reserve.

À CÔTÉ
MEDITERRANEAN $$

(☎510-655-6469; www.acoterestaurant.com; 5478 College Ave; dishes $5-16; ⊙dinner; ⓡRockridge) Small plates are the specialty at this foodie-scenester restaurant, with knockouts like lobster corn fritters. Women can sport high heels without standing out; men can wear jeans and blend in. Great cocktails.

TAMARINDO
MEXICAN $$

(☎510-444-1944; www.tamarindoantojeria.com; 468 8th St; dishes $8-12; ⊙Mon-Sat; ⓡ12th St) The carefully crafted *antojitos* (Mexican tapas) aren't your usual Mexican fare. Expect flavor-packed spins on familiar dishes, like tostadas and tacos (try the shrimp), served in a stylish brick-walled space.

RATTO'S
DELI $

(821 Washington St; sandwiches $5-8; ⊙9am-5:30pm Mon-Fri, 10am-3pm Sat; ⟋; ⓡ8th St & Broadway) Gather picnic supplies at this vintage grocery (c 1897) with deli counter and devoted lunch crowd.

EVERETT & JONES BARBEQUE
BBQ $

(☎510-663-2350; www.eandjbbq.com; 126 Broadway; lunch $7-9, dinner $12-20; ⊙11am-10pm; ⓡ12th St) The smoked pork ribs are damn good at this simple, family-run spot with plastic red-checked tablecloths, occasional live music and slow service (stick around, it's worth it).

HEINOLD'S FIRST & LAST CHANCE SALOON
BAR

(www.heinoldsfirstandlastchance.com; 56 Jack London Sq; ⓡ12th St) Heinold's 1883 bar sits on a tilt from age and earthquakes (hold onto your beer), but its real claim to fame is that author Jack London was a regular – he even brought his school books here to study.

BEER REVOLUTION
BREWERY

(www.beer-revolution.com; 464 3rd St; ⓡBroadway & 3rd St) Fifty beers on tap, 500 by bottle. Bonuses include a sun deck, no distracting TVs, and punk soundtrack played at conversation-friendly levels. Check the website for Sunday barbecues.

☆ ENTERTAINMENT

For more ideas, see the Nightlife Across the Bay boxed text, p211.

YOSHI'S
JAZZ

(☎510-238-9200; www.yoshis.com; 510 Embarcadero West; shows $12-40; ⊙lunch & dinner; ⓡ12th St) The Bay Area's leading jazz club books a full calendar of talent from around the world. There's good sushi and full bar for preshow eats, but the real draws are awesome acoustics and top-flight acts.

PARAMOUNT THEATRE   THEATER
(☎510-465-6400; www.paramounttheatre.com; 2025 Broadway; �🚇19th St) This gorgeously restored art-deco masterpiece hosts rock concerts (Morrissey, Nelly Furtado), the Oakland Symphony and Ballet, and various traveling acts. Theater tours ($5, starting at 10am) available first and third Saturdays every month.

FOX OAKLAND THEATRE   THEATER
(www.thefoxoakland.com; Telegraph Ave & 19th St; ⚅19th St) The 1928 Fox, once the largest cinema west of Chicago, has been dazzlingly restored and hosts the likes of Sonic Youth and Kylie Minogue. Grab a bite before the show at next-door **Rudy's Can't Fail Cafe**, co-owned by Green Day bassist Mike Dirnt.

GRAND LAKE THEATER   CINEMA
(☎510-452-3556; www.renaissancerialto.com; 3200 Grand Ave; adult/child $10/7; 🚌12 AC Transit) One of the last remaining 1920s movie palaces to show first-run films. Some weekend shows are preceded by performances on the Mighty Wurlitzer organ.

Napa Valley

Explore

The most glamorous stretch of farmland in America, Napa Valley is famous for cabernet sauvignon, star chefs, volcanic-mud baths and monuments to ego. It's the most-visited part of Wine Country – Hwy 29 slows to a standstill summer weekends; come midweek if possible. The city of Napa, to the south, has the least-expensive lodging, but lacks charm. Calistoga, in the north, is the least-gentrified town and the location of 19th-century hot-springs resorts. St Helena is the posh, midvalley destination, where traffic snarls. Many wineries require reservations; don't try to see more than three in a day. Book one appointment and plan your day around it. Go north on Hwy 29, then return southward on parallel-running Silverado Trail. Napa can be done as a day trip, but you'd be smart to stay at least one night.

The Best...

➡ **Winery** Frog's Leap (p216)
➡ **Mud Bath Spa** Indian Springs (p219)
➡ **Place to Eat** Oxbow Public Market (p218)

Top Tip

Because of Napa's strict zoning laws, many of the valley's wineries cannot legally receive drop-in visitors. Book well ahead for famous names. Carry your cell phone for last-minute bookings.

Getting There & Away

Car To Napa: take Hwy 101 to Hwy 37 east. At the 121/37 split take Hwy 121 north, which veers east toward Napa. At Hwy 29, turn north. From Downtown, the Bay Bridge is quicker, but less scenic: take I-80E to Hwy 37 west (exit 33), then go north on Hwy 29. Alternatively, to reach Calistoga and bypass the lower- and midvalley, take Hwy 101 to Mark West Springs Rd (exit 494/River Rd) and keep winding east into Porter Creek Rd and Petrified Forest Rd.

Ferry & Bus Possible, but slow: take the Vallejo ferry (p293), then bus 10 Napa Valley Vine (www.nctpa.net).

Need to Know

➡ **Area Code** ☎707
➡ **Location** 50 miles northeast of San Francisco
➡ **Napa Valley Welcome Center** (☎707-260-0107; www.legendarynapavalley.com; 600 Main St; ◷9am-5pm) Tourist office.

⊙ SIGHTS

Small towns with huge reputations line Hwy 29. Tiny Yountville has more Michelin-starred eateries per capita than anywhere else in America. Charming St Helena – the Beverly Hills of Napa – is where traffic always jams, but there's great strolling if you can find parking. Folksy Calistoga – Napa's least-gentrified town – marks the valley's north end, home to hot-spring spas and mud-bath emporiums that use volcanic ash from adjacent Mt St Helena.

Wine Country

When visiting wineries, call ahead for bookings whenever possible – by local law, some wineries require advance reservations and must cap their daily number of visitors.

The sights below are listed in south to north order.

DI ROSA ART + NATURE PRESERVE
ART GALLERY

(☎707-226-5991; www.dirosapreserve.org; 5200 Carneros Hwy 121; ⊙gallery 9:30am-3pm Wed-Fri, by appointment Sat) When you notice scrap-metal sheep grazing Carneros vineyards, you've spotted di Rosa Art + Nature Preserve, one of the best-anywhere collections of Northern California art. Reservations recommended for tours, covering everything from Tony Oursler's grimacing video projections in the wine cellar to million-dollar Robert Bechtel abstracts hung on the living-room ceiling.

VINTNERS' COLLECTIVE
TASTING ROOM

(☎707-255-7150; www.vintnerscollective.com; 1245 Main St, Napa; tasting $25; ⊙11am-6pm) Ditch the car and chill in downtown Napa at this super-cool tasting bar –inside a former 19th-century brothel – that represents 20 high-end boutique wineries too small to have their own tasting rooms.

TWENTY ROWS
WINERY

(☎707-287-1063; www.twentyrows.com; 880 Vallejo St, Napa; tasting $10; ⊙11am-5pm Tue-Sat) Downtown Napa's only working winery crafts light-on-the-palate cabernet sauvignon for a mere $20 a bottle. Taste in the barrel room – essentially a chilly garage with plastic picnic tables – with fun dudes who know their wines. Good sauvignon blanc, too.

HESS COLLECTION
WINERY, ART GALLERY

(☎707-255-1144; www.hesscollection.com; 4411 Redwood Rd, Napa; tasting $10; ⊙10am-4pm)

ALTERNATIVES TO DRIVING IN NAPA

It's hard to get around Napa without a car, but not impossible. The payoffs are no parking hassles or fear of a DUI, but it will take several hours to get here. Read schedules carefully and take the ferry and Napa Valley Vine bus from SF (p293), then switch to adventurous alternative transportation.

Napa Valley Adventure Tours (☑707-259-1833, 877-548-6877; www.napavalley adventuretours.com; Oxbow Public Market, 610 1st St, Napa; 6½hr tour $139) Wine-tasting bicycle trips with lunch and personal introductions to winemakers, artisans and organic farmers along the Silverado Trail. Also rents bikes.

Napa River Vélo (☑707-258-8729; www.naparivervelo.com; 680 Main St, rear of bldg, Napa; bikes per hour/day $10/35) In downtown Napa; organizes weekend guided tours and wine pickup.

Napa Valley Wine Train (☑707-253-2111, 800-427-4124; www.winetrain.com; $89-189) Cushy, touristy three-hour rail trips through the valley, with an optional winery stop.

Calistoga Bike Shop (☑707-942-9687, 866-942-2453; www.calistogabikeshop.com; 1318 Lincoln Ave, Calistoga) Extensive selection of rental bikes from $35 a day, at the valley's quiet northern end. Also organizes self-guided tours that include free tastings and wine pickup.

Blue-chip art and big reds are the pride of Hess Collection, a winery/gallery northwest of downtown Napa that pairs monster cabs with art by mega-modernists like Francis Bacon and Robert Motherwell. Ready yourself for a winding mountain road. Reservations suggested.

DARIOUSH
WINERY

(☑707-257-2345; www.darioush.com; 4240 Silverado Trail, Napa; tasting $18-35; ☉10:30am-5pm) Stone bulls glower from atop pillars lining the driveway of Darioush, a jaw-dropping, over-the-top winery styled after the ancient Persian temples of Persepolis; it's known for monumental merlots, shiraz and cabernet. Very fancy.

REGUSCI
WINERY

(☑707-254-0403; www.regusciwinery.com; 5584 Silverado Trail, Napa; tasting $15-25; ☉10am-5pm) One of Napa's oldest wineries, unfussy Regusci dates to the late 1800s, with 173 acres of vineyards unfurling around a century-old stone winery on the valley's quieter eastern side. Good when traffic up-valley is bad. Great Bordeaux-style blends. No appointment necessary; lovely oak-shaded picnic area.

MUMM NAPA
WINERY

(☑800-686-6272; www.mummnapa.com; 8445 Silverado Trail, Rutherford; tasting $7-25; ☉10am-4:45pm) The valley views are spectacular at Mumm, which makes respectable sparkling wines that you can sample while seated on a vineyard-view terrace – ideal when you want to impress your parents-in-law. No appointment necessary. Check the website for discounted-tasting coupons.

FROG'S LEAP
WINERY

(☑707-963-4704; www.frogsleap.com; 8815 Conn Creek Rd, Rutherford; tour with tasting $20; ☉by appointment; ⊞) Meandering paths wind through magical gardens and fruit-bearing orchards surrounding an 1884 barn and farmstead with cats and chickens roaming the thickets. The family-friendly, down-to-earth vibe is old Napa, with a major emphasis on fun, and the LEED–certified winery makes excellent sauvignon blanc and fine cabernet. Reservations required.

CULINARY INSTITUTE OF AMERICA AT GREYSTONE
COOKING SCHOOL

(☑707-967-2320; 2555 Main St; mains $25-29, cooking demonstration $20; ☉restaurant 11:30am-9pm, cooking demonstrations 1:30pm Sat & Sun) An 1889 stone chateau houses a gadget-filled culinary shop, fine restaurant and weekend cooking demonstrations and wine-tasting classes.

CADE
WINERY

(☑707-965-2746; www.cadewinery.com; 360 Howell Mountain Rd, Angwin; tasting $20; ☉by appointment) Ascend Mt Veeder for drop-dead vistas, 1800ft above the valley, at Napa's oh-so-swank, first-ever all organically farmed

LEED gold-certified winery, owned in part by former San Francisco Mayor Gavin Newsom. Hawks ride thermals at eye level, as you sample all-organic, bright sauvignon blanc and luscious cabernet sauvignon that's more Bordelaise in style than Californian. Reservations required.

PRIDE MOUNTAIN
WINERY

(☏707-963-4949; www.pridewines.com; 4026 Spring Mountain Rd, St Helena; tasting $10; ☺10:30am-3:45pm, by appointment) High atop Spring Mountain, cult-favorite Pride straddles the Sonoma–Napa county border and makes fabulous, well-structured cabernet sauvignon, big merlot and elegant viognier available only at the winery. Picnicking on the unfussy hilltop estate is spectacular, but you must first have a tasting appointment.

CASA NUESTRA
WINERY

(☏866-844-9463; www.casanuestra.com; 3451 Silverado Trail, St Helena; tasting $10, refundable with purchase; ☺10am-4:30pm, by appointment) A peace flag and portrait of Elvis greet you in the tasting barn at this old-school, '70s-vintage, mom-and-pop winery with playful goats beside a little picnic area. The diverse wines include a chenin blanc from 50-year-old organic vines. Call ahead.

CASTELLO DI AMOROSA
WINERY

(☏707-967-6272; www.castellodiamorosa.com; 4045 Hwy 29, Calistoga; tasting $10-15, tour adult/child $32/22; ☺by appointment; ⛟) It took 14 years to build this near-perfect recreation of a 12th-century Italian castle, complete with moat, hand-cut stone walls, catacombs, frescoes hand painted by Italian artisans and torture chamber filled with period equipment. Trust us, take the tour (bring a sweater). Wines include some respectable Italian varietals, including a merlot blend that's great with pizza, and a late-harvest gewürztraminer dessert wine. Make reservations.

LAVA VINE
TASTING ROOM

(☏707-942-9500; www.lavavine.com; 965 Silverado Trail, Calistoga; tasting $10, waived with purchase; ☺10am-5pm; ⛟) Breaking ranks with Napa snobbery, the party kids at Lava Vine take a lighthearted approach to their seriously good wines, all paired with small bites, including some hot off the barbecue. Kids and dogs play outside, while you let your guard down in the tiny tasting room and tap your toe to James Brown. Bring a picnic. Reservations recommended.

OLD FAITHFUL GEYSER
LANDMARK

(☏707-942-6463; www.oldfaithfulgeyser.com; 1299 Tubbs Lane; adult/child $10/3; ☺9am-6pm; ⛟) Calistoga's miniversion of Yellowstone's Old Faithful shoots boiling water 60-to-100ft into the air every 30 minutes. The vibe is pure roadside Americana kitsch, with folksy hand-painted interpretive exhibits, picnicking and a little petting zoo with llamas. It's 2 miles north of town, off Silverado Trail.

ROBERT LOUIS STEVENSON STATE PARK
NATURE RESERVE

(☺707-942-4575; www.parks.ca.gov; admission free) The long-extinct volcanic cone of Mt St Helena marks the valley's end, 8 miles north of Calistoga. The undeveloped state park on Hwy 29 often gets snow in winter. It's a strenuous 5-mile climb to the 4343ft summit, but what a view – 200 miles on a clear winter's day. Check conditions before setting out. Also consider 2.2-mile one-way **Table Rock Trail** (go south from the summit parking area) for drop-dead valley views. Temperatures are best in wildflower season, February through May; fall is prettiest, when the vineyards change colors.

EATING

Napa is the outpost of San Francisco's food scene; plan to have a lingering lunch or dinner. Make reservations whenever possible; even on weekdays in winter, many restaurants sell out. Most Napa restaurants don't serve late – average visitors get too drunk during the daytime to stay up for a 9pm table. There's a **farmers market** (www.sthelenafarmersmkt.org; Crane Park, off Grayson Ave; ☺7:30am-noon May-Oct) Friday mornings in St Helena.

A LOVELY SPOT FOR A PICNIC

Most Sonoma County wineries allow picnicking, but Napa has strict zoning laws prohibiting picnicking at most wineries. Call ahead for spots at Pride Mountain, Casa Nuestra or Lava Vine; or just drop by Regusci. Bring your own food, but be sure to buy a bottle of your host's wine – it's only polite.

FRENCH LAUNDRY   CALIFORNIAN **$$$**

(☎707-944-2380; www.frenchlaundry.com; 6640 Washington St, Yountville; fixed-price menu $270; ☺dinner daily, lunch Sat & Sun) A high-wattage culinary experience on par with the world's best, Thomas Keller's French Laundry is ideal for marking lifetime achievements – a 40th birthday, say, or a Nobel Prize. Book exactly two months (to the day) ahead: call at 10am sharp, or log onto www.opentable.com at precisely midnight. If you can't score a reservation, console yourself at Keller's nearby note-perfect French brasserie, **Bouchon** (☎707-944-8037; www.bouchonbistro.com; 6354 Washington St, Yountville; ☺11:30am-midnight), which is (much) easier to book and makes perfect roast chicken and *steak-frites*.

OXBOW PUBLIC MARKET   MARKET **$**

(www.oxbowpublicmarket.com; 610 & 644 1st St, Napa; ☺9am-7pm Mon-Sat, 10am-5pm Sun) A gourmet food court á la the Ferry Building in SF, Oxbow showcases local, sustainably produced artisinal food, such as Hog Island oysters (six for $15), Pica Pica's Venezuelan cornbread sandwiches ($8) and Three Twins certified-organic ice cream ($4 for a single waffle cone). Come hungry and plan to graze. Tuesday is locals night, with many discounts. Tuesday and Saturday mornings, there's a farmers market. Friday nights bring live music.

AD HOC   AMERICAN **$$$**

(☎707-944-2487; www.adhocrestaurant.com; 6476 Washington St, Yountville; menu $48; ☺dinner Wed-Mon, Sun 10:30am-2pm) Don't bother asking for a menu at Thomas Keller's innovative comfort-food restaurant, where chef Dave Cruz concocts a daily four-course, market-driven menu. No substitutions (unless you mention dietary restrictions), but none are needed – every dish is garden-fresh and spot-on. Monday's fried-chicken night has a religious following; book ahead.

JOLÉ   CALIFORNIAN **$$$**

(☎707-942-5938; www.jolerestaurant.com; 1457 Lincoln Ave, Calistoga; mains $15-20; ☺dinner Tue-Sun) The farm-to-table small plates at chef-owned Jolé evolve seasonally, but may include standouts like local sole with tiny, tangy Napa grapes, caramelized Brussels sprouts with capers, and organic Baldwin apple strudel with housemade burnt caramel ice cream. Yum. Four courses cost $50.

OENOTRI   ITALIAN **$$**

(☎707-252-1022; www.oenotri.com; 1425 1st St, Napa; mains $15-25; ☺dinner, lunch hours vary)

SLEEPING IN NAPA VALLEY

Most lodging in Napa costs well over $200. The following are good midrange choices. If you can't swing the rates in Napa, consider suburban Vallejo, 20 minutes south of downtown Napa on I-80. Motels near the freeway cost $60 to $100 in high season.

Avia Hotel (☎707-224-3900; www.aviahotels.com; 1450 1st St, Napa; r $149-249; ✳@☎) Downtown Napa's newest hotel opened in 2009 and feels like a big-city hotel, with business-class-fancy rooms, styled in retro-'70s chic.

El Bonita Motel (☎707-963-3216, 800-541-3284; www.elbonita.com; 195 Main St, St Helena; $119-179; ✳@☎☷) Book well ahead to score a room at this sought-after motel with up-to-date rooms, hot tub and sauna.

Eurospa Inn (☎707-942-6829; www.eurospa.com; 1202 Pine St, Calistoga; r $139-189; ✳☎☷) Immaculate single-story motel on a quiet side street in Calistoga, with extras like gas-burning fireplaces and afternoon wine hour.

Best Western Ivy Hotel (☎707-253-9300, 800-253-6272; www.ivyhotelnapa.com; 4195 Solano Ave, Napa; r $149-249; ✳@☎☷) Redone in 2011, this smart-looking motel, on the suburban strip north of Napa, has extras like fridge and microwave.

Chablis Inn (☎707-257-1944, 800-443-3490; www.chablisinn.com; 3360 Solano Ave, Napa; r weekday $89-109, weekend $159-179; ✳@☎☷) Another good-value motel with big rooms on Napa's suburban strip.

Calistoga Inn (☎707-942-4101; www.calistogainn.com; 1250 Lincoln Ave, Calistoga; r with shared bathroom midweek/weekend $69/119) Great-bargain inn, upstairs from a lively brewery-restaurant (bring earplugs). No TVs, shared bathrooms. Spas within walking distance.

MUD-BATH SPAS IN CALISTOGA

Celebrated 19th-century author Robert Louis Stevenson said of Calistoga, 'the whole neighborhood of Mt St Helena is full of sulfur and boiling springs...Calistoga itself seems to repose on a mere film above a boiling, subterranean lake.' Indeed, it does. Calistoga is synonymous with the mineral water bearing its name, bottled here since 1924. Its springs and geysers have earned it the nickname the 'hot springs of the West.'

The town is famous for its old-time spas and mud-bath emporiums, where you're buried like a tree root in hot mud, made with volcanic ash from nearby Mt St Helena. Afterward you soak in clear, hot water, then steam, then fall asleep wrapped in blankets. **Indian Springs** (☑707-942-4913; www.indianspringscalistoga.com; 1712 Lincoln Ave; ⊘9am-8pm) is the first-choice classic, and mines its own all-volcanic-ash mud; baths ($85) include free access afterwards to the giant hot-springs-fed pool. Vintage-1950s **Dr Wilkinson's Hot Springs** (☑707-942-4102; www.drwilkinson.com; 1507 Lincoln Ave; ⊘8:30am-5:30pm) is a respectable backup, and uses more peat for lighter mud ($89). Lovely and tiny **Lavender Hill Spa** (☑707-942-4495; www.lavenderhillspa.com; 1015 Foothill Blvd; ⊘10am-6pm Sun-Thu, to 8pm Fri & Sat) uses a much lighter, less-icky lavender-infused mud and offers couples treatments ($85 per person) in a two-room spa with side-by-side claw-foot Jacuzzi tubs. Top-end and contemporary **Spa Solage** (☑707-226-0825; www.solage calistoga.com; 755 Silverado Trail; ⊘8am-8pm) is the fancy-pants choice for DIY paint-on treatments – great for couples – and has a clothing-optional spa pool.

Housemade *salumi* and pastas, and wood-fired Naples-style pizzas are the stars at always-busy Oenotri, a happening downtown restaurant that draws bon vivants for a daily-changing lineup of locally sourced, rustic-Italian cooking, served in a cavernous brick-walled space in downtown Napa.

🍴UBUNTU   VEGETARIAN **$$$**

(☑707-251-5656; www.ubuntunapa.com; 1140 Main St, Napa; dishes $14-18; ⊘dinner daily, lunch Sat & Sun) The Michelin-starred seasonal, vegetarian menu features artfully presented natural wonders from the biodynamic kitchen garden, satisfying hearty eaters with four-to-five inspired small plates, and ecosavvy drinkers with 100-plus sustainably produced wines.

BOUNTY HUNTER WINE BAR   AMERICAN **$$**

(www.bountyhunterwine.com; 975 1st St, Napa; dishes $14-24; ⊘11am-10pm; 🍴) Inside an 1888 grocery store with pressed-tin ceilings and trophy heads on the walls, Bounty Hunter has an old West vibe, a fitting backdrop for superb barbecue, made with house-smoked meats, and a standout whole chicken roasted over a can of Tecate beer. Great for a no-fuss meal in downtown Napa. Ten local beers and 40 wines by the glass.

GOTT'S ROADSIDE/TAYLOR'S
AUTOMATIC REFRESHER   BURGERS **$$**

(☑707-963-3486; www.gottsroadside.com; 933 Main St, St Helena; dishes $8-15; ⊘10:30am-9pm; 🍴) Wiggle your toes in the grass at this 1950s drive-in diner with 21st-century sensibilities: burgers are of all-natural Niman Ranch beef or lean *ahi* tuna, with optional sides of chili-dusted sweet-potato fries. To avoid hunger-inducing waits, avoid peak meal times, or call ahead for takeout and beat the line. There's also a branch at Oxbow Public Market.

Sonoma Valley

Explore

There are three Sonomas: the town, which is in the valley, which is in the county. Think of them as Russian dolls. Anchoring the bucolic 17-mile-long Sonoma Valley, the town of Sonoma makes a great jumping-off point for exploring Wine Country – it's only an hour from San Francisco, and has a marvelous sense of place, with 19th-century historical sights lining the state's largest town square. Halfway up-valley, tiny Glen Ellen is like a Norman Rockwell painting come to life – in stark contrast to Santa Rosa, the valley's northernmost town, notorious for suburban-sprawl and traffic.

Sonoma Highway (Hwy 12) is lined with wineries and runs from the town of Sonoma to Santa Rosa, then to the Russian

JERRY ALEXANDER / LONELY PLANET IMAGES ©

1. Fresh seafood (p234)
Drakes Bay and nearby Tomales Bay at Point Reyes National Seashore are famous for oysters.

2. Muir Woods National Monument (p227)
The closest stand of coastal redwoods to San Francisco.

3. Napa Valley (p214)
Visit wineries on a summer weekend in the most glamorous stretch of farmland in America.

4. Hwy 1 (p235)
The coastal road south of the city is lined with craggy beaches, lighthouses and tiny towns.

River Valley and the coast. Arnold Dr runs parallel to Hwy 12, on the western side of Sonoma Valley, to Glen Ellen; it has less traffic, but few wineries.

The Best...

➡ **Sight** Sonoma Plaza (p222)

➡ **Place to Eat** Cafe la Haye (p223)

➡ **Winery** Kaz Winery (p223)

Top Tip

If you're not up for driving, aim for the town of Sonoma and lollygag around Sonoma Plaza, the sun-dappled town square, where it's legal to drink wine on the grass.

Getting There & Away

Car From San Francisco to downtown Sonoma, take Hwy 101 to Hwy 37 east. At the split take Hwy 121 north, then Hwy 12 to Sonoma town and valley. One hour.

Bus From San Francisco, take Golden Gate Transit (☑511 or 415-923-2000; www.goldengatetransit.org) to Petaluma (90 minutes), then connect with Sonoma County Transit (☑511, 707-576-7433; www.sctransit.com) to downtown Sonoma (30 minutes). Service is infrequent: call for assistance booking the right connections.

Need to Know

➡ **Area Code** ☑707

➡ **Location** 45 miles north–northeast of San Francisco

➡ **Sonoma Valley Visitors Bureau** (☑707-996-1090; www.sonomavalley.com; 453 1st St E; ◷9am-5pm) Tourist office.

◎ SIGHTS

More casual and less commercial than Napa, Sonoma Valley has 70 wineries around Hwy 12 – and unlike Napa, most welcome picnicking. You don't usually need appointments to taste, but call ahead for tours. If you don't feel like driving, find multiple tasting rooms around Sonoma Plaza.

SONOMA PLAZA   SQUARE

(Bordered by Napa, Spain & 1st Sts) Century-old trees cast sun-dappled shade on the plaza, a great spot for a picnic with a bottle of Sonoma wine. Historic buildings line the plaza's north side. Smack at the center, the stately mission revival-style **City Hall** (1906–08) has identical facades on four sides, reportedly because plaza businesses all demanded City Hall face their direction. At the plaza's northeast corner, the **Bear Flag Monument** marks Sonoma's moment of revolutionary glory. Spring through fall, get local flavor at the weekly **farmers market** (◷5:30-8pm Tue; Apr-Oct).

SONOMA STATE HISTORIC PARK   HISTORICAL SITE

(☑707-938-1519; www.parks.ca.gov; adult/child $3/2; ◷10am-5pm) Glimpse early California history at the **Mission Solano San Francisco** (114 E Spain St). Founded in 1823, it once included 10,000 acres, farmed by 900 conscripted Native Californian workers; the East Spain St wing remains largely intact, with a reconstructed chapel. At the adjacent **Adobe Barracks** (20 E Spain St), Sonoma settlers surprised Mexican soldiers in 1850 by declaring an independent republic and raising the Bear Flag (which is now the California state flag). The adjoining **Toscano Hotel** opened as a store and library in the 1850s, then became a hotel in 1886. Peek into the lobby: except for the traffic outside, you'd swear you'd stepped back in time; free tours 1pm through 4pm, weekends and Mondays.

FREE CORNERSTONE   GARDEN

(☑707-933-9474, 707-933-3010; www.cornerstonegardens.com; 23570 Hwy 121; ◷10am-5pm; ⊕) There's nothing traditional about this tapestry of gardens, which showcase the work of 25 renowned avant-garde landscape designers. We especially love Pamela Burton's 'Earth Walk,' which descends into the ground; and McCrory and Raiche's 'Rise,' which exaggerates space. The kids can run around while you explore top-notch garden shops, set up a picnic at the free-to-use tables, sip wine at the on-site **cafe** or gather winery maps at a satellite office of the **Sonoma Valley visitors center** (☑707-996-1090; www.sonomavalley.com; ◷10am-4pm). Look for the giant oversized blue chair, south of town.

JACK LONDON STATE HISTORIC PARK   HISTORIC SITE

(☑707-938-5216; www.jacklondonpark.com; 2400 London Ranch Rd, Glen Ellen; parking $8; ◷10am-5pm Thu-Mon; ⊕) Up Hwy 12 in Glen Ellen, obey the call of the wild at Jack London State Historic Park, where adventure-novelist Jack London moved in 1910 to build his dream house – which burned down on the eve of completion in 1913. His widow built the house that now stands as a **museum** to London. Miles of **hiking trails** (some open to mountain bikes) weave through the park's 1400 hilltop acres; an easy 2-mile loop meanders to a lake, great for picnicking.

HOMEWOOD WINERY

(☎707-996-6353; www.homewoodwinery.com; 23120 Burndale Rd, at Hwy 121/12; tastings free; ⏰10am-4pm) A stripy rooster named Steve chases dogs in the parking lot of this down-home winery, one of the closest to SF, where the tasting room is a garage, and the wine-maker crafts grenache, mourvèdre and syrah – 'Da redder, da better' – and stand-out ports. Dogs welcome, but you've been warned.

GUNDLACH-BUNDSCHU WINERY

(☎707-938-5277; www.gunbun.com; 2000 Denmark St; tasting $10; ⏰11am-4:30pm) Down a country road from downtown, Gundlach-Bundschu dates to 1858 and looks like a storybook castle. Perched in a park-like setting, above a reclaimed-water lake, the solar-powered winery produces legendary tempranillo; riesling and gewürztraminer are the signatures. Great bike-to destination.

BARTHOLOMEW PARK WINERY WINERY, MUSEUM

(☎707-939-3026; www.bartpark.com; 1000 Vineyard Lane; tasting $5-10, museum & park entry free; ⏰tasting room & museum 11am-4:30pm) Gundlach-Bundschu also runs nearby Bartholomew Park Winery, a 400-acre preserve with vineyards first cultivated in 1857 and now certified-organic, yielding citrusy sauvignon blanc and smoky merlot. Another good bike-to destination.

BR COHN WINERY

(☎707-938-4064; www.brcohn.com; 15000 Sonoma Hwy, Glen Ellen; tasting $10, applicable to purchase; ⏰10am-5pm) Picnic like a rock star at BR Cohn. Its founder Bruce Cohn managed '70s superband the Doobie Brothers before moving on to make organic olive oils and good wines – including an excellent cabernet sauvignon, unusual in Sonoma – and throw an annual September benefit concert amid the vineyards and olive groves.

BENZIGER WINERY

(☎888-490-2739; www.benziger.com; 1883 London Ranch Rd, Glen Ellen; tasting $10-20, tram tour adult incl tasting/child $15/5; ⏰10am-5pm; 🖬) If you're new to wine, Benziger provides an excellent crash course in winemaking on its worthwhile (nonreserveable) open-air **tram tour** (⏰half-hourly, 11:30am-3:30pm) through biodynamic vineyards, which includes a tasting afterward.

WELLINGTON WINERY

(☎707-939-0708; www.wellingtonvineyards.com; 11600 Dunbar Rd, Glen Ellen; tastings $5; ⏰10am-5pm) West off Hwy 12, some of Sonoma Valley's best buys await at low-profile Wellington, where the under-$30 wines include hazelnutty white port and peppery zins produced by 100-year-old vines that miraculously survived Prohibition.

KAZ WINERY WINERY

(☎707-833-2536; www.kazwinery.com; 233 Adobe Canyon Rd, Kenwood; tasting $5-10, applicable to purchase; ⏰11am-5pm Fri-Mon; 🖬) Sonoma's cult favorite, always-fun Kaz serves unusual, organically grown wines at a barrel-top tasting bar inside a barn. Discover lesser-known varietals like alicante bouchet and lenoir. Kids get Play-Doh, grape juice and a playground; adults sift through LPs and pop their favorites onto the turntable.

✖ EATING

FREMONT DINER AMERICAN $

(☎707-938-7370; 2698 Fremont Dr/Hwy 121; mains $8-11; ⏰8am-3pm Mon-Fri, 7am-4pm Sat & Sun; 🖬) Lines snake out the door on weekends at this farm-to-table roadside diner, where you order at the counter, then snag a table – outdoors or inside – and feast on ricotta pancakes with real maple syrup, chicken and waffles, oyster po' boys and finger-licking barbecue. Arrive early to beat the line.

CAFE LA HAYE AMERICAN $$$

(☎707-935-5994; www.cafelahaye.com; 140 E Napa St, Sonoma; mains $19-29; ⏰dinner Tue-Sat) Tops for earthy New American cooking, made with produce sourced from within 60 miles. The tiny room is cheek-by-jowl and service borders on perfunctory, but the clean simplicity and flavor-packed cooking

TRAFFIC ALERT

The road to Sonoma passes by Infineon Raceway, which on major race days causes huge traffic backups lasting for miles. Check the calendar at www.infineonraceway.com. Avoid Hwys 121/12 when there's a race; if there is, take Hwy 101 north to Santa Rosa, then drop back down Hwy 12 into Sonoma Valley.

make it foodies' first choice. Reservations essential.

FIG CAFE & WINEBAR   CALIFORNIAN $$

(☎707-938-2130; www.thefigcafe.com; 13690 Arnold Dr, Glen Ellen; mains $15-20; ⊗5:30-9pm daily, 10am-2:30pm Sat & Sun) Sonoma's take on soul-satisfying comfort food – organic salads, Sonoma duck cassoulet and free corkage on Sonoma wines – in a converted living room in the little town of Glen Ellen.

EL DORADO KITCHEN
CORNER CAFE   CAFE $$

(☎707-996-3030; www.eldoradosonoma.com; 405 1st St W, Sonoma; dishes $9-15; ⊗7am-10pm; ☑) Biodynamic salads and gargantuan pastrami sandwiches with parmesan-dusted truffle fries are big enough to split in this sunny corner cafe, but order your own soft-serve ice cream topped with BR Cohn olive oil and sea salt.

VINEYARDS INN BAR & GRILL   SPANISH $$

(☎707-833-4500; www.vineyardsinn.com; 8445 Sonoma Hwy 12, Kenwood; mains $8-20; ⊗11:30am-9:30pm; ☑) There's nothing fancy about this roadside tavern at the valley's northern end, but the sustainably grown food is terrific, including a succulent certified-organic chuck burger on ciabatta. Seafood is wild and line-caught, and most produce comes from chef Esteban's certified-organic and biodynamic Rose Ranch.

RED GRAPE   PIZZA $$

(☎707-996-4103; www.theredgrape.com; 529 1st St W, Sonoma; pizzas $10-16; ⊗11:30am-10pm; ☑☑) Thin-crust pizza with local cheeses and cured meats, plus small-production Sonoma wines by the half-bottle.

🏃 SPORTS & ACTIVITIES

SONOMA VALLEY CYCLERY   BICYCLES

(☎707-935-3377; www.sonomacyclery.com; 20091 Broadway/Hwy 12; bikes per day from $25; ⊗10am-6pm Mon-Sat, to 4pm Sun; ☑) The town of Sonoma is ideal for biking – not too hilly – with multiple wineries in easy reach of downtown. Book ahead weekends.

MORTON'S WARM SPRINGS   SWIMMING

(☎707-833-5511; www.mortonswarmsprings. com; 1651 Warm Springs Rd; adult/child $8/7, reserved picnic & BBQ sites per person $11; ⊗10am-6pm Sat & Sun May & Sep, Tue-Sun Jun-Aug; ☑) Northwest of Glen Ellen, Morton's Warm Springs were believed to have healing properties by native Wappo. Now it's a swim club, with three geothermal mineral pools, hiking trails, volleyball nets and BBQ facilities great for families.

WILLOW STREAM SPA AT SONOMA
MISSION INN   SPA

(☎707-938-9000; www.fairmont.com/sonoma; 100 Boyes Blvd; ⊗7:30am-8pm) Few Wine Country spas compare with glitzy Sonoma Mission Inn, where if you book two treatments – or pay $89 – you'll have free use of three outdoor and two indoor mineral pools, gym, sauna and herbal steam room at the Romanesque bathhouse. Adults only.

Healdsburg & Dry Creek Valley

Explore

More than 90 wineries lie within 30 miles of Healdsburg – Sonoma County's culinary capital – where upscale eateries, wine-tasting rooms and stylish inns ring the town's plaza. It's a straight shot up the Hwy 101 freeway from the Golden Gate. Once a sleepy ag town, Healdsburg now gets jammed on weekends. Consider heading directly northwest to Dry Creek Valley, a landscape of gently undulating hills and small-scale wineries specializing in zinfandel. Dry Creek Rd is the main highway; parallel-running narrow West Dry Creek Rd is better for bicyclists.

East, along Hwy 128, lies the spectacular Alexander Valley, where merlot and cabernet thrive. West of Healdsburg, West Side Rd meanders along the cooler Russian River Valley, where pinot noir grows and visitors get lost on the winding back roads.

The Best...

➡ **Winery** Bella Vineyards (p226)
➡ **Place to Eat** Cyrus (p226)
➡ **Place to Pack a Picnic** Dry Creek General Store (p226)

Top Tip

On busy summer weekends, see downtown Healdsburg first thing in the morning, then head to wineries in the surrounding valleys. Traffic gets worse as the day wears on.

Getting There & Away

Car From San Francisco to downtown Healdsburg, take Hwy 101 for 65 miles to the Central Healdsburg exit. Plan 75 minutes from the Golden Gate Bridge.

Bus From San Francisco, take Golden Gate Transit (☏511 or 415-923-2000; www.goldengatetransit.org) to Santa Rosa (2 hours), then connect with Sonoma County Transit (☏511, 707-576-7433; www.sctransit.com) to downtown Healdsburg (40min).

Need to Know

➡ **Area code** ☏707
➡ **Location** 67 miles north of San Francisco
➡ **Healdsburg Visitors Center** (☏707-433-6935, 800-648-9922; www.healdsburg.org; 217 Healdsburg Ave; ◷9am-5pm Mon-Fri, 9am-3pm Sat, 10am-2pm Sun) Tourist office.

SLEEPING IN SONOMA VALLEY

At the northern end of Sonoma Valley, Santa Rosa offers affordable chain motels along Cleveland Ave, west of Hwy 101.

Beltane Ranch (☏707-996-6501; www.beltaneranch.com; 11775 Hwy 12; r incl breakfast $150-240; 🐾) Surrounded by horse pastures, Beltane is a throwback to 19th-century Sonoma. The cheerful, lemon-yellow-painted 1890s ranch house occupies 100 acres and has double porches lined with swinging chairs and white wicker. Five rooms. No phones or TVs.

Gaige House Inn (☏707-935-0237, 800-935-0237; www.gaige.com; 13540 Arnold Dr, Glen Ellen; r $249-299, ste $299-599; 🅿🐾📶) Sonoma's chicest inn, with Asian-inspired rooms in the historic main house and spa suites with hewn-granite tubs and pebbled meditation courtyards.

Sonoma Chalet (☏707-938-3129; www.sonomachalet.com; 18935 5th St W; r without bath $125, r with bath $140-180, cottages $195-225) Beautiful old farmstead surrounded by rolling hills, with rooms in a Swiss-chalet-style house adorned with country-Americana bric-a-brac. We especially love the free-standing cottages. No air-con in rooms with shared bath.

Sonoma Hotel (☏707-996-2996, 800-468-6016; www.sonomahotel.com; 110 W Spain St, Sonoma; r incl breakfast Nov-Mar midweek/weekend $140/170, Apr-Oct midweek/weekend $170/200; 🅿📶) Charming 1880 landmark hotel on happening Sonoma Plaza, with larger/smaller rooms for $30 more/less; two-night minimum weekends. No elevator or parking lot.

Hillside Inn (☏707-546-9353; www.hillside-inn.com; 2901 4th St, Santa Rosa; s/d Nov-Mar $70/82, Apr-Oct $74/86; 📶📺) One of Santa Rosa's best-kept motels; close to wine-tasting; add $4 for kitchens.

Sugarloaf Ridge State Park (☏707-833-5712, reservations 800-444-7275; www.parks.ca.gov; Adobe Canyon Rd; campsites $30;) North of Kenwood wineries, 50 sites without hookups are nestled in two mellow meadows.

👁 SIGHTS

BELLA VINEYARDS
WINERY

(www.bellawinery.com; 9711 W Dry Creek Rd; tasting $5-10; ⏰11am-4:30pm) At the northern end of Dry Creek, always-fun Bella has caves bored into the hillside, where you taste big reds – zin and syrah – but keep an eye out for the terrific rosé (good for barbecues) and late-harvest zin (great with brownies).

PRESTON VINEYARDS
WINERY

(www.prestonvineyards.com; 9282 W Dry Creek Rd; tasting $5, refundable with purchase; 🅿) Mosey across the road from Bella Vineyards to the 19th-century homestead at Preston Vineyards for picnics of certified organically grown barbera and viognier with home-baked bread, organic fruit and Pug's Leap goat cheese, plus marathon bocce ball games.

TRUETT-HURST
WINERY

(☎707-433-9545; www.truetthurst.com; 5610 Dry Creek Rd; tastings $5, refundable with purchase; ⏰10am-5pm) Pull up an Adirondack chair and picnic creekside at Truett-Hurst, Dry Creek's newest biodynamic winery, which is already producing terrific old-vine zins, petite sirah and Russian River pinots. Everfun weekends, when the winery offers food-and-wine pairings and hosts live music from 1pm to 5pm.

UNTI
WINERY

(☎707-433-5590; www.untivineyards.com; 4202 Dry Creek Rd; tasting $5, waived with purchase; ⏰by appointment 10am-4pm) Pristine biodynamic blends are served inside a fluorescent-lit garage at Unti, but even under harsh lighting, everyone looks gorgeous after a glass or two of such bodacious Brunello-style sangiovese, Châteauneuf-du-Pape–style grenache and voluptuous syrah. Call ahead to sample these stellar wines.

STRYKER SONOMA
WINERY

(☎707-433-1944; www.strykersonoma.com; 5110 Hwy 128; tastings $10, refundable with purchase; ⏰10:30am-5pm) Wow, what a view from this contemporary hilltop concrete-and-glass tasting room, worth the detour to Alexander Valley. Plan to picnic. Standouts are fruit-forward zinfandel and sangiovese.

🍴 EATING

BOVOLO
ITALIAN $$

(☎707-431-2962; www.bovolorestaurant.com; 106 Matheson St, Healdsburg; dishes $6-14; ⏰9am-4pm Mon, Weds & Thu, 9am-8pm Tue, Fri, Sat, 9am-6pm Sun) Fast food gets a slow-food spin at this order-at-the-counter Cal-Ital bistro in the back of a bookstore, with locally grown salads, farm-fresh egg breakfasts and pizza topped with meats cured in-house from heirloom pigs grown by the owner.

SCOPA
ITALIAN $$

(☎707-433-5282; www.scopahealdsburg.com; 109A Plaza St, Healdsburg; mains $12-26; ⏰5:30-10pm Tue-Sun) Call ahead for a spot at this converted barbershop for thin-crust pizza and rustic Italian homecooking, such as nonna's slow-braised chicken melting into a pillow of polenta.

DOWNTOWN BAKERY & CREAMERY
BAKERY

(☎707-431-2719; www.downtownbakery.net; 308A Center St; ⏰7am-5:30pm) Healdsburg's finest bakery crafts scrumptious sweets and fresh bread to round out your picnic basket. Kids like the homemade ice cream.

JIMTOWN STORE
DELI $

(☎707-433-1212; www.jimtown.com; sandwiches $8-14; 6706 Hwy 128; ⏰7:30am-4pm) If you're heading to Alexander Valley, don't miss Jimtown – one of our favorite stopovers – famous for its picnic supplies and sandwiches made using housemade spreads. Check out the little store in back for quirky gifts to take home.

DRY CREEK GENERAL STORE
DELI $

(☎707-433-4171; www.drycreekgeneralstore1881. com; 3495 Dry Creek Rd; sandwiches $8-10; ⏰6am-6pm) When your stomach protests zin before lunch, make a pit stop here for a Toscano-salami-and-manchego sandwich or a classic BLT; snag a spot on the porch beside the throngs of bicyclists.

CYRUS
CALIFORNIAN $$$

(☎707-433-3311; www.cyrusrestaurant.com; 29 North St, Healdsburg; fixed-price menu $102-130; ⏰dinner Thu-Mon, lunch Sat) An ultrachic dining room in the great tradition of the French-country auberge, Cyrus is Sonoma County's top table, expertly preparing luxury ingredients – foie gras, caviar, lobster – with a French sensibility and global spices.

But the local secret is the bar, where dishes are served á la carte with mad-scientist cocktails.

Muir Woods & Muir Beach

Explore

Coastal redwoods are the tallest living things on earth, and exist only on the California coast, from Santa Cruz to just over the Oregon border. Only 4% of the original forest remains, but you can explore a glorious old-growth stand within 30 minutes of San Francisco. You could spend as little as an hour in the woods, following crowds along the main trail, but for perspective on the primordial forest, hike some of the park's longer trails that get you up on ridgelines, above the big trees, with expansive ocean vistas. Afterward, continue to the coast, along Hwy 1, to Muir Beach and explore the pebbly beach – but you'd do well to bring a sweater, not a bikini: chances are it'll be chilly.

The Best...

➡ **Sight** Cathedral Grove (p228)
➡ **Place to Drink** Pelican Inn (p228)
➡ **Trail** Dipsea Trail (p228)

Top Tip

To beat the crowds, come early in the day, late afternoon or midweek; otherwise the parking lot fills up and you'll need to take a shuttle.

Getting There & Away

Car Head north on Hwy 101 across the Golden Gate Bridge, exit at Hwy 1 and continue north along Hwy 1/Shoreline Hwy to Panoramic Hwy (a right-hand fork). Follow that for about 1 mile to Four Corners, where you turn left onto Muir Woods Rd (there are plenty of signs).

Ferry & Bus On weekends and holidays (when the parking lot at Muir Woods overflows) Marin Transit (☑511; www. marintransit.org; round-trip adult/child $3/1; ☺weekends & holidays late May-Sep) operates bus 66, a 40-minute shuttle from the Sausalito Ferry Terminal, timed to connect with four ferries from San Francisco.

Need to Know

➡ **Area code** ☑415
➡ **Location** 15 miles from downtown San Francisco

◉ SIGHTS

MUIR WOODS NATIONAL MONUMENT   NATURE RESERVE
Map p230 (☑415-388-2595; www.nps.gov/muwo; adult/child under 16 $5/free; ☺8am-sunset) The closest stand of coastal redwoods to San Francisco, the old-growth forest dates back to time immemorial. The trees were initially eyed by loggers, and Redwood Creek, as the area was known, seemed ideal for a dam. Those plans were halted when congressman and naturalist William Kent bought a section of Redwood Creek and, in 1907, donated 295 acres to the federal government. President Theodore Roosevelt

---

SLEEPING IN HEALDSBURG & DRY CREEK VALLEY

Demand exceeds supply here, especially weekends. Most hotels don't merit their astronomical rates. The following are midbudget alternatives:

Best Western Dry Creek Inn (☑707-433-0300, 800-222-5784; www.drycreekinn.com; 198 Dry Creek Rd, Healdsburg; r weekday $59-129, weekend $199-259; ❀@☎❀) Healdsburg's spiffiest motel has free laundry and outdoor hot tub.

L&M Motel (☑707-433-6528; www.landmmotel.com; 70 Healdsburg Ave, Healdsburg; r $100-140; ❀☎❀❀) Old-fashioned, kitschy family-owned motel with big swimming pool, sauna, Jacuzzi and grassy barbecue areas good for families.

made the site a national monument in 1908, the name honoring John Muir, naturalist and founder of environmental organization the Sierra Club.

Even at busy times, a short hike will get you out of the densest crowds and onto trails with huge trees and stunning vistas. A little cafe at the park headquarters serves organic goodies and hot drinks that hit the spot on foggy days.

The 1-mile **Main Trail Loop** is easy, leading alongside Redwood Creek to 1000-year-old trees at **Cathedral Grove**; it returns via **Bohemian Grove**, where the park's tallest tree stands at 254ft. The **Dipsea Trail** is a strenuous 2-mile hike to the top of aptly named **Cardiac Hill**, but it's possibly the most beautiful hike for views – a half-mile steep grade through lush, fern-fringed forest leads from the canyon to an exposed ridge, from which you can see Mt Tamalpais, the Pacific and San Francisco. Gorgeous. You can trek to the tiny coastal vacation town of **Stinson Beach** if you're up for a longer stint.

You can also walk down into Muir Woods via trails from Panoramic Hwy (such as Bootjack Trail, from Bootjack picnic area) or from nearby Mt Tamalpais State Park's Pantoll Station campground (via Ben Johnson Trail).

MUIR BEACH BEACH

Map p230 The turnoff to Muir Beach from Hwy 1 is marked by the north coast's longest row of mailboxes (mileage-marker 5.7, just before Pelican Inn). Immediately north there are superb coastal views from the **Muir Beach Overlook**; during WWII scouts kept watch from the surrounding concrete lookouts for invading Japanese ships.

 **EATING**

PELICAN INN PUB, INN

Map p230 (☎415-383-6000; www.pelicaninn. com; 10 Pacific Way; lunch $12-17, dinner $17-34; ☎) Hikers, cyclists and families come for pub lunches at the Tudor-style timbered restaurant and cozy bar, perfect for a pint, game of darts and warming-up fireside. The British fare is respectable, but it's the setting that's magical. Upstairs are seven cushy rooms (from $190), each individually decorated with half-canopy beds.

Sausalito & Tiburon

Explore

Sausalito is the first town over the Golden Gate. Perched above Richardson Bay, it's known for galleries, window-shopping and picture-postcard vistas of SF and Angel Island. And it's often sunnier than San Francisco. However cute, Sausalito becomes a victim of its charm on summer weekends, when day-trippers jam the sidewalks, shops and restaurants. For the locals' scene, wander up Caledonia St. We recommend taking a bike on the ferry from San Francisco to avoid awful traffic.

Tiburon, with its tiny Main St lined with clapboard buildings, isn't at the forepoint of most tourists' minds, and so the town has retained more of its original character than Sausalito. Browse shops on Main St, grab a bite to eat and you've done Tiburon. Friday nights May through October, Tiburon throws its Main St block party, kicking off at 6pm.

The Best...

➡ **Sight** Bay Model Visitors Center (p229)
➡ **Place to Eat** Fish (p230)
➡ **Place to Drink** Wellingtons Wine Bar (p232)

Top Tip

Take the ferry to reach either town. If you drive, weekend traffic from downtown Sausalito to the bridge jams; leave town by going north to the town's second freeway exit.

Getting There & Away

Ferry Golden Gate Ferry (☎415-455-2000; www.goldengateferry.org; one-way $9.25) sails to Sausalito from the Ferry Building. Blue & Gold Fleet (☎415-705-8200; www. blueandgoldfleet.com; Pier 41; one-way $10.50) sails to Sausalito from Fisherman's Wharf; and to Tiburon from Fisherman's Wharf *and* the Ferry Building. Bikes are free.

Car To Sausalito: immediately over the Golden Gate, take Alexander Ave (exit

442). Alternatively, take the Sausalito exit (445A) and drop into town from the north. To Tiburon: take Tiburon Blvd/E Blithedale Ave (exit 450) and follow Tiburon Blvd east and south into town.

Bus Golden Gate Transit (☎415-455-2000; www.goldengatetransit.org; fare $4.25) bus 10 operates daily to Sausalito from Downtown; commute bus 8 operates weekdays between San Francisco and Tiburon.

Need to Know

➡ **Area code** ☎415

➡ **Location** By car, Sausalito is 10 miles north of San Francisco and Tiburon is 17 miles northeast.

➡ **Sausalito Visitors Center** (☎415-332-0505; www.sausalito.org; 780 Bridgeway Blvd; ☺11:30am-4pm Tue-Sun) Tourist office.

➡ **Tiburon Peninsula Chamber of Commerce** (☎415-435-5633; www.tiburonchamber.org; 96b Main St) Tourist office.

SIGHTS

Sausalito's main strip is Bridgeway Blvd, along the waterfront. The ferry terminal marks town center. In Tiburon, the ferry also lands downtown; Main St, aka Ark Row, is where old houseboats have metamorphosed into a few fancy boutiques. Shopping is better in Sausalito.

BAY MODEL VISITORS CENTER   NOTABLE BUILDING
Map p230 (☎415-332-3871; www.spn.usace.army.mil/bmvc; 2100 Bridgeway Blvd; ☺9am-4pm Tue-Fri, plus 10am-5pm Sat & Sun in summer; ❢) Until computers rendered it obsolete,

this enormous 1.5-acre hydraulic scale model of the entire San Francisco Bay and Delta helped scientists understand the effects of tides and currents on the land. A 24-hour period is represented in just 15 minutes. Look in the deepest water – under the Golden Gate Bridge – in order to understand the incredible force of tidal movement. To explore the actual bay yourself, consider renting a kayak at nearby **Sea Trek Kayaking** (Map p230; ☎415-488-1000; www.seatrek.com; Schoonmaker Point Marina; single/double kayaks per hour $20/35), which also offers guided trips.

BAY AREA DISCOVERY MUSEUM   MUSEUM
Map p230 (☎415-339-3900; www.baykidsmuseum.org; adult/child $10/8; ☺9am-4pm Tue-Fri, 10am-5pm Sat & Sun; ❢) Just under the north tower of the Golden Gate Bridge, at East Fort Baker, this excellent hands-on activity museum is specifically designed for children. Permanent, multilingual exhibits include a wave workshop, small underwater tunnel and large outdoor play area with a shipwreck to romp around. A small cafe has healthful nibbles.

FREE **RAILROAD & FERRY DEPOT MUSEUM**   MUSEUM
Map p230 (www.landmarks-society.org; 1920 Paradise Drive, Tiburon; ☺1-4pm Wed, Sat & Sun Mar-Oct) Formerly the terminus of a 3000-person ferry to San Francisco and railroad that once reached north to Ukiah, this late-19th century building showcases a scale model of Tiburon's commercial hub c 1909; the restored stationmaster's quarters are upstairs.

OLD ST HILARY'S CHURCH   CHURCH
Map p230 (☎415-435-1853; 201 Esperanza, Tiburon; ☺1-4pm Wed & Sun Apr-Oct) There are great views from the lovely hillside surrounding this deconsecrated Catholic

---

SLEEPING IN SAUSALITO & TIBURON

➡ **Gables Inn** (Map p230; ☎415-289-1100, 800-966-1554; www.gablesinnsausalito.com; 62 Princess St, Sausalito; r incl breakfast $185-445; @✿) All nine cozy B&B rooms in this swank historic home have massive baths; the more expensive have Jacuzzis, fireplaces and balconies with spectacular views. Evening wine included.

➡ **Waters Edge Hotel** (Map p230; ☎415-789-5999; www.watersedgehotel.com; 25 Main St, Tiburon; r incl breakfast $169-499; ❂@✿) This smart 23-unit hotel extends over the bay. All rooms have balconies (limited views, except in suites); some have fireplaces. Complimentary in-room breakfast and evening wine and cheese.

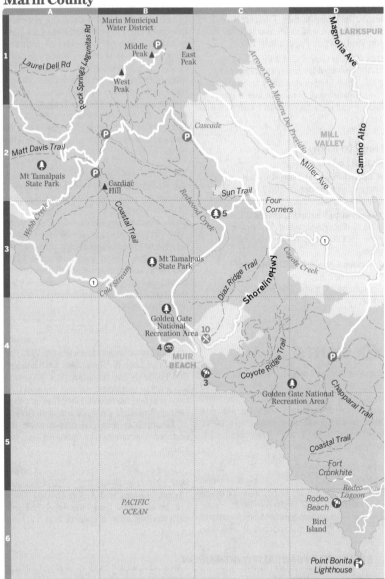

church, one of the country's last examples of Carpenter Gothic architecture still in its original setting. The surrounding hillsides make up **St Hilary's Preserve**, which nurtures a treasure trove of rare wildflowers, best in spring.

EATING & DRINKING

FISH   SEAFOOD $$

Map p230 (☎415-331-3474; 350 Harbor Dr, Sausalito; mains $13-25; ◎11:30am-8:30pm; ⊛) This kid-friendly dockside joint at the end of Harbor Dr hooks locals with sustainable,

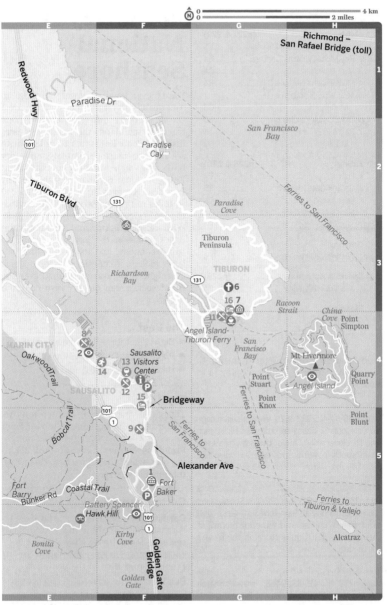

line-caught fish and picnic-table, bayside seating. Sustainability and organics have their price, but it's worth it – especially come salmon season. Chow down on seafood sandwiches, oysters and Dungeness crab rolls. Cash only.

SAM'S ANCHOR CAFE SEAFOOD **$$**

Map p230 (415-435-4527; 27 Main St, Tiburon; dishes $15-25;) Everyone wants an outdoor table, but you can't reserve the bay-front patio at this ever-popular seafood and burger shack – the town's oldest restaurant (look for the trapdoor that was

Marin County

used to spirit booze straight from ship to saloon). Watch for seagulls swooping in to steal your fries.

SUSHI RAN   SUSHI $

Map p230 (☎415-332-3620; www.sushiran.com; 107 Caledonia St, Sausalito; dishes $4-19; ☺lunch Mon-Fri, dinner daily) One of the Bay Area's top sushi spots. A wine and sake bar ease the pain of long waits – reserve ahead.

GOLDEN GATE MARKET   GROCERY $

Map p230 (☎415-332-3040; 221 2nd St, Sausalito; ☺8am-9pm Mon-Sat, 9am-7pm Sun) Grab deli sandwiches, cheese and wine for picnics at this grocery/deli/liquor store on the town's south side.

WELLINGTONS WINE BAR   BAR

Map p230 (☎415-331-9463; www.wellington swinebar.com; 1306 Bridgeway, at Turney St; ☺4-10pm; ⓟ⩟) Cozy up with a glass of wine, before catching the ferry home, at this dockside wine bar and pub with drop-dead vistas across San Francisco Bay. Friendly crowd, great service – you'd not be the first to miss your boat for the fun you're having.

Point Reyes National Seashore

You'd never know you were so close to America's sixth-largest metropolitan area. On an entirely different tectonic plate from the mainland, the windswept peninsula of Point Reyes juts 10 miles out to sea and lures marine mammals, migratory birds and whale-watching tourists. Point Reyes National Seashore, established by President Kennedy in 1963, includes 110 sq miles of pristine ocean beaches, windtousled ridgetops and diverse wildlife. With excellent hiking and camping, Point Reyes is one of the Bay Area's top daytrip excursions, and its surrounding villages make a romantic spot for a quick overnight. Bring warm clothing: even the sunniest days can quickly turn cold and foggy.

....

The Best...

➡ **Sight** Point Reyes Lighthouse (p233)

➡ **Place to Eat** Osteria Stellina (p234)

➡ **Hike** Tomales Point Trail (p223)

....

Top Tip

Though it may seem counter-intuitive, wintertime is the best season to visit Point Reyes for wildlife-spotting – whales breaching just offshore and migratory birds alighting everywhere. In summer, go directly to the Tule Elk Reserve.

....

Getting There & Away

Car From San Francisco, coastal Hwy 1 is twisty, hard on those inclined to carsickness. More direct: Hwy 101 to exit 450B toward San Anselmo; follow Sir Francis Drake Blvd to the peninsula.

Bus West Marin Stagecoach (☎415-526-3239; www.marintransit.org) operates bus 68 from the San Rafael Transit Center to the Bear Valley Visitors Center in Olema. To reach San Rafael, take Golden Gate Transit (☎415-455-2000; www. goldengatetransit.org) bus 70 or 80 from downtown SF.

Need to Know

➡ **Area Code** ☏415

➡ **Location** 40 miles northwest of San Francisco

➡ **Bear Valley Visitors Center** (☏415-464-5100; www.nps.gov/pore; Bear Valley Rd; ⊙9am-5pm Mon-Fri, 8am-5pm Sat & Sun) Tourist office.

➡ **Ken Patrick Center** (☏415-669-1250; www.nps.gov/pore; Drakes Beach; ⊙10am-5pm Sat, Sun & holidays) Tourist office.

➡ **West Marin Chamber of Commerce** (☏415-663-9232; www.pointreyes.org) Tourist office..

◉ SIGHTS

Miles of hiking trails crisscross the peninsula, leading to lovely hidden beaches, but those on the peninsula's western side get hammered by powerful surf and aren't safe for swimming – never turn your back on the ocean at Point Reyes' west-facing beaches.

POINT REYES LIGHTHOUSE   LIGHTHOUSE
(☏415-669-1534; end of Sir Francis Drake Blvd; ⊙10am-4:30pm Thu-Mon) The wild, steep terrain at the peninsula's tip gets buffeted by ferocious winds, and offers the best whale-watching along the California coast. The lighthouse sits 600ft below the headlands, down 308 steps, so that its light can shine below the fog that usually blankets the point. The lens room and clockworks are open as conditions permit.

On weekends during good weather, from 9am to 5:30pm in late December through mid-April, the road to Chimney Rock and the lighthouse is closed to private vehicles. Instead, you must take a shuttle ($5; children under 16 free) from Drakes Beach. Buy tickets between 9am and 3pm at the Ken Patrick Center at Drakes Bay. Shuttles run every 20 minutes from 9:30am to 3:30pm, weather permitting; for daily updates call ☏415-464-5100, ext 2, then press 1.

CHIMNEY ROCK   NATURE RESERVE
(end of Sir Francis Drake Blvd) Nearby Chimney Rock makes a lovely short hike from the lighthouse, especially in spring when wildflowers are blossoming. Look for wild cucumber, purple thistle, bright-orange California poppies and wild grasses tenaciously clinging to the cliffs. A nearby viewing area lets you spy on the park's braying **elephant-seal colony**.

TOMALES POINT & TULE ELK RESERVE   NATURE RESERVE
(end of Pierce Point Rd, north off Sir Francis Drake Blvd) Hike atop high ocean bluffs – through herds of elk – along Tomales Point, the northern finger of Point Reyes, which separates Tomales Bay and the Pacific Ocean. The 4.7-mile, one-way trail is mostly level, and passes through the **Tule Elk Reserve** – keep your distance, lest the animals charge.

SLEEPING IN POINT REYES NATIONAL SEASHORE

Point Reyes has many small inns and unusual B&Bs, from simple to luxe. **Point Reyes Lodging Association** (☏800-539-1872, 415-663-1872; www.ptreyes.com) has a good list.

Motel Inverness (☏866-453-3839, 415-236-1967; www.motelinverness.com; 12718 Sir Francis Drake Blvd, Inverness; r $100-200; ☏) This upmarket motel has wonderful service and spiffy rooms with good beds. Alas, it was built backwards: rooms face the parking lot, but behind there's gorgeous wetlands. No matter – enjoy the view from the lovely main room, with its roaring fire and board games.

Point Reyes Hostel (☏415-663-8811; www.norcalhostels.org/reyes; off Limantour Rd; dm from $24) The only lodging in the park lies in a secluded valley surrounded by hiking trails, 2 miles from the ocean. The one private room (from $68) is reserved for families traveling with a child under six.

Campgrounds (☏415-663-8054; campsites $15) Point Reyes has four campgrounds with pit toilets, untreated water and picnic tables (no fires). Permits are required; reserve at Bear Valley Visitors Center or by telephone three months ahead. All require a 2- to 6-mile hike.

✖ EATING

The little town of Point Reyes Station is the best place to eat; alternatively stop in the tiny town of Inverness, which has a good market.

🍽 OSTERIA STELLINA   ITALIAN $$

(☎415-663-9988; 11285 Hwy 1; mains $15-25; ⊙11:30am-2:30pm & 5-9pm; 🖉) Rustic Italian cooking with a California sensibility – fava-leaf salad, osso bucco, perfect pizzas and homemade pasta, all made with locally sourced, organic ingredients. Osteria is the hands-down best place to eat. Make reservations.

🍽 TOMALES BAY FOODS & COWGIRL CREAMERY   DELI $$

(☎415-663-9335; www.cowgirlcreamery.com; 80 4th St; ⊙10am-6pm Wed-Sun; 🖉) Pick up picnic items, including gourmet cheeses and organic produce at the cafe/market, then watch artisanal cheesemakers demonstrating their craft (tastings $5) at this famous creamery (call ahead for tours).

🍽 PINE CONE DINER   AMERICAN $

(60 4th St, Point Reyes Station; mains $9-13; ⊙8am-2:30pm; 🖉🖐) Big breakfasts and hearty lunches at a retro-cute, small-town diner, with good buttermilk biscuits, chorizo (or tofu) scrambles and fried-oyster sandwiches.

CAFE REYES   PIZZA $$

(☎415-663-9493; www.cafereyes.net; 11101 Hwy 1, Point Reyes Station; dishes $6-15; ⊙noon-9pm; 🖉🖐) A good spot for a quick bite, Cafe Reyes has local oysters and crispy-thin pizza, but best is the view from the big outdoor deck.

PERRY'S DELICATESEN   DELI $

(☎415-663-1491; 12301 Sir Francis Drake Blvd, Inverness Park; sandwiches $6-8; ⊙6:30am-8pm) The great vegetarian sandwiches are made greater with the addition of bacon. Pop one in your backpack and enjoy it midhike from a high promontory.

DRAKES BAY OYSTER COMPANY   SEAFOOD

(☎415-669-1149; www.drakesbayfamilyfarms. com; 17171 Sir Francis Drake Blvd, Inverness; ⊙8:30am-4:30pm) Drakes Bay and nearby Tomales Bay are famous for oysters, which you can sample at this much-loved DIY oyster farm in the park (its future is uncertain; call ahead). Bring your own condiments, plates and drinks from the market at Point Reyes Station or Inverness. They'll shuck the oysters, but provide no utensils. Outdoor picnic tables are first-come, first-served.

🏃 SPORTS & ACTIVITIES

FIVE BROOKS STABLES   HORSEBACK RIDING

(☎415-663-1570; www.fivebrooks.com; trail rides from $40; 🖐) Explore the landscape on horseback with a trail ride through pasturelands or up 1000ft to Inverness Ridge for inland views of Olema Valley. Longer rides go to hidden beaches and waterfalls.

BLUE WATERS KAYAKING   KAYAKING

(☎415-669-2600; www.bwkayak.com; rentals $40-120, guided trips $68-98) The bird-watching at Tomales Bay is superb midwinter. Blue Waters has two locations: one in Inverness, the other in Marshall. Call to confirm opening hours.

HIKING POINT REYES

Gather maps at the Bear Valley Visitors Center, then get an awe-inspiring view on the **Earthquake Trail**, which leads to a 16ft gap between two halves of a once-connected fence line, remnant of the 1906 earthquake. A side trail leads to **Kule Loklo**, a reproduction Miwok village.

Limantour Rd, about 1 mile north of the visitors center, leads to Point Reyes Hostel, the trailhead of several easy walks that lead to bayside beaches. At the end of Limantour Rd is gorgeous, south-facing **Limantour Beach**. The **Inverness Ridge Trail** heads from Limantour Rd up to 1282ft Mt Vision for spectacular views over the entire seashore.

Good day hikes include **Arch Rock** (4.1 miles one-way), **Sky Camp** (2.7 miles one-way), **Wildcat Camp** (6.3 miles one-way) and **Coast Camp** (8.9 miles one-way).

Hwy 1 to Santa Cruz

Explore

The coastal road south of San Francisco is lined with craggy beaches, windswept coastal plains, grassy prairies, lighthouses and tiny towns. Passengers are the lucky ones – heading south they get unobstructed views of the crashing surf. Drivers will be hard-pressed to keep their eyes on the double-yellow line.

Leave time for vista points, and you may spot whales breaching offshore, kitesurfers skimming waves like giant mosquitoes, flocks of shorebirds and the occasional nude sunbather. Half Moon Bay is an easy day trip from the city, but the money shots lie further south. Santa Cruz is good for a long day trip or quick overnight.

The Best...

➡ **Sight** Año Nuevo State Park (p207)
➡ **Place to Eat** Duarte's Tavern (p207)
➡ **Rollercoaster** Giant Dipper (p207)

Top Tip

Take Hwy 1 all the way south from San Francisco, but speed the trip back by taking I-280; cut inland at Half Moon Bay or Santa Cruz.

Getting There & Away

Car Hwy 1 south from San Francisco. Fast route northbound from Santa Cruz: Hwy 17 east, to Hwy 85 north, to I-280 north to SF.

Bus & Train Santa Cruz Metropolitan Transit (☑831-425-8600; www.scmtd. com; ticket/day pass $1.50/4.50) operates from Santa Cruz Metro Transit Center (920 Pacific Ave) and links San Jose ($5), where you catch Caltrain to SF, or Amtrak to Oakland and Berkeley.

Need to Know

➡ **Santa Cruz County** (☑831-425-1234, 800-833-3494; www.santacruz.org; 1211 Ocean St; ☺9am-5pm Mon-Fri, 10am-4pm Sat, 11am-3pm Sun) Tourist office.

◉ SIGHTS

The beauty shots begin 20 miles south of San Francisco, immediately beyond not-so-pretty Pacifica, at infamous **Devil's Slide**, an unstable cliff zone that, after winter storms, often slides into the Pacific. State beaches line the coast; most charge $8 for parking. **Montara State Beach** is a half-mile south and the local favorite for pristine sand. You can spend the night at the **HI Point Montara Lighthouse Hostel** (☑650-728-7177; www.norcalhostels.org/montara; Hwy 1; dm $26-31, r $70-105; @⑦).

Just south at Moss Beach, **Fitzgerald Marine Reserve** (www.fitzgeraldreserve. org; California St, off Hwy 1; admission free; ⑪) protects tide pools teeming with sea life. If you're ready for a beer, follow signs to oceanside **Moss Beach Distillery** (☑650-728-5595; www.mossbeachdistillery.com; 140 Beach Way; ☺noon-8:30pm Mon-Thu, noon-9pm Fri & Sat, 11am-8:30pm Sun), a historic bootleggers' joint with dog-friendly deck and ocean-view drinks.

At **Pillar Point Harbor**, turn off at **Princeton-by-the-Sea**, which has a good brew pub, and climb dunes to **Mavericks**, where in wintertime death-defying surfers ride 40ft-plus swells past rocky cliffs.

Busy **Half Moon Bay** is defined by pretty, 4-mile-long **Half Moon Bay State Beach** (www.parks.ca.gov; per car $10), which has scenic campsites ($35 to $50). To get on the water, visit **Half Moon Bay Kayak** (☑650-773-6101; www.hmbkayak.com; 2 Johnson Dr, Pillar Point Harbor; kayak rentals from $20, tours $65-150). Cafes, restaurants and giftshops for grandma line Half Moon Bay's quaint, five-block-long Main St, just inland from Hwy 1. The town's tastiest seafood shack is **Flying Fish Grill** (www.flyingfishgrill.net; 211 San Mateo Rd, Half Moon Bay; dishes $5-15; ☺11am-8pm); the best picnic-ready sandwiches are at **Garden Deli** (☑650-726-3425; www.sanbenito house.com; 356 Main St, Half Moon Bay; sandwiches $6-8; ☺10am-5pm; ⑪).

Fifteen miles south, **Pescadero State Beach** and **Marsh Natural Preserve** (www. parks.ca.gov; per car $8; ☺8am-sunset) attract beachcombers and birders. Inland Pescadero village is home to famed **Duarte's Tavern** (☑650-879-0464; www.duartestavern. com; 202 Stage Rd; mains $8-35; ☺7am-9pm) – say '*doo*-arts' – where creamy artichoke soup and homemade olallieberry pies are classic crowd-pleasers. For a beach picnic, visit bakery-deli **Arcangeli Grocery Co** (287

Hwy 1 to Santa Cruz

coast and want to spend the night surrounded by state parks and beaches, stop 4 miles further south at **Costanoa** (☑650-879-1100, 877-262-7848; www.costanoa.com; 2001 Rossi Rd; r $99-259; ☎📶), a cushy ecoresort and campground with tent cabins and fireplace cottages (best are the 'Douglas Fir').

Six miles beyond Pigeon Point Lighthouse, **Año Nuevo State Park** (☑tour reservations 800-444-4445; www.parks.ca.gov; per car $10, tour per person $7; ☉8:30am-3:30pm Apr-Aug, 8:30am-3pm Sep-Nov, tours mid-Dec–Mar) is home to the world's largest colony of northern **elephant seals**. Call ahead to reserve space on a 2½-hour, 3-mile guided walking tour, during the cacophonous wintertime birthing and mating season. Off-season, take a self-guided hike, across mesmerizing grassy bluffs, beyond the sound of automobiles.

Ten miles south, **Swanton Berry Farm** (☑831-469-8804; www.swantonberryfarm.com; Hwy 1, Davenport; ☉strawberry-picking 8am-6pm, farmstand 8am-sunset, Apr-Oct; 📶) grows the Bay Area's best organic strawberries (seriously); gorge on delish shortcakes and strawberry lemonade at the old-fashioned, un-manned farmstand, then fill the car with berries.

Santa Cruz is counterculture central, famous for its beaches, surf scene and university. Head directly to the vintage-1907 **Santa Cruz Beach Boardwalk** (☑831-426-7433; www.beachboardwalk.com; 400 Beach St; rides $3-5, all-day ticket $30; ☉daily mid-April–mid-Nov, weekends mid-Nov–mid-April) – the West Coast's oldest beachfront amusement park. It's most famous for the half-mile-long **Giant Dipper**, a vintage-1924 wooden roller coaster, and the **1911 Looff carousel** – both National Historic Landmarks. Parents can laze on the adjacent beach (bring a blanket) while teens go exploring.

Adjacent to the boardwalk, the long **municipal wharf** is lined with restaurants and take-out fish counters. Watch for the **sea lions** braying beneath the pier. Walk southwest from the wharf, along West Cliff Dr, to **Lighthouse Point**, which overlooks **Steamers Lane**, one of California's best, most accessible surf breaks. The lighthouse houses the tiny **Surfing Museum** (☑831-420-6289; www.santacruzsurfingmuseum.org; admission free; ☉noon-4pm Thu-Mon).

Best for sunsets, **Natural Bridges State Beach** (☑831-423-4609) is at the end of West Cliff Dr, 3 miles from the wharf, with

Stage Rd; ☉10am-6pm) and family-owned **Harley Farms Cheese Shop** (250 North St; ☉11am-5pm; 📶), which offers weekend goat-dairy farm tours – a must-see for kids.

Six miles south of Pescadero, on a wind-swept coastal perch, **HI Pigeon Point Lighthouse Hostel** (☑650-879-0633; www.norcalhostels.org/pigeon; dm $24-29, r $72-156; @☎📶) occupies the historic lightkeepers' quarters (book ahead and don't miss the glorious cliff-top hot tub). Though the lighthouse is closed due to storm damage, wander behind it to reach the **whale-watching** viewing platform. If you're falling in love with this magnificent stretch of deserted tide pools and the state's only **monarch-butterfly preserve**, where monarchs roost from November through March.

Downtown Santa Cruz centers around **Pacific Ave**, where boutiques, chain stores and happening cafes draw a wacky mix of characters. Always-packed **El Palomar** (✆831-425-7575; www.elpalomarcilantros.com; 1336 Pacific Ave; meals $10-22; ⊗lunch & dinner; 🖮) serves tasty Mexican staples and good margaritas; **Soif** (✆831-423-2020; www.soif wine.com; 105 Walnut Ave; dishes $4-7, mains $19-27; ⊗dinner) draws food-savvy bon vivants and wine-lovers.

In the hills above town, the **University of California at Santa Cruz** (UCSC; ✆831-459-4008; 1156 High St; www.ucsc.edu) has 13,000 liberal-leaning students, a redwood-studded campus, architecturally interesting buildings, two top-notch galleries and a beautiful **arboretum**.

At day's end, Santa Cruz's best wood-fired pizza is at **Engfer Pizza Works** (✆831-429-1856; www.engferpizzaworks.com; 537 Seabright Ave; pizzas $8-17; ⊗noon-2pm Tue-Fri; 5-9pm Tue-Sun; 🖊🖮), where you can drink beer and play ping-pong; or go for pasta at **Lilian's Italian Kitchen** (✆831-425-2288; 1116 Soquel Ave; mains $8-23; ⊗lunch Tue-Fri, dinner Mon-Sat; 🖮) – the slow-cooked 'Sunday gravy' meat sauce is sublime.

Sleeping

San Francisco is the birthplace of the boutique hotel. You'll find standard-issue chains with good-value rates, four-stars with upmarket comforts and a few palatial five-stars with top-flight luxuries, but it's the little places that stand out – elegant Victorians on neighborhood side streets, artsy downtowners with intimate bars and cozy small inns that smell of freshly baked cookies.

When to Book

Chain hotels routinely overbook when there's a big convention in town. 'City-wide sellouts' happen several times a year. If you haven't chosen dates for your trip, check the SF Convention & Visitors Bureau (www.sanfrancisco.travel/meeting-planners) convention calendar, which shows the expected bed count each convention requires. The city has 33,000 total rooms; if the calendar says a convention (such as Oracle) will require over 10,000 beds, choose other dates or expect to pay a premium.

Room Rates & Fees

Rates in SF fluctuate wildly. To get the best prices at chains, call the hotel during business hours and speak with in-house reservations, rather than the toll-free central reservations line, for the most up-to-date information about inventories and specials. Some hotels have internet specials not available by telephone. When booking online, know that 'best rate' does not necessarily mean the lowest-available rate. When in doubt, call the hotel directly.

Although bright, friendly hostels and budget hotels have opened up around town, rooms are never truly cheap in SF: expect to pay at least $65 at a budget hotel or for a private hostel room, and over $100 at any midrange hotel. Note the hefty 15.5% room tax on top of the quoted rates, and that local telephone calls may cost $1 and wi-fi an extra $10 to $20. Prices run higher from June to August, and drop September to May. If you're staying awhile, ask about weekly rates. On weekends and holidays, rates for business and luxury hotels decrease, but increase for tourist hotels.

Hotels vs Boutique Hotels

The boutique-hotel trend started in San Francisco, but the term has become so overused by marketers that it is nearly meaningless. When we use the term 'boutique hotel' in this book, we're referring to upmarket hotels that generally have fewer than 100 rooms, unique decor and service standards that distinguish them from cookie-cutter chains or other small hotels. Luxury hotels are their own class, too big to be boutique. Some chains, like Kimpton, have branded themselves boutique, but rooms at Hotel Monaco in San Francisco are nearly identical to Hotel Monaco in Denver, so we label them a 'design hotel.' Other chains, like Joie de Vivre, are collections of bona fide indie boutiques; we label them as such. Some charming small hotels listed in this guide could be called B&Bs, but only if they serve breakfast; otherwise we just call them 'small hotels' because they lack the stand-out qualities of real boutiques: style, service and sense of place.

Lonely Planet's Top Choices

Orchard Garden Hotel (p242) San Francisco's first all-green-practices hotel.

Hotel Vitale (p248) Contemporary cool with knockout waterfront vistas.

Hotel Bohème (p246) Artsy boutique charmer in the heart of North Beach.

Hotel Drisco (p247) Stately boutique hotel in civilized Pacific Heights.

Argonaut Hotel (p241) Nautical-themed hotel at Fisherman's Wharf.

Best for Views

Seal Rock Inn (p250)
Sir Francis Drake Hotel (p244)
Westin St Francis Hotel (p242)
W Hotel (p248)

Best for Kids

Hotel del Sol (p241)
Americania Hotel (p248)
Hotel Tomo (p247)
Seal Rock Inn (p250)

Best Pools

Palace Hotel (p242)
W Hotel (p248)
St Regis Hotel (p248)
Phoenix Hotel (p245)
Hotel del Sol (p241)
Americania Hotel (p248)

Best by Budget

$

San Remo Hotel (p246)
Hotel Metropolis (p245)
Pacific Tradewinds Hostel (p246)
Coventry Motor Inn ()
Fitzgerald Hotel (p245)

$$

Petite Auberge (p243)
Hotel Abri (p243)
Golden Gate Hotel (p244)
Crescent Hotel (p244)
Steinhart Hotel & Apartments (p243)

$$$

Mandarin Oriental (p241)
W Hotel (p248)
Palace Hotel (p242)
Hotel Palomar (p242)

Best Boutique Hotels

Hotel Rex (p243)
Inn at Union Square (p242)
White Swan Inn (p243)
Petite Auberge (p243)

Best for a Party Weekend

Phoenix Hotel (p245)
Crescent Hotel (p244)
Hotel Diva (p244)
W Hotel (p248)
Hotel Triton (p243)

Best B&Bs

Inn San Francisco (p249)
Parsonnage (p249)
Belvedere House (p249)
Chateau Tivoli (p250)
Washington Square Inn (p246)
Parker Guest House (p249)

Best Splurges

St Regis Hotel (p248)
Taj Campton Place (p242)
Mandarin Oriental (p241)
Palace Hotel (p242)
Mark Hopkins Intercontinental (p247)

NEED TO KNOW

Prices
Rates quoted here are for double rooms, with bath, in high season (summer); you can sometimes do better, except when there's a convention.
$ under $100
$$ $100–$200
$$$ more than $200

Parking
Parking costs $35 to $50 per night and is rarely included. When there's an on-site self-service lot, we've noted it with P. Hotels *without* parking often have valet parking; call ahead.

Reconfirming
If you're arriving after 4pm, guarantee with a credit card or your reservation may be canceled.

Tipping
Tipping housekeepers in US hotels is standard practice; leave a couple of dollars on your pillow each morning and be guaranteed excellent housekeeping.

Breakfast
Breakfast is not included in the tariff, unless specified.

Websites
Lonelyplanet.com (http://hotels.lonely planet.com) For more accommodation reviews by Lonely Planet authors; you can also book online here.
Priceline (www.priceline. com) Clearinghouse for mid-to-upscale lodging.
Topaz Hotel Services (www.hotelres.com) Hotels in the Bay Area and Wine Country.

SLEEPING

Where to Stay

Neighborhood	For	Against
The Marina, Fisherman's Wharf & the Piers	Near the northern waterfront; good for kids; lots of restaurants and nightlife at the Marina.	Fisherman's Wharf is all tourists; parking at the Marina and Wharf is a nightmare.
Downtown & Civic Center	Biggest selection of hotels; near all public transportation, including cable cars; walkable to many sights, shopping and theaters.	Downtown quiet at night; Civic Center feels rough – the worst area extends three blocks in all directions from Eddy and Jones Sts; parking is expensive.
North Beach & Chinatown	Culturally colorful; great strolling; lots of cafes and restaurants; terrific sense of place.	Street noise; limited choices and transport; next-to-impossible parking.
The Hills & Japantown	Stately, classic hotels atop Russian and Nob Hills; good nightlife and shopping in Japantown and Pacific Heights.	The Hills are steep, hard on the out-of-shape; parking difficult; slightly removed from major sights.
The Mission, SoMa & Potrero Hill	Parts of SoMa are close to major downtown sights; great nightlife and restaurants; flat terrain makes walking easier.	Limited choice in the Mission; distance from sights, especially the Mission; gritty street scene in both SoMa and the Mission.
The Castro & Noe Valley	Great nightlife, especially for GLBT travelers; provides a good taste of local life.	Distance from major tourist sights; few choices; limited parking.
The Haight & Hayes Valley	Lots of bars and restaurants; Hayes Valley near cultural sights; the Haight near Golden Gate Park.	Limited public transportation in the Haight; gritty street scene at night on major thoroughfares; parking difficult.
Golden Gate Park & the Avenues	Quiet nights; good for outdoor recreation; easier parking.	Very far from major sights; foggy and cold in summer; limited transportation.

🛏 The Marina, Fisherman's Wharf & the Piers

TOP CHOICE ARGONAUT HOTEL
DESIGN HOTEL **$$$**

Map p315 (☎415-563-0800, 866-415-0704; www. argonauthotel.com; 495 Jefferson St; r $205-325; P✴🛜🐾; MJones & Beach Sts) The top hotel at Fisherman's Wharf was built as a cannery in 1908, and has century-old wooden beams and exposed brick walls. Rooms sport an over-the-top nautical theme, with porthole-shaped mirrors and plush, deep-blue carpets. Though the amenities are of an upper-end hotel – ultra-comfy beds, stereo CD players – some rooms are tiny and get limited sunlight. Pay extra and get a mesmerizing bay view. Kids love the playful aesthetic and meet other kids in the big lobby.

🍽 TUSCAN INN
DESIGN HOTEL **$$**

Map p315 (☎415-561-1100, 800-648-4626; www. tuscaninn.com; 425 North Point St; r $169-229; P✴@🛜🐾; MBeach & Mason Sts) Staying at touristy Fisherman's Wharf doesn't necessarily mean you have to settle for a plain-Jane chain, like Hilton. The Tuscan Inn – managed by fashion-forward Kimpton Hotels – is just as comfortable, but has way more character, with spacious rooms done in bold colors and mixed patterns. Who says stripes and checks don't match? Kids love the in-room Nintendo; parents love the afternoon wine hour.

🍽 HOTEL DEL SOL
THEME MOTEL **$$**

Map p318 (☎415-921-5520, 877-433-5765; www. thehoteldelsol.com; 3100 Webster St; d $149-199; P✴@🛜🏊🐾; MFillmore & Lombard Sts) The spiffy, kid-friendly Marina District del Sol is a riot of color with tropical-themed decor. A quiet, revamped 1950s motor lodge, with a palm-lined central courtyard, it's also one of the few San Francisco hotels with a heated outdoor pool. Family suites have trundle beds and board games. Free parking.

WHARF INN
MOTEL **$$**

Map p315 (☎415-673-7411, 800-548-9918; www. wharfinn.com; 2601 Mason St; r $139-189; P🛜🐾; MBeach & Mason Sts) This standard-issue, two-story motor lodge at the Wharf has clean, nothing-special rooms, ideal for kids who make a mess. Some rooms are very loud; bring earplugs. Rates fluctuate wildly with the tourist tide. Free parking.

COVENTRY MOTOR INN
MOTEL **$**

Map p318 (☎415-567-1200; www.coventrymotor inn.com; 1901 Lombard St; r $95-145; P✴🛜🐾; MChestnut & Buchanan Sts) Of the scores of motels lining Lombard St (Hwy 101), the generic Coventry has the highest overall quality-to-value ratio, with spacious, well-maintained (if plain) rooms and extras like air-con (good for quiet sleeps) and covered parking. Parents: there's plenty of floor space to unpack the kids' toys, but no pool.

MARINA MOTEL
MOTEL **$$**

Map p318 (☎415-921-9406, 800-346-6118; www. marinamotel.com; 2576 Lombard St; r $149-179; P🛜; MLombard St & Divisadero) Established in 1939 to accommodate visitors arriving via the new Golden Gate Bridge, the Marina has an inviting, vintage Spanish-Mediterranean look, with a quiet bougainvillea-lined courtyard. Rooms are homey, simple and well maintained (never mind the occasional scuff mark); some have full kitchens (an extra $10). Rooms on Lombard St are loud; request one in back. Free parking.

MARINA INN
SMALL HOTEL **$**

Map p318 (☎415-928-1000, 800-274-1420; www. marinainn.com; 3110 Octavia St; r $79-109; 🛜; MChestnut & Octavia Sts) A good deal in the Marina, this vintage 1920s hotel has small, clean (if shabby) rooms with cabbage-rose decor, offering a cozier alternative to a motel. Single-pane glass means street noise; bring earplugs. Close to Union St shopping and bars.

HI SAN FRANCISCO FISHERMAN'S WHARF
HOSTEL **$**

Map p318 (☎415-771-7277; www.sfhostels.com; Bldg 240, Fort Mason; dm $25-30, r $65-100; P@🛜; MVan Ness & North Point) This hostel trades downtown convenience for a glorious park-like setting by the northern waterfront. Dorms range from a manageable four to a whopping 22 beds; some are coed. No curfew, but there's no heat on during the day in winter: bring warm clothes. Limited free parking.

🛏 Downtown & Civic Center

MANDARIN ORIENTAL
LUXURY HOTEL **$$$**

Map p316 (☎415-276-9888, 800-622-0404; www.mandarinoriental.com/sanfrancisco; 222 Sansome St; r $295-375, ste from $875; ✴@🛜; M&🚇Montgomery St, 🚋California St) On the top 11 floors of SF's third-tallest building, the Mandarin has sweeping, unobstructed views from every room. There's nothing risky about the Asian-accented classical decor, but beds are sumptuous – and, oh, those vistas. The room to book: 'Mandarin King' (from $500), with a bathtub surrounded by floor-to-ceiling windows and bird's-eye views of the Golden Gate and Bay Bridges. Alas, no spa or pool – hence the four-star designation – but the service equals, or bests, what you'll get at the city's three five-stars.

TAJ CAMPTON PLACE LUXURY HOTEL $$$

Map p320 (☑415-781-5555, 866-969-1825; www.tajhotels.com; 340 Stockton St; r from $279; ❀@🛜; ⓂSutter & Stockton Sts) Impeccable service sets Campton Place apart – this is where to put your fur-clad rich aunt when she wants discretion above all. Details are lavish, if beige. The cheapest rooms are tiny; pay for the upgrade or be imprisoned in a jewelry box. Excellent on-site formal restaurant.

PALACE HOTEL HOTEL $$$

Map p320 (☑415-512-1111, 800-325-3535; www.sfpalace.com; 2 New Montgomery St; r $199-329; ❀@🛜❀; Ⓜ&ⓇMontgomery St) The 1906 landmark Palace stands as a monument to turn-of-the-20th-century grandeur, aglow with century-old Austrian crystal chandeliers. The cushy (if staid) accommodations cater to expense-account travelers, but prices drop weekends. Even if you're not staying here, see the opulent **Garden Court**, where you can sip tea beneath a translucent glass ceiling in one of Northern California's most beautiful rooms. There's also an on-site spa; kids love the big indoor pool.

HOTEL PALOMAR DESIGN HOTEL $$$

Map p320 (☑415-348-1111, 866-373-4941; www.hotelpalomar-sf.com; 12 4th St; r $199-299; ❀@🛜; Ⓜ&ⓇPowell St) The sexy Palomar is decked out with crocodile-print carpets, stripy persimmon-red chairs, chocolate-brown wood and cheetah-print robes in the closet. Hugh Hefner would definitely approve. Beds are dressed with feather-light down comforters and Frette linens, and there's plenty of floor space to stretch out for in-room yoga (request mats and DVD at check-in). Though the hotel sits smack downtown, rooms have soundproof windows. Our only complaint is sometimes-spotty service. Don't miss drinks at the swank on-site **Fifth Floor** restaurant.

HOTEL MONACO DESIGN HOTEL $$$

Map p320 (☑415-292-0100, 866-622-5284; www.monaco-sf.com; 501 Geary St; r $199-269; ❀@🛜; ⓂGeary & Taylor Sts) The Monaco maintains its playful spirit, though the vintage-1990s rooms are starting to look a touch dated. Still, we love the opulent lobby, the guestrooms' bold colors and fabrics, and the goldfish available on request to keep you company in your room. Front-desk reception could be warmer, but evening wine hour compensates for occasionally lackluster service. Don't miss the lobby's walk-in fireplace, a cool place to sit with a book.

INN AT UNION SQUARE BOUTIQUE HOTEL $$$

Map p320 (☑415-397-3510, 800-288-4346; www.unionsquare.com; 440 Post St; r $229-289, ste $309-359; ❀@🛜; Ⓜ&ⓇPowell St, ⓇPowell-Hyde, Powell-Mason) Traditionalists love the conservative chintz decor and personalized service of this lovely boutique hotel, best for older travelers who appreciate quiet. Extras include twice-daily maid service, and breakfast served fireside. Great location for shopping and theaters.

WESTIN ST FRANCIS HOTEL HOTEL $$$

Map p320 (☑415-397-7000, 800-228-3000; www.westin.com; 335 Powell St; r $209-369; ❀@🛜; Ⓜ&ⓇPowell St, ⓇPowell-Mason, Powell-Hyde) This is one of SF's most storied hotels – Gerald Ford was shot right outside. Tower rooms have stellar views, but feel architecturally generic. We prefer the original building's old-fashioned charm, with its high ceilings and crown moldings. Though Westin beds set the industry standard for comfort, service is decidedly business-class, not first. Don't miss the glass elevators, even if you're not staying here.

TOP CHOICE ORCHARD GARDEN HOTEL ECO HOTEL $$

Map p320 (☑415-399-9807, 888-717-2881; www.theorchardgardenhotel.com; 466 Bush St; r $179-249; ❀@🛜; ⓂSutter & Stockton Sts) San Francisco's first all-green-practices hotel uses sustainably grown wood, chemical-free cleaning products and recycled fabrics in its soothingly quiet rooms. Don't think you'll be trading comfort for conscience: rooms have unexpectedly luxe touches like high-end down pillows and Egyptian-cotton sheets. Don't miss the sunny rooftop terrace – a lovely spot to regroup at day's end.

SLEEPING DOWNTOWN & CIVIC CENTER

KENSINGTON PARK HOTEL
BOUTIQUE HOTEL **$$$**

Map p320 (☎415-788-6400; www.kensington parkhotel.com; 450 Post St; r $189-269; ✲@☎; M&⧉Powell St, ⧉Powell-Hyde, Powell-Mason) The gorgeous vintage-1925 Spanish-Moorish lobby plays a broody counterpoint to the guestrooms' sophisticated mash-up of Queen Anne and contemporary furnishings. Some rooms are small, but have extra touches like down pillows. Downstairs is the top-flight seafood restaurant **Farallon**. Central location, just off Union Square, apart from the sketchy Tenderloin.

HOTEL REX
BOUTIQUE HOTEL **$$**

Map p320 (☎415-433-4434, 800-433-4434; www.jdvhotels.com; 562 Sutter St; r $169-279; P✲@☎; M&⧉Powell St, ⧉Powell-Hyde, Powell-Mason) Strains of French gramophone music fill the intimate lobby and the adjoining dimly lit lounge, intended to conjure New York's Algonquin in the 1920s. Despite their compact size, rooms feel inviting for their sunny colors, hand-painted lampshades and works by local artists. Beds are particularly great, with crisp linens and down pillows. Caveats: most rooms have limited natural light and air-cons installed in the windows.

GALLERIA PARK
BOUTIQUE HOTEL **$$**

Map p320 (☎415-781-3060, 800-738-7477; www.jdvhotels.com; 191 Sutter St; r $189-229; ✲@☎; M&⧉Montgomery) Exuberant staff greet you at this downtown boutique charmer, a 1911 hotel styled with contemporary art and handsome furnishings in soothing jewel tones. Some rooms (and bed sizes) run small, but include Frette linens, down pillows, high-end bath amenities, free evening wine hour and – most importantly – good service. Rooms on Sutter St are noisier, but get more light; interior rooms are quietest.

WHITE SWAN INN
BOUTIQUE HOTEL **$$**

Map p320 (☎415-775-1755, 800-999-9570; www.jdvhotels.com; 845 Bush St; r $159-199; P@☎; MBush & Jones Sts) In the tradition of English country inns, the romantic White Swan is styled with cabbage-rose wallpaper, red-plaid flannel bedspreads and polished Colonial-style furniture. Each oversized room has a gas fireplace – a cozy touch on a foggy night. Hipsters may find it stifling, but if you love Tudor style, you'll feel right at home.

PETITE AUBERGE
BOUTIQUE HOTEL **$$**

Map p320 (☎415-928-6000, 800-365-3004; www.jdvhotels.com; 863 Bush St; r $169-219; ☎; MBush & Jones Sts) Petite Auberge feels like a French country inn, with floral-print fabrics, a sunny yellow color scheme and fireplaces in many rooms. Though cheerfully decorated, several rooms are dark (especially tiny number 22) and face an alley where rubbish collectors rattle cans early in the morning (request a quiet room). Nonetheless, Petite Auberge remains one of Downtown's most charming midprice B&B inns, and we'd happily stay here ourselves. Breakfast and afternoon wine are served fireside in the cozy salon.

HOTEL ABRI
BOUTIQUE HOTEL **$$**

Map p320 (☎415-392-8800, 866-823-4669; www.hotel-abri.com; 127 Ellis St; r $149-229; ✲@☎; M&⧉Powell St) The Abri has an up-to-date design sensibility and snazzy rooms with bold black-and-tan motifs, a pillow-top bed with feather pillows, iPod docking station, flat-screen TV and big desk with cordless phone. Few baths have tubs, but rainfall showerheads compensate. Everything looks fresh and clean, and staff are friendly and accommodating. Request a quiet room, *not* above the Subway sandwich shop to avoid the pervasive smell of baking bread.

STEINHART HOTEL & APARTMENTS
APARTMENT HOTEL **$**

Map p322 (☎415-928-3855, 800-533-1900; www.steinharthotel.com; 952 Sutter St; studio per week $595-665, 1-bedroom apt per week from $1325; ☎; MSutter & Leavenworth Sts) If you're staying in SF for a week or longer, the Steinhart is a great address. It's a glorious early-20th-century building with high ceilings and swank art-deco furnishings. Small studios have galley-style kitchenettes; larger studios and one-bedroom apartments have full kitchens. Rates include weekly housekeeping, free wi-fi and local calls, and use of the backyard patio and grill.

HOTEL TRITON
BOUTIQUE HOTEL **$$**

Map p320 (☎415-394-0500, 800-800-1299; www.hotel-tritonsf.com; 342 Grant Ave; r $169-239; ✲@☎; M&⧉Montgomery St) The Triton's lobby thumps with high-energy music, and pops with color like the pages of a comic book. This was one of SF's first boutique hotels, and every room is different. Some are tiny, but all have an aggressively whimsical design, ecofriendly amenities and shag-worthy beds. Baths have massaging shower heads, but limited space. Suites are decorated in honor of celebs like Carlos Santana and Jerry Garcia. Don't miss the tarot-card readings and chair massages during the nightly wine hour.

SIR FRANCIS DRAKE HOTEL   HOTEL $$$

Map p320 (☑415-392-7755, 800-795-7129; www.sirfrancisdrake.com; 450 Powell St; r $199-279; ❋ @ 🛜; M & 🚋 Powell St, 🚋 Powell-Mason, Powell-Hyde) The city's most famous doormen, clad like clownish Beefeaters, stand sentinel at this vintage-1920s classic. Rooms have less flair and their intentionally mismatched colors feel forced, but were slated for renovation in 2011. Book 16th-to-20th-floor rooms for expansive city views. All have great beds. Ask about the secret room, between elevator platforms, where the hotel operated a speakeasy during Prohibition. Pop into the top-floor, touristy-swank Starlight Room (p94) for cocktails.

HOTEL ADAGIO   BOUTIQUE HOTEL $$

Map p320 (☑415-775-5000, 800-228-8830; www.thehoteladagio.com; 550 Geary St; r $159-249; ❋ @ 🛜) Huge rooms and a snappy aesthetic set the Adagio apart. The hotel's designers placed a premium on style, blending chocolate-brown and off-white leather furnishings with bright-orange splashes. Beds are cushy, with Egyptian-cotton sheets and feather pillows. Baths are disappointing for the price. Still, it's a cool address for a reasonable-ish price. Great bar downstairs.

HOTEL DIVA   BOUTIQUE HOTEL $$

Map p320 (☑415-885-0200, 800-553-1900; www.hoteldiva.com; 440 Geary St; r $159-229; ❋ @ 🛜; M Geary & Mason Sts) Favored by midbudget fashionistas and traveling club kids, the industrial-chic Diva's stainless-steel and black-granite design aesthetic conveys a sexy urban look. Beds are comfy, with good sheets and feather pillows, but poly-fill duvets (a small reminder that this is a midbudget property). If you like hard edges and you're here to party, you'll dig this place.

LARKSPUR HOTEL   BOUTIQUE HOTEL $$

Map p320 (☑415-421-2865, 866-823-4669; www.larkspurhotelunionsquare.com; 524 Sutter St; r $169-199; @ 🛜; M Sutter & Powell Sts, 🚋 Powell St) Built in 1915 and overhauled in 2008, the understatedly fancy Larkspur has a monochromatic, earth-tone color scheme and clean lines. Baths are tiny, but have fab rainfall showerheads. There's nothing risky about the Spartan aesthetic, but it's smartly done and presents a reasonable alternative to Union Square's splashier boutiques.

GOLDEN GATE HOTEL   SMALL HOTEL $$

Map p320 (☑415-392-3702, 800-835-1118; www.goldengatehotel.com; 775 Bush St; r with/without bath $165/105; @ 🛜; M Sutter & Powell Sts, 🚋 Powell St) Like an old-fashioned pensione, the Golden Gate has kindly owners and simple rooms with mismatched furniture, inside a 1913 Edwardian hotel safely up the hill from the Tenderloin. Rooms are small, clean and comfortable, and most have private baths (some with antique claw-foot tubs). Enormous croissants, homemade cookies and a resident kitty-cat provide TLC after a long day sightseeing.

CRESCENT HOTEL   SMALL HOTEL $$

Map p320 (☑415-400-0500; www.crescentsf.com; 417 Stockton St; r $139-179; @ 🛜; M Sutter & Stockton Sts) Built in 1904 and redone in 2009, the Crescent's austere design plays to hip cats on a budget, with some sexy details – smoked mirrors, tufted white-vinyl headboards, black-vinyl fainting couches – in simple small rooms. Alas, pillows are lumpy, baths run small (but look sharp) and the elevator is temperamental, but that's why rates are so good. No air-con means open windows above a loud street (bring earplugs). Not all rooms have been renovated; confirm when you book. Don't miss the downstairs Burritt Room (p89).

HOTEL UNION SQUARE   SMALL HOTEL $$

Map p320 (☑415-397-3000, 800-553-1900; www.hotelunionsquare.com; 114 Powell St; r $150-220; ❋ @ 🛜; M & 🚋 Powell St) The Hotel Union Square looks sharp, with swank design touches complementing the original brick walls. The main drawbacks are lack of sunlight and very small rooms, but designers compensated with cleverly concealed lighting, mirrored walls and plush fabrics. Convenient location, near major public transport – never mind the panhandlers outside. Not all rooms have air-con.

WARWICK SAN FRANCISCO   HOTEL   SMALL HOTEL $$

Map p320 (☑415-928-7900, 800-203-3232; www.warwicksf.com; 490 Geary St; r $129-229; @ 🛜; M Geary & Taylor Sts) If you prefer high heels to hiking boots but can't afford the Ritz, the Warwick presents a (way) less-expensive alternative. Conveying discreet tastefulness, with European antiques and Chinese porcelain. It's an ideal choice for debutantes and royalty on a budget, never mind the scuffed furniture and tight quarters. Beds even have triple-sheeting, but you'll have to request feather pillows.

ANDREWS HOTEL   SMALL HOTEL $$
Map p320 (☎415-563-6877, 800-926-3739; www.andrewshotel.com; 624 Post St; r incl breakfast $109-199; ☂; Ⓜ Post & Taylor Sts, ⒭ Powell St) Just two blocks west of Union Square, this 1905 hotel has friendly, personable staff, small but comfortable rooms (the quietest are in back) and a good Italian restaurant downstairs. Though it's nothing fancy, we love the Andrews' homey feel – it's like staying at your aunt's house, without having to pet the cat.

PHOENIX HOTEL   MOTEL $$
Map p322 (☎415-776-1380, 800-248-9466; www.jdvhospitality.com; 601 Eddy St; r incl breakfast $119-169; Ⓟ ☂ ⛱; Ⓜ Eddy & Polk Sts) The city's rocker crash pad draws minor celebs and Dionysian revelers to a vintage-1950s motor lodge with basic rooms dolled up with tropical decor. The former coffee shop is now the happening, sexy gastro-lounge **Chambers**. Check out the cool shrine to actor-director Vincent Gallo, opposite room 43. One complaint: noise. Bring earplugs. Parking is free, as is weekday admission to Kabuki Springs & Spa (p129).

HOTEL DES ARTS   ART HOTEL $$
Map p320 (☎415-956-3232, 800-956-4322; www.sfhoteldesarts.com; 447 Bush St; r $139-199, without bath $99-149; ☂; Ⓜ & ⒭ Montgomery St) Finally a midbudget hotel for art freaks. All rooms have been painted by underground street artists, and some of the murals are jaw-dropping. Service could be stronger, linens are thin and some sinks have separate hot and cold taps (ask when you book), but the art is incredible – it's like sleeping inside a painting. Note: some rooms are loud; bring earplugs.

HOTEL VERTIGO   SMALL HOTEL $$
Map p322 (☎415-885-6800, 800-553-1900; www.hotelvertigosf.com; 940 Sutter St; r $129-189; ☂; Ⓜ Sutter & Leavenworth Sts) Scenes from Hitchcock's *Vertigo* were shot here – it was the Empire Hotel in the film – and a recent refurbishment nods to the master with Spirograph-like artwork reminiscent of the opening sequence. The snappy aesthetic blends cool colors and low-slung wingchairs beside platform beds dressed with down duvets. Trouble is, they ran out of money during the refurb and parts looks unfinished. The upside? Good deals. It's a 10-minute walk to

get anywhere, but you get more bang for your buck than right at Union Square – and bragging rights to a bit of movie history.

STRATFORD HOTEL   HOTEL $
Map p320 (☎415-397-7080, 888-504-6835; www.hotelstratford.com; 242 Powell St; r incl breakfast $89-149; @ ☂; Ⓜ & ⒭ Powell St) A great value hotel at Union Square, the eight-story Stratford has simple, smallish rooms, with plain furnishing and the occasional scuff mark, but they're clean – as are the baths, which have rainfall showerheads, but no tubs. Rooms on Powell St are loud.

HOTEL METROPOLIS   HOTEL $
Map p320 (☎415-775-4600, 800-553-1900; www.hotelmetropolis.com; 25 Mason St; r $89-125; Ⓟ @ ☂; Ⓜ & ⒭ Powell St) Never mind the streetwalkers outside, the Metropolis has fresh-looking rooms with standard-issue Ikea-like furniture, cushioned windowsills and good amenities in the tiny baths. If you're timid, you'll hate the neighborhood, but if you're an intrepid traveler, these are good digs at great prices.

HOTEL CALIFORNIA   SMALL HOTEL $$
Map p320 (☎415-441-2700, 800-227-4223; www.hotelca.com/sanfrancisco; 580 Geary St; r $149-169; ☂; Ⓜ Geary & Jones Sts) Alas, no pink champagne on ice, but it does provide frosted tequila shots upon check-in and wine and cheese nightly. This bay-windowed, vintage-1920s hotel has small rooms and sometimes-thin walls, but cheery yellow paint jobs, fluffy beds and double-pane windows that generally block street noise (request a quiet room).

FITZGERALD HOTEL   SMALL HOTEL $
Map p320 (☎415-775-8100, 800-334-6835; www.fitzgeraldhotel.com; 620 Post St; s $89-119, d $99-139; @ ☂; Ⓜ Post & Taylor Sts) Upgrade from hostel to hotel at this good-value, vintage-1910 property styled with a quirky mishmash of furniture liquidated from fancier boutique hotels. The old-fashioned building needs upgrades (note the temperamental elevator), and there are occasional scuff marks and torn curtains, but baths are clean, rooms have fridges and microwaves, and staff is friendly. Downstairs there's a cute wine bar.

ADELAIDE HOSTEL   HOSTEL $
Map p320 (☎415-359-1915, 877-359-1915; www.adelaidehostel.com; 5 Isadora Duncan Lane; dm $30-35, r $70-90, incl breakfast; @ ☂; Ⓜ Geary &

Taylor Sts) Down a hidden alley, the 22-room Adelaide has up-to-date furnishings and marble-tiled baths – but the occasional rust stain and dust bunny. Extras include $5 dinners, multiple group activities and two common areas, one quiet. Good service, friendly crowd. Note: your private room may wind up being in the nearby Dakota or Fitzgerald Hotels; of the two, the Fitzgerald is the (far) better choice.

USA HOSTELS   HOSTEL $

Map p320 (☑415-440-5600, 877-483-2950; www. usahostels.com; 711 Post St; dm $30-34, r $73-83; 🛜; ⓜPost & Jones St, 🚋Powell St) Built in 1909, this former hotel was recently converted into a spiffy hostel that draws an international crowd. Private rooms sleep three or four, and you can usually save a few bucks by reserving through the website. The basic cafe here serves inexpensive cafeteria-style dinners every night. Great service.

HI SAN FRANCISCO CITY CENTER   HOSTEL $

Map p322 (☑415-474-5721; www.sfhostels.com; 685 Ellis St; dm incl breakfast $25-30, r $85-100; @🛜; ⓜPolk & O'Farrell Sts) A converted seven-story, vintage-1920s apartment building, this better-than-average hostel has private baths in all rooms, including dorms, and all-you-can-eat pancakes or eggs $1. The neighborhood is sketchy, the edge of the gritty Tenderloin, but there are good bars and cheap eats nearby.

🛏 North Beach & Chinatown

WASHINGTON SQUARE INN   B&B $$$

Map p324 (☑415-981-4220, 800-388-0220; www. wsisf.com; 1660 Stockton St; r incl breakfast $179-329; @🛜; ⓜColumbus Av & Union St) On leafy, sun-dappled Washington Square, this inn looks decidedly European and caters to the over-40 set, with tasteful rooms and a few choice antiques, including carved-wooden armoires. The least-expensive rooms are tiny, but what a stellar address. Wine and cheese each evening and breakfast in bed are lovely extras. No elevator.

TOP CHOICE HOTEL BOHÈME   BOUTIQUE HOTEL $$

Map p324 (☑415-433-9111; www.hotelboheme. com; 444 Columbus Ave; r $174-194; @🛜; ⓜStockton St & Columbus Ave) Our favorite boutique hotel is a love letter to the Beat era, with moody orange, black and sage-green color schemes that nod to the 1950s.

Inverted Chinese umbrellas hang from the ceiling, and photos from the Beat years decorate the walls. Rooms are smallish, some front noisy Columbus Ave (the quietest are in back) and baths are teensy, but the hotel is smack in the middle of North Beach's vibrant street scene. No elevator.

SAN REMO HOTEL   SMALL HOTEL $

Map p324 (☑415-776-8688, 800-352-7366; www. sanremohotel.com; 2237 Mason St; d $65-99; @🛜; ⓜColumbus Ave & Francisco St, 🚋Powell-Mason) One of the city's best values, the San Remo dates to 1906 and is long on old-fashioned charm. Rooms are simply done, with mismatched turn-of-the-century furnishings, and all rooms share baths. Think reputable, vintage boarding house. Note: the least-expensive rooms have windows onto the corridor, not the outdoors. No elevator.

PACIFIC TRADEWINDS HOSTEL   HOSTEL $

Map p324 (☑415-433-7970, 888-734-6783; www.sanfranciscohostel.org; 680 Sacramento St; dm $29; @🛜; ⓜSacramento & Kearny Sts) San Francisco's smartest-looking all-dorm hostel has a blue-and-white nautical theme, fully equipped kitchen and spotless glass-brick showers. The nearest BART station is Embarcadero. Alas, no elevator means hauling your bags up three flights, but it's worth it. Great service, fun staff.

SW HOTEL   HOTEL $$

Map p324 (☑415-362-2999, 888-595-9188; www. swhotel.com; 615 Broadway; r $109-149; P🅿; ⓜStockton St & Pacific Ave) The legendary Sam Wong flophouse underwent a late '90s overhaul that included earthquake retrofitting and updated decor. Now it's simple and respectable, with bland pastel decor. The number-one selling point is location – on the Broadway axis dividing North Beach and Chinatown – but some rooms are incredibly loud: bring earplugs or use the aircon (not available in cheaper rooms). Parking not always available.

GRANT PLAZA   HOTEL $

Map p324 (☑415-434-3883, 800-472-6899; www. grantplaza.com; 465 Grant Ave; r $69-129; 🛜; 🚋California St) Many rooms overlook the blinking neon and exotic street scene of Grant Ave: expect noise. Rooms are generally clean (never mind the heavy air-freshener), but blandly decorated with generic furniture. Baths have soap, but not shampoo. If you want to be in the heart of Chinatown, this is it.

SLEEPING NORTH BEACH & CHINATOWN

🛌 The Hills & Japantown

TOP CHOICE **HOTEL DRISCO** BOUTIQUE HOTEL $$$

Map p328 (☎415-346-2880, 800-738-7477; www.jdvhotels.com; 2901 Pacific Ave; r $209-299; @🖘; MDivisadero & Jackson Sts) The only hotel in Pacific Heights stands high on ridgeline, a stately 1903 apartment-hotel tucked between mansions. We love the architecture, attentive service and fresh, spiffy rooms, with their elegantly simple decor, but the high-on-a-hill location is convenient only to the Marina; anywhere else requires bus or taxi. Still, for a real boutique hotel, it's hard to beat.

HUNTINGTON HOTEL LUXURY HOTEL $$$

Map p326 (☎415-474-5400, 800-227-4683; www.huntingtonhotel.com; 1075 California St; r from $325; ❋@🖘🏊; 🚇California St) Other nearby hotels are showier, but the Huntington is Nob Hill's discrete grande dame, the go-to address of society ladies who prefer the comfort of tradition over the garishness of style. Book a refurbished room, and don't even think of wearing workout clothes in the elegant lobby. The on-site **Nob Hill Spa** is one of the city's best.

FAIRMONT SAN FRANCISCO HOTEL $$$

Map p326 (☎415-772-5000, 800-441-1414; www.fairmont.com; 950 Mason St; r $219-339; ❋@🖘; 🚇California St) One of the city's most storied hotels, the Fairmont's enormous lobby is decked out with crystal chandeliers, marble floors and towering yellow-marble columns. Rooms sport traditional business-class furnishings, but lack the finer details of a top-end luxury hotel. For maximum character, book a room in the original 1906 building.

MARK HOPKINS INTERCONTINENTAL HOTEL $$

Map p326 (☎415-392-3434, 800-327-0200; www.markhopkins.net; 999 California St; r $179-339; ❋@🖘; 🚇California St) Glistening marble floors reflect glowing crystal chandeliers in the lobby of the 1926 Mark Hopkins, a San Francisco landmark. Detractors call it staid, but its timeless Nob Hill elegance is precisely why others (including Michelle Obama) love it. Rooms are done with tasteful furnishings and Frette linens, but the recession has taken its toll: some need updating. The top-floor Top of the Mark (p125) lounge has knockout views and live jazz.

NOB HILL INN INN $$

Map p326 (☎415-673-6080; www.nobhillinn.com; 1000 Pine St; r $125-165, ste $195-275; 🖘; 🚇California St) Situated in a genteel old Edwardian house one block below the top of Nob Hill, the 20 rooms at this inn are classically decorated with antiques, armoires and (some) four-poster beds. It's predominantly a timeshare-hotel, popular with an older crowd (read: quiet). Website specials drop rates as low as $99. Suites sleep four to six and have kitchenettes.

KABUKI HOTEL THEME HOTEL $$

Map p328 (☎415-922-3200, 800-333-3333; www.jdvhotels.com/kabuki; 1625 Post St; r $129-249; P🖘; 🚇Geary Blvd & Laguna St) The Kabuki nods to Japan, with shoji (rice paper screens) on the windows and orange-silk dust ruffles beneath platform beds. The boxy 1960s architecture is plain, but rooms are spacious (if in need of some upgrading). Best details: deep Japanese soaking tubs with adjoining showers, and free weekday passes to Kabuki Springs & Spa (p129).

HOTEL TOMO THEME HOTEL $$

Map p328 (☎415-921-4000, 888-822-8666; www.jdvhotels.com/tomo; 1800 Sutter St; r $119-189; P❋@🖘🏊; 🚇Sutter & Buchanan Sts) Japanese pop culture informs the Tomo's aesthetic, with big-eyed anime characters blinking on the lobby's TV screens. The blond minimalist room furniture and fat-boy beanbags make it feel a bit like a college dorm, but it's great fun for families and anime nuts – if not high-heeled sophisticates.

HOTEL MAJESTIC HISTORIC HOTEL $$

Map p328 (☎415-441-1100, 800-869-8966; www.thehotelmajestic.com; 1500 Sutter St; r $100-175; @🖘; 🚇Sutter & Gough Sts) The 1902 Hotel Majestic holds a torch for traditional elegance – even if its edges are fraying. Rooms are done with Chinese porcelain lamps beside triple-sheeted beds, and while they need some upgrades, we like the old-school vibe. Standard rooms are small but better value than comparable Union Square hotels. The clubby lobby bar is ideal for a clandestine meeting with your paramour.

NOB HILL HOTEL SMALL HOTEL $

Map p326 (☎415-885-2987; www.nobhillhotel.com; 835 Hyde St; r $95-145; @🖘; 🚇Sutter & Hyde Sts) Rooms in this 1906 hotel have been dressed up in Victorian style, with brass beds and floral-print carpet. The twee look borders on grandma-lives-here, but it's definitely not cookie cutter and service is personable. Rooms on Hyde St are loud; book in back.

QUEEN ANNE HOTEL   B&B $$

Map p328 (☑415-441-2828, 800-227-3970; www.queenanne.com; 1590 Sutter St; r incl breakfast $123-169, ste $203-255; P@☎; MSutter & Octavia Sts) The Queen Anne occupies a lovely 1890 Victorian mansion, formerly a girls' boarding school. Though the decor borders on frilly, we love the stately house. Rooms are comfy (some are tiny) and have a mishmash of antiques; some have romantic wood-burning fireplaces.

🛏 SoMa

TOP CHOICE HOTEL VITALE   DESIGN HOTEL $$$

Map p330 (☑415-278-3700, 888-890-8688; www.hotelvitale.com; 8 Mission St; d $239-379; ✳@☎; M&🅡Embarcadero) The ugly exterior disguises a fashion-forward hotel, with echoes of mid-century-modern design enhanced by up-to-the-minute luxuries. Beds are dressed with silky-soft, 450-thread-count sheets. Excellent on-site spa with two rooftop hot tubs. The best rooms face the bay and have spectacular views.

ST REGIS HOTEL   LUXURY HOTEL $$$

Map p330 (☑415-284-4000, 877-787-3447; www.stregis.com/sanfrancisco; 125 3rd St; r from $399; ✳@☎✈; M&🅡Montgomery St) The pinnacle of luxury, the St Regis is one of SF's three five-star hotels (the others are Four Seasons and Ritz-Carlton), and it's our favorite for its art collection, which nods to the neighboring Museum of Modern Art. Rooms have all the latest bells and whistles, including magnificent beds dressed with Pratesi linens and travertine baths with two-person soaking tubs. Alas, the recession has affected service standards, but we still love the oversized rooms, despite their too-beige monochromatic color scheme.

W HOTEL   HOTEL $$$

Map p330 (☑415-777-5300, 877-946-8357; www.whotel.com; 181 3rd St; r from $249; ✳@☎✈; M&🅡Montgomery St) Sexy doormen stand sentinel, looking like bouncers at a disco, and club-kids-turned-conventioneers crowd the lobby, which blares with thump-thump music. Though forced in its cool, the look is sexy – wear black and blend right in. High-floor rooms in the 31-story tower have spec-tacular views; all have upholstered window seats, stereos with chill music and sumptuous beds. Though the concept is definitely corporate, W does a stellar job capitalizing on sex and rock and roll – the drugs are up to you.

HARBOR COURT HOTEL   BOUTIQUE HOTEL $$$

Map p330 (☑415-882-9890, 866-792-6283; www.harborcourthotel.com; 165 Steuart St; r $189-269; ✳@☎✈; M&🅡Embarcadero) Rooms are small at this repurposed, vintage-1928 YMCA hotel, but designers compensated with pull-out drawers under platform beds, and handsome textures and colors. Book a bay-view room (trust us). Downstairs, guests gather fireside in the handsome bayside common area. Just outside are lively bars and restaurants. The adjoining Y has an excellent gym and pool.

BEST WESTERN CARRIAGE INN   DESIGN MOTEL $$

Map p330 (☑415-552-8600, 800-780-7234; www.carriageinnsf.com; 140 7th St; r $129-169; P@☎✈🚶; M&🅡Civic Center) An upmarket motor lodge with bigger-than-average rooms, restyled with classic furniture and disco-ready textiles, the Carriage Inn gives good bang for your buck, but it's on a sometimes-sketchy street. On-site hot tub; pool across the street at the Americania.

AMERICANIA HOTEL   DESIGN MOTEL $$

Map p330 (☑415-626-0200; www.americaniahotel.com; 121 7th St; r $129-169; P@☎✈🚶; M&🅡Civic Center) Rooms at this restyled motor lodge face a central courtyard and look sharp, with a retro-'70s aesthetic incorporating black-and-teal-checked carpeting, white-vinyl headboards, pop art and playful extras. Kids love the outdoor heated pool. Parents love the microbrews at the excellent downstairs burger joint – but may dislike the sometimes-gritty neighborhood

🌿 GOOD HOTEL   DESIGN HOTEL $$

Map p330 (☑415-621-7001; www.thegoodhotel.com; 112 7th St; r $109-169; P@☎✈; M&🅡Civic Center) A revamped motor lodge attached to a restyled apartment hotel, Good Hotel places a premium on green, with reclaimed wood headboards, light fixtures of repurposed bottles, and fleece bedspreads made of recycled soda bottles and cast-off fabrics. The aesthetic is like a smartly decorated college dorm room, youthful and fun. The big drawbacks are a sometimes-sketchy neighborhood and street noise; book in back. Also has bikes for rent. The pool is across the street at the Americana.

MOSSER HOTEL HOTEL $$

Map p330 (☑415-986-4400, 800-227-3804; www.themosser.com; 54 4th St; r $129-159, with shared bath $69-99; @⌨; Ⓜ&ⒷPowell St) A tourist-class hotel with stylish details, the Mosser has tiny rooms and tinier baths, but rates are (usually) a bargain. Service can be lackluster and the building is old, but it's centrally located and rooms are half the price of the neighboring Marriott, a boon for conventioneers on a budget.

⌂ The Mission

Ⓘ INN SAN FRANCISCO INN $$

Map p334 (☑415-641-0188, 800-359-0913; www.innsf.com; 943 S Van Ness Ave; r $175-285, with shared bath $120-145, cottage $335, all incl breakfast; Ⓟ@⌨; ⓂMission & 20th Sts) The stately Inn San Francisco occupies an elegant 1872 Italianate-Victorian mansion, impeccably maintained and packed with period antiques. All rooms have fresh-cut flowers and sumptuous beds with fluffy featherbeds; some have Jacuzzi tubs. There's also a free-standing garden cottage that sleeps up to six. Outside there's an English garden and redwood hot tub open 24 hours (a rarity). Limited parking: reserve ahead. No elevator.

⌂ The Castro & Noe Valley

PARKER GUEST HOUSE GLBT, B&B $$

Map p336 (☑415-621-3222, 888-520-7275; www.parkerguesthouse.com; 520 Church St; r incl breakfast $149-229; Ⓟ@⌨; ⓂChurch & 18th Sts) The Castro's most stately gay digs occupy two side-by-side 100-year-old Edwardian mansions. Details are elegant and formal, but never froufrou. Rooms feel more like a swanky hotel than a B&B, with super-comfortable beds and down comforters. Bath fixtures gleam. The garden is ideal for a lovers' tryst, as is the steam room. No elevator.

BELVEDERE HOUSE GLBT, B&B $$

(☑415-731-6654, 877-226-3273; www.belvederehouse.com; 598 Belvedere St; r incl breakfast $125-190; @⌨; ⓂClayton & Carmel Sts) On a leafy residential street, up a steep hill from the Castro, this B&B is one of the city's best-kept secrets. Six cozy rooms have eclectic art and vintage chandeliers, and the living

room is packed with treasures from the owner's world travels. Though primarily for gay guests, all are welcome – kids get child-sized bathrobes. No elevator.

INN ON CASTRO GLBT, B&B $$

Map p336 (☑415-861-0321; www.innoncastro.com; 321 Castro St; r $165-195, without bath $125-155, incl breakfast, self-catering apt $165-220; ⌨; ⓂCastro St) A portal to the Castro's disco heyday, this Edwardian townhouse is decked out with top-end '70s-mod furnishings. Rooms are retro-cool and spotlessly kept. Exceptional breakfasts – the owner is a chef. Also rents out several nearby apartments. No elevator.

WILLOWS INN GLBT, B&B $$

Map p336 (☑415-431-4770; www.willowssf.com; 710 14th St; r $110-140; ⌨; ⓂChurch St) Willows has the homey comforts of a B&B, without any fuss. None of the 12 rooms has a private bath, but all have sinks. Shared kitchenette. Rooms on 14th St are sunnier and have good street views, but they're noisier; ask when you book. No elevator.

BECK'S MOTOR LODGE GLBT, MOTEL $

Map p336 (☑415-621-8212, 800-227-4360; www.becksmotorlodgesf.com; 2222 Market St; r $95-135; ⌨; ⒷCastro St) Though technically not gay, its placement at the center of the Castro makes it the defacto gay favorite. We don't recommend bringing kids, especially during big gay events, when rooms reserve months ahead. Book a rear-facing unit for quiet, a room in front to cruise with your blinds open. 'Deluxe' rooms have air-con.

24 HENRY GLBT, B&B $$

Map p336 (☑415-864-5686, 800-900-5686; www.24henry.com; 24 Henry St; r $149, without bath $105-110; ⌨; ⓂSanchez & Market Sts) A converted Victorian on a beautiful, quiet side street, 24 Henry's rooms are simply decorated with cast-off ersatz antiques and utilitarian furniture. Best for no-fuss gay travelers. No elevator.

⌂ The Haight & Hayes Valley

PARSONNAGE B&B $$$

Map p329 (☑415-863-3699, 888-763-7722; www.theparsonage.com; 198 Haight St; r $200-250; @⌨; ⓂHaight & Laguna Sts) A 23-room Italianate-Victorian convenient to Market St transit, the Parsonnage retains gorgeous original details, including rose-brass chandeliers and Carrera-marble fireplaces. The spacious, airy rooms are lovely with oriental rugs, period antiques and, in some cases, wood-burning fireplaces. Take breakfast in the formal dining room, from 8am to 10am, then brandy and chocolates before bed. Charming owners. No elevator.

CHATEAU TIVOLI
INN $$

Map p338 (✆415-776-5462, 800-228-1647; www.chateautivoli.com; 1057 Steiner St; r $140-200, r without bath $100-130, ste $250-290; ☎; ⓜFillmore St & Golden Gate Ave) This imposing, glorious chateau on a secondary thoroughfare near Alamo Square has somewhat faded since the time when Isadora Duncan and Mark Twain were guests. Still, you can't pass by without gawking at the two-toned gabled roofs, domed turrets and cornices – all painted maroon and blue with gold accents. The guestrooms are more modest, with no TVs, but the place is full of soul, character and, rumor has it, the ghost of a Victorian opera diva. No elevator.

RED VICTORIAN BED, BREAKFAST & ART
B&B $$

Map p338 (✆415-864-1978; www.redvic.net; 1665 Haight St; r $149-229, without bath $89-129, incl breakfast; ☎; ⓜHaight & Cole Sts) 1968 lives on at the tripped-out Red Vic. Each individually decorated room in the 1904 landmark building pays tribute to peace, ecology and global friendship, with themes like Sunshine, Flower Children and, of course, the Summer of Love. Only four of the 18 rooms have baths; all come with breakfast in the organic **Peace Café**. Reduced rates for longer stays. There's wi-fi in the lobby. No elevator.

STANYAN PARK HOTEL
HOTEL $$

Map p338 (✆415-751-1000; www.stanyanpark.com; 750 Stanyan St; r $140-225, ste $275-350, incl breakfast; @☎; ⓜStanyan & Waller Sts) On the eastern edge of Golden Gate Park, this stately Victorian hotel is up to date, with nary a drafty window or creaky floor. There's nothing risky about the traditional decor, but that's its charm – Queen Anne and Chippendale-style chairs, floral-print wallpaper and dusty-green and pale-pink color schemes. Service could be better, but rooms are lovely. Note: junkies congregate at the nearby McDonald's at nighttime, but the 'hood is generally safe and the hotel secure.

HAYES VALLEY INN
SMALL HOTEL $

Map p329 (✆415-431-9131, 800-930-7999; www.hayesvalleyinn.com; 417 Gough St; s $80-105, d $84-120, incl breakfast; @☎) Like a European pension, this amazingly reasonable find has simple, small rooms with shared baths, a border collie panting in the parlor and staff who want to mother you. The biggest complaints are the street noise and too-few baths. Good shopping nearby. No elevator.

SLEEP OVER SAUCE
B&B $

Map p329 (✆415-252-1423; www.sleepsf.com; 135 Gough St; r $110-155; @☎; ⓡVan Ness) We like the homey vibe of this eight-room, vintage-1906 B&B, set above a pretty good dinner house and bar. Rooms are simple, with dark-wood furniture and nothing froufrou; guests share a big common area with a fireplace. Some rooms have baths across the hall; ask when you book. Easy access to Hayes Valley shopping, the opera and symphony. No elevator.

METRO HOTEL
SMALL HOTEL $

Map p338 (✆415-861-5364; www.metrohotelsf.com; 319 Divisadero St; r $76-120; ☎; ⓜDivisadero & Oak Sts) On a thoroughfare bisecting the Upper and Lower Haight districts, this straightforward, no-frills hotel provides cheap, clean rooms with private bath and an outdoor garden patio. Its location is largely residential, but you can walk to the Haight's bars and restaurants. No elevator.

🛏 Golden Gate Park & the Avenues

SEAL ROCK INN
MOTEL $$

Map p342 (✆415-752-8000, 888-732-5762; www.sealrockinn.com; 545 Point Lobos Ave; s $129-167, d $139-177; ℗☎✼♿; ⓜ48th & Point Lobos Aves) Hunter S Thompson used to stay at this vintage-1950s, ocean-side motel to listen to the seals, which have since migrated to Fisherman's Wharf. Rooms need updating (think 1970s rumpus-room style), but they're big and most sleep up to four. All have refrigerators; some have kitchens. It's good for families who want to spend time at the beach and hiking the coast. Reserve way ahead for the upgraded 3rd-floor fireplace rooms. A heated pool (summer only) and ping-pong keep the kids from getting antsy.

Understand San Francisco

San Francisco Today

Small as it is, this seven-by-seven-mile peninsula looms large in the imagination. The greenest city in America is full of ideas, including urban farms, biotech and social media – plus a lot more that mostly serve as in-box filler. Saloons, food trucks, pop-ups and pot clubs are sprouting up all over SF's 43 hills, while same-sex couples are still on standby, waiting to get hitched. SF has its ups and downs, but as anyone who's clung onto the side of a cable car will tell you, this town provides one hell of a ride.

Best on Film

Milk (2008) Sean Penn won an Oscar for his portrayal of America's first openly gay elected official.

Tales of the City (1993) Laura Linney unravels a mystery in SF's swinging '70s disco scene.

Harold & Maude (1971) Conservatory of Flowers and Sutro Baths make metaphorically apt backdrops for May–December romance.

Chan Is Missing (1982) When Chan disappears, two cabbies realize they don't know Chan, Chinatown or themselves.

Best in Print

Howl and Other Poems (Allen Ginsberg; 1956) Mind-altering, law-changing words defined a generation of 'angel-headed hipsters.'

Time and Materials (Robert Hass; 2007) Every Pulitzer Prize-winning syllable is as essential as a rivet in the Golden Gate Bridge.

On the Road (Jack Kerouac; 1957) Banged out in a San Francisco attic, Kerouac's travelogue set post-war America free.

Slouching Towards Bethlehem (Joan Didion; 1968) Scorching truth burns through San Francisco fog during the Summer of Love.

Green City, USA

In 2011, San Francisco was named North America's Greenest City, and you'll notice that distinction when it comes to choosing what eat and drink, where to sleep, what souvenirs to buy and how to get around town. Pretty much anything you might want to do in San Francisco, you can do with a green conscience – just look for the ✪ designation in this book.

San Francisco is tough on proof of green credentials. Businesses must compost and recycle by law here, so that alone is not enough to merit a special ✪ designation. Practices that might be considered standard-setting elsewhere have gone mainstream here, including electric public buses, restaurants featuring California-grown ingredients or hotels encouraging guests to re-use towels to save water. Only businesses that have gone above and beyond local law and standard SF practices earn a ✪ designation, such as San Francisco city–certified green businesses, LEED–certified green attractions, all-hybrid-car taxi services, and restaurants and bars with a verifiable commitment to using ingredients from organic local farms or foraged ingredients.

Social-Mediated SF

If you're not on Twitter, Facebook, Yelp, Google +, Yahoo Groups or LinkedIn, are you sure you still have a pulse? San Francisco will try to convince you must use one of these Bay Area–based social media platforms in order to validate your existence. After all, a lot of local jobs depend on it.

But there is already a backlash afoot in this technological hub. In a city where telecommuters have turned public spaces into satellite offices for the past decade, cafes have begun removing electrical outlets and unplugging wi-fi routers, and boutiques and restaurants are posting signs saying 'No phone calls. No excuses.'

That's right: even Apple and Google products don't get a pass for being local and seasonal. Conversations are happening offline and off the cuff, and early adopters are now returning social media to its initial use: as a place to briefly touch base and make plans to meet in person.

Extravagant Indulgence

You can blame SF for any number of temptations: chocolate bars, designer jeans, martinis, TV broadcasts, online shopping and LSD. Lately, San Francisco's saloon revival has been putting spitoons and absinthe fountains back into active service – and if there's a video store that hasn't yet been converted into a medical marijuana dispensary, it's only a matter of time. Only a very local and very specific ailment could explain why one of every six San Franciscans has a prescription to the city's 40-odd pot clubs. All those herbal clubs and saloons do help explain the near-ubiquity of food trucks and pop-up restaurants throughout the city, doing a brisk business in cupcakes and curry.

Yet despite their many indulgences and slacker reputations, San Franciscans still hold more patents per capita than any other US city, and they read more books and rack up many more degrees than other Americans. The city has been working up quite a reputation for compassion, too, creating new models for AIDS care, family homeless shelters and more nonprofits than any other US city. In its spare time, this city continues to stretch the limits of free speech in poetry, grow urban gardens, pioneer locavore cuisine, promote civil rights, make new media art and rock Folsom Street Fair getups that may permanently impair your ability to blush.

Always a Bridesmaid

San Francisco was the first city to authorize same-sex marriages back in 2004 – but some 4036 honeymoons were abruptly ended when their marriages were legally invalidated by the state. Court battles ensued, and California voters narrowly passed 2008's California Proposition 8 measure to legally define marriage as between a man and a woman. Counter-suits were initiated, arguing limiting marriage rights runs contrary to civil rights protections in California's constitutions.

Meanwhile, New York passed a law allowing gays to marry in June, 2011 – an event cheered by some 1.2 million San Francisco Pride Parade–goers, many dressed as bridesmaids. But star-crossed San Francisco couples – some of whom have had marriages annulled by the state twice – aren't all booking flights. Many are awaiting the results of the Supreme Court challenge to Proposition 8 that would set a nationwide precedent, and could start the maddest dash for white tulle San Francisco has ever seen.

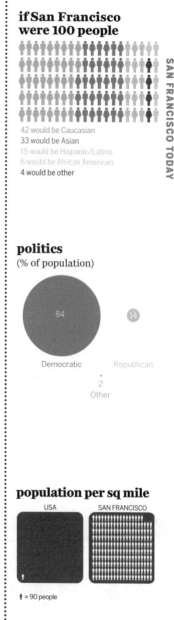

SAN FRANCISCO TODAY

if San Francisco were 100 people

42 would be Caucasian
33 would be Asian
15 would be Hispanic/Latino
6 would be African American
4 would be other

politics
(% of population)

84 Democratic

14 Republican

2 Other

population per sq mile

USA   SAN FRANCISCO

† ≈ 90 people

History

Native Californians had found gold in California long before 1849, but it hardly seemed worth mentioning, as long as there were oysters for lunch and venison for dinner. But once word circulated, San Francisco was transformed almost overnight from bucolic trading backwater to Gold Rush metropolis. One hundred and fifty years of booms, busts, history-making hijinks and lowdown dirty dealings later, San Francisco remains the wildest city in the west – and still dreams of oysters for lunch and venison for dinner.

COWBOYS ON A MISSION

When Spanish cowboys brought 340 horses, 302 head of cattle and 160 mules to settle Mission San Francisco in 1776, there was a slight hitch: the area had already been settled by Native Americans for over 14,300 years. Since there was enough shellfish and wild foodstuffs to go around, the arrival of Captain Juan Bautista de Anza, Father Francisco Palou and their livestock was initially met with no apparent resistance – until the Spaniards began to demand more than dinner.

The new arrivals expected the local Ohlone to build them a mission, and to take over its management within 10 years. In exchange, the Ohlone were allowed one meager meal a day that didn't always materialize, and a place in God's kingdom – which came much sooner than expected for many. Smallpox and other introduced diseases decimated the Ohlone population by almost three-quarters during the 50 years of Spanish rule in California. While some Ohlone managed to escape the short life of obligatory construction work and prayer, others were caught, returned to the adobe barracks and punished.

The mission settlement never really prospered. The sandy, scrubby fields were difficult to farm, fleas were a constant irritation, and the 20 soldiers who manned the local Presidio army encampment were allotted one scanty shipment of provisions per year. Spain wasn't especially sorry to hand over the troublesome settlement to the newly independent nation of Mexico, but Mexico soon made this colony a profitable venture with a

Top 5 Sites for Native History

Mission Dolores (the Mission)

Alcatraz

The Presidio

Rincon Center Murals (Financial District)

TIMELINE	June 1776	1835	1846
	Captain Juan Bautista de Anza and Father Francisco Palou arrive in SF with cattle and settlers. With Ohlone conscripts, they build the Misión San Francisco de Asís (now Mission Dolores).	An emissary of President Andrew Jackson makes a formal offer of $500,000 to buy Northern California, but Mexico testily refuses and tries to sell California to England.	The Mexican–American War breaks out and drags on for two years, with much posturing but little actual bloodshed in California.

bustling hide and tallow trade at Yerba Buena Cove, where the Financial District now stands.

Meanwhile, US–Mexico relations steadily deteriorated, made worse by rumors that Mexico was entertaining a British buy-out offer for California. The Mexican–American War broke out in 1846, and it dragged on for two years before ending with the Treaty of Guadalupe Hidalgo. This treaty formally ceded California and the present-day southwestern states to the USA – a loss that was initially reckoned by missionizing Church fathers in souls, but within months could be counted in ingots.

'GOLD! GOLD! GOLD!'

Say what you will about Sam Brannan, but the man knew how to sell a story. In 1848, the San Francisco real-estate speculator and Mormon tabloid publisher published sensational news of a find 120 miles away near Sutter's Mill, where sawmill employees had found gold flakes in the water. Hoping to scoop other newspapers and maybe sell swampland to rubes back East, Brannan published rumors of the find as solid fact. When San Franciscans proved more skeptical than expected, Brannan traveled to Sutter's Fort and convinced fellow Mormons to entrust him with a vial of gold for the church, swearing to keep their secret. Brannan kept his word for about a day. Upon his arrival, he ran through the San Francisco streets, brandishing the vial and shouting, 'Gold! Gold! Gold on the American River!'

But Brannan's plan backfired. Within weeks San Francisco's population shrank to 200, as every able-bodied individual headed to the hills to pan for gold. Brannan's newspaper folded; there was no one around to read, write or print it. Good thing Brannan had a backup plan: he'd bought every available shovel, pick and pan, and opened a general store near Sutter's Fort. Within its first 70 days, Brannan & Co sold $36,000 in equipment – about $949,000 in today's terms.

Luckily for Brannan's profit margins, other newspapers around the world weren't that scrupulous about getting their facts straight either, hastily publishing stories of 'gold mountains' near San Francisco. Boatloads of prospectors arrived from Australia, China, South America and Europe while another 40,000 prospectors trudged overland, eager to scoop up their fortunes on the hillsides. Prices for mining supplies shot up tenfold, and Brannan was raking in $150,000 a month, almost $4 million in today's terms. Food wasn't cheap, either: a dozen eggs could cost as much as $10 in San Francisco in 1849, the equivalent of $272 today.

When bawdy Jenny Lind Theater became SF's first city hall, competitor Bella Union advertised: 'As sweet and charming creatures as ever escaped a female seminary. Lovely tresses! Lovely lips! Buxom forms! at the BELLA UNION. And such fun! If you don't want to risk both optics, SHUT ONE EYE.'

1848
Gold is discovered near present-day Placerville by mill employees. San Francisco newspaper publisher and full-time big mouth Sam Brannan lets word out, and the Gold Rush is on.

1850
With hopes of solid-gold tax revenues, the US hastily dubs California the 31st state.

RICHARD CUMMINS / LONELY PLANET IMAGES ©

Town center, Placerville

EMPEROR NORTON OF SAN FRANCISCO

The Gold Rush made paupers into kings, but it also made one man a penniless emperor. Joshua Norton arrived in San Francisco from South Africa with $40,000 in 1849, and within months he'd made a fortune, lost it all through speculation and then disappeared. In 1859 he returned to San Francisco a changed man, wearing theatrical gold-braided military attire and grandly proclaiming himself 'Emperor of the United States and Protector of Mexico.' San Francisco newspapers published Emperor Norton's proclamations over 21 years, including decrees dissolving the Democratic and Republican parties, commanding the building of suspension bridges spanning the bay (considered one of his craziest ideas), and outlawing the use of the term 'Frisco' and imposing a penalty of $25 (payable to the Emperor, naturally). Police saluted him in the streets, and some local establishments accepted banknotes issued by the 'Imperial Government of Norton.' When the Emperor's adopted stray dog Bummer departed for that great doghouse in the sky, Mark Twain wrote the epitaph: 'He died full of years, and honor, and disease, and fleas.'

LAWLESS, LOOSE & LOWDOWN

By 1850, the year California was fast-tracked for admission as the 31st state in the Union, San Francisco's population had skyrocketed from 800 a year earlier to an estimated 25,000. But for all the new money in town, it wasn't exactly easy living. The fleas were still a problem and the rats were getting worse – but at least there were plenty of distractions.

Most of the early prospectors (called '49ers, after their arrival date) were men under the age of 40, and to keep them entertained – and fleece the gullible – some 500 saloons, 20 theaters and numerous venues of ill repute opened within five years. A buck might procure whiskey, opium or one of the women frolicking on swings rigged from saloon ceilings. At the gaming tables, luck literally was a lady: women card dealers dealt winning hands to those who engaged their back-room services. In 1851, visiting French journalist (and noted brothel expert) Albert Benard de Russailh reported, 'There are also some honest women in San Francisco, but not very many.'

Wise prospectors arrived early and got out quick – but there weren't very many of those, either. As gold became harder to find, backstabbing became more common, sometimes literally. Successful Peruvians and Chileans were harassed and denied renewals to their mining claims, and most left California by 1855. Native Californian laborers who had helped the '49ers strike it rich were also denied the right to hold claims. Despite San Francisco's well-earned notoriety for free-

1849–51	1851	1861–65	May 10, 1869
San Francisco's waterfront 'Sydney-Town' area becomes an increasing target of resentment and attacks; Australian boarding houses are torched six times by arsonists in two years.	Gold discovery in Australia leads to cheering in the streets of Melbourne and panic in the streets of San Francisco as the price for California gold plummets.	While US Civil War divides North from South back East, SF perversely profits in the West as industry diverted from factories burdened by the war effort heads to San Francisco.	The Golden Spike completes the first transcontinental railroad. The news travels via San Franciscan David Brooks' invention, the telegraph.

wheeling lawlessness, crime was swiftly and conveniently blamed on Australian newcomers. From 1851 to 1856, San Francisco's self-appointed Vigilance Committee tried, convicted and hung suspect 'Sydney Ducks' in hour-long proceedings that came to be known as 'kangaroo trials.' Along with Australians, Chinese – the most populous group in California by 1860 – were at the receiving end of misplaced resentment.

KEEPING THE WEST WILD

As gold, silver and railroad money flowed into San Francisco, the city grew. It didn't exactly blossom at first, though – public works were completely neglected, and heavily populated sections of the city were mired in muck. Eventually the debris-choked waterfront filled in and streets were graded and paved. As soon as Andrew Hallidie made the formidable crag accessible by cable car in 1873, Nob Hill sprouted mansions for millionaires, including the 'Big Four' railroad barons: Leland Stanford, Collis P Huntington, Mark Hopkins and Charles Crocker. Wherever there was green in the city, real-estate speculators saw greenbacks, cleverly repackaging even the flea-plagued cattle pastures of the Mission District and Cow Hollow as desirable residential districts. The Gold Rush was officially over; the land rush was on.

Naturalist John Muir came through San Francisco in 1868, but quickly left with a shudder for Yosemite. However, the early environmentalist organization he founded, the Sierra Club, would eventually find its major backers in San Francisco. The unspoiled wilderness that Muir and his organization successfully lobbied to protect includes one of San Francisco's most popular escapes: Muir Woods.

San Franciscans determined to preserve the city's natural splendors pushed to establish the city's first park in 1867, when squatters were paid to vacate the area now known as Buena Vista Park. With a mandate from San Francisco voters to transform sand dunes into a vast city park, tenacious engineer William Hammond Hall saw the development of Golden Gate Park through to completion from 1870 to 1887 – despite developers' best attempts to scuttle park plans in favor of casinos, amusement parks, hotels and an igloo village. Populist millionaire Adolph Sutro decided that every working stiff should be able to escape Downtown tenements for the sand dunes and sunsets of Ocean Beach, accessible for a nickel on his public railway. Sutro's idea proved wildly popular, and by way of thanks he was elected mayor in 1894.

William Hammond Hall briefly quit his job building Golden Gate Park in 1886 over proposals to convert the park into a racetrack lined with tract homes. When a casino and carnival were established for the 1893 Midwinter's Fair, Hammond Hall fought to get the park returned to its intended purpose.

HISTORY KEEPING THE WEST WILD

GOLDEN GATE PARK

1873 When a nervous driver declines to test the brakes of Andrew Hallidie's 'wire rope railway,' aka cable car, Hallidie jumps in and steers the car downhill as crowds cheer.

1882 The US Chinese Exclusion Act suspends new immigration from China. These racially targeted laws remain until 1943.

1882–1924 The Exclusion Act spurs the passage of parallel Japanese exclusion laws, with ordinances limiting citizenship, marriage, immigration and property rights for Japanese San Franciscans.

California St cable car

THE VIEW FROM GOLD MOUNTAIN

Within a year of the 1849 Gold Rush, Chinatown was already established in San Francisco – better known in Cantonese as 'Gold Mountain.' At first Chinatown wasn't exclusively Chinese at all, but a bachelor community of Mexican, American, European, African American and Chinese miners who bunked, prospected and caroused side by side. Working conditions were often harsh, and in 1852 San Francisco's first labor strike was orchestrated by the Chinatown guild of masons.

The solidarity didn't last. When gold prices came crashing down with the discovery of gold in Australia, miners down on their luck turned their irrational resentments on resident Australians and Chinese. Australian lodging houses were burned to the ground, anti-Chinese riots broke out and Chinese miners' and farmers' land claims were rendered null and void. In 1870 San Francisco officially restricted housing and employment for anyone born in China. Not coincidentally, San Francisco's anti-Chinese laws served the needs of local magnates looking for cheap labor to build the first cross-country railroad. With little other choice of legitimate employment, an estimated 12,000 Chinese laborers did the dangerous work of dynamiting rail tunnels through the Sierra Nevada.

Anti-Chinese riots troubled San Francisco's self-appointed Emperor Norton, who in one instance reportedly stood between the attackers and their intended targets, and recited the Lord's Prayer until the rioters dispersed. But any hope that SF's general populace – composed almost entirely of recent immigrants at the time – would likewise reject xenophobia was dashed when California's discriminatory anti-Chinese laws were extended nationwide in 1882. The US Chinese Exclusion Act prevented new immigration from China, barred Chinese from citizenship until 1943, and spurred the passage of 100 parallel ordinances limiting rights for Japanese San Franciscans.

City officials planned to oust Chinese residents altogether and develop the prime property of Chinatown after the 1906 fire, but the Chinese consulate and rifle-toting Chinatown merchants persuaded the city otherwise. Today Chinatown is a major economic boon to the city as one of its top tourist attractions, yet many residents scrape by on less than $10,000 a year – not exactly a Gold Mountain. Better-off residents tend to leave Chinatown, new arrivals move in, and the cycle begins anew. Each night as the crowds of visitors thin out and the sun sets on Chinatown, ballroom dancers convene in social halls to glide across the floor with practiced elegance, past historic odds.

DOUBLE DISASTER

By the 20th century, San Francisco had earned a reputation for scandal, corruption, earthquakes and other calamities – none of it good for business. To redirect attention from its notorious waterfront fleshpots to its comparatively underexposed urban assets, the city commissioned Chicago architect Daniel Burnham to give San Francisco a beaux arts Civic

April 18, 1906	1910	1913	1914
A massive earthquake levels entire blocks of SF in 47 seconds flat, setting off fires that rage for three days. Survivors start rebuilding while the town is still smoldering.	Angel Island opens as the West Coast immigration station. Over 30 years, 175,000 arrivals from Asia are subjected to months or years of interrogation and prisonlike conditions.	California's Alien Land Law prohibits property ownership by Asians, including Japanese, Koreans and Indians. Lawyer Juichi Soyeda immediately files suit; he wins in 1952, 23 years after his death.	The Red Light Abatement Act prohibits dancing in the city's 2800 bars; police arrest female barkeeps, burlesque dancers and prostitutes.

Center plaza to rival Baron Haussmann's Paris. This elaborate plan had just been finalized in April 1906 when disaster struck – twice.

On April 18, 1906, a quake estimated at a terrifying 7.8 to 8.3 on today's Richter scale struck the city. For 47 seconds, the city emitted unholy groans and crashes as streets buckled, windows popped and brick buildings imploded. Wooden structures were set ablaze by toppled chimneys, and ruptured gas mains spread the fire.

In a matter of minutes, San Franciscans discovered just how many corners had been cut on government building contracts. Unreinforced civic structures – even City Hall – collapsed in ruins. Since city maintenance funds had been pocketed by unscrupulous officials, fire hydrants and water mains didn't work, and there was no way to contain fires Downtown. The sole functioning water source was a fountain donated to the city by opera prodigy Lotta Crabtree. Assembly lines were formed to haul buckets of water from Lotta's Fountain, but the water couldn't reach the crest of steep Nob Hill fast enough. Mansions with priceless Old Master and Impressionist art collections went up in smoke; inhabitants were lucky to escape with their lives.

Federal support was brought in to rescue the flaming city and restore order. Firebreaks were created by dynamiting entire city blocks – but instead of containing the conflagration, the explosions set off new fires. Firefighters couldn't haul equipment and water through the rubble-choked streets, so in a city surrounded by water on three sides, fires continued to rage. Homeless citizens took refuge atop Potrero Hill and Buena Vista Park, and watched their city and its dreams of grandeur go up in smoke.

After three days and two nights, most of the city was reduced to a smoldering black heap. The death toll mounted to an estimated 3000 people, plus an unknown number of prostitutes kept under lock and key. More than a third of the 300,000 people living in the city at the time were left homeless. Thousands left San Francisco for good, convinced its glory days were over.

Built in 1907, soon after the earthquake, the Great American Music Hall still shows the determined flamboyance of post-earthquake San Francisco, with carved gilt decor recalling the city's Gold Rush heyday and scantily clad frescoed figures hinting at other possible backstage entertainments.

THE SHOW MUST GO ON

San Francisco had learned one thing in 50 years of booms and busts: how to stage a comeback. San Francisco was brought back to its feet not by City Hall, but by die-hard entertainers. All but one of the city's 20 historic theaters had been completely destroyed by the earthquake and fire, and theater tents were soon set up amid the rubble. The smoke wafting across makeshift stages wasn't a special effect when the surviving entertainers began marathon performances to keep the city's spirits up – and it wasn't hard to bring down the house when buildings were

EARTHQUAKE

1915	1927	1934	1937
Postquake San Francisco hosts the Panama–Pacific International Exposition. The city cements its reputation as showplace for new technology, outlandish ideas and the arts.	After a year of tinkering, 21-year-old Philo Farnsworth transmits the first successful TV broadcast of...a straight line.	A West Coast longshoremen's strike ends with 34 strikers and sympathizers shot by police. A mass funeral and citywide strike follow; longshoremen win historic concessions.	After four years of dangerous labor in the treacherous Pacific tides, the Golden Gate Bridge is complete.

still collapsing all around them. But in the midst of utter devastation, San Francisco hummed along, and the city was rebuilt at an astounding rate of 15 buildings a day.

In a show of popular priorities, San Francisco's theaters were rebuilt long before City Hall's grandiose Civic Center was completed. Most of the Barbary Coast had gone up in flames (with the notable, highly flammable exception of Hotaling's whiskey warehouse), so the theater scene and most of its red-light entourage decamped to the Tenderloin, where it remains. San Francisco's more highbrow entertainments of opera and classical music began a glorious second act, despite the fact that the world's most famous tenor, Enrico Caruso, vowed never to return to the city after the quake jolted him out of bed at the Palace Hotel. Soprano Luisa Tetrazzini ditched New York's Metropolitan Opera to return to San Francisco, and gave a free performance at Lotta's Fountain for an audience of 250,000 – virtually every last living man, woman and child in San Francisco.

But San Francisco's greatest comeback performance was the 1915 Panama–Pacific International Exposition, held in celebration of the completion of the Panama Canal. Earthquake rubble was used to fill 635 marshy acres of the Marina, where famous architects built elaborate pavilions showcasing San Francisco's Pacific Rim connections, exotic foods and forward thinking. Crowds gasped at pavilions displaying the latest, greatest inventions, including the world's first steam locomotive, a color printing press and a prototype personal typewriter (at 14 tons, a far cry from a laptop). When the party ended, Bernard Maybeck's Palace of Fine Arts was the one temporary exhibit San Franciscans couldn't bear to see torn down. The structure was recast in concrete in the 1960s and in the spirit of the expo it now hosts the Exploratorium, San Francisco's hands-on museum of weird science.

THE LEFT COAST

With the fanfare of the Panama expo and new piers replacing the ragged Barbary Coast, San Francisco soon became the major West Coast port, but the morning lineup at the docks told another story. Only longshoremen known for toughness, speed and readiness to pay bribes were hired to unload heavy cargo onto perilously slippery docks from 8am to midnight – all for pay that hardly put dinner on the table. On May 9, 1934, longshoremen gathered down by the piers and, one by one, refused work.

As shiploads of food spoiled dockside in the summer sun, shipping companies frantically scoured first the bay, then ports all along the West Coast for substitute dockworkers. No one was available: San Francisco's longshoremen had coordinated their strikes with 35,000 work-

February 1942	1957
Executive Order 9066 mandates internment of 120,000 Japanese Americans. The Japanese American Citizens League files civil rights claims.	City Lights wins a landmark ruling against book banning over the publication of Allen Ginsberg's *Howl*, and free speech and free spirits enjoy a reprieve from McCarthyism.

City Lights (p112), North Beach

DIANA MAYFIELD / LONELY PLANET IMAGES ©

ers all along the West Coast. They held out for an unprecedented 83 days, until police, hired guns and finally the National Guard forcibly ended the strike, killing two longshoremen. In the ensuing riots, 34 strikers and sympathizers were shot and another 40 beaten.

In a silent funeral procession that marched down Market St on July 9, thousands of San Franciscans stood shoulder to shoulder with longshoremen. Word of a general strike spread throughout the city, and for four days even San Francisco's nightclubs and movie palaces were closed in solidarity and draped in black. The ship owners met the longshoremen's demands, cementing San Francisco's reputation as the organizing headquarters of the 'Left Coast.'

When WWII brought a shipbuilding boom to town, women and 40,000 African American arrivals claimed key roles in San Francisco's workforce. But with misplaced anxiety about possible attacks from the Pacific, Japanese San Franciscans became convenient targets for public animosity. Two months after the attack on Pearl Harbor, President Franklin Delano Roosevelt signed Executive Order 9066 ordering the relocation of 120,000 Japanese Americans to internment camps. The San Francisco–based Japanese American Citizens League (JACL) immediately challenged the grounds for internment, and it lobbied tirelessly for more than 40 years to overturn Executive Order 9066, gain symbolic reparations for internees, and restore the community's standing with a formal letter of apology signed by President George HW Bush in 1988. By setting key legal precedents from the 1940s onward, JACL paved the way for the 1964 Civil Rights Act.

BEATS: FREE SPEECH, FREE SPIRITS

Members of the armed services dismissed from service for homosexuality and other 'subversive' behavior during WWII were discharged onto the streets of San Francisco, as if that would teach them a lesson. Instead, the new arrivals found themselves at home in the low-rent, laissez-faire neighborhoods of North Beach and the Haight. So when the rest of the country took a sharp right turn with McCarthyism in the 1950s, rebels and romantics headed for San Francisco – including one Jack Kerouac. By the time *On the Road* was published in 1957 chronicling his westward journey, the motley crowd of writers, artists, dreamers and unclassifiable characters Kerouac called 'the mad ones' had found their way to like-minded San Francisco.

San Francisco didn't always take kindly to the nonconformists derisively referred to in the press as 'beatniks,' and police and poets were increasingly at odds on the streets of North Beach. Officers tried to fine

Top 5 for Beats

City Lights (North Beach)

Beat Museum (North Beach)

Vesuvio (North Beach)

Li Po (Chinatown)

Bob Kaufman Alley (North Beach)

1959	January 21–23, 1966	October 1966	January 14, 1967
Mayor George Christopher authorizes crackdowns on cruising areas and gay bars and starts a blacklist of gay citizens.	The Trips Festival is organized by techno-futurist Stewart Brand, and features author Ken Kesey, the Grateful Dead, Janis Joplin, Native American activists and Hells Angels.	In Oakland, Huey Newton and Bobby Seale found the Black Panther Party for Self-Defense, a black-power group that demanded 'Land, Bread, Housing, Education, Clothing, Justice and Peace.'	The Summer of Love kicks off with the Human Be-In, with draft cards used as rolling papers, free Grateful Dead performances and Allen Ginsberg naked as usual.

'beatnik chicks' for wearing sandals, only to be mercilessly taunted in verse by the self-styled African American Jewish anarchist and street-corner poet Bob Kaufman. Poet Lawrence Ferlinghetti and manager Shigeyoshi Murao of City Lights were arrested for 'willfully and lewdly' printing Allen Ginsberg's magnificent, incendiary epic poem *Howl*. But artistic freedom prevailed in 1957, when City Lights won its landmark ruling against book banning.

The kindred Beat spirits Ginsberg described in *Howl* as 'angel-headed hipsters burning for the ancient heavenly connection' experimented with art, radical politics, marijuana and one another, flouting 1950s social-climbing conventions and defying Senator Joe McCarthy's alarmist call to weed out 'communists in our midst.' When McCarthy's House Un-American Activities Committee (HUAC) convened for the fourth time in San Francisco in 1960 to expose alleged communists, UC Berkeley students organized a disruptive, sing-along sit-in at City Hall. After police turned fire hoses on the protesters, thousands of San Franciscans rallied, and HUAC split town, never to return. It was official: the '60s had begun.

On November 20, 1969, 79 Native American activists and their families defied Coast Guard blockades to symbolically reclaim Alcatraz as native land. Hundreds of supporters joined the protest, until ousted by FBI raids on June 11, 1971. Public support for protesters strengthened self-rule for Native territories, signed into law by Richard Nixon.

PROTEST

FLOWER POWER

San Francisco would continue to be a testing ground for freedom of expression in the years to come, as comedian Lenny Bruce uttered the F-word on stage and burlesque dancer Carol Doda bared it all for titillated audiences in North Beach clubs. But neither jokes nor striptease would pop the last button of conventional morality in San Francisco – no, that was a job for the CIA. In a pronounced lapse in screening judgment, the CIA hired local writer Ken Kesey to test psychoactive drugs intended to create the ultimate soldier. Instead, they unwittingly inspired Kesey to write the novel *One Flew Over the Cuckoo's Nest,* drive psychedelic busloads of Merry Pranksters across country, and introduce San Francisco to LSD and the Grateful Dead at the legendary Acid Tests.

After the Civil Rights movement anything seemed possible, and for a while it seemed that the freaky force of free thinking would stop the unpopular Vietnam War. At the January 14, 1967 Human Be-In in Golden Gate Park, trip-master Timothy Leary urged a crowd of 20,000 to dream a new American dream and 'turn on, tune in, drop out.' Free music rang out in the streets, free food was provided by the Diggers and LSD by Owsley Stanley, free crash pads were found all over the Haight, and free love transpired on some very dubious free mattresses. For the duration of the Summer of Love – weeks, months, even a year, depending on who you talk to and how stoned they were at the time – it seemed possible to make love, not war.

1969	November 20, 1969	December 6, 1969	April 16–17, 1977
The first computer link is established between Stanford Research Institute and UCLA via ARPANET. When an unsolicited group message is sent across the fledgling network, spam is born.	Native American activists reclaim the abandoned island of Alcatraz as reparation for broken treaties. The occupation lasts 19 months, until FBI agents forcibly oust the activists.	A free concert at Altamont Speedway goes tragically wrong when Hells Angels on bodyguard duty turn on the performers and audience. Four people are killed.	The Apple II is introduced in SF at the first West Coast Computer Faire, and stuns the crowd with its computing speed (1MHz) – current computers run 2000 to 3000 times faster.

But a chill soon settled over San Francisco, and for once it wasn't the afternoon fog. Civil rights hero Martin Luther King Jr was assassinated on April 8, 1968, followed by the fatal shooting of Robert Kennedy on June 5, right after he'd won California's presidential primary. Radicals worldwide called for revolution, and separatist groups like Oakland's Black Panther Party for Self-Defense took up arms. Meanwhile, recreational drug-taking was turning into a thankless career for many, a distinct itch in the nether regions was making the rounds, and still more busloads of teenage runaways were arriving in the ill-equipped, wigged-out Haight. The Haight Ashbury Free Clinic (p296) helped with the rehabbing and the itching, but the disillusionment seemed incurable when Hell's Angels beat protestors in Berkeley and turned on the crowd at a free Rolling Stones concert at Altamont.

Many idealists headed 'back to the land' in the bucolic North Bay, jumpstarting California's organic farm movement. A dark streak emerged among those who remained, including young Charles Manson, the Symbionese Liberation Army (better known post-1974 as Patty Hearst's kidnappers) and an evangelical egomaniac named Jim Jones, who would obligate 900 followers to commit mass suicide in 1978. By the time Be-In LSD supplier Owsley Stanley was released from a three-year jail term in 1970, the party seemed to be over. But in the Castro, it was just getting started.

PRIDE

By the 1970s, San Francisco's gay community was fed up with police raids, done with hetero Haight squats and ready for music with an actual beat. In 1959, after an opponent accused then-mayor George Christopher of allowing San Francisco to become 'the national headquarters of the organized homosexuals,' Christopher authorized crackdowns on gay bars and started a blacklist of gay citizens.

Never one to be harassed or upstaged, WWII veteran and drag star José Sarria became the first openly gay man to run for public office in 1962, on a mayoral platform to end police harassment of gay San Franciscans. He won 5600 votes. Undaunted, he declared himself Absolute Empress of San Francisco, the widow and true heir of Emperor Norton. When local media echoed the Empress' criticism of the continuing raids, the crackdown stopped – a feat not achieved for years elsewhere, until New York's 1969 Stonewall protests.

By the mid-1970s, the rainbow flag was flying high over gay businesses and homes in the out-and-proud Castro, and the sexual revolution was in full swing at gay clubs and bathhouses on Polk St and South

Best Ways to Revive the Summer of Love

HISTORY PRIDE

Give a free concert on Haight St, or give freely to any local nonprofit

Commune with nature in Golden Gate Park

Walk on the wild side of hippie history on the Haight Flashback walking tour

Read '60s manifestos at Bound Together Anarchist Book Collective

Write your own manifesto, fuelled by soy lattes at Coffee to the People

1977	November 18, 1978	1981	1989
Harvey Milk becomes the first openly gay man elected to US public office. Milk sponsors a gay-rights bill and trend-setting 'pooper-scooper' ordinance before his murder by Dan White.	After moving his People's Temple from SF to Guyana, cult leader Jim Jones orders the murders of Congressman Leo Ryan and four journalists and mass suicide of 900 followers.	The first cases of AIDS are identified. The disease has since taken 30 million lives, but early intervention in SF instituted key prevention measures and established global treatment standards.	Hundreds of sea lions haul out on the yacht slips near Pier 39; state law and wildlife officials grant them squatters' rights, and the beach bums become San Francisco mascots.

of Market (SoMa). Gay San Francisco had arrived; now all it needed was an elected representative.

The Castro was triumphant when Castro camera-store owner Harvey Milk was elected city Supervisor, becoming the nation's first openly gay elected official – but as Milk himself predicted, his time in office would be cut short by an act of extremist violence. Dan White, a washed-up politician hyped on Hostess Twinkies, fatally shot Milk and then-mayor George Moscone in 1978. The charge was reduced to manslaughter due to the infamous 'Twinkie Defense' faulting the ultrasweet junk food, sparking an outpouring of public outrage dubbed the 'White Riot.' But White was deeply disturbed and committed suicide a year after his 1984 release.

By then San Francisco had other matters weighing heavily on its mind. A strange illness began to appear in local hospitals, and it seemed to be hitting the gay community especially hard. The first cases of AIDS reported in 1981 were initially referred to as GRID (Gay-Related Immune Deficiency) and a social stigma became attached to the virus. But San Francisco health providers and gay activists rallied to establish global standards for care and prevention, with vital early HIV/AIDS health initiatives funded not through federal agencies, but with tireless local fundraising efforts. Yet despite ground-breaking progress on treatment for HIV/AIDS, unmarried partners had no legal standing to make lifesaving medical decisions.

Civil rights organizations, religious institutions and GLBT organizations increasingly popped the question: why couldn't same-sex couples get married too? Early backing came from the Japanese American Citizens League, which in 1994 publicly endorsed marriage for same-sex couples as a civil right. Just 45 days into his term in office, San Francisco mayor Gavin Newsom authorized same-sex weddings in San Francisco, in time for Valentine's Day, 2004. The first couple to be married were Phyllis Lyon and Del Martin, a San Francisco couple who had spent 52 years together. California courts ultimately voided theirs and 4036 other San Francisco same-sex marriage contracts, but Lyon and Martin weren't dissuaded: they married again on June 18, 2008, with Mayor Newsom personally officiating. Martin passed away in August at age 83, her wife by her side.

In November 2008, California voters passed Proposition 8, asserting that only marriages between a man and a woman would be legally recognized. Although California courts struck down the 2008 law as unconstitutional in 2010, appeals are still pending.

Best Ways to Show Gay Pride

Join the Pride Parade

Get introduced to fabulous, fearless pioneers at GLBT Historical Society

Peruse petitions at Human Rights Campaign

Shop until there's a cure at AIDS fundraising boutique Under One Roof

Come out and play in the Mission, Castro and SoMa

October 17, 1989

The Loma Prieta earthquake hits 6.9 on the Richter scale and a freeway in SF and a Bay Bridge section collapse in 15 seconds, killing 41. Bridge repairs remain incomplete.

March 10, 2000

After the NASDAQ index peaks at double its value a year earlier, the dot-com bubble pops and share prices drop dramatically. The 'dot-bomb' closes businesses across SF within a month.

DAVID RYAN / LONELY PLANET IMAGES ©

Collapsed buildings after the 1989 earthquake, the Marina District

SAN FRANCISCO 3.0

Industry dwindled steadily in San Francisco after WWII, as Oakland's port accommodated container ships and the Presidio's military presence tapered off. But onetime military tech contractors found work in a stretch of scrappy tech firms south of San Francisco, an area known today as Silicon Valley. When a company based in a South Bay garage called Hewlett-Packard introduced the 9100A 'computing genie' in 1968, a generation of unconventional thinkers and tinkerers took note.

Ads breathlessly gushed that Hewlett-Packard's 'light' (40lb) machine could 'take on roots of a fifth-degree polynomial, Bessel functions, elliptic integrals and regression analysis' – all for the low, low price of $4,900 (about $29,000 today). Consumers didn't know what to do with such a computer, until its potential was explained in simple terms by Stewart Brand, an LSD tester for the CIA with Ken Kesey and organizer of the first Trips Festival in 1966. In his 1969 *Whole Earth Catalog,* Brand reasoned that the technology governments used to run countries could empower ordinary people. That same year, University of California, Los Angeles, professor Len Kleinrock sent the first rudimentary email from a computer in Los Angeles to another at Stanford. The message he typed was 'L,' then 'O,' then 'G' – at which point the computer crashed.

The next wave of California techies was determined to create a personal computer that could compute and communicate without crashing. When 21-year-old Steve Jobs and Steve Wozniak introduced the Apple II at San Francisco's West Coast Computer Faire in 1977, techies were abuzz about the memory (4KB of RAM!) and the microprocessor speed (1MHz!). The Mac II originally retailed for the equivalent today of $4300, or for 48KB of RAM, more than twice that amount – a staggering investment for what seemed like a glorified calculator/typewriter. Even if these computers could talk to one another, pundits reasoned, what would they talk about?

Billions of web pages later, it turns out computers had plenty to say. By the mid-1990s an entire dot-com industry boomed in SoMa warehouses, as start-up ventures rushed to put news, politics, fashion and, yes, sex online. But when venture capital funding dried up, multimillion-dollar sites shriveled into online oblivion. The paper fortunes of the dot-com boom disappeared on one nasty NASDAQ-plummeting day, March 10, 2000, leaving San Francisco service-sector employees and 26-year-old vice-presidents alike without any immediate job prospects. City dot-com revenues vanished; a 1999 FBI probe revealed that a sizable windfall ended up in the pockets of real-estate developers.

But true to shape-shifting form, San Francisco has morphed again with search engines Google and Yahoo based south of the city, plus Web

Top 5 for Weird Technology

Exploratorium (the Presidio)

Musée Mécanique (Fisherman's Wharf)

Audium (Japantown)

SFMOMA (SoMa)

Children's Creativity Museum (SoMa)

2003	2004	February 12, 2004	November 4, 2008
Republican Arnold Schwarzenegger is elected governor of California. Schwarzenegger breaks party ranks on environmental issues and wins 2007 reelection.	Google's IPO raises a historic $1.67 billion at $85 per share. In 2011 the company's worth was valued at $174 billion.	Defying California's same-sex marriage ban, SF mayor Gavin Newsom licenses 4037 same-sex marriages. Courts declare the marriages void, but the civil rights challenge stands.	California voters approve Proposition 8. Opponents of the measure included President Obama, Amnesty International, *San Francisco Chronicle,* Apple, Google and a majority of SF voters.

2.0 social media ventures like San Francisco–based Twitter and Yelp and Palo Alto's Facebook. Recession has slowed the flow of software venture capital, but in shiny new glass towers in Mission Bay, biotech start-ups are hanging out their shingles.

Biotech is nothing new here: in 1976, an upstart company called Genentech was founded over beer at a San Francisco bar, then got to work cloning human insulin and introducing the hepatitis B vaccine. California voters approved a $3 billion bond measure in 2004 for stem cell research, and by 2008, California had become the biggest funder of stem cell research, with SoMa's Mission Bay as its designated headquarters. With the US in recession, it seems impossible that San Francisco could initiate another boom – but if history is any indication, the impossible is almost certain to happen in San Francisco.

2010	2010	2013	2013
California courts declare Proposition 8 unconstitutional due to equal rights protections, but a stay prevents further same-sex marriages pending appeal.	The San Francisco Giants win the World Series title for the first time since 1954. 'Fear the Beard,' 'Rally Thong' and 'Got Heeem' enter the San Francisco lexicon.	The America's Cup sailing race embarks from San Francisco, at a $300 million estimated cost to the city.	The eastern span of the Bay Bridge is due for completion, including the final seismic retrofit after the 1989 earthquake and commuter bike lanes.

Local Cuisine & Drinks

Two secret ingredients have transformed this small city into a global culinary capitol: dirt and competition. Almost anything grows in the fertile farmland around San Francisco, and rocky hillsides yield fine wines in nearby Sonoma and Napa. Add Pacific seafood and coastal pasture-raised meats, and it seems like a no-fail recipe for a feast. But chefs need to work even harder to stand out in San Francisco, where everyone has access to top-notch ingredients, and there's about one restaurant for every 227 people – more than anywhere else in the USA, and 50% more than New York.

Call them spoiled, but San Franciscans expect inventive, sustainable, tasty food at reasonable prices. Anything less, and SF's tech-savvy foodies will tweet, blog or Yelp their distress. No wonder many San Francisco restaurant menus are so heavily footnoted, crediting organic farms, sustainable fish purveyors, even wild food foragers. Mock if you must, but people have been known to move to SF for the food (ahem).

HISTORY

Before San Francisco became part of the US it belonged to Mexico, which established NorCal ranching and farming traditions. Early arrivals to California's Gold Rush came from around the Pacific Rim, and since most were men not accustomed to cooking for themselves, they relied on makeshift restaurants. SF's cross-cultural cravings began with '49er favorites: Chinese chow mein, local oysters and French wines. Between hot meals, miners survived on chocolate bars, invented in San Francisco by Domingo Ghirardelli.

Fishing and farming brought fresh ingredients and new dishes to San Francisco. Before the first Italian restaurant in the USA opened in 1886 at North Beach, Italian fishermen cooked up vats of cioppino (seafood stew) dockside. The 1942–64 US Bracero Program importing Mexican agricultural labor brought local variations on Mexican staples, including megameals wrapped in flour tortillas known as burritos.

After the 1960s, many disillusioned idealists concluded that the revolution was not about to be delivered on a platter – but chef Alice Waters thought otherwise. In 1971 she opened Chez Panisse in a converted house in Berkeley, with the then-radical notion of highlighting the ultrafresh flavors of the Bay Area's seasonal, sustainably produced bounty – and diners tasted the difference for themselves. Today, Waters' call for good, clean, fair food has become a worldwide Slow Food manifesto and a rallying call for Bay Area chefs like Traci Des Jardins.

FOOD SPECIALTIES

California Cuisine

What other cities might call fusion or California cuisine, San Francisco just calls dinner. There's nothing fussy or forced about mixing cuisines here – after 150 years, it's become a reflex. Dishes are prepared with a light touch, highlighting ingredients grown locally with San Francisco's worldly, adventurous eaters in mind: Vietnamese garlic grass, heirloom purple beef-heart tomatoes, Blenheim apricots. But don't be fooled into

---

Top 5 Dim Sum

City View
(Chinatown)

Chairman Bao
food truck

Ton Kiang
Restaurant
(the Richmond)

San Tung
(the Sunset)

Heaven's Dog
(SoMa)

Top 5 for Local & Sustainable Seafood

Tataki
(Pacific Heights)

Benu (SoMa)

Jardinière
(Hayes Valley)

Hog Island Oyster
Company
(Ferry Building)

Ichi Sushi
(the Misson)

TRACI DES JARDINS: CHEF & RESTAURATEUR

What's so special about the food here? You'll notice a lot of Bay Area restaurants proudly name their producers on menus, like we do (at Jardinière; p183). Sometimes farmers introduce chefs to new flavors; sometimes we see an ingredient on our travels we ask them to grow. I grew up on a farm, and I really appreciate that creative partnership with producers.

With such abundance, why the focus on sustainability? In the past five years, a growing awareness among consumers has driven the market for organics. If people are paying attention to what they eat at home, they're going to bring that awareness into restaurants, and demand different choices: organics, fair-trade products, free-range meats, seafood that's not at risk. This makes our collaboration with producers even more important.

What's new on the SF menu? There's been an evolution in the Bay Area style of cooking around local, seasonal produce that Alice (Waters, of Chez Panisse, p209) started. Our food has evolved to be much more simple, with ingredients starring on the plate – it's more of the Italian school of combining five or six ingredients perfectly, instead of an overly layered French style.

Unusual items spotted at local farmers markets? Lately I've seen a lot of Jerusalem artichokes, gem lettuces and all kinds of heirloom carrots – red, white and thumb carrots. We're lucky that almost anything can grow in California, and because there's such a high demand for specialties, some items that used to be hard to find are now really easy to come by.

Where do you take foodie friends? The Ferry Building (p86), followed by a trip to the MH de Young Museum (p193) and Golden Gate Park and Crissy Field (p60) for spectacular views of the Golden Gate Bridge (p59).

Traci Des Jardins is a James Beard Award–winning chef and a restaurateur at Jardinière (p183).

thinking it's easy. A single dish may use knife skills learned from Asian neighbors and cooking techniques borrowed from the Mediterranean, where the climate and soil are similar to the Bay Area's.

Ethnic Comfort Food

Since one out of three San Franciscans is born overseas, SF's go-to comfort foods aren't just burgers and pizza – though you'll find plenty of those – but *pho* (Vietnamese noodles), tandoori chicken, *kim chee* (Korean fermented vegetables), and above all, dim sum and burritos. Anyone attempting to leave San Francisco without trying these last two favorites should be turned back at the airport for their own good – though once you try them, you might not want to leave.

Dim sum is Cantonese for what's known in Mandarin as *xiao che* (small eats); some also call it *yum cha* (drink tea), and there are dozens of places in San Francisco where you'll call it delicious. Waitstaff roll carts past your table with steaming baskets of dumplings, platters of garlicky sautéed greens and, finally, plates of sweet crispy sesame balls and creamy egg custard.

The most hotly debated local dish is the SF burrito, which is nothing like imposters you'll find elsewhere. San Franciscans have religious convictions about correct fillings: beans (pinto, black or, heaven help you, refried), meats (grilled, stewed or, if the gods are smiling upon you, fried pork carnitas) and salsas (tomato-onion *pico de gallo,* tangy green tomatillo or devilishly smoky mesquite). This is all loaded onto a flour tortilla and rolled into a foodstuff the approximate length and girth of a forearm. No one finishes, but leftovers rival cold pizza as SF's guilty-pleasure breakfast.

Seafood

The Pacific offers a haul of seafood to San Francisco diners, but there's trouble in those waters: some species have been overfished, and their extinction could throw the local aquaculture off balance. Monterey Bay Aquarium has been monitoring local fish stock for decades, and its Seafood Watch program helps diners identify best options, good choices and items to avoid on local seafood menus – find out which of your seafood favorites are on the best list at www.montereybayaquarium.org/cr/seafoodwatch.aspx. Delicious, sustainable, local seafood choices found almost year-round include wild Dungeness crab, locally farmed oysters and locally farmed caviar.

Sourdough Bread

San Francisco is famous for its sourdough bread, although the pucker-inducing aftertaste can be an acquired taste. The most famous 'mother dough' in town dates back to 1849, when baker Isidore Boudin hit on a combination of wild yeast and bacteria that's been kept alive ever since. You'll see people eating sourdough bowls filled with clam chowder down at Fisherman's Wharf, but be warned: the combination of starchy, salty glop, crusty carbs and the very occasional clam has yet to be proven digestible.

Vegetarian & Vegan Food

To all you beleaguered vegetarians, accustomed to eating out at places where the only non-animal dish is some unspeakable vegetarian lasagna: you're in San Francisco now. While fine dining chefs elsewhere stake their reputations on French truffle-strewn steaks, California-grown fruits and vegetables are not side dishes to Bay Area chefs, but tasting-menu highlights. On the cheaper side, vegetarian options abound at downtown lunch spots, taquerias, pizzerias, Japanese noodle joints, Thai restaurants, Ethiopian eateries and Middle Eastern places, plus bakeries and groceries. With the most farmers markets of any metropolitan area in the US (20 and counting), you're not about to run out of veggie options anytime soon.

DRINK SPECIALTIES

Wine

Wine bars are the newest, oldest trend on the SF drinking scene. Wine has been the local drink ever since Mission Solano was established in Sonoma with acres of vineyards, more than strictly necessary for communion wine. While Gold Rush miners who struck it rich splashed out for imported champagne at SF bars, others found solace in beverages from Napa and Sonoma vineyards. Some local vines survived federal scrutiny during Prohibition, on the grounds that the grapes were needed for sacramental wines back east – a bootlegging bonanza that kept SF speakeasies well supplied.

Drinking snobbery is reversed in SF: wine drinkers are always game for a glass of something local and good times, while beer drinkers fuss over their monk-brewed triple Belgians and debate relative hoppiness levels. It's not that SF wine drinkers are always so easy to please – the local selection's just that good. Many of the USA's best wines are produced within two hours of the city, including excellent cabernet, zinfandel, syrah, pinot noir, rose of pinot noir, viognier, chardonnay, sauvignon blanc and sparkling wines.

LOCAL CUISINE & DRINKS DRINK SPECIALTIES

Grain alcohols from Korea and Japan (*soju* and sake, respectively) are key mixers in SF bars, partly because they're not yet restricted by SF liquor license laws. But be warned: more than two sake cocktails at Noc Noc in the Haight will knock-knock you off your stool.

Top 5 Wine Bars

RN74 (SoMa)

Terroir Natural Wine Merchant (SoMa)

Barrique (Financial District)

Hôtel Biron (Hayes Valley)

Vinyl Wine Bar (the Haight)

VIP bottle service and Kristal are so LA. There's no reason to get fancy just to get a decent glass of wine in SF, where some bars just roll out the barrels from local wineries and pour the good stuff straight from the tap. At restaurants, many wine lists outsize the food menu and feature cult wines that aren't distributed outside California. Consult your sommelier to help you find daring parings by the glass or bottle, or take tips from Benu's acclaimed sommelier Yoon Ha (p147).

Beer

Blowing off steam took on new meaning during the Gold Rush, when entrepreneurs trying to keep up with the demand for drink started brewing beer at higher temperatures, like ales. The result was a full, rich flavor and such powerful effervescence that when a keg was tapped, a mist would rise like steam. The much-beloved, local Anchor Brewing Company has made its signature Anchor Steam amber ale this way, using copper distilling equipment since 1896. Other favorite local brews include Trumer Pils, and Speakeasy and Boont Amber ales, plus locally microbrewed seasonal beers and ales. Head to the City Beer Store & Tasting Room for a drinkable education, and leave a tipsy connoisseur.

'Researched' Cocktails

The highest honorific for a bartender in San Francisco isn't mixologist (too technical) or artisan (too medieval), but drink historian. Cocktails have appeared on San Francisco happy hour menus since its Barbary Coast days, when they were used to sedate sailors and shanghai them onto outbound ships. Now bartenders are researching old recipes and reviving SF traditions: pouring absinthe from fountains into cordial glasses of Sazerac, including traditional foamy egg whites in Pisco sours as though no one had ever heard of veganism or salmonella, and apparently still trying to knock sailors cold with combinations of tawny port and Nicaraguan rum.

Every self-respecting SF bartender holds strong opinions on the martini, first mentioned in an 1887 bartending guide by Professor Jerry Thomas. Legend has it that the martini was invented when a boozehound walked into an SF bar and demanded something to tide him over until he reached Martinez across the bay. The original was made with vermouth, gin, bitters, lemon, maraschino cherry and ice, though by the 1950s the recipe was reduced to gin with vermouth vapors and an olive or a twist. Today SF's drink historians offer variations on the original, as well as the Sinatra Rat Pack version.

Irish coffee takes the chill off foggy SF nights, and the Buena Vista Cafe is often mistakenly credited with inventing this sweet concoction of whisky, coffee and cream. Even more deliciously inauthentic is the Italian version at Tosca Cafe, made with espresso to leave drinkers slightly toasted and oddly alert.

Top 5 for Researched Cocktails

....

Alembic
(the Haight)

....

Bar Agricole
(SoMa)

....

Smuggler's Cove
(Hayes Valley)

....

Bourbon & Branch
(the Tenderloin)

....

Rickhouse
(Union Square)

Literary San Francisco

You can hardly throw a pebble without hitting a writer in San Francisco, though it might get you cursed in verse. San Francisco has more writers than any other US city and hoards three times as many library books as the national average. The truth of San Francisco is stranger than its fiction: where else could poetry fight the law and win? Yet that's exactly what happened when Beat poet Lawrence Ferlinghetti was arrested for publishing Allen Ginsberg's *Howl and Other Poems*. The 1957 case was a landmark ruling for free speech, and though it may seem anachronistic here in the capitol of new technology, San Franciscans continue to buy more books per capita than other US cities.

REQUIRED READING

Any self-respecting SF bookshelf hosts plenty of poetry (Beat authors obligatory), a graphic novel, nonfiction essays about the San Francisco scene, and at least one novel by a Bay Area author.

Poetry

San Francisco's Kenneth Rexroth popularized haiku here back in the 1950s, and San Franciscans still enjoy nothing more than a few well-chosen words. When the city has you waxing poetic, hit an open mic in the Mission.

Key titles:

➡ *Howl and Other Poems* (Allen Ginsberg) Each line of Ginsberg's epic title poem is an ecstatic improvised mantra, chronicling the waking dreams of the generation that rejected postwar conformity.

➡ *Time and Materials* (Robert Hass) These Pulitzer Prize–winning poems by the Berkeley-based US poet laureate don't seem to have been written so much as released onto the page, where every word finds its wings.

➡ *A Coney Island of the Mind* (Lawrence Ferlinghetti) This slim 1958 collection by San Francisco's poet laureate is an indispensable doorstop for the imagination, letting fresh air and ideas circulate.

Fiction

Many San Franciscans seem like characters in a novel, and after a few days here, you'll swear you've seen Armistead Maupin's corn-fed Castro newbies, Dashiell Hammett's dangerous redheads, and Amy Tan's American-born daughters explaining slang to Chinese-speaking moms.

Key titles:

➡ *Tales of the City* (Armistead Maupin) The 1976 *San Francisco Chronicle* serial follows true San Francisco characters: pot-growing landladies of mystery, ever-hopeful Castro club-goers and wide-eyed Midwestern arrivals.

➡ *The Man in the High Castle* (Philip K Dick) The bestselling Berkeley sci-fi writer presents the ultimate what-if scenario: imagine San Francisco c 1962 if Japan and Nazi Germany had won WWII.

➡ *The Joy Luck Club* (Amy Tan) The stories of four Chinese-born women and their American-born daughters are woven into a textured history of immigration and aspiration in San Francisco's Chinatown.

➡ *The Maltese Falcon* (Dashiell Hammett) In this classic noir novel, private eye Sam Spade risks his reputation on a case involving an elusive redhead, a gold statuette, the Holy Roman Empire and an unholy cast of thugs.

Best for Readings

City Lights
(North Beach)

Booksmith
(the Haight)

San Francisco Main Library
(Civic Center)

City Arts & Lectures
(Civic Center)

Omnivore
(Noe Valley)

Best for Comics & Graphic Novels

Cartoon Art Museum gift shop
(SoMa)

Isotope (Hayes Valley)

Kinokuniya Books & Stationery
(Japantown)

Neon Monster
(Noe Valley)

Green Apple Books
(the Richmond)

Nonfiction & Memoir

People-watching rivals reading as a preferred San Francisco pastime, and close observation of antics that would seem bizarre elsewhere pays off in stranger-than-fiction nonfiction – hence Hunter S Thompson's gonzo journalism and Joan Didion's core-shaking truth-telling.

Key titles:

➡ *Slouching Towards Bethlehem* (Joan Didion) Like hot sun through San Francisco fog, Didion's 1968 essays burn through the hippie haze to reveal glassy-eyed teenagers adrift in the Summer of Love.

➡ *On the Road* (Jack Kerouac) The book Kerouac banged out on one long scroll of paper in a San Francisco attic over a couple of sleepless months of 1951 shook America awake.

➡ *San Francisco Stories: Great Writers on the City* (edited by John Miller) One hundred and fifty years of San Francisco impressions, including Jack London's 1906 earthquake reports and Jack Kerouac's attempts to hold a Downtown day job.

➡ *Hell's Angels: A Strange and Terrible Saga* (Hunter S Thompson) This spare-no-details account of the outlaw Bay Area motorcycle club invented gonzo journalism and scandalized the nation.

➡ *The Electric Kool-Aid Acid Test* (Tom Wolfe) His florid style seems dated, but Wolfe had extraordinary presence of mind to capture the '60s with Ken Kesey, the Merry Pranksters, the Grateful Dead and Hell's Angels.

➡ *Martin Eden* (Jack London) San Francisco's first literary star started out as the Prince of the Oyster Pirates, a waterfront bad boy who got by on his wits in this semi-autobiographical account.

Graphic Novels

Ambrose Bierce and Mark Twain set the San Francisco standard for sardonic wit, but recently Bay Area graphic novelists like R Crumb and Daniel Clowes have added a twist to this tradition with finely drawn, deadpan behavioral studies. For more, don't miss the Cartoon Art Museum.

Key titles:

➡ *Ghost World* (Daniel Clowes) The Oakland-based graphic novelist's sleeper hit follows recent high-school grads Enid and Rebecca as they make plans, make do, grow up and grow apart.

➡ *Long Tail Kitty* (Lark Pien) San Francisco cartoonist/architect Pien brings the poetry of *The Little Prince* and the charm of Hayao Miyazaki's *Spirited Away* to her tales of a heavenly cat.

➡ *American Born Chinese* (Gene Yang) A young-adult graphic novel, combining Monkey King fables with teenage stories of assimilation and alienation.

Zines

The local zine scene has been the underground mother lode of riveting reading since the '70s brought punk, a DIY ethic and V Vale's groundbreaking *RE/Search* to San Francisco. The most successful local zine of all, McSweeney's, is the doing of Dave Eggers, who achieved first-person fame with *A Heartbreaking Work of Staggering Genius* and generously sunk the proceeds into 826 Valencia, a nonprofit publisher and writing program for teens. McSweeney's also publishes an excellent map of literary San Francisco so you can walk the talk.

Spoken Word

San Francisco's literary tradition doesn't just hang out on bookshelves. Allen Ginsberg's ecstatic readings of *Howl* continue to inspire slam poets at Litquake and Beat authors like Kerouac freed up generations of open-mic monologuists from the tyranny of tales with morals and punctuation.

Best for Zines

San Francisco Main Library Zine Reading Area (Civic Center)

Needles & Pens (the Mission)

826 Valencia (the Mission)

Adobe Books (the Mission)

Bound Together Anarchist Book Collective (the Haight)

Best for Spoken Word

Yerba Buena Center for the Arts (SoMa)

Edinburgh Castle (the Tenderloin)

Make-Out Room (the Mission)

Amnesia (the Mission)

Marsh (the Mission)

Visual Arts

Art explodes from frames and jumps off the pedestal in San Francisco, where murals, street performances and impromptu sidewalk altars flow from alleyways right into galleries. Velvet ropes would only get in the way of SF's enveloping installations and interactive new-media art – often provocative and occasionally off-putting, but hardly ever standoffish.

MEDIA & METHODS

San Francisco has some unfair artistic advantages: it's a photogenic city with a colorful past, with 150-year-old photography and painting traditions to prove it. Respected area art schools keep fresh talent coming, yet SF artists remain streetwise and dreamy, more obsessed with Mission asphalt and Pacific horizons than what's selling in New York and Miami. Homegrown traditions of '50s Beat collage, '60s psychedelia, '70s beautiful-mess punk, '80s graffiti and '90s skater-graphics keep San Francisco's art scene down to earth and deeply rooted. At a time when globalized trends are making art fairs as drearily alike as shopping malls, San Francisco adds a refreshing touch of madness to its artistic methods.

Photography

Oh, that new-fangled technology? Interesting, but it'll never catch on as an artistic medium. The San Francisco Bay Area has heard this refrain a few times over the past 150 years, starting with photography. But Bay Area photographers stood behind their cameras, creating masterworks that put photography on the art-world map.

Pioneering 19th-century photographer Pirkle Jones saw expressive potential in California landscape photography, but it was SF native Ansel Adams' photos of Northern California's sublime wilds and his accounts of photography in Yosemite in the 1940s that would draw legions of camera-clutching visitors to San Francisco. Adams founded Group f/64 with Seattle-based Imogen Cunningham and Edward Weston, who also kept a studio in SF and made frequent visits from his permanent base in nearby Carmel. Instead of using the 19th-century tricks of soft focus and tinting, f/64 favored 'straight' photography – pictures that were matter-of-fact yet evocative, like Weston's famous shot of a single green pepper that looks like two lovers entwined.

Dorothea Lange spent many of her most productive years based in San Francisco, photographing Californians grappling with the hardship of the Great Depression and WWII. While she is best known for her searing photographs of desperate Dust Bowl farmers, such as *Migrant Mother, Nipoma, California, 1935,* her images of Japanese Americans forced to leave their San Francisco homes for WWII internment camps have the aching impact of a body blow. This legacy of cultural critique is kept alive today in the full-color suburban dystopias of Larry Sultan and Todd Hido. Hido's desolate tract homes eerily lit by car taillights look like crime scenes in the making, while Sultan's 'In the Valley' series shows sunny California suburbs serving as backdrops for bored porn stars awaiting their extra-close-ups.

Always fascinated by technical novelty and willing to take a gamble, San Franciscans started collecting photographs avidly in the 19th century. As a result of local interest and key donations from private collectors, San Francisco Museum of Modern Art (SFMOMA) has amassed one of the world's best photography collections – including all the above photographers.

Best for Photography

SFMOMA (SoMa)

MH de Young Museum (Golden Gate Park)

Fraenkel Gallery at 49 Geary (Union Square)

Koch Gallery at 49 Geary (Union Square)

Social Commentary

The 1930s social realist movement brought Mexican muralist Diego Rivera to San Francisco – and with him came bold new approaches to public art. The Depression-era Work Projects Administration (WPA) sponsored several SF muralists, and their larger-than-life figures and leftist leanings are reprised in works by Mission *muralistas* from the 1970s to today (see p133). Sculptor Beniamino Bufano made radical statues in granite and steel, including a tribute to Chinese revolutionary Sun Yat-sen at Chinatown's St Mary's Sq and patron saint of the everyman St Francis of Assisi.

Offsetting all this high-minded revolutionary art is gutsy, irreverent SF satire. In the '70s Tom Marioni scandalized gallery audiences who were expecting highbrow entertainment with performances where he would drink beer, urinate from a ladder and repeat until the galleries closed. Tony Labatt's disco balls dangling from his nether regions pretty much summed up the '70s era of Travolta testosterone, and Mads Lynnerup's vigilant camo-clad surveillance of San Francisco from a cardboard-armored SUV sunroof spoofed post-9/11 'orange alerts.' But political satire is not a passing fad here: San Francisco provocateur Enrique Chagoya serves comic relief for banking-crisis hunger pangs with his Warhol-esque 'Mergers, Acquisitions and Lentils' soup-cans at Electric Works.

Best for Provocation

Catharine Clark Gallery (SoMa)

Electric Works (SoMa)

Luggage Store Gallery (Civic Center)

Yerba Buena Center for the Arts (SoMa)

Intersection for the Arts (the Mission)

Abstract Thinking

Art schools in San Francisco attracted major abstract expressionist talents during the vibrant postwar period, when Clyfford Still, David Park and Elmer Bischoff taught at the San Francisco Art Institute. Still and Park splintered off from antiseptic mainstream abstraction to become leading proponents of the somewhat misleadingly named Bay Area Figurative Art, an elemental style often associated with San Francisco painter Richard Diebenkorn's fractured, color-blocked landscapes and the luminous, slippery figures of Oakland painter Nathan Oliveira.

San Francisco's Wayne Thiebaud tilted Sunset street grids into giddy Bay Area abstract cityscapes, but the abstract artist who made the biggest impact on the San Francisco landscape in terms of sheer scale is Richard Serra, as you can see in the rooftop sculpture garden at SFMOMA. With their massive scale, Serra's spare metal shapes begin to take on other dimensions: a prow of a ship, say, or a Soviet factory second.

Best for Murals

San Francisco Art Institute's Diego Rivera Gallery (Russian Hills)

Coit Tower (North Beach)

Rincon Center (SoMa)

Balmy Alley (the Mission)

Clarion Alley (the Mission)

High Concept, High Craft

San Francisco's peculiar dedication to craft and personal vision can get obsessive. Consider *The Rose,* the legendary painting Beat artist Jay DeFeo began in the 1950s and worked on for eight years, layering it with 2000lb of paint until a hole had to be cut in the wall of her apartment to forklift it out. Ruth Asawa started weaving not with wool but metal in the 1950s, creating intricate sculptures that look like jellyfish within onion domes within mushrooms. But SF's most famous obsessive is Matthew Barney, who was raised in San Francisco and made his definitive debut at SFMOMA with his *Cremaster Cycle* videos. Barney seems to delight in making life and art unnecessarily difficult for himself, choosing Vaseline as his major medium and tethering himself for *Drawing Restraint* – but it's hard to argue with the mesmerizing results.

Despite all the effort involved, many standout Bay Area artworks don't seem labored at all. Anna Von Mertens covers army-cot-like beds with gorgeously discomfiting quilts, stitched with abstract patterns drawn from mushroom cloud explosions and WWII bombing raids. Artists Ann Chamberlain and Ann Hamilton coordinated 200 volunteers to collage an entire wall at the San Francisco Main Library with 50,000 cards from the old card catalog, each card with commentary handwritten in one of a dozen locally spoken languages.

Street Smarts

SF skateboard decks and back-alley garage doors were transformed in the 1990s with meticulous and oddly poignant graphics, dubbed 'Mission School' for their storytelling *muralista* sensibilities and graffiti-tag urgency. The Mission School's professor emeritus was the late Margaret Kilgallen, whose closely observed character studies blended hand-painted street signage, comic-book pathos and a miniaturist's attention to detail. Clare Rojas expanded on these principles with urban folk-art wall paintings, featuring looming, clueless California grizzly bears and tiny, fierce girls in hoodies.

Other Mission School work is rougher around the edges: Chris Johanson's crowds of shy hipsters are drawn in endearingly awkward style with dripping paint, and Barry McGee's assemblages include piles of found bottles painted with freckled, feckless characters and jumpy animations shown on beat-up TVs. Some Mission School art is fairly derided as the faux-naive work of stoned MFAs – but when its earnestness works, it hits you where it counts.

New Media

The technological expertise of the Bay Area is hard to match, and it's no surprise that local artists are putting it to creative use. But some of the most compelling new media artists don't show off with lots of bells and whistles, as is the case for Rebecca Bollinger's grouped sketches of images found through a single keyword search on the web. Frame by frame, using specially modified software, Kota Ezawa turned the OJ Simpson trial into the multichannel cartoon animation it actually was.

Technology doesn't always behave the way you expect, especially in new media works. Since the early '80s, Silicon Valley artist Jim Campbell has been building motherboards to misbehave – in one case, a running figure freezes as soon as it senses the slightest motion in the gallery, and like a frightened doe will resume activity only if you stay stock still. There's a certain silent-movie slapstick humor to Scott Snibbe's projections: a plain square of light sits on the wall until approached, when it suddenly recoils like a sensitive jungle fern. But most disconcerting of all is work by John Slepian, recently shown at Catharine Clark Gallery: a hairy rubber nub swaddled in blankets is programmed to sob disconsolately, until you pick it up and pat its posterior. Forget admiring Old Masters from afar: in San Francisco, you're invited to burp the art.

Best for Inspired Abstraction

Haines Gallery at 49 Geary
(Union Square)

Gregory Lind Gallery at 49 Geary
(Union Square)

Heather Marx Gallery at 77 Geary
(Union Square)

Ratio 3
(the Mission)

Eleanor Harwood Gallery
(the Mission)

Best for Experimental & New Media

SFMOMA (SoMa)

di Rosa Art + Nature Preserve
(Napa Valley)

Catharine Clark Gallery (SoMa)

Southern Exposure
(the Mission)

MH de Young Museum
(Golden Gate Park)

VISUAL ARTS MEDIA & METHODS

San Francisco Music

You'll have to excuse San Francisco DJs if they seem schizophrenic: only an extremely eclectic set can cover SF's varied musical tastes. Classical, bluegrass, Latin music and Chinese and Italian opera have survived fire and earthquakes in San Francisco. Music trends that started in the Bay Area never really went away: '50s free-form jazz and folk; '60s psychedelic rock; '70s disco bathhouse anthems; and in the '90s, Oakland's west-coast rap and Berkeley's punk revival. Today, DJ mash-ups put SF's entire back catalog to work, and laptops and Moog machines sitting around Silicon Valley to good use.

CLASSICAL MUSIC & OPERA

The San Francisco Symphony has rated among the finest interpreters of classical music since conductor Michael Tilson Thomas was wooed away from the London Symphony Orchestra to take up the baton here in 1995. Thomas' innovative programming combines American and Russian composers, full-throttle Mahler and Beethoven, and some genuinely odd experimental music. New York critics grouse that their city's renowned classical music scene seems comparatively staid, and they're right – on the bright side, they can always load up on San Francisco Symphony CDs at Amoeba Music. Thomas and the San Francisco Symphony record regularly, producing several Grammy-winning recordings and a number-two hit in the Billboard charts with *S&M,* an album recorded with San Francisco heavy-metal powerhouse Metallica.

The San Francisco Opera is the USA's second-largest opera company. But while New York's Metropolitan Opera is larger in size and reputation, SF takes big, bold risks. You'd never guess San Francisco's opera roots go back to the 19th century from its more avant-garde productions, such as *Dangerous Liaisons, Harvey Milk, Dead Man Walking* and the definitive revival of Puccini's California Gold Rush opera *The Girl of the Golden West* featuring Pavarotti successor Salvatore Licitra. The company has seen its share of megawatt divas: Leontyne Price made her debut here during the '50s, and the recent recurring favorite is Renée Fleming, whose dulcet tones you may recognize from a dozen CDs and *The Lord of the Rings* movie soundtrack.

ROCK

Fire up those lighters, but don't go calling for 'Freebird' as an encore. The San Francisco rock of choice lately is preceded by the prefix alt- or indie at the Mission, Potrero and Polk Gulch venues and music extravaganzas like Outside Lands, Noise Pop and the free Mission Creek Music Festival. SF acts like Rogue Wave, Peggy Honeywell and Joanna Newsom add acoustic roots stylings even when they're not playing the Hardly Strictly Bluegrass Festival, while Black Rebel Motorcycle Club and Deerhoof throw Mission grit into their seismic walls of sound. Metalheads need no introduction to the mighty Metallica, the perpetually hard-rocking innovators and triumphant survivors of a genre slowly smothered in the '80s by its own hair.

And to think that before you arrived, you thought San Francisco's rock scene had ODed long ago, along with Jerry Garcia, Janis Joplin, Jimi Hendrix, various Doors and most of Jefferson Airplane. Fair enough. San

Classical music is accessible and often free in San Francisco – a local tradition started when opera divas performed for free to raise SF's spirits after the 1906 earthquake and fire. For listings of free concerts around town, see www.sfcv.org.

Best for Classical & Opera

San Francisco Symphony
(Civic Center)

San Francisco Opera
(Civic Center)

Stern Grove Festival
(Golden Gate Park)

Zellerbach Hall
(Berkeley)

Francisco has the ignominious distinction of being a world capital of rocker drug overdoses, ranking right up there with Rome. You could do a macabre walking tour (p182) of the Haight to see all the places Janis nearly met her maker, passing by 32 Delmar St, where Sid Vicious went on the heroin bender that finally broke up the Sex Pistols.

No drug was powerful enough to kill Grateful Dead guitarist Jerry Garcia, who survived decades beyond any medically explicable life expectancy only to die in rehab in 1995. But the Grateful Dead carry on in their rambling, shambling fashion on now-digitized mix tapes traded among Deadheads like currency, and Jerry's former band mates still periodically tour under the names the Dead or Furthur.

Baby boomers have kept the sound of San Francisco in the '60s alive, and much of it stands the tests of time and sobriety. After Joan Baez and Bob Dylan had their Northern California fling, folk turned into folk rock, and Jimi Hendrix turned the American anthem into a tune suitable for an acid trip. When Janis Joplin and Big Brother & the Holding Company applied their rough musical stylings to 'Me and Bobby McGee,' it was like applying that last necessary pass of sandpaper to the sometimes clunky, wooden verses of traditional folk. Jefferson Airplane held court at the Fillmore, turning Lewis Caroll's opium-inspired children's classic into the psychedelic anthem 'White Rabbit' with singer Grace Slick's piercing wail.

The '60s were quite a trip, but the '70s weren't a let-down either, at least musically. Crosby, Stills, Nash & Young splintered, but Neil Young keeps 'rockin' in the free world' from his ranch south of San Francisco with his earnest, bluesy whine. Since the 1970s, California-born, long-time Marin resident Tom Waits has been singing in a gruff, after-hours voice with a permanent catch in the throat, giving the world some idea what folk might sound like if it spent a decade working jangly honky-tonks across the West. SF's own Steve Miller Band turned out stoner hits like 'The Joker,' and Mission-born, lifelong San Franciscan Carlos Santana combined a guitar moan and Latin backbeat in 'Black Magic Woman,' 'Evil Ways' and 'Oye Como Va' – and made a crossover pop comeback with 1999's Grammy-winning *Supernatural* and 2005 *All That I Am,* featuring fellow San Franciscan Kirk Hammett of Metallica.

**Best for
Funk &
Hiphop**

Mezzanine (SoMa)

*Elbo Room
(the Mission)*

*Boom Boom
Room
(Japantown)*

*Little Baobab (the
Mission)*

FUNK & HIP-HOP

The '60s were perhaps best summed up by freaky-funky, racially integrated San Francisco supergroup Sly and the Family Stone in their creatively spelled 1969 number-one hit: 'Thank You (Falettinme Be Mice Elf Agin).' San Francisco's '70s funk was mostly reverb from across the bay in Oakland, where Tower of Power worked a groove with taut horn arrangements. All this trippy funk worked its way into the DNA of the Bay Area hip-hop scene, spawning the jazz-inflected, free-form Charlie Hunter Trio and the infectious wokka-wokka baseline of rapper Lyrics Born. Oakland's MC Hammer was an '80s crossover hip-hop hitmaker best known for inflicting harem pants on the fashion world, though his influence can be felt in the bouncing, hyperactivity of E-40. Political commentary and pop hooks became an East Bay hip-hop signature with the breakaway Billboard-chart hits of Michael Franti and Spearhead, Blackalicious and the Coup.

But the Bay Area is still best known as the home of arguably the world's most talented and notorious rapper of all: Tupac Shakur. He became a victim of his own success in Las Vegas in 1996, when an assailant out to settle the increasingly violent East Coast/West Coast gangsta rap rivalry fatally shot him. San Francisco rapper San Quinn got his

**Best for
Rock &
Punk**

Fillmore Auditorium (Japantown)

*Warfield
(Union Square)*

*Bottom of the Hill
(Potrero Hill)*

*Great American
Music Hall
(the Tenderloin)*

*Slim's
(SoMa)*

SF ECLECTIC HITS PLAYLIST

➡ 'Take Five' by Dave Brubeck Quartet (1959)
➡ 'Uncle John's Band' by The Grateful Dead (1970)
➡ 'Me and Bobby McGee' by Janis Joplin (1971)
➡ 'Everyday People' by Sly and the Family Stone (1968)
➡ 'Evil Ways' by Santana (1969)
➡ 'Lights' by Journey (1978)
➡ 'California' by Rogue Wave (2005)
➡ 'Make You Feel That Way' by Blackalicious (2002)
➡ 'Stay Human (All the Freaky People)' by Michael Franti & Spearhead (2007)
➡ 'San Francisco Anthem' by San Quinn (2008)
➡ 'Come Out and Play (Keep 'Em Separated)' by The Offspring (1994)
➡ 'Welcome to Paradise' by Green Day (1992)

start opening for Tupac but takes a less hard line, remixing the 1967 Mamas and the Papas hit 'San Francisco (Be Sure to Wear Flowers in Your Hair)' into his 'San Francisco Anthem' and adding a bougie twist: 'We got the cable car/but my car got cable.'

Search & Destroy was San Francisco's poorly photocopied and totally riveting chronicle of the '70s punk scene as it happened from 1977 to 1979, starting with an initial run financed with $100 from Allen Ginsberg and Lawrence Ferlinghetti, and morphing into V Vale's seminal zine RE/Search in the 1980s.

PUNK

London may have been more political and Los Angeles more hardcore, but San Francisco's take on punk was weirder. The New Wave and punk scene took root in San Francisco in the late 1970s, and Dead Kennedys frontman Jello Biafra ran for mayor in 1979 with a platform written on the back of a bar napkin: ban cars, set official rates for bribery and force businesspeople to dress as clowns. With the slogan 'There's always room for Jello,' he received 6000 votes; his political endorsement is still highly prized in mayoral races.

Biafra was the ringleader of a three-ring circus in the '70s that included the Avengers (founded by San Francisco Art Institute grad Penelope Houston), Crime (whose 1976 song 'Hotwire My Heart' was the first US punk single, later covered by Sonic Youth), and noise/punk innovators Flipper (formed from the remains of Negative Trend, which also yielded post-punk dub masters Toiling Midgets). Post-punk kicked off locally with Marin's precocious proto–New Waver Todd Rundgren and power-popping Flamin' Groovies, whose 1976 cult-hit album *Shake Some Action* critics call the first New Wave album. But for oddity it's hard to top art-rockers the Residents, whose identities remain unknown after three decades and 60 records' worth of strange sounds, all while wearing giant eyeballs over their heads.

Today, punk's not dead in the Bay Area – in fact, it's getting mainstream radio play. The East Bay's one-two punch of ska-inflected Rancid and Berkeley's Green Day brought punk staggering out of the underground and blinking into the glare of the mass-media spotlight in the mid-'90s. Hardcore punks sneered at Green Day's chart-topping hits, but the group won street cred (and Grammys) in 2004 with the dark social critique of *American Idiot* – at least until that album was turned into a Broadway musical in 2010. Since the early success of their gold album *Punk in Drublic,* San Francisco–based NOFX has avoided Green Day–ish derision by staying on an independent label and recording an impressively degenerate show at Slim's called *I Hear They've Gotten Worse Live!*

Punk continues to evolve in San Francisco, with queercore success of Pansy Division, the brass-ballsiness of Latin ska-punk La Plebe, and all-girl, all-badass rockers the Donnas. It may not be 'traditional' punk (isn't that an oxymoron anyway?), but it's very San Francisco.

JAZZ

Ever since house bands pounded out ragtime hits to distract Barbary Coast audiences from bar-room brawls, San Francisco has had a romance with jazz. Today, the SF Jazz Festival is among the nation's best jazz festivals, attracting leading innovators, interpreters and improvisers.

The SF scene was set in the 1950s, with bebop and West Coast jazz innovated by the legendary Dave Brubeck Quartet. Brubeck's groovy, mathematically complex rhythmic shifts, combined with Paul Desmond's laid-back bossa nova saxophone, had San Francisco hepcats finger-snapping their approval, and made *Time Out* one of the best-selling jazz albums of all time. Bebop had its disciples among the Beats, and such is the continued devotion to the work of John Coltrane in particular that he's revered as a saint at the African Orthodox Church of St John Coltrane. San Francisco's '50s jazz scene saw recordings by Miles Davis and frequent tour stops by Billie Holliday, and it's memorably chronicled in Kerouac's *On the Road*.

Starting in the '60s, the SF jazz scene exploded into a kaleidoscope of styles. Devotees of trumpeter Don Cherry followed his work with Ornette Coleman's avant-garde ensemble, while Dixieland band Turk Murphy developed a following with roots jazz fans. At Yoshi's and SF's other jazz clubs, tempos shift from Latin jazz to klezmer, acid jazz to swing. Local jazz innovators like Broun Fellinis regularly share the bill with hip-hop groups, and jazz traditionalists have played Hardly Strictly Bluegrass Festival. Even listeners not familiar with jazz will recognize the work of native San Franciscan Vince Guaraldi, whose score for *A Charlie Brown Christmas* has become the beloved antidote to standard Christmas carols.

Best for Jazz

Yoshi's
(Japantown)

SF Jazz
(Financial District)

Intersection for the Arts
(the Mission)

Yerba Buena Center for the Arts (SoMa)

SAN FRANCISCO MUSIC JAZZ

San Francisco Architecture

Superman wouldn't be so impressive in San Francisco, where most buildings are low enough for even a middling superhero to leap in a single bound. The Transamerica Pyramid and Ferry Building clock tower are helpful pointers to orient newcomers, and Coit Tower adds emphatic punctuation to the city skyline – but San Francisco's low-profile buildings are its highlights, from Mission adobe and gabled Victorians to forward-thinking grass-covered roofs. Just when you think you've seen it all, you'll turn a corner to find a row of Western storefronts, their squared-off, toothy roofline as rakishly charming as a crooked smile.

Debates are rising over SoMa's new high-rise Mission Bay development. Proponents describe it as a forward-thinking green scheme, eliminating commutes to bedroom communities and the after-five desertification of Downtown. Critics argue that such costly real estate attracts only chain stores and high-priced retailers, excluding affordable mom-and-pop businesses and cultural institutions.

DEVELOPMENT

THE MISSION & EARLY SF

Not much is left of San Francisco's original Ohlone-style architecture, beyond the grass memorial hut you'll see in the graveyard of the Spanish Mission Dolores and the wall of the original presidio (military post), both built in adobe with conscripted Ohlone labor. When the Gold Rush began, buildings were slapped together from ready-made sawn timber components, sometimes shipped from the East Coast or Australia – a sign of postwar prefab ahead.

In SF's Barbary Coast days, City Hall wasn't much to look at, at least from outside: it was housed in the burlesque Jenny Lind Theater at Portsmouth Sq. Most waterfront buildings from SF's hot-headed Wild West days were lost to arson, until builders of Jackson Square got wise and switched to brick. But masonry was no match for the 1906 earthquake and fire, which left the waterfront almost completely leveled – with the mysterious, highly explosive exception of the Italianate AP Hotaling's Warehouse, which at the time housed SF's largest whiskey stash. Uphill toward North Beach, you'll spot a few other original 1860s to 1880s Italianate brick storefronts wisely built on bedrock: elevated false facades are capped with jutting cornices, a straight roofline and graceful arches over tall windows.

VICTORIANA

To make room for new arrivals with the gold, railroad and shipping booms, San Francisco had to expand – and fast. Wooden Victorian row houses cropped up almost overnight with a similar underlying floor plan, but with eye-catching embellishments so inhabitants stumbling home after Barbary Coast nights could recognize their homes. Some proved surprisingly sturdy: several upstanding Victorian row-houses remain in Pacific Heights.

The Victorian era was a time of colonial conquest and the culmination of the European Age of Discovery, and Victorians liked to imagine themselves as the true successors of great early civilizations. San Franciscans incorporated designs from ancient Rome, Egypt and the Italian Renaissance into their houses, giving fresh-out-of-the-box San Francisco a hodge-podge instant culture.

Painted Ladies

The city's signature architectural style was labeled 'Victorian,' but demure Queen Victoria would surely blush to see the eccentric architecture perpetrated in her name in San Francisco. Local 'Painted Ladies' have candy-jar color palates, lavish gingerbread woodworking dripping off steeply peaked roofs, and gilded stucco garlands swagging huge, look-at-me bay windows. Grand parlors were decorated to the hilt with gilt flourishes to show off Gold Rush fortunes, and cluttered with exotic objets d'art reflecting the cultural origins and aspirations of the owners. With their rococo-cosmopolitan flourishes, Nob Hill mansions and waterfront bordellos shared a common design sensibility.

The 1906 quake and fire destroyed many of the city's 19th-century treasures and much of its kitschy excess. Only a fraction of the older buildings you'll see in SF were built during Victoria's 1837 to 1901 reign, including steeply gabled Gothic Revivals; the rest are cheerfully inauthentic San Franciscan takes on a vaguely Anglo-Continental style. Of the 19th-century Painted Ladies that have stood the test of trends and tremors, many belong to other architectural categories:

Stick (1880s) In the Lower Haight and Pacific Heights, you'll notice squared-off Victorians built to fit side-by-side in narrow lots, usually with flat fronts and long, narrow windows.

Queen Anne (1880s–1910) Architects pulled out all the stops on Queen Anne mansions, adding balconies, turrets, chimneys, bay windows and gables. Alamo Square has several exuberant examples with fish-scale shingle decoration, rounded corner towers and decorative bands to lift the eye skyward.

Edwardian (1901–1914) Most of the 'Victorians' you'll see in San Francisco are actually from the postfire Edwardian era – art nouveau, Asian-inspired, and Arts and Crafts details are the giveaway. You'll spot original Edwardian stained-glass windows and false gables in the inner Richmond and Castro.

Some Victorian mansions are now B&Bs, so you too can live large in swanky San Francisco digs of yore; see Sleeping options in the Haight, Pacific Heights, Mission and Castro.

PACIFIC POLYGLOT ARCHITECTURE

A trip across town or even down the block will bring you face to facade with San Francisco's Spanish and Mexican heritage, Asian ancestry and California Arts and Crafts roots. Mission St movie-palace facades and Sansome St banks incorporated Spanish and Aztec design influences from Mexico, and the 1920s brought a mission revival acknowledging California's Hispanic heritage.

Distinctive Chinatown deco became a cornerstone of Chinatown's redevelopment initiative after the 1906 quake, when a forward-thinking group of merchants led by Look Tin Eli consulted with a cross-section of architects and rudimentary focus groups to produce a crowd-pleasing, modern chinoiserie look that would attract tourists. The first licensed female architect in California and the chief architect of over-the-top Spanish-Gothic-Greek Hearst Castle, Julia Morgan showed more tasteful restraint and finesse combining cultural traditions in her designs for the pagoda-topped brick Chinatown YWCA (now the Chinese Historical Society of America Museum) and graceful Italianate Emanu-el Sisterhood Residence (now home to San Francisco Zen Center).

Meanwhile, Berkeley-based architect Bernard Maybeck reinvented England's Arts and Crafts movement with the down-to-earth California bungalow, a small, simple single-story design derived from summer homes favored by British officers serving in India. California Arts and Crafts style can be spotted in Bay Area Craftsman cottages and earthy ecclesiastical structures like San Francisco's Swedenborgian Church. Though Maybeck's Greco-Roman 1915 Palace of Fine Arts was intended as a temporary structure, the beloved almost-ruined fake ruin was

Best for Victorians

Alamo Square
(the Haight)

Haight Flashback
walking tour
(the Haight)

Haas-Lilienthal
House
(Pacific Heights)

Octagon House
(Cow Hollow)

Chateau Tivoli
(the Haight)

recast in concrete in the 1960s, and it continues to serve as San Franciscans' favorite wedding-photo backdrop.

MODERN SKYLINE

Once steel-frame buildings stood the test of the 1906 earthquake, San Francisco began to think big with its buildings. The city hoped to rival the capitols of Europe, and commissioned architect Daniel Burnham to build a grand City Hall in the classicizing beaux arts or 'city beautiful' style. Willis Polk was among the city's busiest architects, defining downtown with his striking 1918 Hallidie Building at the Powell St cable car turnaround. The Hallidie's glass-curtain facade was shockingly innovative for the time and remains a little too daring – its balconies and steel stairwells were declared unsafe in 2010 by the SF Department of Building Safety.

Top 5 Low-Profile SF Landmarks

California Academy of Sciences (Golden Gate Park)

MH de Young Museum (Golden Gate Park)

Swedenborgian Church (the Presidio)

Chinese Historical Society of America (Chinatown)

Xanadu Gallery (Union Square)

Flatirons

Chicago and New York were already raising skylines to new heights, and San Francisco borrowed their flatiron style to maximize prime real estate along Market St. Market St cuts a diagonal across San Francisco's tidy east–west street grid, leaving both flanks of four attractive, triangular flatiron buildings exposed to view.

Among the XXX cinemas surrounding Golden Gate Ave, Taylor and Market Sts, you'll find the lacy, white flatiron featured as broody Brad Pitt's apartment in the film *Interview with a Vampire*. On a more respectable block above the Powell St cable car turnaround is the stone-cold silver fox known as James Flood Building, a flinty character that has seen it all: fire, earthquakes and the Gap's attempts to bring back bell bottoms at its ground-floor flagship store. Flood's opulent cousin is the 1908 Phelan Building at 760 Market St, while that adorable little slip of a building on the block at 540 Market St is the 1913 Flatiron Building. Its sunny disposition outshines all the overwrought bank buildings along nearby Sansome St.

Streamlined SF

San Francisco became forward-thinking port city in the 1930s, with Streamline Moderne apartment buildings that looked like ocean liners and its signature art-deco Golden Gate Bridge. But except for Coit Tower, most new buildings kept a low, sleek profile. Until the '60s, San Francisco was called 'the white city' because of its unbroken swaths of white stucco.

The Depression years of the 1930s and the following WWII era brought a bonanza of WPA murals to town, but very little heavy construction. By this time most of the city center flatlands had been fully built up, so the best places to see post-Victorian residential architecture are in hilly neighborhoods such as Diamond Heights and Twin Peaks and the outlying Avenues, where SF's ornate Victorian sensibility was quickly being superseded by toned-down color schemes and streamlined facades.

Skyscrapers

SF's skyline scarcely changed until the early 1960s, when seismic retrofitting and innovations made upward mobility possible in this shaky city. The Financial District quickly became a Manhattanized forest of glass boxes, with one pointed exception: the Transamerica Pyramid.

Recent high-rise construction has sprung up in SoMa around the Caltrain station, as San Francisco braces for booms in biotech and social media. Developers are determined to make the outer reaches of SoMa attractive to businesses but also livable, with slots for shops, con-

BUILDINGS I LOVE (& LOVE TO HATE)
DAVID CROTTY, BAY AREA ARCHITECT

Why should the Painted Ladies and Transamerica Pyramid get all the attention? Some of the most interesting buildings in the city – for better or worse – don't appear on any postcards.

Crown Zellerbach Building (1959, SOM; Map p322; 1 Bush St) – stand on Market St and you can fully understand how the building works. The tall dark tower is the 'core,' with elevators and services, leaving the glassy rectangle for unobstructed office space. Simple and elegant.

MH de Young Museum (2005, Herzog & de Meuron; Map p342) – controversial, academic, beautiful and self-important, this rusty battleship marks SF's entrance into architectural relevance.

SFO International Terminal (2004, SOM) – check out the slick interiors and curvy, sexy exterior. This is the right way to enter our city.

Yerba Buena Gardens (opened 1993; Map p330; 3rd & Mission Sts) – stand in the garden and you can see stunning buildings on four sides: God, art and shopping – all in great buildings! This complex shows successful design on large and small scales.

AT&T Park (2000, HOK Sport; Map p330; 3rd & King Sts) – the architects had such great success in Baltimore they decided to do it again (and again and again). This brick park is a crowd-pleaser and a fun place to see a ball game, but the *Leave It to Beaver* architecture is a lost opportunity.

Marriott Hotel (1989, DMJM; Map p330; 55 4th St) – locals call it the Jukebox, and we hate it. The ugliest building in SF screams for attention with its clumsy massing and flashy materials. Have a drink on the top floor of the hotel so you can see the city with this monster out of view.

dos, restaurants and cafes. These carefully designed 'urban villages' are San Francisco's latest attempt at instant culture, though they're considerably more bland than the city's earlier Victorian attempt.

Prefab

Meanwhile, amid Victorian-prefab row houses in San Francisco neighborhoods, you might also spot some of the sleek, architect-designed, eco-prefab homes innovated in the Bay Area during the 1990s. The exteriors of these new constructions can seem starkly minimal, but the interior spaces make the most of air and light, with open-plan living areas opening into gardens to provide the ready access to nature that makes San Francisco so livable.

Adaptive Reuse

Instead of starting from scratch, avant-garde architects are resolving the differences between San Francisco's eclectic architecture and the needs of a modern city by making creative use of existing structures. Architect Daniel Libeskind's design for the 2008 Contemporary Jewish Museum turned a historic power station into the Hebrew letter for life, with a blue-steel pavilion as an emphatic accent. But the roof has literally been blown off previous standards for adaptive reuse by the 2008 LEED–certified green building for the California Academy of Sciences. Pritzker Prize–winning architect Renzo Piano's incorporated the previous building's neoclassical colonnaded facade, gutted the interior to make way for a basement aquarium and four-story rainforest, and capped it with a domed 'living roof' of California wildflowers perforated with skylights to let air circulate.

Hills & Fog

Seen from space, San Francisco's defining features are surely the Golden Gate Bridge and the city's 43 hills – but astronauts who orbit any closer might also hear the people atop them, gasping in unison. If the climb doesn't take your breath away at hilltop parks, the Golden Gate vistas surely will. Nature has been kind to San Francisco, but it takes San Franciscans to make hilltop moments happen, with pioneering conservation efforts, artistic masterpieces and moments of audible awe.

PEAK EXPERIENCES

Gravity seems unkind as you scale SF's steepest hills, with calf muscles and cable car wheels groaning in unison – but all grumbling ends once you hit the summit. With wind-sculpted trees, Victorian turrets and the world at your feet, the climb was worth it.

Top 5 Hilltop Parks

Telegraph Hill

Sterling Park

Buena Vista Park

Ina Coolbrith Park

Hilltop Parks

The city wasn't exactly planned, with sailors abandoning their ships in the harbor to swim ashore during the Gold Rush. But among the early arrivals were naturalist John Muir, founder of Sierra Club and Muir Woods, and William Hammond Hall, champion of Golden Gate Park, who saw beauty and not just gold in these hills. Today virtually every hilltop in San Francisco has a precious green toupee it wouldn't be seen without, and these hilltop parks give the city its natural charm.

San Francisco voters backed the 1867 creation of Buena Vista Park, and the staggering peak still offers the city's most sweeping panoramas, along with Pacific Heights' Alta Vista Park. Drivers gunning down Lombard St miss spectacular photo-ops of the Golden Gate Bridge through the windswept pines of Sterling Park. Watch a sunset here, and you'll see what inspired poet and park namesake George Sterling to gush: 'Homeward into the sunset/Still unwearied we go/Till the northern hills are misty/With the amber of afterglow.'

Next-level Landmarks

Scandal, artistic masterpieces, enlightenment and a stiff drink await your arrival at the summit of San Francisco's hills. Scenic greenery prevented 1906 fires from devastating Russian Hill, preserving the quaint cottage at 29 Russell St where Jack Kerouac wrote *On the Road* and held up his end of a love triangle. Coit Tower has controversial murals capped with crowd-pleasing panoramas, while Diego Rivera Gallery murals show the Mexican maestro hard at work, capturing a sweeping SF cityscape. Grace Cathedral is illuminated from within by Keith Haring's AIDS Memorial altar of angels taking flight – the artist's last work before death by AIDS in 1990. Across Nob Hill, Top of the Mark offers your choice of 100 martinis with a view over foggy hilltops that'll make you misty.

Hidden Hilltops

Corona Heights Park

Strawberry Hill

The Presidio

Bernal Heights

Stairway Walks

Instead of declaring your love for SF on a T-shirt, shout it from a hilltop – but first you have to get here. Whenever possible, take the stairs. On Telegraph Hill, Filbert St Steps (p101) are flanked with surreal statuary and wild parrots, while the flowering staircases that lead to Ina Coolbrith Park make a perfumed, romantic climb. With its cottage-lined stairway and leafy canopy, Macondray Lane was the model for mysterious 'Bar-

SF'S GREEN OUTLOOK

It's not always easy being green, even in San Francisco. Since local real-estate prices remain among the highest in the US, there's always the fear that San Francisco's scenic hilltop living rooms will be swallowed up by private development. But a motley coalition of neighborhood councils, dog walkers, parrot-feeders, parents, kite-flyers, conservationists and lollygaggers have actively protected San Francisco's urban green spaces for over a century. San Franciscans successfully lobbied for the preservation of Golden Gate Park in the 19th century, and recently convinced the US military to hand over a military base for use as public parkland in the Presidio.

Nature has lavished the city with hilltop parks, gardens and top-notch produce – and the city does its best to repay the favor, with mandatory composting citywide and thoughtful everyday conservation efforts. All around you in San Francisco, you'll notice wild ideas in action with support ranging from green-certified businesses to the Green Party (a power player in city politics). Rooftop vegetable gardens have taken off, and defunct freeway ramps were converted into the nonprofit Hayes Valley Farm (p177). There's even a buzz about public beekeeping, to encourage healthy cross-pollination in urban plant life.

This is one town where you can eat, sleep and cavort sustainably; just look for 🌿 icons throughout this book. All these measures help make San Francisco a livable, breathable city – that urban claustrophobia you get surrounded by New York skyscrapers or Los Angeles freeways isn't a problem here. From the bottom of its heart and the top of its green hills, San Francisco thanks you.

bary Lane' in Armistead Maupin's *Tales of the City*. And never mind the motorists: walking lets you stop and smell the roses along zig-zagging Lombard St.

The Easy Way Up

Top-of-the-world views don't always have to be earned the hard way in San Francisco. Instead of trudging up stairs, elevators whisk you straight to the viewing platform of Coit Tower, SFMOMA's rooftop sculpture garden and cafe, and the wildflower-covered roof of the California Academy of Sciences. Downtown public roof gardens let you picnic with a view, and cable cars offer uphill thrills with your commute.

FOGGY DAYS

Once you've watched the fog lurching into town like a pirate on shore leave, it's hard to imagine San Francisco without it. Minus these mists, the entire San Francisco Bay would be missing its standout scenery: lighthouses wouldn't be necessary, and giant redwoods wouldn't survive the hot sun. Finicky native NorCal ferns would refuse to sprout from the cliffs along Hwy 1 or from shoe planters atop Alamo Square. Sourdough bread starter (technically, *lactobacillus sanfrancisco*) wouldn't start, and pinot noir grapes would shrivel into raisins. But wait, it gets worse: with California sunshine all day, every day, San Francisco might start to look like LA.

The foggy fact of the matter is, no sweeping San Francisco vista is complete without a case of the goose bumps. Sunny days suit most cities just fine, but San Francisco saves its most dramatic view of Golden Gate Bridge for for. When fog swirls around the towers, romantics and photographers rejoice – and you'll swear you see the ghost of Alfred Hitchcock at misty Fort Point, rubbing his hands with glee.

Golden Gate Bridge isn't the only local landmark – though the other one likes to hide. As summer afternoon fog blows in, look westward to Sutro Tower, the double-spiked radio beacon atop Twin Peaks. When the rolling clouds cover its base, the tower magically turns into a double-masted schooner sailing across a sea of fog.

Microclimates

Armies of glam rockers with dry-ice machines can't create the moody, misty effects San Francisco comes by naturally. On sunny summer afternoons, the city skyline can vanish into clouds within an hour. There are two secrets to San Francisco's amazing disappearing act: geography and microclimates.

To understand how fog moves inland, first you need to picture California's geography. The vast agricultural region in the state's interior, the Central Valley, is ringed by mountains, like a giant bathtub. As this inland valley heats up and the warm air rises, it creates a deficit of air at surface level, generating wind that gets sucked through the only opening it can find: the Golden Gate. Suddenly the misty air hovering over the chilly Pacific gets pulled into the bay, and ta-da: the city disappears behind a misty veil.

Rolling fog moves fast, and it's unpredictable: gusty wind is the only indication that it's coming. But even when the fog swallows beaches in the Presidio, the sun is probably still shining in the Mission. Hills block fog, especially at times of high atmospheric pressure, as often happens in summer. When forecasters refer to the Bay Area's 'microclimates,' this is what they mean. These alternating pockets of fog and sun may support different flora, ranging from windswept Presidio pines to Mission palm trees.

Now you know why jackets are a permanent style statement in San Francisco. In July it's not uncommon for inland areas to reach 100°F (38°C), while the mercury at the coast barely reaches 70° (21°C). Even across the city, temperatures can vary by 15 degrees or more. But when the fog has worn out its welcome in the Avenues and the Haight, take a bus to the Castro or the Mission – and when the fog reaches the Mission, hop BART to sunny Berkeley across the bay.

Misty-eyed Sunsets

Surfer hangouts, bargain gourmet meals and unforgettable sunset views over the velvety fog are all good reasons to linger in the Avenues after the fog has sneaked into Golden Gate Park. Above the east end of the park are side-by-side 922ft and 904ft Twin Peaks formerly known as El Pecho de la Chola (the Breasts of the Indian Girl), which are ideal vista points. Climb either one to watch the fog roll in from the ocean around sunset, and see the Oakland Hills glitter with golden afternoon light across the bay. To drive to Twin Peaks, head southwest on Market St as it climbs steeply uphill (it becomes Portola Ave) and then turn right on Twin Peaks Blvd.

Best Fog Views

Facing the Golden Gate Bridge from the dock alongside Crissy Field

Looking down on the city from atop Corona Heights

Overlooking Golden Gate Park from the MH de Young Museum tower

Reading poetry on a hillside bench at Sterling Park

Sprawled naked on Baker Beach... brrrrr

Top 5 Consolations for Foggy Summer Days

Muir Woods

Golden Gate Bridge's rock-star scenery

Sourdough bread

Cool-climate coastal wines

Pigeon Point Lighthouse overnights and cliffside hot tub

Survival Guide

Transportation

GETTING TO SAN FRANCISCO

Service from three Bay Area airports makes getting to San Francisco quick and convenient. Direct flights to SF from LA take about 90 minutes; from Chicago about 4 hours; from Atlanta, 5 hours; and from New York, 5½ to 6 hours. Bargain fares can be found online year-round, but don't forget to factor in additional transit time and costs to get to SF if you're flying into San Jose or Oakland instead of San Francisco.

Consider getting here by train instead of car or plane to enjoy spectacular scenery en route, without unnecessary traffic hassles and excess carbon emissions.

Flights, tours and rail tickets can be booked online at lonelyplanet.com/bookings.

Air

San Francisco International Airport

One of the busiest airports in the country, **San Francisco International Airport** (SFO; www.flysfo.com) is 14 miles south of downtown off Hwy 101 and accessible by BART.

GETTING TO/FROM SAN FRANCISCO INTERNATIONAL AIRPORT

BART (Bay Area Rapid Transit; www.bart.gov; one-way $8) Offers a fast, direct 30-minute ride to/from downtown San Francisco. The SFO BART station is connected to the International Terminal; tickets can be purchased from machines inside the station entrance.

BusSamTrans (www.samtrans.com; one-way $5) Express bus KX takes about 30 minutes to reach Temporary Transbay Terminal in the South of Market (SoMa) area.

Airport Shuttles (one-way $14-17) Depart from baggage-claim areas, taking 45 minutes to most SF locations. For service to the airport, call to reserve a pickup from any San Francisco location at least 4 hours in advance of departure time. Companies include SuperShuttle (☑800-258-3826; www.supershuttle.com), Quake City (☑415-255-4899; www.quakecityshuttle.com), Lorrie's (☑415-334-9000; www.gosfovan.com) and American Airporter Shuttle (☑415-202-0733; www.americanairporter.com).

Taxi Taxis to downtown San Francisco cost $35 to $50, departing from the yellow zone on the lower level of SFO.

Car The drive between the airport and the city can take as little as 20 minutes, but give yourself an hour during morning and evening rush hours. If you're headed to the airport via Hwy 101, take the San Francisco International Airport exit. Don't be misled by the Airport Rd exit, which leads to parking lots and warehouses.

Oakland International Airport

Travelers arriving at **Oakland International Airport** (OAK; ☑510-563-3300; www.oaklandairport.com), 15 miles east of Downtown, will have a little further to go to reach San Francisco.

GETTING TO/FROM OAKLAND INTERNATIONAL AIRPORT

BART The cheapest way to get to San Francisco from the Oakland Airport. AirBART shuttles (adult/child $3/1) run every 10 to 20 minutes to the Coliseum station, where you can catch BART to downtown SF ($3.80, 25 minutes).

Taxi Leave curbside from Oakland airport and average $25 to Oakland and $50 to $70 to SF.

SuperShuttle (☑800-258-3826; www.supershuttle.com) Offers shared van rides to downtown SF for $25 to $30.

Airport Express (☑800-327-2024; www.airportexpressinc.com; ⊙5:15am-9:15pm) Runs a scheduled shuttle every two hours (from 6am to midnight) between Oakland Airport and Sonoma ($34) and Marin ($26) counties.

CLIMATE CHANGE & TRAVEL

Every form of transport that relies on carbon-based fuel generates CO_2, the main cause of human-induced climate change. Modern travel is dependent on aeroplanes, which might use less fuel per kilometer per person than most cars but travel much greater distances. The altitude at which aircraft emit gases (including CO_2) and particles also contributes to their climate change impact. Many websites offer 'carbon calculators' that allow people to estimate the carbon emissions generated by their journey and, for those who wish to do so, to offset the impact of the greenhouse gases emitted with contributions to portfolios of climate-friendly initiatives throughout the world. Lonely Planet offsets the carbon footprint of all staff and author travel.

Norman y Mineta San Jose International Airport

Fifty miles south of downtown San Francisco, **Norman y Mineta San Jose International Airport** (SJC; Map p235; ☎408-501-0979; www.sjc.org) is a straight shot into the city by car via Hwy 101. The VTA Airport Flyer (bus 10; tickets $2; from 5am to midnight) makes a continuous run between the Santa Clara Caltrain station (Railroad Ave and Franklin St) and the airport terminals, departing every 15 to 30 minutes. From Santa Clara station, Caltrain (one-way $9; 90 minutes) runs several trains every day to the terminal at 4th and King Sts in SF.

Bus

Until the new terminal is complete in 2017, SF's inter-city hub remains the **Temporary Transbay Terminal** (Map p330; Howard & Main Sts, SoMa). From here you can catch the following buses:

AC Transit (www.actransit.org) Buses to the East Bay.

Golden Gate Transit (www.goldengatetransit.org) North-bound buses to Marin and Sonoma Counties.

Greyhound (☎800-231-2222; www.greyhound.com) Buses leave daily for Los Angeles ($57, 8 to 12 hours),

Truckee near Lake Tahoe ($33, 5½hrs) and other destinations.

SamTrans (www.samtrans.com) South-bound buses to Palo Alto and the Pacific coast.

Train

Easy on the eyes and carbon emissions too, train travel is a good way to visit the Bay Area and beyond.

Caltrain (Map p330; www.caltrain.com; cnr 4th & King Sts) Caltrain connects San Francisco with Silicon Valley hubs and San Jose.

Amtrak (☎800-872-7245; www.amtrakcalifornia.com) Amtrak serves San Francisco via its stations in Oakland and Emeryville (near Oakland). Amtrak offers rail passes good for seven days of travel in California within a 21-day period (from $159). Amtrak runs free shuttle buses from its stations in Emeryville and Oakland's Jack London Sq to San Francisco's Ferry Building and Caltrain station.

Coast Starlight (LA-Emeryville from $69, Oakland-Portland from $153, Oakland-Seattle from $192, LA-Seattle from $204) A spectacular 35-hour run from Los Angeles to Seattle via Emeryville/Oakland, with meals served on china in the Dining Car, local wines and artisan cheeses served in the Pacific Parlor Car and an Arcade Room to play video games.

California Zephyr (Chicago-Oakland from $292) The California Zephyr takes its time (51 hours), traveling from Chicago through the Rockies and snow-capped Sierra Nevada en route to Oakland.

GETTING AROUND SAN FRANCISCO

When San Franciscans don't have somewhere else to be right quick – and even when they do – most people walk, bike or take Muni instead of a car or cab. Those slackers are smart: this is the best way to take in San Francisco, and helps preserve the city's many all-natural charms by curbing carbon emissions and other pollutants.

Bus, Streetcar & Cable Car

Muni (Municipal Transit Agency; www.sfmuni.com) operates bus, streetcar and cable car lines. Buses and streetcars are referred to interchangeably as Muni and marked in this book with Ⓜ, while cable cars are marked with 🚋. Some areas are better connected than others, but Muni spares you the costly hassle of driving and parking in San Francisco, and it's often faster than driving during rush hour.

SCHEDULES
For fastest routes and the most exact departure times, consult http://transit.511.org. Arrival times can also

be viewed on digital displays or guesstimated by consulting schedules posted inside bus shelters. Nighttime and weekend service is less frequent. Owl service (from 1am to 5am) is offered on a limited number of lines, with departures about every half-hour.

SYSTEM MAPS
A detailed Muni Street & Transit Map is available free online (www.sfmuni.com) and at the Powell Muni kiosk ($3).

TICKETS
Standard fare for buses or streetcars is $2; tickets can be bought on board buses and streetcars (exact change required) and at underground Muni stations. Cable car tickets cost $6 per ride, and can be bought at cable car turnaround kiosks or on board from the conductor. Hang onto your ticket even if you're not planning to use it again: if you're caught without one by the transit police, you're subject to a $100 fine (repeat offenders may be fined up to $500).

TRANSFERS
At the start of your Muni journey, free transfer tickets are available for additional Muni trips within 90 minutes (not including cable cars or BART). After 8:30pm, buses issue a Late Night Transfer good for travel until 5:30am the following morning.

Discounts & Passes

MUNI PASSPORTS
A **Muni Passport** (one-/ three-/seven-days $14/21/27) allows unlimited travel on all Muni transport, including cable cars. It's sold at the Muni kiosk at the Powell St cable car turnaround on Market St, SF's Visitor Information Center (p298), the TIX Bay Area kiosk at Union Square (p35) and from a number of hotels. One-day passports can be purchased from cable car conductors.

CLIPPER CARDS
Downtown Muni/BART stations issue the **Clipper Card**, a reloadable transit card with a $5 minimum that can be used on Muni, BART, AC Transit, Caltrain, SamTrans, and Golden Gate Transit and Ferry (not cable cars). Clipper Cards automatically deduct fares and apply transfers – only one Muni fare is deducted in a 90-minute period.

FAST PASS
Monthly Muni Fast Pass (adult/child $62/21) offers unlimited Muni travel for the calendar month, including cable cars. Fast Passes are available at the Muni kiosk at the Powell St cable car turnaround and from businesses that display the Muni Pass sign in their window.

Bus

Muni buses display their route number and final destination on the front and side. If the number is followed by the letter A, B, X or L, then it's a limited-stop or express service.

KEY ROUTES
5 Fulton From the Temporary Transbay Terminal, along Market and McAllister Sts to Fulton St, along the north side of Golden Gate Park to the ocean.

14 Mission From the Temporary Transbay Terminal, along Mission St through SoMa and the Mission District.

22 Fillmore From Dogpatch (Potrero Hill), through the Mission on 16th St, along Fillmore St past Japantown to Pacific Heights and the Marina.

30 Stockton From the Caltrain Station in SoMa, through Chinatown on Stockton St, from North Beach to Fisherman's Wharf on Colombus, through North Beach on Columbus Ave, and to the Palace of Fine Arts at the Marina.

33 Stanyan From San Francisco General Hospital, through the Mission, Castro and Haight, past Golden Gate Park to Clement St.

38 Geary From the Temporary Transbay Terminal, along Market to Geary Blvd, north of Golden Gate Park through the Richmond district to Ocean Beach.

71 Noriega From the Temporary Transbay Terminal, along Market and Haight Sts, along the southeast side of Golden Gate Park through the Sunset and to the Great Hwy at the beach.

Streetcar

Muni Metro streetcars run from 5am to midnight on weekdays, with limited schedules on weekends. The L and N lines operate 24 hours, but above ground Owl buses replace streetcars between 12:30am and 5:30am. The F-Market line runs vintage streetcars above ground along Market St to the Embarcadero, where they turn north to Fisherman's Wharf. The T line heads south along the Embarcadero through SoMa and Mission Bay, then down 3rd St. Other streetcars run underground below Market St Downtown.

KEY ROUTES
F Fisherman's Wharf and Embarcadero to the Castro.

J Downtown to the Mission, the Castro and Noe Valley.

K, L, M Downtown to the Castro.

N Caltrain and SBC Ballpark to the Haight, Golden Gate Park and Ocean Beach.

T The Embarcadero to Caltrain and Bayview.

Cable Car

In this age of seat belts and air bags, a rickety cable-car ride is an anachronistic thrill. There are seats for about 30 seated passengers, who are often outnumbered by passengers clinging to creaking leather straps. For more on cable car maps, service and history, see p45.

KEY ROUTES
California St Runs east to west along California St, from

the Downtown terminus at Market and Davis Sts through Chinatown and Nob Hill to Van Ness Ave.

Powell-Mason Runs from the Powell St cable car turnaround past Union Square, turns west along Jackson St, and then descends north down Mason St, Columbus Ave and Taylor St towards Fisherman's Wharf. On the return trip it takes Washington St instead of Jackson St.

Powell-Hyde Follows the same route as the Powell-Mason line until Jackson St, where it turns down Hyde St to terminate at Aquatic Park; coming back it takes Washington St.

BART

Throughout this book, venues readily accessible by **BART** (Bay Area Rapid Transit; www.bart.gov; ⊙4am-midnight Mon-Fri, 6am-midnight Sat, 8am-midnight Sun) are denoted by 🚇 followed by the name of the nearest BART. The fastest link between Downtown and the Mission District also offers transit to SF airport, Oakland ($3.20) and Berkeley ($3.75). Four of the system's five lines pass through SF before terminating at Daly City or SFO. Within SF, one-way fares start at $1.75.

Tickets

BART tickets are sold at BART stations, and you'll need a ticket to enter and exit. If your ticket still has value after you exit the station, it is returned to you with the remaining balance. If your ticket's value is less than needed to exit, use an Addfare machine to pay the appropriate amount. The Clipper Card can be used for BART travel.

Transfers

At San Francisco BART stations, a 25¢ discount is available for Muni buses and streetcars; look for transfer machines before you pass through the turnstiles.

Taxi

Fares start at $3.50 at the flag drop and run about $2.25 per mile. Add at least 10% to the taxi fare as a tip ($1 minimum). Credit cards are often accepted, but confirm before getting into the cab.

The following taxi companies have 24-hour dispatches:

DeSoto Cab (📞415-970-1300)

Green Cab (📞415-626-4733; www.626green.com)

Luxor (📞415-282-4141)

Yellow Cab (📞415-333-3333)

Car & Motorcycle

If you can, avoid driving in San Francisco: traffic is a given, street parking is harder to find than true love, and meter readers are ruthless. Gas prices are rising steadily, and driving on these hills means applying brakes often. If you're driving a stick shift (manual transmission), you'd better have your hill-start technique down pat.

Three public bus systems connect San Francisco to the rest of the Bay Area. Most buses leave from clearly marked bus stops; for transit maps and schedules, see the bus system websites.

AC Transit (www.actransit.org) Offers bus East Bay services from the Temporary Transbay Terminal. For public transport connections from BART in the East Bay, get an AC Transit transfer ticket before leaving the BART station, and then pay an additional 75¢ to $1.

Golden Gate Transit (Map p330; www.goldengate transit.org) Connects San Francisco to Marin (tickets $2-3.25) and Sonoma counties (tickets $9.25-10.25), but be advised that service can be slow and erratic.

Samtrans (📞800-660-4287; www.samtrans.com) Runs buses between San Francisco and the South Bay, including bus services to/from SFO. Buses pick up/drop off from the Temporary Transbay Terminal and other marked bus stops within the city.

Traffic

San Francisco streets mostly follow a grid bisected by Market St, with signs pointing toward tourist zones such as North Beach, Fisherman's Wharf and Chinatown. Try to avoid driving during rush hours: 7:30am to 9:30am and 4:30pm to 6:30pm, Monday to Friday. Before heading to any bridge, airport or other traffic choke-point, call 📞511 for a traffic update.

Parking

Parking is tricky and often costly, especially Downtown – ask your hotel about parking, and inquire about validation at restaurants and entertainment venues.

GARAGES
Downtown parking garages charge from $2 to $8 per hour and $25 to $50 per day, depending on how long you park and whether you require in-and-out privileges. The most convenient Downtown parking lots are at the Embarcadero Center, at 5th and Mission Sts, under Union Square, and at Sutter and Stockton Sts; for more public parking garages, see www. sfmta.com.

PARKING RESTRICTIONS

Parking restrictions are indicated by the following color-coded sidewalk curbs:

Blue Disabled parking only; identification required.

Green Ten-minute parking zone from 9am to 6pm.

Red No parking or stopping.

White For picking up or dropping off passengers only.

Yellow Loading zone from 7am to 6pm.

TOWING VIOLATIONS

Desperate motorists often resort to double-parking or parking in red zones or on sidewalks, but parking authorities are quick to tow cars. If this should happen to you, you'll have to retrieve your car at **Autoreturn** (☎415-865-8200; www.auto return.com; 450 7th St, SoMa; ☺24hr; Ⓜ27, 42). Besides at least $73 in fines for parking violations, you'll also have to fork out a towing and storage fee ($393 for the first four hours, $62 for the rest of the first day, $62 for every additional day, plus a $25.50 transfer fee if your car is moved to a long-term lot). Cars are usually stored at 415 7th St, corner of Harrison St.

Rental

Typically, a small car might cost $50 to $60 a day or $175 to $300 a week, plus 9.5% sales tax. Unless your credit card covers car-rental insurance, you'll need to add $10 to $20 per day for a loss/damage waiver. Most rates include unlimited mileage; with cheap rates, there's often a per-mile charge above a certain mileage.

Booking ahead usually ensures the best rates, and airport rates are generally better than those in the city. As part of SF's citywide green initiative, rentals of hybrid cars and low-emissions vehicles from rental agencies at SFO are available at a discount.

To rent a motorcycle, contact **Dubbelju** (☎415-495-2774; www.dubbelju.com; 689a Bryant St; Ⓜ27); rates start at $99 per day. Major car-rental agencies include:

Alamo Rent-a-Car (☎415-693-0191, 800-327-9633; www.alamo.com; 750 Bush St, Downtown; ☺7am-7pm; Ⓜ2, 3, 4, 76; 🚋Powell-Mason, Powell-Hyde)

Avis (☎415-929-2555, 800-831-2847; www.avis.com; 675 Post St, Downtown; ☺6am-6pm; Ⓜ2, 3, 4, 76)

Budget (☎415-292-8981, 800-527-0700; www.budget.com; 321 Mason St, Downtown; ☺6am-6pm; Ⓜ2, 3, 4, 38)

Dollar (☎800-800-5252; www.dollarcar.com; 364 O'Farrell St, Downtown;☺7am-7pm; Ⓜ2, 3, 4, 38)

Hertz (☎415-771-2200, 800-654-3131; www.hertz.com; 325 Mason St, Downtown; ☺6am-6pm Mon-Thu, to 8pm Fri & Sat; Ⓜ2, 3, 4, 38)

Thrifty (☎415-788-6906, 800-367-2277; www.thrifty.com; 350 O'Farrell St, Downtown; ☺7am-7pm; Ⓜ2, 3, 4, 38)

Car Share

Car-sharing is a convenient alternative to rentals that spares you pick-up/drop-off and parking hassles: reserve a car online for an hour or two or all day, and you can usually pick up/drop off your car within blocks of where you're staying. It also does the environment a favor: fewer cars on the road means less congestion and pollution, especially with fuel-efficient and hybrid share-cars.

Zipcar (☎866-494-7227; www.zipcar.com) rents Prius Hybrids and Minis by the hour for flat rates starting at $6.98 per hour, including gas and insurance, or by day for $69.30; a $25 application fee and $50 prepaid usage are required in advance. Drivers without a US driver's license should follow instructions on the website. Once approved, cars can be reserved online or by phone. Check the website for pick-up/drop-off locations.

Roadside Assistance

Members of **American Automobile Association** (AAA; ☎415-773-1900, 800-222-4357; www.aaa.com; 160 Sutter St; ☺8:30am-5:30pm Mon-Fri) can call the 800 number any time for emergency road service and towing. AAA also provides travel insurance and free road maps of the region.

Boat

The opening of the Bay Bridge in 1936 and the Golden Gate Bridge in 1937 spelled the near demise of ferry services across the Bay, but with the revival of the

FURTHER AFIELD: LOS ANGELES & LAS VEGAS

For muscle beaches, celebrity sightings and camera-ready wackiness, head south on coastal Hwy 1 to Los Angeles. It'll take 12 hours depending on traffic and how often you stop. A quicker jaunt is less-scenic Hwy 101 (nine hours); the fastest route is boring inland I-5, which takes about six hours.

Las Vegas, Nevada, is a nine-hour non-stop drive from San Francisco. Cross the Bay Bridge to 580 east, to I-5 south, veering off towards 99 south (at exit 278), to 58 east, then I-15 the last 160 miles. A slower, gloriously scenic option is to go east through Yosemite National Park on Hwy 120 (summer only; verify by calling 800-GAS-ROAD) and south on Hwy 395, east on Hwy 190 through Death Valley National Park then south on Hwy 95 straight into Sin City.

Embarcadero and reinvention of the Ferry Building as a gourmet dining destination, commuters and tourists alike are taking the scenic way across the bay after leisurely Ferry Building meals.

ALCATRAZ
Alcatraz Cruises (☎415-981-7625; www.alcatrazcruises.com; adult/child day $26/16, night $33/19.50) has ferries departing from Pier 33 for Alcatraz every half-hour from 9am to 3:55pm, and at 6:10pm and 6:45pm for night tours.

EAST BAY
Blue & Gold Fleet Ferries (Map p318; ☎415-705-8200; www.blueandgoldfleet.com) operates ferries from the Ferry Building, Pier 39 and Pier 41 at Fisherman's Wharf to Jack London Square in Oakland (one-way $6.25). During baseball season, a Giants ferry service runs directly from the landing at AT&T Park's Seals Plaza entrance to Oakland and Alameda. Ticket booths are located at the Ferry Building and Piers 39 and 41.

MARIN COUNTY
Golden Gate Transit Ferries (Map p318; ☎415-455-2000; www.goldengateferry.org; ⏱6am-9:30pm Mon-Fri, 10am-6pm Sat & Sun) runs regular ferry services from the Ferry Building to Larkspur and Sausalito (one-way adult/child $9.25/4.50). Transfers are available to Muni bus services, and bicycles are permitted. Blue & Gold Fleet Ferries also provides service to Tiburon or Sausalito (one-way $10.50).

NAPA VALLEY
Get to Napa car-free via **Vallejo Ferry** (☎877-643-3779; www.baylinkferry.com; adult/child $13/6.50) with departures from Ferry Building docks about every hour from 6:30am to 7pm weekdays and every two hours from 11am to 7:30pm on weekends;

BIKING AROUND THE BAY AREA

➤ **Within SF** Muni has racks that can accommodate two bikes on some of its commuter routes, including 17, 35, 36, 37, 39, 53, 56, 66, 76, 91 and 108.

➤ **Marin County** Bikes are allowed on the Golden Gate Bridge, so getting north to Marin County is no problem. You can transport bicycles on Golden Gate Transit buses, which usually have free racks available (first-come, first-served). Ferries also allow bikes aboard when space allows.

➤ **Wine Country** To transport your bike to Wine Country, take Golden Gate Transit or the Vallejo Ferry. Within Sonoma Valley, take Arnold Dr instead of busy Hwy 12; through Napa Valley, take the Silverado Trail instead of Hwy 29 to avoid manic drivers U-turning for wineries. The most spectacular ride in Wine Country is sun-dappled, tree-lined West Dry Creek Rd in Sonoma's Dry Creek Valley.

➤ **East Bay** Cyclists can't use the Bay Bridge, so you'll need to take your bike on BART. Bikes are allowed on BART at all hours, but during rush hours some limits apply. Between 6:30am and 9am, people with bikes are only allowed to travel in the 'reverse commute' direction from Embarcadero station in San Francisco to points in the East Bay. From 4pm to 6:30pm, people with bikes can travel only from points in the East Bay to San Francisco, and they must exit at Embarcadero station. During commute hours, you can also travel with your bike across the bay via the **Caltrain's Bay Bridge Bicycle Commuter Shuttle** (☎510-286-0876; tickets $1; ⏱6:20-8:30am & 3:50-6:15pm Mon-Fri), which operates from the corner of Folsom and Main Sts in San Francisco and MacArthur BART station in Oakland.

bikes are permitted. From the Vallejo Ferry Terminal, take Napa Valley Vine bus 10 to downtown Napa, Yountville, St Helena or Calistoga.

Caltrain
From the depot at 4th and King Sts in San Francisco, **Caltrain** (☎800-660-4287; www.caltrain.com) heads south to Millbrae (connecting to BART and SFO, 30 minutes), Palo Alto (one hour) and San Jose (1½ hours). This is primarily a commuter line, with frequent departures during weekday rush hours and less often between non-rush hours and on weekends.

Bicycle
San Francisco is fairly bike-friendly, but traffic Downtown can be dangerous; biking is best east of Van Ness Ave. For bike shops and rentals in SF, see p41; for bike rentals and tours in Wine Country, see p293. Bicycles can be carried on BART, but not in the commute direction during weekday rush hours. If you're bringing your own, bicycles can be checked in boxes on Greyhound buses for $20 to $30; bike boxes cost $10. On Amtrak, bikes can be checked as baggage for $5.

Directory
A–Z

Business Hours

Standard business hours are as follows. Nonstandard hours are listed in specific reviews.

Banks 9am to 4:30pm or 5pm Monday to Friday (occasionally 9am to noon Saturday).

Offices 8:30am to 5:30pm Monday to Friday.

Restaurants Breakfast 8am to noon, lunch noon to 3pm, dinner 5:30pm to 10pm; Saturday and Sunday brunch 10am to 2pm.

Shops 10am to 6pm or 7pm Monday to Saturday and noon to 6pm Sunday.

Customs Regulations

Each person over the age of 21 is allowed to bring 1L of liquor and 200 cigarettes duty-free into the USA. Non-US citizens are allowed to bring in $100 worth of duty-free gifts. Should you be carrying more than $10,000 in US or foreign cash, traveler's checks or money orders, you need to declare the excess amount – undeclared sums in excess of $10,000 may be subject to confiscation.

Discount Cards

Go Card (☑800-887-9103; www.gosanfranciscocard.com; adult/child 1-day $55/40, 2-day

---

PRACTICALITIES

Newspapers & Magazines

➡ **San Francisco Bay Guardian** (www.sfbg.com) SF's free, alternative weekly covers politics, theater, music, art and movie listings.

➡ **San Francisco Chronicle** (www.sfgate.com) Main daily newspaper with news, entertainment and event listings online (no registration required).

➡ **SF Weekly** (www.sfweekly.com) Free weekly with local gossip and entertainment.

Radio

For local listening in San Francisco and online via podcasts and/or streaming audio, check out these stations:

➡ **KQED** 88.5 FM (www.kqed.org) National Public Radio (NPR) and Public Broadcasting (PBS) affiliate offering podcasts and streaming video.

➡ **KALW** 91.7 FM (www.kalw.org) Local NPR affiliate: news, talk, music, original programming.

➡ **KPOO** 89.5 FM (www.kpoo.com) Community radio with jazz, R&B, blues and reggae.

➡ **KPFA** 94.1 FM (www.kpfa.org) Alternative news and music.

Volunteering

➡ **VolunteerMatch** (www.volunteermatch.org) Matches your interests, talents and availability with a local nonprofit where you could donate your time, if only for a few hours.

➡ **Craigslist** (http://sfbay.craigslist.org/vol) Lists opportunities to be of service to the Bay Area community, from nonprofit fashion-show fundraisers to teaching English to new arrivals.

$76/59, 3-day $96/70) Offers unlimited access to the city's major attractions, including cable cars, California Academy of Sciences, Exploratorium, SFMOMA, MH de Young Museum, Aquarium of the Bay and more, plus discounts on packaged tours and waterfront restaurants and cafes. Do the math on entry fees at your desired destinations, and think about how much you can reasonably do in a day; there's no sense tuckering yourself out just to sweeten your Go Card deal.

It pays to be green in SF, with special discounts on Bay Area green-friendly businesses from the **Green Zebra guide** (www.thegreen zebra.org). Some green-minded venues also offer discounts for ticket-bearing Muni riders, including the MH de Young Museum, the California Academy of Sciences and the Legion of Honor.

Electricity

120v/60hz

120v/60hz

Electric current in the USA is 110 to 115 volts, 60Hz AC. Outlets may be suited for flat two-prong or three-prong plugs. If your appliance is made for another electrical system, pick up a transformer or adapter at Walgreens (p296).

Emergencies

Police, Fire & Ambulance (⍾emergency 911, nonemergency 311)

San Francisco General Hospital (⍾emergency room 415-206-8111, main hospital 415-206-8000; www.sfdph.org; 1001 Potrero Ave; MPotrero Ave)

Drug & Alcohol Emergency Treatment (⍾415-362-3400)

Trauma Recovery & Rape Treatment Center (⍾415-437-3000; www.trauma recoverycenter.org)

Internet Access

SF has free wi-fi hot spots citywide – locate one nearby with www.openwifispots. com. Places listed in this guide that offer wi-fi have a

🛜 symbol. You can connect for free at most cafes and hotel lobbies, as well as at the following locations:

Apple Store (www.apple. com/retail/sanfrancisco; 1 Stockton St; 🕘9am-9pm Mon-Sat, 10am-8pm Sun; MPowell St; 🛜) Free wi-fi and internet terminal usage.

San Francisco Main Library (www.sfpl.org; 100 Larkin St; 🕘10am-6pm Mon & Sat, 9am-8pm Tue-Thu, noon-5pm Fri & Sun; 🛜) Free 15-minute internet terminal usage; spotty wi-fi access.

Legal Matters

San Francisco police usually have more urgent business than fining you for picking a protected orange California poppy on public land (up to $500), littering ($100 and up), jaywalking (ie crossing streets outside a pedestrian crosswalk, which can run from $75 to $125) or failing to clean up after your puppy ($30 in some places, plus shaming glares from fellow dog-owners).

Drinking alcoholic beverages outdoors is not officially allowed, though drinking beer and wine is often permissible at street fairs and other outdoor events. You may be let off with a warning for being caught taking a puff on a joint, but don't count on it – possessing marijuana for personal use is still a misdemeanor in this lenient city, though legal with a prescription inside a medicinal marijuana club. In recent years the police have cracked down on park squatters, so maybe you should change your plans if you were hoping to relive the Summer of Love at Golden Gate Park.

If you are arrested for any reason, it's your right to remain silent, but never walk away from an officer until given permission or you could be charged with resisting arrest. Anyone arrested gets the right to make one phone call. If you want to call your consulate, the police will give you the number on request.

Medical Services

Before traveling, contact your health-insurance provider to find out what types of medical care they will cover outside your hometown (or home country). Overseas visitors should acquire travel insurance that covers medical situations in the US, where nonemergency care for uninsured patients can be very expensive. For nonemergency appointments at hospitals, you'll need proof of insurance or cash. Even with insurance, you'll most likely have to pay up front for nonemergency care, and then wrangle with your insurance company afterwards in order to get your money reimbursed. That said, San Francisco has reputable medical facilities as well as alternative medical practices and herbal apothecaries; see following for specific listings.

Clinics

American College of Traditional Chinese Medicine (☑415-282-9603; www.actcm.edu; 450 Connecticut St; ☺8:30am-9pm Mon-Thu, 9am-5:30pm Fri & Sat; Ⓜ18th St) Acupuncture, herbal remedies and other traditional Chinese medical treatments.

Haight Ashbury Free Clinic (☑415-746-1950; www.hafci.org; 558 Clayton St; ☺by appointment;Ⓜ6, 71, N) Services are offered by appointment only, but once you're in, a doctor will see you for free; provides substance abuse and mental health services.

Lyon-Martin Women's Health Services (☑415-565-7667; www.lyon-martin.org; ste 201, 1748 Market St; ☺11am-7pm Mon & Wed, 9am-5pm Tue & Fri, noon-5pm Thu; Ⓜ6, 71, F) Women's clinic with affordable

gynecological, recovery, HIV and mental health services, by appointment only; lesbian- and transgender-friendly.

Emergency Rooms

Davies Medical Center (☑415-565-6000; cnr Noe & Duboce Sts; ☺24hr; Ⓜ6, 22, 24, 71, J, N) Offers 24-hour emergency services.

San Francisco General Hospital (☑emergency 415-206-8111, main hospital 415-206-8000; www.sfdph.org; 1001 Potrero Ave; ☺24hr; Ⓜ9) Provides care to uninsured patients; no documentation required beyond ID.

University of California San Francisco Medical Center (☑415-476-1000; www.ucsfhealth.org; 505 Parnassus Ave; ☺24hr; Ⓜ6, 24, 71, N) Leading medical advances nationwide.

Pharmacies

Pharmaca (☑415-661-1216; www.pharmaca.com; 925 Cole St; ☺8am-8pm Mon-Fri, 9am-8pm Sat & Sun; Ⓜ6, 43, N) Pharmacy plus naturopathic and alternative remedies, and weekend chair massage.

Walgreens (☑415-861-3136; www.walgreens.com; 498 Castro St at 18th St; ☺24hr; Ⓜ24, 35, F) Pharmacy and over-the-counter meds; dozens of locations citywide (see website).

Money

US dollars are the only accepted currency in San Francisco, though barter is sometimes possible on **Craigslist** (http://sfbay.craigslist.org). Debit/credit cards are accepted widely, but bringing a combination of cash, cards and traveler's checks is wise.

ATMs

Most banks have ATM machines, which are open 24

hours a day, except in areas where street crime has proved a problem (such as near the BART stop at 16th and Mission Sts). For a nominal service charge, you can withdraw cash from an ATM using a credit card; check with your provider about applicable fees.

Changing Money

Though there are exchange bureaus located at airports, the best rates are generally at banks in the city. For the latest exchange rates, visit currency converter website www.xe.com.

American Express (AmEx; ☑415-536-2600; www.americanexpress.com/travel; 455 Market St; ☺8:30am-5:30pm Mon-Fri, 9:30am-3:30pm Sat; Ⓜ&ⓇEmbarcadero) Traveler's checks are still a handy cash backup in case your ATM and credit cards inexplicably stop working; the shop exchanges money as well.

Bank of America (☑415-837-1394; www.bankamerica.com; downstairs, 1 Powell St; ☺9am-6pm Mon-Fri, to 2pm Sat; Ⓜ&ⓇPowell St) Though any bank can exchange currency, this branch of the Bank of America is the most centrally located and convenient.

Traveler's Checks

In the US, traveler's checks in US dollars are virtually as good as cash; you don't have to go to a bank to cash them, as many establishments will accept them just like cash. The major advantage of traveler's checks in US dollars over cash is that they can be replaced if lost or stolen.

Organized Tours

Chinatown Alleyway Tours (☑415-984-1478; www.chinatownalleywaytours.org; adult/child $18/5; ☺11am Sat

& Sun) Neighborhood teens lead two-hour tours for up-close-and-personal peeks into Chinatown's past (weather permitting). Book five days ahead or pay double for Saturday walk-ins; cash only.

Fire Engine Tours (☑415-333-7077; www.fireenginetours.com; Beach St at the Cannery; adult/child $50/30; ⊙tours depart 1pm) Hot stuff: a 75-minute ride in an open-air vintage fire engine over Golden Gate Bridge. Dress warmly in case of fog.

Green Tortoise (☑800-867-8647, 415-956-7500; www.greentortoise.com) Quasi-organized, slow travel on customized, biodiesel-fueled buses with built-in berths that run from San Francisco to points across California and beyond, including Bay Area day tours to Half Moon Bay and Santa Cruz; three-day trips to Yosemite or Death Valley; three-to-five-day jaunts to Burning Man and other festivals; and three-to-seven-day coastal trips south to Monterey, Big Sur and LA.

Precita Eyes Mission Mural Tours (☑415-285-2287; www.precitaeyes.org; adult $12-15, child $5; ⊙11am, noon, 1:30pm Sat & Sun) Muralists lead two-hour tours on foot or bike covering 60 to 70 murals in a six to 10 block radius of mural-bedecked Balmy Alley; proceeds fund mural upkeep.

Public Library City Guides (www.sfcityguides.org; tours free) Volunteer local historians lead tours by neighborhood and theme: Art Deco Marina, Gold Rush Downtown, Pacific Heights Victorians, North Beach by Night and more. See website for upcoming tours.

Transported SF (☑415-424-1058; www.transportedsf.com; $23-35) The journey is the destination with these DJ-equipped party buses bound for Sonoma organic wineries, Treasure Island, the Marin Headlands, and nowhere in particular in the

Mission. Departures are twice monthly; see website for upcoming dates and destinations.

Pets

Since San Franciscans have more pets than kids, this town is definitely pet-friendly – although dogs still have to stay on a leash in many parts of town, and you're required by law to clean up your dog's little gifts to nature.

Leash Laws

To check out the best locations for Rover to roam free, see **Urban Hound** (http://sf.urbanhound.com), and bone up on local leash laws at **SF Dog** (www.sfdog.org).

Dog Housing

To find SF hotels that allow dogs, check out www.dogfriendly.com. If you need to go away for a few days, you might check your pet into the swanky **Wag Hotel** (☑415-876-0700; www.waghotels.com; 25 14th St).

Community

There are opportunities galore for pet lovers to connect in SF, including two SF-based websites: www.catster.com and www.dogster.com.

Post

Check www.usps.com for post office locations throughout San Francisco. Following are the most conveniently located post offices for visitors:

Civic Center Post Office (Map p322; ☑415-563-7284; 101 Hyde St; Ⓜ&Ⓡ Civic Center)

Rincon Center Post Office (Map p330; ☑800-275-8777, 415-896-0762; 180 Steuart St; ⊙8am-6pm Mon-Fri, to 2pm Sat; Ⓜ&Ⓡ Embarcadero)

US Post Office (Map p320; ☑415-397-3333; Macy's, 170 O'Farrell St; Ⓜ&Ⓡ Powell St; Ⓡ Powell-Mason & Powell-Hyde) Located at Macy's department store.

Public Holidays

A majority of shops remain open on public holidays (with the exception of July 4, Thanksgiving, Christmas and New Year's Day), while banks, schools and offices are usually closed. For information on festivals and events, see p22. Holidays that may affect business hours and transit schedules include the following:

New Year's Day January 1

Martin Luther King Jr Day Third Monday in January

Presidents' Day Third Monday in February

Easter Sunday (and Good Friday and Easter Monday) in March or April

Memorial Day Last Monday in May

Independence Day July 4

Labor Day First Monday in September

Columbus Day Second Monday in October

Veterans Day November 11

Thanksgiving Fourth Thursday in November

Christmas Day December 25

Safe Travel

Keep your city smarts and wits about you, especially at night at the Tenderloin, South of Market (SoMa) and the Mission. The Bayview-Hunters Point neighborhood south of Potrero Hill along the water is plagued by a high crime rate and frequent violence, and not particularly suitable for wandering tourists. After dark, Mission Dolores Park, Buena Vista Park and the entry to Golden Gate Park at Haight and Stanyan

Sts host drug deals and casual sex hookups.

Taxes

SF's 9.5% sales tax is added to virtually everything, including meals, accommodations and car rentals. Groceries are about the only items not taxed, and unlike European Value Added Tax, sales tax is not refundable. There's also a 14% hotel room tax to take into consideration when booking a hotel room. In response to city laws mandating healthcare benefits for restaurant workers, some restaurants are passing along those costs to diners by tacking an additional 4% charge onto the bill – a slippery business practice mentioned in the menu fine print that may eventually be eliminated, given widespread diner protest on restaurant review websites.

Telephone

The US country code is ☑1, and San Francisco's city code is ☑415. To make an international call from the Bay Area, call ☑011 + country code + area code + number. When calling Canada, there's no need to dial the international access code ☑011. When dialing another area code, the code must be preceded by ☑1. For example, to dial an Oakland number from San Francisco, start with ☑1-510.

Area Codes in the Bay Area

East Bay ☑510
Marin County ☑415
Peninsula ☑650
San Francisco ☑415
San Jose ☑408
Santa Cruz ☑831
Wine Country ☑707

Local calls from a public pay phone usually start at

50¢. Hotel telephones will often add heavy surcharges. Toll-free numbers start with ☑800 or ☑888, while phone numbers beginning with ☑900 usually incur high fees.

Cell Phones

Most US cell phones besides the iPhone operate on CDMA, not the European standard GSM – make sure you check compatibility with your phone service provider. North American travelers can use their cell phones in San Francisco and the Bay Area, but should check with the carrier about roaming charges.

Operator Services

International operator (☑00)
Local directory (☑411)
Long-distance directory information (☑1 + area code + 555-1212)
Operator (☑0)
Toll-free number information (☑800-555-1212)

Phonecards

For international calls from a public pay phone, it's a good idea to use a phone card, available at most corner markets and drug stores. Otherwise, when you dial 0, you're at the mercy of the international carrier who covers that pay phone.

Time

San Francisco is on Pacific Standard Time (PST), three hours behind the East Coast's Eastern Standard Time (EST) and eight hours behind Greenwich Mean Time (GMT/UTC). Summer is Daylight Saving Time in the US.

Toilets

Citywide Self-cleaning, coin-operated outdoor kiosk commodes cost 25¢; there are 25 citywide, mostly located

at North Beach, Fisherman's Wharf, the Financial District and the Tenderloin. Toilet paper isn't always available; there's a 20-minute time limit to avoid lines.

Downtown Clean toilets and baby-changing tables can be found at Westfield San Francisco Centre (p96) and Macy's (p96).

Civic Center San Francisco Main Library (p83) has restrooms, as do public library branches and parks throughout the city.

Haight-Ashbury & Mission District Woefully lacking in public toilets; you may have to buy coffee, beer or food to gain access to locked customer-only bathrooms.

Tourist Information

San Francisco Visitor Information Center (Map p320; ☑415-391-2000, events hotline 415-391-2001; www.onlyinsanfrancisco.com; lower level, Hallidie Plaza, Market & Powell Sts; ⏰9am-5pm Mon-Fri, to 3pm Sat & Sun; Ⓜ&ⓇPowell St) Provides practical information for tourists, publishes glossy tourist-oriented booklets and runs a 24-hour events hotline.

Golden Gate National Recreation Area Headquarters (Map p315; ☑415-561-4700; www.nps.gov/goga; 499 Jefferson St; ⏰8:30am-4:30pm Mon-Fri; Ⓜ19, 30, 47, F; ⒸPowell-Hyde) Find out everything a hard-core hiker needs to know about accessing the outer reaches of the Golden Gate National Recreation Area, including the Presidio, Alcatraz, Fort Point, Fort Funston, the Cliff House, Muir Woods and the Marin Headlands. This is the park's headquarters and visitors center, and offers a wealth of maps and information about camping, hiking and other programs for these and other national parks in the Pacific West region (including Yosemite).

For further tourist information, check out the following websites:

Lonely Planet (www.lonely planet.com)

SFGate.com (www.sfgate. com)

SFist (www.sfist.com)

Travelers with Disabilities

All Bay Area transit companies offer travel discounts for disabled travelers, and wheelchair-accessible service. Major car-rental companies can usually supply hand-controlled vehicles with one or two days' notice. For visually impaired people, major intersections emit a chirping signal to indicate when it is safe to cross the street. For the hearing impaired, many local TV stations include subtitles. Check the following resources:

San Francisco Bay Area Regional Transit Guide (www.transit.511.org/disabled/index.aspx) Covers accessibility for people with disabilities.

Muni's Street & Transit (www.sfmta.com) Details which bus routes and streetcar stops are wheelchair-friendly.

Independent Living Resource Center of San Francisco (☎415-543-6222; www.ilrcsf.org; ⏰9am-4:30pm Mon-Thu, to 4pm Fri) Provides further information about wheelchair accessibility on Bay Area public transit and in hotels and other local facilities.

Visas

Canadians

Canadian citizens currently only need proof of identity and citizenship to enter the US – but check the US Department of State for up-dates, as requirements may change.

Visa Waiver Program

USA Visa Waiver Program (VWP) allows nationals from 36 countries to enter the US without a visa, provided they are carrying a machine-readable passport. For the updated list of countries included in the program and current requirements, see the **US Department of State** (http://travel.state.gov/visa) website.

Citizens of VWP countries need to register with the US Department of Homeland Security (http://esta.cbp.dhs.gov) three days before their visit. There is a $14 fee for registration application; when approved, the registration is valid for two years.

Visas Required

You must obtain a visa from a US embassy or consulate in your home country if you:

➡ Do not currently hold a passport from a VWP country.

➡ Are from a VWP country, but don't have a machine-readable passport.

➡ Are from a VWP country, but currently hold a passport issued between October 26, 2005, and October 25, 2006, that does not have a digital photo on the information page or an integrated chip from the data page. (After October 25, 2006, the integrated chip is required on all machine-readable passports.)

➡ Are planning to stay longer than 90 days.

➡ Are planning to work or study in the US.

Work Visas

Foreign visitors are not legally allowed to work in the USA without the appropriate working visa. The most common, the H visa, can be difficult to obtain. It usually requires a sponsoring organization, such as the company you will be working for in the US. The company will need to demonstrate why you, rather than a US citizen, are most qualified for the job.

The type of work visa you need depends on your work:

H visa For temporary workers.

L visa For employees in intra company transfers.

O visa For workers with extraordinary abilities.

P visa For athletes and entertainers.

Q visa For international cultural-exchange visitors.

Women Travelers

Women should apply their street smarts in San Francisco as in any other US city, just to be on the safe side. SF is an excellent destination for solo women travelers: you can eat, stay, dine and go out alone without anyone making presumptions about your availability, interests or sexual orientation.

The Women's Building (p135) has a Community Resource Room offering information on healthcare, domestic violence, childcare, harassment, legal issues, employment and housing. For more sites and venues geared specifically to women and transgender individuals, see p37.

Behind the Scenes

SEND US YOUR FEEDBACK

We love to hear from travelers – your comments keep us on our toes and help make our books better. Our well-traveled team reads every word on what you loved or loathed about this book. Although we cannot reply individually to postal submissions, we always guarantee that your feedback goes straight to the appropriate authors, in time for the next edition. Each person who sends us information is thanked in the next edition – and the most useful submissions are rewarded with a free book.

Visit **lonelyplanet.com/contact** to submit your updates and suggestions or to ask for help. Our award-winning website also features inspirational travel stories, news and discussions.

Note: We may edit, reproduce and incorporate your comments in Lonely Planet products such as guidebooks, websites and digital products, so let us know if you don't want your comments reproduced or your name acknowledged. For a copy of our privacy policy visit lonelyplanet.com/privacy.

OUR READERS

Many thanks to the travelers who used the last edition and wrote to us with helpful hints, useful advice and interesting anecdotes:
Diana Frattali-Moreno, Petra Kempf, Jan Onno Reiners, Ophelie Vantournout and Luka Vidovic.

AUTHOR THANKS

Alison Bing

Many thanks and crushing California bear hugs to editorial superhero Suki Gear; delightful coauthor, co-conspirator, muse and raconteur John Vlahides; fearless leaders Brice Gosnell and Heather Dickson at Lonely Planet; cartographer Alison Lyall; editor Katie O'Connell; project manager Bruce Evans; the Sanchez Writers' Grotto for steady inspiration; fellow foodies Dee Budney, Sahai Burrowes, Yosh Han, Luke Haas, Mini Kahlon, PT Tenenbaum, Lisa Park, Raj Patel and Cook Here and Now; and above all to Marco Flavio Marinucci, whose powerful kindness and bracing espresso makes anything possible, including romance on a skeevy Muni bus.

John A Vlahides

I owe heartfelt thanks to my commissioning editor, Suki Gear, and co-author, Alison Bing, for their stellar assistance and always-sunny dispositions. Kate Brady, Steven Kahn, Karl Soehnlein, Kevin Clarke, Jim Aloise and Adam Young – you kept me upbeat and laughing when things seemed impossible. And to you, the readers, thank you for letting me be your guide to our wonderful little city. Have fun. I know you will.

ACKNOWLEDGMENTS

Cover photograph: Golden Gate Bridge seen from Marshall Beach, San Francisco, California, United States, Sabrina Dalbesio/ Lonely Planet Images.
Many of the images in this guide are available for licensing from Lonely Planet Images: www. lonelyplanetimages.com.

THIS BOOK

This 8th edition of Lonely Planet's *San Francisco* was researched and written by Alison Bing and John A Vlahides, as was the previous edition. This city guide was commissioned in Lonely Planet's Oakland office, and produced by the following:
Commissioning Editor Suki Gear
Coordinating Editor Gabrielle Innes
Coordinating Cartographer Alex Leung

Coordinating Layout Designer Jacqui Saunders
Managing Editors Bruce Evans, Anna Metcalfe
Managing Cartographers Alison Lyall, Adrian Persoglia
Managing Layout Designer Jane Hart
Assisting Editors Holly Alexander, Janet Austin, Susan Paterson, Tasmin Waby McNaughtan, Saralinda Turner
Assisting Cartographers Ildiko Bogdanovits, Csanad Csutoros, Katalin Dadi-Racz, Valentina Kremenchutskaya

Assisting Layout Designer Frank Deim
Cover Research Naomi Parker
Internal Image Research Sabrina Dalbesio

Thanks to Janine Eberle, Ryan Evans, Chris Girdler, Liz Heynes, Laura Jane, David Kemp, Wayne Murphy, Piers Pickard, Lachlan Ross, Michael Ruff, Julie Sheridan, Laura Stansfeld, John Taufa, Gerard Walker, Clifton Wilkinson

NOTES

Index

Sights p000
Map Pages p000
Photo Pages p000

San Francisco Maps

Map Legend

Sights
- Beach
- Buddhist
- Castle
- Christian
- Hindu
- Islamic
- Jewish
- Monument
- Museum/Gallery
- Ruin
- Winery/Vineyard
- Zoo
- Other Sight

Eating
- Eating

Drinking & Nightlife
- Drinking & Nightlife
- Cafe

Entertainment
- Entertainment

Shopping
- Shopping

Sleeping
- Sleeping
- Camping

Sports & Activities
- Diving/Snorkelling
- Canoeing/Kayaking
- Skiing
- Surfing
- Swimming/Pool
- Walking
- Windsurfing
- Other Sports & Activities

Information
- Post Office
- Tourist Information

Transport
- Airport
- Border Crossing
- BART
- Bus
- Cable Car
- Cycling
- Ferry
- Monorail
- Muni Buses & Streetcars
- Parking
- S-Bahn
- Taxi
- Tram
- Tube Station
- U-Bahn
- Other Transport

Routes
- Tollway
- Freeway
- Primary
- Secondary
- Tertiary
- Lane
- Unsealed Road
- Plaza/Mall
- Steps
- Tunnel
- Pedestrian Overpass
- Walking Tour
- Walking Tour Detour
- Path

Boundaries
- International
- State/Province
- Disputed
- Regional/Suburb
- Marine Park
- Cliff
- Wall

Geographic
- Hut/Shelter
- Lighthouse
- Lookout
- Mountain/Volcano
- Oasis
- Park
- Pass
- Picnic Area
- Waterfall

Hydrography
- River/Creek
- Intermittent River
- Swamp/Mangrove
- Reef
- Canal
- Water
- Dry/Salt/Intermittent Lake
- Glacier

Areas
- Beach/Desert
- Cemetery (Christian)
- Cemetery (Other)
- Park/Forest
- Sportsground
- Sight (Building)
- Top Sight (Building)

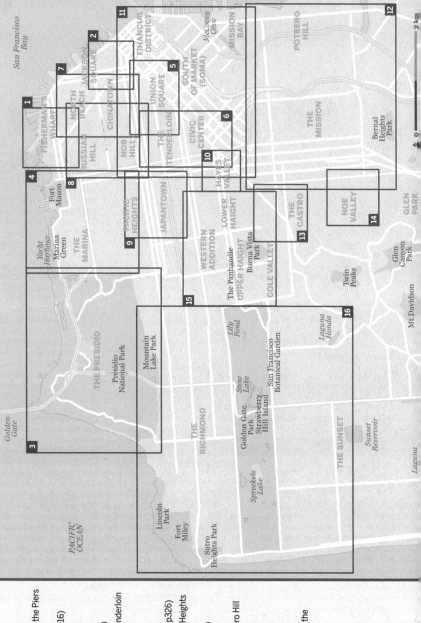

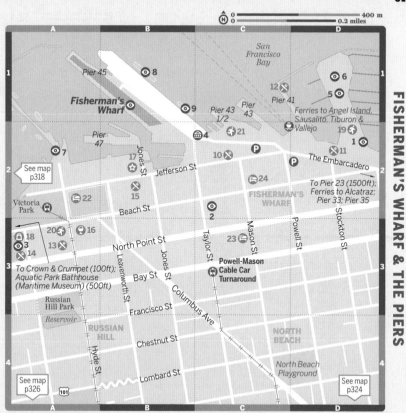

◎ **Top Sights** (p56)
Fisherman's Wharf B1

◎ **Sights** (p62)
1 Aquarium of the Bay D2
2 Beniamino Bufano's St Francis Statue....C2
3 Ghirardelli Square A3
4 Musée Mécanique C2
5 Pier 39 .... D1
6 San Francisco Carousel D1
7 San Francisco Maritime National
  Historical Park A2
8 SS Jeremiah O'Brien B1
9 USS Pampanito B1

◎ **Eating** (p66)
10 Boudin Bakery C2
11 Eagle Café D2
12 Forbes Island C1
13 Gary Danko A3
14 Ghirardelli Ice Cream A3

Grandeho's Kamekyo II .... (see 20)
15 In-N-Out Burger B2

◎ **Drinking & Nightlife** (p70)
16 Buena Vista Cafe A3

◎ **Entertainment** (p70)
17 Lou's Pier 47 .... B2

◎ **Shopping** (p71)
18 elizabethW A3

◎ **Sports & Activities** (p72)
19 Adventure Cat D2
20 Blazing Saddles A3
21 Red & White Fleet C2

◎ **Sleeping** (p241)
22 Argonaut Hotel A2
23 Tuscan Inn C3
24 Wharf Inn C2

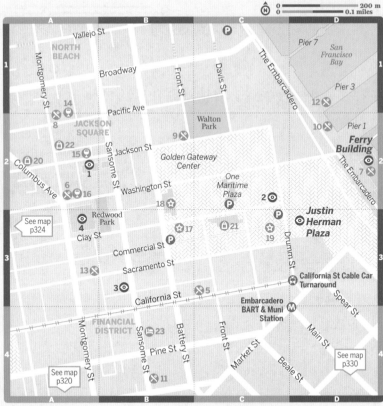

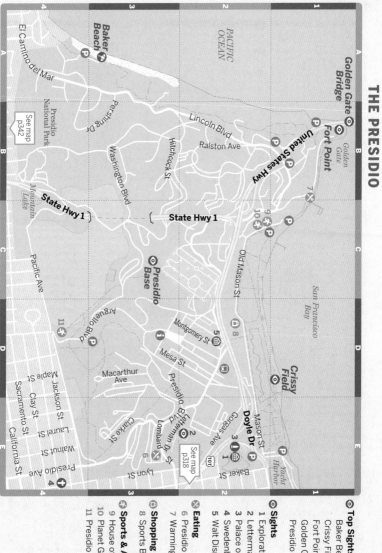

THE MARINA

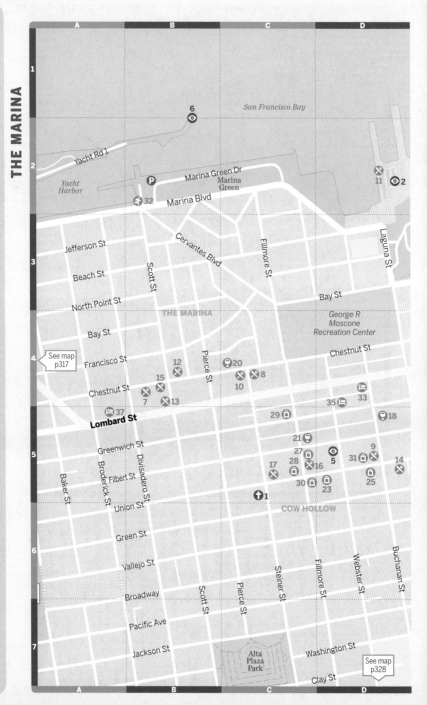

A | B | C | D

1

6

San Francisco Bay

Yacht Rd 1

Yacht
Harbor

Marina Green Dr

Marina
Green

11 · 2

P

32

Marina Blvd

2

Jefferson St

Cervantes Blvd

Beach St

Scott St

Filmore St

North Point St

Bay St

THE MARINA

Bay St

George R
Moscone
Recreation Center

3

Laguna St

See map
p317

Francisco St

12

Pierce St

20

Chestnut St

15

8

Chestnut St

10

7   13

35   33

37

29

18

Lombard St

Greenwich St

21

Baker St

Broderick St

Filbert St

Divisadero St

Greenwich St

27

9

17

28

5

31

14

16

30   23

25

Union St

1

COW HOLLOW

Green St

6

Vallejo St

Steiner St

Filmore St

Webster St

Buchanan St

Broadway

Scott St

Pierce St

Pacific Ave

7

Jackson St

Alta
Plaza
Park

Washington St

See map
p328

Clay St

A | B | C | D

UNION SQUARE

See map p316

See map p330

See map p324

See map p326

0.2 miles

400 m

BatterySt

1st St

Sansome St

Bush St

Stevenson St

2nd St

Minna St

Natoma St

Howard St

FINANCIAL
DISTRICT

Montgomery St
Trinity Pl

Montgomery St BART &
Muni Station

New Montgomery St

3rd St

SOUTH OF
MARKET
(SOMA)

Yerba Buena
Gardens

Mission St

Kearny St

Vermehr Pl

Robert
Kirk La

Grant Ave

Market St

4th St

St George
Al

Maiden La

Stockton St

UNION SQUARE

Joice St

Pine St

Fella Pl

NOB HILL

Bush St

Sutter St

Post St

Powell St

Geary St

O'Farrell St

Ellis St

Powell St BART
& Muni Station

Mason St

Taylor St

Jones St

THE
TENDERLOIN

Leavenworth St

Sights (p78)

1 49 Geary	E2
2 77 Geary	E3
3 Bohemian Club	B3
4 James Flood Building	D4
5 Lotta's Fountain	E3
6 One Montgomery Terrace	D3
7 Powell St Cable Car Turnaround	F2
8 Union Square	D4
9 Xanadu Gallery: Folk Art International	D3

Eating (p85)

10 Bio	D3
11 Boxed Foods	E1
12 Bread & Cocoa	E2
13 Cafe Claude	E1
14 Emporio Rulli	D2
15 Fleur de Lys	B2
16 Gitane	E2
Hecho	(see 55)
17 Johnny Foley's	C4
18 Katana-Ya	C3
19 Lefty O'Douls	C3
20 Mocca on Maiden Lane	D3
21 Muracci's Curry	E1
22 Rotunda	D3
23 Sons & Daughters	C1

Drinking & Nightlife (p89)

Burritt Room	(see 53)
24 Cantina	C2
25 Cellar	B2
Clock Bar	(see 79)
26 Gold Dust Lounge	C3
27 Irish Bank	E1
28 John's Grill	D4
29 Le Colonial	E2
30 Rickhouse	B2
31 Ruby Skye	C3
32 Tunnel Top	D1
33 Vessel	D2

Entertainment (p92)

34 American Conservatory Theater	C3
35 Biscuits & Blues	C3
36 Commonwealth Club	F2
37 Exit Theater	C5
38 Rrazz Room	C4
Starlight Room	(see 74)
39 Warfield	C5

Shopping (p95)

40 Barneys	D3
41 Britex Fabrics	D3
42 DSW	D4
43 Gump's	E2
44 H&M	D4
45 Le Sanctuaire	D2
46 Loehmann's	E2
47 Macy's	D3
48 Margaret O'Leary	E1
49 Original Levi's Store	D2
50 Westfield San Francisco Centre	D5

Sleeping (p241)

51 Adelaide Hostel	B3
52 Andrews Hotel	B3
53 Crescent Hotel	D2
54 Fitzgerald Hotel	B3
55 Galleria Park	E2
56 Golden Gate Hotel	C2
57 Hotel Abri	C4
58 Hotel Adagio	B3
59 Hotel California	B3
60 Hotel des Arts	E1
61 Hotel Diva	B3
62 Hotel Metropolis	C5
63 Hotel Monaco	B3
64 Hotel Palomar	E4
65 Hotel Rex	C2
66 Hotel Triton	E1
67 Hotel Union Square	D4
68 Inn at Union Square	C2
69 Kensington Park Hotel	C2
70 Larkspur Hotel	C2
71 Orchard Garden Hotel	E1
72 Palace Hotel	F2
73 Petite Auberge	B2
74 Sir Francis Drake Hotel	C2
75 Stratford Hotel	D3
76 Taj Campton Place	D2
77 USA Hostels	A3
78 Warwick San Francisco Hotel	B3
79 Westin St Francis Hotel	C3
80 White Swan Inn	B2

See map p322

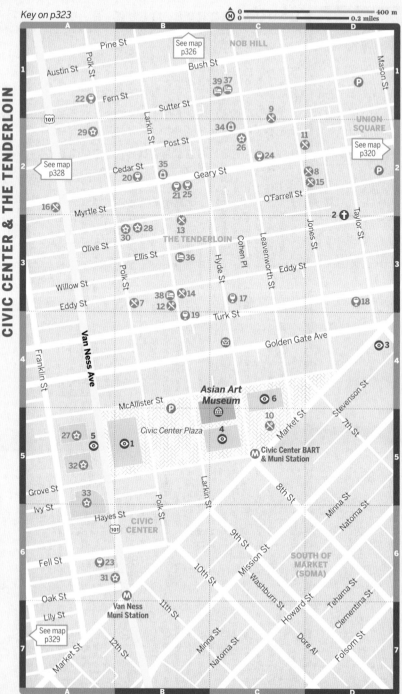

CIVIC CENTER & THE TENDERLOIN

Key on p323

0 — 400 m
0 — 0.2 miles

See map p326

See map p320

See map p328

See map p329

NOB HILL

UNION SQUARE

THE TENDERLOIN

Asian Art Museum

Civic Center BART & Muni Station

Civic Center Plaza

CIVIC CENTER

SOUTH OF MARKET (SOMA)

Van Ness Muni Station

Pine St
Austin St
Polk St
Fern St
Bush St
Sutter St
Larkin St
Post St
Cedar St
Geary St
Myrtle St
Olive St
Ellis St
Willow St
Polk St
Eddy St
Turk St
Golden Gate Ave
McAllister St
Larkin St
Hayes St
Fell St
Oak St
Lily St
Market St
12th St
11th St
10th St
9th St
8th St
Mission St
Washburn St
Howard St
Dore Al
Folsom St
Clementina St
Tehama St
Natoma St
Minna St
Stevenson St
7th St
O'Farrell St
Jones St
Taylor St
Leavenworth St
Hyde St
Cohen Pl
Eddy St
Mason St
Franklin St
Van Ness Ave
Grove St
Ivy St
Natoma St
Minna St

CIVIC CENTER & THE TENDERLOIN

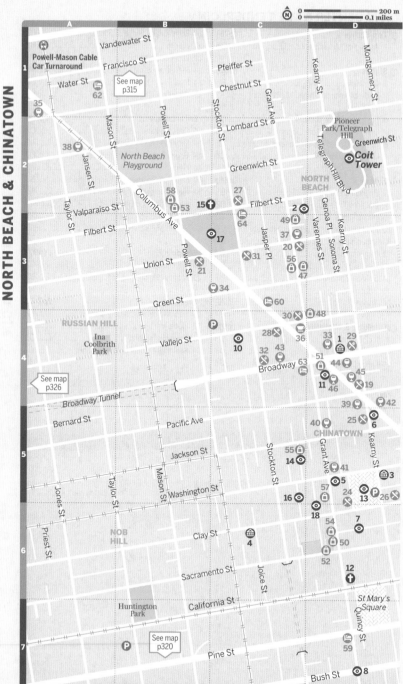

NORTH BEACH & CHINATOWN

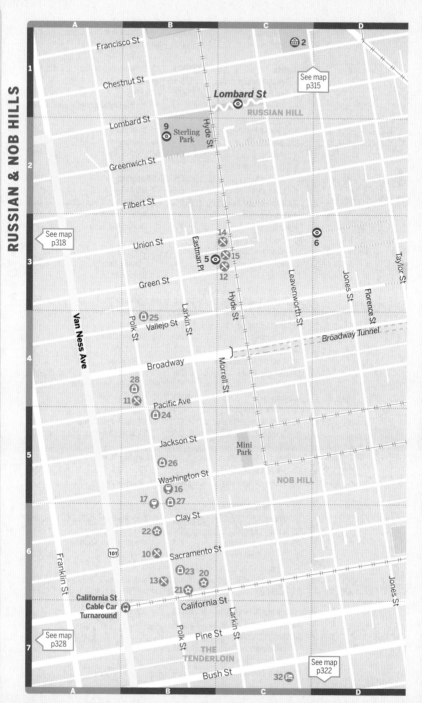

Francisco St

⊕ 2

Chestnut St

See map
p315

Lombard St ⊙

RUSSIAN HILL

Lombard St

9 ⊙ Sterling
Park

Hyde St

Greenwich St

Filbert St

14 ⊗

See map
p318

Union St

Eastman Pl

5 ⊙ ⊗ 15

6 ⊙

Green St

12 ⊗

Leavenworth St

Jones St

Taylor St

Florence St

Larkin St

Hyde St

25 🔒
Polk St
Vallejo St

Broadway Tunnel

Van Ness Ave

Broadway

Morrell St

28 🔒

11 ⊗

Pacific Ave

24 🔒

Jackson St

Mini
Park

26 🔒

NOB HILL

Washington St

16 🏠

17 🏠

27 🔒

Clay St

22 ☆

101

10 ⊗

Sacramento St

13 ⊗

23 🔒

20 ☆

21 ☆

Franklin St

Jones St

California St
Cable Car
Turnaround 🚋

California St

Larkin St

See map
p328

Pine St

Polk St

THE
TENDERLOIN

Bush St

32 🛏

See map
p322

RUSSIAN & NOB HILLS

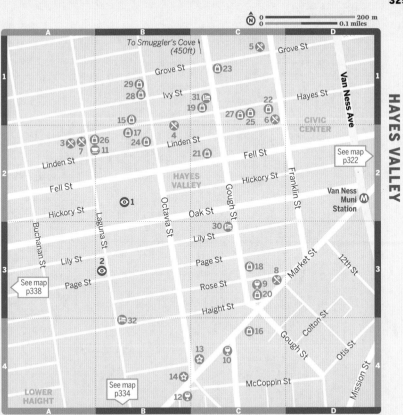

SOMA

Key on p332

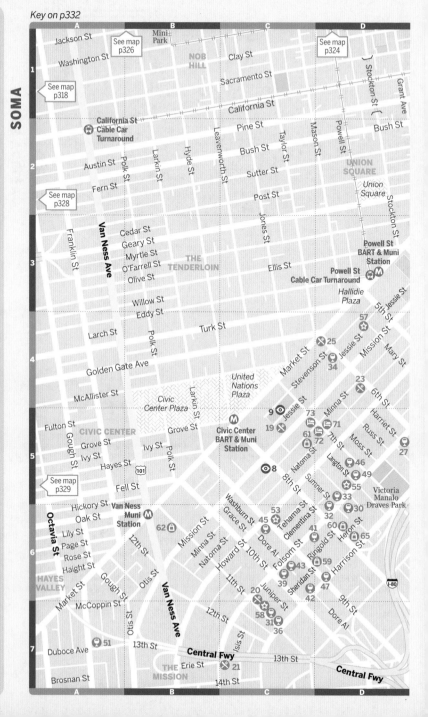

See map
p326

See map
p318

See map
p324

See map
p328

See map
p329

Jackson St

Washington St

Mini
Park

NOB
HILL

Clay St

Sacramento St

Stockton St

Grant Ave

California St
Cable Car
Turnaround

Pine St

Bush St

UNION
SQUARE

Austin St

Polk St

Larkin St

Hyde St

Leavenworth St

Bush St

Taylor St

Mason St

Powell St

Fern St

Sutter St

Union
Square

Post St

Stockton St

Franklin St

Van Ness Ave

Cedar St

Geary St

Myrtle St

O'Farrell St

Olive St

Jones St

THE
TENDERLOIN

Ellis St

Powell St
BART & Muni
Station

Powell St
Cable Car Turnaround

Willow St

Eddy St

Hallidie
Plaza

5th St

Jessie St

Larch St

Polk St

Turk St

57

Market St

25

Stevenson St

Jessie St

Mission St

Mary St

Golden Gate Ave

34

23

6th St

McAllister St

United
Nations
Plaza

Minna St

Harriet St

Fulton St

Gough St

Grove St

Ivy St

Civic
Center Plaza

Larkin St

Grove St

9

Jessie St

73

71

Russ St

Moss St

Civic Center
BART & Muni
Station

19

61

72

7th St

Ivy St

Hayes St

Polk St

8

Natoma St

Langton St

46

27

Fell St

8th St

Sumner St

49

55

33

Victoria
Manalo
Draves Park

Hickory St

Van Ness
Muni
Station

62

Washburn St

Grace St

53

45

Tehama St

Clementina St

32

30

Octavia St

Oak St

Lily St

Page St

Rose St

Haight St

12th St

Mission St

Minna St

Natoma St

Dore Al

41

60

65

Howard St

10th St

Folsom St

Ringold St

Heron St

Harrison St

43

59

I-80

HAYES
VALLEY

Market St

McCoppin St

Gough St

Otis St

Van Ness Ave

11th St

39

Sheridan St

47

Isis St

20

Juniper St

42

Dore Al

9th St

58

31

12th St

36

Duboce Ave

51

13th St

Central Fwy

13th St

Central Fwy

Brosnan St

THE
MISSION

Erie St

14th St

21

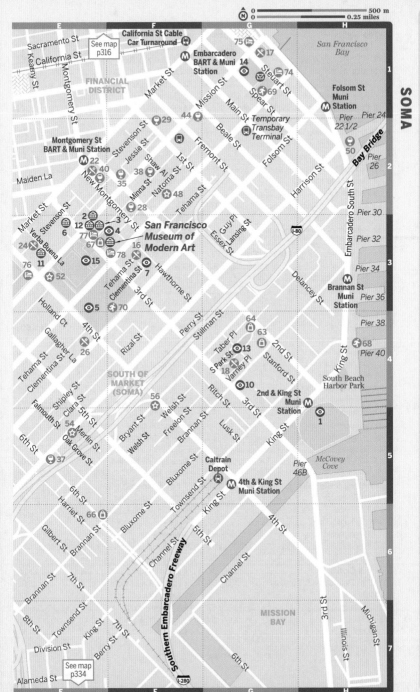

SOMA

See map p316

Sacramento St
Keary St
California St

FINANCIAL DISTRICT

California St Cable Car Turnaround

Montgomery St
Montgomery St BART & Muni Station

Maiden La

Market St

Stevenson St
Jessie St
Shaw Al
Minna St
Natoma St

Market St
Stevenson St
Yerba Buena La

Holland Ct

4th St

Gallagher La

Tehama St
Clementina St
Shipley St
Clara St
5th St
Falmouth St
6th St
Merlin St
Oak Grove St

Embarcadero BART & Muni Station

Market St
Mission St
Spear St

Steuart St

Folsom St Muni Station

San Francisco Bay

Pier 24

Bay Bridge

Pier 22 1/2

Pier 26

Main St
Beale St
Fremont St

Temporary Transbay Terminal

Folsom St

Harrison St

Embarcadero South St

Pier 30
Pier 32
Pier 34

Guy Pl
Essex St
Lansing St

I-80

1st St
Tehama St

San Francisco Museum of Modern Art

Tehama St
Clementina St
3rd St
Hawthorne St

Delancey St

Brannan St Muni Station

Pier 36
Pier 38
Pier 40

King St

South Beach Harbor Park

Perry St
Stillman St

Taber Pl
S Park St
Varney Pl

2nd St
Stanford St

Ritch St

2nd & King St Muni Station

SOUTH OF MARKET (SOMA)

Rizal St

Bryant St
Welsh St
Freelon St
Brannan St

Lusk St

3rd St

King St

McCovey Cove

Pier 46B

6th St
Harriet St

Gilbert St
Brannan St

Brannan St
7th St

8th St
Townsend St
King St
Division St

Bluxome St
Townsend St

Caltrain Depot

4th & King St Muni Station

Channel St

King St
5th St
4th St

Channel St

3rd St

Michigan St

MISSION BAY

Illinois St

Southern Embarcadero Freeway

I-280

Alameda St
Berry St
6th St

See map p334

SOMA *Map on p330*

THE MISSION & POTRERO HILL *Map on p334*

THE MISSION & POTRERO HILL

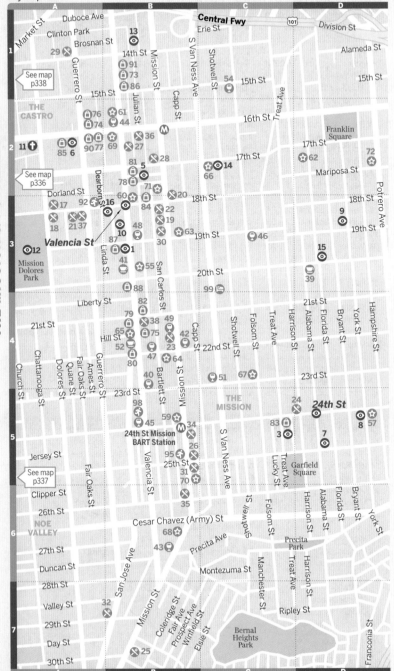

THE MISSION & POTRERO HILL

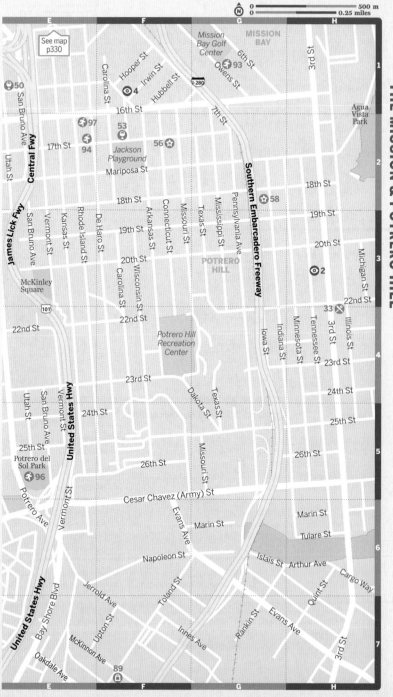

0 — 500 m
0 — 0.25 miles

See map p330

MISSION BAY

Mission Bay Golf Center

Agua Vista Park

POTRERO HILL

McKinley Square

Jackson Playground

Potrero Hill Recreation Center

Potrero del Sol Park

Streets:
Central Fwy
San Bruno Ave
Utah St
James Lick Fwy
San Bruno Ave
Vermont St
Kansas St
Rhode Island St
De Haro St
Carolina St
Wisconsin St
Arkansas St
Connecticut St
Missouri St
Texas St
Mississippi St
Pennsylvania Ave
Southern Embarcadero Freeway
Iowa St
Indiana St
Minnesota St
Tennessee St
3rd St
Illinois St
Michigan St
22nd St
Carolina St
Hooper St
Irwin St
Hubbell St
Owens St
6th St
3rd St
7th St
16th St
17th St
Mariposa St
18th St
19th St
20th St
22nd St
23rd St
24th St
25th St
26th St
Cesar Chavez (Army) St
United States Hwy
San Bruno Ave
Vermont St
Utah St
Potrero Ave
Bay Shore Blvd
Jerrold Ave
Upton St
McKinnon Ave
Oakdale Ave
Toland St
Innes Ave
Evans Ave
Napoleon St
Marin St
Marin St
Tulare St
Islais St
Arthur Ave
Cargo Way
Quint St
Rankin St
Evans Ave
3rd St
Dakota St
Texas St
Missouri St

Map numbers: 50, 4, 97, 94, 53, 56, 93, 58, 2, 33, 96, 89

I-280
101

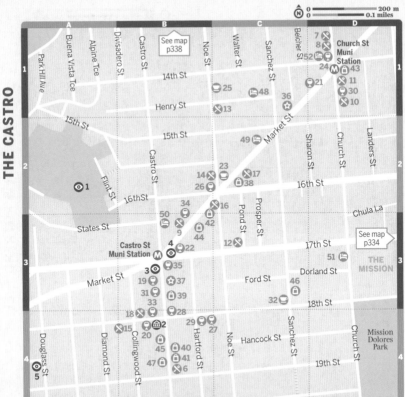

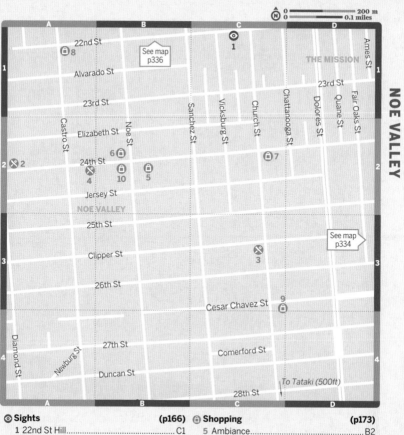

◉ **Sights** (p166)
1 22nd St Hill...C1

✕ **Eating** (p166)
2 Barney's Burgers.......................................A2
3 Lovejoy's Tea Room................................C3
4 Noe Valley Bakery A2

🛍 **Shopping** (p173)
5 Ambiance..B2
6 Global Exchange Fair Trade Craft
   Center B2
7 Isso...C2
8 Neon Monster...A1
9 Omnivore C3
10 PlumpJack Wines.....................................B2

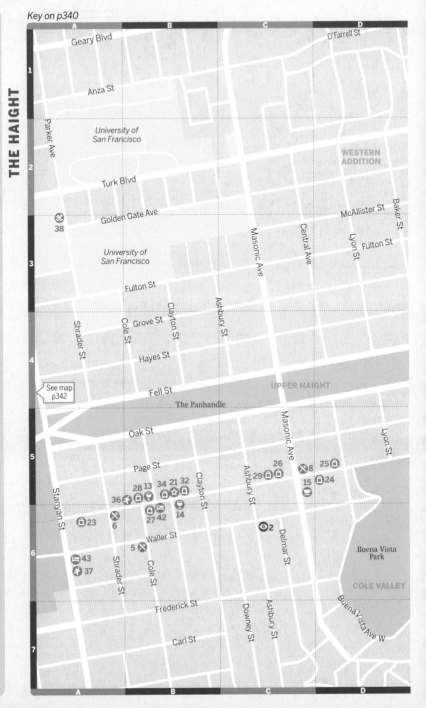

THE HAIGHT

See map
p342

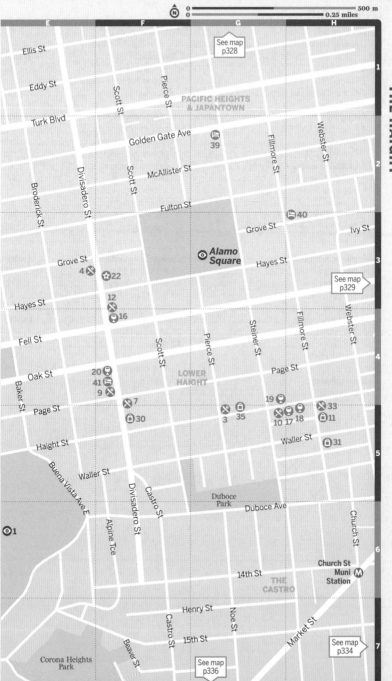

See map p328

See map p329

See map p334

See map p336

PACIFIC HEIGHTS & JAPANTOWN

Alamo Square

LOWER HAIGHT

THE CASTRO

Church St Muni Station

Duboce Park

Corona Heights Park

Ellis St
Eddy St
Turk Blvd
Golden Gate Ave
McAllister St
Fulton St
Grove St
Hayes St
Ivy St
Grove St
Hayes St
Fell St
Oak St
Page St
Haight St
Waller St
Duboce Ave
14th St
Henry St
15th St
Page St
Waller St
Scott St
Pierce St
Fillmore St
Webster St
Broderick St
Divisadero St
Baker St
Steiner St
Buena Vista Ave E
Alpine Tce
Divisadero St
Castro St
Castro St
Noe St
Beaver St
Church St
Market St

39
40
4
22
12
16
20
41
9
7
30
3
35
19
10 17 18
33
11
31
1

THE HAIGHT *Map on p338*

THE HAIGHT

GOLDEN GATE PARK & THE AVENUES *Map on p342*

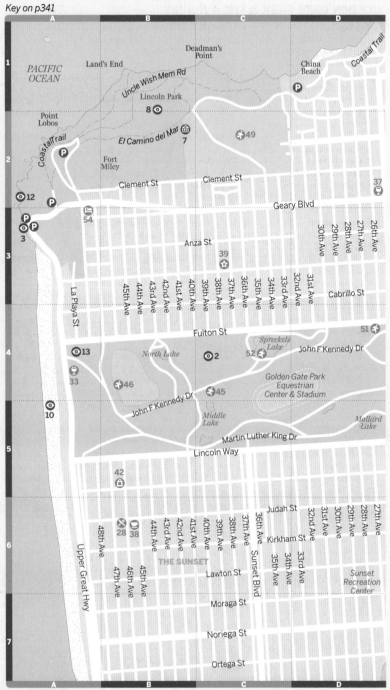

GOLDEN GATE PARK & THE AVENUES

PACIFIC
OCEAN

Deadman's
Point

Land's End

China
Beach

Coastal Trail

Uncle Wish Mem Rd

Lincoln Park

8

Point
Lobos

Coastal Trail

El Camino del Mar

7

49

Fort
Miley

Clement St

Clement St

12

Geary Blvd

37

P

3

54

Anza St

39

30th Ave
29th Ave
28th Ave
27th Ave
26th Ave

45th Ave
44th Ave
43rd Ave
42nd Ave
41st Ave
40th Ave
39th Ave
38th Ave
37th Ave
36th Ave
35th Ave
34th Ave
33rd Ave
32nd Ave
31st Ave

Cabrillo St

La Playa St

Fulton St

51

North Lake

Spreckels
Lake

13

2

52

John F Kennedy Dr

33

46

Golden Gate Park
Equestrian
Center & Stadium

45

10

John F Kennedy Dr

Middle
Lake

Mallard
Lake

Martin Luther King Dr

Lincoln Way

42

Judah St

32nd Ave
31st Ave
30th Ave
29th Ave
28th Ave
27th Ave

28

38

48th Ave
47th Ave
46th Ave
45th Ave
44th Ave
43rd Ave
42nd Ave
41st Ave
40th Ave
39th Ave
38th Ave
37th Ave
36th Ave
35th Ave
34th Ave
33rd Ave

Kirkham St

THE SUNSET

Lawton St

Sunset Blvd

Sunset
Recreation
Center

Upper Great Hwy

Moraga St

Noriega St

Ortega St

Our Story

A beat-up old car, a few dollars in the pocket and a sense of adventure. In 1972 that's all Tony and Maureen Wheeler needed for the trip of a lifetime – across Europe and Asia overland to Australia. It took several months, and at the end – broke but inspired – they sat at their kitchen table writing and stapling together their first travel guide, *Across Asia on the Cheap*. Within a week they'd sold 1500 copies. Lonely Planet was born.

Today, Lonely Planet has offices in Melbourne, London and Oakland, with more than 600 staff and writers. We share Tony's belief that 'a great guidebook should do three things: inform, educate and amuse'.

Our Writers

Alison Bing

Coordinating Author: North Beach & Chinatown, The Mission, SoMa & Potrero Hill, The Haight & Hayes Valley, and Golden Gate Park & the Avenues Over 15 years in San Francisco, Alison has done everything you're supposed to do in the city and many things you're not, including falling in love on the 7 Haight bus and gorging on Mission burritos before Berlioz symphonies. Alison holds degrees in art history and international diplomacy – respectable diplomatic credentials she regularly undermines with opinionated culture commentary for radio, newspapers, foodie magazines and books, including Lonely Planet's *California, USA, Coastal California, California Trips, San Francisco* and *San Francisco Encounter* guides. Alison also wrote the Planning, Understand and Survival Guide chapters.

John A Vlahides

The Marina, Fisherman's Wharf & the Piers, Downtown & Civic Center, The Hills & Japantown, and The Castro & Noe Valley John A Vlahides co-hosts the TV series *Lonely Planet: Roads Less Travelled,* screening on National Geographic Channels International. John studied cooking in Paris, with the same chefs who trained Julia Child, and he's a former luxury-hotel concierge and member of *Les Clefs d'Or,* the international union of the world's elite concierges. He lives in San Francisco, where he sings tenor with the San Francisco Symphony, and spends free time skiing the Sierra Nevada. For more, see www.johnvlahides.com and twitter.com/john vlahides. John also wrote the Sleeping and Day Trips chapters.

Read more about John at:
lonelyplanet.com/members/johnvlahides

Published by Lonely Planet Publications Pty Ltd
ABN 36 005 607 983
8th edition – Feb 2012
ISBN 978 1 74179 923 1
© Lonely Planet 2012   Photographs © as indicated 2012
10 9 8 7 6 5 4 3 2 1
Printed in China